MANAGING HUMAN BEHAVIOR
in PUBLIC
and NONPROFIT
ORGANIZATIONS

2 EDITION

MANAGING HUMAN BEHAVIOR
in PUBLIC
and NONPROFIT
ORGANIZATIONS

2 EDITION

Robert B. Denhardt • Janet V. Denhardt • Maria P. Aristigueta
Arizona State University   *Arizona State University*   *University of Delaware*

SAGE

Los Angeles • London • New Delhi • Singapore

For information:

SAGE Publications, Inc.
2455 Teller Road
Thousand Oaks, California 91320
E-mail: order@sagepub.com

SAGE Publications India Pvt. Ltd.
B 1/I 1 Mohan Cooperative Industrial Area
Mathura Road, New Delhi 110 044
India

SAGE Publications Ltd.
1 Oliver's Yard
55 City Road
London EC1Y 1SP
United Kingdom

SAGE Publications Asia-Pacific Pte. Ltd.
33 Pekin Street #02-01
Far East Square
Singapore 048763

Printed in the United States of America

Library of Congress Cataloging-in-Publication Data

Denhardt, Robert B.
Managing human behavior in public and nonprofit organizations/Robert B. Denhardt, Janet Vinzant Denhardt, Maria P. Aristigueta. — 2nd ed.
       p. cm.
Includes bibliographical references and index.
ISBN 978-1-4129-5667-3 (pbk. : acid-free paper)
   1. Public administration. 2. Nonprofit organizations—Management.
3. Organizational behavior. I. Denhardt, Janet Vinzant. II. Aristigueta, Maria Pilar,
1956– III. Title.

JF1351.D449 2009
658—dc22   2008004783

This book is printed on acid-free paper.

       09   10   11   12   11   10   9   8   7   6   5   4   3   2

Acquisitions Editor:	Al Bruckner
Editorial Assistant:	MaryAnn Vail
Production Editor:	Diane S. Foster
Copy Editor:	Anthony Moore
Typesetter:	C&M Digitals (P) Ltd.
Proofreader:	Scott Oney
Indexer:	Molly Hall
Cover Designer:	Candice Harman
Marketing Manager:	Nichole M. Angress

Contents

Preface

*M*anaging Human Behavior in Public and Nonprofit Organizations is intended as a core text in management and organizational behavior as taught in undergraduate and graduate programs in public administration and nonprofit management as well as courses in educational administration. Faculty in the field of public administration and nonprofit management are increasingly recognizing the importance of teaching basic management skills as part of the public administration curriculum. Indeed, over the past several years, the National Association of Schools of Public Affairs and Administration has listed "organization and management concepts and behavior" as a necessary curriculum component of MPA programs seeking accreditation. For these reasons, nearly every MPA program now requires a course in management and organizational behavior as part of its core curriculum. In addition, many undergraduate and doctoral programs in public administration feature courses in management and organizational behavior.

The same is true in the field of nonprofit management. The Nonprofit Academic Centers Council is an independent organization hosted at the Mandel Center for Nonprofit Organizations at Case Western Reserve University in Cleveland. It is the driver of curriculum standards for the growing nonprofit and philanthropic studies field. Included in its guidelines for nonprofit curricula is attention to management and organizational behavior, both at the undergraduate and graduate level. In fact, there is an entire section of the guidelines on such topics.

Finally, schools and colleges of education are recognizing the importance of principals, superintendents, and other educational administrators at all levels being well-prepared for the human aspects of administration and management. Again, attention to management and organizational behavior is central.

Although the courses offered to meet these needs vary considerably in name and content, there are certain basics that are likely to be included. First, these courses recognize the importance of students developing basic management skills such as communications, motivation, teamwork and group dynamics, decision making, power, influence, and leadership. Second, these courses typically employ a variety of cases, exercises, and simulations to give students some sense of the real-world implications of their actions. Third, the courses typically emphasize continuing to learn from one's own experience, reflection, and insight.

Managing Human Behavior in Public and Nonprofit Organizations covers all of the essential topics in management and organizational behavior, but it does so *from the perspective of public and nonprofit management.* There are three themes that are central: (1) the importance of understanding the behavior, motivations, and actions of *individuals* in the public service; (2) a focus on the distinctiveness of management and leadership in *public and nonprofit organizations;* and (3) an emphasis on students learning not only from reading but also from their own *experiences.*

This book, therefore, seeks the following objectives appropriate for a course in management and organizational behavior:

- To help students develop a thorough understanding of the basic issues that affect behavior in public and nonprofit organizations (including schools)
- To help students understand the value of analyzing management problems from the standpoint of the individual and how that perspective can augment action and analysis at the organizational level
- To increase students' understanding of core behavioral principles on which these personal, interpersonal, and public leadership skills are based
- To help foster competency in critical management and leadership skills—that is, the capacity to act effectively and responsibly under the stress, complexity, and uncertainty of the real world
- To provide cases, exercises, simulations, and evaluative instruments that will enable students to learn both cognitively and experientially

In each chapter, we present a review of the relevant literature related to each of the topics covered, but we also present some specific and immediate ideas and tools that should be of help. We also develop some long-term strategies that students can use to learn from their own experiences and the experiences of others. And we provide a set of learning tools—cases, simulations, and assessment tools—that students can use to develop and practice their emerging skills in management and leadership. Each of the central chapters follows the same organization:

Introductory paragraphs. Each chapter begins with a brief introduction establishing the importance of the topic and how the topic reflects our commitment to and concern for individual action, the distinctive character of public service, and learning from experience.

Where Do We Begin? This section provides several brief self-assessment exercises to give students a sense of where they currently stand with respect to the issue being discussed.

Ways of Thinking. This section introduces students to the basic knowledge that has been accumulated on the topic. It discusses what we know about the particular topic. What does the literature tell us?

Ways of Acting. This section takes the information presented in the previous section and puts it in the context of action, presenting general lessons and behavioral guidelines that might instruct managers' behavior in specific situations.

Thinking in Action. This section presents cases, simulations, and other exercises that give students an opportunity to practice the skills that they have learned.

We thank our many friends and colleagues who contributed to this book, especially Dean Debra Friedman of the ASU College of Public Programs, whose support of this project was essential, and, of course, our colleagues in the School of Public Affairs at Arizona State University and those in the School of Urban Affairs and Public Policy at the University of Delaware, many of whom provided special knowledge and insight.

We also thank a group of dedicated practitioners who helped to substantially enhance our understanding of the work of public organizations. We especially acknowledge the helpful contributions and advice of Larry Bacon, Beverly Daniels, Tom Eichler, Frank Fairbanks, Jay E. Hakes, Barbara Male, Robert O'Neill, John Paron, Phil Penland, Jan Perkins, and James Shuler. We also express special appreciation to Ljubinka Andonoska, who made superb contributions while at Arizona State, and to Donald Coons and Ellen Fanjoy, who provided their technical assistance at Delaware.

CHAPTER 1

Organizational Behavior as a Way of Thinking and Acting

This book is about human behavior in public and nonprofit organizations. Its purpose is to provide information and perspectives that enhance our understanding of our own behavior and our ability to influence the behavior of others. It concerns how public servants interact with others in their organizations and with the public, how they view their work and its importance to their communities, and how they choose to serve their cities, states, and nation. These are people doing extremely important work. They are charged with making our communities and our society better by fostering citizenship, making cities safer, educating youth, healing the sick, protecting the vulnerable, and keeping the country and the world clean, safe, and prosperous. Public servants, of course, do not bear this responsibility alone. Instead, they seek to accomplish these and other critical public goals in collaboration with elected officials, business leaders, citizens, world leaders, and many others. Each and every public employee, from the top of the organization to the front line, bears a responsibility as well as a deeply satisfying opportunity to serve the public interest.

To be effective, public administrators and nonprofit managers—from police chiefs to policy analysts, from agency executives to child protective services workers—must lead and motivate others within and outside of their organizations, function effectively in groups, communicate clearly, think creatively, navigate change successfully, and manage conflict. They must cope with their own and their employees' stress, be self-reflective and open to growth and learning, and renew and reinvigorate their commitment to public service in spite of sometimes unreachable goals, limited resources, and an often hostile public. Thankfully and remarkably, given the

1

challenges they face, thousands of public servants succeed in meeting these challenges every day.

Our intent in this book is to provide information, enhance skills, and broaden perspectives in support of efforts to manage organizational behavior in the public interest. The book builds on the knowledge and skills acquired by successful public administrators, draws from the research and observations of social scientists, and provides opportunities for students to acquire habits of mind that will allow them to reflect on and learn from their own experiences in public organizations. Accordingly, the goals of this book are as follows:

1. To examine what is known about the factors that affect human behavior in public organizations and how these ideas inform the practice of public administration

2. To develop an appreciation of the value of analyzing management problems from the standpoint of individual behavior and how that perspective can augment action and analysis at the organizational level

3. To explore some of the most contemporary approaches to management and leadership

4. To increase understanding of the core behavioral principles on which personal, interpersonal, and public leadership skills are based

5. To foster competency in critical management and leadership skills—that is, to develop the capacity to act effectively and responsibly under the stress, complexity, and uncertainty of the "real world" of public administration

6. To provide cases, exercises, simulations, and evaluative instruments that will enable students to learn both cognitively and experientially

In this book, we examine organizational behavior as a field of study. But we want to make clear at the outset that organizational behavior is not *just* a field of study. It is a way of thinking and acting that is of critical importance and value to people who work in public organizations.

Consider the following scenario. In your 10 years with the state social services department, you have earned a reputation as a problem solver. Because of this reputation, you have just been appointed as the head of a division charged with finding and securing payments from individuals who are not paying their required child support. The previous administrator left in a storm of controversy following a legislative study showing an abysmal track record in payment and widespread dissatisfaction on the part of the parents—both those who were owed money and those who owed money. These citizens complained that they were treated discourteously and that their cases were mishandled. The study was initiated after a popular weekly "newsmagazine" show on television highlighted how much more effective the growing number of private companies were in finding the parents who owed money and securing payments from them.

Understandably, the workers in your division are disheartened. Turnover and absenteeism are high. Workers report feeling unfairly criticized and point to the lack of necessary resources to effectively do their jobs. Yet, as you talk with these individuals, you find that they are bright, committed, and hardworking. The truth is, resources *are* extremely limited, and some of the criticism does seem unwarranted. You believe that you can work with these people to build a stronger, more service-oriented division.

How are you going to handle this challenge? What information will you collect? What decisions will you make? What actions will you take? What will you do first?

There are many important perspectives from which situations such as this can be analyzed and approached. Certainly, those in public agencies deal with personnel issues, technical problems, systems failures, budgetary or policy issues, and performance measurement. But much of what happens in public organizations can best be seen as problems of human behavior in organizations. The ways in which individuals act make a huge difference in the outcomes of public programs. But even here there are different levels of analysis. Look again at the case of the child support collection division. What are the important issues here? Are they concerns that should be framed in terms of individual behavior, group functioning, organizational operations, community considerations, or society at large? Will you respond by dealing with one person at a time, or will you seek some systemwide intervention? Each of these levels of analysis gives us a different perspective on the ways in which our organizations and the people in them work. In turn, each perspective becomes a lens through which we see, interpret, and attempt to respond to the specific organizational circumstances that we confront.

As we change the lenses through which we see a given situation, our definition of the problems that the situation entails and the possible solutions to those problems also will change. For example, if we focus on individual behavior, then we might think of the problem as one of employee motivation, the failure of employees to communicate effectively with citizens, or employees' lack of understanding the broader purposes and goals of the organization. As a result, we might meet and talk with employees; try to understand their needs, desires, and motivations; work with them to set individual and group goals; and seek their input on policy and operational changes that would improve outcomes. Are supervisors managing their units in a manner that supports employee development and performance? Do workers understand the underlying values of the mission of the unit, and are they empowered to serve the public in a manner consistent with these values? Helping individuals to redirect their behavior toward meeting organizational and community goals would be the purpose of our efforts.

At the group level, we might ask whether existing work groups are functioning effectively. Do employees feel like a part of a team, or do they feel alienated from their coworkers and supervisors? Is the culture of existing groups or teams conducive to or counter to division goals? We might form task forces of employees to address particular problems, or we might reconfigure work teams to address certain types of cases. We might work with staff members to improve their group process and leadership skills. Our objective in undertaking these activities would be to strengthen work teams, enhance worker commitment and involvement, and provide the skills and support needed for the employees to achieve their goals.

At the organizational level, we might ask whether the division is structured appropriately to accomplish its tasks. Are management systems, such as goal setting and performance measurement, in place? Is there a strategic plan? Is management information available to guide decision making? Are resources tracked and allocated to areas of high need? Are organizational communications clear, and are policies documented and disseminated? Are the appropriate equipment, technology, and supplies available? Are personnel guidelines for hiring appropriate regarding the skills needed for the job? Is training adequate?

At the systems level, we might question whether the unit is receiving adequate funding and central agency support. How can we work with key legislators as we attempt to implement organizational improvements? We also might consider the problem to be the manifestation of a larger societal issue—perhaps a generally hostile attitude toward government workers that leads to inadequate funding or, alternatively, a lack of cooperation by clients as the employees try to gather information that will help in tracking down nonpaying parents. How then can we improve public relations and our interactions with other groups so that we can demonstrate that an important service is being provided to the public?

Each of these perspectives provides important insights and tools for public administrators as they work to manage their organizations in the public interest. The field of organizational behavior speaks to most of these issues, at least so far as the human dimension is concerned. As will be explored more fully in the sections that follow, organizational behavior is the study of individual and group behavior in organizational settings. Accordingly, the field provides critically important and highly useful perspectives on motivation, leadership, groups, power and politics, culture, and other matters that directly concern individual and group behavior. It also speaks to organizational issues and community issues, but it does so through the lens of individual and group behavior. For example, it is concerned with the following:

- Motivating employees
- Being an effective team member
- Leading and inspiring others
- Communicating effectively within and outside of the organization
- Making effective decisions
- Using power and politics constructively and ethically
- Creating and securing commitment to shared values
- Managing conflict productively
- Using diversity to enhance organizational performance
- Helping people to become more innovative and creative

So, organizational behavior provides the tools, skills, ideas, and strategies for managing human behavior in organizations. But it should be recognized that as the study of organizational behavior spotlights individual and group behavior, it leaves other important concerns and issues at least partially in the dark. Models of organizational behavior cannot tell a manager what type of computer system to buy, nor can they directly address outcome measurement systems and other organizational issues—except in terms of their implications for human behavior. But given the undeniable importance of humans in the public sector, the perspective of organizational behavior offers a particularly important way of thinking and acting that can help public servants to achieve organizational goals more effectively and to serve the public more responsibly. In other words, people in public service are the key ingredient in determining how well government serves its citizens. It also is important to note here that we are not using the word *citizen* in the legal sense. Rather citizens are those we serve, and citizenship is the engagement of individuals in democratic governance, regardless of legal status. Perhaps the easiest, and in some ways the most useful, way of defining organizational behavior in the public sector is to say that it is the study of how people behave in public organizations. Organizational behavior is concerned with how people act, their motivations, and how they interact with others. As we noted earlier, it is concerned with human behavior and social systems. But there are differences of opinion as to where the boundaries of the field actually lie. In particular, the distinction between the studies of organizational behavior and organizational theory can become blurred. Some suggest that organizational behavior is one perspective within the larger field of organizational theory, whereas others conceive of organizational behavior as having a distinct identity as a separate field of study.

This confusion arises because organizational behavior typically is defined as concerned not only with the behavior of the individual and groups but also with the influence of the individual on the organization and the influence of organizational structure, culture, and other factors on the individual. As we have seen, it deals with at least three levels of analysis: the individual, the group, and the organization. If it deals with organizational matters, then how is it different from organizational theory? More important, why does it matter?

We would argue that the distinctiveness and value of organizational behavior as a field of study and as a way of thinking and acting lie in what one chooses as the starting point. Organizational behavior has a different orientation from that of other organizational management perspectives because it has a different focus. In organizational behavior, the starting point is the person. Accordingly, the questions that we consider in this book focus on individual and group behavior, needs, and perceptions. Is the organization meeting the needs of its people so as to allow them to work effectively? Are individual creativity and responsibility being fostered? Are there opportunities for learning and change? Is the "fit" between individuals and the organization a good one? By starting with "people concerns," values such as human dignity, growth, fairness, and participation become paramount.

If we were to begin instead with the organization as the starting point of our analysis, then we would tend to define problems as organizational and seek solutions at that level. We would be most likely to think first about changing the organizational structure and systems so as to make them more rational and consistent with generally accepted models of organization. We also might ask about the role that the organization plays in the larger society and in the governance system. The underlying values at the organizational level might be to achieve rationality, consistency, performance, responsiveness, and efficiency.

So, although organizational behavior concerns topics that it holds in common with organizational theory perspectives, it has a different analytic starting point.

Organizational behavior emphasizes human behavior and individual values rather than organizational structures and organizational values. Accordingly, it leads us to take actions that are aimed at understanding and influencing individual human behavior. In other words, organizational behavior deals with virtually all aspects of organizations and management, but it does so from the perspective of *people.*

In this book, we go a step further. We assert that the management of organizational behavior *in the public sector* must, in fact, consider a fourth level of analysis—that which concerns governance in the public interest. In public service, we must be concerned not only with leading and motivating others but also with doing so in a manner that is consistent with democratic values and the public interest. In the public sector, it is not enough to simply be successful in influencing people to behave in a particular way. Public servants have a responsibility to manage organizational behavior so as to meet public objectives and community needs—and these values are, in fact, more important than the personal needs and desires of managers or workers or organizational values such as stability and structure. Therefore, organizational behavior in the context of public management encompasses both the values inherent in a "people perspective" on organizations and the values that guide public service in democratic government (Figure 1.1).

Organizational behavior in the public sector can be seen as resulting from the interactions and influences among these levels. It is the product of the complex interactions among individuals, groups, organizational factors, and the public environment in which all of this takes place. In part because of the complexity of these interactions, the management of behavior in organizations always will be complex, somewhat unpredictable, and challenging. We cannot control the thinking, much less the behavior, of others. But we can positively influence others, and we can be more successful in working with people to accomplish shared objectives. By gaining a better understanding of our own behavior, the behavior of people and groups in organizations, and the influence of organizational and other environmental factors, our ability to successfully accomplish public objectives will be enhanced.

Perhaps it would be helpful to think about these issues from the perspective of the knowledge and skills needed by successful public servants. That is, what do we need to know, and what do we need to be able to do, so as to act effectively and responsibly in a public organization? These questions were addressed in a classic study conducted by the U.S. Office of Personnel Management (OPM) that sought to identify the skills that are critical to managerial success in government. Based on information collected from a large number of highly effective governmental managers and executives, the researchers developed two categories of competencies: one focusing on management functions (or the "what" of government) and one focusing on effectiveness (or the "how" of government). Those competencies are summarized and paraphrased in Figure 1.2.

The first thing we notice when we look at the list in Figure 1.2 is how many of these competencies require a working knowledge of, and effective skills in, organizational behavior. Certainly, interpreting and communicating, guiding and leading, supervising and promoting performance, and flexibility are all organizational behavior skill areas. But a second look reveals how integral the skills in

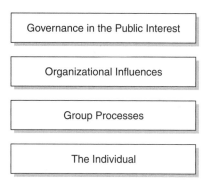

Figure 1.1   Levels of Analysis in Organizational Behavior in the Public Sector

organizational behavior are to virtually every aspect of managerial competence. Look at the list and see whether you see any elements that do not require, or at least could not be strengthened by, an ability to effectively influence, manage, motivate, and lead people.

The need for competencies and skills at multiple levels is reinforced by the diagram in Figure 1.3, again drawn from the OPM study. The OPM framework highlights the need for management competencies at all levels of the organization. For example, it suggests that successful first-line managers must be not only technically competent but also effective communicators who demonstrate personal sensitivity. Their actions also must be consistent with those competencies emphasized at the next level; while having an action orientation and being focused on results, these managers must demonstrate leadership and flexibility. At this level, successful middle-level managers must demonstrate all of these skills and competencies and also work to acquire the characteristics of those at the outer ring—a broad perspective, a strategic view, and environmental sensitivity. If executives at the top levels of government are to be successful, then they must demonstrate the full range of effectiveness characteristics and be especially attentive to their interactions with the organization's environment. Clearly, a wide variety of skills, most notably their ability to work with and through people, will be essential to their success as public managers.

The Roots of Organizational Behavior

The field of organizational behavior is fairly young. Although we have been interested in the behavior of people in organizations for a long time, most early approaches focused on simply controlling workers and manipulating their environment so as to maximize predictability and productivity. Given the importance of employee behavior to organizational success, it might seem somewhat surprising that this topic was not a matter of significant managerial concern until at least the 1940s.

The "What" of Management: Functions

1. *External awareness:* Identifying key agency politics and priorities and/or external issues and trends likely to affect the work unit

2. *Interpretation:* Keeping subordinates informed about key agency and work unit policies, priorities, issues, and trends and about how these are to be incorporated into the unit

3. *Representation:* Presenting, explaining, selling, and defending the work unit's activities to the supervisor in the agency and to persons and groups outside of the agency

4. *Coordination:* Performing liaison functions and integrating the work of various units within the organization and interacting with other organizations

5. *Planning:* Developing long-term goals, objectives, and priorities and deciding on actions

6. *Guidance:* Converting plans to action by establishing schedules and standards

7. *Budgeting:* Preparing, justifying, and administering the budget

8. *Managing materials:* Making sure that the needed supplies, equipment, and facilities are available

9. *Personnel management:* Projecting needs and recruiting, selecting, appraising, and retaining employees

10. *Supervision:* Providing guidance and oversight while working to promote and recognize performance

11. *Monitoring:* Staying up-to-date on the status of activities, identifying problems, and taking corrective action

12. *Evaluation:* Assessing how well program goals are met and identifying ways in which to improve

The "How" of Management: Effectiveness Characteristics

1. *Broad perspective:* Ability to see the big picture and to balance long- and short-term considerations

2. *Strategic view:* Ability to collect and analyze information and to anticipate and make judgments

3. *Environmental sensitivity:* Awareness of the agency in relation to its environment

4. *Leadership:* Individual and group leadership and willingness to lead, manage, and accept responsibility

5. *Flexibility:* Openness to new information, change, and innovation as well as to tolerance for stress and ambiguity

6. *Action orientation:* Independence, pro-activity, calculated risk taking, problem solving, and decisiveness

7. *Results focus:* Concern with goal achievement

8. *Communication:* Effective speaking, writing, and listening

9. *Interpersonal sensitivity:* Self-knowledge and awareness of impact on others—sensitivity to their needs, strengths, and weaknesses; negotiation and conflict resolution skills and the ability to persuade

10. *Technical competence:* Specialized expertise in agency programs and operations

Figure 1.2   U.S. Office of Personnel Management Inventory of Management Skills

From "The Management Excellence Inventory," by L. R. Flanders and D. Utterback, 1985, *Public Administration Review,* 45(3), pp. 403–410.

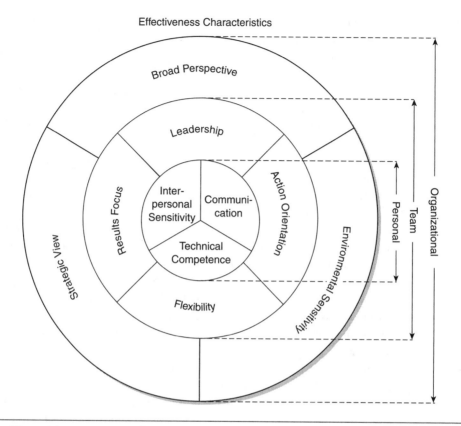

Figure 1.3   Management Excellence Framework

SOURCE: Flanders & Utterback (1985).

Some Early History

From the perspective of early management theorists, people were primarily viewed as extensions of their tools and machines. For example, employee motivation, if it was considered at all, was based on the fear of physical or economic punishment. It was assumed that workers found work to be unpleasant and therefore had to be motivated (or bribed) by money to contribute to the organization. It also was assumed that workers would do what they were told because they would be punished or fired if they did not.

Frederick Taylor, best known as the father of scientific management, is representative of these traditional perspectives on human behavior (Taylor, 1911). He, like other management thinkers of his time, assumed that workers would do what they were told if they were paid to do so. In testimony before Congress in 1912, Taylor boasted, "Under scientific management, the initiative of the workmen—that is, their hard work, their goodwill, their ingenuity—is obtained practically with absolute regularity" (1912/1997, p. 30). Taylor believed that if managers studied the best ways for tasks to be performed and then scientifically selected and trained workers to perform those tasks, then workers would be induced to perform as expected by paying them a "piece rate"—a set amount of money for each task performed or product produced.

But it is important to point out that Taylor did not see this as exploiting employees. To the contrary, his writing made it clear that the design of work and production was the responsibility of management and that if management employed scientific approaches to the study of work tasks, then both employers and employees would benefit. Taylor suggested that "only one-tenth of our trouble has come on the workmen's side" and that instead, "we find very great opposition on the part of those on the management's side to do their new duties and comparatively little opposition on the part of the work men to cooperate in doing their new duties" (1912/1997, p. 31). The point is that motivation per se was simply not a concern.

Taylor's overall purpose was to make people, whom he assumed to be naturally lazy and stupid, more productive. Referring to his efforts to secure greater productivity from men hauling pig iron, Taylor is quoted as saying that it is "possible to train an intelligent gorilla" to do their job (1911, p. 40). Moreover, despite employees' natural tendencies toward laziness, he expected them to obey their superiors without question. Using the analogy of a baseball team, Taylor stated that it is obvious and necessary to recognize the "utter impossibility of winning . . . unless every man on the team obeys the signals or orders of the coach and obeys them at once when the coach give those orders" (1912/1997, p. 32).

There were a few early voices who were more humanistic, people such as Hugo Munsterberg, who urged greater attention to the psychology of workers (Munsterberg, 1913), and Mary Parker Follett, who argued that dynamic administration must be grounded in "our cognition of the motivating desires of the individual and of the group" (Metcalf & Urwick, 1940, p. 9). But such work was largely considered outside the mainstream until the Hawthorne studies, published during the 1930s, pointed the way toward a greater acceptance of the importance of social factors at work (Roethlisberger & Dickson, 1939). In 1927, a group of researchers led by Elton Mayo and F. J. Roethlisberger from Harvard University embarked on a study of worker productivity in the Hawthorne Works of the Western Electric Company in Chicago. The project began as a relatively straightforward examination of "the relation between conditions of work and the incidence of fatigue and monotony among employees" (1939, p. 3). The researchers anticipated that definitive data on this matter could be collected and analyzed within a year. But things did not turn out as they had planned. As they put it, "the inquiry developed in an unexpected fashion" and, as a result, continued for 5 years, from 1927 to 1932 (1939, p. 3).

Although the Hawthorne studies took longer than expected, the findings from this research ultimately would signal a fundamental shift in how employee behavior was to be understood. The Hawthorne findings actually surprised the researchers. In fact, a series of initial experiments to measure the effects of lighting on efficiency were deemed failures. Basically, the researchers could find no direct relationship between changes in illumination and worker efficiency. In fact, short of literally making it so dark that the workers could not see, every change that the researchers implemented seemed to increase productivity. The researchers concluded that "light is only one, and apparently a minor, factor among many which affect employee output" and that "the attempt to measure the effect of one variable had not been successful because the various factors affecting the performance of the operators had not been controlled, and hence, the results could have been influenced by any one of several variables" (Roethlisberger & Dickson, 1939, p. 19). So, in the next phase of their study, the researchers attempted to control for these many variables by isolating a group of workers and systematically and comprehensively studying their behavior and attitudes.

After observing, consulting, and interviewing this group of employees for 5 years, the researchers arrived at two conclusions that would profoundly change research on worker behavior. First, they found that people change their behavior when they know they are being observed (the so-called Hawthorne effect). Second, they concluded that human relationships (including a relationship with the researchers) influenced the behavior of workers and, consequently, that new hypotheses were needed to explain worker behavior. The Hawthorne experiments showed that human behavior and motivation is complex, being influenced by attitudes, feelings, and the meaning that people assign to their work and their relationships at work. As the researchers stated succinctly, "It is [our] simple thesis that a human problem requires a human solution" (Roethlisberger & Dickson, 1939, p. 35). This was a far cry from the types of assumptions that Taylor and his contemporaries had made about worker motivation.

Research conducted over the subsequent few decades confirmed the Hawthorne findings and resulted in a more sophisticated understanding of the relationship between people and organizations. The importance of human cooperation in organizations was emphasized in Chester Barnard's definition of a formal organization as "a system of consciously coordinated activities or forces of two or more persons" (1948, p. 81). For Barnard, the participation of the individual was necessary for cooperation, and indeed, he viewed the need to build cooperation among organizational subunits as the crucial function of the manager. The rationale for including workers in problem-solving and decision-making teams was established later as a result of collaboration between social psychologist Kurt Lewin and anthropologist Margaret Mead in experiments concerning the reduction of civilian consumption of rationed food. Through Lewin's research in this setting, he established a core principle: "We are likely to modify our own behavior when we participate in problem analysis and solution, and [we are] more likely to carry out decisions we have helped make" (Weisbord, 1987, p. 89).

In 1946, Lewin and McGregor started the Research Center for Group Dynamics with the mission of training leaders to become skilled in improving group relations and managing change. McGregor's research on group norms and personal needs underlined the importance of developing the morale of the workforce and encouraging cooperative efforts so as to increase efficiency (Knickerbocker & McGregor, 1942). In *The Human Side of the Enterprise,* McGregor (1960) discussed a highly effective management team studied by researchers. He concluded that "unity of purpose" is the main distinguishing characteristic of the successful unit. Even more important, McGregor discussed the now familiar "Theory X" and "Theory Y," arguing that traditional command-and-control approaches (Theory X)—based on assumptions of people as lazy, uninvolved, and motivated solely by money—actually caused people to behave in a manner consistent with those expectations. His alternative, Theory Y, suggested a much more optimistic and humanistic view of people, emphasizing the inherent worth of individuals in organizations.

In related work, Likert (1961), in *New Patterns of Management,* developed the notion of organizations as a series of interlocking groups and the manager as a "linking pin." Argyris (1964) focused his attention on the personal development of the individual in the context of the organization; organizational effectiveness was a function of the interpersonal competence of team members and the extent to which the organization supported positive norms. Blake and Mouton (1964) provided a model of team excellence and a set of styles useful in understanding team members' contributions through their managerial grid, which may be used to diagnose the team's culture. Through contributions such as these, a particular approach to management and human behavior gained increasing acceptance during the 1960s and 1970s. It is this perspective, and the models and theories that have been built from it over the subsequent decades, that forms the foundation of the field of organizational behavior as explored in this book.

During the past few decades, the field of organizational behavior has benefited from work in a variety of disciplines. Because of its emphasis on individual behavior, contemporary organizational behavior draws heavily from the field of psychology. Psychological theories and models form the basis of our knowledge about perception and learning, human motivation, and small-group or one-on-one interactions. But not all schools of thought within psychology play an equal role in the study of organizational behavior. For example, psychological theories such as those espoused by Sigmund Freud assume that human personality and behavior are largely fixed at a young age. Not surprisingly, such perspectives are not particularly useful to adults in organizational settings. On the other hand, behavioral psychology, with its emphasis on learning and behavior change, is quite useful and important. Likewise, social psychology offers insights into group behavior, conflict, power, and leadership.

Sociology also is an important source of insights into organizational behavior. Sociologists help us to understand organizations and how their structure and function affect individuals. Conflict, adaptation, and the influence of the environment all are issues addressed in the field of sociology. Similarly, anthropology, with its exploration of the role of culture in society, offers important insights into organizational life. Finally, political science contributes to our understanding of organizational behavior by focusing on power, leadership, strategy, and (most important for our purposes here) democratic values and governance.

The influence of these fields is not singular; each of them may provide insights into a particular topic within the field of organizational behavior. For example, our understanding of conflict and power in organizations may be explored from a psychological, sociological, anthropological, or political standpoint. Each of these perspectives may emphasize different aspects of the causes, sources, and manifestations of these phenomena as well as our role in managing and responding to them. In fact, the more different angles and lenses we can use to look at human behavior in organizations, the more likely our actions will be effective.

Values and Assumptions
of Organizational Behavior

There are a number of assumptions and values that underlie the study of organizational behavior and that will guide our examination of the field in the context of public service. In other words, the field of organizational behavior is fundamentally based on certain assumptions about the nature of people and behavior. These assumptions are just that; they are simply things we assume or assert about human behavior that allow us to interpret what people do and why they do it and then to act accordingly ourselves. To the extent that these assumptions do not hold true in a given circumstance, the tools of organizational behavior might be less than completely effective. But in any case, recognizing these assumptions and the values they imply is important in understanding how the perspective of organizational behavior can inform our actions.

The first such assumption is that human behavior is purposeful. That means that a great deal of what we do involves behavior that is intended to accomplish some purpose. That does not mean that *all* behavior is goal oriented, at least not in the conscious sense. Some actions or behavior may be involuntary, and certainly the consequences of our behavior can be unintended. But in terms of organizational behavior, voluntary goal-directed behavior is seen as critical to achieving organizational effectiveness. The field of organizational behavior, in turn, assumes that voluntary and purposeful behavior can be influenced by the behavior of others and through the practices of management.

The second assumption is that behavior is not random—that it is caused. The study of organizational behavior looks for the antecedents and causes of human behavior. It assumes that, by studying behavior and patterns of interaction, we can gain insights into ways of thinking about and influencing the behavior of others.

The third assumption is that behavior can be changed through learning. When people change how they think, they frequently change how they act. Although human learning is not directly observable (because it takes place within the mind of the individual), organizational behavior is based in part on the idea that people will change their behavior in response to their experiences and knowledge. Furthermore, behavior that has favorable consequences or is otherwise reinforced probably will be repeated.

The fourth assumption is that people should be valued simply as humans aside from their contributions to organizational goal attainment. Treating humans with respect and dignity is an important value in its own right. Organizational behavior is fundamentally grounded in the idea that improvements to organizational processes, structure, and performance require "managing through people." Although approaches that ignore or disrespect people may get results in the short term, they do not build responsible, engaged, and civic-minded employees or citizens. And in the long term, they are unlikely to be all that effective anyway.

The final assumption that guides our exploration of organizational behavior in the public sector is that public service is about serving others. There is nothing wrong with meeting our own needs and priorities at work, but in the public service, the needs of others take precedence. We are in the public service to serve others—our country, our community, our fellow citizens (including our employees and coworkers)—and not ourselves. Public servants are people whose motivations and rewards are more than simply a matter of pay or security. They want to make a difference in the lives of others and to serve the public. To be both effective and responsible, organizational behavior in the public sector always must be attentive to the special calling of public service.

Themes and Purposes of This Book

Building on the assumptions described in the preceding section, this book is organized around three themes: (1) the importance of understanding the behavior, motivations, and actions of individuals in the public service; (2) a focus on the distinctiveness of management and leadership in *public* organizations; and (3) an emphasis on students learning not only from reading but also from experience. We can examine each of these points in greater detail.

First, in our view, public administration courses in management and organizational behavior should focus on the individual. We assume that a key to success in public administration is the ability to understand and influence the behavior of individuals and groups. Moreover, we assert that public managers must learn to manage, change, and reflect on their *own* behavior and motivations in developing the capacity to manage others. For this reason, this book focuses on *the individual public servant*—how and why individuals behave as they do, how students can act with greater probability of success in influencing the behavior of others, and how (over time) they can improve their own capacity to act as individual managers and public servants. In other words, the effective and responsible management of organizational behavior requires that public managers understand and develop a capacity to manage their own behavior, influence the behavior of others at the interpersonal and group levels, and act as individual public leaders in their interactions with the public and its representatives.

To manage others, we must start with ourselves; we must learn to manage our own behavior and understand our motivations and perceptions of ourselves. We must know ourselves—our style, our strengths, and our limitations. We must learn to distinguish our motivations, preferences, and worldviews from those of others. We must have a sense of direction, a willingness to explore and take risks, and a good understanding of how we can learn from our administrative experiences over time.

Beyond the personal level, public managers are involved with other people in the organization—bosses, coworkers, and subordinates. To interact effectively with these people, public managers need to develop strong *interpersonal* skills in areas such as communicating with and motivating others, working with and facilitating groups and teams, and understanding and employing power and influence. They need to be culturally aware, especially in a multicultural global society, and capitalize on diverse approaches and talents to improve organizational effectiveness (Hofstede & Hofstede, 2005).

Finally, building on personal and interpersonal skills, effective public managers also must assume the skills of *public* leadership. Public leadership involves not only internal management issues but also the management of critical interactions between organizational representatives and individuals and groups outside of the public organization. Particularly important are skills involved in managing change processes and in effectively representing the organization to the public, to the legislative body, to the media, and to those in other organizations. Again, individual interactions are critical; the way in which individual public servants, whether executives or line-level employees, deal with citizens, reporters, and clients ultimately defines the relationship between the organization and the public it serves.

This issue of "publicness" leads to the second major perspective of the book. We believe that public management is made distinctive by the compelling nature of the political environment and the nature of public service. Specifically, it is our firm belief that organizational behavior in the public sector is different—that public administration is, in many cases, significantly affected both by the particular requirements of public sector work and by the important traditions of democratic participation and a commitment to the public values that underlie work in public organizations. Public managers must be fully attentive to the public service motive that draws people to work in public organizations. For these reasons, leadership and management in public organizations must be understood in the context of public values and public service.

Third, to develop the capacity for action, a different style of learning is necessary. Learning the skills to support effective and responsible action requires not only reading and discussing ideas but also improving people's capacity to act in pursuit of their ideas. For this reason, we try to present a solid foundation of ideas on which you can act, but we also provide opportunities and aids that you can use in developing your own personal, interpersonal, and institutional skills in areas such as creativity, decision making, communication, and group dynamics.

In public administration, as in other skill-based disciplines, practice is required for improvement to occur. So, rather than just talking about organizational behavior, we draw on two types of experiences: (1) those that can be created in the classroom using cases, exercises, and simulations that we provide and (2) those drawn from real life, meaning your own work in public organizations (including internships) or other ongoing groups of which you are a part.

In each chapter, we seek not merely to present a review of the relevant literature related to each of the topics but also to present some specific and immediate ideas and tools that are intended to be of practical assistance. We also develop some long-term strategies or behavioral guidelines that you can use to learn from your own experiences as well as from the experiences of others. And we provide a set of learning tools—cases, simulations, assessment tools—that you can use to develop and practice your emerging skills in management and leadership.

In so doing, we hope to provide information as well as opportunities to enhance your skills and broaden your perspectives in support of efforts to manage organizational behavior in the public interest. Our goal is to provide perspectives and insights that will allow men and women in the public service to do their jobs better, to feel more competent and confident in their interactions with people, to lead others in their work to achieve a better world, and to gain greater satisfaction and joy from the careers they have chosen—all to the benefit of the public they serve.

CHAPTER **2**

Knowing and Managing Yourself

An enlightened organization will encourage its employees to pursue self-discovery. With a sense of purpose and a connection to the organization's mission, employees will become passionate about their work and there will be no limit to what can be accomplished.

—Larry Bacon, senior manager,
John E. Polk Correctional Facility,
Seminole County, Florida

For more than 2,000 years, knowledge of the self has been considered to be at the very core of human behavior. We are all familiar with the ancient Greek admonition to "know thyself." But this time-honored advice still has a great deal of currency. Knowing yourself and being reflective about your own behavior is essential to realizing your potential and having positive relationships with others. Erich Fromm was one of the first behavioral scientists to comment on the close connection between an individual's self-concept and his or her views of others. Fromm (1939) believed, for example, that hatred against oneself is inseparable from hatred against others. Indeed, Carl Rogers argued that the most basic human need is for self-acceptance, which he found in his clinical cases to be more important than physiological needs. According to Rogers (1961), self-acceptance is necessary for psychological health, personal growth, and the ability to know and accept others.

Knowledge of ourselves not only is valuable from a personal standpoint but also is critical to success and satisfaction in our work lives. Many contemporary public organizations are experimenting with new approaches to organizing and managing—approaches that take them far beyond the top-down, rule-bound hierarchies of the past. These changes are not easy for organizations or for the individuals who work in them. Adopting new ways of operating often requires significant changes in our basic thinking about work and our psychological response to it.

For example, most upper-level public sector managers came of age professionally during an era in which success was defined as attaining a position of power and then using that position to direct public programs. Management had a distinctive top-down character; the manager presumably was in a position to know what was best for his or her organization and to control the behavior of the staff so as to achieve the organization's goals. Moreover, success for these managers also was defined in terms of increased budgets and increased personnel. Today, public administration requires a far different mindset for these managers in which measures of success are far more ambiguous. These managers are moving away from top-down management and are finding ways of doing more with less. It is a new ballgame.

Similarly, middle managers are facing changes as they are being given more responsibility to take on assignments that previously were left to upper management. They also are finding new ways of relating to others both within and outside of their organizations. Meanwhile, lower-level personnel are being asked to be more productive, to serve their "customers" better, and (in some cases) to become "empowered." Regardless of level, the changes sweeping public organizations today have created considerable ambiguity, confusion, and stress. More than ever, there is the need for ethical competence, which includes moral reasoning, values management, and prudent decision making (Bowman, West, Berman, & Van Wart, 2004). "Without ethical competence, public managers do not use their political, professional, or task competence in right ways" (Virtanen, 2000, p. 336). Our ability to deal with these difficult times will be greatly enhanced by our understanding of ourselves. And as Larry Bacon mentioned in the quote at the beginning of this chapter, the organization also will gain from our self-knowledge.

According to Sluss and Ashforth (2007, p. 9), a major breakthrough in research on identity occurred with Brewer and Gardner's 1996 "contrast of the three levels of self": The *individual level* focuses on oneself as a unique being, and self-esteem derives from interpersonal comparisons of traits, abilities, goals, performance, and vision. The individual is essentially independent and autonomous, and its basic motivation is self-interest. The *interpersonal level* focuses on role relationship, such as supervisor–subordinate and colleague–colleague. At this level, the individuals are interdependent, and a premium is placed on the nature of the interaction, the potential for personal connection, and intimacy. The basic motivation at this level is that welfare and self-esteem derive from fulfilling one's role-relationship obligations. The final level is the *collective,* where the focus is on oneself as a prototypical member of a group, such as the organization, or of a social category, such as gender. Self-esteem derives from intergroup comparison, and the basic motivation is the welfare of the group.

We maintain a sense of self from all three levels, and cognitive shifts between the levels are generated by situational cues, such as names, rewards, and uniforms. However, "changes in levels of self-categorization reflect not only differences in views of the self but also different worldviews," including goals, values, and norms

(Brewer & Gardner, 1996, p. 91). The focus of this chapter is on the individual level of self, or what we refer to as the intrapersonal.

Where Do We Begin?

Life Experiences

Whereas attaining self-knowledge is an ongoing lifelong process, the following are some exercises designed to help you reflect on the experiences, values, and perspectives that shape who you are. Obviously, our personal culture, our life experiences, and our interactions with others affect our self-concepts and our views of the world. What events and relationships have influenced you? Make some notes in response to the following:

What world or national events have taken place during your lifetime?

- Which of these influenced your life most dramatically?
- How was your life influenced by those events?

   (Examples might include 9/11 and Hurricane Katrina. More positive influences might have come from an admired leader or public figure.)

Are there local events that have been particularly influential in your life?

- Were there cultural opportunities or political events in your hometown that were particularly influential?

   (Examples might include activities in a local theater, library, sports team, or government.)

What were your most important educational experiences?
Which personal relationships influenced you the most?

- What roles have these individuals played in your life?

   (Examples might include relationships with grandparents, parents, teachers, siblings, spouses, or children.)

Your Lifeline

On the chart in Figure 2.1, plot the major events and relationships of your life and then draw your lifeline. On the horizontal axis, fill in the years beginning with your birth and ending with the current year. On the vertical axis, use a 5-point scale with 0 as the midpoint (5, 4, 3, 2, 1, 0, −1, −2, −3, −4, −5) to represent the level of significance of each event or relationship and whether it had a positive or negative impact. This timeline should represent people and events that have had an impact in formulating your values, your style, and your orientation to life. This information might help you later in answering questions regarding your motivation for change and capacity for decision making.

	Birth	Childhood	Adolescence	Young Adult	Now
5					
4					
3					
2					
1					
0					
−1					
−2					
−3					
−4					
−5					

Figure 2.1   Lifeline of Experiences and Relationships

Ways of Thinking

A summary of organizational and psychological literature by Holmer (1994) suggests that the extent to which we actually practice what we preach as good management is, in large measure, a function of the competence with which we respond to emotional challenges. The term *emotional challenge* refers to any real or perceived threat to our security, self-image, or sense of self-worth that stimulates our instinctive self-protective tendencies to either withdraw or become aggressive. Holmer and Adams (1995) asserted that emotional challenges in organizations usually are interpersonal in nature. Interestingly, in these relationships, we often focus on trying to change or control the behavior of other people. The truth is that we can control only one person in a relationship—ourselves. If we can enhance our understanding of ourselves and how our values influence our behavior, if we can gain insight into how our attitudes and behaviors affect others, and if we can accept that how we view the world is not necessarily how others view the world, then we can build our capacity to handle emotional challenges and to maintain positive and productive relationships.

Even though we recognize that self-awareness and self-understanding are strongly related to our sense of well-being, the health of our interpersonal relationships, and our general success in life, sometimes we still avoid learning about ourselves. Maslow noted,

> We tend to be afraid of any knowledge that would cause us to despise ourselves or to make us feel inferior, weak, worthless, evil, [or] shameful. We protect ourselves and our ideal image of ourselves by repression and similar defenses, which are essentially techniques by which we avoid becoming conscious of unpleasantness or dangerous truths. (1962, p. 57)

The opposite also is true; we fear our highest potentials or abilities—what Maslow (1962) termed our personal "struggles against our own greatness." Nonetheless, being honest with ourselves despite these fears is the first step in becoming who we want to be.

Understanding ourselves might be particularly important in public organizations. Diamond (1993), Harvey (1988), Senge (1990), and others have explored the organizational consequences of failures to develop emotional and interpersonal capacities in leaders, work groups, management teams, and organizations. For example, Denhardt and Denhardt (1999) found that city managers known for their ability to manage change place a premium on knowing themselves and their values. Conversely, managers who lack the maturity and self-confidence to act independently are likely to be ineffective in managing others and in serving the public. Moreover, they might suffer personal psychological damage, especially as they are subjected to the stress and complexity that are virtually unavoidable in contemporary public organizations.

The type of knowledge that helps us to cope productively with these challenges operates at multiple levels, involving both cognition and behavior. Denhardt and Aristigueta (1996) suggested that focusing on skill development is a useful way of thinking about these multiple aspects of self-awareness and knowledge. Think about the way in which people learn any skill-based discipline, whether it be sports, art, music, or management. The first level of skill development in any discipline involves *cognitive knowledge* or an intellectual understanding of the basic technical skills that the discipline requires, such as a correct bat swing, a proper brush stroke, a perfect vibrato, or a proper approach to organizational change. But cognitive understanding alone is not enough. People also must develop the *behavioral skills* needed to accomplish these technical moves on every occasion. They not only must know how to swing the bat or mix colors but also must be able to do so time after time. For the athlete or artist, this requires extensive practice or rehearsal. The same is true of managers, although in their case the most important skills are not swinging a bat or mixing colors but, rather, becoming effective in terms of interpersonal skills. For managers, these skills are developed through watching and modeling others—through workshops, simulations, case studies, and (most important) experience.

But even those who fully understand their discipline and have acquired the necessary behavioral and technical skills through practice and experience might not always follow the correct course of action. The baseball player might strike out, or the musician might suffer from stage fright. Of course, public administrators face similar challenges. For example, any modern manager knows the importance of involving employees in organizational change. But even managers who have done so effectively in the past might—under conditions of complexity, uncertainty, and stress—fail to consult and involve others. Something beyond cognitive knowledge and behavioral practice is needed. Like athletes and artists, public and nonprofit managers need not only cognitive knowledge and behavioral skills but also a certain moral and psychological grounding to enable them to act with consistency and integrity. Their actions must be based on a strong sense of self and the capacity to learn from experience and self-reflection. In our view, a strong sense of self provides the core from which we can cultivate a personal vision, be more creative, and deal with ambiguity and change. To become more effective managers, we must engage in learning about ourselves and in gaining greater maturity and self-confidence based on self-reflection and personal learning. It is clear, then, that *people who seek to manage others must first learn to manage themselves.* Indeed, those who master "self-leadership practices are far more likely to be successful in gaining higher leadership positions and in being considered more effective in those positions" (Van Wart, 2005, p. 364).

Technical ability and intelligence are not enough for success; emotional intelligence—a term coined by Goleman in 1995—is also required. Examine the situation of someone with technical and professional expertise getting promoted to a managerial job and failing. The failure may be attributed to management tasks such as planning, organizing, and controlling the use of resources. But it is likely that it is due to a failure to manage personal relationships as a leader. This is often attributable to a lack of understanding of the individual's own emotions and an inability to appreciate the emotions of the people with whom he or she works (Armstrong, 2004). Emotional intelligence is the key to understanding others' perspectives and needs, resolving conflicts, and wielding influence (Lubit, 2006).

Improving Your Sense of Self

But how can you learn more about yourself and improve your sense of self? Let's begin by examining the four components of emotional intelligence identified by Goleman (adapted from Armstrong, 2004, pp. 75–76).

- Self-management—the ability to control or redirect disruptive impulses and moods and regulate your own behavior, coupled with a propensity to pursue goals with energy and persistence. The seven competencies associated with this component are self-control, trustworthiness, integrity, initiative, adaptability and comfort with ambiguity, openness to change, and a strong desire to achieve.
- Self-awareness—the ability to recognize and understand your moods, emotions, and drives as well as their effect on others. Competencies include self-confidence and knowing yourself.
- Social awareness—the ability to understand the emotional makeup of other people and skills in treating people according to their emotional reaction. This is linked to six competencies: empathy, expertise in building and retaining talent, organizational awareness, cross-cultural sensitivity, valuing diversity, and service to stakeholders.
- Social skills—proficiency in managing relationships and building networks to get the desired result from others, reach personal goals, build rapport, and find common ground. The five competencies associated with this component are leadership, effectiveness in leading change, conflict management, influence/communication, and expertise in building and leading teams. All of these competencies will be discussed in this book.

Please refer to the exercise in Appendix 2.E to evaluate you emotional intelligence.

The following subsections offer some guidance on gaining self-awareness, first by noting the importance of having a clear vision and then by moving to more specific methods and techniques.

The Power of Vision

There are several dimensions of self-awareness. The first is vision. Whereas we all have an implicit vision about the direction of our lives, many psychologists and experts in management stress the importance of consciously creating a personal vision. Just as an organization might create a statement of vision or values, we can do the same thing for ourselves. Creating a vision for ourselves provides us with a sense of direction and helps us to clarify our values. One way of assisting that process is to think in terms of images. Try the following experiment. Stop reading for a moment, and think about the city of Paris. What immediately comes to mind? Most people will think of the Eiffel Tower, the Arc de Triomphe, the Seine, Notre Dame, good food, wine, romance—all images of real places and real sensations. People do not mention the square kilometers, population, or gross domestic product of France. Human memory stores images and senses, not numbers. What implications does this have for our personal vision? It means that to envision the future, "we must draw upon that very natural mental process of creating images" (Kouzes & Posner, 1995, p. 102).

Developing a vision also can help in clarifying our core values, the "deep-seated, pervasive standards that influence every aspect of our lives: our moral judgments, our responses to others, our commitments to personal and organizational goals" (Kouzes & Posner, 1995, p. 212). People who are unsure of their values tend to drift when they are unsure or confused about how to behave. Values help us to determine what to do and what not to do when we are unsure or conflicted about a situation. When we have a clear sense of our values, it becomes easier to make decisions about our lives and to become aware of circumstances in which our behavior is inconsistent with our values. Clarifying our values also serves as the first step in recognizing that many of the ideas we hold dear are values rather than facts. Value clarification, in turn, opens the door to the acceptance of the views and values of others.

We also might ask what our personal vision says about the importance of relationships with others. In today's global economy, leaders must be sensitive to a broad range of political, cultural, organizational, and human issues. But Kanter (1994) emphasized the need to nurture relationships as an essential managerial skill. In her view, public managers are the human connectors in a wired world, and unless they possess relationship-building skills, there is little hope for local, let alone global, alliances.

Where does trust fit into our personal vision? Do we see ourselves and others as trustworthy? Building and maintaining trust is a central issue in human relationships, and in today's contracting environment for service delivery, it is at the heart of efforts to foster collaboration. People who do not trust others often are viewed by others as untrustworthy themselves. Furthermore, psychologists have found that people who are trusting are more likely to be happy and psychologically well adjusted than are those who view the world with suspicion and disrespect. Psychologists also have found that individuals who are willing to self-disclose—to share personal information and feelings with others—are viewed as more trustworthy than those who are not willing to share of themselves. This requires that we let others know what we stand for, what we value, what we want, what we hope for, and what we are willing or not willing to do.

Assessing Yourself

There are a number of well-known and thoroughly researched assessments or inventories available to the individual interested in self-knowledge. Here we discuss six such tools that may be helpful on the journey to self-awareness: personal values (to provide personal standards and moral judgment), personality style (to assist in the acquisition and evaluation of others), interpersonal orientation (to measure interpersonal needs), locus of control (to assess attitudes toward control of an individual's own destiny), career orientation (to match the individual with the organization), and self-disclosure (to reveal ourselves to others).

Personal values lie at the core of a person's behavior and play a significant role in unifying his or her personality. Values are the foundation upon which attitudes and personal preferences are formed and the basis for crucial decisions, life directions, and personal choice. Building on earlier work suggesting that individuals sometimes lose touch with their values, Whetten and Cameron (1998, p. 53) state that "not being cognizant of one's own value priorities can lead to misdirected decisions and frustration in the long term." We will be discussing two areas influenced by values in this section: value development as it refers to moral judgment and values as a source for career choice.

Behavior displayed by individuals is believed to be a product of their values maturity (Whetten & Cameron, 1998). Value maturity is sometimes referred to as virtues that are believed to be internal but are not innate and have outward consequences. Oakley and Cocking (2001, p. 18) explain that "virtues are character traits which we need to live humanly flourishing lives." Aristotle's virtue theory prioritized the good over the right, a distinction that remains important today (see Mangini, 2000; Oakley & Cocking, 2001). For example, as a school administrator you may instruct your kitchen staff to donate the leftover lunches to the homeless shelter in your community, although throwing away the food may save the staff time and effort. Using Kohlberg's model discussed below, we may say that this virtuous person who made the decision on the personal value of providing for the hungry is operating at the postconventional stage of moral development.

We differ in our level of value maturity, so different instrumental values, values that prescribe desirable standards of conduct or methods for attaining an end, are held by individuals at different stages of development. Kohlberg's (1971) model of moral development focuses on the kind of reasoning used to reach a decision with value or moral connotations. At the *preconventional level,* moral reasoning and instrumental values are based on personal needs or wants and on the consequences of these acts. For example, cheating on an exam is considered OK at this stage because it achieves the personal need of passing the exam and it does not hurt the person whose paper one copied. At the *conventional level* of moral development, people behave morally by conforming to standards as determined by society, and respect from others is valued. Cheating on an exam is wrong because there are rules against it, and respect for one's ability will be lost from the professor and peers. Denhardt and Denhardt (2005b) explain that this level has two stages: one where we simply meet the expectations of others and a second where we learn the conventional rules and laws of society. Most adults continue to operate at this level of moral development. The third and final stage is the *postconventional.* In this stage, right and wrong are judged on the basis of the internalized principles of the individual. Thus, cheating on the exam continues to be wrong, but not because of rules and regulations or respect, but because one has developed this principled judgment. According to Kohlberg, few individuals reach this level of moral maturity. You will have the opportunity to relate the model to a case in this chapter.

What we value has a direct bearing on the decisions we make, whether we are at work or at home. The inventory that we will discuss in this section is for determining the individual values as related to career choice. For example, a person who is financially oriented might be better suited for a sales position than for a position as a caseworker in a social service agency. The opposite would be true for a person with a human orientation, who likely would find the caseworker's assignment to be highly motivating and would not like the sales position. Reddin's (1978) Personal Values Inventory describes six different value orientations:

- *Theoretical:* Interested in ordering and systematizing knowledge, likes to reason and think, and is rational and analytical
- *Power oriented:* Interested in the use, implications, and manifestations of power
- *Achievement oriented:* Practical, efficient, and concerned with obtaining results
- *Human oriented:* Views people and relationships in a positive manner, a humanitarian
- *Industry oriented:* Likes to work and sees work as an end in itself
- *Financial oriented:* Interested in the power of money and in rewards for effort and personal gain

A copy of Reddin's inventory is provided in Appendix 2.A. Using this inventory to identify our values allows us to make career decisions that might be more in line with our personal preferences. The inventory contains instructions for answering the statements. (Remember that there are no right or wrong values here.) Once you have completed the statements, score your answers using the form at the end of the survey. Be sure to add your subtotals to compute your total factor score. When you add up all of your factors, your score should equal 84. The highest scored factor is your preference. For example, if Factor F is your highest total factor score, then you are interested in the power of money and in reward for effort and personal gain. On the other hand, if Factor D is your highest factor score, then you place a higher value on people and relationships. Consider your scores and, if possible, discuss them with someone else.

Personality style refers to the manner in which individuals gather and process information. Swiss psychologist Carl Jung described several aspects of the human psyche based on the way in which we take in and process information (Jung, 1971).

For example, information may be acquired through our senses or though our intuition. Information then is processed through rational processes or through feelings. Jung's framework also includes our orientation to the external world (extroverts) and those oriented toward the internal world (introverts) as well as two modes of decision making, one relying on perception and the other relying on judgment. Over time, individuals become more dependent on one way of collecting and processing information than on other ways. They also come to depend on one orientation to the external world and on one decision-making style. That is not to say that one way is better than another way, and indeed, we all possess all of these capacities to some degree. But over time, we become more comfortable with one approach and come to rely on that approach. Our preferences are then reflected in our personalities.

Our personality types, then, affect the way in which we see the world and, consequently, the way we act. (We typically do not change these preferences unless we make a concerted effort to do so.) For example, those who rely on "sensing" are likely to focus on specific data and what is immediately present; those who rely on "intuition" are more likely to focus on the future, to see the potential in a situation, and to be highly creative. Imagine two people looking in the window of a house they are thinking about buying. One (the sensing type) might see all the flaws—torn carpets, peeling paint, and so on. The other (the intuitive type) might think in terms of possibilities (e.g., "We could do great things with this house"). Two people can look at the same situation and see it in completely different ways.

The Myers-Briggs Type Inventory is a widely used, self-administered inventory to assess an individual's Jungian personality types. David Keirsey has a similar instrument available online through his Web page (www.keirsey.com). After the inventory is scored, information is included on the meaning of the preferences identified. After taking the inventory, you will be able to read about your personality profile online. The Keirsey inventory first identifies you as one of four basic temperaments: artisan, guardian, rational, or idealistic. Figure 2.2 includes some typical characteristics for the types.

Again, there are no right or wrong answers in this inventory; it is simply intended to give us insights about our perspectives and preferences. Again, we all possess all of the orientations that Jung described: extroversion and introversion, intuition and sensing, thinking and feeling, and perception and judgment. Some people prefer one style, whereas others prefer other styles. But all of the types are necessary for success in organizations. Tosi, Mero, and Rizzo provided us with examples of how the different types reinforce each other:

> The sensing type needs an intuitive to generate possibilities, to supply ingenuity, to deal with complexity, and to furnish new ideas. Intuitives add a long-range perspective and spark things that seem impossible.

> The intuitive needs a sensing type to bring facts to inspect, to attend to detail, to inject patience, and to notice what needs attention.

> The thinker needs a feeling type to persuade and conciliate feelings, to arouse enthusiasm and to sell or advertise, and to teach and forecast.

Artisans (SP)
Tend to be
- Playful
- Optimistic
- Sensual
- Unconventional
- Daring
- Impulsive
- Excitable
- Adaptable

Guardians (SJ)
Tend to be
- Responsible
- Helpful
- Hardworking
- Sociable
- Loyal
- Stable
- Traditional
- Law-abiding

Rationals (NT)
Tend to be
- Pragmatic
- Skeptical
- Analytical
- Independent
- Strong-willed
- Logical
- Even-tempered
- Curious

Idealists (NF)
Tend to be
- Enthusiastic
- Romantic
- Intuitive
- Kind-hearted
- Intense
- Authentic
- Symbolic
- Inspiring

Figure 2.2   Personality Types

NOTE: SP = sensation, perceiver; SJ = sensation, judging; NT = intuitive, thinker; NF = intuitive, feeler.

SOURCE: *Please Understand Me II,* by D. W. Keirsey, 1998, Del Mar, CA: Prometheus Nemesis Books. Used with permission.

The feeling type needs a thinker to analyze and organize, to predict flaws in advance, to introduce fact and logic, to hold to a policy, and to stand firm against opposition. (2000, p. 50)

Interpersonal orientation refers to behavior and interpersonal relationships, not just personal and psychological inclinations regarding others. Moreover, it identifies the underlying tendencies that the individual has to behave in certain ways regardless of circumstances or presence of others. Schutz's (1958) classic theory of interpersonal orientation states that three interpersonal needs must be satisfied if the individual is to function effectively and avoid unsatisfactory relationships: the need for inclusion, the need for control, and the need for affection. These needs have two aspects: a desire to express the behavior through the individual's own actions and a desire to receive the behavior from others. It is healthy to have consistency in what we desire in terms of expressed and received behavior. For example, if we value working alone and would prefer not to be included, then we might find ourselves highly frustrated in an environment that promotes and requires inclusion. These preferences and tendencies may be assessed through Schutz's

Fundamental Interpersonal Relations Orientation–Behavior (FIRO-B) inventory, which is included as Appendix 2.B. Again, there are no right or wrong answers, but if you can become more aware of your preferences and the way in which your behavior exhibits your preferences, then you will be more likely to understand the way in which others respond to you.

Locus of control refers to our attitudes toward the extent to which we have control of our own destiny. An internal locus of control reflects the belief that what happens in our lives is the result of our own actions (e.g., "I am personally responsible for the grade that I receive in this class"). An external locus of control reflects the belief that what happens is the product of outside forces (e.g., "The poor grade on the exam was the result of the teacher not explaining the material"). Locus of control studies indicate that those with internal locus of control are more likely to (a) be attentive to aspects of their environment that provide useful information for the future, (b) engage in actions to improve their environment, (c) place greater emphasis on striving for achievement, (d) be more inclined to develop their own skills, (e) ask more questions, and (f) remember more information (Rotter, 1966; Seeman, 1962). In North American culture, people who interpret information about change as if they are in control of it and who perceive themselves to be in charge of their own performances and outcomes are more likely to be successful managers (Hendricks, 1985; Spector, 1982). In the workplace, internal locus of control is correlated with better adjustment to work in terms of satisfaction, coping with stress, job involvement, and promotability (Anderson, 1977). Employees with internal locus of control also have less absenteeism and are more involved at work (Blau, 1987). The Locus of Control inventory is included as Appendix 2.C.

Career orientation is a self-perceived talent, motive, or value that serves to guide, stabilize, and integrate a person's career (Schein, 1978). In any organization, we are likely to find very different types of people with different goals, lifestyles, talents, and values. According to Schein,

> Sometimes these differences are masked by titles or by stereotypes of what kind of person we expect to see in any given kind of job. Yet if the organization and societal policies are to be realistic in terms of human needs, greater attention must be paid to the real differences that arise as we enter our careers. (1978, p. 165)

Schein described eight typical "career anchors" or different orientations to those things that a person desires from his or her career. These career anchors reflect the underlying needs, values, talents, and motives that the person brings into adulthood, but they develop largely through the work experience. According to Schein,

> It is in the process of integrating into the total self-concept what one sees oneself to be more or less competent at, wanting out of life, one's value system, and the kind of person one is that begins to determine the major life and occupational choices throughout adulthood. (p. 171)

The eight anchors are as follows:

Technical/functional competence: The person is driven by the opportunity to apply skills and continues to develop those skills to an ever-higher level.

General manager competence: The person desires to climb to a leadership level in an organization so as to enable integration and coordination of the efforts of others.

Autonomy/independence: The person needs to be able to define his or her own work and needs to do it in his or her own way. Flexibility is the key.

Security/stability: The person needs security or tenure in a job or an organization.

Entrepreneurial creativity: The person desires the opportunity to create an organization or enterprise of his or her own—built on the person's abilities—and is willing to take the necessary risks and obstacles.

Service/dedication to a cause: The person is driven by a desire to pursue work that achieves something of value, such as helping others.

Pure challenge: The person needs work that requires the opportunity to solve seemingly unsolvable problems.

Lifestyle: The person requires the opportunity to balance and integrate his or her personal and family needs as well as the requirements of the career.

Understanding our own career anchors will help us to make good decisions about our careers. The identification of career anchors early in our careers is helpful in moving through our careers. It also can be useful for managers to become aware of their subordinates' career anchors so that the appropriate career moves can be fostered by the organization. Schein (1978) designed a Career Orientation Inventory that assesses the career anchor of the individual. This inventory is included as Appendix 2.D.

Self-disclosure requires that we reveal ourselves to others through verbal or nonverbal means. We disclose our beliefs, values, and desires not only through conversation but also through artifacts and nonverbal communication. For example, the pictures that we have in our offices speak of our families, preferred landscapes, places we have traveled, and so on. We become human by sharing our interests and desires with others. Self-disclosure also affects the way in which others see us. For example, studies have shown that people are more likely to trust leaders who are self-disclosing (Kouzes & Posner, 1995).

To practice self-disclosure, spend an evening with a relative or close friend discussing the results of your personal assessment instruments and their implications. Your relative or friend might want to complete the instruments in this chapter as well. Use questions such as the following: Who am I? What are my values? What are my strengths? What are my weaknesses? What will be necessary for me to be happy in a career or in my personal life? What changes do I need to make in my life? What legacy do I want to leave?

In addition to employing instruments such as those included in this chapter, we can enhance our self-awareness by being attentive to feedback that we receive from others either informally through personal conversations or formally through performance evaluations. The information gained through these interactions can provide us with knowledge about how we are perceived by others and, therefore, offer opportunities for improvement. For example, we might find that others perceive us as concentrating so strongly on the details that we lose sight of the overall mission with which we have been charged. Or our lack of participation in the organization's activities might be viewed as a lack of interest in others. We might not always like the information that we learn through feedback and self-discovery, but that information can be quite valuable. The key is to use the newly acquired information to enhance our personal growth and competence.

Whatever its source, self-knowledge is essential to your productive personal and interpersonal functioning, especially understanding and empathizing with others. Based on your experiences, feedback from others, information from the inventories, and your personal vision, are there skills and competencies that you would like to enhance? Did you gain knowledge that you will draw on in making important career decisions? What changes in your life do you want to make as a result of your increased knowledge?

Ways of Acting

Although strategies for learning about yourself and enhancing self-knowledge remain somewhat less fully developed than strategies for building cognitive knowledge and behavioral skills, there are several suggestions that you might consider.

1. *Focus on learning from your administrative experience.* To learn from your experience, you must engage in self-reflection and self-critique. Your past experiences must be translated into an action agenda for personal development. Annual evaluations at work may be a good place to begin the journey, but other means also are available. These include asking or surveying others about your work performance as well as the attitudes and values you express. Schön's (1983) classic term "reflective practitioner" nicely sums up what your aspirations should be as you learn about yourself from your administrative experience.

2. *Keep a journal.* A journal allows you the opportunity to engage in self-reflection and self-critique over a sustained period of time. Writing in a journal also gives structure to your examination of events. See Denhardt (2000) for a suggested format for the administrative journal.

3. *Talk regularly with people you trust.* In addition to self-reflection and self-critique, the insights and support of trusted friends can be a great boost to developing your confidence and self-esteem.

4. *Watch and read how others handle change.* Learning from the experiences of respected managers and leaders also is helpful. In the rapidly changing world in

which we live, it is important to be able to handle change. Others who have been successful before us provide important lessons toward this end.

5. *Strive for balance and insight.* As we will see in Chapter 4, although the pressure to perform might seem overwhelming, effective performance can be undermined by excessive "Type A" behavior. It also can be harmful to your health. Take time to relax and to participate in activities that are not work related. Relaxation will provide for renewed energy with which to improve productivity and creativity.

6. *Set an example.* As a manager, you should not only be concerned with developing your own maturity and self-confidence; you should also encourage and energize others to develop theirs. Such an understanding of yourself not only helps you as an employee but also can help the organization.

7. *Carefully examine the explanations that you give.* You might refuse an assignment by saying, "I am too busy to take on this assignment," when, in fact, the assignment simply might not be of interest to you. Recall Reddin's (1978) Values Inventory and Schein's (1978) career anchors. Although we all have aspects of our jobs that are less enjoyable, knowing our values and preferences can help us to make prudent job choices.

8. *Look for several causes.* When attempting to interpret behavior, look for various causes that might have triggered the behavior. For example, if someone takes too long to complete an assignment, do not be too quick to determine that the person was uninterested in completing the assignment in a timely manner. Perhaps the delay was due to faulty equipment, pressures from peers to complete other assignments, or other external forces.

9. *Account for individual differences.* Try to account for individual differences and do not overgeneralize or project your own preferences onto others. For example, you might like to be publicly recognized for your achievements, but a highly introverted employee might be quite embarrassed by such public recognition.

10. *Use past behavior as an indicator, but not necessarily a predictor, of future behavior.* How someone behaved in the past might indicate how he or she will behave in the future, but you should not ignore the possibility of change. For example, if someone has not been timely in producing necessary work, then you might assume that he or she will continue to delay the process. But the person might decide that it is in the best interest of everyone concerned to turn in the next assignment on time.

11. *Recognize personality differences.* Consider personality differences when selecting assignments. For example, recall the Locus of Control inventory. There are some people who will be much more internally motivated than others. If you are one of these individuals, then you might prefer to work in autonomous situations. On the other hand, if you are an externally motivated individual, then you might function best in team assignments.

12. *Celebrate diversity and what contributions diversity brings to the organization.* We are working in an environment with increasing differences in age, race, gender, nationality, political views, and religion. Rather than fearing or judging differences, evaluate how those differences may add to the organization.

Thinking in Action

In this section, we make use of what we have learned through exercises and case studies.

Increasing Self-Knowledge

This is an exercise that may be used as a class assignment or project paper. Students will increase their self-knowledge by answering the following questions:

Where have I been? The timeline described earlier in the chapter will help in answering this question. Develop a 5- to 10-page autobiographical sketch that will assist you in improving your sense of self by reflecting on the past and how it will influence the future.

Where am I going? Develop interview guides and interview several individuals in positions to which you might aspire. Following are some examples of questions to include:
  – How would you describe your typical day at work?
  – What are the most critical skills you draw on during a typical workday?
  – What qualities do you see as necessary for your line of work?
  – If you had to find someone to replace you, on what key abilities would you focus?

Do I have what it takes in terms of ability, motivation, and personal traits to get there? This question may be answered through inventories or evaluations or through questioning others who are familiar with your abilities.

Do not be afraid to engage in self-disclosure. "Several studies have shown that low self-disclosers are less healthy and more self-alienated than high self-disclosers. College students give the highest ratings for interpersonal competence to high self-disclosers" (Whetten & Cameron, 1998, p. 51).

Write out an action plan for implementation to help you accomplish your vision.

A Vision Statement

Work with close friends and colleagues to determine what your personal lifetime vision might look like. Try to focus on what you believe an ideal future would look like, or consider looking back on your life and career at an advanced age. What are the things that you would like to have done? Write your vision statement:

Write down a set of values that are important to you. Ask family members and friends to encourage you to live according to your values.

Describe key areas of your life that are important to you, and write down one or two goals in each major area.

Select one or two goals and imagine the goal(s) being achieved to your full satisfaction. How does this goal, or how do these goals, relate to your vision? Experience the achievement of your vision in every way possible.

Develop a detailed action plan to achieve this vision, and make commitments for particular actions necessary to bring your vision to fruition.

Valuing Diversity

In managing a diverse workforce it is important that we understand our own feelings and the messages that we convey about our value of diversity. Reflect on how you and the organization that you work for react in terms of accepting differences and otherness (adapted from Deep & Sussman, 2000):

1. Do others see you acting comfortable around colleagues with nontraditional demographics (examples include others of a different age, education, ethnicity, gender, race)?

2. Do colleagues of nontraditional demographics provide evidence that they feel comfortable around you?

3. Do these same employees report that their differences are respected?

4. Do you actively solicit the opinions, feelings, and suggestions of all colleagues, regardless of demographics?

5. Do you receive a relatively equal amount of opinions, feelings, and suggestions from all employees?

6. Does the organization that you work for hire and promote in such a way that employee diversity reflects the diversity of society?

7. Do the organization's social activities reflect diversity?

8. Do the organization's fringe benefits reflect diversity?

9. Are there consequences for colleagues who engage in demeaning or prejudicial behavior toward others?

10. Does your organization maintain a committee charged with improving the working climate for all employees?

Cases

Privatizing the Cafeteria. Ramon Smith is city manager of a midsize town in Louisiana. The city that he is managing has run its own cafeteria for many years. The staff has been with the city for 20 to 30 years and is in their forties and fifties. The city's evaluation unit at his request has conducted a study showing that great saving would be available to the city by privatizing the cafeteria services. Ramon knows the staff well, and their level of skill would make it very difficult for them to attain jobs in the same industry with the pay and benefits that the city currently pays them.

Employing Kohlberg's model of moral development, answer the following questions:

1. What decisions would a city manager at the *preconventional* level be expected to make?

2. What reaction would you expect of employees at the *preconventional* level?

3. What decisions would a city manager at the *conventional* level be expected to make?

4. What reaction would you expect of employees at the *conventional* level?

5. What decisions would a city manager at the *postconventional* level be expected to make?

6. What reaction would you expect of employees at the *postconventional* level?

7. What reaction will you make as the city manager?

8. How will you explain your decision to the city council?

Laura's Employment Dilemma. Laura Gomez just completed her MPA program at the University of Southern California. She entered the program as a midcareer student after spending 12 years as a state employee in Sacramento. During those 12 years, she worked in a budget office, where she found the work to be tedious and routine. She wanted a change and thought that the best way of going into the job market was to have an MPA in hand. During her academic program, she concentrated on public management. At home, she is a single parent with two children, 8 and 10 years of age. She feels a great deal of responsibility for these children and wants to be available to participate in their lives on a daily basis.

Laura has been interviewing, and with her experience and education she has had several job offers. The first came from a management consulting firm in the Midwest. The management consulting firm is interested in more work in the public sector, and Laura's experience in a state budget office was viewed as highly valuable. The salary is higher than she had been expecting to receive as an entry-level MPA graduate. She would be expected to travel the Midwest approximately 80 percent of the time.

The second job offer came from a nonprofit organization in Los Angeles. This nonprofit has been in existence for about 5 years and now is in the position of hiring someone to handle all aspects of its finances, including fundraising. Laura does not have experience in fundraising but has been recommended to the organization as a quick learner. The salary is lower than what she was making before she returned to school 2 years ago. There are expectations that, with successful fundraising, her salary would increase. The office location is 3 miles from her current residence. The job would require very little traveling.

The third job offer came from the federal government in Washington, D.C. In this position, Laura would be fully trained to work in evaluation for the Department of Health and Human Services. This is not an area in which she has worked before, but she is known to pay a great deal of attention to detail, to have good interpersonal skills, and to be a fast learner. The salary is higher than what she was making prior to entering the MPA program but not as high as that offered by the consulting firm in the Midwest.

You are Laura Gomez. Given what you know about yourself from information in this chapter, respond to the following questions:

1. Which position would you take?

2. Why?

3. How does this fit with your preferences, career anchors, and values?

4. Is your choice different from that which you would recommend to Laura?

5. If yes, then why?

APPENDIX 2.A
Reddin's Personal Values Inventory

INSTRUCTIONS FOR ANSWERING

Read the first set of three statements (A, B, C) and decide to what extent you agree with each. Assign exactly three points among the three statements. The more points you give a statement, the more you agree with it.

EXAMPLE 1: Suppose that you agree with Statement A but not at all with any of the others; then, you would distribute your points in this way:

STATEMENT A
STATEMENT B
STATEMENT C

A3	B0	C0			

EXAMPLE 2: Suppose that in another group of statements, you agree somewhat with Statement B, disagree with Statement C, and do not totally disagree with Statement A; then, you would distribute the three points this way:

STATEMENT A
STATEMENT B
STATEMENT C

A1	B2	C0			

SURVEY

1. A. Examples and events of history press down on the mind the weight of truth.
   B. As wealth is power, so all power will draw wealth to itself.
   C. Success is always achievement.

A	B	C			

2. A. By what means can the man please who has no power to confer benefits?
   B. A manager's only job is to be effective.
   C. What will money not do?

	A	B			C

3. A. The worst of faces is still human.
   B. Never put off to tomorrow what you can do today.
   C. Money answers all things.

			A	B	C

4. A. Everything includes itself in power.
   B. Life teaches us to be less severe with ourselves and others.
   C. It is pretty to see what money will do.

	A		B		C

5. A. Truth is always strange—stranger than fiction.
   B. It is not enough to do good; one must do it well.
   C. Work keeps at bay three great evils: boredom, vice, and need.

A		B		C	

6. A. The smallest atom of truth represents some man's bitter toil and agony.
   B. We never do anything well till we cease to think about the manner of doing it.
   C. All work is noble; work alone is noble.

A		B		C	

7. A. The father aims at power, the son at independence.
   B. The only way to have a friend is to be one.
   C. Money is indeed the most important thing in the world.

	A		B		C

8. A. All truths begin as blasphemies.
   B. The ornament of a house is the friend who frequents it.
   C. There are few sorrows in which good income is of no avail.

A			B		C

9. A. Disinterested intellectual curiosity is the lifeblood of real civilization.
   B. Labor conquers everything.
   C. Money is like a sixth sense—and you cannot make use of the other five without it.

A				B	C

10. A. God gives to some men despotic power over other men.
    B. He who attempts to do all will waste his life doing little.
    C. Instead of loving your enemies, treat your friends a little better.

	A	B	C		

11. A. A man of words and not of deeds is like a garden full of weeds.
    B. Man's happiness is to do a man's true work.
    C. If you mean to profit, you are wise.

		A		B	C

12. A. The only means of strengthening one's intellect is to make up one's mind about nothing.
    B. To know the pains of power, we must go to those who have it.
    C. If you have one true friend, you have more than your share.

A	B		C		

13. A. The prize of the general is not a bigger tent but command.
    B. The reasonable man adapts himself to the world; the unreasonable man tries to adapt the world to himself.
    C. No man is born into the world whose work is not born with him.

	A	B		C	

14. A. The highest intellects, like the tops of mountains, are the first to catch and reflect the dawn.
    B. A man should keep his friendship in constant repair.
    C. Work brings its own relief; he who is most idle has most of the grief.

A			B	C	

15. A. Man is a social animal.
    B. Actions speak louder than words.
    C. Wherever I found a living creature, there I found the will to power.

		A	B	C	

16. A. There are many wonderful things in nature, but the most wonderful of all is man.
    B. The shortest answer is doing.
    C. Irrationally held truths may be more harmful than reasoned errors.

		A	B		C

17. A. Every man's work is always a portrait of himself.
    B. To know the pleasure of power, we must go to those who are seeking it.
    C. To think is to live.

	A			B	C

18. A. Go to your work and be strong.
    B. The great end in life is not knowledge but action.
    C. Guns will make us powerful; butter will only make us fat.

	A		B	C	

19. A. The mind of a man is cheered and refreshed by profiting in small things.
    B. All work is as seed sown; it grows and spreads, and it sows itself anew.
    C. Life is not long, and too much of it must not pass in idle deliberation over how it shall be spent.

A	B		C		

20. A. There is no substitute for hard work.
    B. The highest duty is to respect authority.
    C. Knowledge is capable of being its own end.

A	B		C		

21. A. Ill blows the wind that profits nobody.
    B. Genius is 1 percent inspiration and 99 percent perspiration.
    C. Logical consequences are the scarecrows of fools and the beacons of wise men.

A	B				C

22. A. Time is money.
    B. The true science and study of mankind is man.
    C. Bustle is not industry.

A		B	C		

23. A. In all labor, there is profit.
    B. Human existence always is irrational and often painful, but in the last analysis it remains interesting.
    C. He who has the longest sword is the leader.

A		B		C	

24. A. Money speaks in a language that all nations understand.
    B. To cultivate kindness is a valuable part of life.
    C. A good catchword can obscure analysis for 50 years.

A		B			C

25. A. They say that knowledge is power, but they meant money.
    B. Every man is the architect of his own fortune.
    C. Make a model before building.

A			B		C

26. A. It is a bad bargain where nobody gains.
    B. In the country of the blind, the one-eyed man is king.
    C. It requires a very unusual mind to undertake the analysis of the obvious.

A				B	C

27. A. What we have to learn to do, we learn by doing.
    B. It is more blessed to give than to receive.
    C. Whatever is worth doing at all is worth doing well.

	A	B	C		

28. A. Doubt can be ended by work alone.
    B. To err is human, to forgive is divine.
    C. Power is a grand objective.

	A	B		C	

VALUES INVENTORY: SCORING

A_1 = 1A + 5A + 6A
= ___ + ___ + ___   = ___ = A_1

B_1 = 1B + 2A + 4A + 7A
= ___ + ___ + ___ + ___   = ___ = B_1

C_1 = 1C + 2B + 5B + 6B
= ___ + ___ + ___ + ___   = ___ = C_1

D_1 = 3A + 4B + 7B
= ___ + ___ + ___   = ___ = D_1

E_1 = 3B + 5C + 6C
= ___ + ___ + ___   = ___ = E_1

F_1 = 2C + 3C + 4C + 7C
= ___ + ___ + ___ + ___   = ___ = F_1

A_2 = 24C + 25C + 26C
= ___ + ___ + ___   = ___ = A_2

B_2 = 23C + 26B + 28C
= ___ + ___ + ___   = ___ = B_2

C_2 = 22C + 25B + 27C
= ___ + ___ + ___   = ___ = C_2

D_2 = 22B + 23B + 24B + 27B + 28B
= ___ + ___ + ___ + ___ + ___   = ___ = D_2

E_2 = 27A + 28A

= ___ + ___   = ___ = E_2

F_2 = 22A + 23A + 24A + 25A + 26A

= ___ + ___ + ___ + ___ + ___   = ___ = F_2

A_3 = 8A + 9A + 12A + 14A

= ___ + ___ + ___ + ___   = ___ = A_3

B_3 = 10A + 12B + 13A

= ___ + ___ + ___   = ___ = B_3

C_3 = 10B + 11A + 13B

= ___ + ___ + ___   = ___ = C_3

D_3 = 8B + 10C + 12C + 14B

= ___ + ___ + ___ + ___   = ___ = D_3

E_3 = 9B + 11B + 13C + 14C

= ___ + ___ + ___ + ___   = ___ = E_3

F_3 = 8C + 9C + 11C

= ___ + ___ + ___   = ___ = F_3

A_4 = 16C + 17C + 20C + 21C

= ___ + ___ + ___ + ___   = ___ = A_4

B_4 = 15C + 17B + 18C + 20B

= ___ + ___ + ___ + ___   = ___ = B_4

C_4 = 15B + 16B + 18B + 19C

= ___ + ___ + ___ + ___   = ___ = C_4

D_4 = 15A + 16A

= ___ + ___   = ___ = D_4

E_4 = 17A + 18A + 19B + 20A + 21B

= ___ + ___ + ___ + ___ + ___   = ___ = E_4

F_4 = 19A + 21A

= ___ + ___   = ___ = F_4

NOTE: The scoring sheet was developed by Donald Coons.

WHAT DO THE ANSWERS MEAN?

Add up your subtotals for all of the factors, and your score should equal 84. The highest single factor is your preferred value:

Factor A   *Theoretical:* Interested in ordering and systemizing knowledge, likes to reason and think, and is rational and analytical

Factor B   *Power oriented:* Interested in the use, implications, and manifestations of power

Factor C   *Achievement oriented:* Practical, efficient, and concerned with obtaining results

Factor D   *Human oriented:* Views people and relationships in a positive manner; a humanitarian

Factor E   *Industry oriented:* Likes to work and sees work as an end in itself s

Factor F   *Financial oriented:* Interested in the power of money and in rewards for effort and personal gain

---

SOURCE: From *Values Inventory*, by W. J. Reddin, 1978, La Jolla, CA: Learning Resources.

APPENDIX 2.B
Fundamental Interpersonal Relations
Orientation (FIRO)–Behavior

Instructions. For each statement below, decide which of the following answers best applies to you. Place the number of the answer to the left of the statement. When you have finished, turn to the scoring key.

Rating Scale

1—Usually	4—Occasionally
2—Often	5—Rarely
3—Sometimes	6—Never

1. ___ I try to be with people.
2. ___ I let other people decide what to do.
3. ___ I join social groups.
4. ___ I try to have close relationships with people.
5. ___ I tend to join social organizations when I have an opportunity.
6. ___ I let other people strongly influence my actions.
7. ___ I try to be included in informal social activities.
8. ___ I try to have close, personal relationships with people.
9. ___ I try to include other people in my plans.
10. ___ I let other people control my actions.
11. ___ I try to have people around me.
12. ___ I try to get close and personal with people.
13. ___ When people are doing things together, I tend to join them.
14. ___ I am easily led by people.
15. ___ I try to avoid being alone.
16. ___ I try to participate in group activities.

Instructions. For each of the next group of statements, choose one of the following answers:

Rating Scale

1—Most people	4—A few people
2—Many people	5—One or two people
3—Some people	6—Nobody

17. ___ I try to be friendly to people.
18. ___ I let other people decide what to do.

19. ___ My personal relations with people are cool and distant.

20. ___ I let other people take charge of things.

21. ___ I try to have close relationships with people.

22. ___ I let other people strongly influence my actions.

23. ___ I try to get close and personal with people.

24. ___ I let other people control my actions.

25. ___ I act cool and distant with people.

26. ___ I am easily led by people.

27. ___ I try to have close, personal relationships with people.

28. ___ I like people to invite me to things.

29. ___ I like people to act close and personal with me.

30. ___ I try to strongly influence other people's actions.

31. ___ I like people who invite me to join in their activities.

32. ___ I like people to act close toward me.

33. ___ I try to take charge of things when I am with people.

34. ___ I like people to include me in their activities.

35. ___ I like people to act cool and distant toward me.

36. ___ I try to have other people do things the way I want them done.

37. ___ I like people to ask me to participate in their decisions.

38. ___ I like people to act friendly toward me.

39. ___ I like people to invite me to participate in their activities.

40. ___ I like people to act distant toward me.

Instructions. For each of the next group of statements, choose one of the following answers:

Rating Scale

1—Usually	4—Occasionally
2—Often	5—Rarely
3—Sometimes	6—Never

41. ___ I try to be the dominant person when I am with people.

42. ___ I like people to invite me to things.

43. ___ I like people to act close toward me.

44. ___ I try to have other people do things I want done.

45. ___ I like people to invite me to join their activities.

46. ___ I like people to act cool and distant toward me.

47. ___ I try to strongly influence other people's actions.

48. ___ I like people to include me in their activities.

49. ___ I like people to act close and personal with me.

50. ___ I try to take charge of things when I am with people.

51. ___ I like people to invite me to participate in their activities.

52. ___ I like people to act distant toward me.

53. ___ I try to have other people do things the way I want them done.

54. ___ I take charge of things when I am with people.

SCORING KEY

To derive your interpersonal orientation scores, refer to the following table. Note that there are six major columns, each with separate columns for items and keys. Each column refers to an interpersonal need. Items in the column refer to question numbers on the questionnaire; keys refer to answers on each of those items. If you answered an item using any of the alternatives in the corresponding key column, circle the item number on this sheet.

Expressed Inclusion		Wanted Inclusion	
Item	Key	Item	Key
1	1-2-3	28	1-2
3	1-2-3-4	31	1-2
5	1-2-3-4	34	1-2
7	1-2-3	37	1
9	1-2	39	1
11	1-2	42	1-2
13	1-2	45	1-2
15	1	48	1-2
16	1	51	1-2
Expressed Control		Wanted Control	
Item	Key	Item	Key
30	1-2-3	2	1-2-3-4
33	1-2-3	6	1-2-3-4
36	1-2	10	1-2-3
41	1-2-3-4	14	1-2-3
44	1-2-3	18	1-2-3

Expressed Control	
Item	Key
47	1-2-3
50	1-2
53	1-2
54	1-2

Wanted Control	
Item	Key
20	1-2-3
22	1-2-3-4
24	1-2-3
26	1-2-3

Expressed Affection	
Item	Key
4	1-2
8	1-2
12	1
17	1-2
19	4-5-6
21	1-2
23	1-2
25	4-5-6
27	1-2

Wanted Affection	
Item	Key
29	1-2
32	1-2
35	5-6
38	1-2
40	5-6
43	1
46	5-6
49	1-2
52	5-6

TABLE FOR SUMMARY SCORES

When you have checked all of the items for a single column, count up the number of circled items and place that number in the corresponding box in the chart. These numbers will give you your strength of interpersonal need in each of the six areas. The highest possible score is 9; the lowest possible score is 0. Refer to the explanations in the chapter to interpret your scores and for some comparison data.

	Inclusion	*Control*	*Affection*
Expressed			
Wanted			

SOURCE: Schutz, W. C. (1958). *FIRO: A Three-Dimensional Theory of Interpersonal Behavior* (3rd ed.). New York: Holt, Rinehart & Winston.

INTERPRETING RESULTS

Schutz's (1958) classic theory of interpersonal orientation states that three interpersonal needs exist that must be satisfied if the individual is to function effectively and avoid unsatisfactory relationships: the need for inclusion, the need for control, and the need for affection. Each of these needs has two aspects: the desire to express the behavior and the desire to receive the behavior from others. It is healthy to have consistency in what we desire in terms of expressed and received behavior. The closer the scores in each of the need areas, the greater the consistency. If you add up all of the scores, then you will come up with your social interaction index representing your interpersonal need level. The highest possible score is 54; the higher the score, the greater the need for interaction. The opposite also is true; the lower the score, the lesser the need for interaction. Interpersonal compatibility is determined by comparing your score with the scores of others.

APPENDIX 2.C
Locus of Control

Instructions. This questionnaire assesses your opinions about certain issues. Each item consists of a pair of alternatives (*a* or *b*). Select the alternative with which you most agree. If you believe both alternatives to some extent, then select the one with which you agree most strongly. If you do not believe either alternative, then mark the one with which you disagree least strongly. Because this is an assessment of opinions, there obviously are no right or wrong answers. When you have finished all of the items, turn to the scoring key for instructions on how to tabulate the results and for comparison data.

1. a. Leaders are born, not made.
   b. Leaders are made, not born.

2. a. People often succeed because they are in the right place at the right time.
   b. Success is mostly dependent on hard work and ability.

3. a. When things go wrong in my life, it is generally because I have made mistakes.
   b. Misfortunes occur in my life regardless of what I do.

4. a. Wherever there is war or not depends on the actions of certain world leaders.
   b. It is inevitable that the world will continue to experience wars.

5. a. Good children are mainly the products of good parents.
   b. Some children turn out bad no matter how their parents behave.

6. a. My future success depends mainly on circumstances I cannot control.
   b. I am the master of my fate.

7. a. History judges certain people to have been effective leaders mainly because circumstances made them visible and successful.
   b. Effective leaders are those who have made decisions or taken actions that resulted in significant contributions.

8. a. To avoid punishing children guarantees that they will grow up irresponsible.
   b. Spanking children is never appropriate.

9. a. I often feel that I have little influence over the direction my life is taking.
   b. It is unreasonable to believe that fate or luck plays a crucial part in how my life turns out.

10. a. Some customers will never be satisfied no matter what you do.
    b. You can satisfy customers by giving them what they want when they want it.

11. a. Anyone can get good grades in school if he or she works hard enough.
    b. Some people are never going to excel in school no matter how hard they try.

12. a. Good marriages result when both partners continuously work on the relationship.
    b. Some marriages are going to fail because the partners are just incompatible.

13. a. I am confident that I can improve my basic management skills through learning and practice.
    b. It is a waste of time to try to improve management skills in a classroom.

14. a. More management skill courses should be taught in business schools.
    b. Less emphasis should be placed on skills in business schools.

15. a. When I think back on the good things that happened to me, I believe that they happened mainly because of something I did.
    b. The bad things that have happened in my life have resulted mainly from circumstances beyond my control.

16. a. Many exams I took in school were unconnected to the material I had studied, so studying hard did not help at all.
    b. When I prepared well for exams in school, I generally did quite well.

17. a. I sometimes am influenced by what my astrological chart says.
    b. No matter how the stars are lined up, I can determine my own destiny.

18. a. Government is so big and bureaucratic that it is very difficult for any one person to have any impact on what happens.
    b. Single individuals can have a real influence on politics if they will speak up and let their wishes be known.

19. a. People seek responsibility in work.
    b. People try to get away with doing as little as they can.

20. a. The most popular people seem to have a special inherent charisma that attracts people to them.
    b. People become popular because of how they behave.

21. a. Things over which I have little control just seem to occur in my life.
    b. Most of the time, I feel responsible for the outcomes I produce.

22. a. Managers who improve their personal competence will succeed more than those who do not improve.
    b. Management success has very little to do with the competence possessed by the individual manager.

23. a. Teams that win championships in most sports usually are the teams that, in the end, have the most luck.
    b. More often than not, teams that win championships are those with the most talented players and the best preparation.

24. a. Teamwork in business is a prerequisite to success.
    b. Individual effort is the best hope for success.

25. a. Some workers are just lazy and cannot be motivated to work hard no matter what you do.
    b. If you are a skillful manager, you can motivate almost any worker to put forth more effort.

26. a. In the long run, people can improve this country's economic strength through responsible action.
    b. The economic health of this country is largely beyond the control of individuals.

27. a. I am persuasive when I know I am right.
    b. I can persuade most people even when I am not sure I am right.

28. a. I tend to plan ahead and generate steps to accomplish the goals that I have set.
    b. I seldom plan ahead because things generally turn out okay anyway.

29. a. Some things are just meant to be.
    b. We can change anything in our lives by hard work, persistence, and ability.

SCORING KEY

Count up the number of items you selected of those listed below:

2a	5b	9a	12b	16a	20a	23a	28b
3b	6a	10a	13b	17a	21a	25a	29a
4b	7a	11b	15b	18a	22b	26b	

Total Score _____

SOURCE: Whetten, C., and Cameron, K. S. (1998). *Developing Management Skills* (4th ed.). Reading, MA: Addison-Wesley.

INTERPRETING RESULTS

The higher the score, the more the external locus of control. The lower the score, the more the internal locus of control. An internal locus of control reflects the belief that the reinforcements one receives are the result of one's own actions (e.g., "I am personally responsible for the grade that I receive in this class"). An external locus of control reflects the belief that reinforcement is the product of outside forces (e.g., "The poor grade on the exam was the result of the teacher not explaining the material").

APPENDIX 2.D
Career Orientation Inventory

The purpose of this questionnaire is to stimulate your thoughts about your own areas of competence, your motives, and your values. This questionnaire alone will not reveal your career anchor because it is too easy to bias your answers. However, it will activate your thinking and prepare you for the discussion with your partner.

Try to answer the questions as honestly as you can and to work quickly. Avoid extreme ratings except in situations where you clearly have strong feelings in one direction or the other.

HOW TO RATE THE ITEMS

For each of the next 40 items, rate how true that item is for you in general by assigning a number from 1 to 6. The higher the number, the more that item is true for you. For example, if the item says "I dream of being the president of a company," then you would rate that as follows:

1 if the statement is never true for you

2 or 3 if the statement is occasionally true for you

4 or 5 if the statement is often true for you

6 if the statement is always true for you

Please begin your self-report by writing the appropriate rating in the blank to the left of each item.

____   1. I dream of being so good at what I do that my expert advice will be sought continually.

____   2. I am most fulfilled in my work when I have been able to integrate and manage the efforts of others.

____   3. I dream of having a career that will allow me the freedom to do a job my own way and on my own schedule.

____   4. Security and stability are more important to me than freedom and autonomy.

____   5. I am always on the lookout for ideas that would permit me to start my own enterprise.

____   6. I will feel successful in my career only if I have a feeling of having made a real contribution to the welfare of society.

____   7. I dream of a career in which I can solve problems or win out in situations that are extremely challenging.

____   8. I would rather leave my organization than to be put into a job that would compromise my ability to pursue personal and family concerns.

____ 9. I will feel successful in my career only if I can develop my technical or functional skills to a very high level of competence.

____ 10. I dream of being in charge of a complex organization and making decisions that affect many people.

____ 11. I am most fulfilled in my work when I am completely free to define my own tasks, schedules, and procedures.

____ 12. I would rather leave my organization altogether than accept an assignment that would jeopardize my security in that organization.

____ 13. Building my own business is more important to me than achieving a high-level managerial position in someone else's organization.

____ 14. I am most fulfilled in my career when I have been able to use my talents in the service of others.

____ 15. I will feel successful in my career only if I face and overcome very difficult challenges.

____ 16. I dream of a career that will permit me to integrate my personal family and work needs.

____ 17. Becoming a senior functional manager in my area of expertise is more attractive to me than becoming a general manager.

____ 18. I will feel successful in my career only if I become a general manager in some organization.

____ 19. I will feel successful in my career only if I achieve complete autonomy and freedom.

____ 20. I seek jobs in organizations that will give me a sense of security and stability.

____ 21. I am most fulfilled in my career when I have been able to build something that is entirely the result of my own ideas and efforts.

____ 22. Using my skills to make the world a better place to live and work is more important to me than achieving a high-level managerial position.

____ 23. I have been most fulfilled in my career when I have solved seemingly unsolvable problems or won out over seemingly impossible odds.

____ 24. I feel successful in life only if I have been able to balance my personal, family, and career requirements.

____ 25. I would rather leave my organization than accept a rotational assignment that would take me out of my area of expertise.

____ 26. Becoming a general manager is more attractive to me than becoming a senior functional manager in my current area of expertise.

____ 27. The chance to do a job my own way, free of rules and constraints, is more important to me than security.

____ 28. I am most fulfilled in my work when I feel that I have complete financial and employment security.

____ 29. I will feel successful in my career only if I have succeeded in creating or building something that is entirely my own product or idea.

____ 30. I dream of having a career that makes a real contribution to humanity and society.

____ 31. I seek out work opportunities that strongly challenge my problem-solving and/or competitive skills.

____ 32. Balancing the demands of personal and professional life is more important to me than achieving a high-level managerial position.

____ 33. I am most fulfilled in my work when I have been able to use my special skills and talents.

____ 34. I would rather leave my organization than accept a job that would take me away from the general managerial track.

____ 35. I would rather leave my organization than accept a job that would reduce my autonomy and freedom.

____ 36. I dream of having a career that will allow me to feel a sense of security and stability.

____ 37. I dream of starting up and building my own business.

____ 38. I would rather leave my organization than accept an assignment that would undermine my ability to be of service to others.

____ 39. Working on problems that are almost unsolvable is more important to me than achieving a high-level managerial position.

____ 40. I have always sought out work opportunities that would minimize interference with personal or family concerns.

At this point, look over your answers and locate all of the items that you rated highest. Pick out the *three* items that seem most true for you and give each of those items an additional *four* points. You now can score your questionnaire, but the scales will not have a real meaning for you until you have read the text in the next sections.

SCORING INSTRUCTIONS

In the next section, you will find blank spaces for all 40 items, arranged in order so that you can easily transfer the numbers from your rating sheets onto the scoring sheet. After you have transferred all of the numbers, add up the columns and divide by five (the number of items) to get your average score for each of the eight career anchor dimensions. Do not forget to add the extra four points for each of your three key items before you total and average your scores.

SCORING SHEET

The following blanks represent the items you have just rated. Transfer your previous answers to these blanks. Do not forget to add the four points for the three items that were most true for you. Total the numbers in each column and then divide that total by five (the number of items in the column). The resulting average is your self-assessment of how true the items in that scale are for you.

Explanations of the columns are provided on the next page [in the original source].

	TF	GM	AU	SE	EC	SV	CH	LS
	1___	2___	3___	4___	5___	6___	7___	8___
	9___	10___	11___	12___	13___	14___	15___	16___
	17___	18___	19___	20___	21___	22___	23___	24___
	25___	26___	27___	28___	29___	30___	31___	32___
	33___	34___	35___	36___	37___	38___	39___	40___
Total: (divide by 5)	___	___	___	___	___	___	___	___
Average:	___	___	___	___	___	___	___	___

SOURCE: From *Career Dynamics: Matching Individuals and Organizational Needs,* by E. H. Schein, 1978, Reading, MA: Addison-Wesley.

APPENDIX 2.E
Emotional Intelligence

Instructions: Ask yourself how often you respond in a healthy way when severely disappointed, verbally attacked, or treated unfairly by analyzing these attitudes and behaviors:

1. When I am upset, I respond rationally, so that I can remain analytical and solve the problem or otherwise make the best of the situation.

2. I reject the harm than can result from reacting emotionally when I am upset and getting angry or feeling battered.

3. When verbally attacked, I allow for the likelihood that the attackers might never have learned how to respond when their needs aren't met.

4. When verbally attacked, I allow for the probability that the attack is prompted by pain or fear.

5. When verbally attacked, I keep my role as a manager separate from my identity as a person.

6. I resist the temptation to feel entitled to better treatment and to lose emotional control.

7. I understand that victims of my outbursts will remember my accusatory statements and name-calling long after I have calmed down.

8. I accept that others cannot make me angry without my full cooperation. In other words, I control my anger.

9. When I get angry, I talk about my feelings to calm myself down, rather than focus on what the other person did.

Interpreting Results

The first two behaviors lay a firm foundation for emotional intelligence. Behaviors 3–5 are proven strategies for staying in control when under attack. Regardless of the root of your anger, deal with it as suggested in 6–9.

These prescriptions will take practice, and it will help to have a positive role model share how they deal with these difficult situations.

SOURCE: Adapted from *Act on It! Solving 101 of the Toughest Management Challenges* (p. 33), by S. Deep and L. Sussman, 2000, Cambridge, MA: Perseus Publishing. Reprinted with permission.

CHAPTER 3

Fostering Creativity

Creativity is perhaps the most important concept in public administration.

—Marshall Dimock (1986, p. 3)

Creativity is one of the hallmarks of leadership and is a central component in the science and, most particularly, the *art* of public administration. Goodsell (1992) stated, "The concept of creativity infuses and transcends . . . the values and lessons of artisanship for the everyday tasks of administration" (p. 252). The notion of creativity suggests innovation and originality—the ability to see old problems in novel ways and to devise new ways of thinking, analyzing, and doing. Creativity is critical to organizational success as it helps people and organizations to respond to new challenges and opportunities for change. As Denhardt (1993) said, "Today's problems are different—more than anything else, they require creativity. . . . Rigid and unchanging organizations are more likely to fail while those promoting change and innovation succeed" (pp. 131–132). How can we foster creativity in ourselves and others? How can we manage people in public organizations in a manner that enhances and encourages their creativity consistent with public values and accountability?

The creative process is intuitive, is fluid, and thrives on the freedom to think and act outside of normal procedures. For these reasons, some may suggest that creativity is antithetical to government. Certainly, some of the common stereotypes concerning the so-called creative types as artistic, eccentric, and unpredictable stand in stark contrast to the stereotypes of government bureaucrats as rule bound, inflexible, and rigidly unchanging. But both stereotypes are wrong. It is not necessary to be artistic, eccentric, or mentally unusual to be creative. We all have the capacity to be creative, so in a sense we all are the creative type (Rawlinson, 1981; West, 1997). As we explore in this chapter, there are different types of creativity, all of which can help organizations to solve problems and work better. Furthermore, creativity and innovation are alive and well in the public sector (West & Berman, 1997). For example, Denhardt and Denhardt (1999) found in their case studies of leading change in Fairfax, Virginia; Altamonte Springs, Florida; and Fremont, California, that city managers and their teams of executives had successfully developed a culture of creativity and innovation with tremendous benefits for the cities and citizens they serve. It is important to build on and enhance this creativity if public organizations are to meet their goals and serve the public well.

Where Do We Begin?

Rate yourself on a scale of 1 to 10 (1 = *not skilled at all*, 10 = *very skilled*) on the following dimensions of creativity:

Perceiving problems

Thinking intuitively

Developing lots of ideas

Being imaginative

Visualizing my thoughts

Creating new combinations of ideas

Communicating ideas

Reconceptualizing problems

Relaxing and allowing my mind to wander

Discovering new ways of doing things

Seeing things from multiple perspectives

Based on this inventory, think about the following questions:

1. What are your creative strengths?

_____

_____

_____

2. What are your challenges in the creative process?

_____

_____

_____

3. What do you do to stimulate and support the creativity in others?

_____

_____

_____

Ways of Thinking

What is creativity? There is no single, commonly accepted definition of creativity. Perhaps this lack of agreement on a single definition is appropriate given the nature of creativity, but it is nonetheless useful to look at what various writers and scholars have written about the concept. Creativity has been described as "any form of action that leads to results that are novel, useful, and predictable" (Boone & Hollingsworth, 1990, p. 3); as "seeing things that everyone around us sees while making connections that no one else has made" (Wycoff, 1995, p. 21); as "a process or change from what is and has been to what might be" (Singh, 1985, p. 108); and as "the entire process by which ideas are generated, developed, and transformed into value" (Kao, 1996, p. xvii). Definitions and interpretations of creativity differ, in part, because they are emphasizing different aspects of creativity in different settings. As shown in Figure 3.1, these varying perspectives can be grouped according to whether they focus on the personal characteristics or attributes of individuals, the possession of a group of conceptual abilities, the demonstration of particular

Perspective on Creativity	Main Points	Practical Implications
Creativity as a trait	People have innate characteristics that predispose them to be creative.	Some people have traits that make them naturally creative; such people probably will be creative wherever they are situated.
Creativity as cognitive skills and abilities	Creativity is based on conceptual skills and abilities such as divergent and abstract thinking.	Creativity can be enhanced by learning and improving certain cognitive skills.
Creativity as behavior	Creativity is whatever results in the formation of new ideas or solutions that are useful.	The value of the creativity lies in what useful outcomes are produced.
Creativity as a process	Creativity is a process of generating and testing ideas.	The creative process may or may not yield a new product or process; individuals can play different roles in the process.
Integrated views of creativity	Creativity is a function of the interaction among the person, the environment, and the task.	Some types of tasks and organizational environments can be more or less conducive to creativity.

Figure 3.1   Alternative Views of Creativity

behaviors, or creativity as an integrated process (Gundry, Kickul, & Prather, 1994). As discussed in what follows, each of these perspectives provides insights and has practical implications for how we view creativity in ourselves and others.

Characteristics of Creative Individuals

One way of looking at creativity is in terms of the traits, attributes, or characteristics that predispose a person to be considered "creative." In this view, if a person possesses these traits, then he or she is deemed to be creative. The trait perspective also assumes that personal characteristics are more important than the nature of the organizational environment in which the person works. In other words, creative people probably will be creative wherever they are situated. Conversely, in this view, people who do not have these characteristics will not be creative, regardless of where they are situated. For example, some people are said to be naturally intuitive in that they do not amass facts and test theories; they simply "sense" things and therefore are thought of as creative. Creativity also has been described as synonymous with originality. People who demonstrate originality also have been found to be more intelligent and to have a preference for complexity— traits that also are associated with creativity (Foundation for Research on Human Behavior, 1958; Gundry et al., 1994).

This trait approach to creativity also has included attention to the personalities of creative people. For example, Gough (1979) developed and tested a creative personality scale based on the types of adjectives that people used to describe creative individuals. Some of the adjectives used that were positively correlated with creativity were *capable, clever, confident, humorous, original, reflective, resourceful,* and *self-confident.* Some of the adjectives used that were negatively associated with creativity were *affected, commonplace, conventional, submissive,* and *suspicious.* Others have emphasized personality characteristics of creative people, such as sensitivity, high energy, independent judgment, tolerance for ambiguity, self-confidence, and broad interests (Barron & Harrington, 1981). Traits such as persistence, curiosity, energy, intellectual honesty, and internal locus of control also have been suggested (Amabile, 1988).

Those who see creativity as residing in the personal characteristics of the individual would not deny that we all have some creative potential. This view of creativity suggests that although we all can exercise a certain degree of creativity, some of us simply have greater innate creative potential, in the same way as we all can learn to express ourselves artistically even though only some of us will become artists. But there are limits to this approach. As with trait theories of leadership (which we examine in Chapter 7), trait theories of creativity give us only part of the picture. Creativity involves more than simply the presence of certain traits; it also involves certain skills, motivations, behaviors, and environmental factors. Nonetheless, an understanding of the traits associated with creativity provides a partial explanation for why some of us feel more comfortable expressing ourselves creatively and why others of us might have to exert more effort to access our creative potential.

Conceptual Skills and Abilities

Creativity also has been described as involving the use of a particular set of conceptual skills and abilities. This perspective differs from trait approaches in that it focuses more on cognition than on personality characteristics. Koestler (1964), for example, suggested that creativity is based on the ability to think on more than one plane or more than one level at a time. As Dimock (1986) characterized it, "The more adept a person is at rising from lower applied areas to higher intellectual and imaginative planes, the more creative such a fortunate individual is likely to become" (p. 5). This manifestation of creativity can take many forms. For example, a creative person such as Jan Perkins, city manager of Fremont, California, might liken organizational change to successive waves of the ocean, drawing from that metaphor to better understand the ebb and flow of the change process (see the case study in Chapter 12). Creative people are said to possess cognitive skills in divergent thinking and ideational fluency (the ability to generate alternatives or a stream of ideas), linguistic ability, and a strong ability to find associations between things or ideas (Barron & Harrington, 1981).

Although there is a degree of overlap between views of creativity that rely on personal characteristics and those that emphasize conceptual and cognitive skills, there is an important distinction. Skills can be learned, whereas characteristics cannot. Accordingly, in this view, we all can learn to be more creative by expanding and enhancing our conceptual and cognitive abilities.

Creativity as Behavior

The behavioral view of creativity focuses on actions and activities that result in the development of something new. Thus, creativity is something a person does rather than what the person is. Amabile (1983), for example, suggested that creativity is behavior that results in a novel and useful response to a problem or situation. Amabile (1997) also stated, "The ideas must be novel—different from what's been done before—but they can't be simply bizarre; they must be appropriate to the problem or opportunity presented" (p. 40). But the emphasis is on the behavior, not on the innate characteristics or cognitions of the individual. So, a person who designs an innovative and useful new approach to neighborhood crime prevention is creative because he or she has engaged in behavior that resulted in a creative response to a problem. Here, the focus is on the creative product rather than on the personality or skills of the person who developed it.

This view of creativity focuses on the outward behavioral manifestations of creativity and places them in context. Importantly, this view of creativity adds the element of usefulness, thereby distinguishing creativity from simply bizarre, erratic, or unusual behavior. Accordingly, creativity not only brings forward new ideas; it is a process that results in actions or behaviors that are functional and useful in a given situation. In that sense, it is not nonconformity for its own sake but rather nonconformity with a purpose.

Creativity as a Process

Creativity also can be seen as a process. In this view, creativity is a highly complex phenomenon involving multiple phases and stages. Torrance (1988), for example, described creativity as a process of sensing problems, making guesses, formulating hypotheses, and communicating ideas. Drazin, Glynn, and Kazanjian (1999) defined creativity as the engagement of a person in a creative process where the person "behaviorally, cognitively, and emotionally attempts to produce creative outcomes" (p. 290). The emphasis here is on the process rather than on the outcome. The creative process involves both the generation of ideas and the testing of ideas. As such, creativity in the generation of ideas may or may not result in creative outcomes. This process perspective on creativity is useful for thinking about the stages in the creative process and about the roles that different individuals might play in each of these stages.

An Integrated Perspective on Creativity

Finally, some have suggested that creativity is best viewed as encompassing all of these views. For example, Amabile (1997) offered what she called a componential theory of creativity that takes into account expertise in a particular domain, creative thinking ability, and the intrinsic motivation of the individual in a particular work or social environment. Similarly, Woodman, Sawyer, and Griffin (1993) linked individual, group, and organizational factors to creative outcomes. They indicated that creativity can be viewed as the development of a valuable and useful new product, service, process, or procedure by people working together in a complex social system.

This integrated perspective is illustrated in Figure 3.2, which indicates the mutual influence of personal factors, environmental characteristics, and the nature of the task. Some integrated perspectives, in particular, emphasize the intrinsic motivation of an individual in a particular context. In this case, the focus is shifted from what levels and types of creativity people are capable of to what they are willing to do. That is, people are most likely to be creative when they love what they do and do what they love (Amabile, 1997; Drazin et al., 1999). Intrinsic motivation is included as part of an integrated perspective because it involves not only the personal interests and personalities of individuals but also how interesting the problems or tasks are.

This approach is a useful one for public administrators and students of organizational behavior. It recognizes that we all are potentially creative, although some of us might be more naturally suited to some parts of the creative process than others. It suggests that we can learn skills that will enhance our own creativity and that we can support creativity in others. It recognizes that creativity takes place in context and that creativity must be useful and appropriate to the setting or problem at hand. It leads us to think about ways in which the organizational environment may enhance or impede the development of creative ideas and solutions to problems. Finally, it suggests that creativity is an important component of a larger process of change and innovation (a subject that is dealt with in more depth in Chapter 12).

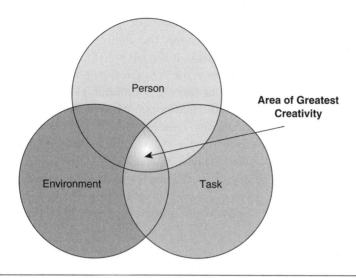

Figure 3.2   An Integrated View of Creativity

Why Do We Need Creativity in Public Organizations?

Before continuing our examination of creativity, it is important to first ask some fundamental questions. What are the consequences of creativity for public organizations? Why should public servants strive to be creative and to support the creativity of others? How do individuals respond to opportunities to be creative in the workplace? The answers to these questions provide insights about both the nature of creativity and the importance of creativity to the public service.

For public organizations to be effective, they must craft and facilitate creative responses to increasingly complex societal problems. Organizations and the individuals who work in them must innovate and change as community needs and demands shift. Meeting these challenges requires the full use of all human and mental resources available. Among the most important of those resources is creativity—the capacity to think of old problems in new ways, to change our perspectives, or to create novel and useful approaches to making our organizations work better and serve the needs of citizens. To fail to do so is wasteful to individuals and organizations and is inconsistent with the values of public service. It is incumbent on all of us, then, to use our imaginations and expertise as we work to achieve public goals.

Creativity is directly and positively linked to organizational effectiveness and to improvements in quality and productivity. It increases the quality of solutions to organizational problems, helps to stimulate innovation, revitalizes motivation, and promotes team performance (Raudsepp, 1987). Creativity helps organizations respond to challenges, demands, and opportunities for change.

There are other benefits to creativity as well. There is evidence that the opportunity to be creative is important for employee motivation and retention. There is evidence that employees and potential employees strongly value the chance to use their creativity. For example, in a poll conducted by Louis Harris and Associates of the class of 2001, the top-ranked qualities desired in a job were committed coworkers, creativity, responsibility, and the ability to work independently ("Committed Co-workers," 1998, p. 14). It also has been found that managers who are creative and have opportunities to use their creativity on the job are less likely to want to leave their organizations (Koberg & Chusmir, 1987). It even has been demonstrated that innovation and creativity can reduce workplace stress. Helping people to become more innovative and creative "not only makes the work environment less stressful but also leads to the introduction of procedures which enhance productivity and quality of work" (Bunce & West, 1996, p. 210).

Creativity allows public organizations to be responsive and to develop new and better ways of serving citizens and using resources wisely. The opportunity to be creative can help to motivate people, keep them interested in and committed to their work, and reduce stress. So, creativity is not just something for "creative types" or a matter of a "flight of fancy" if people happen to have some extra time. It is a critical component of managing organizational behavior and achieving public service goals.

The Creative Process

Creativity is more than a flash of insight. Instead, creativity can be thought of as a process with five identifiable steps or stages: preparation, concentration, incubation, illumination, and verification (Boone & Hollingsworth, 1990). These stages are illustrated in Figure 3.3.

Preparation is the first step in the creative process. In the preparation stage, all parts of the problems are thoroughly investigated. This includes consciously gathering and examining information, defining the problem, and generating alternative ideas for addressing the problem. The purpose is to ensure that all parts of the problem are fully understood. In the preparation stage, a person not only searches for facts but also searches for ideas and alternative perspectives. Preparation is a conscious mental activity. Therefore, most efforts at enhancing creativity are focused on this stage of the creative process.

In the *concentration* stage, the energy and resources of the person (or of the organization) are focused on solving the problem. The individual, in essence, concentrates his or her efforts on the problem or situation. There is a choice to engage with the process and a commitment to find a solution. This stage is not so much a matter of mental activity as it is a matter of choice.

The *incubation* stage is a largely unconscious phase of the creative process. It is, in essence, the "black box" of creativity. There is an internalization and subconscious ordering and reordering of information gathered in the preparation stage. The person cannot force this process; the best that he or she can do is attempt to relax and allow the subconscious to work and ideas to surface. This may involve the combination of previously unrelated thoughts and a subconscious struggle between what is and what might be. Conscious thought and effort probably interfere, rather than help, in this stage.

Illumination is the "Eureka!" of the creative process. This is the moment of insight or discovery when the answer simply seems to arrive in the person's conscious mind

Verification
"It really works!"
"How can I get people interested?"

Illumination
"I've got it!"

Incubation
"I'll relax and let my subconscious mind work."

Concentration
"I will focus on and solve this problem."

Preparation
"What is the problem?"
"What has been done?"
"What are the alternatives?"
"Who can I discuss them with?"

Figure 3.3   Steps in the Creative Process

from his or her subconscious mind. It has been called an epiphany, a revelation, or a brainstorm—a sudden realization of something new or novel. But when viewed as part of the creative process, such insights actually occur after the individual has gathered information and gone through a period of subconscious mental activity during which the brain has "worked on" the problem.

The final stage of the creative process is *verification*. This involves testing and verifying the idea or insight as viable. In other words, the creative solution is evaluated against some standard of appropriateness or acceptability, and the creator seeks corroboration and acceptance of the idea.

In addition to these identifiable stages, Foster (1995) provided a useful summary of the characteristics of the creative process, including the following:

- Long rather than short in duration
- Ambiguous rather than certain and concrete
- Information rich rather than based on "existing" information
- Involving multiple mental models rather than a particular point of view
- Oriented to defining problems rather than finding short-term fixes
- A continuing process rather than a one-time event

Recognition of the steps in and characteristics of the creative process is important from several perspectives. First, creativity does not just "happen." It is a process that can be observed, nurtured, and supported over time. It is a process that requires an investment in time, a search for information, a commitment to openness, and a tolerance for uncertainty and ambiguity. Second, we do not all have to be highly skilled at all stages of the creative process; some of us might be better at generating ideas, others might be skilled at synthesizing concepts, some might be good information gatherers, and still others might be excellent "validators" of others' insights. Thus, we can play different roles in the creative process—an idea that is elaborated in the sections that follow. Third, not all of the stages of the creative process are amenable to conscious mental effort. As a result, most techniques and training to improve creativity are focused on the preparation stage when conscious mental activity is dominant. Such techniques and training activities, which have been shown to be highly effective, are described in later sections of this chapter.

Roles in the Creative Process

Because there are different stages in the creative process, and because we differ from one another in terms of personality and preferences, it can be useful to think of the different roles that people can play in the various stages of creativity. As Filipczak (1997) pointed out, "Once you understand that all employees are creative, the next step is finding out which part of the creativity spectrum each employee occupies" (p. 34). One way of thinking about roles in the creative process is to consider the different types of creativity. Hollingsworth (1989) defined four types:

- *Innovation:* Seeing the obvious before anyone else does (e.g., some states have innovated by offering multiple services at one site such as offering kiosks in shopping malls or one-stop service centers)
- *Synthesis:* Combining ideas from various sources into a new whole (e.g., a city police department, a state social service agency, and the courts might create a multi-agency approach to dealing with child sexual abuse investigations and prosecutions)
- *Extension:* Expanding an idea to a new application (e.g., many jurisdictions have taken the fast-food idea and created drive-through services such as book drops in libraries)
- *Duplication:* Copying a good idea from others (e.g., as cities have experimented and had success with photo-radar technologies in traffic control, other cities have learned from those experiences and followed suit)

Although these are organizational-level examples, all of these types of creativity ultimately stem from the work and insights of individuals. But as we saw in our discussion of the Jungian psychological types in Chapter 2, there are different types of individuals. Similarly, different individuals might be more or less adept at various types of creativity or might play varying roles in the creative process. Kirton's (1976) Adaptation/Innovation Inventory helps us to understand where different individuals might fall on the creativity spectrum. Kirton described *adaptors* as the type of people who try to find better ways of doing their work. These are the people who make improvements in existing practices, devise ways of cutting costs, and develop approaches to modify programs so as to better meet citizens' needs. Goldsmith (1989) found that adaptors prefer short-term efficiency, seek consensus, and value conformity to rules and group norms. *Innovators,* on the other hand, are the dreamers and big thinkers. They have an ability to take two previously unrelated ideas of things and combine them in a new way. Innovators seek change-oriented solutions, look for new paradigms, are less tolerant of rules, and prefer big changes over small ones. In simple terms, adaptors do things better and innovators do things differently.

Obviously, organizations need multiple types of creativity and people who fall on both ends of Kirton's (1976) adaptor/innovator scale. The key is to find a balance. Too much innovation can result in organizations being in constant flux, thereby failing to secure and perfect improvements before changing to something else. The goal may be creativity, but too much innovation can lead to chaos. On the other hand, if creative efforts are limited to making only small improvements and changes to the status quo (as preferred by adaptors), then organizations might stagnate. Sometimes incremental improvements simply are not enough; in all organizations, there are times when quantum change is needed. According to Kirton (1989), when innovators and adaptors collaborate, adaptors provide stability, order, and continuity; are sensitive to people; help to maintain cooperation; and provide a safe foundation for the innovators' riskier ideas. Innovators, on the other hand, bring to such collaborations the task orientation and dynamics needed to bring about change.

Social and Structural Connections

Perry-Smith and Shalley (2003) relate creativity with the social connections within and outside the organization. "Communication with others in the domain should enhance one's understanding of the area and facilitate the generation of approaches that are feasible and appropriate, but also unique" (p. 91). When individuals connect with other people, they exchange information and ideas, increasing the likelihood that new approaches and solutions will be created.

The degree of creativity fostered by these social connections, according Perry-Smith and Shalley, will depend on the "strength and the position" of the relationship. Under some circumstances, weak ties can actually facilitate creativity more than strong ties. When the relationship is strong, the "parties truly like each other and are concerned about one another, see each other relatively frequently, and have similar perspectives and outlooks on the importance of their relationship" (p. 92). Since the parties involved in a close relationship often share very similar points of view, they may be less likely to challenge ideas. Weak ties, on the other hand, may give individuals more information and "the exposure to different approaches and perspectives" (p. 94).

There is a limit, however, to how many of these social connections a person can effectively and productively handle. When an individual has too many weak ties, he or she may spend too much time exchanging and processing information. This can result in higher levels of stress and conflict rather than in higher levels of creativity. So, weak relationships may foster creativity up to a point, beyond which the number of ties may even constrain creativity at work. The position of the person in the relationship is also very important. The people who have the greatest potential for creativity are those who occupy what the authors call "peripheral network positions." People in these positions have enough connections within the organizations to stay informed and gain organizational knowledge, but their outside connections give them the opportunity to hear something new.

Impediments to Creativity

There are a number of common impediments or barriers to creativity (Gundry et al., 1994). Removing these barriers can be the first step in fostering creativity in ourselves and others. Each of these impediments is considered in the following subsections.

Defining the Problem Incorrectly

If the problem is defined incorrectly, incompletely, or inappropriately, then creative approaches to solving it will be misplaced. One of the ways in which this can occur is when individuals engage in what de Bono (1992) called *vertical thinking*. Vertical thinking occurs when a problem is defined in a single way and there are no deviations or alternative definitions considered until the solution is reached. For example, an organizational problem might be defined as one of excessive costs in a particular service unit. If there are no challenges to this definition of the problem, then people will logically pursue cost-cutting efforts such as reducing hours of service, laying off staff, decreasing the variety of services, and postponing purchases of equipment and supplies. But such approaches might make the problem worse if it is later discovered that the real problem was failure to understand and respond to changes in citizens' needs (which had reduced the effectiveness of existing approaches and caused unproductive uses of staff time). The cost-cutting measures might even result in the development of new and more serious problems. If the problem were redefined, then it might be possible to come up with new approaches that would not only reduce costs but also provide services better tailored to citizens' needs.

Ironically, language also can be a barrier to problem definition. If people are accustomed to, and limited by, using only certain terms and language in defining a problem, then they will think about that problem only in a manner that the terms will allow. In this way, language actually can serve as a barrier between the thinker and reality (Koestler, 1964). In addition to verbal language, there are other languages, such as symbolic, emotional, sensory, and visual languages. In other words, sometimes it is useful to represent problems or ideas using symbols or drawings (to consider their emotional aspects) or even to express them in terms of touch, smell, or sensation. In some cases, people can seem stuck not only with verbal language but also with a particular set of organizationally sanctioned terms. For example, if people in police organizations were to consistently and exclusively use the language of "crime" and "criminals" to understand their roles and responsibilities, then they might be less likely to consider factors such as citizens' perceptions of safety; a sense of neighborhood and community; the roles of other institutions such as schools, churches, and social services; the physical environment; and aesthetic and quality-of-life issues—all of which might influence the roles of police officers and the nature of their relationship with community members. For example, it might lead them to ask what citizens would like their neighborhoods to look like or to feel like.

Judging Ideas Too Quickly

People often reject ideas that are inconsistent with their current thinking. We all have heard people defend current practices by saying, for example, "We've always done it that way." Although constancy and consistency might be a human need and a virtue in certain circumstances, blind adherence to the status quo in organizations is not. As Allison (1971) argued in his analysis of the Cuban missile crisis, sometimes organizations (and the people in them) try to fit problems into particular organizational routines, whether or not the situation really calls for a novel response.

Stopping at the First Acceptable Idea

Because people often are under pressure to come up with solutions to problems, sometimes the response is to accept the first good idea that comes along. Time pressures, different problems competing for our attention, or simply lack of recognition that other ideas might be better can lead us to choose alternatives too quickly. Obviously, this can result in forgoing what might have been a later—but better—idea.

Lack of Support

Creative ideas can wither on the vine. If someone comes up with an interesting and original idea but no one listens or considers it, then the idea probably will not go anywhere. We might learn over time that curiosity and questioning are not welcome in our work environment. Sometimes we are not creative because it takes a great deal of mental energy, and the demands of our daily jobs simply consume all of our reserves. Moreover, thinking does not *look* like working. We might be concerned with appearing busy and engaged with our work and, as a result, become mentally and creatively lazy. The truth is that it often is easier and less demanding to keep doing things and thinking about things in the way we always have.

Hostility to Sharing Knowledge

In some organizations, there is not only a lack of support but also an outright hostility to creativity and the sharing of ideas. In such cases, Michailova and Husted (2003) suggest that "it is unrealistic to expect or assume that individuals are basically willing to share knowledge even when incentives are introduced" (p. 60). For example, if there is an organizational norm that employees should not know more than their managers, it is unreasonable to expect any initiative from the lower levels. If managers believe that they are solely responsible for innovation, "competition" from someone who is at a lower level in the organizational hierarchy may be unwelcome. Creativity is also thwarted in organizations where mistakes are taboo. When mistakes are punished, employees will avoid risk and are often scared to admit when they make a mistake. Finally, Michailova and Husted suggest that what they call the "NIH syndrome" (Not-Invented-Here Syndrome) can be deleterious to creativity. In organizations with the NIH syndrome, things that come from outside the organization are considered less valuable than the things that come from the inside. This obviously limits a potentially important source of information and inspiration for creativity.

Other Ways of Thwarting Creativity

Morgan (1968) suggested 12 tongue-in-cheek "rules" for killing creativity that we have adapted and reduced to 9 rules for the public sector manager:

1. Drag your feet. Just keep going through the idea over and over until people lose interest.

2. Say yes, but do not act on the idea. That way, people will be momentarily pleased and will leave you alone.

3. Wait for full analysis. Who can argue with this logic? This will give you lots of time because public sector problems rarely can be *fully* analyzed.

4. Do not follow up. Drop the idea on your associates and see whether anything happens.

5. Call many meetings. This will kill time and interest.

6. Put the idea into channels and forget about it. Anything novel or original will not go far.

7. Boost the cost estimates. Public organizations never have much money, and you will be the hero for saving some by vetoing the idea.

8. Wait for someone else to try the idea first. Why put yourself out in front?

9. Stick to standard operating procedures and rules. They still will be there long after the idea has died.

Although these "rules" are, of course, written with a humorous edge, they remind us of how easy it can be to stifle creativity. Public organizations often are underfunded and overextended while being asked to simultaneously meet multiple and conflicting goals. It is not all that surprising that we sometimes can lose track of the importance of creativity, imagination, innovation, and renewal to organizational success. Fortunately, there are a number of things we can do to foster such efforts.

Fostering Creativity in Organizations

A supportive organizational environment can enhance and encourage individual creativity. If people are to choose to exercise their creative abilities, then they have to be motivated to do so. That motivation resides in part within individuals, but it also is influenced by people's social environment.

A positive climate can create an atmosphere in which creativity and innovation flourish, whereas a negative one can squash such efforts. Scott (1965) stated, "Creative behavior, a product of the creative individual in a specifiable contemporary environment, will not occur until both conditions are met. . . . An unfavorable contemporary environment will inhibit creative behavior no matter how talented the individual" (p. 213). It is also necessary to have the capacity to adapt and use innovations developed elsewhere (Chesbrough, 2003). Innovation requires resources and time, and organizations do not possess limitless amounts of either. This does not suggest deemphasizing internal innovations but creating an organization that can benefit from a combination of internal and external innovations.

What can we do to create a climate that encourages creativity? Three organizational factors seem particularly important: challenging work, supportive supervision, and an organizational/work group culture that supports and encourages creativity.

Challenging Work

As suggested previously, intrinsic task motivation is an important component of creativity. Intrinsic task motivation is driven by "deep interest and involvement in the work, by curiosity, enjoyment, or a personal sense of challenge" (Amabile, 1997, p. 44). Intrinsic motivation is the motivation to work on something because a person wants to—because it is exciting, satisfying, involving, challenging, and personally interesting. A key factor in this regard is choice. Research has shown that if a person chooses to do something just because he or she wants to, then that person will approach the task more creatively than if he or she were given external incentives or rewards (Amabile, 1997; Kruglanski, Friedman, & Zeevi, 1971). Obviously, then, intrinsic motivation is heavily influenced by an individual's preferences, values, interests, and attributes. But it also has to do with the nature of the task. Even the most curious, committed, and creative individual might not exhibit these talents if placed in a repetitive, rigid, and uninteresting job. Moreover, the individual probably will be miserable. With a high level of intrinsic motivation, on the other hand, the individual will be more likely to fully engage his or her expertise and creative thinking abilities. Intrinsic motivation can be so powerful that it even can make up for deficiencies in expertise, knowledge, and creative thinking skills because it drives people to look to other domains or to exert the effort to acquire those skills (Dweck, 1986; Harter, 1978).

Job design is critical in this respect. Amabile (1997), one of the leading researchers on creativity in organizations, stated,

> Because a positive sense of challenge in the work is one of the most important predictors of creativity, it is imperative to match people to work that utilizes their skills, stretches their skills, and is clearly valued by the organization. As much as possible, all work should be designed to maximize intrinsically motivating aspects. (p. 55)

Challenging jobs with complex tasks, high levels of autonomy, skill variety, significance, and feedback are associated with higher levels of motivation and creativity than are jobs that are simple and routine (Deci, Connell, & Ryan, 1989; Hackman & Oldham, 1980). When jobs are designed to be interesting and challenging, people are more likely to be excited about and willing to invest themselves in their work in the absence of external controls and constraints (Oldham & Cummings, 1996). It also has been found that intrinsic interest and creativity can be enhanced by designing jobs in a way that gives people choices about how to perform their job tasks (Woodman et a1., 1993). Intrinsically creative jobs, then, are jobs in which there is a measure of worker control and freedom in deciding what work to do and how to do it.

Supportive Supervision

How you interact with your employees can have a significant effect on their creativity at work. Supervision that is supportive of employees fosters their creative achievement, whereas supervision that is controlling usually diminishes it (Cummings & Oldham, 1997). Supervisors can be supportive by demonstrating concern for employees' feelings, encouraging employees to voice their concerns and needs, providing positive and information-rich feedback, and facilitating worker skill development (Deci & Ryan, 1987). Doing so can bolster workers' feelings of self-determination and control, which in turn can positively influence intrinsic motivation and creativity.

Because intrinsic motivation is enhanced by offering people more choices in what they do, participative decision making also is important in creating an organizational climate supportive of creativity. Plunkett (1990), for example, found that workers who believed that they had meaningful input into organizational decision making were more creative than those who did not. Thus, management and supervisory approaches that increase opportunities for participation can enhance creativity.

Conversely, supervision that is controlling and limiting, sometimes called *micromanaging*—where employees are closely monitored, allowed few choices, denied opportunities to participate in decisions, and pressured to think, act, or behave in particular ways—can easily thwart creativity. Supervision that is overly controlling undermines intrinsic motivation and shifts workers' attention away from the job itself and toward external concerns (Deci & Ryan, 1987).

Organizational and Work Group Culture

In addition to supervision, creativity is influenced by overall organizational culture and climate. Hollingsworth (1989) identified the following key elements of a creative organizational climate:

Trust: People are allowed to suggest and try new things without fear of reprisal.

Open communication: Everyone in the organization feels free to put forward ideas and is kept informed of needs and goals.

Diversity: The organization provides for the presence of different personalities and recognition of the varying contributions that each can make to the creative process.

Change: The organization values innovation and change, and it recognizes their importance to organizational success.

Rewards: The organization rewards creativity including both the development and the implementation of new and useful ideas.

Similarly, Amabile (1997) described creative cultures as those in which there is fair and constructive evaluation of ideas, reward and recognition for creativity, mechanisms for developing new ideas, and a shared vision. An organization with a climate or culture that supports and enhances creativity might express these values in a number of ways. In addition to supervisory attitudes and practices discussed in the preceding subsection, organizations can cultivate these values, for example, by talking about the values of creativity, developing a shared sense of organizational vision, providing time and opportunities to develop new ideas, offering special recognition and rewards for creative solutions to problems, providing creativity training and education, and other activities and actions that reflect an attitude or mindset that is receptive to creative efforts. The climate of an individual's work group also can have a positive effect. When group leadership is democratic and collaborative, the structure is flexible, and the group is composed of people with diverse backgrounds, creativity is enhanced (King & Anderson, 1990).

Cultural artifacts are also important in communicating and reinforcing a culture of innovation. Higgins and McAllaster (2002) suggest that cultural artifacts "shape the attitudes and behavior of new as well as veteran employees" (p. 77). In order to create a culture of innovation, organizations often have to modify or even create new myths and stories, language, and metaphors. Telling success stories about innovation can reinforce those cultural values and make the employees feel free to express their ideas. Value systems and behavioral norms are also powerful tools that can enhance innovation. If innovation is rewarded over time, employees can become more aware that the organization values such behavior. Physical artifacts and surroundings can be important in fostering creativity as well. Higgins and McAllaster also suggest that the shape and the size of the office, the building itself, the amenities around the building—sport courts, parks, and so forth—not only encourage creativity but also can increase overall productivity of the organization (2002).

Workload Pressures and Resources

The effect of workload pressure on creativity is difficult to gauge. On the one hand, excessive workload demands can undermine creative efforts. On the other hand, some degree of pressure or urgency can have a positive influence, particularly when it arises out of the nature of the problem itself (Amabile, 1988). Similarly, some time pressure can enhance creativity, but too much can stifle it (Andrews & Farris, 1967). Part of the issue seems to be whether the time and workload pressure is externally imposed as a form of control (in which case it would tend to hamper creativity) or the urgency and challenge come from the person's perception of the problem or the work itself (in which case creativity can be enhanced).

The resources allocated to a project also can affect creativity. The obvious effect of extreme resource restriction is to limit what people can accomplish. However, if an organization does not commit adequate resources to a particular project or task relative to others, then that also can have a psychological effect in that it may lead to the belief that the work is not valued or considered important by the organization (Damanpour, 1991). Of course, money is not the only resource that can be invested in creative efforts. Another way in which organizations can emphasize creativity is to provide the time needed to think about problems and to develop innovative solutions (Redmond, Mumford, & Teach, 1993).

Positive Emotions

Emotions also play an important role in creativity. Put simply, positive emotions foster creativity and creativity fosters positive emotions. Amabile, Barsade, Mueller, and Staw (2005) have found that "Creative activity appears to be an affectively charged event, one in which complex cognitive processes are shaped by, co-occur with, and shape emotional experience" (p. 367). Their research showed that positive emotions can lead people to discard time-tested ideas and think in novel ways. They also found that individuals who are successful with creative problem solving often experience positive emotions as a result. Conversely, individuals who could not develop appropriate solutions often had negative feelings (anger, dissatisfaction, etc.). In fact, positive affect and creativity can happen at the same time. Individuals may start some process of solving a problem, and as they feel satisfied or pleased with the progress, their creativity may increase even more. This can produce an "organizational affect-creativity cycle . . . whereby influences at any point can begin a dynamic pattern of increasing or decreasing positive affect and creativity" (Amabile et al., 2005, p. 386). This suggests that when people have opportunities to exercise creative problem solving, and have success in doing so, they can experience positive emotions, which can lead to more creativity.

Fostering Creativity—Putting It All Together

Taken together, job design, supervision, organizational climate, and the allocation of adequate time and resources can have a potent and synergistic effect on individual and organizational creativity. When people have interesting and challenging jobs, when they are supervised in an open and supportive manner, and when they work in an environment that encourages and rewards creativity, they are more likely to respond with creativity and enthusiasm (Amabile, 1987; Gundry et al., 1994; Oldham & Cummings, 1996).

But it should be remembered, as we will see in Chapter 6, that motivation—including the motivation to be creative—resides within the individual. Although it can be influenced, it cannot be directly controlled. In other words, despite environmental conditions designed to promote creativity, different individuals will respond in varying ways. Furthermore, we can unintentionally and unwittingly contribute to inhibiting our own creativity by blaming others or by blaming the organization for producing conditions that discourage creativity (Wesenberg, 1994). In this case, our own defense mechanisms might lead us to blame the organization for our lack of creativity, to avoid change, and to deny the importance and intrinsic value of public service work. It is important to remember that just as all of us are products of our work environments, we also contribute to shaping those environments. So, as we work to foster creativity in others, we also need to be self-reflective and take responsibility for the levels of enthusiasm, creativity, and energy that we invest in our work.

Techniques for Improving Creativity

Creative skills can be enhanced by learning and practicing. Both business and government organizations use creativity training to build and foster creativity approaches and skills. In the following subsections, a sampling of some of the tools used in organizations to enhance creativity is offered.

The Idea Box or Matrix Analysis

In matrix analysis, a two-dimensional "idea box" is used to explore new ideas or alternatives (Miller, 1987). There are four steps to generating an idea box: (1) specifying your purpose or what you are trying to accomplish, (2) identifying the parameters of the problem, (3) listing variations, and (4) trying different combinations. Consider a situation in which your purpose is to gain citizen input and involvement in the city's recreation department, but you are not sure how to do it and resource limitations are such that you will be limited in the number of approaches you can use. You could begin by asking yourself what the parameters of the problem might be. For example, perhaps you could consider methods of input, timing or frequency, subjects, and target groups as your parameters. For each of those parameters, you would develop options. Methods of input might include citywide open meetings, neighborhood forums, mailed questionnaires, or suggestion boxes. For target groups, you might think about seniors, teenagers, preschool children, and businesspeople. The resulting table might look something like this:

	Input	*Timing*	*Subject*	*Target Group*
1.	Meeting	Once	Programming	Seniors
2.	Forum	Quarterly	Facilities	Teenagers
3.	Questionnaire	Semiannually	Access and hours	Preschoolers
4.	E-mail	Ongoing	Volunteering	Business

Using the idea box, you then would randomly combine one item from each column (e.g., a forum held semiannually on volunteering for seniors, a questionnaire mailed quarterly on facility construction to businesspeople). The matrix, or idea box, provides a structure to combine and recombine ideas to develop new alternatives. The 4 × 4 box depicted yields 1,024 different combinations—a far greater number than you are likely to generate without the aid of such a structure. Of course, it is not necessary to consider all of these combinations. The purpose of the idea box is simply to get you to start thinking about multiple options.

Synectics

Synectics is a technique developed by Gordon (1961) for improving creative problem solving. The word *synectics* means joining together different and apparently unconnected or irrelevant elements. In synectics, problems are defined by "making the strange familiar," and ideas are sought by "making the familiar strange" (Gordon, 1961, p. 33). In the former case, the aim is to understand or define the problem using terms that are familiar to you. In the latter case, the purpose is to make the familiar strange by purposely distorting, inverting, or transposing the problem to something unfamiliar. This can "transpose both our usual ways of perceiving and our usual expectations about how we or the world will behave" (Gordon, 1961, p. 36). Synectics uses four types of metaphors in this process: (1) the personal analogy, (2) the direct analogy, (3) the symbolic analogy, and (4) the fantasy analogy.

In using a *personal analogy,* you actually imagine yourself as the object or problem. For example, if the purpose is to reduce the incidence of panhandling on city streets, then you might want to imagine yourself as a panhandler. Or if the purpose is to reduce pollution in a lake, then you might want to imagine yourself as the water. This might sound far-fetched, but such an exercise probably will increase the number of ways that you think about the problem. As Gordon pointed out, even Einstein used visual and muscular analogies in understanding mathematical constructs. The *direct analogy* is similar to the problem or issue in terms of facts, knowledge, or technology. For example, in organizational theory, we often talk about organizations functioning as organic systems, using a biological metaphor where there are inputs, a conversion process, outputs, and a feedback loop. The *symbolic analogy* uses an image or symbol to represent the problem. For example, developing a work team might be thought of as analogous to creating a collage with a common theme, or your role as a supervisor might be thought of as analogous to the role of a conductor, a coach, a gardener, a teacher, or a tugboat. Finally, in a *fantasy analogy,* you might ask yourself, "What is my wildest fantasy about how to make this work?" The purpose is to imagine the best of all possible worlds or outcomes. This frees you to think about problems without becoming prematurely limited by present constraints and limitations.

Playing with analogies as a means to making the familiar strange and the strange familiar can lead us to think about problems and solutions in new ways. By thinking about the problem in the form of a metaphor, new insights about the nature of the problem and possible solutions can emerge. For example, imagine that the problem is a work group with low levels of creativity and innovation. You might ask yourself what this problem reminds you of or how it makes you feel:

> Is it like working underwater? If so, then how can you create bubbles that will allow ideas to float to the surface? Ensure that people have flippers and oxygen tanks? Build islands of dry land? Drain the pool?

> Is it like trying to open a rusted lid on a jar? If so, then how can you loosen the lid? Remove the rust? Prevent rust? Break the jar?

> Is it like going to the mall but finding that all the stores are closed? Where else can you go to get what you need? Plan ahead and time your trips differently? Get

the shopkeepers to open their stores? Make the items yourself? Use what you already have? Shop on the Internet instead?

Does it look like a bleak winter landscape? How can you add color? Change the season? Get yourself out of hibernation?

What if our work group became the nationally recognized model for creativity? Business experts and public executives from all over the world would visit us and seek our advice. What would they see when they arrived? What would we tell them? What would we do that is unique? How would we be organized? How would people behave? How would they feel?

Mindmapping

Mindmapping is a technique designed to help us think visually and spatially about issues and problems. Mindmaps help to guide us through mental explorations in much the same way as ordinary maps help us in our travels (Rickards, 1988). Mindmapping uses pictures and images to define a vision, a problem, or a situation. It can be a simple representation intended to be used as a memory trigger or as a detailed representation of a situation, process, or "territory." Wycoff (1995) suggested that a mindmap should begin with a central image in the middle of the page. Then colors, pictures, and symbols should be used to map the situation, using only one key word per image. All lines branch from the central image. Mindmapping can be done individually or in a group. One possibility is to draw individual maps and then pair people off to explain their maps to each other and create a shared map. The map can be a depiction of a process, a goal, an interaction, or the multiple facets of a complex problem. Wycoff suggested the following questions to get the process going:

How can we visually describe our goals?

What metaphors might describe how we work together?

How would we like to see ourselves?

What is the environment we are trying to create?

What are some of the possible scenes from our future?

Figure 3.4 contains a mindmap created at a policy retreat in 1994, when Wycoff worked with the U.S. Department of Agriculture.

Mindmapping can be a highly useful tool for organizing information, generating and communicating ideas, and creating a framework for solving problems. There are a number of variations, such as a tree and a fish bone map. Using a tree, some dominant idea or problem is linked to a set of its components or branches. In fish boning (a technique popular in Japan), problems are diagrammed in terms of cause and effect. The head of the fish is the problem, and the fish bones are labeled as the various causes of the problem. Whatever type of picture or representation is used, a map does not need to stand alone. It can be used as a supplement to other forms of idea generation, communication, and presentation.

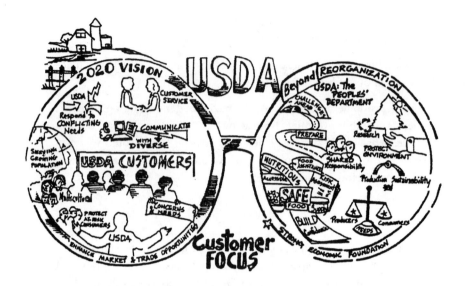

Figure 3.4   U.S. Department of Agriculture Mindmap

SOURCE: From *Transformation Thinking,* by J. Wycoff, 1995, New York: Berkley. Copyright © 1995 by Joyce Wycoff. Used by permission of Berkley Publishing Group, a division of Penguin Putnam, Inc.

Enhancing Your Personal Creativity

In our efforts to create a positive climate for others to be creative, it also is important to think about how to support our own creativity. Miller (1987) made a number of suggestions, summarized and adapted in the following paragraphs, for individuals to improve their own creative process. Many are analogous to the types of things that help to foster creativity in others, but it also is worthwhile to think about them as things that we can do for ourselves.

Be aware. To be creative, it often is necessary to have an understanding of the current situation. What are the facts? What information is available? In the public sector, this means not only being well-versed in current practices in our own and other jurisdictions but also being knowledgeable about the legal parameters, community concerns, political considerations, and other factors that might be important in our understanding of the issue. By immersing ourselves in a particular subject, we ground our creativity in reality. After all, as noted earlier, creativity is the development of novel and useful ideas. How can we know what is novel or useful if we do not know how things work at present?

Be persistent in your vision and values. Applying consistent energy in a particular direction increases the probability of realizing your goals. A vision, or purpose or goal, guides our efforts and motivates us to be persistent. Creativity is, at its core, a personal enterprise in that it brings forth something that you, as an individual, value. Maintaining a vision requires self-reflection, the creation of a clear idea or picture of what you want to accomplish, and a conscious investment of energy.

Consider all of your alternatives. Dream up as many ideas as you can. Do not rush to find a solution. Avoid mental idea killers such as when we say to ourselves, "Oh, that will never work," "That's dumb," or "We already tried that and it didn't work." Keep your evaluation of alternatives separate from your development of ideas and alternatives.

Entertain your intuition. Allow your intuition to give the answers that you are seeking. Relax and allow your mind to work. Creativity involves hard work, but the importance of the intuitive part of the creative process cannot be overlooked. Your intuitive self compiles information and creates new images and symbols that can lead to new inspirations.

Assess your alternatives. In evaluating your alternatives, two factors are critical. First, be open to the best solution. Let go of your ego, hidden agendas, desire for a convenient solution, and even self-interest in considering what the best solution might be. Second, use not only your analytical abilities but also your intuition (or "gut feelings") in evaluating alternatives. Are you excited about the idea? Does it feel right?

Be realistic in your actions. If your creation is to be realized, then it usually requires you to take action. Even the greatest idea will be unlikely to go anywhere unless someone sells it, works out the details, and implements it. Even Einstein had to defend his data and ideas. New ideas have to be supported within formation and then effectively communicated to others. Once you are committed to an idea, share that commitment with others and figure out how to accomplish, or put into practice, what you have envisioned.

Evaluate your results. Many of us want external praise and rewards for our creative efforts. It also is important to set up constructive feedback for yourself. For most of us, the creative process needs a point of completion when we acknowledge what we have accomplished and the results we have achieved. Even if things do not turn out as we hoped they might, self-reflection allows us to evaluate the parts of the process that did and did not work well.

Ways of Acting

Everyone has creative potential. Creativity is more than simply novelty; it involves the development of new, useful, imaginative, and appropriate approaches to meeting challenges and solving problems. Because creativity is one of the greatest and most important personal and organizational resources, it should be nurtured, supported, and encouraged. There are a number of practical steps that can be taken to bolster your own creativity as well as to encourage the creativity of others in organizations. These methods are highlighted in what follows.

1. *Debunk the myths of creativity.* All people have creative potential; it is not limited to the artistic, eccentric, or unusual among us. Moreover, different people can

contribute to the creative process in different ways, all of which are important and constructive for organizations and the people who work in them. Moreover, creativity need not be feared as too risky for public service. Creativity involves the development of novel and *useful* or *appropriate* ideas. To be creative in organizations, we need not embrace or implement the bizarre or unusual for its own sake. Rather, creativity is about using imagination to make things work better.

2. *Change your vocabulary.* Nothing squashes creativity faster than a negative response. Killer phrases such as "Yes, but . . . ," "We already tried that and it didn't work," and "We can't do that" can be substituted with phrases such as "Yes, and . . . ," "How could we . . . ?," "What could we . . . ?," and "Let's build on that to . . ." Remember that it is important not only to use these creativity-building phrases with others but also to use them in our "self-talk." Do not fall into the trap of being overly critical of your own ideas. Instead, consciously invite yourself to suspend judgment and be mentally receptive to your own ideas.

3. *Use participatory management approaches.* Using these approaches can increase intrinsic motivation and allow you to actively encourage creative thinking as part of the decision-making process. Creative collaboration is enhanced when everyone understands that a democratic process for generating ideas can lead to something unexpected and valuable. This means that the contributions of people at all levels of the organization can be useful, regardless of rank, seniority, or position. Overcontrolling supervisory approaches have been shown to hamper creativity. Open participatory approaches can encourage creativity and a willingness to try new things.

4. *Make time and information available for creative efforts.* Information fuels creativity by triggering the imagination and providing the foundations of innovation. Make sure that people have the information they need to think creatively, but also realistically, about finding new and better ways of doing their jobs and meeting organizational and community challenges. Individuals and groups also need time to be creative. Time pressures are undeniable and often unavoidable. But unless it is absolutely necessary, demanding that a task be done or a problem be solved immediately might cost time and money in the long run if it hampers the development of more creative and effective approaches. When possible, give yourself and others some time and room to think about new and appropriate ideas.

5. *Analyze your organizational climate.* Ask yourself the following questions. Does your organizational climate encourage or hinder creativity? Are interactions between people characterized by trust and respect? Are new ideas welcomed and encouraged? Do people feel safe in asking questions and making suggestions? Are they treated as capable and competent adults? Is supervision characterized by control and micromanagement or by guidance, support, and openness? Are people allowed to follow their interests? Does the organization provide enough flexibility to take advantage of differing talents, abilities, and interests? Within a framework of a shared vision and organizational goals, are people encouraged to do what they love and to love what they do? Are you doing what you can to create an environment that is conducive to creativity?

6. *Relax and let your mind work.* There is a point in the creative process when you just need to allow the mind to work, letting your subconscious make new connections and recombinations of ideas. This means that taking a short walk, doodling, or simply taking a "breather" or mental break can be important in allowing creative ideas to emerge in your mind. Laughter also can be a good way of breaking down barriers and relaxing your mind. It is not only OK to laugh and have fun at work; it actually can help you to work more effectively and creatively.

7. *Use techniques and tools to foster creativity.* Use techniques and tools to foster your own creativity as well as that of others. A sampling of techniques discussed earlier in this chapter included idea boxes, mindmapping, and synectics. These and other tools can help you and others to stimulate your creativity. Training programs also are available to build creative thinking skills. When using these techniques and tools, do so within the overall framework of fostering trust, mutual respect, collaboration, and support for the creative process.

8. *Identify problems that need creative solutions.* Identify problems that need creative solutions, and challenge yourself and others to find answers. Creativity requires a willingness to look at what is and consider what might be. This willingness can be encouraged by explicitly identifying issues and problems and by asking people to contribute creative energy to addressing them. If your behavior and language convey the idea that the current way is the best way, then people might be hesitant to make suggestions or ask questions. So, ask people to be creative and to imagine what could be new solutions to existing problems or how to make a good processor service better.

9. *Make work interesting and do not oversupervise.* Ask yourself what you can do to make your work and your employees' work more complex, challenging, and interesting. Creativity is enhanced when people have choices in their work and when they feel challenged to do complex and important tasks. Allowing workers to have some flexibility and discretion in how they will accomplish work tasks creates situations that invite innovation, experimentation, and creative approaches. Too much routine and repetition can drive the creative impulse underground. So, try to avoid unnecessarily controlling or overspecifying *how* someone must accomplish a particular objective. Leave room for innovation and improvement.

10. *Challenge yourself and others to be creative.* Public service demands and challenges us to be creative. It is important to periodically remind yourself and others of the significance of what public servants do for their communities, their states, and their country. Public sector organizations are not charged with solving easy problems. Rather, public service is focused on addressing some of the messiest, most difficult, and most complicated problems that society faces. We would suggest that, despite their complexity and difficulty, these problems are the most important ones. In the middle of work demands, deadlines, and routines, it is important not to lose sight of the fact that public service is intrinsically valuable and important to making our communities and world a better place in which to live. In other words, what we do matters—and it deserves and demands our most creative, energetic, and imaginative efforts to do it well.

Thinking in Action

Go back and review your answers to the questions in the section titled "Where Do We Begin?" at the beginning of the chapter. Do you have any new ideas about what you might do to enhance or develop your creativity? How might you help others to be more creative? Try the following exercises.

Mindmapping Exercise

Think about a goal that you have for your career or education. Spend a few minutes visualizing the goal. Then create a mindmap that represents how you see the process for achieving that goal. Be attentive to choosing a central image that you think best captures your goal. What has to occur for you to reach that goal? Who and what is involved? What is the nature of the goal? What are the consequences of achieving it? What are the barriers and obstacles? How do you view the future? What factors will influence your efforts? Include pictures, images, and symbols for as many facets of the process and the goal as you think are important.

Sometime after completing your mindmap, go back and look at it again. What can you see that might help you to think differently about your approach to the goal? What does the map tell you about the key factors involved? What are the barriers to reaching the goal? What are the things that might contribute to its attainment? What do you want to change? Does the map satisfy you as a depiction of how to reach the goal? What would you like to add? What would you like to erase? What can you learn from the process?

Using Analogies

Think about your present role in an organization. It can be work, school, family, or any other organization or group with which you are involved. Identify a problem that you encounter in this role that you would like to resolve. Using the following as a guide, take a piece of paper and write down some ideas and create some doodles using four types of analogies:

1. *Personal analogy:* If you were this problem, what would you look like? How would you feel?

2. *Direct analogy:* What is the problem like? What metaphors could you use to describe it?

3. *Symbolic analogy:* What symbol or image best captures what this problem looks like? Feels like? Sounds like?

4. *Fantasy analogy:* What is your wildest fantasy about how to solve this problem? How would solving the problem change the future? What is the best possible outcome?

Now go back and think about your analogies and their implications. If the problem you are trying to resolve actually *was* one of these analogies, then what would you do? For example, if you compared the problem with your present organizational role to a flower that was not blooming, then how could you actually make a flower bloom? Fertilizer? Water? Sunshine? What ideas does that give you for addressing the problem?

A Creativity Challenge

You have just received a promotion to become the supervisor of the public information office for your agency. You are thrilled about your new job and are anxiously awaiting the opportunity to work with your staff of seven people both to improve how your agency responds to requests for information and to create new avenues for communication between your agency and citizens.

At the conclusion of your first staff meeting, you ask your staff to help you begin identifying what they think are some of the problem areas and opportunities that the unit can and should address. The silence that follows is very unsettling to you. Nonetheless, you wait for someone to speak. Finally, the most senior staff member says, "There is never any money around here to try anything new." Another comments, "What's the point? Our unit isn't a priority. Everything we've tried has been shot down." Another adds, "Citizens don't respond to our efforts to communicate with them. They are completely apathetic." After a few more similar comments, you conclude the meeting by expressing appreciation for their comments and your hope and vision that things will change for the better. Still, you feel rather discouraged.

Later, in private meetings, you talk with your staff about your desire to approach problems creatively and to come up with some new and innovative approaches to achieving the unit's mission. In the course of these discussions, you learn that the prior supervisor not only did not solicit ideas but also routinely shot them down if they were raised. His favorite response to suggested innovations was, "We tried that once and it didn't work." Staff confided that they had learned a long time ago that they just needed to keep their heads down and do their jobs. One commented, "Besides, it's enough to just keep up with all the requests we get. We don't have staff to do anything else!"

What are some of the characteristics of the past management practices and organizational climate that are thwarting creativity? What are some measures that you can take to begin to foster creativity in the individuals you work with and in your unit as a whole? What tools might be helpful?

Adapting Innovations

One of the best ways to fuel your creativity is to seek out ideas from other individuals and organizations. For example, the Alliance for Innovation has a Web site that describes innovative practices in local governments. Go to www.transformgov .org/govnews.asp and choose one of the examples that you think might or should be adapted and adopted in your community. Then answer the following questions:

1. What particularly intrigues you about this innovation? Why do you think it is needed and might or might not work in your community?

2. In what ways might the innovation be adapted to your particular community characteristics or needs? How can you build from or depart from what is already being done in another community?

3. Where and how would you begin to work toward getting such an innovation implemented? What factors do you think will support its adoption? What might be the significant barriers?

CHAPTER 4

Managing Stress

I just don't know if I can do the job.

—Anonymous and tearful city manager
at home the day before assuming his
very first city manager's position

J ust a month ago, Susan was very excited about her appointment as assistant city manager for South Suburbia. She had moved from a similar position in a small town in a neighboring state, and although the move required her to leave her family and friends, the new job was a terrific opportunity to use her experience and learn new skills. But as she sat at her desk with her pounding head in her hands, she wondered whether she had made the right decision. She was deeply committed to public service, but there was so much to do. The city manager was asking for her to present strategic plans within 2 weeks for the units that reported to her. The previous night, she had managed to anger a member of the city council by strongly recommending a project that, unbeknownst to her, he was on record as firmly opposing. She glanced at her phone and saw the two lights that still were blinking. Two citizens were on hold, both demanding that she immediately attend to their problems (a pothole in the street and an unspecified "police incident") or else they would call the local newspaper. She already had a stack of phone messages to return, four of which were from the mayor's office. On top of all that, she was due at a public meeting in 15 minutes, where she was supposed to facilitate a discussion about economic development and growth—a topic that recently had triggered controversy and angry conflict in the community. The final blow was the note she held in her hand; her boyfriend's mother was coming to town and wanted to stay with her this weekend. Not only did she not know this woman, but she had to work.

Anyone who has worked in the public service knows that it can be stressful for a variety of reasons. As public servants, we tackle a broad range of difficult and important problems, often under less than ideal circumstances. Controlling crime, educating children, protecting the environment, securing our national defense, and delivering health care and myriad public programs and services create difficult challenges for the public servants who are charged with their delivery. In working to do so, for example, we sometimes are asked to achieve goals that are conflicting or ambiguous. At the same time, we are responsible to elected officials, citizens, our supervisors, and our peers—all of whom might expect different things from us. There often is more to be accomplished than seems humanly possible. Our programs often are underfunded and understaffed. Working conditions for some public sector jobs can be unpleasant, and sometimes they even can be dangerous. And after all of that, the public we serve might not always appreciate us.

All of these stressors are, of course, compounded by the realities of everyday life during the 21st century. Traffic, noise, family issues, health problems, time pressures, and all of the other everyday stresses and strains of living can take their toll. Two-income families, changing role expectations, the divorce rate, and changing demographics all challenge our sense of family, not to mention our free time. We are bombarded with information and new technology demanding that we change our ways of communicating and even our ways of thinking.

But before throwing up your hands in despair, you should recognize that stress is a part of being human. You can experience stress anytime you are put in the position of having to adapt or change. Thought of in this way, it is difficult to imagine a meaningful existence that does not include some level of stress. So, eliminating stress is not only bad for you but impossible; life requires that we adapt to changes that occur and respond to demands that are encountered. To put it bluntly, to have no stress, we probably would have to be dead.

In fact, the stress response can contribute to our sense of well-being, motivation, and performance. As Vaillant (1977) put it, stress does not kill people; rather, it is the capacity of people to adapt to the demands of life that enables them to live. Stress that is too intense, too frequent, or poorly managed can be personally and organizationally destructive (Quick, Quick, Nelson, & Hurrell, 1997). The key, of course, is to manage stress both in our personal lives and in the public organizations where we work so that it is a mostly constructive force rather than a mostly destructive one. Although we concentrate on organizational stress, it is important to recognize from the outset that we cannot completely isolate work-related stressors from stresses arising from factors outside of the organization. The reality is that we experience stress as individuals who must respond to demands that arise in both our private and professional lives. In other words, we cannot seal off the workplace from stresses that we experience from other aspects of our lives. For example, if we have a sick relative or are going through a difficult divorce, then we probably will not be able to entirely check those feelings at the workplace door. At a minimum, during those types of life events, we might be more vulnerable to stressors at work. And, of course, bringing those stresses to work might dramatically influence our ability to perform at our best level. Fortunately, if we can understand stress, recognize its effect on us and those around us, and learn ways of coping with it, then there will be both personal and organizational benefits.

This chapter considers ways of meeting this challenge. It begins by considering the consequences and costs of unchecked stress in the workplace. It then describes the stress reaction and identifies some sources of work-related stress. The remainder of the chapter is devoted to strategies for increasing our resiliency to stress, strategies for reducing unnecessary stress, and ways of coping with stress when it occurs. The intent is to provide insights that will allow us to both manage our own stress better and understand how our actions may cause stress in the work lives of others. In addition, organizational-level issues with regard to workplace stress are discussed so that we can become more aware of how organizations can modify their practices to increase the likelihood that stress will be a productive, rather than a destructive, force in public organizations.

Where Do We Begin?

Are you stressed? That might seem like a ridiculous question, particularly because many of you are in school at the same time as you are working and handling family and other responsibilities. Of course you are stressed, you might say. The truth is that all of us experience stress at some level. But it is important to know when we might be exhibiting the symptoms of stress that is too frequent or too intense. Such stress often is exhibited in physical symptoms. The items in the following subsection represent some of the most common symptoms associated with stress (Smith, 1993). It is important to remember that there might be other causes for such symptoms and that an extremely broad array of physical changes and maladies can be stress related.

Symptoms of Stress

With these caveats in mind, look at the following list and ask yourself how often you feel or experience these symptoms:

- Dry mouth
- Heart beating too fast or irregularly
- Feeling restless and fidgety
- Backaches and tense muscles
- Watery eyes
- Hurried or shallow breathing
- Perspiring heavily or feeling too warm
- Headache
- Stomach upset
- Loss of appetite
- Fatigue and exhaustion
- Anxiety and tension
- Cold or sweaty hands
- Lump in throat

Stress Inventory

If you are experiencing such symptoms on a regular basis, then do not panic. Recognizing the symptoms of stress overload is the first step in finding ways of coping with and managing stress more effectively. The next step is to figure out the sources of stress. That can be a difficult task given that we can experience stress arising from virtually any aspect of our lives or experiences. We can experience stress while on vacation, in our homes, on the freeway, with our friends, in the hospital, at the park, or anywhere else. Furthermore, as a practical matter, the cumulative effects of stress cross the boundaries of all the personal and professional aspects of our lives. What follows is a stress inventory originally developed by Holmes and Rahe (1967). Next to the mean value, mark the life events that you have experienced during the past year.

Rank	Life Event	Mean Value
1	Death of a spouse	100
2	Divorce	73
3	Marital separation	65
4	Jail term	63
5	Death of a close family member	63
6	Personal injury or illness	53
7	Marriage	50
8	Fired from job	47
9	Marital reconciliation	45
10	Retirement	45
11	Change in health of family member	44
12	Pregnancy	40
13	Sex difficulties	39
14	Gain of a new family member	39
15	Business readjustment	39
16	Change in financial state	38
17	Death of a close friend	37
18	Change to a different line of work	36
19	Change in number of arguments with spouse	35
20	Mortgage more than $10,000	31

Rank	Life Event	Mean Value
21	Foreclosure of mortgage or loan	30
22	Change in responsibilities at work	29
23	Son or daughter leaving home	29
24	Trouble with in-laws	29
25	Outstanding personal achievement	28
26	Spouse beginning or stopping work	26
27	Beginning or ending school	26
28	Change in living conditions	25
29	Revision in personal habits	24
30	Trouble with boss	23
31	Change in work hours or conditions	20
32	Change in residence	20
33	Change in schools	20
34	Change in recreation	19
35	Change in church activities	19
36	Change in social activities	18
37	Loan less than $10,000	17
38	Change in sleeping habits	16
39	Change in the number of family get-togethers	15
40	Change in eating habits	15
41	Vacation	13
42	Religious holiday (e.g., Christmas, Hanukkah)	12
43	Minor violations of the law	11

SOURCE: Reprinted from "The Social Readjustment Rating Scale," by T. H. Holmes and R. H. Rahe, 1967, *Journal of Psychosomatic Research, 11*, pp. 213–218. © 1967. Used with permission from Elsevier Science.

Holmes and Rahe suggested that the higher the mean score, the more likely the individual is to experience major physical or mental health problems. But for our purposes, look at the life events you checked and evaluate for yourself how they affected you, particularly looking at the year as a whole. Did you have some "high-scoring" events over the past year? Did you have a great many "low-scoring" events? Was it a fairly uneventful year? In any case, did you subjectively experience the year as stressful? How does stress tend to manifest itself in your life?

Sources of Stress

Although in this chapter we primarily concentrate on the sources of stress that are work and job related, as you read, it is important to remember that all types of life events and changes can lead to stress. Furthermore, it is not only big changes and life events that cause stress. In addition to events such as major job moves, shifts in responsibilities, and organizational changes, the day-to-day realities of work can make you feel stressed. What ongoing stresses do you experience at work? Circle the number that indicates the degree to which each item represents a source of stress for you in your job (0 = *no stress*, 5 = *extremely stressful*).

Too much work	0	1	2	3	4	5
Conflicts with coworkers	0	1	2	3	4	5
Too much e-mail	0	1	2	3	4	5
Irate citizens	0	1	2	3	4	5
Unreasonable demands	0	1	2	3	4	5
Travel or commuting problems	0	1	2	3	4	5
Telephone interruptions	0	1	2	3	4	5
Trouble with supervisor	0	1	2	3	4	5
Problems with employees	0	1	2	3	4	5
Unpleasant working conditions	0	1	2	3	4	5
Job interferes with family life	0	1	2	3	4	5
Not enough to do	0	1	2	3	4	5
Tasks are boring	0	1	2	3	4	5
Lack of resources to do job	0	1	2	3	4	5
Unproductive meetings	0	1	2	3	4	5
Goals are not reachable	0	1	2	3	4	5
Too many objectives at once	0	1	2	3	4	5
Unclear guidance	0	1	2	3	4	5
Family life interfering with work	0	1	2	3	4	5
Deadlines	0	1	2	3	4	5
Difficult work	0	1	2	3	4	5
Lack of advancement	0	1	2	3	4	5
Not enough training	0	1	2	3	4	5
Lack of input on decisions	0	1	2	3	4	5
Too little autonomy	0	1	2	3	4	5
Too many hours	0	1	2	3	4	5
Unsatisfying work	0	1	2	3	4	5

Your cumulative score is less important than any item that you scored at the upper end of the stress scale. In looking at the things that stress you the most, can you identify common themes?

Coping With Stress

Now let us look at how you cope with stress. For each of the following items, circle the number that indicates how often you respond to conditions of high stress in this manner (0 = *never*, 5 = *always*).

1.	Skipping meals	0	1	2	3	4	5
2.	Talking with friends	0	1	2	3	4	5
3.	Setting priorities	0	1	2	3	4	5
4.	Sleeping less to work more	0	1	2	3	4	5
5.	Increasing alcohol consumption	0	1	2	3	4	5
6.	Getting angry	0	1	2	3	4	5
7.	Crying	0	1	2	3	4	5
8.	Eating healthy	0	1	2	3	4	5
9.	Exercising	0	1	2	3	4	5
10.	Deep breathing and relaxation	0	1	2	3	4	5
11.	Spending less time with family	0	1	2	3	4	5
12.	Distancing self from the stress	0	1	2	3	4	5
13.	Problem solving	0	1	2	3	4	5
14.	Smoking more	0	1	2	3	4	5
15.	Withdrawing from others	0	1	2	3	4	5
16.	Confronting those responsible	0	1	2	3	4	5

What are your preferred coping mechanisms? Note that Items 2, 6, 7, 12, and 15 may be considered primarily emotional coping strategies. Items 3, 13, and 16 may be seen as focused on problem solving. Items 1, 3, 4, and 11 may be viewed as attempts to manage and control time. Attempts to cope with the physical symptoms of stress may be manifested in the behaviors described in Items 5, 8, 9, 10, and 14. Although all of these coping mechanisms are "normal" in the sense that they are things that people do under conditions of stress, some are healthy and effective, whereas others (e.g., skipping meals, smoking, drinking, cutting oneself off from friends, getting insufficient sleep) most certainly are detrimental in the long term. As you read this chapter, try to think about the things that cause you stress, reflect on how you typically respond, and (if appropriate) consider how you might respond more positively and effectively in the future.

Ways of Thinking

The word *stress* is an everyday part of our vocabulary. If you talk about being "stressed out" at work, you are likely to elicit knowing nods and personal stories of feeling overworked, overpressured, and overwhelmed. Everyone seems to know about stress and can relate their personal experiences with it at one time or another. Some might claim to be immune to it, and others might claim to be almost paralyzed by it, but seemingly everyone knows what it is. To understand how to manage stress constructively, it is helpful to begin by examining in more detail what exactly happens to us when we become overly stressed. By doing so, it becomes clear that stress is not just "all in our minds," as some people seem to suggest.

Hans Seyle (1974), the so-called father of stress research, defined stress as the "nonspecific response of the body to any demand made upon it" (p. 27). So, although many people consider stress to be a psychological or mental response, Seyle's definition refers to the response of the body. That is not to say that there is not a cognitive and psychological component to stress; rather, to understand stress, it is necessary to understand its physiological basis. The word *stress* is derived from the Latin word *strictus,* which means tight or narrow (Cartwright & Cooper, 1997). Subjectively, stress sometimes can feel like being internally constricted. But the actual physiological changes associated with stress are much more complex.

Smith (1993) explained that the stress response begins in the core of a person's brain in the hypothalamus, sometimes called the "stress trigger." The hypothalamus plays a regulatory function related to eating, drinking, sex, hormones, and the coordination of activities among our various organs. Given its central role in our physiology, it also is key in understanding the physical changes that occur because of stress. When a person is stressed, the hypothalamus sets off a type of alarm to the nervous and endocrine (hormonal) systems. This often is called the "flight or fight" response. Heart rate and blood pressure go up as the body readies itself for an emergency. Blood rushes to the heart, muscles, and brain while it rushes away from the intestines, skin, and other organs. Stored fats are broken down, and the liver produces more glucose to fuel the body's response. The breathing rate increases, and bronchial tubes dilate to facilitate an increased flow of oxygen. The pupils of the eyes enlarge to enhance vision. At the same time, the adrenal gland is stimulated to produce adrenaline.

Seyle (1956) suggested that stress occurs in three major stages that, together, he referred to as the general adaptation syndrome. After the alarm stage described previously, there is a countershock phase in which the body's defenses are mobilized. Initially, the person might feel energized to find ways of dealing with the situation. Under ideal circumstances, the individual successfully adapts to the demand and the body returns to normal functioning.

But if the stressors persist or the individual is unable to cope, then he or she enters what Seyle called the resistance stage. In this stage, the signs of the alarm reaction reappear and energy becomes depleted. Eventually, adaptive mechanisms collapse and exhaustion occurs, as depicted in Figure 4.1.

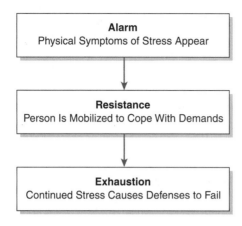

Figure 4.1   General Adaptation Syndrome

While in the alarm stage, bodily changes enhance our capacity to fight or flee, but there also are other physical consequences, particularly when stress becomes chronic and exhaustion sets in. For example, under stress, the hypothalamus stimulates the pituitary gland to produce corticoids that regulate metabolism and release fatty acids in the bloodstream. Over time, these fatty acids can accumulate in the arteries and ultimately compromise the body's ability to deal with injury and infections. Other hormones are released that increase anxiety, feelings of fatigue, and other mental and psychological responses to stress. As our bodies are bombarded with stress-related chemicals over time, all types of health problems can emerge, ranging from migraines to muscle tension, heartburn to rashes, and coughing to tremors.

You might be asking yourself why all of this physiological mayhem results from a late report, an unexpected presentation, or a bad traffic jam. The reason, again going back to Seyle's definition, is that stress is a *nonspecific* bodily response to anything that places a demand on us. In other words, in terms of physical reaction, our bodies do not distinguish between a crisis at work and a car accident, between being physically assaulted and being verbally attacked, or between running from a wild animal and trying to meet an impossible deadline. Even more surprising to some, stress can occur with both happy and sad events. As indicated in the stress inventory at the beginning of this chapter, both marriage and divorce, as well as both getting promoted and getting fired, can be stressful. As Seyle (1974) stated, "It is immaterial whether the agent or situation we face is pleasant or unpleasant; all that counts is the intensity of the demand for readjustment or adaptation" (pp. 28–29). In short, from a physical, biochemical, and medical standpoint, it is all the same.

Although the physical and chemical responses to stress are the same, there is some evidence that men and women may behave differently in reaction to these changes. For example, Taylor et al. (2000) found that the "fight-or-flight" response described above is the dominant behavioral response among males, but that females are more likely to engage in what they called "tend and befriend" behaviors in response to stress. Nuturing and befriending behaviors among females have been beneficial under conditions of stress, and through the process of evolution and natural selection, those responses have been reinforced. So, humans appear to have a broader repertoire of responses to stress, including affiliative, protective, and caretaking behaviors. Yet, research to date has focused almost exclusively on the fight-or-flight response among men. In this context, the authors point out that "there may be value in thinking about the fight-or-flight response as only part of a range of equally flexible male responses" (p. 423).

The Consequences and Costs of Stress

The consequences and costs of stress to individuals, to organizations, and to society at large are nothing short of enormous. It has been estimated that more than 10 million American workers suffer from stress-related problems (West & West, 1989). These stress-related problems can be behavioral, medical, or psychological. For example, increased smoking and alcohol consumption have been associated with stress. Job stress also has been linked to illicit drug use on the job as well as to absenteeism due to drug use (Beehr, 1995; Quick et al., 1997). Eating disorders also may be a response to stress. Each of these behaviors has obvious health risks attached. For example, smoking causes cancer, emphysema, chronic bronchitis, and a host of other medical problems. Excessive alcohol use is a major factor contributing to motor vehicle fatalities and homicides, suicides, liver disease, and birth defects. Eating disorders can lead to organ damage and, ultimately, to death.

Stress can lead to behavior that interferes with our relationships with others. We might become irritable, less patient, angry, or withdrawn. We might lash out at others or react out of proportion to the situation. We are less able to deal with situations calmly, effectively, and appropriately. Obviously, this can affect the nature of our relationships with our supervisors, our employees, citizens, and our peers, families, and friends. Ask yourself, would you rather work with someone who is constantly stressed and "on edge" or with someone who manages his or her stress successfully? In other words, being an effective manager or leader requires us to manage our own stress, not only for our own benefit but also for the benefit of the people working with us and the citizens we serve.

Stress also can make us accident-prone. Peterson (1984) suggested that high stress levels are an important element in work-related accidents. The National Safety Council (1990) estimated the annual cost of work accidents to be $48.5 billion. Stress can make us hurry through tasks, making us more apt to make mistakes. Stress can decrease our reaction time and attention and also can distort cognitive processes. When applied to many public service occupations that involve caring for the sick, apprehending criminals, driving cars and piloting planes, and responding to emergencies of every type, the implications are obvious and potentially very serious.

In extreme cases, stress also can lead to workplace violence. In the United States in 1994, violence in the workplace resulted in the murders of 1,071 people and in injuries to another 160,000 (Elias, 1996). Violence has been found to be the cause of 12% of all occupational deaths. Between 1980 and 1989, it was the leading cause of death in the workplace among women (Pastor, 1995).

Whereas these behavioral consequences of stress have serious implications for our health, there also are other medical issues associated with stress. Stress compromises our immune systems, making us generally more vulnerable to illness and disease. It disrupts our sleep patterns, leading to impaired concentration, memory, and alertness (Quick et al., 1997). Heart attacks, strokes, cancer, ulcers, hypertension, headaches, back troubles, and arthritis all have been linked to or found to be worsened by stress.

Stress also affects us psychologically. Unchecked stress can lead to depression, low self-esteem, and anxiety. Stress can provoke feelings of fear, frustration, conflict, pressure, hurt, sadness, guilt, loneliness, or confusion (Cavanaugh, 1988). Job dissatisfaction is linked to stress as well (Crampton, Hodge, Mishra, & Price, 1995). Job "burnout," characterized by exhaustion, cynicism, and disengagement, often is related to stress (Beehr, 1995). Burnout among human service workers, police officers, and medical workers has been well documented but can affect individuals in a wide variety of professions and job classes.

Obviously, the implications of poorly managed stress for organizations are profound. The financial costs of health care, lost time, and decreased productivity are enormous. It has been estimated that more than 70% of absenteeism is stress related (Adams, 1987). Rosch and Pelletier (1987) estimated that 1 million workers are absent every day primarily due to stress disorders. Stress can lower productivity, compromise effectiveness, deaden creativity, and decrease the quality of work life.

Stress: Good, Bad, and Ugly

So, why do we not avoid stress at all costs? There are two answers to this question. The first is relatively simple: We cannot avoid stress while still living normal lives. The second is that we would not want to do so even if we could. This second answer is somewhat more complex and deserves more explanation. Despite all of its negative consequences and costs, some stress can be very beneficial. It can increase our energy, motivation, and drive. Too little stress can lead to impaired attention, boredom, and apathy. The results of too much and poorly managed stress already have been described. But appropriate levels of stress help us to focus our attention, make our awareness more acute, and promote sound decision making.

What makes the situation even more complicated is the fact that individuals may respond to the same set of circumstances differently. Stress is subjective, and people respond to it in various ways. One person might see a situation as highly motivating and energizing, whereas another might become quite distressed. It is important to remember, then, that what causes stress for others might not be what causes you to feel stress. Conversely, something that you find to be very stressful might be seen as an invigorating challenge to others, or they might not notice it at all.

This distinction between the positive and negative aspects of stress was expressed by Seyle (1975) as the difference between *eustress* (*eu* is the Greek root for "good") and distress. Eustress is healthy stress that is experienced positively with constructive outcomes. Rather than feeling overwhelmed, people feel challenged and motivated.

One way of looking at the variable effects of stress is expressed in what is known as the Yerkes–Dodson law (Yerkes & Dodson, 1908). The Yerkes–Dodson law suggests that the relationship between performance and arousal can be depicted as an inverted U, as shown in Figure 4.2. This model suggests that when stress levels are too low, performance will suffer. Too little stress leads to apathy, boredom, and impaired attention. As stress (arousal) increases, performance improves. People might feel challenged and exhilarated. Their attention becomes more focused, and their senses become more acute. Decision-making capacity and judgment are enhanced. But as stress continues to increase, performance declines. People might withdraw, become overwhelmed, and experience the negative physical and mental symptoms of stress. Although this model may provide a useful way of thinking about the variable effects of stress, it is important to remember that the point at which stress levels become a positive force varies from individual to individual based on circumstances, personality, and other factors.

Sources of Stress on the Job

As explained previously, stress occurs in response to some demand or need to adapt. There are a number of situations or conditions at work that can evoke a stress response. Job stress occurs when job-related factors interact with the worker's individual characteristics in a way that either enhances or disrupts the worker's psychological or physiological functioning (West & West, 1989). There are a variety of job-related factors that may play a role. Some of the most common ones are discussed in the following subsections. When reading about these potential stressors, keep in mind that they are just that—potential. Not all people will respond to these factors in the same way, and the existence of a stress response does not necessarily mean that it is altogether negative. Remember that some stress, when managed appropriately, is an important factor in professional success. Many public servants have found ways of coping successfully and creatively with the challenges they face, to their own and their organizations' advantage. Some of those coping strategies are discussed in a later section of this chapter. But for now, it is useful to explore some of the factors at work that may trigger the stress response in the first place.

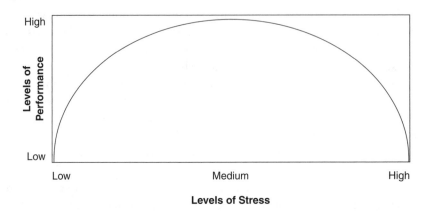

Figure 4.2   The Relationship Between Performance and Stress

Interpersonal Relationships

Although working with people can be a great source of satisfaction, work also can become stressful when we encounter interpersonal conflicts. Both the quality of relationships and the availability of support from peers, supervisors, and others in the organization can influence stress levels (Riley & Zaccaro, 1987). If people believe that they are being treated inappropriately or rudely by coworkers, supervisors, or others, then interpersonal difficulties can arise. These conflicts can be manifested in a variety of ways. In any case, it is not uncommon for such conflicts to cause stress for the people involved. Competitiveness may play a role in encouraging such conflict. Forsyth (1990) suggested that interpersonal conflict is more likely to occur under competitive work conditions, whereas Swap and Rubin (1983) said that some people are just naturally more competitive and less cooperative than others.

Role Ambiguity and Conflict

Role ambiguity and role conflict also can be work-related stressors. Organizational roles can be thought of as a set of expectations about what an individual should do. Role conflict occurs when compliance with one role makes it impossible to comply with another role or when individual needs conflict with role demands (Vasu, Stewart, & Garson, 1990). Role conflict has been found to be associated with tension, anxiety, and poor performance (Jackson & Schuler, 1985). When faced with role conflict, individuals may withdraw, change their personal values, rationalize, or become aggressive.

Given the nature of public sector work, with competing demands and multiple lines of accountability, role conflict is not unusual. Vinzant (1998), for example, found significant role conflict among child protective service workers. Because of the origins of the social services and the training of many workers, the expectations and roles of protective service workers are influenced, at least to some extent, by the norms, values, and orientations of the social work profession. Many of the workers, in fact, defined themselves as social workers, despite the fact that their jobs required them to act as investigators. In addition, workers were expected to simultaneously meet the competing expectations of parents, supervisors, the community, law and regulation, their peers, and the children. As a result, they often felt pressured to play the roles of counselor, enforcer, investigator, and social worker at the same time and were frustrated that they could not do so.

Workload

Workload, or (more accurately) perceptions of workload pressures, can cause stress for people in the workplace. Workload demands can vary not only with the amount of work but also with the difficulty of the work. Very low work complexity can lead to boredom, and very high work complexity can lead to fatigue, anxiety, and stress (Xie & Johns, 1995). At some point, you might have experienced the stress that can occur when you believe that your talents and energies are being wasted in a boring and repetitive job. On the other hand, stress also can result from job requirements and demands that exceed people's abilities or skill levels. Or, as sometimes occurs in the public sector, despite the fact that *nobody* knows how to accomplish a particular public service goal, public servants might be asked to keep trying anyway. Particularly stressful, of course, are those jobs in which both the amount of work and the difficulty of the task become overwhelming. Numerous public service jobs come to mind—police officers in high-crime areas, executives in highly politicized positions, emergency room workers, and social workers with heavy caseloads. But nearly all public service workers have experienced the pressure of not only having too much to do but also feeling like they simply cannot accomplish the tasks for which they are responsible.

Intrinsic Nature of the Work

Some public service jobs involve tasks that are inherently stressful. West and West (1989), for example, studied nurses, police officers, and air traffic controllers. They found that these workers, who have high levels of responsibility for life-and-death consequences coupled with a variety of organizational constraints and environmental factors, exhibited significant physical, psychological, and behavioral symptoms of stress. The occupation of local government manager also was found to be inherently stressful because of the lack of job security, high level of public scrutiny, and conflict and ambiguity that characterize the work (Green & Reed, 1989).

In general, the jobs that are perceived to be most stressful are those in which the workers believe that they have the least amount of control (Jex, 1998). When workers lack a sense of control, because of either the lack of autonomy or the lack of opportunity to participate in decisions that affect them, stress often is the result. It is not difficult to imagine becoming stressed under conditions where you have important responsibilities but lack the freedom to make choices or the opportunity to influence how the work is done. Secretaries, for example, may exhibit stress symptoms when they have little or no control over their work, particularly if they perceive that they are expected to do everything for everyone with no say in how or when it is to be done.

Working Conditions

Working conditions also can exacerbate stress. Noise, lighting, smells, temperature, physical discomfort, and danger can influence our overall mental state (Cooper & Smith, 1985). Long working hours also take their toll on worker stress levels. Some jobs involve travel—either short or long distances—that can involve traffic jams, frustration over incorrect addresses, and delayed flights, buses, or trains. Shift work also has been connected with stress reactions due to the disruption of sleep patterns and personal lives (Cartwright & Cooper, 1997; Riley & Zaccaro, 1987). Heat, the degree of danger, and even the design of the rooms in which individuals work can be important variables (Riley & Zaccaro, 1987). Finally, physical danger is a reality for some public servants, such as firefighters, police officers, and soldiers. Such physical danger can, of course, make people feel threatened, anxious, or stressed.

Organizational Justice

The perception that you are being treated unfairly can also be a source of stress. Greenberg (2004) suggests that people are attentive to multiple types of justice: distributive justice (the fairness of the outcome or decision), procedural justice (the fairness of the process used in making the decision), and interactional justice (the nature of communication and how a person is treated). With regard to distributive justice, if employees feel that they do not receive what they deserve, especially if they think that others in the organization receive more than they do, this can lead to anxiety and stress. But if there are clear reasons and procedures that justify the inequity, it will be less likely to provoke anxiety. What is key here is whether the worker knows the procedures and the manager has openly, fully, and respectfully communicated how the process works (interactional justice). So, it is not necessary to treat everyone exactly the same way, but it is important that the reasons for the differences are clearly and respectfully communicated and understood.

Organizational Environment

The organizational environment of work also can influence our stress levels. Office politics, lack of participation or involvement in decisions, and poor communication can result in worker stress. Ferris and colleagues (1996), for example, found that although politics may be an inherent part of organizational life, the higher the perceived level of politics, the higher the stress for employees. This may occur when people experience politics as a threat to their positions, their resources, and their sense of organizational security. Unfortunately, stress might make them even less able to cope with organizational politics successfully (James & Arroba, 1990). Poor communication and low levels of participation can make people feel powerless, frustrated, and stressed. For example, during times of significant organizational change, poor communication might cause increasing levels of uncertainty, fear, and stress. Moreover, ineffective communication can exacerbate stress caused by role ambiguity and conflict. When a job has some level of role conflict or ambiguity built into the nature of the work, as many public service positions do, poor communication and a lack of guidance only make the problem worse by creating more uncertainty and conflict.

Home to Work and Back

The tensions and problems that workers bring home may affect their families and associates, and the tensions and problems associated with workers' personal lives can affect their work (Riley & Zaccaro, 1987). Child care, elder care, and the everyday demands of living can place strains on workers, many of whom are in dual-career relationships. Green and Reed's (1989) study of local government managers found that family-related issues, particularly those associated with mobility, played a role in producing stress.

The sources of stress related to home–work connections may vary, in part, based on the life stages of individuals. Schott (1986) suggested that certain issues can be expected to present themselves for resolution by employees at specific stages of life. For example, the major issues facing employees during early adulthood are establishing careers and finding personal intimacy. During midlife years, employees may encounter opportunities for growth and change including experiencing a shift from a concentration on external concerns to a concentration on internal or self-oriented ones. During later life, employees may be focused on the search for meaning and ego integrity. This suggests that there are patterns of adult development that will influence the psychological set that employees bring to the workplace. This psychological set will determine how central organizations are to the lives of the individuals. Although there will be variations from individual to individual, the life cycle model highlights the importance of personal growth and development in understanding how people might react differently to work stresses at particular times and under particular circumstances.

But just because employees place high importance on personal issues and interests outside of the job does not necessarily imply high stress levels. For example, a study of female executives in the federal government found that the most stressed were those who were focused solely on the job, whereas the least stressed were those who placed a high priority on self-actualization and considerations outside of the job (Rogers, Li, & Ellis, 1994). On balance, then, it appears that the issues, tensions, and stresses we bring to the job influence how we handle demands on the job. That influence can be positive or negative, depending on the circumstances.

Coping With and Managing Stress

Recognizing and evaluating how stress is influencing both our own performance and that of others is the first step in using stress constructively and avoiding its destructive aspects. As a starting point, we need to be sufficiently self-aware to know when we might be getting into the unproductive and destructive ends of the stress curve. We also need to be aware of how stress may influence others. As noted previously, if we have too little stress, then we might feel bored, apathetic, or unable to stay focused. But it seems that the more common situation in public service jobs is that of too much stress. As described at the beginning of this chapter, symptoms in these situations may include feeling anxious or irritable, having difficulty in sleeping, being unable to concentrate, and overreacting to everyday situations. From a physical standpoint, we might notice an increased heart rate, increased perspiration, headaches and stomach troubles, dizziness and blurred vision, aching and tight neck or shoulders, rashes, or more than the usual number of illnesses.

The question, then, is how we can best use the constructive aspects of stress while minimizing its negative physical and behavioral effects. From an organizational and personal standpoint, managing stress has a lot in common with what we would consider to be some of the basics of good management practice—establishment of clear goals, development of resources and support, effective communication, and self-awareness. In the following subsections, a variety of strategies that might be useful in managing and controlling stress are discussed. As suggested previously, individuals and organizations have at least two purposes in managing stress: (1) preventing unnecessary and destructive levels of stress and strain so that they are motivated and equipped to meet the challenges they confront and (2) responding to and effectively coping with stress as it occurs. To accomplish these purposes, individuals have to be attentive to their responsibilities and capabilities for managing their own personal stress and also be cognizant of the role of their organizations in effective stress management. In other words, individuals and organizations both play roles in creating work environments characterized by eustress rather than distress.

Lifestyle Adjustments

Perhaps one of the most important things we can do for ourselves in managing stress and enhancing our ability to deal with it constructively is to consider our lifestyles. Lifestyle decisions play a significant role in influencing our physical health and well-being as well as our ability to cope successfully with the demands, challenges, and stresses of our work. As explained earlier, stress is a nonspecific bodily or physical response to demands. It only makes sense, then, that one of the most important and effective ways in which we can manage stress is to maintain our physical health. To be effective public servants and leaders, we need to be healthy enough to cope with the demands and challenges we face and to deal with the physical manifestations of stress when we experience them.

So, although it might seem obvious, it is worth reminding ourselves in this context that it is important to eat a balanced diet, get enough sleep, and exercise regularly. As our mothers might have told us, moderation is the key. Following these tried-and-true prescriptions for a healthy life helps to prevent some of the negative manifestations of stress and to cope with stress-related symptoms. Exercise is particularly important, in part because of chemicals that are released in our bodies during the "fight-or-flight" response that stress can evoke.

These chemicals are intended, from an evolutionary standpoint, to aid physical strength and stamina so that we can either win a fight or successfully run away. By physically fighting or running, the chemicals and hormones associated with a stress response do their job and then recede to more normal levels. But in the contemporary world, physically running away from stress might be inappropriate, or at least embarrassing. Certainly, engaging in a "fight" response by getting into a physical altercation with someone in response to stress is not recommended.

More typically, when we feel that rush of adrenaline and hear our pounding hearts, we try to hide, mask, or swallow these feelings. Although it might be perfectly appropriate to curb our desire to run, and although it certainly is appropriate and necessary to avoid physical fights, the result often is that there is no release of the physical energy for which our bodies are so well primed. Exercise provides that outlet and counteracts the negative effects of the chemical changes associated with stress. A regular exercise program, then, is a central component of stress management. Exercise also can be used as a more immediate antidote when we begin to feel stressed. For example, by taking a brisk walk during our lunch hour, we might be able to better handle a tense meeting or the pressures of a deadline.

In considering lifestyle questions, it also is constructive to evaluate and make appropriate changes to maintain a balance between work and outside interests. As noted previously, those whose whole lives revolve around work and work-related issues seem to experience more stress. In this way, leisure and recreational time not only is important to quality of life but also may contribute to enhanced work performance. By having outside interests and activities, we are better able to keep our perspective and cope with the demands of our public service careers. Put more bluntly, working "24/7" not only is bad for our physical and mental health as individuals but also is unlikely to be an effective or productive strategy for making professional or organizational contributions. Although there might be times and circumstances that demand extra hours and personal sacrifices, as a long-term approach, such demands are not likely to be good for us or our organizations.

Learning progressive relaxation, controlled breathing, biofeedback, and similar approaches also may be helpful in coping with stress reactions. By consciously letting go of physical tension and relaxing our muscles, we might be able to avoid some of the uncomfortable and unhealthy consequences of stress. As an added benefit, such approaches might teach us to be more aware of the early signs of stress, allowing us to "short-circuit" these responses before we get overwhelmed by them.

Attitude Adjustment

In a survey of human resources managers in 400 public and private organizations, 94% of the respondents said that "healthy attitudes" helped people to increase their tolerance for stress. This might seem somewhat ironic given that stress is a bodily response and not "all in your head." Although this is true, it also is the case that our perceptions and attitudes can make a difference in how we respond to potentially stressful situations as well as alter our subjective experiences of stress when it occurs. This is not a matter of simply ordering ourselves or others to "pull yourself together and get back to work." As suggested previously, individuals may respond to the same demands in very different ways. Part of this difference lies in the fact that some people might interpret a particular situation as threatening, whereas others might see the same situation as an opportunity. Our cognitive appraisal of a situation, then, influences whether or not we will experience it as stressful (Lazarus, DeLongis, Folkman, & Gruen, 1985).

Remember that depending on how we handle it, stress can be good for us and make us better able to handle future challenges. In fact, developing psychological "resilience" is only developed by having problems, challenges, and failures. Resilient individuals have "the skill and capacity to be robust under conditions of enormous stress and change" (Contu, 2002, p. 52). Contu suggests that people can become more resilient by facing the realities of a particular situation or problem. Realistic optimism is better than misguided optimism. Only by honestly and pragmatically assessing what is happening can we develop realistic and constructive responses. Second, resilience is enhanced by having a strong value system that helps us set priorities and make sense of the challenges we face. Finally, Contu suggests resiliency is fostered by ingenuity—by improvising and being creative with the resources that are available to us. At the core, resilient people "turn challenges into opportunities"

(Harland, Harrison, Jones, & Reiter-Palmon, 2005, p. 4). Accordingly, it makes sense to become more aware of our attitudes toward demands for change and adaptation in the work environment. As we become more attentive, we might discover ways of thinking that could use some reappraisal. How might we think about problems as challenges or about demands as opportunities? This cognitive reappraisal can be aided by "self-talk." For example, we might find it helpful to consciously ask ourselves how we might see a potentially stressful situation in a more positive light. Or we might find it useful to remind ourselves of how we have handled such challenges successfully in the past. Some people might even find it helpful to ask themselves what the worst outcome of a stressful situation would likely be. After thinking through the worst-case scenario of failure (loss of relationship, goal not met, loss of job, bypassed for promotion, etc.), most people conclude that they could indeed survive it. Ironically, doing so might even take away some of the fear and lead them to take constructive action to avoid the worst outcome.

As with many areas of organizational behavior and leadership, self-knowledge is critical (see Chapter 2). Knowing our strengths and weaknesses, and evaluating our ambitions in light of them, helps to keep us focused on realistic goals. For example, if you are a perfectionist, then you might have a number of unspoken assumptions that cause stress. You might think, either consciously or unconsciously, that you must (a) do all things for all people at all times, (b) avoid failure while trying new things, (c) always make everyone completely happy, and (d) do more than is humanly possible. An acceptance of the fact that none of us can be perfect can go a long way toward avoiding unnecessary levels of stress associated with unrealistic self-expectations. If, on the other hand, you find on reflection that you try to avoid having high expectations for yourself, avoid all risks, or find yourself bored and dissatisfied at work, then you might want to find ways of increasing the demands and stresses of your job. Try new things, seek out new challenges, set goals, and take some measured risks. Remember that some stress is a normal and beneficial part of life.

Social Support

People are social beings. From a medical standpoint, in fact, social isolation is a major risk factor in human morbidity and mortality. For example, research has shown that our personal relationships are linked to our immune function and our ability to fight disease (Quick et al., 1997). Similarly, one of the key mediating factors in determining how well people cope with stress is the amount and quality of social support that they receive. Positive relationships with and support from the people we work with can act as a buffer or mediator to job-related stress. Relationships with our supervisors, our employees, or our coworkers can provide structural, functional, emotional, and tangible support, thereby enabling us to ameliorate the potentially harmful effects of stress in the workplace (Beehr, 1995). Structural social support comes from being embedded in and connected to a network of people who we know can potentially provide support. Social support also can be advantageous in that it may serve a particular function in our lives, such as self-esteem, companionship, information, or even humor, that enables us to better cope with the demands of our work. Emotional support can take the form of understanding and sympathetic listening, which in turn can reduce anxiety. Tangible support might take the form of helping with a task or providing resources or assistance to someone at a stressful time (Jex, 1998).

The importance of structural, emotional, and functional social support has implications for both what we can do for ourselves as individuals and what we can do to help others in our organizations. The evidence would suggest that making social connections with others at work can help us to do a better job and cope with stresses as they arise. Accordingly, it makes sense to get to know the people we work with and to be attentive to connecting with others. At the same time, it is important to understand how our support—be it emotional, tangible, or functional—can strongly influence other people's capacity to cope with the stresses and strains of organizational life. Listening sympathetically to others, offering assistance, and reminding others of their contributions and strengths helps them to become more resilient when faced with organizational stressors at the same time as it benefits us by strengthening our connections to them. In short, everyone benefits when people in organizations are mutually supportive and helpful, particularly during times of stress. That is not to say that social needs and contacts ought to take precedence over work tasks and goal accomplishment. Rather, it simply reinforces today what the researchers in the Hawthorne experiments found during the 1940s—that people have social needs at work and respond to their social environment. We all need a little help from our friends.

Emotional Regulation

All of us regulate our emotions to a greater or lesser extent under different kinds of circumstances. Particularly at work, we may choose to conceal or alter the external display of our emotions for our own reasons or because the employer has set up certain rules for behavior. While emotional regulation can cause stress, it can also be important to smoothing the cycles of social interaction. It is not hard to imagine how the lack of emotional regulation, resulting in all people expressing all their emotions at all times, might make social interaction quite difficult.

Accordingly, the assumption may be that emotional regulation is bad for the person but good for the organization. But Côté (2005) argues that the effects of emotional regulation are actually quite complex, in part because emotional regulation occurs in a social context. If emotional regulation results in improved social interaction, it is less likely to cause stress. Specifically, Côté discovered that "surface acting" (what is displayed compared to what is the real emotion) increases strain when "inauthentic displays of emotion evoke adverse responses from receivers" (2005, p. 522). But not all emotional regulation evokes negative responses. If, for example, in an interaction a person conceals his or her frustration or stress and tries to appear relaxed, and the other person responds pleasantly, this might reduce the level of stress. Côté's conclusion is that although there are situations in which the workers feel stressed because of emotion regulation, managers can have an important role in reducing it. He points out that training programs that emphasize the importance and quality of social interaction could significantly reduce workers' stress.

Taking Control of Your Time

Time pressures coupled with too much to do are a major source of stress. What can you do to manage your time better and take control of how your time is spent? At its core, effective time management involves establishing and reaffirming priorities, taking stock of how you spend your time, and then organizing your time to better reflect your goals, plans, and commitments. It does not mean that you have to become a slave to the clock or become compulsive about planning and consulting your calendar. Time management for some individuals might include detailed scheduling, but for many others, a less-structured approach might work best.

Effective time management gives us a sense of control over our days. It is not just a matter of completing all of the tasks presented to us. In fact, at the end of the day, after we have done everything that everyone has asked and that we were expected to do, we still might experience stress if we have not made time to do things that we judge to be the most important. So, the first step is to determine what your priorities are. You might find it helpful to draw a pie chart and assign to the chart different-sized slices of your time that you think ought to be devoted to your various roles and tasks. (Although this exercise is described here in terms of work tasks and responsibilities, it also can be very useful as a "whole" life exercise.) Alternatively, Lakein (1973) recommended listing all of your tasks and responsibilities and using an "ABC" system in which high-priority items are assigned an A and moderate- or low-priority items are assigned a B or C. Either way, after making your priorities explicit, you evaluate how you actually spend your time. You might well discover that the actual allocation of your time does not always match your priorities and the degree of importance you assign to each of your responsibilities.

The next step is to plan your time accordingly. This is where the ubiquitous "to do" list comes in. But according to Lakein's scheme, before plowing through the list, you need to assign an A, B, or C priority to each item—reserving only the top two or three items for an A categorization. Those are the tasks that should be tackled and finished first. C items often can be postponed or ignored. If you have trouble in giving any of the items less than an A, try asking yourself the following questions. What would happen if I did not do this task? Could or would someone else be able to do this task? Could I do this task less often? What are the alternatives to doing this task? You might be surprised by how often the truthful answer to the first question is "Nothing."

In planning your time, it also is very important to allocate some part of the day for reflection, rest, creativity, and social contact. The first three of these (reflection, rest, and creativity) might involve setting aside time when you will not be interrupted, whereas the last of these (social contact) might involve forcing yourself out of your office. Although it might not be possible to "do it all" every day, it *is* possible to do the things that are most important. Doing so increases your feelings of accomplishment and control and, as a result, reduces stress while increasing your effectiveness.

Job Redesign

Some stress arises from the nature of the work itself. By modifying and redesigning jobs, some sources of work-related stress can be ameliorated. Although this is largely an organizational issue, it also might be possible for us to make some changes to our own jobs—or how we approach them—that will make positive differences. As will be suggested in Chapter 6, jobs that have skill variety, task identity, and task significance are intrinsically more motivating. Such jobs increase satisfaction, give a sense of meaning to our work, and reduce stress (Quick et al., 1997, p. 165). We feel as though we are responsible for an identifiable and interrelated set of tasks and that our work produces results.

On the other hand, jobs with great responsibility and little autonomy can cause high levels of stress. Job redesign and enrichment—including efforts to increase control and autonomy, participation in decision making, and feedback on outcomes—can help to reduce the stress associated with these jobs. The benefits of participative management styles will be discussed from a variety of perspectives in this book. Here it is important to note that allowing people to participate in the decisions affecting their work gives them a greater sense of control. Quick and colleagues (1997) stated, "Increasing participation and autonomy leads to greater freedom of action, still within defined limits, which enables individuals to channel and release stress-induced energy more naturally" (p. 173). A study by Bunce and West (1996) demonstrated that, in the long term, providing opportunities for employees to develop innovative responses to work stressors by changing work methods and modifying working relationships was more effective than traditional stress management interventions.

Although most of us are not free to redesign our jobs, there might be small changes and adjustments made in our work to reduce stress. What are the major stressors in your job? How might you increase your sense of control over the tasks for which you are responsible? If goals are lacking, then can you talk with your supervisor about the goals you would like to pursue? Perhaps making a schedule of work in which you set some of the priorities could help. Ironically, sometimes asking for more responsibility for the "whole job" actually can reduce stress. Although there are some constraints on the expansion of job responsibilities and on the nature of tasks to be performed in public sector jobs, sometimes even modest changes can help a great deal.

Other Organizational Factors

In addition to what we can do for ourselves and others, there are a number of organizational-level considerations related to stress management. As West and West (1989) concluded based on their study of job stress in the public sector, organizations must be attentive to preventive strategies in recruiting, selecting, and socializing employees. They suggested that because stress is, in part, a consequence of the "fit" between people and their organizational environment, recruitment and selection should be seen as an opportunity to ensure better person–organization matches. For example, if people are given accurate and complete information about the nature of the work prior to hiring, then they are more likely to have realistic expectations and higher levels of job satisfaction. Taking time to carefully analyze what the job requirements are and assessing candidates in light of those demands also help to decrease the likelihood of mismatches between people and organizational environments.

Organizational actions also can help employees to deal with stress after the initial hiring period. Again emphasizing the person–organization match, West and West (1989) pointed out that public organizations often are not involved in helping their employees with career planning and development. Such programs can help employees and their managers to identify needed skills, training, and development opportunities so that the person–organization match can be enhanced as employees grow and their abilities and goals change within their organizations.

Furthermore, organizations can consciously foster social support and connections among employees. Organizations and their leaders should seek to build a culture characterized by mutual respect, support, and courtesy among all employees. When faced with high stress levels brought about by increased workload and fewer employees, the Minnesota Department of Transportation used a team-building approach to develop a code of personal conduct based on "how we treat each other on a daily basis" (Armour, 1995, p. 127). Its purpose was to create a more positive work environment in which openness, encouragement, and cooperation were the norm. A survey after the development and voluntary implementation of the code reported that half of the respondents thought that the climate had improved "quite a bit," whereas the rest reported that it had improved "somewhat." Such changes can bring about positive results in reducing stress and creating a positive climate for work.

Health promotion programs can encourage employees to engage in behaviors promoting a healthy lifestyle, and employee assistance programs (EAPs) can provide assistance or refer employees to outside resources when troubles arise. Health promotion programs can offer classes and information on diet, exercise, and a variety of approaches to achieving and maintaining wellness. The scope and responsibilities of EAPs can vary from jurisdiction to jurisdiction. Some offer counseling and referral for drug and alcohol abuse and mental health problems, whereas others also deal with broader issues of career development, retirement, and relocation. In addition, EAPs can provide useful information on developing problems in high-stress areas or offer stress management training to employees.

Wright and Cropanzano (2004) argued that workers' performance can be positively influenced by promoting their psychological well-being and happiness. Their research suggested that happier workers cope with stress more efficiently than their unhappy counterparts, and as a result they are more productive. Although a person's psychological well-being remains relatively stable over time, managers can have a positive influence. Wright and Cropanzano suggested training programs that will help employees to cope with stress in a positive way, emphasizing the importance of happiness. Happy workers not only are more pleasant companions but also are more willing to work and better motivated, and they usually outperform those who feel unhappy and overly stressed.

As noted previously, good management is critical to the management of stress. Anyone who has ever worked in a poorly managed organization knows how stressful such environments can be. Information is scarce, decisions are not made or are made poorly, people are not valued, roles are unclear, and goals are lacking. People might feel helpless, frustrated, uncertain, and distressed. On the other hand, management practices that make people feel valued, that provide clear goals, that communicate well, and that offer opportunities for workers to participate and grow reduce feelings of anxiety, uncertainty, and role conflict; increase feelings of control and responsibility; and increase the likelihood that employees will feel equipped and confident that they can meet the challenges they confront.

All of these approaches and actions should be considered as part of a general effort to value, support, and develop the people on which the public service depends. Stress is a fact of organizational life. Although in moderation it has positive effects, it also can negatively affect employee health, well-being, and productivity, thereby compromising both individual and organizational capacities for effective public service. So, all of us, as well as the public organizations for which we work, need to carefully consider how to develop our human resources and build our capacity to constructively manage stress and meet the challenges we face.

Ways of Acting

Whereas a significant portion of the preceding section focused on action strategies, it is useful to review how we can use all of the information in this chapter to take action to prevent and cope with stress so as to improve personal and organizational effectiveness.

1. *Take charge.* Identify the major stresses in your life and evaluate which you can control or influence and which you cannot. For those things that you cannot change, accept them and use coping skills such as relaxation and exercise to counteract the negative effects of stress. For those things that you can change, think of strategies for eliminating or reducing the stress that they cause. For example, if you are experiencing stress because of a lack of clear objectives for your job, then develop some of your own and propose them to your supervisor. Within your own area of discretion, set personal goals for work accomplishment and then reward yourself when you attain your goals. If you are stressed by the confusion at work, then find ways of getting organized and find mental or physical places of clarity or simplicity. If you are bothered by interruptions, then take charge by setting some time aside each day when you will not be interrupted by phone calls or drop-by visitors. The message: Do not wait for your life and work to become calmer or simpler; change the things you can to make things better.

2. *Take care of yourself.* Keeping yourself healthy makes you more resilient in the face of stress and stress-related health problems. Use relaxation techniques, eat well, exercise, and get enough sleep. Remember that the stress response is physiological. Fight back by being physically rested, well nourished, and healthy.

3. *Reach out to others.* Time with friends at work or outside of work will help you to cope with stress and keep you mentally healthy. Do not forget to laugh and enjoy yourself. It is hard to feel stress and tension when you are laughing and having fun with your family or friends. When the pressure mounts and you find yourself becoming stressed, find a trusted person with whom you can talk. Sometimes the best person to talk with is a friend, sometimes it is a family member, and sometimes the objectivity of a counselor might be what is needed. Whoever it is, ask for help and support if you need it. Helping others also is a great stress reducer. Remember that you are not the only one who experiences stress. Support others and offer assistance when possible. A little encouragement, a favor, or an offer of assistance can go a long way when someone is feeling overwhelmed. As an added bonus, it can make you feel better about yourself. When you find yourself experiencing the negative signs of excessive stress, such as depression, anger, anxiety, health problems, and excessive drinking, consult a professional. Seek out assistance through your EAP, consult your doctor, or find an appropriate program or counselor on your own. Do not be afraid to get help.

4. *Find a balance.* If work is your whole life, then you and your work probably will suffer. Those who seem to handle stress best are those who have interests outside of work. It is possible and appropriate to be a dedicated, hardworking, extremely effective public servant while still having other interests. Pursue a hobby, nurture your family, or do something new. Find things that relax or distract you. Listen to music, get involved in sports, start a garden, take up photography—do anything that gives you an opportunity to express yourself, relax, enjoy your time, access your creativity, or learn new things.

5. *Be prepared.* It is helpful to try to be well organized so that you can keep up with things. Planning ahead and setting priorities, thinking ahead, and gathering needed information will help to give you a sense of control and avoid being caught unprepared and ill equipped. Whereas many situations are difficult to predict, many can be thought out in advance and allow for some preparation.

6. *Build your competence.* Feeling like you are not doing your job well can be very stressful. Build your competence and confidence by enhancing your skills, abilities, and knowledge. Honestly assess your strengths and weaknesses on the job. Explore training and educational opportunities that can capitalize on your assets and enhance your skills in areas that are weak. Find a mentor and seek his or her advice and guidance. Learn all that you can about your job, your agency, and your profession.

7. *Get creative.* Find ways of innovating on the job. What can you change to make your work more manageable, more satisfying, and more interesting? What can you reformulate? What can you delegate? How can you better use time? (See Chapter 3.)

8. *Adjust your attitude.* Remember that although stress is not "all in your head," how you perceive situations affects how stressed you become. Pay particular attention to

your self-talk. Are you sabotaging yourself with negative messages? Do you tell yourself that you are unable to cope and that you never will be able to solve the problems you confront? Try telling yourself that problems can be seen as challenges and that demands can offer opportunities. Then figure out some strategies for taking advantage of the challenges and opportunities that you encounter. Do you beat yourself up for not being able to do it all and do it perfectly? Remind yourself that being normal and happy is better than being perfect.

Thinking in Action

Now that you have read this chapter, go back to the self-assessment instruments in the "Where Do We Begin?" section and respond to the following questions.

1. What are the major sources of stress in your life? What are the major sources of stress at work? Write down three sources of stress for which you can take some sort of action to change.

2. Review the material on coping mechanisms. How might you substitute positive coping strategies for negative ones? Are your preferred coping strategies of a particular type (e.g., emotional, physical)? How might you build a more balanced and healthy repertoire of coping skills?

Building Resilience

Look back at some of the major challenges and problems that you have faced in your work and personal life. What have these experiences taught you? Identify a specific instance in which you faced a challenge in a manner that left you stronger and better able to handle such problems in the future. Then answer the following questions:

1. How do you think and feel about the challenge now, and how did you at the time you faced it?

2. What did you do in response to the challenge? How did your responses improve your ability to cope or make you stronger, more flexible, or capable?

3. How might you apply these learnings to the challenges you face currently?

Distress at DES

Your friend Diane works at the Department of Economic Security (DES) as a child protective service worker. You have known Diane personally and professionally for a number of years, and she has asked you to advise her on managing stress. She told you that she admires the way in which you seem to handle stress in your own job at the Department of Motor Vehicles, and she wants advice and counsel for reducing stress where possible and coping with the rest.

Because you are such a good friend, you have decided to set aside an afternoon to talk to Diane. You begin by asking her to simply talk about the sources of stress in her life. She tells you the following:

"First let me say, I love my job. I really think I am making a difference in the lives of children and their families. It's not that it isn't frustrating—it is. Sometimes the system just won't let me do what I think is best. I do care about my work and want to stay in the job, but I guess the stress is getting to me. I can't figure out what the problem is. After all, I've been on the job for 3 years. But I feel terrible, I can't sleep, I'm anxious, my stomach hurts, and my blood pressure is up. I even have this annoying rash that seems to appear on my neck when things get tense.

"I have a new supervisor. She's part of what is making me crazy. According to my training and what I have been taught here, I am a social worker. I am supposed to help families and kids the best I can. By law, my first priority is preserving families, which means that sometimes I have to make some pretty tough judgments between protecting the kids and keeping the family intact. This new supervisor says we're just supposed to investigate, not do social work. As she puts it, 'we don't have time to babysit or be neighborhood do-gooders.' This, she says, will free us up to increase our workload by a third.

"My husband has been so supportive. But he has gone back to school, you know. That means I have to be at the day care at exactly 6 o'clock every day of the week. Morgan, our 4-year-old, can't seem to shake the ear infections. The doctor has suggested surgery. I don't know when we're supposed to fit that in, but I guess we have to get it done.

"But back to the job. I am in the car half the day, going from case to case. I can't even tell you how often I have incomplete information. Sometimes it's a wrong address, but the bigger problem is that I just don't know what I'm walking into. We don't routinely share information with the police. Sometimes I walk into dangerous situations; sometimes it's just a nuisance call from a crazy neighbor. But I can't predict. Three weeks ago, an angry father threatened me. It normally wouldn't have bothered me so much, but I just have felt vulnerable lately.

"When I get back to my office, I have a mountain of paperwork, and of course the phone rings constantly. I used to try to have lunch sometimes with some of the other workers—talk about cases and let off some steam—but I have felt too pressured to do that in the last several months. I've got to catch up on the paperwork!

"So, I've been doing this job for a while. Why am I feeling so stressed all of a sudden? What's wrong with me? What should I do?"

Respond to the following questions.

1. What will you say to Diane? Are there additional questions you would like to ask?

2. What advice will you give her? What do you think are some of the sources of her stress? How will you work with her to develop strategies for reducing her stress?

3. What are your recommendations for coping with the stress that Diane is experiencing? What will you caution her not to do?

4. What actions have you taken in the past that have helped you to cope success-fully with stressful circumstances? Could any of these approaches be useful to Diane?

Life Balance Exercise

1. Draw a circle on a sheet of paper. Then divide the circle into sections repre-senting the importance of each of the following in your life:
   - Work
   - Family and friends
   - Intellectual pursuits
   - Spiritual life
   - Recreation and physical exercise
   - Creative and cultural activities

2. Now draw another circle. Divide this circle into sections representing the rel-ative amount of time and energy you *actually devote* to each. Compare the size of the sections in each circle. How does the relative importance of each compare with the time that you actually spend?

3. If some adjustments are in order, then first consider how you might eliminate some activities or time spent on doing things that are less important or out of balance. Then identify some specific activities that you can do to enhance your growth and development in neglected areas. For example, if you find yourself neglecting recreation and exercise, and if that is important to you, then you might find that you can schedule a brisk walk at lunch if you batch phone calls (and limit their duration) at work. Or you might find that read-ing a new and important book that you have been wanting to read, rather than going to the gym for the fifth time this week, will make you feel less pressured. The key is balance. What do you want your "life circle" to look like, and what changes can you make to more closely align the activities in your life with the values, priorities, and ideals it represents?

Finding Happiness

Being happy helps us handle stress, stay healthy, and improve the quality of our lives and the lives of others—including our coworkers and the people we serve. Accordingly, being happier can help make us better public servants. Finding happi-ness can be thought of as a deep, philosophical life quest similar to finding "the meaning of life." Or it can be thought of as a simple practice of learning to enjoy everyday things, people, situations, and activities. Think about simple things that you do, or could do, to make yourself and others happy. Make a list, if that makes you happy. In any case, do these things more often.

CHAPTER 5

Decision Making

If you properly identify the problem and respond as the situation demands, you are not making a decision. You are only making a decision when a paucity of data ensures you have a good chance of being wrong; rationally, you ought to seek every opportunity to avoid making a decision. Therefore, you must spend lots of energy determining the characteristics of the problem, the physical, bureaucratic, economic, and political environments in which it exists, and the level of performance required for the response to achieve an acceptable resolution. Through this mechanism, you avoid making a decision and instead just execute a rational response to the known situation. To do otherwise is to chance your professional life—and sometimes more.

—Captain John R. Paron, U.S. Navy fighter pilot (retired)

Public administrators face numerous responsibilities and choices. Some of their decisions have limited impact, primarily within their organizations. But others may affect the lives of thousands of people (or more) on a daily basis, and they are decisions that just seem to cascade on one another. Imagine the situation faced by transportation officials in the Northeast Corridor when they discovered that a major section of Interstate 95 (I-95) between Philadelphia and Wilmington, Delaware, had been undermined and that repairs would require completely shutting down a 10-mile section of the highway for several months. The decision to do so was itself a major move, affecting not only the incredibly high volume of traffic between New York and Washington, D.C. (and between New York and Baltimore, Maryland) but also those who commute from Wilmington to Philadelphia to work every day. And think of the decisions that flow from that. How do they reroute traffic? In so doing, what impact will the action have on businesses and residential neighborhoods adjacent to the detour? How can they minimize the difficulty? Can they encourage alternative modes of transportation, perhaps working with Amtrak to add additional commuter trains? What do they do with the cars that people would now want to park at the train station? And after all that, they discover that the parking lot nearest to the station has just been converted to long-term parking only.

Of course, not all decisions are, or should be, treated alike. Some require quick action, whereas others allow more time to decide. Imagine the difference in the I-95 example if, instead of being able to plan several months for the shutdown, transportation officials were awakened in the middle of the night to learn that the highway was closed by a sudden gas explosion and needed to be shut down immediately and for the next several months. Of course, as we saw in Chapter 4, adding time pressures to already difficult situations makes them even more difficult. And as we know, in an increasingly complex world with high-speed information systems, decision makers must respond to events of enormous complexity within minutes or even seconds. Whatever the size and shape of the required decision, it is naive to think that time always is available for decision making to undergo a calculated process. By the same token, it also is a mistake to think of decision making as simply a random process (Hall, 1999).

Let's begin by defining organizational decision making as taking place when a person in authority identifies an important issue and carries out a process to make a choice that produces outcomes with consequences (Nutt, 2005). Earlier research has found the process to unfold in a sequence of actions that includes intelligence gathering, direction setting, the regeneration of alternatives, selection of a solution, and solution implementation (Witte, 1972; Mintzberg, Raisinghani, & Theoret, 1976; Bryson, Broiley, & Jung, 1990; Eisenhardt & Zbaracki, 1992).

There are several ways of thinking about the different types of decisions that public administrators must make. Some researchers have divided decisions into two types: (1) programmed decisions (which are repetitive and routine and for which a procedure or decision rule has been established or may be easily specified) and (2) nonprogrammed decisions (which occur infrequently and are poorly structured). For nonprogrammed decisions, there is no apparent decision rule, and administrators are required to engage in difficult problem solving (Simon, 1977).

Interestingly, these different types of decisions are found more frequently at different levels of the organization, leading to another way of characterizing decisions. Decisions that take place at the top of the organization typically are labeled strategic or high-risk decisions. Strategic decisions may involve gathering intelligence, setting directions, uncovering alternatives, assessing these alternatives to choose a plan of action, or implementing the plan (Eisenhardt & Zbaracki, 1992; Harrison & Phillips, 1991; March, 1994). In a public or nonprofit organization, these decisions might involve starting a new program (e.g., community policing) or a new service (e.g., an immunization program). High levels of uncertainty and even the possibility of conflict often characterize these decisions, and choices often are shaped by external events.

On the other hand, low-risk decisions involve less uncertainty and occasionally permit a degree of delegation. For example, imagine that a change in an organization's benefits package seems advantageous. Such a change might come about by asking the human resources department to research available benefits and provide a recommendation to be approved by top management. Or there might even be more delegation. The human resources department might gather information from representatives of various stakeholder groups (including employees) invited to serve on a "benefits committee." The final recommendation might even be left to the consensus reached by the committee. Figure 5.1 shows the types of decisions that we might expect to be made at different levels of the organization. From this figure, we may conclude that the more uncertain the conditions surrounding the required decision, the higher up in the organization the decision making is likely to take place. Or, to put it differently, nonprogrammed decisions are more likely to be found at the higher levels of the organization, and programmed decisions are more likely to be found at the lower levels.

Another issue is the relationship between decision making and problem solving. As we were reminded by Captain Paron's quote at the beginning of this chapter, decisions often can be avoided if problems are solved. In support of Paron's point, Starling (1993) provided the following illustration:

Effective decision makers know that very few problems or events are unique. Most are manifestations of underlying problems. Therefore, before attempting a quick fix on Problems A, B, C, and D, they will try to find the basic problem, E. Once E is solved, A, B, C, D, and any future problems stemming from E are eliminated. Thus, effective decision makers make few decisions (p. 245). Indeed, Starling indicated that administrators often make more decisions than they need to make. Because the underlying causes of problems are not always obvious, problems are treated as

Top Management
Nonprogrammed and
uncertain decisions

Middle Management
Nonprogrammed and
programmed decisions;
risky and certain decisions

Lower Management
Programmed and
certain decisions

Figure 5.1   Types of Decisions Made at Different Levels of Organizations

SOURCE: From *The Management of Organizations,* by J. B. Barney and R. W. Griffin, 1992, Boston: Houghton Mifflin. Copyright ©1992 by Houghton Mifflin Company. Used with permission.

unique. This results in administrators treating symptoms rather than identifying and treating the root causes (Morehead & Griffin, 1992). It is important to remember that all problems require decisions, but not all decisions will require problem solving.

Finally, we should note that public managers face a particular difficulty in that their decisions often are (necessarily) made in clear public view. Certainly, the prospect of scrutiny increases as decision making moves from private to public organizations (Millett, 1966; Stahl, 1971; Nutt, 1999a). "Sunshine" laws often force the conduct of the public's business into the open, requiring such organizations to make decisions in front of interest groups, stakeholders, and the media. "Even when sunshine laws do not apply, mechanisms of accountability and oversight make all actions in public organizations, even contingency plans or hypothetical scenarios, subject to review and interpretation by outsiders" (Nutt, 1999a, p. 313). Blumenthal (1983) used the term "fishbowl management" to refer to the way in which public organizations must make strategic decisions.

Nutt's (2001) work adds to our understanding of the issue of decision making by introducing the concept of what he terms decision debacles, decisions that go so wrong that they are reported by the media. In fact, he finds that half of all decisions fail (Nutt 1997, 1999b, 2002). Not all failed decisions lead to media attention, but three common elements are found in debacles and failed decisions: faulty decision practices, premature commitments, and misallocation or resources (such as time and money spent on analyses to justify the wrong problem). Nutt also found that the context has less influence on the selection of decision-making practices than previously thought. In other words, best practices can be followed regardless of the decision to be made and the circumstances surrounding it. The prospects of success also improve when managers work to uncover hidden concerns, take steps to manage the social and political forces, identify results, encourage innovation, and estimate risk (Nutt, 2001).

Where Do We Begin?

Generating Alternatives

Think of a situation that you currently are experiencing at work, at home, or at school. Or just use the following example. You have been offered a data-entry job in a local bank. The job pays well; in fact, it might pay better than the social service job you have been planning on for the past 3 years. You have been working hard to complete your degree so as to pursue a career in social services. Going to work at the bank would mean at least postponing graduation.

Why is a choice necessary? Needing to choose implies that a gap exists between what is happening and what you would like to see occur. What alternatives exist in the situation that you are experiencing? The variations to the decision gap might look something like this:

Something is wrong and needs to be corrected.

Something is threatening and needs to be prevented.

Something is inviting and needs to be accepted.

Something is missing and needs to be provided.

Were you able to come up with an action that would close the gap? For example, were you able to justify taking or not taking the job? Through this process, we can say that the decision-making process begins with the perception of a gap and ends with the action that will close or narrow the gap (adapted from Arnold, 1978).

The Horse Grooming Case

The city of Rochester recently created a mounted police unit within the city's police department. The mounted police were to be used to patrol large gatherings, particularly in downtown areas. The city purchased the horses, trained the police officers to patrol on the horses, and rented the stables in which to keep the three newly acquired animals. One issue remained—how to groom the horses.

Andrea Alvarez, a management analyst from the police department's budget office, was asked to look into the situation. She had no idea as to the type of care the horses needed, and she knew that she must begin by learning what was required. She visited stables where horses were kept and talked to their owners, who referred her to the horse groomers. Horses require daily grooming, with several benefits (including the horses' health). Preferably, the grooming would take place in the stables where the horses were housed. Andrea learned that horse groomers could be hired full-time, part-time, or on an hourly basis, depending on the needs of the city.

Andrea was asked by the chief of police, Chief Lewis, for a recommendation to help him make the hiring decision. He was concerned about the cost of these horses and did not want to add to it, but at the same time he understood the need for care of the animals. After interviewing members of the mounted police, horse owners, and horse groomers, learning the costs and benefits of horse grooming, and reviewing the needs of the horses in the city, Andrea determined that there were four options available:

1. Hire a full-time horse groomer to care for the horses. This person would be fully trained to meet the grooming needs of the horses and also would be able to identify health needs when they arose. Of course, this would involve the highest cost, as this person would be a full-time city employee with city benefits.

2. Hire a part-time horse groomer to care for the horses. There currently were only three horses on the force. The horse groomer could be hired for 4 hours a day to come in and groom the three horses. Additional grooming would need to be done by the police officers, who also would be responsible for identifying health needs. The cost of a part-time horse groomer would be lower, but the officers might be taken away from patrol to groom the horses.

3. Contract a horse groomer on an hourly basis to care only for the city's horses. This person would require an hourly rate but would not receive city benefits. The availability of the horse groomer would have to be negotiated at the time of the contract negotiations.

4. The horses were in rented stables with groomers available, and the groomers could be added to the rent of the stables. Because some of the other horse owners who used the stables had experience with the groomers, the quality of the groomers' work could be checked. The cost would be expected to be less than that of using a separately contracted horse groomer because these people already were in the stables.

You are the management analyst who needs to make recommendations on the alternatives to the chief of police. Based on your knowledge, which option would you recommend? Why?

Ways of Thinking

An effective public manager is one who is able to identify which problems are within the scope of managerial decision making and then make an effective and responsible decision. A good decision in terms of effectiveness is one that is high in quality, is timely, and is both understandable and acceptable to those whose support is needed for implementation (Schermerhorn, Hunt, & Osborn, 1994). A good decision in terms of responsibility is one that is consistent with the public interest and offers the greatest value for the public's money. In the public sector, good decision making must meet both criteria. Time must be spent early in the decision-making process to uncover hidden or ethical concerns (Nutt, 2002). Ethical dilemmas may go undetected while decisions are made and surface later. This can be avoided if the decision maker takes steps to allow the exploration of ethical questions about a decision to be voiced as the decision-making effort unfolds (Nutt, 2001).

As a public or nonprofit manager, you must be aware of two initial steps in the decision-making process. First, you must identify the problem and its elements. In the problem-identification phase, you might ask questions such as the following. Is the problem easy to deal with? Might the problem resolve itself? Is this your decision to make? Is this a solvable problem within the context of the organization? In this process, you probably will want to keep in mind some appropriate models of decision making. Second, you will need to manage the involvement of others in the decision-making process, taking into account tradeoffs between quality and speed. If quality is most important and you are seeking a decision that is accurate, creative, and likely to be accepted by others, then you probably will want to engage various individuals and groups in the decision-making process. In this way, you will be able to have more people contributing ideas, you can divide up complex tasks, you can conduct a more thorough search for alternatives, and you probably can generate more alternatives and stimulate greater interest. But if efficiency is paramount and defined in terms of how quickly the decision is made, then you probably will have to resort to making the decision on your own. In the following subsections, we examine three aspects of the decision process: models of decision making, who should be involved, and what techniques are available.

Models of Decision Making

In 1971, Graham Allison published *The Essence of Decision,* in which he analyzed the Cuban missile crisis that President Kennedy faced during the early 1960s. Although Allison's specific example today is somewhat dated, the categories he developed to understand the decision process in this case remain extremely helpful and can be applied to other situations. Essentially, Allison suggested that there are three perspectives that one might use to analyze a major governmental decision: the rational model, the organizational process model, and the governmental politics model. (These sometimes are identified as Model I, Model II, and Model III, respectively.) Allison's basic argument was that, depending on which model or perspective you employ to understand the decision process, you see different things.

As an illustration, Allison described someone watching a chess match. Initially, most observers would assume that the chess players are moving the pieces in a strategic fashion toward the goal of winning the match. This way of understanding the situation—focusing on the goal as well as strategies and tactics to reach that goal—is consistent with the rational model. But someone else might look at the same match and conclude that the players were not single individuals and that, instead, the game was being carried out by a loose alliance of semi-independent "organizations," each moving its pieces (e.g., rooks, bishops, pawns) according to some standard operating procedures. This view would be consistent with the assumptions of the organizational process model. Finally, still another observer might watch the chess match and assume that the game was the result of a number of distinct players, with separate objectives but with shared power over the individual pieces, operating through a process of collegial bargaining (Allison, 1971, p. 7). This view would be consistent with the governmental politics model. In any case, Allison described the three models as conceptual lenses that magnify, highlight, and reveal but that also distort or blur our vision. He called for greater awareness of our choices among the three approaches.

In the following subsections, we organize our discussion around these three perspectives of decision making: the rational model, the organizational process model, and the governmental politics model. In each case, we examine the basic premises of Allison's approach as well as some of the prior thinking that led to Allison's formulation. Then we note some more recent interpretations of decision making that at least loosely correspond to Allison's three models.

The Rational Model

We begin with a general and familiar description of how decision making takes place, either in organizations or for individuals. Within the organizational context, decision making is the process by which "courses of action are chosen (from among alternatives) in pursuit of organizational goals" (Murray, 1986, p. 10). From an individual perspective, decision making can be expressed as a course of action chosen from among alternatives in pursuit of personal goals. Basically, when we think of decision making, we tend to think of a process involving the following five phases (Elbing, 1970; Harrison, 1975; Murray, 1986; Pressman, 1973):

Pre-analysis phase: Situations are defined.

Analytic phase: Situations that affect goals are perceived, and information about them is gathered.

Design phase: Options are crystallized to deal with the situation.

Choice phase: Alternatives are evaluated, and the optimal choice is selected.

Implementation phase: The alternative that is chosen to meet the specific situation is implemented.

In the rational model, these phases for decision making are performed deliberately and consciously, relying on the rationality of the decision maker's thoughts and behaviors. Allison (1971) proposed the rational model as the classical and dominant orientation to decision making. This model assumes "human purposeness both in individual behavior and in the broader scope issues such as foreign policy" (p. 30). Moreover, it assumes that individuals and groups behave rationally in decision making and when they take other actions. And to behave rationally generally is understood to mean that people try to maximize the value they receive in any situation. That is, they make value-maximizing choices.

There actually are several variations on the theme of rationality. The classic "economic man" argument suggests that people consider all available alternatives and then make choices that maximize the values they receive. For example, if you are buying a car, then you get complete information on all cars that meet certain minimum criteria and then make the choice that provides the best value—the best combination of price, features, and quality that you desire. But Herbert Simon, in his classic *Administrative Behavior,* argued that real people cannot quite handle all of the information that is available and that they do not have the decision-making prowess required to fit the assumptions of economic man (Simon, 1976).

Instead, Simon suggested that, as humans, we have cognitive limits. Because we cannot deal with all of the possible aspects of a problem or process all of the information that might be available, we do the next best thing; we choose to tackle meaningful subsets thereof and make decisions that might not maximize value but are at least satisfactory. As Simon put it, we "satisfice." In the example of buying a car, instead of searching out all of the information available and making a purely rational decision, you are more likely to look at different cars until you find one that meets your minimum criteria. Then you buy that car. But note that you still are seeking a rational decision; you just are limited in your capacity to achieve such a decision in all cases. Although what Simon called "administrative man" cannot attain the same degree of rationality as can economic man, administrative man does the best with what he has.

Allison also equated the "rational man" with the classical economic man or at least with its variant, administrative man. In either case, our goal is to make value-maximizing choices to the extent that we can. Also included in the rational model are the assumptions that decisions are orderly (not disorderly), intentional (not unintentional), purposeful (not random), deliberate (not chaotic), consistent (not inconsistent), responsible (not irresponsible), accountable (not unaccountable), explainable (not unexplainable), and rational (not irrational). The result is a decision model characterized by rational calculation of the costs and benefits of various alternatives. Both Allison and Lindblom provided similar interpretations of the rational decision-making model. Allison (1971, pp. 29–30) viewed the process as having the following four steps:

1. Translate goals and objectives into payoffs and utility.

2. Choose among alternatives.

3. Consider the consequences.

4. Select the alternative whose consequences have the greatest utility.

Similarly, Lindblom (1959, 1979) suggested that the rational decision-making process involves the following:

1. All related values are prioritized (e.g., full employment, healthy children, adults with health insurance).

2. Then all possible policy outcomes are rated as more or less efficient in achieving these goals.

3. All possible alternatives are outlined and require a systematic comparison to determine which one would result in the greatest value.

4. The choice that maximizes values is chosen.

Regardless of whether the assumptions of the rational model actually are carried out in practice, the model is attractive as a way of thinking about problems. Indeed, because it is so useful for explaining and predicting behavior, it is the model most familiar to us. Allison and Zelikow (1999) illustrated the pervasiveness of the model by asking individuals to react to another nation's unexpected behavior. They specified three occasions: the expansion into Eastern Europe by Hitler, the transfer of missiles into Cuba by the Soviet Union, and the invasion of Kuwait by Iraq. The overwhelming response of those questioned was to make sense of what happened, to develop reasons and motivations, to explore the intentions of various actors, and to assume a careful and deliberate calculation of the consequences of various outcomes. In other words, they tried to fit these aggressive and risky situations into the rational model and assumed that the government action was primarily the result of a single actor behaving under the assumptions of rational behavior. So, even when other models might be more appropriate for explanation and prediction, we tend to rely on the rational model to make sense out of decisions. In a recent study of almost 400 nonroutine organizational decisions, Nutt (2005) found that "a rational, goal-directed approach was the most effective way to search" for solutions to problems. Setting goals clears ambiguity and increases the decision makers' chance of success. Conversely, "problem-directed searches were seldom successful, no matter what protocol was used to uncover a solution" (p. 870).

The modern rational choice models introduce the element of self-interest, which seeks to explain the inconsistencies between the rational goal of the organization and the individual interests of the actor (Glaser, Aristigueta, & Payton, 2000). The notion of self-interest acknowledges that rationality is just one of the many potential influences on the decision-making process. Think back to the 2000 presidential election. A very close race left the final count of votes in the state of Florida critical to the election of Al Gore or George W. Bush as president of the United States. Early accusations of self-interest were made by both the Democrats and the Republicans. The Democrats blamed the Republican secretary of state, Katherine Harris, for acting out of self-interest in certifying the election before all avenues had been contested. The Republicans blamed the Democrats for not wanting to bring the election to closure, which they considered to be in the best interest of the American people (in this case, it also would be in the Republican candidate's favor). The secretary of state, by imposing deadlines and requirements in the counties, believed that she was acting rationally in ruling that the votes could be certified. Was the secretary of state acting out of self-interest, or was she being rational? Or should we say that rationality and self-interest coexist?

Examples of other public decision debacles include the British Millennium Dome and Euro Disney. The Dome, which opened on January 1, 2000, was hyped as a futuristic, flashy, and high-tech project to usher in the new millennium. Within weeks of opening, the project became a national embarrassment with high admission fees and lower than forecast attendance. Politicians argued over who was to blame. The government put 785 million pounds into the project and 175 million more to keep it afloat. Now, bidders plan to bulldoze the building and use its picturesque location on the river Thames to build something else (Nutt, 2001).

Euro Disney is another example of decision failure resulting from the building of the Disney park in France without, among other things, taking culture into consideration. An American park in the United States made "Americana" accessible to Europeans; yet in Europe it was less appealing. Disney applied its old formulas, replete with historical and cultural assumptions. It limited its downside cost risk but did not consider how to adapt to European culture to ensure revenues would cover the cost. Warning signs were ignored, although expressed at the press conference. Estimates of park and hotel use were overoptimistic, which suppressed the true risk of the project (Nutt, 2001).

How do decision debacles happen? Are they preventable? Can the risks and the magnitude of the losses be foreseen? Can a debacle be headed off with a midcourse correction? What lessons might we learn from experiences?

There is a growing wave of criticism of the rational model. One part of this criticism is the recognition that values and feelings also play an important role in decision making (Etzioni, 1988). In addition, habits, moral feelings, and values that have nothing to do with rationality may guide our behavior (Camic, 1985). Finally, Janis and Mann (1977) criticized the rational approach for its disregard of a holistic picture of human nature, which for us would include culture. Assuming consistency, intentionality, purposefulness, and rationality on the part of individuals invariably leads to misunderstanding and possibly false assumptions. Choosing other models as alternative conceptual lenses avoids this trap and can offer different insights by highlighting different aspects of the decision process.

The Organizational Process Model

An alternative to the rational model sees government as composed of many loosely allied organizations, each with its own set of leaders. One individual leader rarely can control the behavior of so many different organizations. To accomplish the necessary complex tasks, the behavior of a large number of individuals must be coordinated (Allison & Zelikow, 1999). According to Allison and Zelikow, Model I (the rational model) "examines the logic of consequences," whereas Model II (the organizational behavior model) "explains the logic of the action" (p. 146). The latter model includes the possibility of multiple agents in the decision-making process. But under this model, decision makers are constrained by standard operating procedures that tend to make decision outcomes somewhat predictable.

We can think of an organization as the pattern of communication and relationships in a group that provides each member with information and assumptions, goals, and attitudes that enter into his or her decisions. These patterns mean that individual members develop standard ways of reacting to situations they confront. "A sales manager reacts like a sales manager because he occupies a particular organizational position, receives particular kinds of communications, is responsible for particular sub-goals, and experiences particular kinds of pressure" (Simon, 1976, p. xix). More generally, an organization's influence on decision making is exercised by (a) dividing tasks among its members, (b) establishing standard practices, (c) transmitting objectives throughout the organization, (d) providing channels of communication that run in all directions, and (e) training and indoctrinating its members with the knowledge, skills, and values of the organization (Beach, 1990).

Allison and Zelikow (1999, p. 145) outlined five characteristics of the organizational behavior model:

1. Individuals must be organized in a structured way to achieve an objective.

2. Organizations create capabilities for performing tasks that otherwise would be impossible.

3. Existing organizations and programs constrain behavior.

4. An organizational culture emerges that shapes the behavior of individuals within organizations.

5. Organizations form a sort of technology in which groups of individuals work together in developing procedures to complete designated tasks.

Incrementalism, an alternative to the rational model offered by Lindblom, is the key to the organizational process model. Lindblom rejected the notion that most decisions are made by rational processes. Instead, he found that decisions are dependent on small incremental choices made in response to short-term conditions.

His theory suggests that decision making is "controlled infinitely more by events and circumstances than by the will of those in policy-making positions" (as quoted in Shafritz & Russell, 2000, p. 52). According to Lindblom, the bargaining process characteristic of government produces incremental "muddling through" that is quite different from the comprehensive choices of a centralized authority acting according to the dictates of rationality. Inevitably, the analysis of alternatives for action and the choice of values and goals that inform the decision become so intertwined that they are indistinguishable.

Criticisms of the organizational process model include the fact that decision makers are prevented from forecasting the future and acting on the basis of a predetermined vision. Decision makers are forced to make incremental changes based on standard operating procedures. Critics also point out that organizations create their own institutionalized rationality (Fligstein, 1992). A study of hospitals and their use of cesarean sections illustrates this point. In an empirical study, Goodrich and Salancik (1996) found that the rates of cesarean sections for childbirth in hospitals were not related to best medical practice but rather were based on organizational standards of procedure. This case provides a vivid illustration of the concerns presented by using standard operating procedures instead of what is in the best interest of the mother's health.

A related model emphasizes the legal aspects of decision making. In its most simple and direct form, law is concerned with the conduct of individuals in the context of the social, political, and economic order (Murray, 1986). The legal model consists of the sum total of principles and procedures that a society has adopted and relies on to function properly. In using this model for decision making, the law is used as a guiding principle, requiring reasoned decisions and fundamental fairness. Legal models are viewed as administrative tools in that "they aid in decision making, enhance efficiency, reduce arbitrariness, improve morale, and provide defenses when agencies' actions are challenged" (Cooper, 1996, p. 134). The legal model looks to the Constitution, laws, courts, and contractual obligations for specificity on procedures, requirements, and responsibilities. Under this model, the law is an essential device for accomplishing the responsibilities entrusted to public and nonprofit administrators.

The Governmental Politics Model

This model acknowledges that decisions in government (and other institutions) are made through a collaborative process that, in reality, bears little resemblance to a single executive making a rational choice. Under the governmental politics model, decisions are group efforts that involve bargaining among players with different and competing interests. According to Allison (1971), "To explain why a particular formal governmental process was made, or why one pattern of governmental behavior emerged, it is necessary to identify the games and players; to display the coalitions, bargains, and compromises; and to convey some feel for the confusion" (p. 146). Similarly, Wilson (1989) emphasized the important role that constituents play in government, referring to them as "the principal source of power" (p. 204).

The governmental politics model is most readily understood by defining what it is not. First, it is not a model with a single unitary decision maker; rather, it involves a number of actors with their own agendas, priorities, and timetables. Second, this model does not focus on single strategic issues at stake in a decision but rather recognizes complex multilevel issues being considered by groups of actors with multiple interests and agendas and operating in different social spheres simultaneously. For example, a cabinet secretary in a state department is responsible to the governor, departmental staff, the various interests served by the department, the public, and the secretary's own profession and career. The decisions that the secretary makes will affect and be affected by multiple stakeholders, as will the subsequent actions taken. Third, this model does not describe a single rational choice; instead, it offers "the pulling and hauling that is politics" (Allison, 1971, p. 144). Bargaining actually is a collection of decisions that often is assembled more haphazardly than logically. Most issues—for example, the Asian economic meltdown, the proliferation of nuclear weapons, or trade with China—emerge piecemeal over time, one lump in one context, a second in another (Allison & Zelikow, 1999). Hundreds of issues compete for players' attention every day. Each player is forced to fix on the relevant issues for that day, deal with each on its own terms, and rush on to the next. Thus, the character of emerging issues and the pace at which the game is played converge to yield government "decisions" and "actions" as collages (p. 257).

According to Nutt (2005), political explanations have three premises. First, important decisions are thought to stem from compromises made by a coalition. Bounded rationality is overridden by conflict of interests. Furthermore, when feeling pressure from stakeholders that have conflicting interests, "decision makers claimed to seek a politically safe choice and adjust their preferences accordingly" (p. 872). In a study of 343 decisions, Nutt found that only 14% involved delegation of the choice to a coalition, suggesting that this is not the dominant means of decision making in organizations.

The major contribution of the governmental politics model is that it places the actor within a context. Each person is influenced by his or her position, perceptions, practices, and priorities. How problems are defined and how agendas are set are critical considerations in explaining decisions and their results. Issues originate from a variety of sources, ranging from pragmatic considerations to strategic goals and values. For example, a potential increase in tuition at a state university involves various actors—the board of regents, state legislators, perhaps even the governor. How the potential increase is received will vary among the many actors affected by it—the parents or students paying tuition, employers covering employees' educational expenses, the faculty and administration of the university. What would be the reaction of these actors? Can you think of additional actors on both the decision-making and receiving ends of the decision process?

Another popular approach to decision making bearing some resemblance to the governmental politics model is what has been called the "garbage can model." The garbage can model was developed by Cohen, March, and Olsen (1972), whose original work focused on universities as a form of "organized anarchy." "These organizations could then be viewed as having a collection of choice opportunities, solutions looking for problems, and participants looking for work" (Takahashi, 1997, p. 92). *Choice opportunities* are occasions when organizations are expected to produce decisions. For example, in the university setting, a university program might be asked by the administration to decide whether it would like to implement a Ph.D. program in the School of Public Administration. *Participants* are characterized in terms of the energy they have available for problem solving. The school director would determine which faculty members would be available to work on the issue and interested in doing so. The faculty members would be asked to participate in the decision-making process. *Problems* are characterized by how much energy will be required to make a choice. After selecting the faculty members, a committee chair would be assigned. The committee would decide on the issues that must be addressed, such as the curriculum, additional faculty, recruiting of students, and the energy required to supervise doctoral students. *Solutions* recognize the potential energy that is necessary to solve a problem. The committee would then make a decision, given to the department head, on whether or not to consider adding a doctoral program based on the resources that are available.

Under this model, decision processes are affected by the timing of problems, solutions, participants, and choice opportunities, all of which are assumed to be independent. The choice opportunity is viewed as the garbage can in which problems, solutions, and energy are dumped by the participants. Once the garbage can is full, or once all of the alternatives associated with it have been exhausted, it is removed from the decision-making process. Each of the following three scenarios would lead to a full garbage can in that a decision could be made (Takahashi, 1997, p. 92).

Decision making by resolution. The choice resolves problems after some period of time working on them. In the university example just cited, we could say that the decision was reached by resolution. The committee wrote an action plan to address the proposal for the Ph.D. program.

Decision making by flight. When the choice resolves no problems after some period of time working on them, the decision can be made if the problems leave the choice opportunity. The decision could have been made by flight if the committee had not been able to reach consensus on the need or interest for a Ph.D. program in public administration.

Decision making by oversight. If there is effective energy available to make the new decision before problems become activated, then the decision will be made with minimal energy. On the other hand, the decision could have been made by oversight if the school director, after consulting with faculty, had decided that it was in the best interest of the school to develop a proposal for a Ph.D. program and took it upon him- or herself to do so.

Takahashi's empirical research revealed that "decision making by flight is a regular feature of the usual decision processes of white-collar workers in Japanese firms" (1997, p. 106). Takahashi found that an increase in workload increases the use of flight when an organization has a high degree of anarchy. He was not surprised by his findings and did not find the high flight ratio to mean failure in an organization with competent organizational workers. "In fact, it is directly [the] responsible managers for efficiency who have the high flight ratio in comparison with the others in Japanese firms" (p. 106). This is attributed to bounded rationality, where the heavy workload makes it difficult for the organization to operate smoothly and satisfactorily (March & Simon, 1958; Simon, 1976).

In addition, critics have noted that because, in this model, managers make decisions in small increments that make sense to them, they may simply generate actions that will make them look good (Starbuck, 1983) or protect them from looking bad. In fact, an analysis of decision making during the Cuban missile crisis led to the conclusion that decisions were made to avoid failure rather than to achieve success (Anderson, 1983). Perhaps a similar statement could be made of political decisions during the war in Vietnam.

Finally, how people actually choose from among alternatives was studied by Mintzberg et al. (1976), who developed a content analysis of 25 strategic decisions. They found that judgmental, bargaining, and analytical approaches were used to evaluate alternatives. *Judgment* was evidenced by decision makers in applying their intuition to select among courses of action without explaining the reasoning or rationale. *Bargaining* was said to occur when parties to the decision negotiated to reach an agreement. *Analysis* was used to produce factual evaluation. Mintzberg and colleagues found that judgment was the method used most frequently and that analysis was the method applied least frequently. Bargaining was used when opposition arose.

Who Should Be Involved?

A second major area of decision making addresses the question of who should be involved in the decision process. In this regard, there are three basic methods of decision making. *Authoritative* decisions are those made by an individual alone or on behalf of the group. *Consultative* decisions also are decisions made by an individual, but in this case they are made after seeking input from or consulting with members of the group. *Group* decisions are those made by all members of the group, ideally through consensus. Naturally, there are advantages and disadvantages to each approach. As we noted earlier, involving many people in the process may result in a better decision because many will have had the opportunity to think of the pros and cons and therefore will be more likely to support a decision in which they have been involved. On the other hand, involving many also may sacrifice efficiency given that the more people who are involved, the more time-consuming the decision-making process becomes. In group decision making, the process is slower than if an individual were to make the decision. Nutt (2005) found that in group decision making, goal setting was more important than selecting the team's members or the solution protocol to be used. This has implications for teams and will be discussed further in Chapter 10.

Moreover, there is the possibility of "groupthink," a mode of thinking that occurs when people are deeply involved in a cohesive group and their desire for unanimity offsets their motivation to appraise alternative courses of action. Janis (1971) wrote,

"My belief is that we can best understand the various symptoms of groupthink as a mental effort among group members to maintain . . . emotional equanimity by providing social support to each other" (p. 174). For example, imagine a college classroom near the end of the period. A couple of students still have questions, but as they look around the room, they see their classmates packing to leave. Rather than ask their questions, they conform to the class standard and head for the door. The goal of learning has been displaced by the power of the group. Figure 5.2 provides a prescription for the prevention of groupthink. That prescription requires critical thinking on the part of individuals and groups to avoid contamination of the process or goal displacement. Contamination of the process or goal displacement is encountered when the cohesion of the group overcomes the process for decision making or the goal for the assignment.

An extremely detailed formulation of the issue of participation was put forward by Vroom and Yetton (1973) and further developed by Vroom and Jago (1988). The Vroom–Yetton model focuses on the question of when or under what circumstances managers should involve others in decision making. In this model, the matter of participation is viewed as more complex than simply having subordinates participate or not. Rather, there are five different levels of participation that are included in the model and listed in Figure 5.3. This leads to the question: Which of these levels of participation is appropriate in any given situation? (Note that for some situations, two or more participation levels are likely to produce decisions that lead to successful results.)

Leader

    Assign everyone the role of critical evaluator.
    Be impartial; do not state preferences.
    Assign the devil's advocate role to at least one of the group members.

Organization

    Set up several independent groups to study the same issue.
    Train managers and group leaders in groupthink prevention techniques.

Individual

    Be a critical thinker
    Discuss group deliberations with a trusted outsider; report back to the group.

Process

    Periodically break the group into subgroups to discuss the issues.
    Take time to study external factors.
    Hold second-chance meetings to rethink issues before making a commitment.

Figure 5.2   Prescriptions for Prevention of Groupthink

SOURCE: From *Groupthink: Psychological Studies of Policy Decisions and Fiascoes* (2nd ed.), by I. L. Janis, 1982, Boston: Houghton Mifflin. Copyright 1982 by Houghton Mifflin Company. Adapted with permission.

Symbol	Definition
AI	You solve the problem or make the decision yourself using the information available to you at the time.
AII	You obtain any necessary information from subordinates and then decide on a solution to the problem yourself. You may or may not tell subordinates the purpose of your questions or give information about the problem or decision on which you are working. The input provided by them clearly is in response to your request for specific information. They do not play a role in the definition of the problem or in generating or evaluating alternative solutions.
CI	You share the problem with the relevant subordinates individually, getting their ideas and suggestions without bringing them together as a group. Then you make the decision. The decision may or may not reflect your subordinates' influence.
CII	You share the problem with your subordinates in a group meeting. In this meeting, you obtain their ideas and suggestions. Then you make the decision, which may or may not reflect your subordinates' influence.
GII	You share the problem with your subordinates as a group. Together you generate and evaluate alternatives and attempt to reach agreement (consensus) on a solution. Your role is much like that of a chairperson—coordinating the discussion, keeping it focused on the problem, and making sure that the critical issues are discussed. You can then provide the group with information or ideas that you have. But you do not try to "press" group members to adopt "your" solutions, and you are willing to accept and implement any solution that has the support of the entire group.

Figure 5.3   Levels of Participation in Decision Making

SOURCE: Reprinted from *Leadership and Decision Making,* by V. H. Vroom and P. W. Yetton, 1973, Pittsburgh, PA: University of Pittsburgh Press. © 1973. Reprinted by permission of the University of Pittsburgh Press.

To answer this question, the leader is advised to work through the decision tree presented in Figure 5.4. The decision tree initially appears complex but, in fact, is easy to use. One begins under Point A by asking Question A. (All questions must be answered with a *yes* or *no*. No answers of *maybe* or *sometimes* are allowed.) Depending on the answer, one proceeds to either Question B (for a *yes* response to Question A) or Question D (for a *no* response to Question A). One continues answering questions as indicated on the decision tree until reaching an endpoint. Each endpoint is numbered and is followed by a listed set of participation levels. (These refer to the participation levels listed in Figure 5.3.) This is a "feasible set," meaning that each of the levels listed in the set is likely to result in a successful outcome.

A. Does the problem possess a quality requirement?
B. Do you have sufficient information to make a high-quality decision?
C. Is the problem structured?
D. Is acceptance of the decision by subordinates important to effective implementation?
E. If you were to make the decision by yourself, is it reasonably certain that it would be accepted by your subordinates?
F. Do subordinates share the organizational goals to be attained in solving the problem?
G. Is there likely to be conflict among subordinates over preferred solutions?

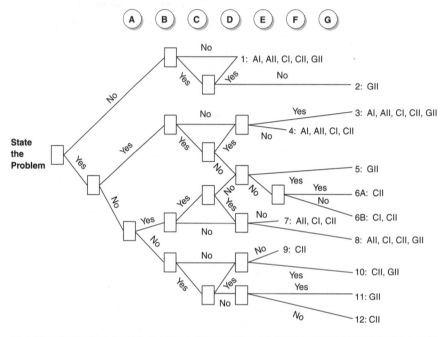

Figure 5.4   Decision Tree for Determining Levels of Participation

SOURCE: Reprinted from *Leadership and Decision Making,* by V. H. Vroom and P. W. Yetton, 1973, Pittsburgh, PA: University of Pittsburgh Press. © 1973. Reprinted by permission of the University of Pittsburgh Press.

But this does not mean that there is no reason to pick one style over another within the set, for the styles are ordered in terms of the amount of time it will take to reach a decision. The fastest approach is listed first, then next fastest is listed second, and so on. Again, the model takes into account the type of decision being made (a process aided by the decision tree) and then offers a level of participation that is most likely to be successful.

There is one more question to consider when reviewing who should be involved: are the decisions that we are making representative of the demographics of stakeholders? Let's examine why diversity should be considered in decision making.

Diversity and Decision Making

The focus on diversity in the workplace results in part from demographic shifts of racial and ethnic minorities, women, and older workers in the domestic workforce, and pressures of globalization (Wentling & Palma-Rivas, 2000); but more important, it is crucial for a representative democracy. As Mosher (1968) argued, "representativeness concerns the origin of individuals and the degree to which, collectively, they mirror the whole society" (p. 15). Mosher viewed diversity as being crucial for decision making and policy: "persons drawn from diverse groups . . . will bring to bear upon decisions and activities different perspectives, knowledge, values, and abilities. And the products of their interaction will very likely differ from the products where they are all of a single genre" (p. 16). This enhances the organization, as a diverse work environment provides an increased awareness of global opportunities, a more cogent approach to problem identification and solution, and a check on the insidious effects of groupthink (Esser, 1998; Larkey, 1996; Milliken & Martins, 1996; Morehead, Neck, & West, 1998; Watson, Johnson, & Merritt, 1998; Dunphy, 2004).

Management of diversity may be seen as a new organizational paradigm where differences are recognized, valued, and engaged (Gilbert, Stead, & Ivancevich, 1999; Pless & Maak, 2004). The goal of managing diversity is to increase awareness of ethical questions related to difference in the workplace and to help managers engage in dialogue to solve complex moral issues (Kujala & Pietilainen, 2007). Effectively managing diversity increases creativity in decision making, reduces diversity-related conflict, improves cross-cultural understanding, and provides more functional interpretation of pluralistic differences (Combs & Luthans, 2007; Cox, 2000; Cox & Beale, 1997; Dass & Parker, 1996). Europeans, Africans, Native Americans, Asians, and other racial groups possess unique cultural norms and values that affect their decisions (White & Rice, 2005).

What Techniques Are Available to Assist You?

There are a variety of techniques to assist you in various aspects of the decision-making process. In this section, we examine two popular techniques for securing more information and then discuss several others for choosing from among alternatives.

Focus Groups

Focus groups are a popular method for receiving input from a large number of individuals, serving as "group interviews" (Morgan, 1997, p. 1). A typical focus group consists of 10 to 12 people brought together to discuss a particular topic, usually with the help of a trained facilitator. Focus groups may be used for problem identification, planning, implementation, or assessment. The data gathered from these meetings are then used by managers to make decisions.

Focus groups require careful planning. Indeed, Morgan (1998) recommended that the planning occur throughout the whole project. He described the focus group process as consisting of four basic steps:

Planning: This step requires the anticipation of major decisions that will need to be made.

Recruiting: Having well-targeted participants is as important as asking good questions or using a skilled facilitator. "Problems with recruitment are the single most common reason why things go wrong in focus group projects" (p. 4).

Moderating: Effective recruiting and good questions will greatly aid the facilitator or moderator in the focus group endeavor.

Analysis and reporting: The information gathered during the focus group is finally analyzed and reported so that it can be used in the decision-making process.

Focus groups can be used in many ways. For example, a federal agency wanted to learn why its national health promotion campaign was having little effect. Focus groups indicated that the message in the existing advertising was too complex and then considered simpler ways of expressing the same ideas. A large nonprofit organization wanted to increase its activities in the African American community. Through a nationwide series of focus groups, the organization learned that it was virtually unknown, despite an advertising campaign that it thought was geared to African Americans. A state agency that was facing major cutbacks wanted to provide a job counseling program that would be of practical use to its former employees. Focus groups revealed the need for different programs for those who wanted jobs that were similar to their old ones as opposed to those who wanted to pursue new careers.

Brainstorming

Originally developed during the 1930s in the advertising industry, brainstorming is a method of generating a large number of ideas in a short period of time (Rawlinson, 1981). More specifically, brainstorming typically is used to create ideas and generate alternatives. Brainstorming is one of the most widely used and, unfortunately, misused techniques for fostering creativity. The key concept behind brainstorming is to increase creative thinking and generation of solutions by prohibiting criticism. Its misuse most commonly takes the form of participants failing to understand or adhere to its ground rules. Brainstorming works best when the following guidelines are followed:

1. State the problem clearly and neutrally. It can be helpful to restate the problem using the phrase "How can I/we . . . ?" Post the stated problem where it can be easily seen.

2. Generate ideas using these ground rules: There is no judgment made about the ideas as they are being generated, the objective is to generate the greatest quantity (not quality) of ideas, all ideas (even wild ones) are welcomed, and it is appropriate to embellish, or "piggyback," on ideas.

Group brainstorming sessions tend to work best when someone takes on the role of facilitator. The facilitator reminds the group of the ground rules and helps the group to enforce them, for example, by stopping participants who might begin evaluating other people's ideas. Rawlinson (1981) suggested that these ground rules are so important to successful brainstorming that they always should be put on display during the brainstorming session. Wycoff (1995, p. 130) suggested a number of additional ways of enhancing group brainstorming sessions:

1. *Allow time for individual idea generation.* Allow 3 to 5 minutes of silent individual brainstorming before beginning the group brainstorming session. This can reduce anxiety and prevent a "follow the leader" type of thought process.

2. *Alternate between small groups and large groups.* Groups of three or four can make it easier for people who are too shy or reticent to participate in larger groups. Larger groups can provide greater diversity and generate more laughter, which can serve as a catalyst to creativity.

3. *Realign groups frequently.* This can help groups to equalize participation and avoid the development of rigid roles.

4. *Use activities and humor.* Movement, participation, and humor can help to break down barriers to communication and creativity.

When used appropriately, brainstorming can be a highly useful technique for generating a large volume of ideas and triggering creative solutions to problems. Brainstorming also can be used effectively in conjunction with other techniques such as focus groups.

Cost–Benefit and Cost-Effectiveness Analysis

After gathering facts and suggestions, the decision maker should begin assessing the various alternatives. A variety of analytical tools are available for decisions that require this level of analysis. Because the cost of public programs usually is an issue of major concern to the public administrator, here we provide a quick overview of cost–benefit and cost-effectiveness techniques.

Cost–benefit analysis. This technique is used by government agencies to plan programs, allocate resources, evaluate outcomes, and assess the efficiency of organizational processes. "The general approach is to identify and quantify both negative impacts (costs) and positive impacts (benefits) of a proposed project and then to subtract one from the other to determine the net benefit" (Sylvia, Sylvia, & Gunn, 1997, p. 145). All costs and benefits must be expressed in monetary terms, so this technique is useful if we are interested in the efficiency of a program. However, we also can consider tangible and intangible items as well as direct and indirect benefits and costs.

These sometimes are fuzzy, requiring the analyst to pass judgment. Starling (1993) provided an example of an indirect cost: "A frequent indirect cost in government programs is compliance costs or simply red tape. For example, a new federal law designed to safeguard employee pension rights can cause small firms to terminate their plans because of paperwork requirements" (p. 253). An example of an intangible benefit is the prestige that a neighborhood might gain by the addition of a new city park. To measure the effectiveness of a program that includes nonmonetary items, the analyst must use cost-effectiveness analysis.

Cost-effectiveness analysis. This technique is used to compare the program's output to the costs encountered. Costs consist of expenditures of money and other resources (e.g., personnel, facilities, equipment) to maintain a program. (Again, some of the "cost" measures might be qualitative.) The costs are then compared with how the program is meeting the goals and objectives that have been established. The steps for cost-effectiveness analysis include the following (Hatry, Blair, Fisk, & Kimmell, 1987, p. 94):

1. Identify the objectives of the work activity and corresponding criteria to assess whether the objectives are being met.

2. Examine the current cost and level of quality of the service activity.

3. Based on this evidence and on observations of the way in which the current activity is performed, identify alternative ways of doing the activity. Consider ways of eliminating unnecessary tasks and new procedures.

4. Assess the cost and service quality effects of each alternative.

Nominal Group Technique

This technique was developed to ensure that every group member has equal input in the process (Guzzo, 1982, pp. 95–126). The process for the nominal group technique is as follows. First, each participant, working alone, writes down his or her ideas on the problem to be discussed. These ideas usually are suggestions for a solution. Second, the group conducts a round-robin in which each group member presents his or her ideas to the group. The ideas are written down on a blackboard for all of the participants to see. No discussion of the ideas occurs until every person's ideas have been presented and written down for general viewing. Third, after all ideas have been presented, there is an open discussion of the ideas for the purpose of clarification only; evaluative comments are not allowed. This part of the discussion tends to be spontaneous and unstructured. Fourth, after the discussion, a secret ballot is taken in which each group member votes for preferred solutions. This results in a rank ordering of alternatives in terms of priority. As desired, the third and fourth steps can be repeated to add further clarification to the process.

Logic Models

Increasingly, what are called "logic models" are being constructed and used to explain program logic and assist with evaluation and decision making. Logic models require systematic thinking yet allow decision makers the flexibility to run through many possible alternatives before determining what is best. The most basic logic model is a picture of how the program is anticipated to work from initial inputs through end outcomes.

It typically consists of inputs and activities, intermediate outcomes, and end outcomes. Hatry (1999) suggested that users of logic models should consider beginning from the desired outcome and work backward, something that he believes will expand the decision makers' creativity and innovative thinking. Hatry suggested that moving in the other direction—starting from existing activities and identifying outcomes that flow from those activities—might limit the user to the existing activities.

To illustrate how a logic model might be used in decision making, consider the problem of children's access to health care, with the end outcome of healthy children. Intermediate outcomes may include immunization of children, medical treatment when necessary, and education for a healthier lifestyle. Activities may include making sure that children have access to health insurance, health centers, and health education. A logic model for this issue is illustrated in Figure 5.5. Additional alternatives to address the same problem could be generated and depicted through an extension of this model or through the development of alternative models. Once the problem is depicted in this way, decision makers might have a clearer picture of the relationship among various elements of the problem and be able to arrive at a more well thought out position.

Discretion in Decision Making

There are times when you will be asked to act without special decision-making tools or normal operating procedures. These situations will call for reasonableness in the application of administrative discretion. Discretion is part of the broad continuum of decision-making processes that involve the act of making choices; these choices may be made by bureaucrats at the street level or by managers exercising administrative discretion (Vaughn & Otenyo, 2007). Administrative discretion is "about judging about competing values, choosing a best possible solution, and

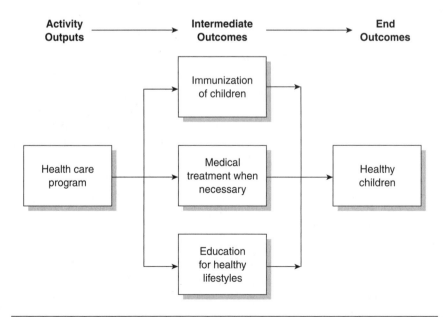

Figure 5.5   A Logic Model

being free to extend the rights and duties of office" (Vaughn & Otenyo, p. xii). This definition takes us beyond the street level and includes discretion at all levels of government involved in management of the public organization, or what will be termed in this chapter *managerial discretion.*

Decision making by discretion requires caution and the inclusion of key administrative values such as representation, economy, efficiency, effectiveness, equity, fairness, and transparency. An ethically sound decision will require evaluation on whether it is right and just (Burke, 1996). When discretion is at odds with political accountability, democratic governance, especially the rule of law, is jeopardized. Earlier we talked about street-level leadership (Vinzant & Crothers, 1998). Related to that idea are street-level bureaucrats, a term coined by Lipsky in 1980. Whether called leaders or bureaucrats, these people are called to make decisions as they are implementing policy. A study by Maynard-Moody and Musheno (2003) reiterated the significance of street-level bureaucrats in the political process, asserting that street-level workers "actually make policy choices rather than simply implement the decisions of elected officials" (p. 3). They also claim, based on a study of 48 street-level state employees in two states, that "workers' beliefs about the people they interact with continually rub against policies and rules" and that the prejudices of the street-level bureaucrats influence their treatment of stakeholders (p. 3).

Dillman (2002) contends that discretion is often necessary for things to get done in emergency situations requiring efficiency and effectiveness. In disaster management, the prevention of loss of life, recovery of life and property, security, public safety, relief, and reconstruction, to name a few, become paramount in the decision-making process, and unnecessary adherence to federal and state policies may slow down the response, a criticism encountered by the governor of Louisiana in her response to the 2005 Hurricane Katrina ravaging of the Gulf Coast. Governors of several affected states were viewed as more proactive by using managerial discretion to prepare and implement their states' relief and evacuation services. In Tennessee, the governor issued an executive order to suspend certain laws and rules in order to provide relief to victims of Hurricane Katrina as part of the state's Emergency Management Plan. Under Tennessee's state law, the governor is authorized to "suspend the provisions of any law, order, rule, or regulations prescribing the procedures for the conduct of state business or the orders or rules of any state agency, if strict compliance with the provisions of any such law, order, rule or regulations would in any way prevent, hinder, or delay necessary action in coping with the emergency" (Vaughn & Otenyo, 2007, p. 67). This included pharmacists assisting evacuees and certain kinds of restricted vehicles permitted to use interstate highways. Other examples of governors using managerial discretion include Alabama, where the governor established an uncompensated care pool that allowed state officials regulatory flexibility in providing medical care for Katrina evacuees. In Arkansas, the governor issued a state of emergency order in specific jurisdictions that permitted school and city buses to be moved into the disaster areas. A Hurricane Recovery Fund was established by the governor of Mississippi to serve as the state's central clearinghouse for corporations, organizations, and individuals making donations for residents who were recovering and preparing to rebuild (Vaughn & Otenyo, 2007).

Summary

To summarize, we can think in terms of building blocks for effective decision making (Arnold, 1978). Building Block No. 1 is to *smoke out the issue.* Ask yourself *why* a decision is necessary. Recognizing and defining a problem is an important first step in problem solving and decision making. The answer to this first step not only provides you with a definition for the problem at hand but also clarifies whether there is a problem at all. If there is a problem, then keep asking why until all issues have been determined. It is possible to deceive yourself with superficial answers. By asking why repeatedly and verifying the answers, you are able to expose the real issue, which will aid in making the correct decision.

What *is* or *is not* the problem? This question helps to define the problem as precisely as possible by separating the mere symptoms from the root cause. Asking what the problem is not, through the process of elimination, might help to uncover a truth or eliminate barriers to a problem. For example, Bryson (2004), in reviewing mandates for public and nonprofit organizations, recommended that the strategic planner consider what is not limited by the mandates. Sometimes we believe that the restraints are greater than they really are.

What is, should be, or could be happening? This question is a supplement or may serve as a substitute to what is or is not the problem. Asking what is, what should be, or what could be requires that we examine the differences among reality, expectation, and desire or conceivability.

Building Block No. 2 is to *state your purpose.* The statement of purpose is the most critical step in the decision-making process, yet it is a step that often is neglected. The neglect comes from not wanting to waste time on examining purpose when time could be spent on solutions. Unexamined statements of purpose frequently mask the real problems. For example, a new assistant professor at a research institution might enjoy teaching so much that she neglects her requirements to contribute to knowledge through research and publication. Examining her purpose at these institutions, she might learn not only that research is a requirement of the position but that it would enhance her teaching as well.

Building Block No. 3 is to *set your criteria.* Setting criteria requires answers to the following three questions, which will be used to judge possible solutions: What do you want to *achieve* by any decision you make? What do you want to *preserve* by any decision you make? What do you want to *avoid* by any decision you make? To illustrate the point using the example discussed in the preceding paragraph, we could say that the assistant professor wants to achieve the following: to provide the best education possible to students, to contribute to knowledge so as to meet the tenure and promotion requirements, and to provide service to the community. She wants to preserve a job at a university she really likes and to remain in a field for which she has prepared. And she wants to avoid having to look for another position.

Building Block No. 4 is to *establish your priorities.* This step requires that you refine your criteria by setting your priorities. In most decisions, not all criteria are of equal importance. Starting with the list of things you want to achieve, preserve, and avoid, you begin by separating the items into categories of relative importance (e.g., very high, high, medium, and low). This will help you to decide which ones are absolute requirements and which ones are desirable objectives. Assigning the values to the criteria is not easy. Some of the criteria might not be as important to you as you originally had thought, or you might discover that you have not stated them correctly or completely. Now is the time to restate, refine, and reevaluate the criteria. When restating the criteria, be as specific as possible.

Building Block No. 5 is to *search for solutions.* After determining your purpose and defining your criteria and priorities, you begin your search for solutions by asking the following questions: How can you meet the criteria you have set? What are the possible courses of action? Answering these questions requires brainstorming. You do not want to limit yourself to the obvious alternatives. Let your criteria generate your alternatives; this will facilitate fresh solutions and provide several alternatives. The alternatives might then need to be combined or modified to fit your criteria and priorities.

Building Block No. 6 is to *test the alternatives.* Testing the alternatives requires answering the question, how well do the alternatives meet each criterion? Each alternative is matched against the criteria, and a choice is made.

Building Block No. 7 is to *troubleshoot your decision.* This final building block is perhaps the most critical and the least practiced. This step helps you to take action to prevent, minimize, or overcome the possible adverse consequences by asking the question, what could go wrong with the solution that I have chosen? Make a list of all the possible problems, and then make a rough calculation of the likelihood of each problem occurring and the likely impact if it did occur. Finally, take preventive action to cope with each potential problem.

Ways of Acting

In this chapter, we learned that there are different types of decisions that we will be faced with in the workplace and that different decisions call for different strategies and actors. We also discussed the difference between decision making and problem solving and learned that there are times when we can rely on previous patterns for decision making and other times when the problem requires new and perhaps innovative solutions. In addition, we learned several models that may be used to help us frame the problems, develop alternatives, and ultimately formulate solutions. We also looked at the question of who should be involved in organizational decisions. Finally, we discussed techniques that are available to the decision maker in examining alternatives. The following behavioral guidelines might help in implementing these various methods correctly.

1. *Define and verify the problem fully and accurately.* You must overcome the temptation as a group or an individual to try to define the problem too quickly. Problem definition is difficult. Problems are not always clear. For example, you might initially attribute turnover in the workplace to a lack of opportunity for promotion. Interviews with those who have left the organization, and with those who have remained, might suggest instead that turnover is due to the lack of resources available to complete the work required.

2. *Use the problem to generate solutions.* You might find that well-defined problems have implied solutions. For example, if the problem is dissatisfaction in the workplace and the problem includes inadequate facilities, then the alternative solutions will begin with how to improve the inadequate facilities.

3. *Prevent premature evaluations of solutions.* Continue brainstorming until all possible alternatives have been generated. When alternatives are evaluated, the idea generation for possible solutions typically ceases.

4. *Provide a climate that values disagreement.* As we will see in Chapter 11, healthy conflict is helpful in generating ideas. Make sure that you seek input from those who disagree with you as well as those who agree with you. Consider all alternatives equally.

5. *Provide a climate that values diversity.* Creativity in decision making will be enhanced and groupthink will be diverted in valued and well-managed diverse environments.

6. *When possible, gain consensus from all of those affected while avoiding premature consensus building.* Solutions will be much more likely to be accepted if all of those affected have been involved in the decision-making process. For example, you might find that the solution to the facilities problem requires moving to a new location. Employees will be more satisfied with the move if they have been kept informed of the options and have contributed to the decision.

Thinking in Action

A Decision-Making Framework

Using a community service project, an internship, or a work experience, use the following framework adapted from Philip (1985, pp. 84–91) to analyze the process of decision making.

1. Clarify your objectives.
   - Describe the situation on which you are working. State your precise objective.

2. Consider the factors that will influence your choice of action.
   - List the factors that are important to you and to those affected by the decision.
   - Extend the factors into statements that specify the results expected, resources available, or constraints that might exist.
   - Classify the statements that will have to be regarded as essential.
   - Assess the importance of the remaining factors and list them in descending order of importance.
   - Generate the options that could be compared with your specifications. Do not forget to include the status quo and inaction as options.
   - Compare your options with your essential factors.

3. Collect information with regard to the benefit and risk factors for the remaining options and assess the degree of satisfaction that each option provides.
   - Identify the benefit–risk area for each option to be considered.
   - Describe your best balanced choice.

New Charter School

Jannell Adami is the new principal of a recently inaugurated charter school. She has many challenges ahead of her given that she is working in a community with many needs. Her board has given her a series of priorities to implement during her first year, and she has promised to make a difference in the lives of as many children as possible. Her first priority is to address the educational needs of the children in her community, but she recognizes that she cannot address the educational needs without getting to know the community better. Because she has limited funds, she would like to maximize her resources by determining the most critical and prevalent needs that affect the children in this community. Before the beginning of the school year, she will go to the community and ask what the critical needs are before making decisions on programs to implement. Through a variety of sources, she is able to identify 20 individuals who would serve as a starting point for the discussion. She likes the idea of using focus groups to generate ideas with the community groups. She has asked you for advice. What recommendations would you provide her in setting up the focus groups?

Using the Decision Tree for Levels of Participation

Max Herbert heads a unit of the state transportation department charged with developing a new traffic flow design for the busiest intersection in the largest city in the state. Max earned an MPA and had several years' experience in the state's budget office before moving to the transportation department, where he has worked for a year and a half. His staff consists primarily of traffic engineers and planners, most of whom are considerably older than Max and have far more experience in transportation that he does. Max recognizes their expertise, although he believes that his staff members have become a bit tradition bound, tending toward "safe" solutions to traffic problems. He recognizes that different staff members are likely to have different approaches to solving the problem they face, although he also believes that in the end they will arrive at an acceptable compromise and probably one that is "safe."

Delays and bottlenecks caused by the current traffic pattern have made the issue of a new design a fairly high-profile issue, so Max is concerned about his group producing a high-quality product, one that will be technically sound as well as politically acceptable. Although he is not a traffic engineer, Max has done his homework and learned a lot about transportation issues during his time in the department. Following a recent conference in London, Max went on a study tour of several European cities, during which he developed some ideas that he considers forward-looking and certainly workable in this particular city. Although he is not prepared to do the technical details and drawings necessary to support his idea, he has a concept in mind that he thinks will work. At the same time, he is concerned that if he forces his idea on his staff, they will "rebel" and not do as good a job as they might otherwise do in completing the follow-up details and drawings.

Using the Vroom–Yetton diagram in Figure 5.4, discuss how Max should approach the question of developing the overall concept for the city's new traffic pattern.

CHAPTER 6

Motivating Yourself and Others

Relationships are the key to effectiveness.

—Jan Perkins, former city
manager, Fremont, California

All organizations need motivated employees. People who are motivated to consistently, creatively, and energetically work toward the attainment of organizational goals are the key to organizational success. Motivation also is critical to our own personal success. The more motivated we feel to do our best, to accept new challenges, and to help others accomplish their goals, the more satisfied and successful we will be in our work.

Whereas motivation is important in all types of organizations, it can be argued that motivation is particularly important in governmental organizations. In fact, Behn (1995) asserted that motivation is one of the three "big questions" of public management. Behn asked, "How can public managers motivate public employees (and citizens, too) to pursue important public purposes with intelligence and energy?" (p. 319). Behn's question is important for two reasons. First, the fact that motivation is one of only three issues in public management that he emphasized highlights its significance in the field. But even more important is the acknowledgment that motivation in the public sector is *aimed at the achievement of public purposes.* In other words, motivating ourselves and others in the public service is critical if we are to fulfill our responsibilities to the citizens and communities we serve. In a very literal sense, the quality of our neighborhoods, communities, and world depends on it.

Despite its importance, the conventional wisdom is that it is difficult, and perhaps even impossible, to develop and maintain highly motivated government employees. There is a persistent and widespread belief that people who work in the public sector are fundamentally lazy and unmotivated. There are a number of reasons given for such a supposition. First, the rewards and incentives available for use by public sector managers, particularly in terms of pay and promotion, might be limited. Behn characterized public managers as frequently complaining about "their inability to motivate their subordinates" and to "get anything done" because of civil service rules that they believe prevent them from firing or rewarding anyone (1995, p. 318). Second, many believe that people who pursue public sector careers are less achievement oriented and are primarily attracted to public service by job security. The assumption is that public employees are, by their very nature, not a very highly motivated group. Third, motivation is said to be more complex in public organizations because the goals often are more ambiguous than those in the private sector, where the clear and fundamental goal is profit.

It turns out that these myths are just that: They are not true. The research on public sector motivation generally suggests that public sector employees are, in fact, no less motivated than their private sector counterparts. Baldwin (1984), for example, found no significant differences in motivation between private and public managers. Furthermore, Guyot (1960) reported that public managers had a significantly higher level of achievement motivation than did their business sector counterparts. Despite these research findings, the perception that public servants lack motivation is persistent. This *belief* might be troubling in and of itself. Kilpatrick, Cummings, and Jennings (1964), for example, interviewed students and government and nongovernment employees about their views on motivation in the public and private sectors. The majority of those questioned reported that they *thought* that government employees lacked drive and initiative.

As public servants, if we also believe that our fellow workers, our employees, and we ourselves lack drive, ambition, and motivation, then we might be led to act and think in ways that only exacerbate the challenges that face *any* manager in working to motivate him- or herself and others. The belief that public employees lack motivation can become a self-fulfilling prophecy as people live up (or down) to their expectations. As this chapter will show, public service offers distinct opportunities for motivating people to do excellent and often extraordinary work. For example, research suggests that public service motivations such as the desire to serve the public, achieve societal goals, and make communities better places in which to live can have a very positive and important role in creating and maintaining a vital and productive public workforce and in enhancing personal motivation, commitment, and satisfaction with public service work (Balfour & Weschler, 1990; Perry & Wise, 1990; Vinzant, 1998).

Beyond these public service motivations, there are many tools and perspectives that are helpful to public sector managers in working to motivate themselves and others. Many of the negative stereotypes about motivating themselves and others in the public sector just do not make sense in light of what we have learned about what does and does not motivate people at work. For example, during the era of scientific management, it was assumed that people would not work unless managers made them work. Accordingly, if managers could not at least maintain a threat of firing them, then people would not be expected to work productively. Since that time, we have learned that motivation is much more complex; people are motivated by a variety of factors having to do with the nature of the work, the quality of relationships, inner needs and drives, and a number of other factors. So, the idea that managers cannot motivate public employees because they cannot fire them not only is insulting but also is not supported by research.

But that does not make motivating yourself and others an easy task. In fact, it remains one of the most challenging and important parts of managing and working with people in organizations. For example, imagine yourself as the newly appointed supervisor of a unit that interviews applicants and processes the paperwork for unemployment applications. You have inherited eight employees whose experience varies from 3 months to more than 40 years, each with his or her own strengths and weaknesses:

> Susan is extremely careful and rarely makes mistakes. She is courteous and professional but takes about twice as long as the average employee to interview an applicant and process the paperwork.

> Marilyn is much faster but is quite brusque with clients, sometimes resulting in complaints.

> Mark's work is average; he handles an appropriate number of cases and makes few errors. But he has been having open, hostile, and time-consuming conflicts with his coworkers over seemingly small matters such as their fans blowing the papers on his desk and the odor of their lunch wrappings in the wastebaskets.

> Tom, the newest employee, is fresh out of college. He is young, energetic, and eager to please but does not always use good judgment in handling clients. Last week, he allowed someone who complained to move ahead in line, rightfully angering the other people who were waiting. Still, he does excellent work and seems willing and ready to learn from his mistakes.

> Sheri is an outstanding employee. She is quick, efficient, and professional, and she has excellent "people skills." She seems to be a natural leader among her coworkers, and they often seek her advice on difficult matters. She has been invaluable to you in providing constructive suggestions on how to make the application process work more effectively.

> Ralph is the most senior employee. Although he has an excellent record, he is going through a very difficult divorce and is only 1 year away from retirement. He has become increasingly preoccupied with these matters. As a result, his work has suffered substantially in terms of both amount and quality.

> Toni is the social organizer and spends much of her day planning potlucks and bowling nights, gossiping with coworkers and clients, bringing in balloons and donuts, and playing practical jokes on everyone. Although a little socializing is good, you think that she crosses the line to the point where she spends more time on those activities than on assigned tasks.

Hank hates his job and you in equal measure. He complains constantly to all who will listen. He pins up slogans in his office such as the one this week that says, "Only insecure supervisors refuse to delegate." This followed a meeting in which he presented you with a proposal that he be allowed to work from home and that the other employees could handle all of the interviews. When you told him that such an arrangement was not feasible, he accused you of not trusting him. As he walked out of your office, he turned and asked snidely, "Haven't you ever had any supervisory training?"

You have just received word from the central office that the geographic area your office serves has doubled and that your office will need to serve the increased numbers of clients with no increase in staff. In addition, the central office has put you on notice that the error rate in paperwork processing has increased 20% over the past 6 months and that your new goal is to decrease it by 10% per quarter for the next three quarters. How will you motivate your staff to take on this new work-load and to do so while achieving a decrease in error rate? How can you motivate yourself and your employees to do their best in terms of serving the public?

As you can see, motivation is critically important in achieving organizational success. It also is important to your own personal achievement and commitment to organizational and public service values. What motivates you and others to behave as you do at work? How can these motivations change? How can you influence motivation in a way that is positive and constructive for you, your coworkers and employees, the organization, and those you serve? This chapter focuses on these types of questions and challenges, with an emphasis on some particular opportunities for improving motivation in the public service. It begins with some exercises to help you reflect on your own motivations and beliefs about what motivates those around you. It then reviews what has been learned about motivation in the workplace and competing models for understanding what motivates employees. Finally, it provides practical action strategies for enhancing motivation in yourself and others as well as cases and exercises to practice your skills.

Where Do We Begin?

There are several reasons for beginning our discussion of motivation with ourselves. First, to enhance our own experience at work, it is important to understand what motivates us. Second, if we are highly motivated, then that can influence others in a constructive way. For example, working for or with someone who lacks motivation would make it more difficult to maintain our own motivation. Third, understanding what motivates us can help us to make prudent career choices that allow us to work in organizational settings that keep us excited about and interested in our work.

The final reason for beginning our examination of motivation with a look inward requires a bit more explanation. Put simply, looking inward helps us to resist the temptation to assume that what motivates us is what motivates others. Psychologists call this process *projection*. Projection is a mental process in which we attribute or assign our own feelings, motives, or qualities to other people. We are particularly likely to project those feelings that we are not conscious of or are not comfortable with. For example, if one of your employees has not been completing his or her assignments, then you might assume that this person has lost interest in the job. This might be true, but it also might be true that *you* have lost interest in *your* job and that you have not confronted those feelings. To deal with those feelings, you project them onto someone else.

Projection is a mental shortcut that makes it seem as though understanding other people's behavior is much simpler than it actually is. It is natural for us, when confronted with other people's behavior, to ask ourselves, "What would make *us* behave in that way?" Although it might be natural, it also is generally a mistake. As we become more self-reflective about our own motivations, it becomes easier to see how and when we might be projecting those motives onto others. As we begin to understand and separate our own needs and motives from those of others, it makes us better employees, managers, and leaders.

The following are some exercises that can begin to help you think about your motivations. Remember as you work through these exercises that motivation is multifaceted; it is influenced by our work situations, our life stages, our personalities, and many other factors. As a result, individual motivations change over time and from situation to situation.

What Motivates You Now?

Read through the following statements. Then select those eight items that are most important in terms of motivating you in your present (or most recent) work environment.

1. A positive working relationship with my boss

2. Good pay

3. Lots of freedom on the job

4. Praise for a job well done

5. Interesting and challenging work

6. People with whom I enjoy working

7. Knowing that there will be consequences for poor performance

8. A clearly written job description

9. Chance for promotion

10. A nice office

11. Personal respect

12. A generous retirement program

13. Performance evaluations

14. Doing important work

15. Time off from work

16. Serving the public and making the community a better place to live

17. Regular hours

18. Knowing "inside" information about what is going on at work

19. Opportunity for learning and growth

Keep your answers. When we discuss "need theories" later in the chapter, we will come back to score this instrument.

What Will Motivate You in the Future?

You have been invited to interview for your dream job. At the time the interview was scheduled, you were asked to be ready to discuss what factors would be most important in motivating you in this position. What will you say? Compare what would motivate you in your dream job with what motivates you in your current job. Are there differences? Why?

Ways of Thinking

What Is Motivation?

Before reviewing different perspectives on motivation, it is useful to consider what is meant by the term *motivation*. Put simply, motivation is what causes people to behave as they do. But the term is used by different people in different ways. In fact, Kleinginna and Kleinginna (1981) found 140 different definitions of motivation. Atkinson (1964) stated that "the study of motivation has to do with the analysis of the various factors which incite and direct an individual's action" (p. 1). Pinder (1998) described work motivation as the set of internal and external forces that initiate behavior and determine its form, direction, intensity, and duration. If we were to review all of the available definitions, then we might conclude, as Brown (1961) did, that the concept of motivation is "scandalously vague." Although this probably is an overstatement, it is important to remember as we review what has been learned about the topic of motivation that not all researchers define motivation in exactly the same way.

Despite the lack of a single commonly accepted meaning, there are some common themes across many of these definitions that prove to be useful from the standpoint of managing organizational behavior. First, as Lawler (1973) suggested, motivated behavior is goal-directed behavior. This means that when we are motivated to accomplish some purpose, we have made a voluntary choice to do so. It also means that motivation does not necessarily explain all behavior. For example, some behavior might be better understood as a manifestation of instinct or reflex. Second, motivation theories seek to explain the process through which goals are pursued and achieved. In other words, the motivation process includes more than just the initial spark or impetus for a particular behavior; it also concerns how behavior or choices are sustained or altered as we seek goal attainment. Third, motivation is "limited and directed by the situations and environments in which people find themselves" (Pettinger, 1996, p. 94). In other words, motivation takes place in a particular context, and the characteristics of that context influence motivation and behavior. Our context here, of course, is the public sector.

In addition to thinking about what motivation *is*, it is important to talk about what motivation *is not*. The following paragraphs give specific examples of what motivation *is not*.

Directly observable. Motivation is an internal state that causes people to behave in a particular way to accomplish particular goals and purposes. It is possible to observe the outward manifestations of motivation but not motivation itself. As Pinder (1998) put it so succinctly, *motivation is invisible.*

The same as satisfaction. It is possible to be very satisfied but not motivated and to be very unsatisfied but highly motivated. As Lawler (1990) pointed out, "Motivation is influenced by forward-looking perceptions concerning the relationship between performance and rewards, while satisfaction refers to people's feelings about the rewards they have received" (p. 32). Put simply, satisfaction is past oriented, whereas motivation is future oriented. Although the terms are not synonymous, satisfaction is a concept that is closely related to motivation. If motivation arises from a desire to meet a particular need or goal, then people will engage in behavior that they think will satisfy that need or meet a particular objective in a given circumstance. So, motivation may involve people's attempts to gain satisfaction of some need or desire.

Always conscious. People are not always aware of what is motivating them to behave in a particular manner. They might do some things out of habit or be motivated by subconscious needs. For example, if people have low self-esteem, then they might subconsciously need to fail so as to reinforce their low opinions of themselves.

Directly controllable. Motivation is not something that people do to others. Motivation occurs within people's minds and hearts. Managers can influence the motivational process, but they cannot control it.

Changing Perspectives on Motivation

As we saw in Chapter 1, the study of motivation was not a central part of early management theorizing in the United States. But during the decades following the Hawthorne experiments (published during the 1930s), a number of different perspectives offered alternative views of motivation. Although these models do not necessarily represent mutually exclusive views on motivation and the motivational process, it is useful to categorize them by which part of motivation they emphasize— human needs, the goals people seek to attain, the factors people consider in choosing behavior, the effect of cognition on motivation, the characteristics of people that may influence the motivational process, and the influence of rewards. These perspectives are considered in the sections that follow.

Need Theories

Among the most influential and intuitively appealing approaches to understanding motivation are the theories that describe behavior as being directed toward the satisfaction of human needs. The theoretical foundation for many of these approaches is found in the works of Maslow. Maslow, a clinical psychologist, published in 1943 "A Theory of Human Motivation," which remains one of the best-known and most widely cited works on motivation. In simple terms, Maslow argued that people are motivated to behave in ways that will satisfy their needs. Maslow conceptualized human needs in an ascending hierarchy from lowest level needs to highest level needs. In this model, different levels of human needs are aroused in a specific sequence, and as each lower-level need is substantially satisfied, the person is motivated to seek to satisfy the next higher level of need. This hierarchy of needs is depicted as a pyramid in Figure 6.1.

Maslow (1943) suggested that the needs that motivate human behavior can be categorized as follows, moving from the bottom (the most basic) to the top of the pyramid:

Physiological needs: Called the most "prepotent" of needs, these address basic biological drives for food, air, water, and shelter.

Safety needs: Once basic physical needs are met, humans seek to gratify their needs for safety, security, and freedom from danger.

Love needs: If both physiological and safety needs are substantially satisfied, then love, belongingness, and social needs will emerge.

Esteem needs: These needs speak to our desire to have the recognition and attention from others that support positive self-esteem and a positive self-image.

Self-actualization: The highest level needs are those that cause us to seek self-fulfillment and "to become everything that one is capable of becoming" (p. 382).

A basic assumption of this model, according to Maslow, is that "man is a perpetually wanting animal" (1943, p. 395). In other words, as we satisfy one type of need, other needs then occupy our attention. Furthermore, although Maslow

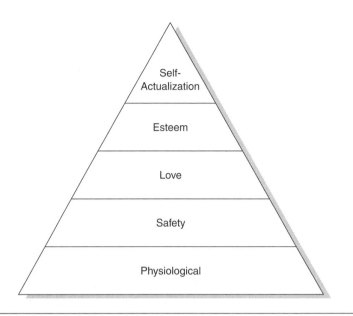

Figure 6.1   Maslow's Hierarchy of Needs

argued that most people tend to experience these needs in the order that he described, for some people the so-called higher-level needs will dominate lower-level needs. It also is important to emphasize that Maslow did not suggest that each level of need has to be fully satisfied, only that it must be partially and adequately satisfied. Maslow stated, "Most members of our society who are normal are partially satisfied in all their basic needs and partially unsatisfied in all their basic needs at the same time" (1943, p. 388). As we reach increasingly higher levels of satisfaction for a particular need, that need decreases in potency as a motivator. Put simply, we no longer will seek food when our hunger is adequately satisfied.

Maslow's work served as the point of departure for McGregor, another highly influential management thinker. As we saw in Chapter 1, although McGregor was not a motivation theorist, he used Maslow's hierarchy of needs to capture the dramatic shift in management thinking that was occurring based on changing conceptions of human motivation and the needs of people at work. In an article titled "The Human Side of Enterprise," McGregor (1957) contrasted the conventional view of "management's task in harnessing human energy" (which he called Theory X) with a "new theory of management" (which he called Theory Y). Theory X is based on conventional assumptions about worker motivation such as those represented in the works of Taylor. Conversely, Theory Y is based on the recognition that people need opportunities at work to satisfy not only lower-level needs for wages and decent working conditions but also higher-level social and ego needs. The Theory X assumptions about workers can be summarized as follows:

People are naturally lazy and work as little as possible.

Workers lack ambition, avoid responsibility, and prefer to be led.

Employees are interested only in their own needs, not the needs of the organization.

People are resistant to change.

Workers are basically gullible and not very bright.

By contrast, the Theory Y assumptions about workers can be summarized as follows:

People are not passive by nature and are capable of self-control and self-direction.

Work is natural and pleasurable.

Workers are not resistant to change and will work toward organizational goals.

People seek and accept responsibility.

McGregor argued that the responsibilities of managers change as the managers change their beliefs about workers. Theory Y assumptions require management to accept responsibility for arranging "organizational conditions and methods of operation so that people can achieve their own goals best by directing their own efforts towards organizational objectives" (1957, pp. 88–89). McGregor suggested strategies such as delegation, job enlargement, and participative management as consistent with Theory Y assumptions. The implication is that if workers are not motivated, then it is because of poor management practices that do not allow people's natural positive attitudes toward work to emerge.

Two other theorists, Aldefer and Herzberg, later refined and built on Maslow's hierarchy. Whereas Maslow's hierarchy of needs was based primarily on his observations in a clinical setting and analysis of biographies of self-actualized people, Aldefer (1972) studied worker behavior in organizations. He suggested that Maslow's hierarchy be collapsed from five levels to three types of needs: existence, relatedness, and growth. He further argued that all three types of needs can motivate behavior at the same time.

Herzberg (1968), who also studied motivation in work settings, took a different approach. In his two-factor or motivation–hygiene theory, he suggested that the factors that produce job satisfaction or motivation are different from the factors that lead to dissatisfaction. Motivating or intrinsic factors are those associated with the nature of the work itself—achievement, recognition, challenging work, responsibility, and growth. These are analogous to Maslow's higher-level needs. Herzberg argued that the satisfaction of lower-level needs, which he called hygiene or extrinsic factors, does not lead to motivation; it only leads to the absence of dissatisfaction. In other words, hygiene factors such as pay or working conditions, supervision, interpersonal relations, status, and security can cause dissatisfaction. But satisfying these needs will not lead to motivation. Only when the work itself is satisfying will workers be motivated.

Now we can return to the self-assessment exercise presented earlier in the chapter in the "Where Do We Begin?" section. Compare your questionnaire answers to Herzberg's categories as shown here:

Maintenance Factors	Motivating Factors
Items 1, 2, 6, 7, 8, 9, 10, 12, 13, 14, 15, 17, and 18	Items 3, 4, 5, 11, 16, and 19

What do your answers tell you about what motivates you? What do your answers tell you about your levels of satisfaction, dissatisfaction, and motivation in your present work environment? Remember that, according to need theories of motivation, we are most preoccupied with unmet needs. What do you need to be motivated? Herzberg (1968) recommended that jobs be redesigned and enriched so as to become more intrinsically motivating. Hackman and Oldham. (1980) suggested that the following elements contribute positively to the motivating potential of a job:

Skill variety: The job requires varying skills, activities, tasks, and talents.

Task identity: The job allows completion of a whole and identifiable piece of work or work product.

Task significance: The work is important and has a positive impact on others in the organization or outside of it.

Autonomy: The workers have a degree of discretion and control over their work.

Feedback: The work provides direct and clear information on the effectiveness of performance.

Although there are important differences among these approaches, Maslow, Aldefer, and Herzberg all emphasized the innate needs that people have in common. McClelland (1985), on the other hand, suggested that some important needs in the workplace are learned and differ from individual to individual. Over the course of his career, he looked at three learned needs: the need for achievement, the need for power, and the need for affiliation. McClelland suggested that people have different motive dispositions that he defined as a "current concern about a goal state that drives, orients, and selects behavior" (p. 183). According to this model, the need for achievement drives some of us, whereas the need for affiliation might be more important for others. As a result, the same set of incentives or circumstances in a particular work environment may cause different people to react in different ways. McClelland found that those with high achievement needs perform better when they are working on moderately difficult tasks, want feedback on how well they are doing, and take personal responsibility for their performance. Because they seek challenges, they try new and more efficient ways of doing things.

McClelland also found that individuals with high power needs, on the other hand, are more sensitive to power-related stimuli, recall more "peak" experiences in terms that involve power, strive to be assertive, are risk takers, and gravitate to careers in which they can exercise power and influence. Such individuals tend to be motivated by the symbols of power or the acquisition of "prestige possessions." Still others, according to McClelland, seem to be motivated primarily by the desire to affiliate or be with other people. People with a strong affiliation motive will do better on tasks if the incentives are social in nature. They want to please others, learn social relationships more quickly, "read" people well, and tend to engage in more dialogue with others. They prefer having friends rather than experts as work partners, and they avoid conflict whenever possible.

Expectancy Theories

Instead of focusing on individual needs, expectancy theories suggest that people will be motivated when they expect that their efforts will result in desirable outcomes. Expectancy theories hold that before people exert effort, they engage in a rational calculation of expected performance and rewards and an assessment of how much those outcomes matter to them.

According to Vroom (1964), there are three concepts important to understanding human motivation: valence, expectancy, and force. Valence refers to the strength of a person's desire for a particular outcome. Expectancy is the association that a person makes between actions and outcomes. As Vroom stated,

> Whenever an individual chooses between alternatives which involve uncertain outcomes, it seems clear that his behavior is affected not only by his preferences . . . but also by the degree to which he believes these outcomes to be probable. (p. 71)

The combination of valence and expectancy, according to Vroom, results in the motivational "force on a person to perform an act" (1964, p. 71). The stronger the valence or value of the reward, and the stronger the expectancy that a person's efforts will be successful and result in the reward, the stronger the motivational force to engage in the behavior.

Porter and Lawler (1968) refined Vroom's model to suggest that, although employee effort is determined by both the value placed on certain outcomes and the degree to which people believe that their efforts will lead to these rewards, effort does not always lead to task accomplishment. They suggested that two other factors need to be considered: employee ability and role clarity. A person might be highly motivated, but if that person does not have the ability to perform the job or task and a clear understanding of how to direct his or her efforts in a manner that is appropriate to the person's organizational role, then the task might not be accomplished.

Again, expectancy theories suggest that if people believe that they possess the skills and abilities needed, that their hard work will result in good performance, that their performance will be rewarded, and that they want that reward, then they will be more likely to exert the required effort. If any one of these factors is not present, then motivation will suffer. For example, if people believe in their ability to get the job done but do not believe that the reward will be forthcoming or do not want the reward, then they will be less likely to put forth much effort. A number of researchers have found that expectancy theories do predict behavior (Burton, Chen,

Grover, & Stewart, 1992–1993; Mastrofski, Ritti, & Snipes, 1994; Smith, Hindman, & Havlovic, 1997).

Expectancy theories go beyond need-based theories of motivation in several respects. First, they introduce a cognitive aspect to motivation—that people at work think about the expected payoffs for their efforts. Second, they suggest that motivation involves not just the individual but also opportunities, rewards, and incentives in the work environment. Third, they remind us that different people have different skills and abilities and that people will tend to exert more effort in those areas where they believe they are more likely to perform well.

Expectancy theories suggest that motivations can be enhanced in three ways. First, managers can choose rewards or outcomes that are of value to a particular worker or group of workers. Second, managers can work to change the expectancy of existing outcomes so that the link between hard work and rewards is strengthened. Third, managers can attempt to change the valence of existing outcomes. As Hackman and Porter (1968) pointed out, the first two ways, which involve changing the situation or organizational circumstances, probably are more amenable to influence than the third way, which would require manipulating how much people value a particular outcome.

Goal-Setting Theories

As was stated in Chapter 1, much of the theoretical base of the field of organizational behavior assumes that behavior is purposeful or goal directed. As Locke (1978) pointed out, "Goal setting is recognized, explicitly or implicitly, by virtually every major theory of work motivation (p. 594). Locke and others also have suggested that goal setting and the existence of goals, in and of themselves, can motivate behavior. During the 1960s, Locke (1968) did a series of laboratory experiments demonstrating that individuals who were assigned difficult goals performed better than those who were assigned easy or moderately easy goals. Latham and Baldes (1975) took Locke's findings and applied them to the logging industry, where they found that

> the setting of a goal that is both specific and challenging leads to an increase in performance because it makes clear to the individual what he is supposed to do. This in turn may provide the worker with a sense of achievement, recognition, and commitment. (p. 124)

The idea behind goal-setting theories is that goals motivate people because they compare people's current performance with the level of performance required to meet the goal. If their current performance falls short, then people will feel dissatisfied and will work harder to achieve the goal. In a review of 87 studies on goal setting as a motivational technique, there was strong empirical support for the idea that goals that are difficult and specific work better than goals that are not challenging and are stated in general terms (Tubbs, 1986). In other words, it is better to state a specific goal than to simply urge workers to do their best.

The research supports goal setting as a motivational technique (Locke & Latham, 1990; Wofford, Goodwin, & Premack, 1992). In fact, goal setting has been found to enhance performance about 90% of the time (Locke, Shaw, Saari, & Latham, 1981). But for goal setting to be effective, people have to feel committed to the goal. Goal setting is particularly effective when feedback is provided that allows people to monitor their progress toward goal attainment.

Eden (1988) suggested that goal setting and expectancy theories are compatible approaches to increasing motivation. He argued that goal setting raises expectations and enhances feelings of self-efficacy. Self-efficacy is defined as people's judgments of their capabilities. In other words, it is our assessment of what we can do with the skills we possess (Bandura, 1986, p. 641). Positive self-efficacy translates into a belief that we can do something—a belief that can become a self-fulfilling prophecy (Eden, 1988). People with high self-efficacy tend to set high personal goals and to perform well (Locke & Latham, 1990). Eden pointed out that because goal setting can raise expectations and trigger productive self-fulfilling prophecies, worker motivation will be enhanced. Put in the language of expectancy theories, as workers' "expectancy," or judgment that their efforts likely will pay off, is increased, they will be more likely to choose to exert more effort toward goal attainment.

Equity Theories

Equity theories present another model of motivation based on the notion of social exchange. They suggest that people make choices based on their assessments of particular situations before exerting effort to achieve organizational goals. Equity theories suggest that people evaluate this exchange based on what they perceive to be fair or advantageous compared with what others receive or the effort required. Adams (1965) argued that people's expectations about what is fair or equitable are learned through a process of socialization and comparison of their experiences with those of others. The "equity norm" suggests that those who contribute more to an organization should receive more rewards (Goodman, 1977).

Motivation, according to this model, is a consequence of perceived inequity. Adams also argued that perceived inequity creates tension in proportion to the magnitude of the inequity. People can either feel guilty because they think they are paid too much (overpayment inequity) or be angry because they believe they are paid too little (underpayment inequity). Individuals will be motivated to reduce this tension by either changing what they do or changing what they think. Adams suggested six ways of reducing tension and achieving a sense of equity: (1) altering effort, (2) altering outcomes, (3) changing how people think about effort or outcomes, (4) leaving, (5) trying to affect the efforts or outcomes for others, and (6) changing the standard of comparison.

The research evidence on equity theories generally is strong. Mowday (1993) argued that, although equity theories have been used primarily to understand employees' reactions to pay, they also have broader applications. Mowday suggested that equity theories also can be applied to social exchange relationships in organizations and that the relationships between superiors and subordinates are characterized by "reciprocal-influence processes" (p. 128). In other words, he urged us to think about interactions at work as a sort of bargaining process "in which the terms of exchange are established to the satisfaction of each party" (p. 128).

Although it might be a mistake to reduce our understanding of all interpersonal interactions at work to a type of social exchange or bargaining, equity theories may provide important insights into understanding how people believe they are treated at work. Research on equity theories also has provided important information on the influence of pay on motivation and on how people look to others to evaluate whether they think they are treated fairly.

Reinforcement, Reward, and Punishment

The literature on motivation is replete with references to rewards and reward systems, particularly the use of money as a reward. Given the importance of rewards in several of the perspectives already discussed, particularly expectancy and equity theories of motivation, it is useful and important to enhance our understanding of how people respond to organizational incentives and inducements.

But at a more basic level, there is a model of human behavior suggesting that behavior is learned and that our motivations and behavior can be changed by manipulating rewards and punishments. Skinner (1971) is perhaps the person most closely identified with this idea. His work focused on what he called "operant behavior," or behavior that is controlled by the individual. The question that Skinner posed was how operant behavior can be conditioned so that desired outcomes occur. He suggested four approaches. The first two types of operant conditioning involve reinforcement. Reinforcement refers to those consequences of a particular action that either increase or decrease the likelihood of the behavior being repeated. For example, receiving praise for good performance may increase the likelihood of similar work being done in the future. Positive reinforcement involves a positive reward, and negative reinforcement refers to the removal of a negative consequence. For example, having an unpleasant assignment taken away might be considered a negative reinforcement.

The third type of operant conditioning is punishment. Punishments are consequences that reduce the likelihood of a behavior being repeated. For example, a stern lecture or reprimand may serve as a form of punishment for some workers. The final type of operant conditioning suggested by Skinner is extinction. Extinction involves the removal of a previously valued consequence. For example, a manager can ignore a worker who previously had responded positively to personal attention. Punishment was found to be the least effective approach to operant conditioning because it has undesirable side effects (e.g., resentment, anxiety) and because it does not shape new desired behavior. Skinner also looked at reinforcement schedules and found that intermittent reinforcement works better than giving reinforcement every time a positive behavior occurs.

This suggests that behavior followed by pleasant consequences is more likely to be repeated, whereas actions followed by unpleasant consequences are less likely to be repeated. The use of positive reinforcement has been shown to be successful in a variety of organizational applications (Luthans & Kreitner, 1985). But remember that rewards do not always (or even usually) have to be monetary. Other rewards such as recognition, access, more responsibility, awards, and praise can be very important to employee motivation.

Financial rewards and incentives have been considered as a primary motivator for a very long time. Depending solely on financial incentives, however, may be an oversimplistic and even ineffective approach to motivation. Durant, Kramer, Perry, Mesch, and Paarlberg (2006) argue that financial incentives can motivate employees, but their effect is limited and they only work when other organizational conditions are favorable. The authors find, in fact, that the typical individual financial incentive programs, such as pay-for-performance, are usually unsuccessful. They conclude that in order to motivate workers in a way that will improve performance and the quality of work, public managers must consider other motivational factors such as attention to job design and work schedules, fostering participation, and setting goals that are challenging and creative.

Participation as a Motivator

Likert (1967) argued that an overall philosophy of management that emphasizes a participative approach is positively related to employee motivation and performance. He characterized management approaches on a continuum from authoritarian (System 1) to democratic (System 4). In System 4, management has complete confidence and trust in workers. Workers are motivated by participating in goal setting and the development of rewards, improving methods, and evaluating goal attainment.

Lawler (1990) is a well-known advocate of participative or "high involvement" approaches to management. He found that participation influences motivation because it increases the amount of information that people have on the expected outcomes of performance, it helps to ensure that rewards have high valence for workers, and it helps people to see the relationship between performance and outcomes. In similar work on goal-setting theories, Locke (1996) found that participation in setting individual goals enhanced goal commitment and, as a result, increased motivation to achieve one's goals. (We return to this issue in Chapter 12.)

Motivation and Life Stages

Interest in adult life stages has been strong in studies of human behavior and motivation during recent decades. Although life cycle theories are a relatively recent development in terms of management theory, concern with adult developmental psychology can be traced back much further. For example, during the 1950s, Erikson (1959) argued that there are identifiable stages of adult psychological development. In Erikson's view, each of these stages presents a crisis or choice that must be dealt with before progressing to the next stage. If the crisis is not resolved, then the individual might regress to an earlier stage.

Schott (1986) looked at the application of adult life-stage theories in public organizations. Based on adult life-stage theories, certain issues can be expected to present themselves for resolution during the different life stages of employees. For example, the major issues facing employees during early adulthood are the establishment of careers and finding personal intimacy. During middle life, employees encounter opportunities for growth and change, and they experiences a shift from concentration on external concerns to concentration on internal or self-oriented concerns. During later life, employees search for meaning and integrity.

Schott argued that these findings are critical to an understanding of organizational behavior and motivation for a number of reasons. First, they suggest that there will be predictable patterns of development, depending on age and stage in the life cycle, that will largely determine the psychological set that employees bring to the workplace. This psychological set will determine how central the organization is to the lives of individuals. Second, the life stage of employees will have an effect on satisfaction and morale. Particularly satisfaction and morale will be lowest during the beginning of people's careers, build until and then plummet during the midlife-crisis period, and build again and then fall during the preretirement period. Finally, life-stage theories have important implications for the career development and job design strategies that will be most effective for individual employees.

Schott (1986) noted that the entry phase and midlife stage are particularly important and that organizations should offer support in the form of mentors and staff psychologists to help employees during these transitions. He also suggested that using mentors who themselves have successfully passed the midlife crisis is mutually beneficial to both mentors and young adults. He noted that, during stages other than the entry and midlife stages, employees are likely to be more receptive to rewards and to want challenging assignments.

Kanfer and Ackerman (2004) also argue that life stage influences an individual's motives and cognitive and intellectual capabilities. In the early stages of their careers, young adult individuals have fluid intellectual abilities, which are most associated with "working memory, abstract reasoning, attention, and processing of novel information" (p. 442). In middle age, they tend to suffer the loss of these abilities. Instead, the authors point out, middle-aged workers gain occupational and avocational (hobbies, music, art, culture) knowledge, which may be very useful for the organization. The authors suggest that not only do skills change, but motives change as well. While in early career it is important for the individual to look for future opportunities, to require novel information and promotion, middle-aged workers have preferences for "job security, salary, and opportunities for skill utilization" (p. 446).

Job satisfaction and overall motivation for both groups of employees will also be influenced by factors not directly related to the work, such as educational background and the position held by the employee. The authors suggest that some types of job positions, such as air traffic controller, require employees that have primarily fluid intellectual abilities, but others, such as those for teachers and writers, require occupational knowledge. Kanger and Ackerman conclude that because going from one life stage to another changes abilities, motivation, and to some degree the values of the individual, managers have to be aware of these changes if they want to maintain and increase the motivation of the people over time.

Life cycle theories have been criticized (Timney-Bailey, 1987) for being based on false assumptions regarding lifetime tenure in organizations beginning at 20 years of age and for enshrining ageism and sexism. Critics note that there are many different lifestyles and paths through life that do not conform to what they claim is a lockstep deterministic model of adult psychological functioning. Furthermore, as Zeitz (1990) noted, the effect of life stage on satisfaction can be situational. He found, for example, that satisfaction varied with age according to situational factors such as position in the organization, location in the organization, and perception of organizational climate. He suggested that, in using life cycle theories to understand employee behavior, the emphasis be placed on providing informational cues so as to create a positive climate for employee–organization relationships regardless of life stage.

Public Service Motivation

As Perry and Wise (1990) described it, "Public service motivation may be understood as an individual's predisposition to respond to motives grounded primarily or uniquely in public institutions and organizations" (p. 368). In other words, this model suggests that there are particular motives that are associated with the nature of public service work. Perry and Wise suggested that public service motives fall into three categories: rational, norm based, and affective. These motives speak to why individuals might be drawn to public service work and, once they are employed, why they might find satisfaction in it. Rational public service motives have to do with individual utility maximization. In other words, some individuals seek public service as a means of satisfying their own needs. These needs might be based on personal identification with a program, a desire to advocate for a special interest, or a desire to participate in policy making because of the excitement or the image of self-importance that it may reinforce (Perry & Wise, 1990).

But public service motivation is most commonly considered from a normative standpoint. Norm-based public service motives are centered on the desire to serve the public and the public interest. These motives are related to factors such as loyalty, duty, citizenship, and values such as social equity. Finally, Perry and Wise (1990) suggested that affective public service motivation may arise from individuals' personal convictions or commitment to the importance of a governmental program, policy, or function. In other words, affective public service motivation is grounded in people's feelings, ideals, and emotions regarding the objectives of a program and the notion of serving society. For example, Frederickson and Hart's (1985) "patriotism of benevolence," which they described as a combination of the love of regime values and love for others, would be an affective-based public-service motive.

In short, some literature suggests that there are rational, norm-based, and affective motives that are particular to public service. Balfour and Weschler (1990), Perry and Wise (1990), and Vinzant (1998) suggested that there is support for the idea that public service motivation will increase the likelihood that people will seek public employment and that, once people are employed, public service values will remain an important factor influencing organizational commitment, motivation, and behavior. Further, Houston (2005) found that public employees don't only "talk the talk" of public service motivation, they also "walk the walk," being more likely to volunteer and become involved with charitable activities than their private sector counterparts. The existence and importance of public service may explain why "the motivational tools common in private management may not be as effective in public organizations" (p. 84). This also suggests that recognizing and building on public service motivation is vitally important. Reminding employees of the importance and value of their role in serving citizens and communities can go a long way in helping keep them energized and excited about their work.

Other Motivation Theories

Steel and König (2006) have tried to integrate multiple perspectives into one overarching motivation theory, which they call the temporal motivation theory (TMT). These authors use the framework of time (or the temporal dimension) to integrate four theories: picoeconomics, expectancy theory, cumulative prospect theory, and need theory. At the most basic level, the TMT model reminds us that not only do people have different needs and value expected rewards differently, but they may be more or less sensitive to time delays in meeting those needs and receiving those rewards.

Picoeconomics, as the authors explain it, emphasizes the idea that when people make decisions, they tend to underestimate the value of benefits that will occur in the future. As already noted, in the expectancy theory of motivation, people engage in behaviors that they think will lead to particular outcomes that they value. TMT adds a time dimension. Put simply, how long a people have to wait to receive a benefit matters to them. So, TMT relates the expectancy of a person that a particular action will be rewarded, and the amount of the payout that will be received, with how long that person is willing to wait to receive the expected payout.

The model also integrates cumulative prospect theory and need theories of motivation. Cumulative prospect theory differs from expectancy theory in the way that values are interpreted by an individual. It suggests that people value "losses and gains in reference to some status quo or baseline" (Steel & König, p. 894). In other words, expected consequences or benefits are not considered in the abstract. Rather, they are considered based on what the person already has. Finally, need theory suggests that different people will respond differently to the same set of circumstances based on their individual needs such as safety needs, social needs, and self-esteem needs.

Taken together, TMT combines all of these elements to explain how individuals make decisions and what affects their actions. The most important element of this model is the "effect of time," which includes a person's sensitivity to "the time required to realize an outcome" and the anticipated losses and gains (Steel & König, p. 899). Because people have differing sensitivities to time as well as different desires and needs, they will not react the same way to a given set of circumstances. For example, all students from one class will have the same amount of homework and assignments required to complete the class. But not all students will do their work at the same time or in the same way. Those who value high grades, are willing to work toward such a reward in the future, and have high achievement needs will likely begin working hard right away. For others, final grades may seem less important or seem too far in the future to worry about. These people may not begin their work until later in the semester, or they may work less intensely.

There are other motivation theories that focus more on emotions in explaining what may motivate people to behave in ways that are not considered "rational." But as Seo, Barrett, and Bartunek (2004) remind us, the effect of emotions on motivation are complex and situational. Their model is based on the idea of "core affect." They define core affect "as momentary, elementary feelings of pleasure or displeasure and of activation or deactivation" (p. 446). Core affective feelings, according to the authors, include two independent dimensions: degree of pleasantness and degree of activation. Pleasantness refers to subjective experience (good/ bad, pleasant/ unpleasant, positive/negative), and activation refers to the energy expended in order to achieve something. What Seo, Barrett, and Barunek found is that pleasant feelings do not always cause people to act and that unpleasant feelings do not always deactivate the person. In fact, some level of unpleasant feelings, such as being tense or nervous, tend to "move" the individual to act and react (often defensively), but also some pleasant feelings, such as being relaxed or calm, can make a person less likely to act. Another interesting perspective on motivation looks at whether people are motivated when they are "energized" or if they are surrounded by people who have positive energy. Cross, Baker, and Parker (2003) see positive energy as a very important source for motivation. They categorize people as "energizers" who by their appearance, attitude, and actions increase the positive attitude in the organization or as "de-energizers" who always have negative predictions about the possible outcomes. Energizers are people who see opportunities in any situation, take into account others' opinions and ideas, have charisma that attracts others, and, most important, show appreciation for others' efforts and stick to what they say. In their study of seven large organizational networks, Cross, Baker, and Parker found that people want to be around energizers and they usually feel energized themselves by the enthusiasm of those people.

"Anti-motivation" Theories

Some recent literature has suggested that when we ask how to motivate employees, we actually are asking the wrong question. Marcum (1999), for example, argued that motivation theory is "a way of thinking that essentially amounts to manipulation" (p. 43). Marcum suggested that motivation theory and practice is fundamentally flawed for the following reasons:

It seeks to cause or stimulate action, assuming that there was none prior to the initiative.

As a consequence, it is incidental, not continuous. Therefore, it must be reinitiated as often as action is desired.

It is founded on a paternalistic assumption—that a protagonist of greater status, experience, intellect, or responsibility is seeking to motivate a second party, presumably of lesser status. The relationship between the two parties is unequal.

It can be critiqued as too narrow, piecemeal, and mechanistic in its assumptions.

It relies too heavily on rewards to achieve objectives. (p. 44)

Marcum also emphasized the idea that rewards actually might destroy people's natural interest in work because people know that if they have to be rewarded to do something, then the action must not be worth doing for its own sake. Marcum suggested that we think in terms of voluntary engagement with work activities rather than in terms of what he characterized as "carrot and stick" motivational approaches. Two essential elements of engagement theory are learning and involvement. The idea is that if people are allowed a degree of self-determination, they will become voluntarily engaged in work that is interesting and enjoyable to them. People will choose work that they are good at, and once they are engaged, people will challenge themselves and be persistent. The acquisition of more and better knowledge is a primary goal. The result, according to Marcum, is self-determination and continuous engagement with work activities rather than episodic motivation. According to this perspective, we should think about partnerships rather than about subordinates, negotiate projects rather than give assignments, and scan for interests and competencies rather than merely track past performance.

Although this might seem to be a rather radical approach, Marcum's (1999) arguments challenge us to think about the nature of work and the assumptions about workers that influence how we behave. In a sense, he asked us to return to the notion of McGregor's Theory Y and to think critically about what those assumptions actually mean in terms of organizational behavior. Marcum also challenged us to think about our own motivations and to reflect on those circumstances when we felt most connected, excited, and enthusiastic about what we were doing. Was it when we chose the activity and became voluntarily committed to it?

Ways of Acting

The preceding sections presented an almost dizzying array of perspectives on motivation and behavior. The reader might be left wondering what might be the best way of understanding behavior. Is it need satisfaction? Based on learning and reinforcement? Shaped by our values and personality? Influenced by rewards? Affected by different management approaches? Intrinsic in the nature of the job? Based on a rational calculation of effort, performance, and expected outcomes? Influenced by our life stages? Based on our assessments of fairness? Grounded in public service values?

The short answer to all of these questions is *yes*. Depending on the situation, it can be useful to think about motivation from all of these perspectives. As we stated at the beginning of the chapter, motivation is complex, and the models developed to explain it represent a complicated and varied theoretical foundation on which to base our attempts to influence our own motivation as well as that of others. But as we also suggested, the various models presented here are not necessarily mutually exclusive. Particularly when we think about the action orientations that are suggested in looking across the varied perspectives, several commonalities emerge. Although motivation is complicated, in general it may be useful to think about the following.

1. *Be self-reflective and proactive about your own motivation.* It is difficult, if not impossible, to motivate your employees if you lack motivation yourself. Carefully

consider the factors that motivate you and keep you motivated. Are you motivated by challenging goals? A sense of serving others? Promotion? Achievement? Whatever your answer, do what you can to create situations for yourself that keep you excited and motivated about your work. Your attitudes and behavior can be an important and positive contributing factor in the overall motivational climate.

2. *Be aware that what motivates you is not necessarily what will motivate others.* Talk with your employees and listen carefully to what they say about the motivational factors that are important to them. Help them to clarify their goals, desires, and needs. There is no "one size fits all" approach to motivating people. Be cognizant of the differences among people in terms of what they need from you and the organization to motivate them. People differ in terms of needs, personality, attitudes, and values. For example, some employees might want a great deal of freedom and autonomy, whereas others might respond better to closer supervision and feedback. Some might be motivated by promotional opportunities, whereas others might value the opportunity to continue to work with members of a work group that they enjoy.

3. *Have realistic expectations about the extent to which you can influence the motivation of others.* Certainly, there were many things suggested in this chapter that have been shown to positively influence motivation. But it also is important to remember that motivation is internal to the individual. As a manager, you cannot motivate everyone. There might be people who, despite your best efforts, simply are not motivated to work toward organizational goals. In those cases, it might just be a poor fit between the organization and the individuals. Likewise, if you find yourself in a position where your motivation is consistently lacking and, despite your best efforts, the situation does not appear likely to change, then it might be best for you to find organizational circumstances in which your public service contribution will be more positive.

4. *Participate in setting clear and challenging goals.* Goal setting is important from several perspectives. Particularly if established in a participative process, goal setting clarifies shared objectives, provides an opportunity for communication, enhances self-efficacy and commitment, and provides the basis for tracking performance. It is particularly important in the public sector because public organizations often do not have clearly defined and singular goals. Public organizations often are charged with meeting multiple and conflicting social goals, so spending time with employees establishing specific objectives and relating those objectives to the personal goals of individuals is very useful. It is not enough to simply establish goals. Once goals are established, you should provide information so that people can track their progress and know when and how well they have reached the goals. This information can be motivating in and of itself for some people. Feedback is particularly important to people with a high achievement need, but in general, people who participate in the formation of goals and become committed to them want information so that they can assess their progress in achieving the goals.

5. *Think about the salience of various rewards.* Because different people are motivated by different things, different rewards will have more or less value to them. Do not assume that the rewards that would be meaningful for one person (or for yourself) will be the same for everyone else. Ask people about their plans, personal goals, and aspirations. Talk to them about what makes their work rewarding for them. Ask them what they want from you so that they will do their best. Listen to what they tell you about what makes them enthusiastic, discouraged, or energized. Then do what you can to provide rewards that are valuable to them. Also make clear the connections between performance and rewards. Let people know what they will need to accomplish to earn the rewards they desire. Talk with employees about their abilities and interests, and jointly identify the resources, training, and experience they need to feel confident about meeting goals. Be generous in your positive feedback when the situation calls for it. But also remember that your attention itself can be a reward. If you are giving a lot of attention to someone who is performing poorly, then ask yourself whether it is possible that your continued attention actually is reinforcing the undesirable behavior.

6. *Be honest with people about what rewards are possible and what rewards are not.* If you promise more than you actually can deliver, then you might end up doing more damage than good. Particularly in the public sector, it is critical to be clear about what you can and cannot do in terms of monetary rewards, promotions, changes to assignments, and other matters over which you might not have complete control. If there is something that is important to a particular employee, then explain clearly what you can and cannot do in that regard. For those things that you cannot control, try to work creatively with the employee. For example, although an immediate promotion might not be possible, it might be feasible to assign a person to manage a task force or special committee so that he or she can gain supervisory experience. If you work hard to help your employees secure the rewards they desire, then they are more likely to work hard to achieve them. For many people in the public sector, a strong self-expressed commitment to helping people and serving the public seems to be an important and powerful motivator. Recognize the contributions that various individuals make to the community and help them to see how their jobs fit into the overall public service mission of the organization. Some public employees do not receive a lot of appreciation from citizens, either because they do not have direct interaction or because their interactions might not always be positive (e.g., police officers). But it is clear that public service motivations are strong and important for many people. Letting employees know that you appreciate their contributions in this regard can be very important.

7. *Although people might be different in terms of personality, wants, goals, and needs, they also want to be treated fairly.* Employees do not work in a vacuum. They make comparisons. When employees think that there is an inequity, they might well act to correct it. Rewards, consequences, and outcomes need not be the same for everyone, but they should be perceived by employees as fair and equitable relative to how their

inputs compare with the inputs of others. Listen to what people say in this regard. Do they believe that they are being treated unfairly? Compared with what? Be open about the variety of factors that can influence pay, working conditions, and other rewards or factors that people might view as inequitable. It might not be possible to avoid all complaints of inequity, both because people value outcomes differently and because of the variety of factors that influence compensation and other rewards. But with these limitations, it is important to treat people as fairly and equitably as possible.

8. *Motivation is not just about the characteristics of people; it also is about the work that you ask them to do.* To maintain motivation, the work itself needs to be satisfying and meaningful. Jobs that are repetitive, lack variety, allow little autonomy, or have little effect on others are inherently unsatisfying, not to mention boring. It makes sense, then, to work with employees to make their work as interesting and satisfying as possible. But we should mention a cautionary note: Make sure that people *want* to enrich their jobs. Ask them what they would like to see changed. Cherrington and England (1980) found that people who were asked and expressed an interest in enriching their jobs were more likely to respond positively to such approaches. If people are interested, then work with them to create "whole" jobs so that they can use a variety of skills and abilities to accomplish something important and tangible. Where practical, create connections between workers and their clients (be they citizens or other people in the organization) and open feedback channels so that people can see the results of their efforts and the impact of their work on others.

9. *It can be helpful to think about the life stages of the people you work with as a means of understanding the challenges they face and offering appropriate support.* But as critics note, life-stage theories cannot be applied unthinkingly or used as the only means of understanding what motivates behavior. It is important to recognize the roles of other factors such as lifestyle, gender, cultural differences, and changes in family structure as well as the influence of factors related to the organizational context such as perceptions of climate and the positions and levels of employees. If used as one of several approaches to understanding employee motivation and behavior with the intent of providing support and help with those psychological issues faced by employees that may influence their performance in the organization, life-stage theories can provide a relevant and useful perspective on needs and motivations.

Thinking in Action

SOS in DHS: A Problem of Motivation

About 18 months ago, Jess Johnson was appointed to direct a newly authorized and funded unit in the state's Department of Human Services (DHS). Shortly thereafter, she interviewed and hired six new employees to staff the unit. The name of the unit is Service Outreach for Seniors (SOS). Its purpose is to coordinate services for the vulnerable elderly. This is Jess's first supervisory position.

Susan Jones and Bob Martin were two of the new employees hired by Jess. Initially, both were very productive, enthusiastic, and industrious. Bob had taken the initiative to work closely with several prominent private service providers to ensure their cooperation and involvement in the new program. Susan had done a terrific job of producing publications and other materials describing the goals of the unit and explaining SOS services to the elderly. But since this initial spurt of activity and enthusiasm, both Susan and Bob have become less-than-ideal employees in Jess's estimation.

Within 6 months of his hiring, Bob developed what Jess considers to be poor work habits (e.g., very long lunches and coffee breaks, tardiness, absenteeism). Bob demonstrates little interest in or enthusiasm for his work. Although he generally accomplishes, at least in a minimal manner, those tasks that are directly assigned to him, he rarely volunteers ideas or takes the initiative. From Jess's perspective, employees who take initiative and demonstrate creativity are critical in helping the unit to establish itself politically and to create a service where none had existed before.

Susan, on the other hand, has become quite "creative" in the sense that she has ceased to check with Jess (or anyone) on important policy matters before speaking to external groups and individuals. On several occasions, she has promised things to representatives of organizations and to elected officials that the SOS program simply could not deliver. On other occasions, she has misrepresented her role as a staff member, instead leaving the impression that she was directing the unit. This has embarrassed Jess and her supervisors more than once. Despite Susan's apparent desire to be "in the limelight" in the political and community arena, she has developed an open disdain for the regular workload in her area. She routinely misses deadlines and fails to complete important paperwork.

Jess has met with Bob and Susan separately to discuss her dissatisfaction with their performance. Being a matter-of-fact person, Jess simply told them that their work was not up to par and that she expected them to improve. For a week or so, things seemed to get better. But the same problems quickly resurfaced.

The other four employees hired by Jess are doing well. They have what she considers good work habits: They usually are on time and are willing to work hard to help the new unit succeed. They seem to be eager to do well. She can count on them to complete assigned tasks and meet deadlines. Each of them, in his or her own way, also has demonstrated a willingness to go "above and beyond" and to make positive suggestions for improving the operations and services of the unit.

But the problems with Susan and Bob are beginning to drag down the morale of the other employees and certainly are causing Jess's attitude toward work to suffer. Jess has not talked to either of them about these problems for several weeks because she has not been able to figure out what to do or say. But at different times this morning, both Susan and Bob came to Jess's office asking her to recommend them for promotion to a position that opened up recently in the Child Welfare unit similar to SOS. Jess does not know how to handle these requests. More troubling, she does not know how to address the longer term problems of motivating all of her employees to do well.

1. Define the problem(s) in this case, using as many theories of motivation from this chapter as you think might apply.

2. Discuss the practical implications for each of the models you use. In other words, what do these models suggest the supervisor should *do or say* as a consequence of defining the problem from that perspective?

3. What are some of the perspectives on organizational behavior that could explain the apparently high levels of motivation among the four employees? What models might explain Jess's motivation?

4. Which of the theories or models do you think fit best with which employees and why?

5. What conclusions can you draw, or what observations can you make, about motivation theory and research?

Staying Motivated

For this exercise, focus on some aspect of your job where you do not feel motivated. Then go over the following steps.

1. Identify the barriers to motivation. Is the work challenging? Do you feel competent to perform the work? Are you getting needed feedback? Do you understand the expectations? Do you have the time and resources needed to perform well? What other problems, obstacles, and unmet needs do you confront?

2. Formulate a plan, including action steps, for overcoming the barriers to motivation. Discuss the plan with affected parties and get commitments from them (if appropriate).

3. Implement the action steps. After a reasonable time period, assess the results. Has your motivation increased? Has your interest, satisfaction, or performance improved? What else might you do to stay motivated?

Being an Energizer

Recall that in this chapter we talked about how Cross and colleagues (2003) see positive energy as a very important source for motivation. Over the next week, observe people in your organization that act as "energizers" and "de-energizers." How do you respond to these people? Then carefully observe how often you are an energizer or a de-energizer at work and how people react to you. Over time, consciously and authentically adopt a more positive attitude and engage in energizing behaviors such as seeing opportunities for positive action, taking into account others' opinions and ideas, and openly showing appreciation for others' efforts. As you continue to practice this behavior, can you observe any changes in the behavior and attitude of the people around you? How do those changes, if any, influence you?

7

Leadership in Public Organizations

A leader is best
When people barely know that he exists,
Not so good when people obey and acclaim him,
Worst when they despise him.
"Fail to honor people, they fail to honor you";
But of a good leader, who talks little,
When his work is done, his aim fulfilled,
They will all say, "We did this ourselves."

—Lao-tzu, circa 600 BC

L eadership is becoming one of the most widely debated but least clearly understood concepts in the study of public and private organizations these days. There are frequent calls for enhanced leadership in organizations of all types because, as Behn (1991) put it, "leadership counts." Yet no one seems exactly sure what constitutes leadership, where it comes from, or how it might be developed. Certainly, there is agreement that the traditional top-down models of leadership that we associate with groups such as the military are outdated and unworkable in modern society—even in the military. Today's society has been described as (a) highly turbulent, subject to sudden and dramatic shifts; (b) highly interdependent, requiring cooperation across many sectors; and (c) greatly in need of creative and imaginative solutions to the problems facing us. Under these conditions, public and private organizations need to be considerably more adaptable and flexible than in the past. Yet the traditional command-and-control form of leadership does not encourage risk and innovation. Quite to the contrary, it encourages uniformity and convention. For this reason, many people now argue that a new approach to leadership is desirable. Under these circumstances, as we think about leadership and how we might exercise it in groups and organizations, there are several issues that we need to keep in mind.

Certainly, we need to understand how leadership has been studied and practiced in the past to understand the context in which modern discussions of leadership are taking place. Studies of the lives and careers of outstanding leaders and related efforts to draw up lists of the qualities or characteristics of those leaders that made them successful provide an important backdrop to our study of leadership today. Similarly, studies suggesting that different leaders exhibit different styles help us to understand the range of options available to us. And those explorations of the various contexts or situations in which leadership takes place, along with the suggestion that different approaches might be more effective in different circumstances, will help us to situate our own efforts to lead.

At the same time, we should understand that leadership is changing in many ways, and we should be attentive to those changes. First, we should understand that, in today's world and certainly in tomorrow's world, more and more people are going to want to participate in the decisions that affect them. In the traditional top-down model of organizational leadership, the leader was the one who established the vision of the group, designed ways of achieving that vision, and inspired or coerced others into helping to achieve that vision. But increasingly, those in organizations want to be involved; they want a piece of the action. Moreover, clients or citizens also want to participate, as well they should. As Bennis (1983) correctly predicted two decades ago, "Leadership . . . will become an increasingly intricate process of multilateral brokerage. . . . More and more decisions will be public decisions; that is, the people they affect will insist on being heard" (p. 16).

Second, leadership is increasingly being thought of not as a position in a hierarchy but rather as a process that occurs throughout organizations (and beyond). In the past, a leader was considered the person who held a formal position of power in an organization or a society. But increasingly we are coming to think of leadership as a process occurring throughout organizations and societies. Leadership will not just be something reserved for presidents, governors, mayors, and department heads; instead, it will become something that everyone throughout our organizations and society will become involved in from time to time. Indeed, there are many who argue that such a shift in the distribution of leadership will be necessary for our survival. John Gardner (1987), the former cabinet secretary and founder of Common Cause, stated,

> In this country, leadership is dispersed among all elements of society and down through all levels, and the system simply won't work as it should unless large numbers of people throughout society are prepared to take leader-like action to make things work at their level. (p. 1)

It is safe to predict that, over the coming years, we will see more and more instances of what we term "shared leadership" in public organizations, both within the organizations and as administrators relate to their many external constituencies. As Helgesen (1996) put it, leaders in the future will be found "not only among those at the top, the 'lead horses,' but also among those who constitute what in the industrial era we called the rank and file" (p. 21). And, as we will see, the notion of shared leadership is especially important in the public sector as administrators work with citizens and citizen groups of all types. In these efforts, public administrators will need to develop and employ new leadership skills that include important elements of empathy, consideration, facilitation, negotiation, and brokering.

Third, we should understand that leadership is not just about doing things right; it is about doing the right things (Bennis & Nanus, 1985). In other words, leadership inevitably is associated with important human values, including the most fundamental public values, such as freedom, equality, and justice. Through the process of leadership, people working together make choices about the directions they want to take; they make fundamental decisions about their futures. Such choices cannot be made simply on the basis of a rational calculation of costs and benefits. They require a careful balancing of human values, whether those reflected in the direction in which an organization chooses to move or as citizens and governmental officials work together in the development of public policies. Leadership, as we will see, can play a "transformational" role in this process, helping people to confront important values and, indeed, to grow and develop individually and collectively in the process of such confrontations. Accordingly, a number of recent writers on leadership have urged that we examine the "servant" role of leadership (Greenleaf, 2002) and that we be attentive to "leading with soul" (Bolman & Deal, 1995).

In this chapter, we consider these important and evolving issues, but we also consider how these considerations might affect the way in which you go about trying to improve your own leadership capabilities. We examine traditional approaches to leadership, contemporary approaches to leadership, and some special considerations related to leadership in the public service. We then explore the implications of these ideas for leadership development. We begin by examining the way in which you think about leadership now.

Where Do We Begin?

The following exercises will help you think through your current ideas about leadership and the way in which you approach leadership situations.

What Makes a Good Leader?

Think of a person who you think is an excellent leader. This could be someone you know personally, someone you have watched from afar, or someone you have only read about or otherwise studied. It could be someone living today or someone from another time and place. What are the 10 qualities that make you think highly of that person's leadership?

1. _____

2. _____

3. _____

4. _____

5. _____

6. _____

7. _____

8. _____

9. _____

10. _____

Consider a specific incident in which you thought this person exercised exceptional leadership skills. Which of the preceding characteristics (or others) were most important in this particular case of leadership? Why?

_____

_____

_____

_____

_____

_____

What five characteristics do you consider your best leadership qualities or traits?

1. _____

2. _____

3. _____

4. _____

5. _____

If we asked your friends to list your best leadership qualities, what do you think they would say?

1. _____

2. _____

3. _____

4. _____

5. _____

6. _____

What Is Your Leadership Style?

The following questionnaire will help you to assess your leadership style. Read each item and think about how often you engage in the described behavior. Indicate your response to each item by circling one of the five numbers to the right of each item (1 = *never*, 2 = *seldom*, 3 = *occasionally*, 4 = *often*, 5 = *always*). We discuss the results of the questionnaire later in the chapter.

1.	Tells group members what they are supposed to do	1	2	3	4	5
2.	Acts friendly with members of the group	1	2	3	4	5
3.	Sets standards of performance for group members	1	2	3	4	5
4.	Helps others to feel comfortable in the group	1	2	3	4	5
5.	Makes suggestions about how to solve problems	1	2	3	4	5
6.	Responds favorably to suggestions made by others	1	2	3	4	5
7.	Makes his or her perspective clear to others	1	2	3	4	5
8.	Treats others fairly	1	2	3	4	5
9.	Develops a plan of action for the group	1	2	3	4	5
10.	Behaves in a predictable manner toward group members	1	2	3	4	5
11.	Defines role responsibilities for each group member	1	2	3	4	5
12.	Communicates actively with group members	1	2	3	4	5
13.	Clarifies his or her own role within the group	1	2	3	4	5
14.	Shows concern for the personal well-being of others	1	2	3	4	5
15.	Provides a plan for how the work is to be done	1	2	3	4	5
16.	Shows flexibility in making decisions	1	2	3	4	5
17.	Provides criteria for what is expected of the group	1	2	3	4	5
18.	Discloses thoughts and feelings to group members	1	2	3	4	5

19.	Encourages group members to do quality work	1	2	3	4	5
20.	Helps group members to get along	1	2	3	4	5

Scoring. The style questionnaire is designed to measure two major types of leadership behavior: task orientation and relationship orientation. Score the questionnaire by first summing the responses on the odd-numbered items; this is your task score. Then sum the responses on the even-numbered items; this is your relationship score. We discuss the question of leadership style later in the chapter.

  Total scores: Task _____   Relationship _____

Interpretation.

  40–50 = High
  30–39 = Moderate
  10–29 = Low

SOURCE: From *Leadership: Theory and Practice* (2nd ed.) (pp. 51–52), by P. G. Northouse, 2001, Thousand Oaks, CA: Sage. Used by permission.

Ways of Thinking

Whereas most of the knowledge we have concerning *organizational leadership* has come from studies of business organizations, a great deal has been learned about leadership more generally from the political and governmental realms. In this section, we examine both traditional and contemporary approaches to organizational leadership. Then we examine several important studies of leadership in the public sector. What we find is that some of the most innovative approaches to leadership today are, in fact, taking place within government organizations and specifically within public organizations. This suggests the opportunity for students of public administration to be at the forefront of leadership development during the coming decades.

But before reviewing what we know about leadership and leadership skills, think for a moment about what we mean by the term *leadership.* One review of major studies in leadership pointed out that there are nearly as many definitions of leadership as there are people trying to define it and that many of the definitions are ambiguous (Bass, 1990, p. 11). Moreover, as we noted earlier, the way in which we think about leadership is changing, meaning that the way in which we should define leadership is changing as well. In the past, students of leadership focused most of their attention on the activities of formal leaders. For the most part, leaders were people in formal positions of power and authority and people who used their power and authority, as well as other forms of influence, to direct others toward goals and objectives that they had established in advance. Consequently, leadership was defined either in terms of the characteristics or traits that leaders possess or in terms of the way in which leaders exert power in relation to others in organizations. Put simply, the leader's role was to (a) come up with good ideas about the direction that the group should take, (b) decide on a course of action or a goal to be accomplished, and (c) exert his or her influence or control in moving the group in that direction.

But as we have noted, the way in which we think about leadership is changing. Leadership no longer is simply what those in leadership positions do. Rather, it refers to a process by which one individual influences others to pursue a commonly held objective. Where leadership is present, something occurs in the dynamics of a group or organization that results in change. Whether leadership comes from someone in a formal position of "leader" or from someone else, we can say that leadership has occurred only when the group has been stimulated to move in a new direction. To move a group in this way, a person does not necessarily need to exercise power or control. Indeed, power actually can be destructive to leadership in the long term. Rather, the potential leader must understand the group or organization and find ways of stimulating or moving it. But the earliest studies of leadership were quite different from this emerging view.

Traditional Approaches to Leadership

The Trait Approach

Leadership, of course, has been a subject of discussion for many centuries, with most of that discussion focusing on the leadership of major public figures—from Julius Caesar, to Adolf Hitler, to John F. Kennedy. Originally, commentators tried to address the question of what constitutes effective leadership and what personal characteristics are associated with successful leaders through biographical studies of well-known leaders. The lives and careers of leaders were studied to try to determine what qualities set leaders apart from others. Are leaders smarter than others? Do they have more highly developed verbal skills? Are they taller or more masculine? (Note that most of the subjects of these discussions, as well as the subjects of the earliest formal studies of leadership during the early 1900s, were men, a fact that many have suggested might have biased the early study of leadership toward a particular model of leadership behavior.)

In any case, Stogdill (1948) analyzed some 124 studies of leadership traits that had been conducted between 1904 and 1947. His synthesis of these studies suggested that leaders are indeed different from others in a group or organization in several ways. For example, most of the studies showed that leaders tended to be more intelligent, more dependable or responsible, and more active in social situations than other group members. On the other hand, factors such as age, height, weight, and appearance seemed to have little to do with leadership (as some had thought earlier). Moreover, leaders had a strong capacity for organizing and generating cooperative behavior. Those traits that Stogdill associated with this capacity included "intelligence, alertness to the needs of others, [and] insight into situations, further reinforced by such habits as responsibility, initiative, persistence, and self-confidence" (1974, p. 65).

But Stogdill's (1948) study suggested that whatever characteristics might be associated with leadership, simply possessing these qualities did not ensure that one would become a leader. Rather, leaders stand in relation to a group, an organization, or "followers," and the nature of that relationship is more determining of the pattern of leadership than is the possession of certain traits. Moreover, leaders that perform well in one situation might fail in another. Therefore, leadership is determined not by possession of certain traits but rather through a relationship between the leader and members of a group "in which the leader acquires status through the active participation and demonstration of his capacity for carrying tasks through to completion" (1974, p. 65).

In the 1974 study, Stogdill reviewed another 163 studies completed after his first study. Based on these studies, he suggested that leaders are characterized by (a) a strong drive for responsibility and task completion, (b) considerable vigor and persistence in the pursuit of goals, (c) creativity and originality in problem solving, (d) the exercise of initiative in social situations, (e) self-confidence and a strong sense of personal identity, (f) a willingness to accept the consequences of their decisions and actions, (g) a capacity for absorbing stress, (h) a willingness to tolerate frustration and delay, (i) the ability to influence the behavior of others, and (j) a capacity to organize groups to achieve the purpose at hand (p. 81). These characteristics were found to distinguish leaders from others, effective leaders from ineffective leaders, and higher-level leaders from lower-level leaders. But again, Stogdill pointed out that the possession of certain traits is not as determining of leadership as the interaction of personality and social situations. Moreover, he noted, those traits that are associated with leadership may vary from culture to culture and from time to time. But despite these reservations, Stogdill concluded that personality is indeed a factor—although not the only factor—in differentiating leaders from others.

Leadership Styles

The suggestion that leadership is determined through the interaction of leaders and situations led researchers to consider the *behavior* of leaders, not just their traits. During the late 1940s, a group of researchers at Ohio State University undertook a series of studies of leadership behavior, largely basing their work on a questionnaire that asked people in the military, in educational institutions, and in industrial settings about the behavior that their leaders exhibited (Bass, 1990, pp. 511–543). (A short version of this questionnaire appeared at the beginning of this chapter.) Two factors emerged from the Ohio State studies: consideration and the initiation of structure.

Consideration describes the extent to which the leader is concerned for the welfare of those in the group. A considerate leader might compliment people on their work, emphasize the importance of job satisfaction, help to put employees at ease, and so on. The idea of consideration is primarily focused on *relationships. Initiation of structure,* on the other hand, describes the extent to which the leader initiates activity in the group, organizes the group, and defines the way in which the work is to be done. A leader focusing on initiation of structure would be concerned with maintaining standards, meeting deadlines, and securing compliance. The idea of initiation is primarily focused on *tasks.* (Note that the questionnaire at the beginning of this chapter yielded a score for task and another score for relationship. Which one did you prefer?)

A similar set of ideas about leadership came from researchers at the University of Michigan (Cartwright & Zander, 1960; Katz & Kahn, 1966; Likert, 1961). Cartwright and Zander, for example, suggested that leaders help to guide two central group functions: contributing to the achievement of group goals and maintaining or strengthening the group itself. (Other studies used the terms *employee orientation* and *job or production orientation*. But in all cases, the essential distinction was between tasks and relationships.) Initially thinking that these were at odds with one another, the researchers pointed out that some leaders are so attentive to maintaining the group that the focus of the group on accomplishing its goals is undermined, whereas other leaders might concentrate so much on task achievement that they destroy the group's morale. Later studies suggested that leaders can be attentive to both tasks and relationships.

One of the most recognizable of these approaches is the managerial (or leadership) grid, which first appeared during the 1960s but has been refined several times since (Blake & McCanse, 1991; Blake & Mouton, 1964). The grid has two key dimensions: concern for production and concern for people (essentially the task and relationship distinction once again). *Concern for production* might be expressed in a focus on results, performance, and the "bottom line," whereas *concern for people* might be expressed in a focus on job satisfaction, working conditions, and wages and salary. Each of these concerns is found in differing degrees in different people, and indeed these concerns are found to differ from time to time in the same person. These degrees are represented on a scale from 1 to 9 and, when they are combined, yield the grid shown in Figure 7.1.

The various combinations of low and high concern for production and concern for people generate five key leadership styles. The 9, 1 style might be characterized by phrases such as "nice guys finish last," "produce or perish," and "results driven." The 1, 9 style might be associated with phrases such as "don't worry, be happy," "see no evil," and "can't say no." The 1, 1 style might be recognized in phrases such as "sorry, but it's not my problem" and "hands off." The 5, 5 style might be characterized by phrases such as "I can live with that" and "that's acceptable progress." Finally, the 9, 9 style might be associated with phrases such as "all for one, and one for all" and "interdependence and shared values." Although there is some implication that each style has a place, the obvious preference is the 9, 9 style. Blake and McCanse wrote, "An organization can maximize its members' contributions by applying these principles daily, which in turn helps ensure relationships among members based on mutual trust and respect. It then becomes possible to maximize the use of financial, technical, natural, and other resources" (1991, p. 265).

The Context of Leadership

Several approaches to leadership relate leadership style and leadership behavior to the context within which leadership occurs. One of the most widely known approaches to leadership behavior is what is called "situational leadership," an approach developed by Hersey and Blanchard during the late 1960s and further refined since that time (Hersey & Blanchard, 1988, chap. 8). Basically, the idea of situational leadership is that different situations require different styles

Figure 7.1   The Managerial Grid

SOURCE: From *Leadership Dilemmas: Grid Solutions,* by R. R. Blake and A. A. McCanse, 1991, Houston, TX: Gulf Publishing. Used with permission.

of leadership and, correspondingly, that leaders need to be able to understand key characteristics of the organizations they lead and then adapt their own behavior to fit the situation. The emphasis in situational leadership is on the relationship between the leader and his or her followers. (Although Hersey and Blanchard used examples drawn from hierarchical organizations, they claimed that the situational leadership approach will work no matter whether you are attempting to influence a subordinate, a boss, a friend, or a group.)

According to the model, the leadership style that should be used by the potential leader depends on the "readiness" level of the people whom the leader is attempting to influence. The styles that are available to the leader again are based on the distinction between task behavior and relationship behavior. Task behavior is defined as "the extent to which the leader engages in spelling out the duties and responsibilities of an individual or group. These behaviors include telling people what to do, how to do it, when to do it, where to do it, and who is to do it" (Hersey & Blanchard, 1988, chap. 8). Relationship behavior, on the other hand, is defined as "the extent to which the leader engages in two-way or multi-way communication" such as listening, facilitating, and supporting. Using a low-to-high difference in task behavior on one dimension and a low-to-high difference in relationship behavior on another, Hersey and Blanchard came up with four possible leadership styles: S1 (high task and low relationship), S2 (high task and high relationship), S3 (high relationship and low task), and S4 (low relationship and low task) (Figure 7.2).

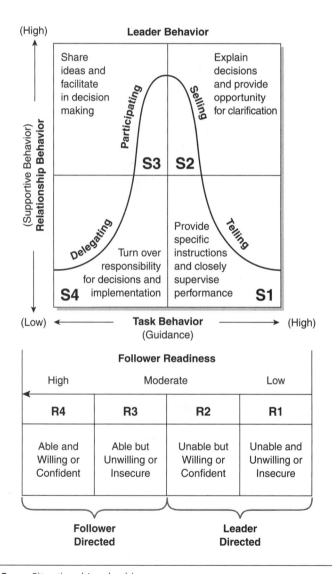

Figure 7.2   Situational Leadership

SOURCE: From *Management of Organizational Behavior* (5th ed.), by P. Hersey and K. H. Blanchard, 1988, Englewood Cliffs, NJ: Prentice Hall. Reprinted with permission from the Center for Leadership Studies.

Again, the key to understanding the situation is understanding the followers, given that whether someone leads is determined by whether anyone follows. At the outset, the leader has to determine the objectives or task-specific outcomes that are desired. Without knowing the objectives, the leader cannot determine the "readiness" of potential followers. The readiness of potential followers is not dependent on their personal characteristics; rather, it has to do with how ready they are to perform a particular task. In this view, a social worker might be very responsible in interacting with clients but less interested in completing the paperwork needed for keeping appropriate records. In such a case, the leader should take a somewhat hands-off approach to the social worker's interactions with clients but should supervise very closely the completion of the necessary paperwork.

The readiness of an individual or a group to perform a specific task depends on the *ability* and *willingness* or confidence to perform the task. There can be various combinations of ability and willingness: R1 (unable and unwilling or insecure), R2 (unable but willing or confident), R3 (able but unwilling or insecure), and R4 (able and willing or confident). Figure 7.2 shows the relationship between follower readiness and the optimal leader behavior. To use the chart, the leader would identify the follower's level of readiness on the continuum at the bottom and then draw a perpendicular line up into the chart to the point where it intersects with the curved line. This line represents the ideal combination of task and relationship behavior that the leader should employ with this particular individual or group—telling, selling, participating, or delegating. In any case, the key to understanding situational leadership is to understand that different approaches to leadership are appropriate in different situations.

This same basic premise underlies several other approaches. For example, Fiedler's (1967) contingency model of leadership suggests that the effectiveness of a group is contingent on the relationship between the style of leadership and the degree to which the situation enables the leader to exert influence. That is, some situations are more favorable for some leaders, and other situations are more favorable for others. Based on extensive empirical research involving a scale called the Least Preferred Coworker (LPC) scale, Fiedler identified two now familiar leadership styles: the task-oriented leader (who is quite efficient and goal oriented) and the relationship-oriented leader (who derives satisfaction from successful interpersonal relationships). Both types of leaders will be concerned with tasks and will engage in interpersonal relationships, but the *task-oriented* leader will be concerned with interpersonal relationships to complete the task at hand, whereas the *relationship-oriented* leader will be concerned with tasks to have successful interpersonal relationships (p. 46).

The next question becomes how the group or organization affects the leader's ability to lead, that is, to motivate others and coordinate their efforts. Three characteristics of groups or organizations are most important: (1) position power, (2) task structure, and (3) the personal relationship between the leader and members of the group. *Position power* refers to the degree to which the position enables the leader to get others to comply with his or her directions. It is the power that the group builds into the situation and is reflected in things such as having an official title (and the perquisites of high office) and having the authority to hire and fire or to give raises in rank and pay. The leader with great position power does not have to spend time convincing others that they should follow; rather, there are stable roles and expectations built into the situation. The leader with high position power can get others to perform their tasks more readily than can a leader with low position power.

Task structure refers to the degree to which the task undertaken by the leader and group is structured or unstructured. Tasks that are highly structured give the leader more control, whereas those that are less structured give the leader less control. Precisely stated tasks allow followers little room for discretion, whereas more vague tasks permit wide latitude on the part of followers. For example, processing driver's license applications is a fairly structured job in which there are exact steps that must be taken and little room for "creativity." Designing a new public park, on the other hand, is a highly unstructured task and could be done in many ways. In very basic terms, "the structured task is enforceable, while the unstructured ambiguous task is difficult or impossible to enforce" (Fiedler, 1967, p. 28).

Position power and task structure are decided on by the organization, according to Fiedler, but the leader's *personal relationship* with members of the group is something that the leader can influence through his or her own personality. Some leaders will be respected and well liked, whereas others will not be. Some will gain that respect through showing wisdom and making good decisions, whereas others will be liked simply based on their charming or likable personalities. In either case, a good relationship between the leader and members of the group will lead to a greater proportion of the leader's ideas being accepted. Of course, the group's effectiveness may or may not be improved simply by a more effective relationship between the leader and the group. The leader still will need to have good ideas. But the chances that the leader's ideas and directions will be accepted improve if the relationship is a good one.

The contingency model, then, suggests that certain leadership styles are more effective in certain situations. The three factors of group life just discussed can be put into eight categories, ranging from those that are favorable to leaders to those that are unfavorable to leaders. For example, the combination of good relationships with the group, high task structure, and strong power would be most favorable. Situations with poor relationships, low structure, and weak power would be most unfavorable. Other combinations would fall in between these two extremes. Task-oriented leaders will be most effective in highly favorable situations (i.e., where things are going along smoothly) or in highly unfavorable situations (i.e., where things are completely out of control). Relationship-oriented leaders will be most effective in moderately favorable situations. But whatever the leader's style, if it does not match the situation that the leader is in, then he or she will not likely succeed as a leader.

Another approach suggesting that a leader needs to select a style meeting the needs of subordinates is called "path–goal theory" (House & Mitchell, 1974). This approach is based on expectancy theory, which was covered in Chapter 6 and, as you might recall, suggests that people are satisfied with their work if they believe it will lead to things that are highly valued and that they will work hard if they believe their effort will lead to things that are valued. Somewhat like contingency theory, the path–goal approach suggests combinations of leadership styles and subordinate attitudes or expectations. The leadership styles are (a) directive leadership (much like task-oriented leadership), (b) supportive leadership (much like relationship-oriented leadership), (c) participative leadership (a style that involves consultation with subordinates and a serious consideration of their ideas before the leader makes a decision), and (d) achievement-oriented leadership (where the leader sets challenging goals and high expectations, continually seeks improvements in performance, and expresses confidence that the group members will put forth the effort required to succeed). These leadership styles are contrasted with three subordinate attitudes or expectations: (1) the attitudes or orientation of subordinates, (2) the subordinates' acceptance of the leader, and (3) the expectations of subordinates that their efforts will result in achievement and that their achievements will be valued (House & Mitchell, 1974, p. 83).

The theory, then, suggests that a *directive* leadership style will be most effective in situations where employees themselves are somewhat dogmatic, where the demands of the task are ambiguous, and where rules and procedures are unclear. In these situations, the directive leader will provide the guidance and structure that the subordinates want and expect. A *supportive* leadership style, on the other hand, will be most effective in situations where subordinates are engaged in work that is stressful, frustrating, or unsatisfying. In these cases, the supportive leader can provide necessary encouragement and help to the subordinates. A *participative* leadership style seems to work best in situations where tasks are ambiguous and where subordinates have a great sense of autonomy and need more control over their work. The participatory leader will engage employees in working out the details of the task and will allow subordinates to meet their need to be involved. Finally, the *achievement-oriented* leadership style works best where subordinates are performing ambiguous nonrepetitive tasks. In these cases, the higher the achievement orientation of the leader, the more subordinates are confident that their efforts will pay off. The bottom line is that the leader should help subordinates to establish goals and set the appropriate paths to those goals and then should work with employees to encourage them in task completion and to remove obstacles that might stand in the way of their success.

Contemporary Approaches to Leadership

From Traits, to Skills, to Strategies

Despite questions that were raised about the ability of trait theory to predict leadership effectiveness, there continues to be considerable interest in defining the traits or characteristics that are associated with successful leadership. Most contemporary works along these lines assume that there are traits that a leader possesses to a greater degree than do others in the organization. Most also agree that these traits can be developed if they are not initially present in the individual. In this sense, to respond to the question of whether leaders are born or made, the contemporary consensus seems to be that leaders may be born but that they also can be made—or at least improved on.

But there also has been an interesting recent twist in this approach. Increasingly, in addition to describing traits of leaders, scholars are focusing on the skills, competencies, and strategies associated with leadership. (Recall the Office of Personnel Management study we examined in Chapter 1.) Thinking in these terms allows us to say that leadership initially builds on the skills of management—the ability to use power and influence effectively, the ability to communicate with and motivate others, and the ability to work in and among diverse groups. Leaders build on these basic skills or competencies in important ways. For example, some have argued that there are sharp distinctions between leaders and managers. In an important article in the *Harvard Business Review*, Zaleznik (1977) argued that leaders and managers ultimately are different types of people. Whereas managers adopt impersonal or even passive attitudes toward goals, leaders are more active or even visionary with respect to the future. Whereas managers excel in problem-solving skills and in work design, leaders seek out opportunities and rewards even if doing so involves risk. Managers prefer to work with people in carefully orchestrated and controlled ways, whereas leaders are much more passionate about what they do and are likely to create more turbulence along the way. Finally, whereas managers see themselves as conservators or regulators of existing institutions, leaders seek to profoundly reorder human, economic, and political relationships; leaders are concerned with vision and judgment, not just mastering routines. To this list of distinctions, Bennis and Nanus added an important "value" dimension: "Managers are people who do things right, and leaders are people who do the right thing" (1985, p. 21).

Various writers have developed different lists of traits, competencies, or skills required of leaders (Bennis & Nanus, 1985; Hitt, 1993; Northouse, 2001; Yukl, 1998). For example, Bennis offered 10 traits of "dynamic leaders," stating that they (1) possess self-knowledge, responsibility, and accountability; (2) are open to feedback; (3) are eager to learn and improve; (4) are curious risk takers; (5) show strong concentration at work; (6) learn from adversity; (7) balance tradition and change; (8) have an open, approachable style; (9) work well with systems; and (10) serve as models and mentors (1997, chap. 12). Similarly, Van Wart (2005; see also 2007) talks about 10 general leadership traits, which are either innate or learned early in life, but which can be improved by training, education, and experience. Six of the 10 characteristics are classified as "personality characteristics: self-confidence, decisiveness, resilience, energy, flexibility, and emotional maturity" (p. 93). The willingness to assume responsibility and the need for achievement are classified as motivational drives; personal integrity and service mentality, as value orientations. Van Wart suggests that these traits should be balanced and that excessiveness in any of these characteristics has negative aspects as well. For example, self-confidence is very important for the leader in providing the "sense that the things are under control" (p. 94). However, overconfidence, Van Wart argues, may lead to "lack of caution, micromanagement, and arrogance" (p. 94).

Whereas others have offered other qualities, certain traits or competencies seem to stand out in the literature. Among these, we would suggest the following (Figure 7.3).

1. *Intelligence and self-understanding.* Intellectual ability seems to be positively associated with leadership success, although substantial differences in the verbal or conceptual ability of leaders and members of the organization might interfere with

---

Intelligence and Self-Understanding

Self-Confidence and Self-Esteem

High Energy and Determination to Succeed

Sociability (Interpersonal Awareness)

Integrity

Figure 7.3   Leadership Traits or Competencies

---

effective communications. Leaders need a strong capacity for conceiving possibilities that might be hidden within a situation, the ability to articulate their ideas clearly and persuasively, and the intelligence to understand the context in which those ideas are to be played out. Leaders must be intelligent with respect to the outside world, but they also must be adept at self-understanding. Indeed, the process of leadership development is seen by many as merely one aspect of personal development. "The process of becoming a leader is much the same as the process of becoming an integrated human being" (Bennis, quoted in Hitt, 1993, p. iii).

2. *Self-confidence and self-esteem.* Obviously, those who aspire to leadership must have a certain degree of confidence that they will succeed. They must feel sure of their own abilities as well as the abilities of their followers. Indeed, leaders who have high expectations for themselves are likely to inspire high expectations for subordinates as well (Kouzes & Posner, 2007, chap. 9). The issue of self-confidence is especially important during a time when we are experimenting with new forms of organizational empowerment and shared leadership. Leaders who engage in sharing power give up some control of the situation; they put themselves at risk. Undertaking that risk requires a strong base of self-esteem. Self-confidence is important, but it also is tricky. Too little self-confidence might cause a potential leader to be indecisive and vague, whereas too much self-confidence might cause the person to be arrogant and intolerant of criticism. But there is no question that the most effective leaders have a high level of maturity and self-esteem.

3. *High energy and determination to succeed.* Leaders have been shown to have greater energy, physical stamina, and tolerance for stress than do others. Leadership is demanding hard work, so physical vitality and emotional resilience are quite helpful characteristics for leaders to possess (Yukl, 1998, p. 244). In addition, leaders need to exhibit high degrees of initiative and drive to get things done. They not only must be willing to commit to putting in long hours but also must make a deep psychological commitment to the task at hand. Leaders also believe that they can influence their own destinies, and they take greater responsibility for their actions than do others. They show energy and enthusiasm for what they are doing, and their energy and enthusiasm inspire others.

4. *Sociability (interpersonal awareness)*. Generally speaking, leaders like to interact with others and tend to be warm, friendly, outgoing, and diplomatic in their relations with others. They have good interpersonal skills and generally are able to achieve cooperative relationships with others. But we should note that there are exceptions to this rule, often among leaders with strong task orientations. Again, this issue cuts in different ways. Leaders who have a strong need to be liked by others might not allow work to interfere with good interpersonal relationships. On the other hand, those with low needs for affiliation might tend to spend too much time by themselves and not engage with others. In any case, leaders need to be sensitive to the social and psychological needs of those around them; they need to exhibit "interpersonal awareness."

5. *Integrity*. Integrity refers not only to knowing the right course of action but also to being able to pursue that course, even under pressure not to do so. Leaders with integrity are honest, principled, and ethical in their dealings with others. They are scrupulously honest and act on principle. They can be trusted to do what they say they will do and to follow up on promises made. They can be trusted to keep their commitments. In acting with integrity, they command the respect of others who recognize the leaders' sense of responsibility. Most important, their actions will match their words; they will act in accord with their principles and will "walk the walk." Being a good leader requires not only excellent technical and professional competence, but also an ethical orientation (including a sense of social responsibility) and a completely engaged personal sense of fulfillment and meaningfulness (Barendsen & Gardner, 2007, p. 21).

Moving from a discussion of traits and skills to a discussion of what leaders do, how they act, and what strategies they employ, we may examine one popular approach to the question of leadership practices—an approach developed by Kouzes and Posner (2007) in their book *The Leadership Challenge*. Kouzes and Posner began their work by surveying thousands of managers in the United States, asking the question, "What values (personal traits or characteristics) do you look for and admire in your superiors?" The most frequent responses were that superiors be honest, competent, forward-looking, and inspiring. Kouzes and Posner noted that these categories were surprisingly similar to those used by communication experts in assessing the believability of sources of communications such as newscasters and salespeople. In such studies, qualities such as trustworthiness, expertise, and dynamism were associated with greater credibility. Kouzes and Posner (2007) concluded that, more than anything else, we want leaders who are *credible*.

> Above all, we must be able to believe in our leaders. We must believe that their word can be trusted, that they will do what they say, that they have the knowledge and skill to lead, and that they are personally excited and enthusiastic about the direction in which we are headed. (p. 23)

If credibility is the foundation of all leadership, then what are the things leaders do that enhance their credibility? Kouzes and Posner (2007) answered that leaders establish their credibility through their actions, specifically through five "practices" that they engage in when they are at their best and that are available to anyone who wishes to accept the leadership "challenge." These include the following.

1. *Challenging the process.* Leaders accept the challenge of change. The specific challenge may come in a number of ways—from trying to introduce a new program of quality service to citizens, to implementing a new program, to turning a decaying organization around. Leaders are willing to step out into the unknown and explore new ideas and approaches. They encourage risk and innovation—in themselves and in others. And they learn from both their successes and their failures.

2. *Inspiring a shared vision.* Leaders look into the future, explore its possibilities, and dream about what the future might be like. This vision or mission represents an important change—a desire to make something happen that is new, different, and hopefully better. But leaders not only have to articulate the vision; they also have to inspire others to buy into that vision, something that is partly dependent on leaders' own energy and enthusiasm in carrying the vision forward.

3. *Enabling others to act.* Leaders cannot carry forward important projects on their own. They need the help and assistance of people throughout the organization. Successful leaders encourage, empower, and enable others to act. They promote teamwork and collaboration throughout the organization, and they model the importance of teamwork in their own behavior. They want people throughout the organization to buy into the vision, to feel a sense of ownership in what is happening, and to feel that their work is being fully supported.

4. *Modeling the way.* The most successful leaders are those who "practice what they preach." These are the leaders who have a clear idea of their beliefs and values and who constantly sharpen their understanding of those beliefs and values. They are people who have a clear sense of their own behavior—what they are doing and how it is affecting the group. And they are people who are able to make sure that their behavior is consistent with their principles. These leaders are role models for those in the organization. They are consistent and persistent—consistent with their values and persistent in pursuit of their goals.

5. *Encouraging the heart.* The most successful leaders encourage others to do their very best and to recognize and celebrate their successes. Leaders are in part cheerleaders, boosting the spirits of those with whom they work and cheering them on to greater accomplishments. The means of "encouraging the heart" may vary widely, from establishing large-scale employee recognition systems or events to simply stopping in the hall to tell employees that they are doing a good job. The best leaders generally are quite enthusiastic about what they are doing, but they also recognize that they cannot do the work on their own and that other people need to know they are doing well and that their efforts are appreciated.

Leadership theorists talk about the traits, skills, behaviors, and styles that make for successful leadership. But who evaluates the leaders? Who can tell whether the leader is good or bad? First, leaders can evaluate their own work through self-reflection and self-critique or through evaluating short-term and long-term improvements (Van Wart, 2005, p. 435). But leaders are also evaluated by their subordinates, because they are directly affected by the leader's actions and behaviors. Leaders can also be evaluated by their superiors, the body to whom they report, or, in the case of political leaders, even to the voters. The stakeholders outside the organization (clients, vendors, partner agencies, indirect consumers of services) may also evaluate the leader. And finally, time, Van Wart argues, is "the toughest and subtlest evaluator of all" (p. 436). Time will say whether the contribution of a particular leader will be remembered by the group, the organization, or the society.

The Transformational Approach

Whereas most of the material on leadership that we have covered to this point has been largely drawn from studies of leadership in business organizations, it is interesting that perhaps the most powerful formulation of leadership in the modern era—the idea of "transformational leadership"—has its roots in studies of political and governmental leadership. Transformational leadership is the key concept in a classic study by Harvard University political scientist James MacGregor Burns titled simply *Leadership* (1978). In this monumental work, Burns did not merely try to understand the dynamics of leadership in terms of getting things done or meeting organizational objectives. Instead, he sought to develop a theory of leadership that would extend across cultures and across time. Specifically, Burns sought to understand leadership not as something that leaders do to followers but rather as a relationship between leaders and followers—a mutual interaction that ultimately changes both:

> The process of leadership must be seen as part of the dynamics of conflict and power; that leadership is nothing if not linked to collective purpose; that the effectiveness of leaders must be judged not by their press clippings but by actual social change . . . ; that political leadership depends on a long chain of biological and social processes, of interaction with structures of political opportunity and closures, of interplay between the calls of moral principles and the recognized necessities of power; that in placing these concepts of political leadership centrally into a theory . . . , we will reaffirm the possibilities of human volition and of common standards of justice in the conduct of people's affairs. (p. 4)

Burns started by noting that although historically we have been preoccupied with power in organizations and in society, there is an important difference between power and leadership. Typically, power is thought of as carrying out one's own will despite resistance. But such a conception of power neglects the important fact that power involves a relationship between leaders and followers and that a central value in that relationship is *purpose*—what is being sought, or what is intended, by both the one who is exercising power and the one who is on the receiving end. In most situations, the recipient has some flexibility in his or her response to an attempted exercise of power, so the power that one can exercise is dependent on the way in which both parties view the situation. Power wielders draw on their own resources and motives, but these must be relevant to the resources and motivations of the recipient of power.

Leadership, according to Burns, is an aspect of power, but it is a separate process. Power is exercised when potential power wielders, acting to achieve goals of their own, gather resources that enable them to influence others. Power is exercised to realize the purposes of the power wielders, whether or not those purposes also are the purposes of the respondents. Leadership, on the other hand, is exercised "when persons with certain motives and purposes mobilize, in competition or conflict with others, institutional, political, psychological, and other resources so as to arouse, engage, and satisfy the motives of the followers" (1978, p. 18). The difference between power and leadership is that power serves the interests of the power wielder, whereas leadership serves both the leader's interests *and* those of the followers. The values, motivations, wants, needs, interests, and expectations of both leaders and followers must be represented for leadership to occur.

There actually are two types of leadership, Burns argued. The first is *transactional* leadership, which involves an exchange of valued things (e.g., economic, political, psychological) between initiators and respondents. For example, a political leader might agree to support a particular policy in exchange for votes in the next election, or a student might write a superb paper in exchange for an "A" grade. In the case of transactional leadership, the two parties come together in a relationship that advances the interests of both, but there is no deep or enduring link between them. *Transformational* leadership, on the other hand, occurs when leaders and followers engage with one another in such away that they raise one another to higher levels of morality and motivation. Although the leaders and followers initially might come together out of the pursuit of their own interests or because the leader recognized some special potential in the followers, as the relationship evolves, their interests become fused into mutual support for common purposes. The relationship between leaders and followers becomes one in which the purposes of both are elevated through the relationship; both parties become mobilized, inspired, and uplifted. In some cases, transformational leadership even evolves into *moral* leadership as leadership raises the level of moral aspiration and moral conduct of both leaders and followers. Moral leadership results in actions that are consistent with the needs, interests, and aspirations of the followers but that fundamentally change moral understandings and social conditions.

Burns (1978) provided the most compelling moral interpretation of leadership that we have encountered so far. In this view, leadership is not merely something that occurs within the context of a particular group or organization seeking its own interests. Rather, leadership (especially transformational or moral leadership) has the capacity to move groups, organizations, or even societies toward the pursuit of higher purposes. Burns added an important element of change and transformation to our understanding of leadership.

Unfortunately, some who have adopted the phrase *transformational leadership* have used it for more narrowly defined purposes. Bernard Bass, for example, developed a model of transformational leadership more confined to the relationships of superiors and subordinates in complex organizations (1985; Bass & Avolio, 1994). Bass used the terms *transactional* and *transformational* as Burns did but in somewhat different ways. The *transactional* leader, according to Bass, exchanges rewards for services rendered so as to improve subordinates' job performance. To accomplish this, the leader

> 1) recognizes what it is we want to get from our work and tries to see that we get what we want if our performance warrants it, 2) exchanges reward and promises of reward for our effort, [and] 3) is responsive to our immediate self-interests if they can be met by getting the work done. (Bass, 1985, p. 11)

The *transformational* leader, rather than focusing on how the current needs of subordinates might be met, concentrates on arousing or altering their needs. Such a transformation can be achieved in one or more of three ways:

> 1) by raising our level of awareness, our level of consciousness about the importance and value of designated outcomes, and ways of reaching them; 2) by getting us to transcend our own self-interest for the sake of the team, organization, or larger polity; [and] 3) by altering our need levels ... or expanding our portfolio of needs or wants. (Bass, 1985, p. 20)

In revising Burns's (1978) work in this way, Bass narrowed the moral basis on which transformational leadership previously stood. Although Bass advised managers that it would be in their long-term interest to act according to moral principles, in his view, transformational leadership does not imply a moral element. Indeed, to illustrate this point, Bass used a classic example—the leadership of Adolf Hitler. Whereas Burns would say that Hitler's leadership was not transformational because it did not further good in the society, Bass contended that Germany still was transformed by Hitler's leadership and, indeed, that Hitler's influence still is felt today. Because Germany was transformed, according to Bass, Hitler was a transformational leader.

In any case, transformational leaders, according to Bass, achieve good results by employing one or more of four strategies: (1) idealized influence (transformational leaders are admired and respected by their followers, and they act as role models or positive influences), (2) inspirational motivation (transformational leaders communicate high expectations for subordinates and encourage them to aspire to high performance), (3) intellectual stimulation (transformational leaders encourage their followers to be creative and innovative and to try new solutions to old problems), and (4) individualized consideration (transformational leaders provide a supportive climate in which individuals are encouraged to grow and develop) (Bass & Avolio, 1994, pp. 3–4). Generally speaking, according to this interpretation, transactional leaders achieve expected outcomes, whereas transformational leaders move the organization beyond expectations. But clearly, the element of moral leadership so central to Burns's work is missing in this interpretation.

Transforming Organizations

The interest in transforming organizations, whether in the broader or narrower sense, has led to increased attention on the part of scholars and practitioners to the relationship between leadership and change. The question has two parts. First, how can leaders stimulate specific policy and program changes? Second, how can they help to develop a culture of change or innovation in their organizations? How can leaders "transform" their organizations? How can they bring about change? How can they encourage innovation, even if it involves risk?

Tichy and Devanna (1986) suggested that bringing about change in organizational settings is not something that happens randomly or something that requires a charismatic leader. Rather, leaders can bring about change by engaging in specific disciplined steps. These steps occur within the context of a drama that symbolizes the many tensions and dilemmas involved in the change process. For example, there typically is a tension between tradition and innovation. Although organizations must adapt to new and changing conditions, they also must maintain some stability so as not to "spin out of control." This tension is reflected in the way that some individuals within organizations fear change, while others are more positive and hopeful that the future will bring about improvements. Sometimes it also is reflected in tension between managers (who typically are forces for stability in organizations) and leaders (who are forces for change). During the change process, leaders must present a positive and attractive view of the future of the organizations while, at the same time, providing the emotional support for those who are most affected (and perhaps most troubled) by the anticipated changes.

Tichy and Devanna (1986) portrayed the change process as a drama involving three "acts," with each act affecting both the organization and individuals. Act I involves "recognizing the need for revitalization." In this stage, events in the environment trigger or signal a need for change, which the effective leader accepts as an impetus for transition and begins to communicate throughout the organization. Because many people will have difficulty in disengaging from past patterns of behavior and will have emotional attachments to the old ways of doing things, the leader in this stage will provide people with the support they need for letting go of the past and grasping the future. In this stage, "Leaders should encourage employees to accept the failures [of the past] without feeling as if they had failed" (Tichy & Devanna, 1986, p. 32).

Act II involves "creating a new vision." In this stage, according to Tichy and Devanna, leaders will need to create a vision or a new way of thinking about what the organization does and how it should go about its work. This vision may be developed in a variety of ways—some fairly directive, others much more participatory—but in the end the vision will have to be appealing to a critical mass of the organization's members. In this stage, individuals will continue to work through their sense of loss with respect to the past but also will begin to understand and accept the new vision of the organization and how they might fit into that vision.

Act III involves "institutionalizing change." In this stage, the new vision begins to become reality as specific programs and policies are institutionalized throughout the organization. Again, leaders have to be attentive not only to the design and implementation of these new ideas but also to the psychological needs that must be met during this period. "Change invokes simultaneous personal feelings of fear and hope, anxiety and relief, pressure and stimulation, threats to self-esteem and challenges to master new situations" (Tichy & Devanna, 1986, p. 31). The most effective leaders will provide support as individuals work through these difficult issues. (Other writers interested in the process of leading change have elaborated on the various stages of transformation. One popular version of leading change [Kotter, 1996, p. 21] suggests an eight-stage process: [1] establishing a sense of urgency, [2] creating a guiding coalition, [3] developing a vision and strategy, [4] communicating the vision, [5] empowering broad-based action, [6] generating short-term wins, [7] consolidating gains and producing more change, and [8] anchoring new approaches in the culture. [See also Kotter & Cohen, 2002.])

Tichy and Devanna's approach stands out for its identification of the emotional and psychological forces at play during the process of leading change, a theme that has been put forward by others. For example, Diamond (1993) argued that unconscious expectations and desires affect organizational life in general and alter the relation between leaders and followers in particular. Especially where they are involved in change efforts, leaders and followers exhibit deep-seated psychological needs that lead them into psychologically complex relationships. First among the patterns examined by Diamond was *recognition and approval,* a limiting type of "mirroring" relationship in which leaders require devotion and honor, whereas followers wish to be led by individuals they can idealize. This pattern results in excessive dependency and tends to reinforce hierarchical systems that are impervious to change. Second is *membership and affiliation.* Many people enter organizations looking for friendship and collegiality or the company of like-minded people. Such tendencies, when extended too far, limit organizations' capacity to deal with novel or conflicting information, both of which are necessary for change to occur. Third, Diamond pointed to conflicting patterns of *compassion, sympathy,* and *retribution.* Many people enter organizations feeling victimized by previous experiences and seek compassion and sympathy in their organizational work, but they also desire to "get even" by projecting their previous experiences into their current organizational situations. Not only does this complicate the leader–follower relationship, but it also may lead to either aggression or depression in these organizations.

In Diamond's view, dealing effectively with these and other defensive reactions in organizations requires a mixture of collaborative and therapeutic leadership styles. "The collaborative leadership of change requires a willingness to experiment with different ideas and feelings, a team player mentality, a sharing of tasks between and among members, and a view of confronting conflict as an opportunity for learning and enhancing organizational effectiveness" (1993, p. 226). Therapeutic leaders recognize that change often is experienced as loss and encourage followers to work through their feelings of grief and separation as a prelude to learning new patterns of behavior. In either case, all members of organizations will need to get past the view that those in authority by themselves can solve the problems we face and will need to select leaders who involve everyone in solving problems (Maccoby, 1981).

Similarly, Hirschorn (1997) described the changing psychodynamics of the leader–follower relationship in contemporary society. Whereas leaders once could "order" followers to do certain manual tasks, the types of activities required for today's organizations to be successful—creativity, flexibility, commitment to the organization, and a capacity for informed decision making—do not lend themselves to top-down authority. To the contrary, these demands cry out for a culture of openness. But for people to be open with one another, they need a sense of security, and in today's organizations (marked as they are by cutbacks and other reconfigurations) there actually is less security for employees than ever before. These contradictory positions mean that the psychological relationship between leaders and followers is cut through by tension and the potential for great antagonism. How, then, can leaders create conditions in which employees can contribute openly and still be assured that they will be protected? Hirschorn suggested building new organizations and new styles of leadership that enable people in organizations to connect with one another, to engage at a very personal level, and (importantly) to be willing to forgive when things go wrong.

Values-Based Leadership

The importance of morality and values in defining leadership has been central in several more recent studies. Robert K. Greenleaf (1998, 2002), a longtime AT&T management development specialist turned consultant and writer, emphasized the role of the spirit and the spiritual in his concept of "servant leadership." The idea is that leadership begins with a commitment on the part of the potential leader to serve others. The leader does not pursue his or her own self-interest but rather is primarily concerned with serving others.

> The servant-leader is servant first. . . . It begins with the natural feeling that one wants to serve, to serve *first.* Then conscious choice brings one to aspire to lead. . . . The difference manifests itself in the care taken by the servant—first to make sure that other people's highest priority needs are being served. The best test, and the most difficult to administer, is: Do those served grow as persons? Do they, *while being served,* become healthier, wiser, freer, more autonomous, more likely themselves to become servants? *And,* what is the effect on the least privileged in society? Will they benefit or, at least, not be further deprived? (Greenleaf, quoted in Frick & Spears, 1996, pp. 1–2)

In this view, the organizational "bottom line" is less important than the leader's capacity for honesty, integrity, character, or spirit. Although there is the implication that, in the long run, the servant-leader will help the organization accomplish its work more effectively, the first priority is service to others—citizens, clients, customers, or the community.

Followers of Greenleaf's ideas have identified a number of characteristics that are central to the development of servant-leaders. For example, servant-leaders are admonished to listen carefully so as to understand the will of the group as well as the leaders' own inner voices. They are urged to empathize with others and to engage in healing broken relationships and broken spirits. Servant-leaders are urged to assume "stewardship," a term that Block (1993) defined in his book

Stewardship as "to hold something in trust for another" (p. xx). Stewardship requires that we be accountable for what our institutions do without defining goals and objectives for others, without controlling others, and without even "taking care" of them. Consistent with this view, Greenleaf argued that leaders hold institutions "in trust" for the greater good of society. Their ultimate goal is the betterment of the human condition.

The idea of approaching leadership "from the inside" (i.e., by beginning with the leader's own personal commitments and values) has been echoed in several other works. O'Toole (1995) contrasted values-based leadership with contingency or situational approaches, arguing that all such approaches ultimately involve an effort on the part of the leader to impose his or her will on followers without regard to their own needs or interests and often without even consulting them, something that O'Toole called "the ultimate in disrespect for individuals" (p. 12). By contrast, the leader must understand why people resist change and make the personal investment required to overcome this resistance, typically by offering a new system of beliefs that resonates with followers so that they come to adopt it as their own. A part of this new belief system is to recognize that people do not follow leaders just because they are right; rather, they follow leaders who act with integrity, listen to the concerns of followers, show respect for and trust in others, and act with their needs and interests in mind. O'Toole suggested that, to develop a theory of leadership that has more substance than "it depends," values and morality need to be at the center. "If the goal is to bring about constructive change, values-based leadership is, yes, always more effective" (p. 15). Leadership is built on the moral principle of respect for followers.

Importantly, values-based leadership requires that leaders begin by changing themselves—that is, by revising their own concept of leadership and the values that support bringing about change. For example, Quinn (1996) held that leaders must engage in an intensely personal struggle to sort out their own lives and commitments before undertaking the task of trying to lead others. Bolman and Deal (1995) told the story of an executive who was led through a series of important self-discoveries to lead with "soul"—that is, to recognize that leadership must come not only from the head but also from the heart. Covey (1991) described several principles on which "principle-centered leadership" might be built—trustworthiness, character, competence, maturity, self-discipline, and integrity. As if to summarize, Hesselbein (1996) wrote,

> Leadership is a matter of how to be, not how to do. We spend most of our lives mastering how to do things, but in the end it is the quality and character of the individual that distinguishes the great leaders.

Leadership and Emotions: The Art of Leadership

Complementary to this work is more recent work that focuses on the connection between leadership and the emotions and then suggests that there is indeed an art of leadership. Daniel Goleman (1995), journalist and behavioral scientist, offered the phrase "emotional intelligence" to refer to "the sense in which there is intelligence in the emotions and the sense in which intelligence can be brought to emotions" (p. 40). The idea is that personal or emotional intelligence, understanding oneself and others and acting wisely in social situations based on clarity with respect to one's own emotions, has a great deal to do with the ability to lead a successful life. Goleman explores five dimensions of emotional intelligence:

Knowing one's emotions. The ability to recognize one's own feelings or emotions is a keystone to self-understanding and gives us a better sense of how we really feel.

Managing emotions. Handling feelings appropriately—that is, recognizing and then doing something positive with one's emotions, is essential to effective interactions with other.

Motivating oneself. Emotional self-control, the capacity to use one's emotions in a productive fashion, is related to one's effectiveness and productivity.

Recognizing emotions in others. People who are empathetic—that is, people who understand the deep-seated, though rarely verbalized, needs and concerns of others—have exceptional emotional intelligence.

Handling relationships. "The art of relationships is, in large part, skill in managing emotions in others. These are the abilities that undergird popularity, leadership, and interpersonal effectiveness" (pp. 43–44)

In *Primal Leadership,* Goleman and his colleagues Richard Boyatzis and Annie McKee (2002) applied the notion of emotional intelligence to the study of leadership, arguing that "great leadership works through the emotions" (p. 3). That is, a leader needs to be fully attuned to the emotional as well as intellectual impact of what he or she is saying and doing. People will react to the emotional "signals" the leader gives off, and where those signals "connect," individuals resonate with the leader. As opposed to dissonance, which is created when there is a lack of harmony between potential leaders and followers, the successful leader stimulates resonance among those who follow. The leader and the followers are on the same "wavelength," they are "in sync," and there is less "noise" in the system. People get along better and work together more effectively. Most of all, the leader's skill in understanding his or her own values and emotions as well as those of others leaves people feeling encouraged, excited, and uplifted, even in difficult times (Goleman et al., p. 20; see also Pescosolido, 2002).

From recognition of leadership as connected to the emotions, recognition that leadership is an art was not far behind. For example, Kouzes and Posner (2007) write that "Leadership is a performing art . . . [in which leaders] enact the meaning of the organization in every decision they make and in every step they take toward the future they envision" (p. 84). Similarly, Bolman and Deal (1997) argue that managers who would lead in the future will require high levels of personal artistry to respond to the ambiguous and paradoxical changes they will face. "Artists interpret experience and express it in forms that can be felt and understood, and appreciated by others. Art allows for emotion, subtlety, ambiguity" (p. 17).

Other works have even more explicitly drawn parallels between leadership and art, especially music. Max De Pree (1992), chairman emeritus of Herman Miller, Inc., in *Leadership Jazz*, draws an analogy between the leader of a jazz group and leaders in industry, an analogy that is also explored by Robert Denhardt (2000) in *The Pursuit of Significance*. Denhardt argues that leaders are rarely able to write and conduct a "symphony" that others play. More often they are called on to be fully integrated into the performance themselves, to play along with others, like the leader of a jazz ensemble improvising a tune:

> By establishing the theme, the leader of the ensemble . . . can chart the basic pattern and direction in which the performance will move. By setting the tone and the tempo, the leader gives focus to the spirit and energy of the group. By modeling effective and responsible performance in their own solos, leaders can energize and articulate the performance of others. But it is the performance of others that is critical. (pp. 180–181)

These are but a few of the allusions to the parallels between art and leadership found in the literature. But even these are typically brief and passing metaphors, acknowledgments that some leadership skills are extremely difficult to describe in rational terms. And while each of these authors proceeds to examine certain approaches or behaviors that are rightfully described as artful, at least in the sense that they can't be explained scientifically, the art of leadership is not developed in any detail. Moreover, these works fall short of suggesting that leadership may in fact share even more with art than the simple metaphor of leadership as an art might suggest.

That step was taken by Robert and Janet Denhardt (2005a) in their recent book *The Dance of Leadership*. Since most leaders would say that leadership is an art rather than a science, the Denhardts decided to take seriously the notion that leadership is an art. They began by interviewing artists, musicians, and especially dancers—not about their leadership, but about how they approach their art. Armed with lessons about how people approach art, the Denhardts then interviewed prominent leaders in the world of business, politics, the military, higher education, and even sports to see if they approach leadership in the same way. From these interviews they confirmed that leaders do in fact approach their work using categories very similar to those in art—rhythm and timing, communicating in images, symbols, and metaphors, improvisation, and focus and concentration.

Based on this work, the Denhardts asked what it is that leaders do that causes others to follow. The answer: Leaders connect with others emotionally in a way that energizes them and causes them to act, and leaders provide the assurance that we need to pursue important values. Leadership is about action and leadership is about change. People must be stimulated to act, and they must be comfortable that the changes they are making are okay.

According to the Denhardts, developing an artistic approach to leadership simply involves looking at the work of leaders through a different lens, an artistic lens. It requires building a new vocabulary, an artistic vocabulary. But once you understand that leadership is an art, it's not hard to see how your artistry can be built. For example, while rhythm is typically associated with dance or music, leaders work with the rhythms of groups and organizations to move them forward. "Rhythm . . . extends throughout the human experience, connecting the vital aspects of that experience in meaningful and recognizable ways" (2005a, p. 49). Not only individuals, but also groups and organizations have their own rhythm. Good leaders intuitively understand or learn the dynamics or the rhythm of their group and organization and are able to "play" with it. "Leading involves drawing energy forward, organizing that energy, and stimulating its movement through time and space in a rhythmic way—that is, in a smooth and coordinated fashion characterized by ease and efficiency" (2005a, p. 77).

In summary, there are seven lessons that will help you build an artistic approach to leadership:

Leaders need to understand how the rhythms of groups and organizations energize people.

Leaders need to be able to improvise with creativity and spontaneity.

Leaders need to speak and listen in a way that inspires.

Leaders need to see the "big picture" but act "at arm's length."

Leaders need to "be present to the moment."

Leaders need to be totally dedicated and committed to what they are doing.

Leaders need to learn from their experiences.

Leadership in Culturally Diverse Organizations

The question of what traits, qualities, and behaviors are most important for leaders to be effective will have different answers in different countries and different cultures. A leader who is effective in Japan might not fit well in an American organization. Indeed, according to some of the most highly respected students of cultural difference, "Asking people to describe the qualities of a good leader is a way of asking them to describe their culture" (Hofstede & Hofstede, 2005, p. 268).

With the increased trend toward globalization, leaders and managers have to learn how to lead people from different cultures, handling and appreciating diversity in the organizations. They have to posses attributes acceptable to people who come from myriad cultures, but they also have to know how to understand the behavior of these people. Understanding cultural differences and managing conflicts that arise from cultural diversity are very important for contemporary leaders in today's globalized world. Leaders in different cultures are not immune to the predominant values and practices of their cultures, so their characteristics and behavior will be dependent on these values and practices.

One of the most recent and most extensive studies of leadership is the Global Leadership and Organizational Behavior Effectiveness (GLOBE) study, which is based on completed questionnaires from approximately 17,000 middle-level managers and 951 organizations in 62 nations (House, Hanges, Javidan, Dorfman, & Gupta, 2005). This worldwide project was designed to provide answers to many questions related to leadership and leadership practices in different cultures. The researchers were interested in whether there are some leadership characteristics and behaviors that are accepted or rejected universally, in every culture. The authors developed nine cultural dimensions and identified several they call "global leader behaviors (leadership dimensions)," which are more or less common to every culture.

The nine cultural dimensions comprising GLOBE's model are performance orientation, power distance, future orientation, gender egalitarianism, assertiveness, institutional collectivism, in-group collectivism, uncertainty avoidance, and human orientation. How one's culture is scored on each of these dimensions will determine the specific behaviors that people from that culture will prefer and will also determine how the leaders from that culture will act.

For example, members of cultures that score high on performance orientation, such as the United States, Singapore, and Japan, as well as their leaders, will expect more demanding targets, will give emphasis to results, will value initiative, will believe that education and hard work are crucial for success, will be more direct and explicit in communication, and will value people for what they do, not for who they are (House et al., 2005, p. 245). Similarly, in cultures that have high scores on human orientation, people (and their leaders) will value kindness, generosity, and personal and family relationships, and they will have a greater need for belonging and affiliation (p. 570).

Although there are great differences among the traits and practices preferred by the world's cultures, GLOBE's researchers believe that there are certain leader behaviors that are universally endorsed by every culture. Charismatic/Value-Based Leadership, according to the authors, is one of the "global leadership behaviors" that is desired by almost every culture, and it "reflects the ability to inspire, to motivate, and to expect high performance outcomes from others on the basis of firmly held core values" (House et al., 2005, p. 675). The other five global leader behaviors, defined by GLOBE researchers, are team-oriented, participative, humsan-oriented, autonomous, and self-protective leadership. These types of leadership, or leadership dimensions, GLOBE authors argue, are more or less desirable and acceptable universally.

Trompenaars and Wooliams (2003) give practical guidelines for the leaders and managers who work with and across different cultures. They suggest that leaders have to recognize, respect, and reconcile cultural differences. "Different cultural orientations and views of the world are not right or wrong—they are just different" (p. 28). Leaders have to be able to reconcile cultural dilemmas, defined as "two prepositions in apparent conflict," or "a situation whereby one has to choose between two good or desirable options" (p. 30). The ability for reconciliation of cultural dilemmas will help leaders to avoid unwelcome behaviors such as ignoring other cultures, abandoning their own orientation, or even compromising. The capacity to reconcile cultural dilemmas within varying cultures is the key to "transcultural competence" or what we might call "transcultural leadership."

Leadership in the Public Service

Although most of the social scientific research on organizational leadership has focused on private organizations, students of leadership have been attentive to the special demands of leadership in the public service as well (Tucker, 1995). Certainly, the American presidency has proven to be a major focus for studies of political leadership (Burns, 1984; Edwards & Wayne, 2005; Greenstein, 1988; Lowi, 1985; Neustadt, 1960, 1990; Pfiffner & Davidson, 2006), although studies also have focused on governors (Beyle & Williams, 1972), mayors (Holli, 1999; Svara, 2008), city managers (Caro, 1974; Watson & Watson, 2006), and a variety of other public administrators (Doig & Hargrove, 1987). In general, these studies have examined both the personalities of leaders and the ways in which they engaged their particular historical situations. As Neustadt (1987) wrote, "Leadership in one context becomes frustration in another" (p. viii). With that advice in mind, we should ask whether leadership in the public sector (i.e., leadership in the policy process or in public agencies) is different from leadership elsewhere.

Leadership in the Policy Process

Leadership in the public realm is concerned not only with the conduct of organizations but also with establishing policies on a variety of important social, economic, and political issues. Public leaders help to create a vision for their community, state, or country; help to build the public policy agenda; mobilize public opinion with respect to policy proposals; and play an important role in shaping and implementing those programs and policies that government undertakes. Recent studies of political leadership have shown some of the ways in which leaders in the public sector go about their work. These studies also have demonstrated the importance of involving communities in collaborative decision-making processes.

Recall Burns's (1978) analysis of transformational leadership, largely based on his studies of political leaders. Burns argued that leaders must be sensitive to the needs and aspirations of followers so that both leaders and followers can grow and develop. Such a view not only moved those who studied organizational leadership away from their standard approaches; it also represented a move away from the traditional "power" orientation that political scientists had long employed. That is, it suggested that politics is not just about power but also about leadership. And the two are different (Tucker, 1995, chap. 1).

This theme was developed in Heifetz's (1994) *Leadership Without Easy Answers*, largely based on his examination of both elected and appointed leaders in the public service. Heifetz noted that people sometimes are described as leaders just because they are able to gather followers or exert influence on a group or an organization. But such a values-free notion of leadership, according to Heifetz, fails to recognize that when we talk about leadership, we inevitably talk about the roles and responsibilities that members of a community hold. Because these basic human values always are at play in the relationship between leaders and followers, to speak of a values-neutral approach to leadership simply would not make sense. Heifetz pointed out the difference between saying "leadership means influencing the community to follow the leader's vision" and saying "leadership means influencing the community to face its problems" (p. 14). Leaders challenge and mobilize communities to face problems and tackle tough issues. For this reason, values are at the core of the exercise of leadership.

Many scholars and practitioners now define leadership not as a position but as an activity. The president can lead, but as we will see, so can a frontline social worker. What is critical is not their offices but rather the types of work that people do. For Heifetz, the notion of service is important, but it is a particular type of service that the leader offers. The notion of "adaptive work" is central. Leadership as adaptive work consists of learning how to "address conflicts in the values people hold or to diminish the gap between the values people stand for and the reality they face" (1994, p. 22). Adaptive work involves changes in values, attitudes, and beliefs, and such basic changes are as difficult for communities or organizations as they are for individuals. The leader's role is to employ various resources to help individuals and groups test reality and confront value conflicts that need to be resolved.

In a more recent work, *Leadership on the Line* (2002), Heifetz and Linsky make a useful distinction between technical work and adaptive work. In technical work, the approach is for authorities to apply current know-how to the problem at hand. In adaptive work, the people with the problem have to learn new ways of operating. Technical work is the work of routine management, whereas adaptive work is the work of leadership. Heifetz and Linsky comment, "Indeed, the single most common source of leadership failure we've been able to identify—in politics, community life, business, or the nonprofit sector—is that people, especially those in positions of authority, treat adaptive challenges like technical problems" (p. 14).

In adaptive work, influence and authority are helpful but do not define leadership. Like Burns, Heifetz (1994) argued that Hitler did not really exercise leadership in Germany during World War II. He pointed out that Hitler held a position of authority and exercised influence in German society. Hitler even acted in a way that was consistent with the needs and interests of many Germans. But Hitler's work did not elevate his society, as Burns's (1978) notion of transformational leadership would require. Nor did it help Germany in adapting to the social and political realities of the time. Instead, Hitler avoided tough realities and relied on illusions of grandeur and the creation of various internal and external scapegoats to get around the hard work of adaptation. The work of adaptation instead requires several conditions that we tend to associate more with democratic rule. Heifetz observed, "In addition to reality testing, these include respecting conflict, negotiation, and a diversity of views within a community; increasing community cohesion; developing norms of responsibility taking, learning, and innovation; and keeping social distress within a bearable range" (1994, p. 26).

Although leadership in the private sector involves values, the dramatic interplay of values that is so much a part of leadership today is even more apparent in the public sector. In addition, public sector leadership must take into account the fact that public problems today do not easily confine themselves to one organization. Policy issues such as building the local economy and protecting the welfare of children and youth involve many different government agencies as well as many groups outside of government. They cross organizational boundaries and even jurisdictional boundaries. No one group or organization can exercise power unilaterally; indeed, the interconnected nature of most public problems means that coordinating many different groups and interests is the main task of policy leadership today.

For those who would seek to assert leadership in situations involving many groups and interests, the traditional skills of organizational management—motivating, delegating, and so on—are less applicable than is a new set of skills, in negotiating, brokering, and resolving conflict. These leadership skills will be particularly important in situations in which no one is in charge and leadership must be shared (Crosby & Bryson, 2005). What has been called "shared leadership" moves beyond the traditional model in which leadership is conceived around a single individual wielding power and influence in a unilateral and largely downward fashion. Shared leadership instead connotes "a dynamic interactive influence process among individuals in groups in which the objective is to lead one another to their achievement of group or organizational goals" (Pearce & Conger, 2003, p. 1). As such, shared leadership at some times involves peer or lateral influence and at others upward or downward influence. In any case, leadership is broadly distributed among members of the group, the organization, or the society.

In a world of diverse interests, all expecting to weigh in on major policy issues (see Chapter 13), this form of leadership will increasingly be essential to the collaborative process. Those who Luke (1998) called "catalytic leaders" will need to be able to think and act strategically and to stimulate others to do the same. They will need to be able to encourage productive interactions among many different players (something requiring excellent skills in facilitation, negotiation, and mediation). And they will have to develop strength of character, a passion for results, and immense personal integrity. Especially in the public sector, but throughout society, we must pay greater attention to "the ethics of leadership—that is, the obligations of leaders to promote justice, fairness, trust, and the conditions necessary for people to live well in communities that flourish" (Knapp, 2007, p. xii).

Howard Gardner, whose early work on multiple intelligences underlies more recent work on emotional intelligence, reinforces this view. In *Five Minds for the Future* (2006), Gardner speculates that the changes in our world today and into the future will require five specific "kinds of minds" in order to cope and to thrive. The *disciplined mind* is that which has mastered a single discipline, craft, or profession. It provides a foundation for the work of other minds. The *synthesizing mind* is able to bring together information and ideas from many different sources in a way that makes sense, "new" sense. This mind is especially valuable to leaders of the future who must sort through amazingly complex information to make decisions. The *creating mind* comes up with new ideas and concepts and is helpful in breaking new ground. The *respectful mind* recognizes and celebrates the differences among individuals. And the *ethical mind* moves beyond self-interest to make decisions based on a sense of social responsibility. All of these minds, Gardner argues, are important to people throughout society, but especially to those who would lead (Chapter 1).

Leadership in Public Agencies

Whereas much of the material already covered having to do with organizational leadership is applicable to the public sector, there are several important studies that show how leadership in the public service is different. Terry (2002), for example, suggested that leaders in public bureaucracies watch over institutions that embody important social ideals and, for that reason, bear a special responsibility to maintain the integrity of those institutions. The leader's role is, in large part, to "conserve" the public service values that are part of the public organization. The "administrative conservator" may be called on to play different roles at different times, sometimes engaging in "initiating leadership" (pursuing innovative courses of action) and, at the other end of the continuum, sometimes engaging in "protecting leadership" (maintaining the strength, identity, and traditions of the organization). Specifically, the administrative conservator, in Terry's view, is called on to conserve or protect the mission and goals of the organization, to protect the values that give the organization its distinctiveness, and to maintain both external and internal support:

> The conservator not only should be responsive to the various constitutional matters but also [should] preserve the executive and non-executive authority invested in public bureaucracies, maintain commitment among the executive cadre to core agency values, and sustain support among key external constituents and internal interest groups. (2002, p. 172)

Ultimately, Terry argued, administrative conservatorship actually is a form of statesmanship balancing professional expertise, political skills, and the values of democratic governance.

Whereas others have focused on executive-level leadership in public organizations, Vinzant and Crothers (1998) argued in *Street-Level Leadership* that leadership occurs throughout public agencies, even at the front line. At this level, public servants such as police officers and social service workers engage in extremely difficult and unpredictable tasks, and they often have considerable discretion in how they act. They may be called on to apprehend violent criminals, to determine how to deal with questions of domestic violence, to decide when to reunite troubled families, to curb gang activity, or to assist victims of child abuse. In carrying out these tasks, frontline public servants have to make choices, and they eventually are evaluated with respect to the appropriateness of their choices. Their exercise of discretion or power must be found to be legitimate.

Based on the direct observation of about 100 street-level public servants (mostly police officers and social workers), Vinzant and Crothers (1998) argued that these frontline workers exercise leadership in their relationships with clients and others. As the situational model of leadership would suggest, street-level public servants make choices within the context of the particular situations in which they find themselves. As the transformational model would suggest, they exercise influence but also are influenced by and accountable to others. In either case, the legitimacy of their exercise of power and discretion can be better understood by using a leadership model. "Such workers are, or at least can be, leaders as they do their jobs, and the legitimacy of their actions can be evaluated through standards expressed in the concept of leadership" (Vinzant & Crothers, 1998, p. 142).

Some Concluding Notes

Increasingly, the skills needed for leadership in the public service will be the skills of shared leadership. Shared leadership focuses not on the leader but rather on clusters of individuals working and growing together. Leadership is seen as a function that operates within a group—not the property of a single individual but rather an activity in which many can participate. Leadership refers to the actions of an individual only as he or she interacts with others in a group, an organization, or a society. We can define this new approach to leadership in the following way: Leadership occurs where the action of one member of a group or an organization stimulates others to recognize more clearly their previously latent needs, desires, and potentialities and to work together toward their fulfillment. In other words, leadership *energizes*. Leadership is exercised by the person in the group who energizes the group, whether or not he or she carries the title of "leader."

As we have seen, leadership is not power. Although it is obviously the case that many leaders exercise power, it is not their exercise of power that makes them leaders. Rather, there is something in the way that leaders relate to the groups, organizations, or societies of which they are a part that distinguishes their actions from the actions of others. Where leadership occurs, something occurs in the dynamics of the group that leads to change. That something need not be a display of power. Indeed, there are reasons to believe that continued efforts by leaders to control actually are destructive of leadership. As Burns (1978) wrote, "Leadership mobilizes, naked power coerces" (p. 439).

But when the direction of the group, organization, or society is selected through a process that gives priority to the needs and desires of its members, leadership is much more likely to be constructive and enduring. Therefore, an argument for improved leadership is not an argument for improved rulership; instead, it is an argument for an expanded notion of leadership and for the extension of leadership—its skills, capacities, and responsibilities—to all levels of the group, organization, or even society.

In the traditional view of leadership, a particular person holds the position of leader and wields the power associated with that position to bring about change. The traditional leader was expected to (a) come up with good ideas about the direction that the group should take, (b) decide on a course of action or a goal to be accomplished, and (c) exert his or her influence or control in moving the group in that direction. The new leadership is exercised by a person who (a) helps the group, organization, or society to understand its needs and potential; (b) integrates and articulates the vision of the group, organization, or society; and (c) acts as a "trigger" or stimulus for group action. Leadership today is viewed quite differently from how it used to be viewed.

Leadership must develop through an open and evolving process in which the values and interests of all members of the group are equally valued. For the energizing effect of leadership to be felt most strongly, leadership must reflect the interests of many in the group. This way of thinking about leadership suggests a reciprocal relationship through which members of the group express, in word or deed, the shared interests of all in an open and visible process. As opposed to a leader who pursues private interests, this type of leadership is quite public, involving many and open to all. Consider the way in which city manager Camille Cates Barnett (1984) described shared leadership:

We must use our power to empower others; we must change behaviors while staying in tune with existing values; we must act as though we are in charge and be aware that we are not; our logic must be guided by our intuition; we must create a vision of the future that already exists in the minds of others. (p. 526)

Ways of Acting

One remaining question is how leadership skills can be developed. Although there is general agreement that leadership skills can be built or at least improved on, there are differences in how one might seek improvements. We offer the following suggestions.

1. *Examine the traits, skills, and commitments associated with leadership and try to assess your own strengths and weaknesses.* As we have seen, the lists of traits and skills vary, but there are some areas of agreement (see Figure 7.3). There also are a variety of assessment surveys (a couple of which are included at the end of this chapter) that will give you some idea of the traits and skills that you value most. You also might ask others who know you and perhaps work with you to complete an assessment form *about you.* This will give you some extra feedback and might point to some areas that you did not recognize as areas in need of work. With this information about your leadership style and your skill levels, you can then begin a program to develop those areas that seem most important.

2. *Learn about leadership by observation; study examples of leadership excellence.* Identify people who you think are excellent leaders. Talk with them about how they approach their leadership activities or simply watch them carefully as they interact with others. How do their actions reflect some of the ideas that we have talked about in this chapter? How would you describe their leadership styles? Look especially carefully for the role of values in their leadership activities. What are the deep-seated commitments that seem to underlie their work? Look also for the way in which these leaders enter into psychological or emotional relationships with followers. What can you say about the complex dynamics that might underlie the leader–follower relationship? In addition to identifying leaders whom you actually can observe, you might read the biographies or autobiographies of well-known leaders. Look especially for information about those influences that shaped their approaches to leadership. What is it about their backgrounds or experiences that might help to explain their approaches? Novels are another good source of leadership lessons. You also might watch films such as *Patton, The Caine Mutiny, Norma Rae, Twelve Angry Men,* and *The Mission* and look for leadership lessons. Take notes as you watch the films and then discuss the leadership lessons they contain.

3. *Experiment with your own behavior.* As in other areas discussed in this book, such as motivation and communication, you should use the classroom to try out alternative ways of approaching leadership situations. Some students already will have had extensive leadership experience in schools, in churches, on sports teams, and so on. Others will have had relatively little. In either case, the classroom provides a "safe"

place in which you can try out various approaches to leadership. Perhaps you would like to see what would happen if you were a little more assertive (or even more aggressive) than usual, or perhaps you would like to see what would happen if you were less demanding and more supportive. Classroom exercises can give you an opportunity to try out different behaviors and practice those that are most effective.

4. *Model important values.* As we have seen, values play an important role in leadership in any organization. But values are especially important in the public service. Public leadership activities, whether at the executive level or at the street level, affect people's lives in important ways. As we develop policies, programs, or organizations to pursue public purposes, we inevitably encounter difficult moral and value choices, both for leaders and for followers. Those in the public service have a special responsibility to maintain and extend democratic principles throughout society and to deal with citizens and other public servants with dignity and respect. Those who exercise leadership in the public service typically do so because they want to make a difference in society, and that is a noble purpose. But because their acts of leadership do change lives, they must be especially sensitive to issues of trust and confidence, justice and equity, and fairness and due process in all that they do. Consider carefully the personal commitments that you are willing to stand by as a public servant and leader.

5. *Assume leadership.* One of the best ways in which to develop as a leader is through engaging in leadership experience. You can gain leadership experience by becoming involved in clubs and other organizations, by engaging in service projects in your community, by accepting internships or other related experiences, or simply by doing your job. The experience itself will teach you important lessons about leadership, but you will get much more out of your experience if you take time to reflect critically on what occurs in your group or organization. For example, you might want to keep a journal of leadership experiences—your own as well as those of others. What seemed to make a difference in your capacity to energize others? What approaches to persuasion or communication did you use in conjunction with your efforts to lead? When were you most successful? When were you least successful? What specific lessons about leadership can you use in future situations?

Thinking in Action

The following cases and exercises will help you to develop your leadership skills.

Developing a Leadership Autobiography

Trace the history of your personal development as a leader. In a 10-page essay, consider the major influences on your understanding of what it means to be a leader and those that helped to shape the development of your particular leadership style. You might consider questions such as the following to guide your writing. What were your most influential models of leadership? What were your earliest leadership experiences like? What qualities of leadership do you find most attractive? Why do you think you chose these particular qualities? How would you rate yourself in terms of these qualities? What other leadership traits might you develop? What leadership styles or strategies do you employ most frequently? What were the influences that led you to use these approaches as opposed to others? How would you like to grow in terms of your capacity for leadership? How do you think you will? What will be necessary for this to occur? What are the issues that you believe leaders of the future will have to confront? What is your philosophy of leadership?

A Debate Topic

Earlier, we wrote,

Whereas Burns would say that Hitler's leadership was not transformational because it did not further good in the society, Bass contended that Germany still was transformed by Hitler's leadership and, indeed, that Hitler's influence still is felt today. Because Germany was transformed, according to Bass, Hitler was a transformational leader.

In your view, would it be proper to call Hitler a transformational leader? Would it even be proper to call Hitler a leader? Develop a classroom debate on this question, with half of the class taking one position and the other half taking the other.

Transactional Versus Transformational Leadership

Instructions. For each of the following 10 pairs of statements, divide 5 points between the two according to your beliefs and perceptions of yourself or according to which of the two statements characterizes you better. The 5 points may be divided between the *a* and *b* statements in any one of the following ways: 5 for *a*, 0 for *b*; 4 for *a*, 1 for *b*; 3 for *a*, 2 for *b*; 1 for *a*, 4 for *b*; and 0 for *a*, 5 for *b*. They cannot be divided equally (2.5 for each) between the two. Weigh your choices between the two according to the one that better characterizes you or your beliefs.

1. a. As a leader, I have a primary mission of maintaining stability.
    b. As a leader, I have a primary mission of change.

2. a. As a leader, I must cause events.
    b. As a leader, I must facilitate events.

3. a. I am concerned that my followers are rewarded equitably for their work.
    b. I am concerned about what my followers want in life.

4. a. My preference is to think long range—what might be.
    b. My preference is to think short range—what is realistic.

5. a. As a leader, I spend considerable energy in managing separate but related goals.
    b. As a leader, I spend considerable energy in arousing hopes, expectations, and aspirations among my followers.

6. a. Although not in a formal classroom sense, I believe that a significant part of my leadership is that of teacher.
    b. I believe that a significant part of my leadership is that of facilitator.

7. a. As a leader, I must engage with followers at an equal level of morality.
    b. As a leader, I must represent a higher morality.

8. a. I enjoy stimulating followers to want to do more.
    b. I enjoy rewarding followers for a job well done.

9. a. Leadership should be practical.
    b. Leadership should be inspirational.

10. a. What power I have to influence others comes primarily from my ability to get people to identify with me and my ideas.
    b. What power I have to influence others comes primarily from my status and position.

Scoring. Circle your points for Items 1b, 2a, 3b, 4a, 5b, 6a, 7b, 8a, 9b, and 10a and add up the total points you allocated to these items; enter the score here: Tf = _____. Next, add up the total points given to the uncircled Items 1a, 2b, 3a, 4b, 5a, 6b, 7a, 8b, 9a, and 10b; enter the score here: Ta =_____.

Interpretation. This instrument gives an impression of your tendencies toward "transformational" leadership (your Tf score) and "transactional" leadership (your Ta score). Refer to the discussion of transactional and transformational leadership in the chapter to interpret your scores.

Assessing Your Leadership Style

One assessment device was produced by David Campbell (n.d.), the H. Smith Richardson Senior Fellow at the Center for Creative Leadership (CCL). CCL, a nonprofit educational institution founded in 1970, develops models of effective managerial practice and applies them as guides for assessment and development. Following are the categories that Campbell uses for assessing leadership capacities, categories that you can use in your own informal examination of your leadership capacities. Rate yourself, and have others rate you, on a scale of 1 to 5 for each category. Try to think of specific examples of how you have displayed each characteristic.

- Leadership
    Ambitious: Determined to make progress, likes to compete
    Daring: Willing to try new experiences, is risk oriented
    Dynamic: Takes charge, inspires others, is seen as a leader
    Enterprising: Works well with the complexities of change
    Experienced: Has a good background
    Farsighted: Looks ahead, plans, is a visionary
    Original: Sees the world differently, has many new ideas
    Persuasive: Articulate and persuasive in influencing others

- Energy/Affability
    Affectionate: Acts close, warm, and nurturing
    Considerate: Thoughtful, is willing to work with others
    Empowering: Motivates others and helps them to achieve
    Entertaining: Clever and amusing, enjoys people
    Friendly: Pleasant to be around, smiles easily

- Dependability
    Credible: Open and honest, inspires trust
    Organized: Plans ahead and follows through
    Productive: Uses time and resources well
    Thrifty: Uses and manages money wisely

- Resilience
    Calm: Has an unhurried and unruffled manner
    Flexible: Easily adjusts to changes
    Optimistic: Positive, handles personal challenges well
    Trusting: Trusts and believes in others

SOURCE: Reprinted by permission of NCS London House.

Leadership When No One Is in Charge

Read and discuss the following case:

A small work team consisting of Eddie, Cyndi, Gina, Jennifer, and Ralph was asked to meet after work to come up with a theme for the company picnic, to be held the third of July at a park on the outskirts of town. No one had a great deal of enthusiasm for this project—or the idea of staying after work.

All were silent for the first few minutes, each probably hoping someone else would come up with an idea that would make this chore go away. When it was apparent that no one was going to take the lead, Gina said, "None of us wants to be here. Let's just make it a Fourth of July party and be done with it."

A couple of heads nodded, but Ralph responded, "I'd love to get out of here, too, but couldn't we come up with something a little more inventive than that? You know, the boss will be paying attention to this."

"Well, Mr. Brown-nose," Cyndi laughed, "still after that raise you didn't get last quarter?" Several members of the group smiled, although they could sense an underlying tension between Ralph and Cyndi.

Eddie came to the rescue: "We'd all like that raise, wouldn't we? What about giving this just a few more minutes and see if we can come up with something?"

Jennifer stood up, opened her cell phone, and walked out of the room. Gina mumbled, "Fourth of July."

"Let me try once again," Ralph said. "What about a Fourth of July party?"

"That was Gina's idea," Cyndi reminded the group, unnecessarily.

"And it was a good idea, too," said Eddie. "But what about building on that idea by thinking about a different kind of celebration—maybe something like a circus?"

"That's not bad," said Gina. "We could do costumes and have a parade . . . "

"I like clowns," said Ralph.

"You *are* a clown," said Cyndi.

"No, really," Ralph said. "We could have a parade with clowns, and animals, and all that stuff."

"Sure," said Eddie, "circus in July!"

Suddenly energized, the group started making plans in earnest and even assigned responsibilities for carrying the idea forward.

Analysis. Think through the pattern of leadership exhibited in this case. There was no formal leader, but several people exercised leadership—some effectively, some not so effectively. Who was the leader of the group? What made him or her the leader? What behaviors were most helpful to the group? Which were least helpful? Someone has said, "Leadership energizes." What happened to energize this group? How much involved rational intelligence? How much involved emotional intelligence? What does your experience tell you about leadership in groups when no one is in charge?

CHAPTER **8**

Power and
Organizational Politics

Power is America's last dirty word. It is easier to talk about money—and
much easier to talk about sex—than it is to talk about power.

—Rosabeth Moss Kanter (1979, p. 65)

Most students of public administration will readily recognize the importance of politics in the practice of public management. After all, it is through the political process that public organizations are created and funded. Political institutions enact the laws that we are charged with implementing, establish missions, and express the values and norms that guide our behavior as public administrators. But we also need to recognize that public organizations themselves are political entities as well. As Pfeffer (1992) put it, to understand organizations "one needs to understand organizational politics, just as to understand governments one needs to understand governmental politics" (p. 29).

But for most of us, our feelings about and reactions to power politics in organizations are ambivalent. Certainly, we do not want to be powerless. Yet, we are equally uncomfortable with the idea of becoming unwitting victims of other people's power plays. We recognize the need to influence others to work positively toward organizational objectives, to successfully defend our programs, and to obtain opportunities and recognition for our employees. We also recognize that power can be used to hurt others, to pursue goals not sanctioned by the organization, and to fulfill personal needs for control and even retribution.

Although many people are uncomfortable talking about power, and although there certainly are disagreements about the moral and practical implications of the use of power, power politics are, at least to some extent, inescapable in organizations. All types of organizations, from churches to professional associations, small companies to large corporations, elementary schools to private universities, and families to large social groups, as well as governmental organizations at all levels, involve people using power and politics in attempts to influence others. People form coalitions and alliances, bargain and strategize, and engage in other forms of organizational politics to influence decision making and organizational outcomes. The problem, of course, is that sometimes politics and power are used for things that organizations (or we as individuals) support or need, whereas other times they are used for things that we judge to be less desirable. Nonetheless, we must recognize that organizational politics, in all of its forms, can and will occur in organizations.

Accordingly, an awareness and understanding of power politics helps us to understand some important facets of organizational behavior and can contribute to our success in groups and organizations. People who acquire and use power appropriately and well are persuasive, have a positive influence on others, and are better able to obtain necessary support and resources for programs, people, and priorities. So, although there might be a seamy side to power, it can be a positive and necessary force as well. As Coates (1994) stated, "Education in the politics of organizations in the positive sense of the word, reciprocal obligations, is crucial to the personal development of any successful manager and absolutely central to the long-term success of any senior executive" (p. 261).

Where Do We Begin?

How do you currently think about and use power? Indicate for each of the following whether you think the statement is true or false.

1. It is important to get along with everyone in organizations, even people you do not like.

2. Organizational politics should have no role in the administration of public programs.

3. You can gain power by making others feel important.

4. The simplest and best long-term strategy for getting others to do what you want is to let them know that you are the boss.

5. It often is a good idea to make others dependent on you for your expertise and knowledge.

6. To maintain power, you should not compromise, even when an issue is of minor importance to you.

7. It is advisable to do favors for people whenever possible.

8. Empowerment requires delegation; if your boss does not give it to you, then it is not possible to make it happen.

9. Power and politics can be destructive forces in organizations.

10. If you have good relationships with the people in your unit, then it is not necessary to have good relationships with people in other parts and levels of the organization.

11. As a manager, it is necessary to have organizational power just to do a good job with the tasks assigned to you.

12. It is advisable to always tell people everything you know about a situation.

13. You always should try to make a good first impression.

14. Reaching organizational goals requires that organizational politics and power be avoided whenever possible.

15. On very controversial issues, it often is best to delay or avoid your involvement as long as possible.

16. If you have very little power in an organization, then there is basically nothing you can or should do about it.

17. Gaining power often involves making friends rather than making enemies in the organization.

18. If you have power, then people will dislike and fear you.

19. It is not a good idea to become dependent on one person in an organization.

20. The best way of handling power and organizational politics is to stay away from it.

Scoring. Give yourself 1 point for every odd-numbered statement you marked *true* and every even-numbered statement you marked *false.* You can interpret your scores based on the following scale:

17–20: You have an excellent grasp on power and politics in organizations. You appreciate that power and politics can be both constructive and destructive. You have a strong grasp of some of the tactics and strategies of politics, and you understand how they can be used in a positive manner.

13–16: You have a good sense of power and politics. You have an appreciation for some of the aspects of power and politics in organizations but perhaps do not yet fully understand some of its manifestations.

9–12: Your success in organizations might be enhanced by gaining a greater appreciation for power and organizational politics in its many forms. You might want to think about how your power can be enhanced and used constructively in organizations.

8 or less: You might be uncomfortable with notions of power and politics. Enhancing your understanding of how power and politics work in organizations might be important in your career development, and it might give you some important insights into organizational behavior.

Regardless of your score, as you read this chapter, think about your own experiences with power and organizational politics. How can you gain and use power in your organization in a manner that benefits you, the people you work with, your organization, and the people you serve? How can you respond to organizational politics constructively? How can you become an organizational politician in the best sense of the word?

Ways of Thinking

Power and organizational politics are closely related concepts, and for the purposes of this chapter they are considered together. Power has been defined as "the latent ability to influence others' actions, thoughts, or emotions" (Ott, 1989a, p. 420). Politics, on the other hand, generally refers to the use of power and authority to influence organizational outcomes. In simple terms, power is the potential for influence, whereas politics is the exercise or use of that power.

These appear to be relatively straightforward definitions of organizational phenomena that all of us have encountered at one time or another. But the nature, sources, desirability, and conditions for the exercise of power have been the subject of debate for many hundreds of years. This debate forms the foundations not only for how we think about power and organizational politics but also for how we feel about it (at least in some sense).

So, our examination of power and organizational politics leads us to first look at how societal attitudes about the nature of power have changed over time. Although at one time workers might have willingly accepted the use of power and force by their supervisors, our society has undergone a significant change in how we view power. Ideas about who has a right to power and how that power should be used have shifted as we have changed our ideas about organizations, the nature of people, and authority. In today's organizations, rarely is it the best strategy to simply order or openly coerce someone to do something. Power and organizational politics in the contemporary environment often are more subtle and are exercised in relationships that are more egalitarian and involve the use of shared power. The following subsections trace these changes, beginning with three early voices.

Early Voices

Much of our understanding about the nature of power and politics in organizations is derived, to a greater or lesser extent, from the early literature on governmental politics and political rulers. Although these writings did not speak directly to the power and politics in organizational behavior, they nonetheless formed many of the foundations of current perspectives. For that reason, it is useful to begin our examination of power with Machiavelli's *The Prince,* written during the early 16th century (Machiavelli, 1947). There are three basic themes in this often-cited and well-known book. First, Machiavelli considered people to be "ungrateful, fickle, and deceitful" (p. 48). Second, he argued that the state and patriotism come before all else. Third, he asserted that the purpose of political leadership must be to gain and maintain power.

In Machiavelli's view, the strength of a leader's power is measured by the degree to which he or she is independent of others and maintains domination over the people. Machiavelli also stated that politics and power are human enterprises and not in the hands of God or fate, as was commonly believed at the time. Machiavelli argued that because the state is paramount, whatever means are necessary to per- petuate the power of the state must be undertaken by the leader. The leader should be ruthless if necessary. "A prince should care nothing for the accusation of cruelty so long as he keeps his subjects united and loyal" (1947, p. 47). Accordingly, Machiavelli's work is perhaps most commonly known for the philosophy of "the end justifies the means."

Machiavelli's legacy with regard to his notions of power in politics, but also in organizations, is pronounced. We still talk of some people who use power in orga- nizations as being "Machiavellian," meaning that they are power hungry and self- serving or, as *Webster's Ninth New Collegiate Dictionary* defined it, "characterized by cunning, duplicity, or bad faith" (Merriam-Webster, 1987). But Machiavelli's influ- ence can be seen in other ways as well. He introduced the notion of power as a function of dependency and independence and of politics as a natural human enterprise. He articulated a view of power as a desirable and necessary end, an idea later denounced by Bertrand Russell and others but nonetheless generally recog- nized as one manifestation of power through history and in contemporary settings.

It also is interesting to see how Machiavelli's view of power hinges on the assump- tion that people are ungrateful, fickle, and deceitful—assumptions that most students of organizational behavior would reject. Yet, Machiavelli might have some useful lessons for us, particularly the idea that leaders often need power to do their jobs. He pointed out that during his day (as well as now), powerless leaders could do little to ensure the protection and well-being of the people for whom they were responsible.

But what type of power is needed, and how should it be used? This was a ques- tion explored by many key writers and thinkers. For example, most students of public administration know Max Weber from his writings on bureaucracy, but he struggled with fundamental questions about power as well. Weber wrote broadly about society, government, and organizations but was particularly concerned about the nature of power and the question of why people obey others or are willing to be controlled by them. He suggested that there are three types of power or domina- tion: charismatic (where power and control are derived from the personal magnet- ism of the power wielder), traditional (where power is granted through family lineage from one generation to the next), and legal–rational (where laws and con- stitutional processes create legitimate authority). Weber argued that the last of these, the *legal–rational* form of authority, was superior to other forms of power. It was superior, he said, because in this form authority and power were institutional- ized and depersonalized in bureaucratic organizations where their exercise was controlled by rules, hierarchy, and reporting relationships (as cited in Gerth & Mills, 1946).

Although Weber argued that organizations founded on legal–rational grounds were technically superior, his writings also suggested a pessimism about the effect of their power over the behavior of humans. He predicted that people would become trapped by the legalistic and rule-bound structure. Furthermore, he predicted that because the power of bureaucratic organizations derived from their expertise and efficiency, they would conflict with, and possibly prevail against, the power of politicians. Yet, his writing suggested that bureaucratic forms of power, or power based on formal grants of authority, remained superior to alternative forms and sources of power.

Certainly, we still can see the influence of Weber's perspectives today. Many of us might believe that power in organizations ought to reside with the position held, rather than with the person, and that the power that is exercised should be within that person's official authority to act. In other words, we may readily accept the power and influence of the director of an agency, but we question or feel uncomfortable with power derived from personal magnetism, deal making, or family position. So, we are ambivalent. When people in particular positions use power, it may be seen as good and necessary; when others exercise power, it may be viewed as unfair and inappropriate.

During the 1930s, Russell clearly expressed this American ambivalence toward power. Russell introduced the idea that power as a means to an end can be virtuous but that power as an end (as the goal itself) is inherently undesirable. His writing reflected a concern for the control of power in organizations, particularly government, as a protection against its arbitrary use for personal gain. Russell argued that one of the characteristics that separates humans from animals is the insatiability of some human needs. Chief among those needs is the desire for power and glory. Whereas for some the need for power is suppressed because of inherent timidity or personality, for others the quest for power is all-important.

Russell (1938) defined power as "the production of intended effects" (p. 35) and suggested that it takes several forms. Traditional power is that which is characterized by habit, mostly passive assent to institutional authority such as with priests and kings. Power that is not based on assent or agreement is called "naked power" or coercion. Revolutionary power is based on active dissent so as to unseat traditional power. Russell also considered a number of secondary or derivative forms of power. His distinctions among different types and forms of power are something that contemporary authors have continued to explore.

In examining the organizational framework through which power is exercised, Russell asserted that an organization has power over the individual but that it still is in the individual's interest to be a part of an organization. In other words, for an individual to gain the advantages of joining an organization, he or she submits to the power of that organization. Russell was particularly concerned about the ethics of power. He pointed out that although power can be used for the collective good, it also can be used for evil. He claimed that the difference is the purpose for which power is used. When gaining and using power becomes the end or the goal in itself, it is wrong. When power is used as a means to accomplish something desirable, it can be a positive force.

Again, the influence of Russell's work can be seen today. He provided a framework for understanding both the positive and negative sides of power and our continuing ambivalence toward it. He suggested that the use of power as a means of accomplishing a desirable end can be a good thing—a distinction that remains in our minds as a guide to appropriate and ethical behavior.

Changing Perspectives on Workers and Organizations

Our perspectives on power and organizational politics continued to evolve. Whereas early voices such as those of Machiavelli, Weber, and Russell were focused principally on power as exercised by a single executive or official over members of an organization, by the 1950s power had become a subject of interest in social psychology, where it was recognized as a phenomenon found throughout organizations. Building on earlier works, writers during this era refined and reevaluated how power worked. For example, Bierstedt (1950) viewed power as a sociological phenomenon, not just a political or economic one. Bierstedt argued that, when viewed from a sociological standpoint, the concepts of force and authority were useful in defining power as follows: "1) power is a latent force; 2) force is manifest power; and 3) authority is institutionalized power" (p. 733). Put simply, Bierstedt was suggesting that power is the *potential* to influence or control, that power can be exercised through the use of force, and that power can be formalized by granting someone the authority for its exercise.

The idea that power always is latent is particularly important. In this view, when power is used, it becomes something else, such as authority, force, or coercion. So, power is not necessarily open coercion, influence, or control; more accurately, it is the perception of others that the power wielder could exercise coercion, influence, or control if he or she chose to do so. In a very real sense, how much power a person has depends in large measure on how much power people think the person has.

Writing during the same era, Dahl (1957) suggested that most people have an intuitive sense of power as based in a relationship between people such that "A has power over B to the extent that he can get B to do something that B would not otherwise do" (pp. 202–203). Dahl said that power can be compared between actors but that the comparison must be based on the "responses they are capable of evoking . . . rather than on the attributes of the actors" (p. 206). Again, the idea is that power is a latent potential or capacity, not an action or attribute.

Questioning Power and Authority

The 1960s were not only a period of political unrest in the United States but also an era that called into question the nature of power and authority and who should have the "right" to tell people what they could or could not do. In organizations, attitudes about the types of power that individuals were willing to grant their "superiors" underwent a marked shift. The human relations movement during the 1960s and 1970s challenged the idea that the job of management was to manipulate workers for the benefit of organizations and promoted the idea that organizations should meet both individual and collective needs. During the early stages of the organization development movement (see Chapter 12), the nature and desirability of traditional hierarchical authority relationships came under particularly heavy fire. In short, people began to openly question authority and the power that accompanied it.

When writers during the 1960s asked the same question that Weber had asked decades earlier—"Why do people do what they are told?"—they came up with very different answers. For example, Haire (1962/1989) argued that traditional conceptions of authority had become outmoded and counterproductive. He suggested that executive authority traditionally had been based on ownership; the owners of factories had the right to use power to control the people who worked in them. As a result, authority became "grounded in the process of managing itself" (p. 456). Later, ownership became separate from organizational management. Still, the assumption that power and authority are an inherent right of management remained.

But Haire argued that our conceptions about management and the nature of people must change. He pointed out that much of classic organizational theory has a pessimistic view of people as lazy, shortsighted, selfish, and stupid. He suggested that people might exhibit these behaviors because of outmoded organizational forms and authority relationships. Haire concluded by suggesting that we embrace a more optimistic view of people, that authority in organizations be made more participative, and that power be equalized consistent with this enlightened view.

It is important to recognize, however, that people of different cultures may view power and authority differently. In Chapter 5, we examined differences in national culture. Among those differences was what Hofstede and Hofstede (2005) call "power distance." Power distance is "the extent to which the less powerful members of institutions and organizations within a country expect and accept that power is distributed unequally" (p. 46). In countries that score low on power distance (the United States, Canada, the Netherlands, Great Britain, Australia, Luxembourg, Germany, Norway, Sweden, Costa Rica), subordinates are more likely to disagree with their bosses and desire a "consultative style" of management. Employees in the countries which score high on power distance (Malaysia, Venezuela, Guatemala, Arab countries, Russia, Romania, Panama, Serbia, Slovenia) are willing to accept more autocratic bosses, and they rarely disagree with their managers.

With this cultural context in mind, it is also important to recognize the evolution in theory about the nature of organizations themselves. The work of Cyert and March (1963), for example, discredited the then prevailing view of organizations as economically rational in their decision-making process and promoted the idea that organizations were political entities. Likewise, Thompson (1967) saw organizations, and the people in them, as acting politically. One of his basic premises was that organizations seek to reduce uncertainty and dependency. Thompson suggested that because power is the opposite of dependency, organizations will seek to minimize dependency arising from the environment by maintaining alternatives, seeking prestige, engaging in cooperative strategies, contracting, and co-opting those who impose environmental threats. He then applied these propositions to the behavior of people in organizations and argued that individuals behave in much the same way as organizations by seeking to minimize dependence, forming coalitions, and attempting to acquire power. Like others, Thompson suggested that the traditional idea that one person could hold absolute authority had ceased to make a lot of sense. "An individual can be powerful . . . and can exercise significant leadership . . . only with the consent and approval of the dominant coalition" (p. 142). In this view, the power of individuals is not derived, nor should it be derived, solely from their positions.

In a particularly compelling look at the political nature of organizational decision making, Allison (1971) used the Cuban missile crisis to demonstrate how an overreliance on rational theories could lead to distortion and incomplete understanding of the way in which organizations actually operate. He did so by explaining the crisis using three alternative models or lenses: the rational actor model, the organizational process model, and the governmental politics model. It is the third model that is of particular interest in exploring the subject of power in organizations.

The governmental politics model conceptualizes governmental behavior as a result of numerous political actors engaging in a bargaining game. It assumes no single strategic goal; rather, it assumes differing perceptions on the part of the players, who engage in a struggle for preferred outcomes. Under this model, "it is necessary to identify the game and players [and] to display the coalitions, bargains, and compromises" (Allison, 1971, p. 146). Allison described and demonstrated the use of this model in explaining organizational behavior as the outcome of power struggles between key actors over preferred outcomes.

So, by the 1970s, writers were suggesting that we should hold a more egalitarian and optimistic view of people when we consider questions of power and organizational politics and that we should recognize organizations as political entities. Yet then and now, most of us remain ambivalent about power and organizational politics. In examining a survey of managers by Gandz and Murray (1980), this ambivalence is clear. Note in Figure 8.1 that although nearly 90% of respondents thought that politics are common and that successful executives must be good politicians, and although only 16% agreed that powerful executives do not act politically, more than half also thought that politics in organizations are detrimental to efficiency and that organizations free of politics are happier. Nearly half thought that management ought to get rid of politics, whereas more than 40% thought that politics help organizations to function effectively. Apparently, we admit that politics are a part of organizational life, but we still do not always like it very much.

So, although we might prefer to think that organizations should not be political and that we should not have to deal with political issues, such issues are, in large measure, unavoidable. Organizations are, by their nature, political entities, and to be successful in them we must become politically aware. To do so, we need to understand the sources of power, recognize when and how power is exercised, gain an appreciation for the tools and strategies of politics, and understand the positive and negative effects of power and politics on people and organizations.

Sources of Power

How do people in organizations acquire power? One of the best known and most cited attempts to understand the sources of power is French and Raven's (1959/1989) "The Bases of Social Power." These authors defined power from

Statement	Percentage Expressing Strong or Moderate Agreement
The existence of workplace politics is common to most organizations.	93.2
Successful executives must be good politicians.	89.0
The higher you go in organizations, the more political the climate becomes.	76.2
Powerful executives do not act politically.	15.7
You have to be political to get ahead in organizations.	69.8
Top management should try to get rid of politics within the organization.	48.6
Politics help organizations to function effectively.	42.1
Organizations free of politics are happier than those in which there is a lot of politics.	59.1
Politics in organizations are detrimental to efficiency.	55.1

Figure 8.1   Managers' Feelings About Workplace Politics

SOURCE: "The Experience of Workplace Politics," by J. Gandz and V. Murray, June 1980, *Academy of Management Journal*, p. 244. Copyright © 1980 by Academy of Management. Reproduced with permission of Academy of Management via Copyright Clearance Center.

a psychological standpoint, emphasizing power as a means of influencing or causing psychological change in others. As such, they were primarily concerned with explaining power in terms of its effect on people. Influence on a person is measured as the amount of change that occurs as the result of a social agent, which could be "a person, a role, a group, or a part of a group" (p. 441). The amount of power correlates with the persistence of change. But like Bierstedt and Dahl, French and Raven argued that power has the property of potentiality. That is, it does not have to be used in full capacity under all circumstances. Within this general framework, they proposed a five-category classification of the sources or bases of power: legitimate power, reward power, coercive power, referent power, and expert power.

Legitimate Power

Legitimate power arises from people's values and beliefs that someone has the right to exert influence over them and that they have an obligation to comply. These values and beliefs may be culturally instilled, reinforced by social or organizational structure (e.g., hierarchy), or designated by a legitimating agent or process (e.g., elections). In public organizations, this type of power often is derived from people's positions or job titles. Although most organizations use position titles to designate levels of authority, some organizations rely on position power more than do others.

For example, military and police organizations use symbols (e.g., uniforms) to convey differences in position. But even in these organizations, power is derived from other sources as well. Not all people with the title of "director" have the same amount of power—even within the same organization. This is so because, in most organizations, a reliance solely on position power is inadequate and inadvisable. Positively influencing others usually requires drawing on other sources of power as well such as those described in the subsections that follow.

Nonetheless, legitimate power is important. We are influenced by the positions or titles that people hold in organizations, particularly with regard to the legitimacy that others will be likely to accord those people in the use of power. As a practical matter, then, it makes sense to pay attention not only to other people's titles but to our own as well. Although in government there can be limited flexibility in changing position titles, it is worthwhile to consider the title of your position as one of the factors that can influence how others will respond to you. For example, if you take on project responsibilities, then it might be possible to negotiate a "working" title that will communicate to others the authority and responsibility you hold in relation to the project.

Reward Power

Reward power is just what the label implies—power arising from our ability to reward other people for behaving as we want them to. Reward power involves influencing others by providing positive outcomes and preventing negative ones. Reward power is similar to positive reinforcement. When managers recommend promotions, give positive performance evaluations, give desirable assignments, provide recognition, offer support, and so on, they gain power. Effective managers use reward power to highlight good work and to reinforce behavior that reflects and advances organizational values. We might not think of rewarding others as giving us power. But if we provide rewards that people want, then it makes sense that we can influence their behavior. If used appropriately, this can help employees to learn and grow and can help organizations to attain their objectives.

It is not necessary to be a manager to use reward power. By sincerely praising others, bringing the good work of coworkers to your supervisor's attention, or providing positive feedback to others, you not only are being a "good person" but also are creating a situation in which you are likely to be able to influence those people in the future. The use of reward power typically engenders cooperation and minimizes resistance. Furthermore, its use can support others, enhance the organizational environment, and reflect positively on you.

Coercive Power

Coercive power is the opposite of reward power. Coercive power is based on our ability to apply sanctions or punishments for the failure to behave as we desire. Using coercive power involves exerting influence through the use of punishments or the threat of punishments. Punishments, of course, can take many forms. They can be as subtle as ignoring others or as open as blocking pay raises. Supervisors can use coercive power by controlling assignments, initiating transfers, giving poor performance evaluations, oversupervising, or providing criticism. Punishments can go in the other direction as well. Employees can punish supervisors by refusing to work hard, ignoring them, or making them look bad by withholding information or embarrassing them.

It is easy to see how using coercive power can have its pitfalls. Particularly if punishments are dispensed without also offering rewards, negative consequences can result. For example, coercive power typically produces more resistance than does reward power. Nonetheless, coercive power has its place in organizations. If a public employee is not performing, is behaving inappropriately with coworkers or citizens, or has engaged in wrongdoing, then negative consequences are appropriate. If other employees see negative behavior as having no consequences, then this can, in turn, affect their behavior in an undesirable manner. But again, the use of coercive behavior by itself as the sole means of influencing others is not recommended.

Referent Power

Referent power is based on the psychological identification between people. Its strength depends on the degree to which others desire to have a relationship or identify with us. Put simply, we are influenced by people we like or admire. When we admire other people, we are apt to see what they do in a favorable light, de-emphasize their mistakes, and seek their approval. We want to do what they want us to do because we want to please them and have them continue to like us. Simply having the positive regard and respect of others, then, is a potential source of power. It is interesting to note that French and Raven (1959/1989), in distinguishing between reward power and coercive power, pointed out that the use of reward power tends to increase referent power, whereas the use of coercive power tends to diminish referent power. Although this might appear to be just good sense, it is important to remember that rewarding people will increase their positive regard for us, thereby giving us more capacity to positively influence them in the future. Conversely, if we coerce others to comply, then our referent power will diminish, leaving us with fewer tools for positive influence.

In practical terms, we gain influence through referent power by being liked, admired, and respected. The best way of doing that is by being genuinely likable, admirable, and respectable. In other words, being nice to gain power generally is pretty transparent. These are not just attitudes to try on when it is convenient to do so. We have to actually earn people's respect and admiration the hard way—by consistently treating them well. Behaving in a manner that is professional, kind, respectful, caring, and interested is desirable in its own right. It also gives us the power to influence others to our own benefit, to their benefit, and to the organization's benefit.

Expert Power

French and Raven (1959/1989) defined expert power as power based on our knowledge and expertise, in the opinion of others, thereby giving us credibility.

Expert power is drawn from having a special expertise that is needed or valued in an organization. This may take the form of technical expertise (e.g., computer skills), may be grounded in a person's insights with regard to the legislative process, or may even be based on someone's connection with and knowledge of an influential person. If you know or understand something important that other people in the organization do not, then this gives you expert power.

This suggests, from a practical standpoint, that you should "do your homework," so to speak. Whether you are a line-level staff member or an executive, being an "expert" in your area of work gives you an edge. If you work in the budget office, then learn all you can about the budget. If you work in personnel, then study personnel systems and become knowledgeable about innovative practices. If you are involved with issuing building permits, then talk to contractors, builders, home owners, and developers to learn what their needs and concerns are. Becoming knowledgeable in a manner that helps your organization to function better and to serve the public more effectively makes you more valuable, more persuasive, and more powerful.

Kotter (1977) expressed similar ideas about how managers, in particular, can gain power positively and successfully. He suggested that effective managers create and maintain power in four different ways. The first way is by doing favors for people, thereby creating a sense of obligation or a perception that these people owe return courtesies. The second way is by building reputations as experts in given areas, resulting in the deferral of others on matters relating to those areas. The third way is by using their images and reputations to foster psychological identification, thereby encouraging others to emulate and defer to managers. The fourth way is by creating and reinforcing the perceived dependency of others on managers for rewards, assistance, and protection. Kotter saw formal authority as a tool that managers use to strengthen and develop each of these four types of power.

Recognizing Power and Organizational Politics

Recognizing the exercise of power and politics in an organization is important to understanding its influence on organizational behavior and in protecting ourselves from some of its negative consequences. But this can be difficult. Just as power comes from a variety of sources, its exercise can take a number of forms. Pfeffer's (1981) analysis of the conditions for the use of power and its sources suggested that the use of power increases when there are high levels of decentralization and interdependence among subunits, a scarcity of resources, disagreement on goals, and uncertainty about technologies. Similarly, Salancik and Pfeffer (1977/1989) suggested that power is most likely to be used to influence organizational decisions under conditions of scarcity, criticality, and uncertainty. So, when the stakes are high, resources are limited, or goals and processes are unclear, power politics can be quite likely.

Sometimes power still can be difficult to recognize because it is not always overt or directly observable. How can we recognize and, consequently, better respond to the use of power? How can we evaluate whether it is legitimate? These questions are important not only to the power wielder but also to the observer or "recipient" of power politics. Because the use of power is not always easy to recognize, our evaluation and reaction to it might be inaccurate and inappropriate. So, how do we become better observers and interpreters of organizational politics?

It is helpful to think about the different forms that power can take. On the one hand, overt power is easily observed. In this "first face" of power (Lukes, 1974), power is a direct exchange between actors in which one of the actors exerts more control over the outcome than does the other actor. This type of power is easy to recognize in that it involves a relationship in which one person has potential control over another person because of dependency, knowledge, skill, or some other source of power. Individuals with more power, whatever its sources, can be expected to be relatively more successful in achieving their goals than those with less power. The use of power in this case is overt. For example, imagine that you want a promotion and that your boss controls the promotion. She assigns you a project that you disagree with and do not want to do, but she makes the promotion contingent on you doing the project. You might be angry and resentful, but because you want the promotion, you do it.

But the use of power often is more subtle and complicated than that. For example, it is not always in the interest of those with power to engage in an open struggle. When individuals engage in a power struggle, one side typically loses. From the perspective of those with established positions, any visible losses erode their latent power or their ability to prevail in future struggles. So, logically, it makes sense for those with relatively established power to work to systematically avoid or exclude challenges. These exclusionary actions have been termed power's "second face" (Lukes, 1974).

For example, imagine that you are one of three assistant directors. One of the other assistant directors is making a proposal for something you think is inadvisable, unnecessarily costly, and potentially damaging to the organization. You have tried to talk with her about it, to no avail. Rather than openly challenging and fighting against a fellow supervisor's proposal (the first face of power), you might choose to speak privately with the director and other key decision makers, providing information and background that will make them less likely to support the proposal. Alternatively, consider a hypothetical situation in which an employee openly challenges you and refuses to cooperate on a group project. Rather than responding in a coercive manner, the second face of power might suggest that you simply isolate that person from the group or reassign him or her. Better yet, you might choose project participants more carefully in the first place.

There also is a "third face" of power in which the power wielder convinces others that what they really want is what the power wielder wants. As Lukes (1974) put it,

> A may exercise power over B by getting him to do what he does not want to do, but he also exercises power over him by influencing, shaping, or determining his very wants. . . . This may happen in the absence of observable conflict, which may have been successfully averted. (p. 23)

The successful use of power's third face, then, might insulate the powerful from challenge simply because the powerful are able to convince potential challengers that there is no reason to challenge them in the first place.

In its positive form, the third face of power might be evidenced in a situation where the manager designs a necessary, but potentially difficult or controversial, project so that the project goals and the goals of individuals working on that project are compatible. The manager does so primarily by convincing the workers through incentives, persuasive communication, or other strategies that it is in their interest for the project to be successful. A less positive use of the third face of power would be misinforming an employee who comes to you for career advice. To keep this individual in your unit, you might intentionally mislead him or her about what might in fact be a great opportunity for the individual to advance. Thus, you do not force the person to stay; you create a situation where he or she no longer wants to leave.

In short, power in organizations can take many forms, some overt and others much more subtle. The advantages of the more subtle forms are that they are less likely to be met with open resistance. People tend to balk at open power plays. So, using these cons and third faces of power can help you to accomplish organizational objectives without coercing people to cooperate. Unfortunately, when power becomes covert and less visible, it also is somewhat easier to hide its potentially destructive aspects. Being sensitive to the multiple faces of power can help you to better understand and respond to organizational situations.

Balancing Power

In addition to having many forms, power in today's organizations is not unidirectional. Most people in contemporary settings do not unquestioningly accept the power of their "superiors." Although this does not always take the form of open rebellion, people often will attempt to balance power relationships. That is, individuals' power may be confined to certain spheres and balanced by the influence of others in different spheres (Wrong, 1968). Politics, then, involves efforts both to gain power and to limit or balance the power of others.

There are four styles or ways in which people with less power can act to equalize or balance power in a relationship, all based on the idea that dependence reduces power and independence increases it. To increase power, people can (1) decrease their needs or demands (need less or be less dependent); (2) increase their alternative sources of getting what they want, thereby gaining independence; (3) increase other people's needs or demands for us, thereby making them more dependent; or (4) decrease other people's alternative sources, again making them more dependent (Emerson, 1962).

These power-balancing operations, then, either decrease dependence (Styles 1 and 2) or increase the dependence of other people (Styles 3 and 4). Because Styles 1 and 2 decrease our dependence on the organization, they can be less desirable for the organization. Because Styles 3 and 4 increase the dependence of other people while not decreasing our dependence on the organization, they can result in increasing our involvement in the organization and, at the same time, making us more valuable to it.

For example, consider this hypothetical situation. You very much want praise and positive feedback from your supervisor, but it is not forthcoming. As a result, she has potential power over you by denying something that you want. If you do nothing, then you might end up being resentful, unhappy, and unproductive. There are several ways to change or balance the effect of this potential power. First, you could decide to rely on your own self-assessment of your performance and not to make your professional self-image so dependent on feedback from your boss. This decreases your dependence by changing what you want from her. Second, you could look for other sources of positive feedback, thereby increasing your alternatives and decreasing your dependency. Third, you could work to make your work more central to the unit's success, thereby increasing your boss's dependence on you. When you ask for more positive feedback, her dependency on your performance would make her more likely to provide it. Fourth, you could gain special expertise that no one else in the unit has, again making yourself less dependent on the supervisor and making her more dependent on you. The first and second options might result in a sort of psychological distancing from your supervisor and the organization, whereas the third and fourth options might result in a stronger commitment on your part.

You might ask yourself, isn't what has been described really just a matter of manipulating your supervisor to get something you want? The answer is yes, it is, at least in some sense. But it is important to remember three things. First, relationships are becoming more egalitarian in organizations, with positive consequences for individuals and the organizations themselves. You are more valuable to your organization if you have the power to influence others, act independently, and be self-reliant than if you are powerless and dependent. But at the same time, creating psychological distance between yourself and your organization might be detrimental to both. Second, gaining expertise and knowledge that are critical to organizational success not only is helpful to you but also can help the organization to better accomplish its public service mission. Third, as a public manager, it is important for you to recognize that although you might have organizational authority and other sources of power at your disposal, your employees have a number of sources of power as well. This is an appropriate and positive situation in which there cognition of your mutual dependency with others can foster mutual respect and cooperation.

Wrong (1968) pointed out that all social interaction, by definition, involves a measure of mutual influence and control. In relationships involving power, this influence is "asymmetrical in that the power holder exercises greater control over the behavior of the power subject than the reverse" (p. 673). But the mutuality of the influence is not necessarily destroyed given that power can be exercised in different spheres. Thus, you might have power in relation to another person regarding certain situations, whereas the other person might have power over you in other situations. Therefore, power relationships need not be hierarchical and unilateral, even if one person has more power in a particular area.

But there is another way to look at mutual dependency and power relationships. Wrong (1968) called unilateral power "integral," whereas "intercursive" power occurs where there are differing spheres of influence between parties. Wrong suggested that integral, or "one-way," power often causes people to attempt to limit or resist it. These attempts can take the form of creating countervailing power (thereby transforming it to an intercursive power relationship); setting limits on the extent, comprehensiveness, and intensity of power; destroying the power altogether; or taking measure to supplant the power wielder by self-regulation. Wrong argued that the idea that politics is a struggle for power is incomplete because it does not consider efforts to limit or resist the power of others.

While the subject of negotiation is considered more fully in Chapter 11, it is important to note here that negotiation involves this type of power dependency and balancing. In negotiations, it is important that we accurately assess our power potential in order to either effectively use the power we have or work to balance power, if necessary. Kim, Pinkley, and Fragale (2005) remind us that many times we will have a different perception about our own power position than will others. If we have the perception that our power position is higher or lower than what others perceive it to be, our actions will depend on *our* perceptions, not the perceptions of others. If we have the perception that our power position is lower than our counterpart's, we are more likely to use power-balancing tactics such as described above. If, on the other hand, you believe that you are more powerful in the negotiation process than the other person, Kim et al. suggest that you are more likely to use "power-use" tactics such as consultation, personal appeal, or rational persuasion, for example. This suggests that it is very important to carefully and accurately assess our power position, keeping in mind that it may be less important how we perceive our power than it is to understand how other people perceive us.

Structural Aspects of Power

Power and organizational politics are, at least in part, a function of organizational structure (Pfeffer, 1981). There is a degree of power that goes along with one's position in the organizational structure. But beyond this position power, the farther up the organizational ladder you go, the better access you have to information, people, and resources. Once this structure is established, it becomes resistant to change because it is in the interest of those in power to keep the structure that gave them power in the first place. After all, why change a structure that reinforces your power and political influence?

The structure of power touches many aspects of organizational life. One of the major issues of the past several decades has been the representativeness of the workplace and the assimilation of new groups into organizational life. This assimilation can be seen, at least in part, as an issue of structural power. Kanter (1977), for example, argued that the behavior of members of certain groups (particularly women and minorities) can be explained by structural factors in the organization rather than by the stereotypical attributes of those groups. More specifically, she suggested that powerlessness, and structural characteristics of organizations that perpetuate such powerlessness, result in counterproductive behavior. She indicated that by changing the structure of rewards and opportunities, feelings of powerlessness will diminish and the negative behavior associated with these groups will decrease.

Kanter also argued that men and women behave differently in organizations not because of gender differences but rather because of the structural characteristics of their roles. Women tend to be clustered in low-power, dependent, and low-mobility positions. Furthermore, those women and minorities who are placed in other roles find that their lack of numerical representation and their inability to command resources make them powerless tokens. This powerlessness leads to ineffective management behavior (e.g., refusal to delegate, lack of concern for tasks and goals). Kanter suggested that White men behave similarly when placed in low-power, dependent, and low-mobility jobs.

In short, Kanter argued that structural determinants—opportunity, mobility, perceived political power, dependency, influence in garnering resources and rewards for subordinates, and numerical representation—are critical to understanding the influence of power in organizational behavior. She concluded that, to correct this, organizations must seek to expand opportunity and mobility, empower people, and balance numerical representation.

Is Power a Positive Force or a Destructive Force?

So far, we have talked about changing attitudes toward power and authority, sources of power, balancing power and empowerment, the structural aspects of power, and power and organizational learning, but we have not fully explored the question of whether power is a positive and constructive force in organizations or a negative and destructive one. Unfortunately, as with many other facets of human behavior, there is not a clear yes/no answer. Power and organizational politics can be a positive and constructive force or a negative factor in organizations.

First, on the positive side, Salancik and Pfeffer (1977/1989) pointed out that, although political power in organizations often is considered an unfair, unjust, and generally undesirable phenomenon, political processes "tend toward the realistic resolution of conflicts among interests" (p. 470). In their view, power is not only necessary for positive organizational functioning but also a vital and critical force in ensuring organizational survival. They argued that power and political processes in organizations help organizations to adapt to and interact with their environments appropriately. Effective managers must recognize, acquire, and use power to achieve organizational ends.

Salancik and Pfeffer suggested that power also is a positive force because those organizational subunits "most able to cope with the organization's critical problems and uncertainties acquire power" (1977/1989, p. 471). This "strategic-contingency" theory of power suggests a positive and desirable picture of power in organizations. The reason subunits or persons who deal with critical problems acquire power is because these subunits or persons play a critical role in organizational success. Accordingly, the power of these units is functional and positive in terms of organizational goal attainment. Moreover, power appropriately plays a role in the selection of executives. Power, in this view, helps to ensure that organizations will protect the survival of their most critical components and select executives best able to deal with environmental contingencies.

Kotter (1977) suggested that power and politics are a positive and necessary force in organizations. He argued that dependency is an inherent part of a manager's job because of the division of labor (creating dependence on others for the completion of tasks) and limited resources (creating dependence for financial and other types of support). Furthermore, according to Kotter, "All the people on whom a manager is dependent have limited time, energy, and talent, for which there are competing demands" (p. 127). As a result, he argued, using power to manage these dependencies is a critical part of the managerial process.

Wilson (1995) stated that, in the public sector, "to successfully implement policy which serves [the] public interest . . . requires power" (p. 102). In her study of federal executives, Wilson found that when leaders use power in a positive manner, it enhances organizational commitment. Managers who use power in this way are focused on building and supporting the confidence and skills of followers. They use their power and "clout" to provide employees with needed information, to obtain necessary resources, to bargain with other organizational actors, and to deal with other impediments to goal attainment. Such managers delegate authority, share information, and promote employee involvement in decision making. Wilson found that managers who use power in this way "uplift" their employees and enhance the motivation, self-control, and commitment of those employees.

Power, according to Pfeffer (1992), is a necessary and healthy aspect of organizational functioning and, in fact, is a critical component of leadership. The problem in most situations is not the use of power but rather powerlessness. Powerlessness leads us to say "I don't know what to do," "I don't have the power to get it done," or "I can't really stomach the struggle that might be involved." As such, it is "a prescription for both organizational and personal failure" (Pfeffer, 1992, p. 49). Without power, we are forced to rely on solely hierarchical authority, an approach that is fraught with difficulties. Not only are people likely to resist it, but it also ignores the need for cooperation, participation, persuasion, and other influence processes. Pfeffer argued that managing with power is absolutely necessary for effective implementation. Attention to the question of power is needed to establish and get buy-in on goals, to identify dependencies and strengths, to identify key actors who support or oppose implementation, and to choose approaches and strategies that will increase your influence over the outcome.

It has also been suggested that power and organizational politics are necessary components of organizational learning. "Organizational learning is a multilevel process that begins with individual learning, that leads to group learning, and that then leads to organizational learning" (Lawrence, Mauws, Dyck, & Kleysen, 2005, p. 181), and this sequence involves the use of different types of power. Organizational learning involves four processes (4I's): "intuiting, interpreting, integrating, and institutionalizing" (p. 181). "Intuiting" happens when individuals develop new ideas, and "interpreting" occurs when these ideas are communicated or explained to others. "Integrating" involves translating the new ideas into coordinated actions. The last phase, "institutionalizing," refers to the incorporation of new ideas and insights into organizational practice.

Lawrence et al. argue that organizational learning requires the effective use of power. They further suggest that the types of power and tactics used will vary based on the phase of organizational learning: Intuition is linked with discipline, interpretation with influence, integration with force, and institutionalization with domination. For instance, in the interpreting phase, an individual's actions to influence or persuade others will affect how an idea is received. Integration, on the other hand, may involve the use of force more than persuasion. "This might involve restricting the consideration of alternative practices, restricting issues for discussion on formal and informal agendas, and removing/transferring opponents of the innovation" (Lawrence et al., 2005, p. 186). The politics of institutionalization most often involves the use of systemic power, such as changing procedures or rules, to overcome resistance (p. 186). Most important, the authors conclude that "having smart employees with great ideas is not enough. Managers who want to foster learning require a slate of employees with appropriate political skills and resources." Without political behavior, "new ideas may be generated by individuals, but organizations will never learn" (p. 190). In contrast to these positive views on the role of power in organizations, others urge caution in advocating power politics in organizations. For example, Vrendenburgh and Maurer (1984) cautioned that to exclude the dark or selfish side of power is an overcompensation. They suggested that political activities are, by definition, not formally sanctioned by organizations. In short, they suggested that in the rush to recognize the positive role of political processes in organizations, power politics in organizations is, by nature, a self-serving process. They categorized definitions of power as falling into one of two categories: those focused on using power to affect organizational decision making and those emphasizing power as self-serving or nonsanctioned by the organizations. They suggested that power in organizations includes the attributes of both categories. Organizational politics is both an individual phenomenon and a group phenomenon that is undertaken to influence others in the direction of the actor's or group's goals. In political situations, these goals are either not sanctioned or unofficially sanctioned by the organization. "A group's or [an] individual's goals or means are political to the extent that they are not positively sanctioned by an organization's formal design or to the degree [that] they are positively sanctioned by unofficial political norms" (Vrendenburgh & Maurer, 1984, p. 50). This makes organizational politics more likely to result in destructive outcomes than in positive ones.

We also need to remember that power can be abused in organizations. Vrendenburgh and Brender (1998) cautioned that hierarchical, interpersonal abuse of power is a danger in organizations. Power can be used in a manner that negatively affects others' sense of dignity and self-respect in both style and substance. Such abusive power interferes with employee job performance and might block deserved rewards. Certainly, it is easy to see that power used in this manner is destructive to both individuals and organizations.

Milgrom and Roberts (1988) suggested that members of organizations invest a significant amount of time in trying to influence decisions in which they have personal stakes. Whereas this is rational for individuals, these attempts to influence impose costs on organizations. For example, because individuals might find it in their interest to manipulate or distort information so as to influence decision makers in a manner that benefits their interests, organizations must make decisions based on imperfect and incomplete information. This decreases the quality of the resulting decisions and diverts time and energy away from more productive pursuits. Therefore, Milgrom and Roberts suggested that organizations employ strategies to discourage organizational members from engaging in such influence activities. They described three such methods: (1) limiting participation and access to decision makers, (2) altering the decision criteria to favor good performers, and (3) offering financial incentives to discourage political activity.

So, we are left with no clear answer. Politics and power are an organizational fact of life, and they can have both positive and negative consequences. If we manage our dependencies and are sensitive to political issues, then we can go a long way toward avoiding the negative aspects of power. But there are other things we can do as well. There are a number of tools and approaches for managing power to which we now turn our attention.

Managing Power and Organizational Politics

Remember that organizational politics are most likely to occur when the stakes are high, resources are limited, or goals and processes are unclear. Although there might be relatively few things that we can do to change the importance of an issue, or the uncertainty and resource scarcity that might surround it, goal ambiguity is something that we can influence. By seeking clarification of goals, or by developing a shared sense of direction and purpose through dialogue and interaction, some of the negative consequences of power politics can be moderated. At a minimum, when there is greater agreement on goals, it is easier to distinguish organizational politics that is primarily focused on organizational and shared goal achievement from organizational politics that is largely self-serving. When goals are unclear and conflicting, it is much easier for individuals to claim and convince others that their agenda is the "right" one for the organization.

In addition to clarifying goals, people who are successful and influential in organizations use various tactics and strategies to gain power, exercise influence, and balance the power of others. Fairholm (1993) listed a number of such tactics commonly used in organizations, a sampling of which are summarized in what follows. As you read them, remember that each of these tactics can be used ethically and appropriately as well as unethically and inappropriately, depending on the means employed and the goals being sought.

- *Controlling the agenda:* Determining in advance what issues will and will not be discussed or decided on
- *Controlling information and using ambiguity:* Keeping communications and meanings unclear so that others will be less able to act; not divulging all information, particularly information that can be used against you
- *Forming coalitions:* Securing alliances with people who are willing to support or agree with you
- *Co-optation:* Involving those who potentially oppose you in the decision making, thereby attempting to secure their commitment to the outcome
- *Using outside experts:* Using an outsider's expertise or reputation to legitimize a position or to avoid having to take a potentially controversial position yourself
- *Developing others:* Increasing the capacity of those around you, thereby increasing overall power
- *Deal making:* Securing quid pro quo agreements or tradeoffs with others
- *Incurring obligations:* Doing things for people knowing that such favors will create an obligation for them to repay the favors
- *Selecting decision criteria:* Controlling the criteria by which decisions are made, allowing you to influence the outcome without personally deciding

Another tactic that is used is "impression management," which is an attempt to influence how others perceive us. Zivnuska, Kacmar, Witt, Carlson, and Bratton (2004) found that when employees perceive a high level of uncertainty in a highly political organization, they will not expect rewards to be based on an actual performance. In such situations, employees will have lower expectations for rewards and will adjust their behavior accordingly, with obvious negative consequences for the organization. Rather than being motivated to work toward rewards based on performance, employees are apt to rely on impression management tactics and self-promotion. The challenge in managing politics, of course, is to choose strategies and tactics that are both legitimate and effective in a given circumstance. Yates (1985), for example, took a contingency approach to the management of politics in organizations. He advised, "The manager of political conflict will be more effective if his or her responses and strategies fit the problems in his or her environment" (p. 91). Yates recommended that managers assess their resources, diagnose the situation, and find the desired fit between strategies and the environment. He pointed out that managers possess a range of resources including "authority, force, persuasion, symbolic rewards, personal style, bargaining techniques, negotiating and mediating skills, coalition-building approaches, and allocations of benefits" (p. 91). He suggested that, in choosing the appropriate approach, managers consider the nature of the problem and the organizational environment. For example, if there is conflict between two people with equal power, then negotiating makes more sense than using force. Conversely, if there is a "yes/no" conflict between you and someone who works for you, then the use of authority might be more effective than engaging in a long negotiation. Power is a scarce resource. The use of power involves time, energy, and the depletion of the amount of power available over time. In other words, we need to choose our battles.

Kotter (1977) argued that managers should use power to influence the behavior of others in a manner that will allow managers to get things done. Power is a quick and efficient means of influencing others. Kotter suggested that effective managers use all of the different methods of acquiring and using power in both direct and indirect ways. He said that effective managers recognize the role of power in the managerial process, are sensitive to organizational norms concerning what is legitimate in terms of the acquisition and use of power, and are responsible in its exercise.

Empowerment: More Than Delegation

There is a significant amount of recent literature suggesting that the issue of power in organizations should be focused on creating conditions that foster the development of personal power and the empowerment of others to accomplish their goals. Conger and Kanungo (1988) suggested that although the concept of empowerment has been popular in recent management literature, there is some confusion and lack of clarity regarding what empowerment actually is. They argued that empowerment often is oversimplified and treated primarily as a management technique. But these authors viewed the root construct of empowerment as based on a different view of power than is suggested in most of the literature on organizational politics. Conger and Kanungo grouped existing views on power into two categories: relational constructs (where power is a function of the relative dependence or inter-dependence of the actors, a view reflected in much of the literature reviewed in this chapter) and motivational constructs (which are found primarily in the psychology literature and based in the idea that "power and control are used as motivational and/or expectancy belief states that are internal to individuals" [p. 473]). In *relational constructs,* the empowerment process becomes one of delegation or sharing of power. In other words, managers empower workers by delegating to them. By contrast, in *motivational constructs,* empowerment is an enabling process aimed at creating conditions that increase motivation and the development of feeling or personal efficacy.

Conger and Kanungo (1988) suggested that the motivational view of power is superior to the relational view because the process of delegating power is only one means by which empowerment may (or may not) result. They described the process of moving from powerlessness to empowerment as consisting of five stages: (1) conditions leading to feelings of powerlessness, (2) the use of managerial strategies to increase personal efficacy and motivation (e.g., participative management, modeling, job enrichment), (3) feedback and the removal of conditions found in Stage 1, (4) reinforcement of the empowerment experience, and (5) persistence of new behavior.

Creating conditions that foster empowerment requires us to consider our assumptions about power in organizations and the behavioral consequences of these assumptions. Tjosvold and Sun (2006) suggested that power in the organizations can be viewed by managers as either "fixed sum" or "expandable." If power is perceived to be "fixed sum," managers will believe that when employees gain power, they do so at the manager's expense. Managers will likely behave in ways that thwart the empowerment of others, because they believe that doing so protects their own power. In more empowering environments, power is viewed "expandable." Managers that view power as expandable will act on the belief that their power will be increased if their employees' performance is high, or in other words, "the success of employees can make them successful" (Tjosvold & Sun, p. 219). These managers are more apt to empower, encourage, help, and support their employees. There are a number of things that we can do to foster people's willingness to empower themselves. When we encourage workers to participate in decision making, treat workers with respect, provide opportunities for growth and development, and reward initiative and responsibility, we can foster empowerment. Equally important is how we treat mistakes and failure. If someone who works for us takes appropriate responsibility and initiative to solve a problem or address an issue and it does not work, then we need to gauge our response carefully. (It might be helpful to first ask ourselves whether anything we have ever tried has failed to work out as planned.) Some of the key questions we should ask ourselves in responding to mistakes or even flat-out failures include the following:

Did the person take the initiative to understand the issue and gather needed information?

Was the person thoughtful about the alternatives, and did he or she make a reasonable and appropriate choice given the information available?

Was there an effort to involve the appropriate people?

Is the person willing to deal with the consequences?

Are there lessons that can be learned from the experience that will inform future practice in a positive manner?

If the answer to most of these questions is yes, then it would be a mistake to respond punitively by seizing control of the situation. It would be more constructive to sit down with the person and try to understand what went wrong and determine how you will proceed, both individually and collectively. Imagine, for example, that an employee identified a problem with gaining citizen input on a particular program. With your buy-in, this employee looked into options by examining practices in other cities and consulting with other staff in your organization. When this employee came to you with a proposal to have rotating neighborhood meetings, the proposal seemed well thought out, and the potential benefits seemed worth the risk and expense. You told the employee to implement the idea. Unfortunately, no one came to the first meeting.

What will happen if you respond in a manner that communicates that the employee has done a bad thing, that you no longer trust him or her, and that you will now take over? The most likely result will be that the person will be less likely to take responsibility and initiative in the future. On the other hand, if you provide support and allow the person to learn from the experience, then everyone concerned is likely to benefit.

If we do not foster empowerment, then it can lead to feelings of powerlessness and a dampening of initiative. In his book *The Empowered Manager,* Block (1987) reminded us of the negative consequences of powerlessness and suggested that the answer is an individual and largely psychological remedy rather than a change in management behavior or organizational structure. According to Block, although empowerment can be fostered by organizational conditions, it is primarily achieved through the decisions of individuals to change their self-images and belief systems. Empowerment, in this view, is not something granted from the outside but rather something we give ourselves.

In fact, Block suggested that "the process of organizational politics as we know it works against people taking responsibility" (1987, p. xiii). He said that traditional organizations have fostered the development of a bureaucratic management mentality that emphasizes caution, compliance, patriarchal supervisory styles, and narrow self-interest. Block argued that a more desirable management style, which he called entrepreneurial, can be fostered through the use of political processes in organizations. Through empowerment, Block called for enlightened self-interest based on service and contribution to organizations. The empowered manager is a "Theory Y" individual—creative, committed to organizational goals, and willing to take risks and shoulder the responsibility for consequences. Power, in this view, is acquired through the alteration of a person's state of mind.

As a part of this self-empowerment process, Block (1987) urged managers to model this behavior for others. He considered such modeling to be political in that it is intended to create, and therefore redistribute, power in organizations.

He suggested that, in this modeling, managers adopt the belief that they are their own authority (rather than looking to their superiors), engage in and encourage self-expression in others, and make personal commitments to achieving results.

To make this empowerment and enlightened self-interest possible, organizations must reflect and express values about work, achievement, and community that can be affirmed by organizational members. This sense of organizational values is expressed as visions for the future. Once managers create these visions, they must then engage in political processes such as negotiating for support and building coalitions. From there, they must recognize and build on healthy interdependencies balanced with autonomy. In short, they need to avoid sticking their heads in the proverbial sand about organizational politics. Understanding the need for power and influence, and taking action based on that knowledge, is a path that sometimes requires courage and conviction. But the alternative—to use their dependence on others as a manipulative tool or to simply throw their hands in the air and claim to be powerless to make things better—might be worse.

Power and the Public Service

As the subject of power has been debated throughout history, notions of the role and rightness of power have evolved and changed. In general, although there has been a growing acceptance and recognition of power as a facet of organizational behavior, Americans are ambivalent about its exercise in the absence of authority and standards of legitimacy. As Burns (1978) asserted, the world lacks moral leaders, not power holders. Power alone, without moral purpose and reasoned values, will not satisfy the need for compelling and creative leadership. In short, whereas power can be explored empirically and debated pragmatically, it appropriately remains a philosophical and moral issue as well.

Public leadership can involve the exercise of power, but it must be used appropriately and legitimated in reference to some larger set of values or purposes. As Russell (1938) argued, power as an end is inherently undesirable, but power as a means can be desirable. The problem, of course, is determining when power as a means is appropriate. This is a particularly problematic issue in the case of public servants because they are, and should be, accountable to a broad array of organizational rules, laws, norms, and values.

Power is pervasive and multifaceted. Effective and appropriate public service involves the use of power, but it must be a legitimate use. In other words, power must be legitimated through reference to external standards, norms, and values before its use can be considered to be a dimension of public service and leadership. If it is not, then it is simply manipulation, coercion, or something else.

Because power can take so many forms, and because its use by public servants can profoundly influence the meaning of law, justice, and governance in everyday life, it is important to focus on the legitimacy of its use in that context. Particularly in the public sector, Friedrich (1963) argued that the authoritative exercise of power must be based on legitimacy and grounded in reason and values. "Power thus reinforced by authority acquires the capacity to create law that is right and just by making it legitimate" (p. 204). In the same way, our use of power in public organizations should be based on the achievement of shared goals and legitimate purposes. Clearly, public servants at all levels exercise power in and outside of their organizations. The public service ethic demands that in political situations we ask ourselves the question: What are we trying to accomplish and for whose benefit?

Ways of Acting

1. *Enhance your personal power by considering all of its possible sources.* Just because you lack the title of a person in authority does not mean that you do not need or cannot gain power and influence. Power is derived from many sources—expertise, admiration and respect for others, doing things for other people, giving rewards and recognition, and so on. Anything that makes people more dependent on you, or that makes you less dependent on them, increases your capacity to influence people. Such dependencies can be highly positive for both parties and the organization. Even if you are in a position of authority, relying solely on position power is not advisable. To get things done in an organization, you need to be able to engender cooperation, persuade others, and negotiate solutions to problems. These are political skills that are needed at all levels of the organization, regardless of position.

2. *Make yourself visible and indispensable.* It is important to remember that being highly skilled and competent in your job and taking on responsibilities that are critical to your unit make for a positive political strategy. Again, power is in part a matter of dependency. If the people at work learn that you are knowledgeable about and skilled in matters that are critical to your organization's success, then they are more likely to listen to and be influenced by you. But in addition to being an expert on key matters, you must make yourself visible enough so that people know that to be the case. This suggests that taking on visible assignments, speaking at meetings, and being clear and accurate about your contributions to key projects not only can help you career-wise but also can help you to be more influential in your present position.

3. *Take charge of your own empowerment.* Claiming to be powerless sometimes is an excuse for not taking responsibility. Empowerment is more about changing the way in which you think than a formal delegation of authority from your boss. Although empowerment can be fostered by management behavior or organizational conditions, it is primarily a matter of deciding to change your self-image and belief system. You can empower yourself to be creative, be committed to organizational goals, take calculated risks, and shoulder the responsibility for consequences. Doing so requires that you ask yourself how you can take initiative and responsibility when confronted with problems. For example, when you encounter a difficulty or problem, do not simply take it to your supervisor for his or her resolution. Instead, take responsibility for formulating some potential strategies for solution. When you see your supervisor, explain the problem, briefly describe the alternative solutions, and recommend the one you judge to be the best. Or, if you have the authority to act, simply solve the problem.

4. *Use power constructively and effectively.* Remember that not all sources of power and political strategies are created equal in terms of their effect on individuals and the organization. Leadership at all levels of the organization should be fundamentally based on respecting the dignity and worth of people, a commitment to organizational goals, and an ethic of public service. When you acquire power and use it to serve your own needs and agendas, or simply for the "thrill" of feeling as though you are in control, you are not using power constructively. Doing so is destructive to the organization, the people you interact with, and ultimately yourself. Power and political acumen are necessary ingredients for personal and organizational success. But each of us needs to be self-aware and self-reflective about how we are using power and for what purpose. It also is important to remember that some political strategies are more consistent with humanistic and democratic values than others. Developing your employees, or what Wilson (1995) called "uplifting" others (i.e., fostering their participation, listening carefully to their values and interests, and building and supporting their confidence and skills), is a constructive use of power. Doing so also enhances your reserve of referent power. In using that power to secure needed information, to obtain necessary resources, or to bargain with other organizational actors, you increase the likelihood of being successful in attaining organizational goals. That is not to say that other strategies such as using hierarchical authority, punishment, secrecy, and so on are not sometimes appropriate. But they often are less effective in the long run because they tend to result in resistance and do not build the positive regard of others.

5. *Devote time and energy to clarifying goals.* In one sense, political behavior occurs because different people have different goals. They try to gain power and use their influence to have their goals take precedence over competing goals. In the public sector, this can be particularly problematic because our mandated goals can be ambiguous and sometimes conflicting. Remember that political behavior is most likely to occur when goals are unclear and resources are scarce—conditions that are common in the public sector. It also should be kept in mind that one of the key differences between the constructive and destructive aspects of power in organizations is whether the power is used in pursuit of organizational or personal goals. Accordingly, clarifying and building shared goals reduces the likelihood of political behavior that does not positively contribute to the organization or, at a minimum, makes that political behavior easier to recognize as negative. If no one agrees on the goals, then it is difficult (if not impossible) to sort out what is positive influence and what is self-serving manipulation.

6. *Support and foster the empowerment of others.* Although empowerment is principally something you can do for yourself, there are several things that management and the organization can do to foster people's willingness to empower others. By providing opportunities to become involved in decision making, showing respect, giving trust, and allowing people to grow, you can enhance people's development and reward their efforts in taking responsibility. Equally important to these steps is how you treat mistakes and failure. If someone who works for you takes appropriate responsibility and initiative to solve a problem or address an issue and their approach does not work, then you need to gauge your response carefully.

7. *Think about, plan for, and maintain your awareness of political issues in management and in the implementation process.* Being successful in organizations is not always about being "right." Effective public service is accomplished through the dedication, hard work, and cooperation of people. It is a difficult thing to accept sometimes that your perception of what is right is not going to be the same as everyone else's. So, the idea that effective organizational politics is about forcing others to conform and bend to your will is both ineffective and inconsistent with the values of the public service, even if you are absolutely convinced that you have discovered the "one best way." In the public sector, there always are many competing values and interests, both within and outside of the organization, that successful public administrators must navigate to accomplish organizational objectives. Democratic values demand that you allow people's voices and perspectives to be heard and that public interest values be paramount. As a practical matter, public organizations cannot operate successfully in any other way. There are too many opportunities in the public sector to stop or impede successful implementation of policy. Employees not only must understand but also must internalize public service values and support organizational goals if they are to be effective in accomplishing public purposes. This cannot be accomplished by coercing and over-controlling people, nor can it be accomplished by naked power plays that undermine trust. But public purposes can be accomplished and, in fact, must be accomplished through compromise, persuasion, positive influence, and compromise. (Incidentally, such approaches do not make you less powerful; rather, they make you more powerful and influential.) Serving the public requires that you be attentive to, and plan for, the political aspects of your job. Consulting others, building alliances, persuading others, and providing information often are essential to accomplishing your objectives. Put simply, you not only need power to get things done but must devote the time and energy to use that power and influence in an appropriate and timely fashion.

8. *Whenever possible, be nice.* This final way of acting flows from everything else that we have discussed. Being nice is not about being mealy-mouthed, weak, or ineffectual. In fact, when we talk about being nice, we are trying to reinforce the idea that being kind, considerate, and respectful toward others builds mutual trust and respect. It enhances your influence, power, and persuasiveness. It helps you to accomplish your objectives. It models the sort of treatment that you want public servants to emulate in their dealings with citizens. It fosters the empowerment of others. And it makes organizational life a more pleasant experience for everyone involved. Being nice not only is the good and right thing to do for its own sake but also is a good political strategy.

Thinking in Action

The following exercises will help you to think through some of the questions we have raised concerning power and politics.

Politics and MBO: A Case Study

John was thrilled when, after completing his MPA degree, he was hired to work as a management analyst in the state office of management and budget. During his first year on the job, John impressed his supervisor and coworkers with his excellent analytical and writing skills. Even though his time on the job was short, he had proven himself to be an intelligent, hardworking, and reliable employee. At his 1-year performance review, he received an "excellent" overall rating.

Shortly after his 1-year anniversary on the job, a new governor was sworn into office. She had many innovative ideas and changes that she wanted implemented to improve the efficiency and effectiveness of state government. One of the vehicles she instituted to achieve these changes was the introduction of a statewide "management by objectives" (MBO) program to be administered out of John's office. Although John was relatively inexperienced, the unit director believed that his excellent work qualified him to serve as the coordinator for the MBO program for all social service and education programs. Two other staff members were assigned to split the remaining functional areas of state government including transportation, natural resources, staff departments (e.g., purchasing, personnel), and so on. But social service and education programs were the new governor's top priority and were expected to receive the most attention.

It was John's job to help the agencies to develop goals and objectives and set up data collection strategies to obtain information on performance against those goals. He was to personally advise the governor on the progress of the MBO program on a periodic basis and to make a formal presentation with agency officials to the governor's office four times a year. John quickly learned that achieving agency cooperation was going to be very difficult. The agency representatives he worked with were openly hostile to the ideas of measurable objectives, did not get reports completed on time, and were generally uncooperative with the effort. These agency staff viewed John as an inexperienced, naive, and intense young man who presented an organizational annoyance that probably would disappear in time. Although the agency heads were publicly supportive of the program, John was finding it nearly impossible to work with agency staff to complete his tasks.

In response, John attempted to coerce the agency staff to cooperate, threatening to "expose" them and punish them (and their agency) for their lack of support and involvement. When he had his first meeting about the MBO program with his supervisor, he expressed his outrage at how difficult and obstinate the agency representatives were as well as anger at his mistreatment and the lack of respect he was being shown. He dismissed his supervisor's suggestions about how he might develop a more cooperative positive working relationship with the agency representatives, saying that they were simply "dead-wood" in the bureaucracy and should be fired. "The governor wants this, this is the right approach to take, and if they aren't going to cooperate, I say they should be fired," he said. Shortly thereafter, John was reassigned to an internal, lower priority project.

Respond to the following questions.

1. What do you think has happened here? Who, and in what way, are the various participants responsible for the outcome? How does John's experience relate to questions of organizational power and politics?

2. Assuming that, after his reassignment, John might have become more open to suggestions on his behavior, how might you advise him?

3. If you were John and had the benefit of hindsight, how might you have handled the situation differently? How could you use power and organizational politics to gain the respect and cooperation you need to accomplish the governor's objectives?

Observing Organizational Politics

1. Think of the most effective and successful organizational politician you know. From what sources of power does this person draw?

2. What strategies does this person employ? What strategies have been the most effective and why?

3. Are these strategies used constructively to enhance organizational goal attainment? Are these strategies used for self-serving purposes? Explain.

4. Do you have power relative to this person? Why or why not? Do you need or want more power in this case? If yes, then what are some of the ways in which you might increase your influence and power?

5. What can you learn from this person that will help you to gain power and use it constructively for your own benefit and for the organization's benefit? (In some cases, this might involve learning from behavior and strategies that you want to avoid rather than emulate.)

Assessing Your Power Potential

How powerful and influential are you? Probably not as powerful as you could be. Think about the sources of power outlined by French and Raven and the power-balancing techniques described in this chapter. Are there specific areas where you feel less powerful than you would like to be? What specifically might you do to increase your capacity to influence others and create more balanced power relationships in your relationships at work? Most important, how will you use that power in the public interest?

9

Communicating Effectively With Others

Three Englishmen were riding on a bus. At the first stop, one man says, "Is this Wembley?" "No," says the second man, "this is Thursday." "So am I," says the third man. "Let's have a drink."

What we have here is a failure to communicate.

—*Cool Hand Luke* (film)

Mary Lou Cooper, head of an internal audit agency in state government, sees signs of fatigue in John Carter, one of her best employees. Being concerned about his health, she suggests that he take some time off. John, on edge because of an illness in his family, already is worried that he is not doing his job as well as he can and takes Mary's suggestion as an effort to get him out of the way. Concerned that he might lose his job, he does not follow Mary's advice and instead works even harder—at some risk to his health and psychological well-being. Meanwhile, Steve Jackson and Phil Dexter, two very close friends, hear rumors of a new and very attractive management position for which they both would be eligible. In a lunchroom conversation, Steve happens to comment on a recent mistake Phil made in an important project. Phil hears of the comment from someone else, takes offense at Steve's "negative campaigning" for the new job, and isolates himself from Steve. The two friends soon become intense rivals or even enemies. Then they hear that John has been working especially hard recently. They assume that he also wants the new job, so they both begin to shape their conversations to disparage John. Suddenly the organization is in chaos. People are hurt, friendships are damaged, and the actual work of the organization is pushed to a back burner.

Obviously, clear and constructive communication within public organizations is essential not only for the organizations to accomplish their tasks most effectively and responsibly but also for people in the organizations to live happier and more satisfying lives. But communicating effectively with others is not easy. What would seem to be a simple process of speaking, listening, and understanding actually is enormously complex. Moreover, there are a number of important barriers to effective communication in organizations, many of which we examine in this chapter. But there also are some lessons we can learn about communication that will enable us to communicate more effectively with others, and we examine several of these techniques as well. Finally, there are some special communication issues that those in public organizations often face—how to counsel employees in a supportive fashion, how to conduct meetings, and how to write good memos, reports, and proposals. These demand our attention as well.

It is helpful to begin by thinking through what is involved in the communication process. Communication can be defined most simply as the transmission of information from one party to another. In its classic formulation, communication appears to be quite straightforward. First, there is the *sender,* or the one who initiates the communication by sending some type of *message.* That message is transmitted through various *channels* or *media*—speech, body language, e-mail, and so on. The message goes to the *receiver,* who then may or may not provide *feedback.* In this formulation, communication is successful when the receiver understands what the sender intended (Figure 9.1).

In practice, communication is much more complicated than this simple model implies. Imagine that Anne, the dean of the School of Public Affairs at a major midwestern university, wants to encourage faculty to contribute to the college's endowment fund, especially because this would provide a model for those outside who might be asked to give. The first problem that Anne faces is how to formulate the message. Anne knows what she wants and what she means to communicate, but she also knows that faculty might resent her request. For this reason, she wants to choose just the right words to express her meaning clearly and carefully. She also must make a decision about what channel to use to communicate her message. In the best of all possible worlds, she would like to talk with each faculty member individually so that she could gauge the individual's response and shape her message to that reaction. But time limitations make that impossible. So, she is left with other alternatives, such as making an announcement in a meeting of the school faculty and sending a memo or an e-mail to everyone in the school. Whatever her choice, when the message is received it will be interpreted differently by different faculty members. Some might recognize the importance of having solid internal contributions from those in the organization prior to undertaking an external fundraising campaign. Others might believe that the university's recent raises have been so small that for someone to ask for money is simply ludicrous. In response to Anne's message, some faculty members might send contributions. Others might send back sharply worded letters complaining about the dean's cruel and ruthless arm-twisting tactics.

As our example shows, what is critical in any communication is what the sender meant and what the receiver understood. When Anne began to think about her communication problem, she knew what she meant, but she also recognized the difficulty of putting that meaning into words. Similarly, the receivers of the message

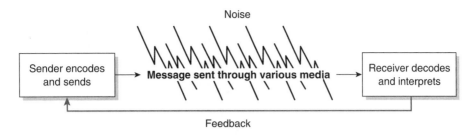

Figure 9.1   The Process of Communication

will interpret the message differently based on their own perceptions (of the situation, of the dean, and even of themselves). They need to translate the message into
terms meaningful to them. Communication, then, not only is concerned with
transmitting information but also is concerned with establishing common meanings. (After all, the root of the word *communication* is derived from the Latin word
communis, meaning "common.")

But the process of establishing common meaning raises several other issues.
First, as we already have seen, the sender has to *encode* the intended meaning, and
the receiver has to *decode* the meaning. Communication involves creating meaning,
transmitting meaning, and deciphering meaning. But the different parties involved
in the process do so in terms of their own particular circumstances. We view the
world through different lenses shaped by our accumulated perceptions, attitudes,
beliefs, and interpretations. Using different lenses, we see (or hear) different things.

The classic illustration of this point is the image presented in Figure 9.2. As you
look at this picture, what do you see first—a well-dressed young woman or an old
woman with a scarf over her head? Some will see the former, and others will see the
latter. Actually, both are present. The young woman is facing left and slightly away
from you; you can barely see her nose at the left of the picture. The old woman also
is facing left, almost in profile, with her left eye fully showing just below her hair.
Which figure you see first obviously is a result of your perceptions, and people differ with respect to their perceptions.

If we are to fully understand the communication process, we need to understand
the enormous complexity of what is involved in communicating human meaning.
A more complete understanding of the communication process recognizes that
communication is not merely a mechanical exercise in transmitting information
but also an effort to establish shared meaning. This raises a number of important
issues for us to keep in mind as we explore the communication process.

1. Some messages are *unintentionally* ambiguous with respect to their meaning.
The sender believes that the appropriate meaning has been expressed, and the
receiver thinks that he or she understands what has been said, but both of them are
wrong. The sender meant one thing, and the receiver heard another. For example,
Ronald Reagan was reported to have decided to offer George Schultz the position
of secretary of state, but in his call to Schultz, Reagan said, "I'd be interested in

Figure 9.2   What Do You See?

having you join my cabinet." Schultz, who wanted to be secretary of state but had heard that he was being considered for the treasury secretary position (which did not interest him), thought that Reagan was talking about the treasury position and turned the president down.

2. Other messages, especially in organizations, are *intentionally* ambiguous. Eisenberg (1984) laid out several conditions under which people are likely to use *strategic ambiguity*. These include situations in which (a) people are faced with multiple and possibly conflicting goals, (b) conditions are volatile and likely to change, (c) relationships are tenuous, and (d) elite positions are threatened. A delightful example of the latter was contained in Whyte's (1952) *Is Anybody Listening?*: "All you have to remember is . . . let the language be ambiguous enough that if the job is successfully carried out, all credit can be claimed, and if not, a technical alibi can be found" (p. 52). More seriously, some degree of ambiguity might be necessary because of the particular circumstances of the communicator. For example, listen to the White House press secretary briefing the press. Listen for potentially ambiguous statements (and recognize that they often will not appear ambiguous at all on the surface).

3. Meaningful communication, or communication that carries meaning, is not merely rational; it also is laden with emotions. We often ask about a person's intentions in his or her communication: "What did you mean by that?" Or we sometimes believe that it is important to explain our own intentions to others: "That's really not what I meant to say." Although our intentions are important, communication does not operate only at that rational level. We communicate emotions as well as words, and often the emotions that others perceive in our communications are not

those that we intend. Yet they have an impact, one that might not later be corrected as we try to explain what we really meant. In this sense, communication is not always just a rational or technical matter; it often is highly emotional, often more symbolic than "real," and subject to widely varying interpretations.

4. Communication depends on one's frame of reference. It is difficult enough to communicate what we intend, but in fact, many of the messages that we send we do not even know we are sending. Others perceive that we are trying to communicate something completely different from what we intend. For example, wearing formal clothes on a "casual Friday" might be taken as a sign of protest or an effort to intimidate others (when in fact the person simply realized that he or she would not have time to change before the opera after work). If your frame of reference places high value on organizational rules and conventions, then you might see this as a sign of protest. If your primary value is getting to the opera quickly after work, then wearing more formal clothes to work makes perfectly good sense. Recognizing and clarifying unintended communications is quite difficult but often necessary.

5. Messages serve different functions. We all are familiar with the examples of extreme bureaucratic language that occasionally are paraded by the popular press. These examples of "bureaucratic gobbledygook" typically are seen by the public as either humorous or outlandish. And that certainly is understandable if the intent of the communication is to inform an audience. But in many cases, the intent of the language is to regulate behavior, and that must be done with the utmost attention to precision and detail. Although such messages might seem excessively detailed and even convoluted to those on the outside, their language often is necessary to state positions thoroughly and correctly. Again, to understand the meaningfulness of communications, you need to understand the context within which the communications occur.

6. Communication is shaped by relationships of power in organizations as elsewhere. That is, we tend to shape our conversations depending on the people with whom we are talking. That shaping of conversations is particularly evident in situations where there is an imbalance of power between those involved in the communication. Stohl (1995, p. 54) described four levels of communication: (1) what you would really like to say if you were completely free to do so (e.g., "Boss, you really don't know what you are talking about."), (2) what you decide you should say ("There might be some flaws in that plan."), (3) what you actually do say ("That's an interesting possibility."), and (4) what the message means to the receiver ("Possibility? I would have expected a little more support than that. I'll remember that when it comes to giving raises."). The power relationship involved in this example is perhaps too obvious, but the same shaping of conversations occurs much more subtly.

7. Some of the more elementary explanations of the process of communication, such as the sender/channel/receiver/feedback model presented earlier, make that process seem rather mechanical; communication becomes merely transmitting information from one person to another. But as we noted earlier, a more contemporary perspective would recognize the role of meaning in communication and the

resulting complexity that it engenders. In this view, communicating always expresses a certain tension that exists in all human relationships but that is especially apparent in complex organizations—a tension between creativity and constraint (Eisenberg & Goodall, 1993, pp. 29–40).

In this view, communication does not merely take place in organizations; rather, communication creates and sustains organizations. Individuals within organizations are constantly trying to work out satisfactory interpretations of their lives and their work. It is through the process of communication that they are able to arrive at and maintain particular ways of looking at the world. Those versions of reality are seen in the norms, attitudes, and beliefs that constitute organizations and constrain the behavior of people within organizations. These people's "social construction of reality" provides a certain amount of security because it lets people know where they stand, but it also restricts the range of actions in which they engage. But just as realities are socially constructed, they also can be changed through social interaction. Any effort to change the way in which organizations and the people within them act must necessarily start with changing the beliefs and attitudes of organizations' members. That involves an element of creativity, and it is through the process of communication that new realities are constructed. It is the constant interaction of creativity and constraint that makes organizations what they are—and what makes the people within them who they are. The process of communication, for this reason, cannot be viewed merely as an instrument for achieving organizational goals; communication also must be seen as an avenue to organizational learning, growth, and development.

Where Do We Begin?

How would you respond to the following statements? Choose one of the alternative responses or just fill in the blanks. Then discuss your responses with classmates.

1. [From the head of your agency] "I've heard some disturbing rumors about the way you treat our clients."
   a. "That's ridiculous."
   b. "You can't believe everything you hear."
   c. "Could you please be more specific?"
   d. _____

2. [From a coworker] "I'm terribly afraid that the mistake I made in the Harris confirmation hearing means that the boss is going to transfer me to the end of the world."
   a. "That's stupid. He hates Harris."
   b. "You shouldn't be so worried. He'll get over it."
   c. "So you're worried that your position may be in jeopardy?"
   d. _____

3. [From your subordinates] "We really think that we deserve more money for doing this job."
   a. "That's silly. You're really not worth what we're paying you now."
   b. "You know that the legislature won't give us any more money."
   c. "Why don't we sit down and think through our salary structure together?"
   d. _____

4. [From a legislator or a member of the city council] "I want to see all the information we have on the new construction project, and I want it in my office in one hour."
   a. "That's none of your business."
   b. "That's impossible. I'll need at least three hours to get it together."
   c. "It will be very difficult for me to get it together that quickly. But could we set an appointment for later this afternoon?"
   d. _____

5. [From a citizen] "Can you tell me who to talk with about a junk car that I'd like to have removed from the vacant lot next door?"
   a. "That's not my department."
   b. "Ask the secretary over there."
   c. "That would be the public works department. Let me show you where they are located."
   d. _____

Ways of Thinking

Studies have shown that people generally spend some 70% to 80% of their waking hours engaged in communication, with about 40% of that time spent speaking and writing (i.e., sending messages) and about 60% of the time spent reading and listening (i.e., receiving messages). For managers, the percentage spent in the latter category—receiving messages—is even higher (Tracey, 1988). If communication plays such an important role in public organizations, then it is important to understand ways in which communication can be improved. Fortunately, there are some specific guidelines that can be employed that will help considerably in the transmission not only of information but also of meaning among those in public organizations.

Improving Interpersonal Communication

As we know too well, even though we spend so much time "practicing" communication, there often are breakdowns that threaten the work of the organization and even endanger people's lives. In this section, we examine the various ways in which communication fails as well as some specific ways in which we can improve our capacity for effective and responsible communication, both in speaking and in listening. (Some examples of breakdowns are provided in Figure 9.3.) We then examine several "special" communication issues in contemporary public organizations such as nonverbal communication and the effect of electronic media on communication.

Barriers to Effective Communication

In the simple model of communication that we present in Figure 9.1, there are several obvious places where communication might break down and *distortion* might occur. (Distortion refers to the difference between the meaning that was intended by the sender and the meaning that was decoded by the receiver.) First, the sender must express the intended meaning in symbols, usually words. There are many words available, but only a few of these words can be used in any statement, meaning that almost any communication is incomplete. For example, think of a 10-second segment of a television show that you recently watched. Chances are good that you could describe that segment in 25 words or less. But a skilled novelist, intent on conveying the incident as completely as possible, might write several pages. In many conversations, listeners might think that they heard what was intended, but they actually "hear" only an abbreviated version of the meaning that was intended.

What the Manager Said	What the Manager Meant	What the Employee Heard
There's a position open in the budget office that might give you valuable experience in understanding the budget process.	This would be a good opportunity for someone from our office to learn budgeting and then come back and really help us out.	I'm being pushed out.
You've met the standards for satisfactory work performance this year.	You are barely getting by, and you really need to improve your work.	Wow! I'm doing great!
I'd like for you to have the new personnel classification report ready as soon as possible.	I need the report for a meeting in 10 days.	I'd better drop everything and get that report completed today.
You sure have been putting in a lot of hours lately.	I'm worried about your health; you might be getting overloaded.	Sounds like a hint. I'd better get to work.
The legislature is considering a bill that would eliminate our division.	I think we can counter this move if we build an effective case for our division to be continued.	I'd better polish my résumé.

Figure 9.3   Examples of Communication Failures

And there always is the question of *semantics.* The sender must encode the message in words. But most words mean many different things. For example, any fairly comprehensive dictionary will list dozens of meanings for the word *round.* Indeed, according to a study of word meanings, the *Oxford English Dictionary* gives an average of 28 different definitions for each of the 500 most used words in the English language (David & Newstrom, 1985, p. 431). In addition, all organizations, and especially public organizations, seem to depend heavily on *jargon,* a specialized "shorthand" language often composed of specialized terminology and acronyms known to insiders but often mystifying to others. Relying excessively on jargon may serve to further obscure one's language. In any case, a poor choice of symbols or words can distort the intended message.

One's intended meaning also can be subject to *filtering.* Filtering involves manipulating the information that is being sent so that it will be received more favorably by the receiver. Earlier, we noted the relationship between power and communication. Filtering is especially prevalent where one party to the conversation has more power than the other, as in cases where lower-level employees are sending information to upper-level employees. Many executives have complained that they often are given the answers that people think they want rather than the answers that are most honest and, typically, most helpful.

Second, the sender must choose the correct channel or medium to send the message. Although oral communication allows the possibility for feedback and interaction, a message transmitted orally also might be misinterpreted as words pass by quickly and soon are forgotten as people move on to other things. Oral communication also is particularly susceptible to "noise"—either *actual noise* or *social noise.* The possible interference from actual noise is obvious. If you are trying to talk with someone while others are talking nearby or while a fire engine is passing by outside, then both you and the other person might be distracted and the message might not be heard clearly. Social noise refers to the way in which individuals involved in more complex communications may alter their messages as they transmit them to others. Remember the old game in which one person starts a message by telling one person in a group, that person passes it on to someone else, and so on around the circle. At the end, the message almost always is quite different from the original message.

Written communication, on the other hand, has the advantage of permanence (and you can come back to it later for possible clarification). But the formal character of written communication might be considered inappropriate for many types of messages. One way of deciding whether to use written communication is to think about the purpose of the communication. A formal memo might be necessary if the purpose is to establish procedures or regulations. But if the purpose is merely to inform people of new developments, then conversations, staff meetings, or even e-mail might provide a better mode of communicating. Of course, as we note later in this chapter, electronic communication is rapidly changing the way in which we communicate in organizations. One of the biggest challenges for managers is to know when to employ e-mail and other electronic forms of communication and when to rely on more traditional channels of communication.

Third, as the receiver decodes the message, there is an additional possibility for breakdown. As we noted earlier, the receiver will understand, or at least seek to understand, the message through the lens of his or her biases and perceptions. Different people perceive the world in different ways, and the differences in their perceptions make an important difference in the ways in which they interpret messages that they receive. For example, people with different backgrounds, experiences, interests, preferences, and motivations are likely to hear messages differently. This phenomenon often occurs in problem-solving situations, where the accountant will see the problem as an accounting problem, the economist will see it as an economic problem, and so on. Those who receive messages also might project their expectations of others into what they hear, as in *stereotyping*. If an interviewer expects a female applicant to put family before work, then that interviewer might hear such a preference even if the interviewee is trying very hard to communicate the opposite.

But the way in which the receiver decodes the message may be affected by even more mundane circumstances. Certainly, the emotional state of the receiver may affect the communication. For example, if you are particularly angry or upset when you hear a message, then your emotions probably will affect the way in which you hear the message. Rather than hearing the message rationally and objectively, you are likely to read considerable emotion into the message. There also are personal characteristics that affect the way in which the receiver decodes messages that he or she receives. For example, the receiver might have poor listening habits—something we explore later in the chapter. Or the receiver might have a short attention span and be unable to absorb lengthy or complex messages. Or the receiver might simply not have certain information that would be necessary to understand the message. For example, if you are told that "the data previously entered on Line 17 no longer are necessary," then it would be helpful to know what previously was entered on Line 17. And of course, decoding a message, especially a complicated one, requires careful thought. But in the rush of day-to-day work, individuals sometimes do not give sufficient attention to incoming communications and miss the messages.

Finally, the psychological state of the recipient of the message will affect what is heard and what is missed. Well-known psychologist Carl Rogers (1991) argued that the main obstacle to effective communication is people's tendency to *evaluate*. People have a natural urge to judge—to approve or disapprove of—what others say. If someone says that your state would be better off with a governor from the other political party, then your first reaction probably will be evaluative. You will find yourself either agreeing or disagreeing. You might find yourself making some judgment about the person speaking—for example, "She has really good judgment" or "How absurd!" Rogers argued that the effectiveness of communication can be enhanced if people can avoid the tendency to evaluate.

A variation of the tendency to evaluate, and one of the psychological conditions most affecting organizational communication, is *defensiveness*. Defensive behavior occurs when a person feels or anticipates some sort of threat (Gibb, 1961). It can be stimulated by the character of the message itself, or the message can touch a particularly sensitive area in the receiver and trigger a reaction. For example, messages that appear to "judge" other people, those that are used to "control" others, those that appear to be based on "hidden agendas," those that convey an attitude of superiority or disdain, and those that seem lacking in concern for others might provoke defensiveness on the part of recipients. On the other hand, messages might simply "strike a nerve" in receivers, and those people might react defensively. For example, a person receiving a performance evaluation that is generally quite positive might "hear" the one negative part of the message as the most important, dwell on that single part of the message, and react quite defensively to the entire evaluation. As we will see in Chapter 12, dealing with defensiveness often is a central issue as managers try to change their organizations.

In sum, even though we all speak the same language—English—we often do not really speak the same "language." Our use of certain words varies, we filter what we are saying based on what we think others want to hear, we use the wrong channels of communication, and we misinterpret the intent of others (for a variety of reasons). Although we tend to assume that all of our communications are clear and effective, this assumption is not always correct. But there are ways in which we can improve the process of communication so that, as individuals and as members of public and nonprofit organizations, we can be more effective and more responsible.

Supportive Communication

Effective communication in public organizations, as elsewhere, aims at transmitting information accurately, honestly, and in such away that the receiver will understand, accept, and use that information. But effective communication also must help to develop and maintain interpersonal relationships, specifically by enabling people to express and accept differences in how they feel. Supportive communication refers to an approach to communicating with others that recognizes both of these purposes of communication: to convey needed information *and* to enhance interpersonal relationships in the group or organization. Engaging in supportive communication probably will engender a happier and more pleasant work environment, and it also probably will lead to greater productivity. Research has shown that organizations that foster positive interpersonal relationships among their members are more productive, are more effective at problem solving, produce higher quality outcomes, and have fewer conflicts than organizations that do not. Supportive communication has the characteristics shown in Figure 9.4.

1. *Supportive communication is problem oriented, not person oriented.* Supportive communication focuses on problems and their solutions rather than on the individual. For example, a manager practicing supportive communication would say, "Let's work together to improve our work" rather than "Your laziness is really the problem." The reason for this approach is that people rarely can change their personalities, but they can change their behavior. Focusing on the problem rather than on the person opens opportunities for positive and constructive change. Imputing motives to others or criticizing them directly is likely to bring about defensive reactions and very little change. Connecting the conversation to specific behaviors and to expected standards of behavior not only acknowledges the other individual personally but also gives the person receiving the message more to work with.

1. Problem oriented, not person oriented

2. Descriptive, not evaluative

3. Specific, not general

4. Conjunctive, not disjunctive

5. Validating, not demeaning

6. Owned, not disowned

7. Two-way, not one-way

Figure 9.4   Attributes of Supportive Communication

2. Supportive communication encourages being descriptive, not evaluative. Similarly, providing information that is descriptive rather than evaluative avoids making a judgment or placing a "label" on the other person and is, therefore, less likely to be met with a defensive reaction. For example, a manager practicing supportive communication might say, "You have been late to work three days this week" rather than "You really messed up this time." To engage in descriptive communication does not mean that you ignore the issue at hand; rather, it means that you approach it in a more positive, action-oriented way. For example, a manager engaging in descriptive communication might work through the following stages in a discussion with an employee. First, the manager should describe the event or behavior in objective and verifiable terms (e.g., "We have received two complaints from prominent legislators that your report was late"). Second, the manager should focus on the specific behavior and his or her own reaction, as opposed to attributes of the other person (e.g., "I'm concerned that our credibility with the legislature may be called into question"). Third, the manager should talk about solutions (e.g., "Could you please talk with the two legislators and see exactly what information they need and how we can provide it in a timely manner?") (Whetten & Cameron, 1998, p. 203).

3. Supportive communication is specific, not general. The more specific a statement is, the more helpful it will be. For example, a manager practicing supportive communication might say, "There were three factual errors and five grammatical mistakes in your report" rather than "You are really sloppy." General statements often are extreme and might make the person feel incompetent or insignificant. Under these conditions, there is little reason to expect anything to change. Similarly, you should avoid "either/or" statements (e.g., "Either improve your writing or you'll be assigned less important work"). Both extreme statements and either/or statements reduce the range of possible actions that might be taken to correct the problem and, therefore, reduce the likelihood that anything positive will be done.

4. Supportive communication is conjunctive, not disjunctive. Conjunctive statements clearly relate to what was said previously and move the conversation forward.

Disjunctive statements are not connected and often create a roadblock interfering with effective communication. They tend to be final. For example, a manager practicing supportive communication might say, "Let me try to build on what you just said" rather than "That's not important. Let's move on." Effective communicators recognize that it is important for people to take turns speaking and do not dominate conversations; they want to listen to others, not just to themselves. They also recognize that they need to connect to what was said immediately before or at least to something said earlier in the conversation; they need to maintain a sense of context for their comments. And they recognize that moving to a new topic must be (at least implicitly) agreed to by all parties or else someone might get lost. The shift should not occur too abruptly or appear to be an exercise of control.

5. *Supportive communication is validating, not demeaning.* Supportive communication helps people to feel recognized, understood, accepted, and valued, whereas negative or demeaning comments make people feel inadequate, incompetent, and insecure. A demeaning message or a message expressed in a demeaning tone, even if unintended, can cause serious damage to effective interpersonal relationships. It creates a barrier between people that might remain in place for a long period of time. A supportive communicator might say something like, "I understand your position even if mine is slightly different" rather than "You simply aren't making any sense." There are various types of communications that people consider demeaning. One is taking a superior attitude or giving others the impression that you think you know everything and that they know very little. This may occur through "put-downs" (where the communicator tries to make himself or herself look good by making others look bad) or through "one-upmanship" (where the communicator tries to elevate him- or herself in the eyes of others). But invalidation also can be expressed through rigid communications (i.e., communications that are not open to question), communications that express indifference toward others, or communications that do not acknowledge the feelings and values of others. Validating communication, on the other hand, acknowledges the importance of others, including their feelings and values, and is characterized by respect and flexibility.

6. *Supportive communication is owned, not disowned.* Supportive communication also is owned in the sense that the speaker takes responsibility for what is being said. Someone communicating supportively might say, "I have decided to deny your application" rather than "They have decided to deny your application." Communication that is not owned puts the person receiving the message at a psychological distance from the speaker and inhibits building a strong interpersonal relationship. Communication that is attributed to another person or that is ambiguous with respect to the source of the information also makes it difficult for the receiver to pursue the issue further, and that can be very frustrating.

7. *Supportive communication is two-way, not one-way.* Supportive communication also involves listening carefully and receiving feedback from the other person. A manager practicing supportive communication might say, "That's my understanding of the issue. What's yours?" rather than "Here's my position." Whereas we

discuss specific listening techniques later in this chapter, we should note here that effective listening is essential to receiving accurate feedback, which in turn is essential to supportive communication.

Speaking

Despite the recent dramatic increase in electronic communication, much of the public manager's communication time is spent in face-to-face oral communication, either one-on-one, in relatively small groups, or in presentations to larger audiences. Whereas we will address the question of formal presentations in Chapter 13, there are several helpful guidelines to keep in mind when you are speaking with others. Conversational speaking is particularly useful in situations where immediate feedback is important or where those engaged in the conversation need to "brainstorm" or build on the ideas of others. But where the content of the communication is very lengthy, technical, or complex, using written communication or at least following up a conversation by putting matters in writing may be helpful.

In thinking about oral communication, remember that when you speak, you transmit both rational and emotional messages. For example, regardless of the substance of your message, your tone of voice will send an emotional message to the receiver. If you speak loudly or with the slightest hint of sarcasm, then your message might seem to be angry, regardless of how neutral the actual words you use might be. Similarly, a highly formal or stilted tone will convey a far different emotional message from one delivered in a friendly and good-natured way. Of course, there may be situations in which either of these tones could be appropriate. The trick is to pick the right tone of voice to communicate what you wish to communicate in that particular situation.

Obviously, a great deal of the public manager's communication time is spent imparting information to others or giving directions to others. The key to effective speaking in either case is the ability to put yourself in the position of the person who will receive the information or instructions. Ideally, you want to give exactly the right amount and type of information—neither too much nor too little—but if you depart from the ideal, then giving more information rather than less obviously is more desirable. There are two questions that you can ask in situations such as these. First, what does the other person need to know? Second, what does the other person want to know? (Incidentally, the capacity to put yourself in the position of the other person is an argument for promoting from within. Those who have held lower positions in an organization might have a better understanding of exactly what information is needed by subordinates than those who have not.)

Making sure that your content, tone, and approach fit the situation is aided by being fully attentive to yourself and to others. Often, and especially when we are very busy, we speak carelessly, with little concern for the context of the communication. But to the extent to which we can become sensitive to the thoughts and feelings of others, as well as to our own thoughts and feelings, we will communicate more effectively. Sensitivity to others involves understanding "where they are coming from"; it requires *empathy,* or the capacity to put yourself in the place of others. But it is difficult to be sensitive to others if you are not sensitive to your own needs and desires.

One way in which you can contribute to an organizational culture where people are more willing to reveal their deeper feelings and emotions is through *self-disclosure.* Disclosing to others what you think and how you feel about deep-seated personal matters—those things you like and those you hate, those things that appeal to you and those that scare you, and so on—may help to establish a situation in which others are willing to do the same, thereby making communication easier for all. But there are dangers in self-disclosure. If you try to engage in self-disclosure in a hostile work environment, then your efforts might be seen as inappropriate or even manipulative, causing others to react defensively. Self-disclosure is far easier in a trusting work environment, where it may act to extend trust even further.

Persuasive Communication

A public manager might wish to persuade an audience to accept a particular point of view. A policy analyst might want to persuade a decision-making group, either within the agency or in the legislature, of the soundness of a particular proposal. Or an agency's executive might want to persuade the budget office that a particular item is necessary for the agency to do its job. In any case, the ability to move others to one's position can be tremendously helpful. Again, we may think about persuasive communications in terms of the sender, the character of the message, and the receiver.

Research clearly has shown that the key to effective persuasion is the *credibility* of the source. (Recall from Chapter 7 that a key component of effective leadership is credibility; we suspect that there is a connection.) A sender with strong credibility is more effective in changing the beliefs and attitudes of others than a sender with low credibility (Cherrington, 1994, pp. 537–542; see also Kouzes & Posner, 2003). Credibility, in turn, is aided by two characteristics: expertise and trustworthiness. Someone who is considered an expert will be taken more seriously than someone who is thought to know little about a subject. For example, a research scientist who has extensively studied the effects of tobacco on smokers' health is presumed to know more about that issue than the average person on the street. But the question of trustworthiness may cut in a different direction. In some situations, a person who actually has experienced lung cancer as the result of smoking might be far more persuasive. In general, if the issue is one of facts (e.g., how many smokers die from lung cancer each year), then expertise will be the more important factor in persuasion; if the issue is one of values (e.g., whether people feel better after they stop smoking or even whether they should stop smoking), then the most effective communicator might be one who shares characteristics or experiences with the intended audience.

The character of the message also can affect how persuasive it is. Kipnis and Schmidt (1985) argued that, although we think of persuasive messages as involving rationality and objectivity, there also are emotional elements that enter into the process of persuasion, and these elements can be addressed through either a "hard sell" approach or a "soft sell" approach. The approach that is chosen may depend on several factors. For example, people frequently rely on soft tactics—flattery, praise, acting humble, and so on—when they want something (e.g., time off) from another person, especially from a supervisor. But when they want to persuade the supervisor or to endorse a request for a new piece of equipment, then they are likely to be more rational. In some cases, they might even resort to hard tactics such as going over the supervisor's head. Similarly, tactics depend on the relative power positions of those involved. Kipnis and Schmidt explained,

> The greater the discrepancy in clout between the influencer and the target, the greater the likelihood that hard tactics will be used. At first, most simply request and explain. They turn to demands and threats (the iron fist lurking under the velvet glove of reason) only when someone seems reluctant or refuses to comply. (pp. 45–46)

Finally, people use different approaches based on their expectations about whether they will be successful. When they believe that their requests will be granted, they are likely to use softer tactics; when they anticipate resistance (and when they have power), they use hard tactics. But Kipnis and Schmidt made one other interesting point: The use of hard tactics might indicate a lack of confidence or low self-esteem on the part of the individuals involved. Such people might believe that others will not listen unless they are treated harshly, an assumption that often is self-defeating.

Finally, the effectiveness of an effort at persuasion is affected by characteristics of the receiver. People seem to have a *range of acceptance*—that is, a range within which they are willing to entertain beliefs or attitudes different from their own. Arguments falling in that range often are accepted, but when arguments fall outside of that range, people may well react by moving even further from that position. Similarly, the way in which people process information affects their willingness to accept attempts to persuade. For example, a highly educated audience would be expected to respond to attempts at persuasion in a different manner than would a group with less education. But the results are mixed. Highly intelligent people are more receptive to communications, perhaps because they have a greater range of comprehension. But they also are more resistant to influence, perhaps because they recognize a wide range of counterarguments (Larson, 1992).

Active Listening

Listening is the single most important communication skill, consuming more time than any other aspect of communication. Indeed, as we saw earlier, managers spend as much as 30% to 40% of their time listening. Moreover, listening clearly affects the success of managers. Not only are managers who listen well able to pick up more and better information; they are also likely to encourage and motivate employees, most of whom appreciate managers "who really listen." Yet despite the obvious benefits of listening more carefully, listening has been called the "neglected skill" of management because it is the least practiced and least understood. But studies have shown that managers differ widely in their listening abilities (Brownell, 1990). For example, women are perceived as better listeners than men, younger managers are considered better listeners than older managers, and managers who are new to their current positions are perceived to be better listeners than managers who have been in their positions for longer periods of time. Most important for our purposes, managers who have had training in listening skills and managers who try harder to listen well seem to be perceived as better listeners. This means that there is a good chance that you can improve your listening skills by learning new techniques of listening and by consciously practicing these skills from day to day.

You certainly can improve your listening capacity by being conscious of the barriers to effective communications that we discussed earlier. Beyond that, the conversational role you play can be a much more active one than just hearing what is said. *Active listening* is an approach to listening that involves the one who is on the receiving end of a communication engaging in a series of conscious actions intended to clarify and confirm the meaning of the message being received (Rogers & Farson, 1976). The active listener shows empathy and understanding for the other person and confirms his or her own comprehension of the message by restating what has been said, summarizing major points, and listening not only to the words being said but also to the emotional tone and the accompanying nonverbal cues being transmitted (Knippen & Green, 1994). Active listening can be a central element in an effort to improve your listening skills, an effort that might include the basics shown in Figure 9.5.

Have a reason or purpose for listening. To listen most effectively, you must be motivated to listen. Having a reason or purpose to listen increases your motivation to listen well. One must be motivated to listen; it does not just happen. Think carefully about why it is important that you listen effectively in a particular situation. Is it because this is material that will be on the next test? Because this is material that will help you on the job? At first, the reason or purpose might not be at all clear. If you cannot immediately think of a reason to listen, then search for one. Ask yourself, "How can this information help me do my job better?" or "How can I use this information in some way, either on the job or elsewhere?" Finding a reason or purpose to listen will help you to focus on all of the other principles and techniques listed here.

---

1. Have a reason or purpose for listening.

2. Suspend judgment initially.

3. Resist distractions.

4. Wait before responding.

5. Rephrase what you hear in your own words.

6. Seek important themes.

7. Use the thinking–speaking differential.

Figure 9.5   Principles of Effective Listening

Suspend judgment initially. Earlier, we noted Rogers's suggestion that communication can be improved by avoiding our natural tendency to evaluate. Rogers (1991) counseled that we should try to listen with empathetic understanding—that is, understanding *with* a person rather than *about* the person. "This means seeing the expressed idea and attitude from the other person's point of view, sensing how it feels to the other person, [and] achieving his or her frame of reference about the subject being discussed" (p. 106). Of course, at some point, you might need to evaluate the material that you listen to, but you should first be clear about the complete message. Obviously, this can be very difficult, especially in the public arena, where policies and positions are hotly debated. For example, during an election year, if we know a candidate's party, then we are likely to evaluate what the candidate is going to say before he or she even begins speaking. But effective communication requires listening to the message fully and completely before judging or responding.

Resist distractions. As we noted earlier, there are many things that can distract us as we try to communicate with others, but those distractions can be resisted. Some distractions are a part of the environment. For example, a noise outside the window, such as a fire truck or an ambulance going by, or simply the voices of others talking in the same room, may well interfere with effective communications. But the distraction might be closer to home, as in the case of trying to listen to someone who has mustard on his or her coat; seeing the mustard might draw our attention away from what is being said. Similarly, there might be something unusual about the way in which the speaker talks; the speaker might have a particularly raspy voice or speak with an unfamiliar accent. Regardless of the source of the distraction, the answer is to try to increase your concentration. By increasing your concentration, you can resist distractions that you would have thought were impossible to overcome. This principle is especially important as people from different cultures and even different countries are brought together in work situations. Even if everyone in a group speaks English, there likely will be variations in accents and figures of speech that make some speech difficult to follow. In effect, hearing an unfamiliar accent becomes a distraction. But simply concentrating harder on what is being said often will help considerably. In addition, using the speaking–thinking differential (discussed later) may permit you to recognize unusual figures of speech. But the key is concentration.

Wait before responding. There is a strong tendency to respond to someone's statement before he or she is finished, especially if you believe that you already have received the gist of the person's message. This can occur in a couple of ways. First, even while the person is still talking, you begin to formulate your response, and if the person continues talking long enough, then you may begin to practice your response in your head. Second, you may simply interrupt the other person and state your opinion. The "response" principle suggests that, in either case, you relax and wait for the natural opportunity to speak instead of jumping into the conversation immediately. When you are overly eager to contribute to a conversation, you become so excited about your own anticipated contribution that you tune out the other person. You stop concentrating on what the other person is saying. The response principle suggests that you wait for an appropriate opportunity to respond. Try to flow with the conversation as an event rather than disrupting it by speaking prematurely.

Rephrase what you listen to in your own words. This is a key principle of active listening—that you occasionally take time to restate or paraphrase what you understand the other person to have said before making your own contribution. You might say, "What I understand you to be saying is that the budget projections are incorrect because the initial information was compromised." By restating the other person's comments without evaluation, you almost have to enter into the person's frame of reference and to understand the context of his or her comments. Moreover, if your understanding of these comments is inconsistent with the person's intended meaning, then he or she will have a chance to try to clarify that meaning. Finally, taking time to clarify the meaning of communication in this way tends to reduce the emotional level of the conversation and allows more reasoned communication. Obviously, to restate or paraphrase every statement in a conversation produces a very stilted and awkward conversation, although it is an extremely good exercise. Moreover, this type of immediate feedback to another person can be threatening to both parties because what they hear might make them change. But if used judiciously and accompanied by comments that let the other person know exactly what you are doing (e.g., "Just so I'm sure I understand your position, let me try to state my understanding"), this aspect of active listening can be extremely helpful. A variation of this approach is to use a third party who can listen with understanding to each party to the communication—each person or group—and then clarify the views and attitudes of each. Rogers (1991) summarizes the benefits of this approach in this way:

> Gradually, communication grows. It leads to a situation in which I see how the problem appears to you as well as to me, and you see how it appears to me as well as to you. Thus accurately and realistically defined, the problem is almost certain to yield to intelligent attack, or if it is in part insoluble, it will be comfortably accepted as such. (p. 107)

Seek the important themes. This principle suggests that listening for the main ideas in a message is more important than listening for specific facts. Understanding the major themes of the message gives you a framework for organizing the facts, thereby making the facts themselves easier to remember. For example, research has shown that students who listen for the main ideas in a lecture are more likely to receive better grades than those who merely listen for the facts. Apparently, it is much easier to fit specifics into the "big picture" than to construct the big picture based only on a few facts.

Use the thinking–speaking differential. People think much faster than they speak. Although the rates vary by region, people in the United States speak at a rate of about 150 words per minute. But they think at a rate of about 500 words a minute, more than three times as fast as they speak. This differential can offer a temptation to do things that interfere with effective listening, such as daydreaming, thinking about something completely apart from the conversation, and practicing your response in advance. But it also can provide an opportunity to listen more effectively. Most important, it provides the opportunity to reflect on what the other person is saying and to try to find the major themes or meanings in his or her comments. Although the speaking–thinking differential can be used improperly to prepare for your own speaking, when it is used for more careful listening, it can be a great help in understanding what others are saying.

Nonverbal Communication

Nonverbal communication, or *body language,* sends messages that are every bit as important as those transmitted orally or in writing. Any movement of your body can communicate something to the outside world and may do so more honestly than your spoken words. For example, a person frowning might be displaying disapproval, and someone folding his or her arms might be indicating withdrawal. Obviously, someone who is good at reading body language receives a more complete message than someone who is not. But you have to be careful not to react to just a single clue or to read too much into someone's body language. For example, the frown might just mean that the person has a headache, and some people do just like to fold their arms.

Nonverbal communication is becoming an especially important topic as people from different cultures interact more frequently but have different culturally approved ways of expressing themselves nonverbally (Nahavandi & Malekzadeh, 1999, pp. 421–425). For example, facial expressions and eye contact (*occulesics*) and body language (*kinesics*) vary widely from culture to culture. People from North America and Europe tend to maintain eye contact when speaking with others, whereas people from Asia avoid eye contact (especially if they are speaking with people of higher status). People in the West consider eye contact a sign of honesty and openness, whereas people in the East consider it a lack of respect. Similarly, animated hand gestures are commonplace in more emotionally expressive cultures, whereas they are considered overly emotional or even disrespectful in more restrained cultures. And, of course, specific gestures might mean quite different things in different places. For example, for many people, holding two fingers upright symbolizes "victory" or "peace," whereas in England and Australia doing so with the palm and fingers facing inward means "up yours!" (Axtell, 1991, pp. 51–52).

Similarly, variations in the ways in which we speak (*paralinguistics*)—in our tone of voice or in its pitch, expression, or rate of speed—have an effect on our credibility. We tend to respond more positively when someone speaks in a clear and confident tone and at a moderate speed. But again, there are cultural differences affecting the use of paralinguistics. For example, North Americans and Australians tend to talk more loudly and with greater apparent confidence than the more quiet and self-effacing Thai or Japanese. Similar differences might exist between men and women. For example, Tannen (2001) argued that "women speak and hear a language of connection and intimacy, while men speak and hear a language of status and independence" (p. 42), and this leads to different conversational styles or dialects.

Proxemics refers to the use of space and distance between people; the type of relationship we have with others determines to what extent we let them encroach on our *personal space*. According to Hall (1966, pp. 108–122), in the United States, the intimate zone extends out almost 2 feet and is reserved for close family and friends. The personal zone goes out to about 4 feet and is accessible to other friends and more distant family members. Social distance extends 7 to 12 feet and is where most social interaction takes place. Public distance, or the distance we tend to maintain in the presence of major public figures, is somewhere between 12 and 30 feet. In any of these cases, if you stand too close you might be considered intrusive or rude; if you stand too far away, you might be considered distant or shy.

Again, there are important cultural differences. In general, people from Latin America, the Middle East, and southern Europe tolerate close social distances more than do people from North America and Asia. For example, if a Saudi talking with a German starts inching closer, then the German will tend to back away (Nahavandi & Malekzadeh, 1999, pp. 422–423). Similar cross-cultural differences are found with respect to timing and scheduling. For example, Europeans will schedule fewer events in the same time period and will reserve more time for interpersonal relationships than will Americans (Hall, 1966, p. 124).

Finally, touching behaviors (*tactiles*) are an important part of communication. But the social and cultural rules governing when touching is considered appropriate are extremely complex. "The basic meaning of touch is that an interpersonal bond is being offered or established. . . . However, touch also carries the implication of invasion of privacy" (Argyle, 1988, p. 226). Touch can express warmth, but touch also can express dominance. In fact, in many organizations, those with power are more likely to touch than those with less power. More generally, touching clearly is permitted, or even encouraged, in greetings and farewells, in congratulations, and in certain ceremonies. But touch that implies sexual intimacy is entirely inappropriate in the workplace and may lead to charges of sexual harassment. Once again, there also are cultural differences. Those from Latin America and the Middle East seem more comfortable touching others than do the English and the Japanese. But even here, touching typically occurs between those of the same gender and social status (Nahavandi & Malekzadeh, 1999, p. 425). Clearly, touch must be initiated with great care and very clear meaning.

Electronic Communication

Obviously, communication in public organizations, as elsewhere, has been dramatically affected by new forms of electronic communication. The emergence of electronic mail (e-mail), voice mail, facsimile (fax), computer conferencing, audio- and videoconferencing, management information systems, group decisions support systems, local and wide-area networks, and the Internet have revolutionized organizational communication. These new forms of communication have certain advantages over older forms. They typically are much faster. They allow communication among geographically dispersed people and permit information to be "broadcast" to many people at once. They have much greater capacities for memory, storage, and retrieval. And they permit asynchronous communication—that is, communication that occurs at different points in time.

There are, however, a number of questions that have been raised about how these new technologies will affect human communication in organizations. For example, O'Connell (1988) developed the following six hypotheses about the influence of electronic technology on communication in organizations:

1. Opportunities for face-to-face contact will be diminished, and information from nonverbal cues will be reduced. Consequently, opportunities for random spontaneous information sharing will be reduced.

2. More informal messages and "short-circuiting of the hierarchy will occur. . . ." Organization structure and formal information flow will be redefined.

3. Messages of affect and value will decrease. Ambiguity in interpreting information will increase. Managers will have to seek new ways of communicating the affective component of messages.

4. Trust develops with shared experience, values, give-and-take, and the result of human communication. Satellites, electronic mail, and networks could reduce the dimensions of trust to which we are accustomed.

5. The computer imposes a discipline of linear thinking. Organizations . . . will need to find ways to encourage and protect nonlinear thinking and communicating.

6. Expectations of work performance may be machine driven. Employees in some organizations will perceive this as dehumanizing and coercive. (pp. 480–481)

SOURCE: From "Human Communication in the High Tech Office," by S. E. O'Connell, in *Handbook of Organizational Communication* (pp. 480–481), by G. M. Goldhaber and G. A. Barnett (Eds.), Norwood, NJ: Ablex Publishing. © 1988 by Ablex Publishing. Reprinted with permission of Greenwood Publishing Group, Inc., Westport, CT.

Certainly, electronic forms of communication create the possibility of flattening organizations. In the past, a line employee wishing to make a proposal to his or her city manager would have to go through several levels of the organization (and numerous secretaries and administrative assistants) just to get an appointment. Today, that same employee can simply send an e-mail to the city manager and attach the proposal. Not only does this process avoid the delays and confusion of messages that move up the hierarchy, but it also establishes a record of accountability. Use of e-mail in this way may dramatically change organizational structures, reporting relationships, and communication with clients and citizens.

One other question that has been raised about electronic communication is where such communication will fit into the array of channels available to managers to communicate with their employees. That is, which channel of communication would be best for reminding employees of a meeting as opposed to, say, settling a dispute between members of a group? To address this question, Daft and Lengel (1984) suggested that organizational communication tasks vary in their levels of *ambiguity* (i.e., the existence of multiple or conflicting interpretations) and that communication channels vary in terms of (a) the availability of instant feedback, (b) the use of multiple cues, (c) the use of natural language, and (d) the personal focus on the medium. Those communication channels that have all or many of these attributes are called *rich* media, whereas those that have few are called *lean* media. On a continuum of media richness, face-to-face communication would be considered most rich, and impersonal media (e.g., flyers, computer-generated reports) would be considered most lean. Between these endpoints, from rich to lean, would be telephone, e-mail, and personal written communication. Daft and Lengel claimed that managers who are able to match the level of ambiguity with the right type of communication channel will be most successful. So, when facing a highly ambiguous issue, the manager would choose the richest possible medium.

But other theorists have pointed out that messages contain both data and symbols, and managers must consider both aspects in selecting communication channels. For example, the manager who needs to remind employees of a meeting faces a relatively unambiguous task and might choose e-mail for the reminder. But the manager might believe that daily interpersonal contact is important because of the strong symbolic value of face-to-face communication and might, therefore, choose to visit each employee to remind him or her of the meeting (Miller, 1999, p. 285). At this point, it appears that managers must not simply choose electronic media because they carry information quickly and easily; managers need to keep the symbolic importance of other, more traditional forms of communication in mind.

Specialized Forms of Communication

There are several specialized forms of communication that those entering the public service will do well to consider. In this section, we review several of these: personal counseling, conducting effective meetings, and writing memos, reports, and proposals.

Personal Counseling

Occasionally, you might find it necessary to discuss work problems with individual employees. You might notice a decrease in an employee's performance or productivity. The employee might be in violation of a rule or policy. There might be conflict with other employees. Or you might just suspect that personal problems are negatively affecting the employee's work. For example, the employee might be exhibiting increased tardiness, absenteeism, increased use of sick days, irritability, increased or decreased talkativeness, depression, or signs of substance abuse (DeVoe, 1999b, p. 92). These types of cases call for employee counseling. "Counseling is the continuous process of monitoring employee performance and behavior and of identifying and addressing problems by determining and implementing courses of action through one-to-one communication with affected employees" (McConnell, 1997, p. 77).

The primary purpose of counseling is to address work-related issues at an early stage so as to prevent their growing and further affecting the work of the organization, although occasionally counseling may involve assisting an employee in addressing outside problems that might be affecting his or her work. In any case, the hope is that through counseling the employee's behavior will be changed so that he or she once again becomes a productive member of the organization. There can be several objectives of counseling: (a) to correct performance problems before they escalate, (b) to motivate employees toward more effective performance, (c) to provide guidance in areas such as career counseling and retirement planning, and (d) to provide assistance or, better yet, referrals to employees who reveal personal concerns affecting their work. Importantly, counseling should address problems as early as possible. "Employee counseling should be considered primarily preventive in nature. Its primary purpose is to identify and correct problems before they reach crisis proportions and require possible drastic action" (McConnell, 1997, p. 82).

Before conducting the counseling session with the employee, collect all the facts so that you are clear on the specific problem, who is involved, when, where, and so on. You may even want to prepare notes so that you can keep the details straight and keep the conversation focused. You should meet with the employee as soon as possible after the problem has been identified, but do not rush through the meeting and do not hold the meeting if you are angry. Take time to calm down before starting the conversation. During the conversation, try to keep the discussion focused on the specific problem with which you are concerned. The employee, quite naturally, might want to deflect the blame or shift the focus of attention to someone else.

If a personal problem is revealed, then do not let it shift the focus of the meeting. Stay work centered.

> What an employee does or is involved in outside of work is—legally—none of the supervisor's business. The only aspect that does become the supervisor's business is the effect the outside circumstances have on performance; that is, the supervisor must deal exclusively with the job performance issues and stay clear of inquiring into whatever difficulty the employee may be experiencing external to the organization. (McConnell, 1997, p. 80)

In dealing with personal concerns that do arise, you certainly should be sympathetic, but not so sympathetic that the work issues are ignored. Where it is necessary and appropriate, you should provide referrals to the employee assistance program or other sources of help. But remember that it is the employee's responsibility to take care of whatever personal issues are affecting his or her performance (Cook, 1989, p. 5).

In any case, be as specific and clear as possible. For example, state the problem in explicit and factual terms. Instead of just saying, "You've been abusing the sick leave policy," you might say, "You left work early last Monday because you said you hurt your back, but you were later seen dancing at Club Tango." Specify exactly what is expected of the employee and what actions will result if the employee does not meet expectations. Naturally, you should be consistent, applying the same approach and expectations to each employee. Establish a follow-up meeting or plan, and then summarize what was accomplished and agreed on. After the meeting, you might want to document in writing what occurred in the meeting and what was agreed on. "Properly written counseling ensures a supervisor strong grounds if it becomes necessary to fend off a union grievance or court case" (Cook, 1989, p. 4). And remember to follow through with what was agreed on. Following these guidelines will make your counseling sessions much more productive—and comfortable.

Conducting Effective Meetings

Meetings have developed an awful reputation. People see most meetings as dragging on endlessly and accomplishing little (if anything). By some recent estimates, the average manager spends the equivalent of about 20 weeks a year in meetings—and 6 weeks worth are a complete waste of time (Sandwith, 1992, p. 29). Think about the typical meeting. The meeting is set for 9 A.M., but people drift in slowly and nothing begins until about 10 or 15 minutes later. The person conducting the meeting, who we will call Belinda, makes a short speech about how she knows that everyone is busy but reminds everyone that having meetings like this is very important. Then she starts through a list of loosely connected bits and pieces of information, often interrupted by silly questions and unrelated comments. Soon the conversation begins to drift as people try to work their own "agendas." There are frequent disagreements, some of which get a little personal, but nothing ever seems to be resolved. Finally, Belinda gets a message from her secretary and leaves the room to return a call. By the time she returns, most of those in attendance have slipped away, and most who have remained are deeply involved in conversations about topics ranging from the lottery, to cable television, to the latest online auction. Belinda, feeling frustrated about the whole thing, throws up her hands and says, "Well, that's all for today." Those in the room think to themselves, "It's about time."

Fortunately, meetings actually can be productive, or even inspiring, although it takes a person with great skills to move a group successfully through the many pitfalls of "meeting behavior." It helps, at the outset, to have a good idea of what meetings actually are all about. Most meetings, of course, have goals or objectives—information to be transmitted, problems to be solved, assignments to be worked out, and so on. Meeting these *functional* purposes can build the competence of the group and move the larger organization in a positive direction. But meetings also serve *symbolic* purposes. The purposes to be achieved and the way in which the meetings are run both send messages to employees. They help to establish norms and values, as well as communication patterns, that continue to develop even after the meetings are over (Sandwith, 1992, p. 30). If the people conducting meetings are attentive to both the functional and symbolic purposes of the meetings, then great things can be accomplished and people can leave with an even greater commitment to the organization and its work.

There actually are some specific steps that you can take to make a meeting both more productive and more meaningful. First, you should decide whether the meeting is even necessary. If a memo or an e-mail would accomplish the same or better results, then you should choose one of those avenues. Second, if you decide to hold the meeting, then develop a clear purpose for the meeting and communicate that purpose to those who will attend. Keep the purpose of the meeting clear and do not try to accomplish more than should be expected in the time allocated for the meeting. Keep the meeting focused on a few key objectives and be clear in advance about how long the meeting will take or, better yet, exactly when it will end. Third, develop an agenda, seeking suggestions from others about what should be on the agenda. (Sometimes it is helpful to rank items in terms of importance so that you are sure you will have time for the most important items.) Distribute the agenda in advance so that participants can think about the topics, form their own ideas, and prepare for any material they will be expected to present or comment on. Be clear with individuals about what they will be expected to bring to the meeting or to do in the meeting.

When the meeting time arrives, you already should be there and should start on time. "Waiting for latecomers only communicates to those who are punctual that you don't value their time and that it doesn't pay to be punctual" (Group, 1997, p. 77). As you go through the meeting, you should stick carefully to the agenda and keep the focus of the conversations on the topics at hand. Try to control interruptions and "side conversations." You should try to prevent one or two people from monopolizing the meeting time and instead should attempt to solicit comments from everyone in attendance. Remember that people who are asked to participate in decision making are likely to feel better about the meeting and also are more likely to help implement the resulting decisions. Although meetings often must focus on very serious topics, if the situation allows, try to maintain some informality. Some social conversations and informal discussions can be helpful in building the spirit of the group. And, of course, give people the chance to be funny. "The ability to identify the humor or absurdity of a situation is a wonderful way to maintain energy and build group camaraderie. Sharing funny stories and anecdotes about work-related subjects is a terrific way to build bridges of understanding among meeting participants" (Hawkins, 1999, p. 57).

When you have accomplished the objectives of the meeting, it is time to end the meeting. On the other hand, if the time you told people the meeting would end gets close, then you should either poll the attendees to see whether they can continue for a few more minutes or adjust the agenda to end at the time you said. At the end of the meeting, it might be helpful to summarize what has been accomplished and exactly what the next steps will be. (This also can be done at the end of each individual item on the agenda.) "A truly effective meeting ends conclusively. Progress has been made on some issues; other issues have been completely resolved" (Sandwith, 1992, p. 31). Summarize the progress you have made, remind participants of assignments they have received, and (if appropriate) tell people when the next meeting will be. After the meeting, prepare and distribute the minutes as soon as possible so that people will be reminded of what they are supposed to do next. Hopefully, people will look back on the meeting with a feeling of accomplishment and pride and will give you credit for conducting a good meeting.

The Power of Dialogue

Recently a great deal of attention has been given to the idea of dialogue as a special case of group and intergroup communications. Dialogic processes have been tried in a variety of settings, from schools to businesses to public and nonprofit orga-nizations. Dialogue has examined natural resources issues, development assistance, border concerns, multiethnic conflicts, and community development plans, among other topics. The idea of dialogue is often contrasted with other forms of commu-nications. To get a clearer understanding of what makes dialogue special, Daniel Yankelovich (quoted in Roberts, 2002, p. 7) contrasts dialogue with debate and dis-cussion. In debate, people counter arguments with other arguments in order to win "points." Each claims their view of the world is right and the other is wrong. In dia-logue, participants work toward a mutual understanding. They listen carefully and try to explore the special meanings that others bring to the table. Similarly, discus-sion tends to emphasize differences rather than commonalities. Yankelovich suggests that true dialogue can only occur where participants feel equal and not coerced, where they listen empathetically, and where they probe assumptions.

Roberts makes a similar distinction among solving problems by competitive strategies, authoritative strategies, or collaborative strategies. The most complex problems we face today are characterized by the fact that we not only can't agree on a solution. We can't even agree on what the problem is. We can compete, we can sub-mit to authority, or we can collaborate. The process of dialogue is intended to achieve collaboration. Through a series of carefully guided (facilitated) phases, par-ticipants in the dialogue are encouraged to listen and really hear, to try to understand differences rather than magnify them, and to build relationships of trust and respect. Dialogue, then, is "the co-creation of new meaning through mutual understanding and reciprocal communications between two or more parties" (Roberts, 2002, p. 6).

While there are many ways in which dialogues can be structured, ranging from small to very large groups, from situations that are strictly conversational to those mediated by technology, there are some typical patterns to dialogues:

1. Dialogue is a process, not an event.

2. Dialogue is about relationship building and thoughtful engagement about difficult issues.

3. Dialogue requires an extensive commitment.

4. Dialogue takes place face-to-face.

5. Dialogue takes place best in an atmosphere of confidentiality, and issues of sponsorship and context are important to its success.

6. Dialogues often focus on race, but they also address multiple issues of social identity that extend beyond race.

7. Dialogue focuses on both intergroup conflict and community building.

8. Dialogues are led by skilled facilitators.

9. Dialogue is about inquiry and understanding and the integration of content and process.

10. Dialogue involves talking, but taking actions often leads to good talking, and dialogue often leads to action (Schoem, Sevis, Chester, & Sumida, 2001, pp. 6–14).

Writing Memos, Reports, and Proposals

Public administrators often are called on to produce memos, reports, and other forms of written communication ranging from proposals to personnel evaluations. You might be called on to develop a written analysis of a policy proposal. You might be asked to write a grant proposal. Or you might be asked to develop a lengthy memo laying out the circumstances under which an employee received disciplinary action. In any of these cases, your ability to write clearly and communicate effectively will be tested.

Writing memos or reports is different from giving oral communications for several reasons. Obviously, in written communications you cannot use gestures or a special tone of voice to convey your intent, and the audience cannot ask questions of you (at least initially). For these reasons, written communication may be more difficult. On the other hand, as we noted earlier, written communication has the advantage of greater permanence. What you write will remain "on the record" for a longer period of time than oral comments, so people can come back to your writing to check what you said. Written documents can be saved, duplicated, distributed, filed, retained, and referred to later. But your audience is likely to have higher standards for written communication.

> When you speak, the people around you know the circumstances and take them into account. They know you don't have the time to organize what you want to say, to choose the right words. When you write, you've got the time— or at least people around you assume you've got more time. (Sparks, 1999, p. x)

Others will expect better organization, more accurate information, and clearer expression. These considerations make style and clarity especially important in report writing or any other form of written communication.

Writing requires several basic steps. You must know exactly who your audience is and be clear about the purpose of what you are writing. Are you trying to communicate the facts in an objective fashion, or are you trying to persuade someone to adopt your position? Also, you must research the topic thoroughly and gather all of the information needed to meet your purpose. What do you need to know to communicate your message? Then you must organize your material into an outline. "A fragmented approach results in a disjointed report; you may be in danger of emphasizing the areas you found most interesting while neglecting other, equally important issues" (Hearty & Oakes, 1986, p. 87). Once you have carefully organized your material, you are ready to begin writing.

Effective writing takes years of study and practice, but there are a number of guidelines that you can follow to improve your writing. For example, Sussman and Depp (1984) offered six rules for effective managerial writing, what they called the "six C's." The six C's provide a useful way of organizing our discussion of guidelines for good writing.

Clarity. To be clear, you must put yourself in the reader's position. Write in the active voice (e.g., "Dave painted the house") rather than the passive voice (e.g., "The house was painted by Dave"), and use the positive form rather than the negative form (e.g., "Lucy is happy" rather than "Lucy isn't sad"). Avoid jargon, and use simple words wherever possible. "Avoid the four- or five-syllable word when one or two syllables convey the idea just as well" (Venolia, 1998, p. 86). On the other hand, be sure to use the most precise word available to convey your meaning. Remember that government memos are noted for their jargon and obfuscation; do not contribute to that impression.

Courtesy. Courtesy involves knowing your readers, adapting to their mood, and writing at their level, providing neither too much nor too little information.

Conciseness. This is the rule of brevity; be short and to the point. For example, be specific by saying "pizza" rather than "food" or by saying "golden retriever" instead of "pet." Be concrete by saying "Absenteeism was reduced by 40% when the company built an employee gym and offered child care services" rather than "The new health and family programs improved employee performance" (Venolia, 1998, p. 85). Sometimes you might want to repeat something for emphasis, but remember the following general rule: The shorter, the better. Think of it this way: Which are you more likely to read, a 50-word memo or a 10-page report? You are likely to read the 50-word memo on the spot, whereas the 10-page report will go into the pile that you will "get to when you can."

Confidence. Always write with confidence. Confidence really is a matter of judgment on the writer's part, based on the writer's knowledge of his or her readers. Judgment is especially important in avoiding two extremes: being overbearing (too confident) or being wishy-washy (not confident enough).

Correctness. You must be correct in grammar and composition—the technical rules of writing that include spelling and punctuation. Inaccurate spelling is especially conspicuous. Proofread carefully for proper spelling, grammar, and punctuation. These technical details can completely obscure your meaning so that your message is lost. (And remember that your computer's spell-checker does not know, for example, whether you meant "their" or "there." You might have correctly spelled the wrong word.) If possible, ask someone else to look over the report before submitting it.

Conversational tone. To achieve a conversational tone, try to write in the same way as you talk, and try to imagine one specific person to whom you are writing. As Strunk and White (1979) advised, "Write in a way that comes naturally" (p. 70). Thinking of a specific individual rather than an abstract category makes it much easier to write. It is much easier to write to John Jones than to "all economics professors." Occasionally, conversational writing calls for violating some formal rules of grammar, but this breach often makes things smoother and, therefore, more understandable and easier to follow.

You also should be attentive to creating a neat and orderly final product. No matter how well your report or proposal is written, if it is presented in a sloppy manner, then it will not communicate effectively. Keep your paragraphs relatively short, typically between four and eight sentences. Avoid excessive use of italics and capital letters that may clutter your presentation. And be careful in your use of graphics and visuals. Use visuals only when they will enhance readers' understanding of the material. Choose the appropriate visual (e.g., graph, table) and place it close to the text that corresponds to it.

One final consideration is to avoid bias in the language that you are using. Venolia (1998, p. 92) suggested four guidelines in this regard. First, do not mention race, gender, age, or disability unless it is pertinent. Second, avoid stereotypes and labels that reveal bias. Third, give parallel treatment (e.g., "Mr. Waxman and Ms. Stone," not "Mr. Waxman and Linda"). Fourth, find substitutes for words that may be considered insensitive or confusing, such as masculine pronouns. Again, asking someone else to review your work will help to catch errors that might creep into your writing. In all cases, being sensitive to the needs and concerns of those who constitute your audience is the key to effective writing.

Exploring Diversity and Intercultural Communication

One of the clear trends in today's public organizations is the increasing diversity of the workplace. That trend is augmented by the emergence of a global society in which the capacity for cross-cultural communications is greater than ever. In this section, we explore both of these trends and then suggest some ways in which individuals can become more culturally aware and organizations can more effectively serve people from different cultural backgrounds. (See Estlund, 2003; Mor Barak, 2005; and Konrad, Prasad, & Pringle, 2006.)

Clearly, the demographics of the workforce are rapidly changing and altering the labor market and the pool of employees for the public and private sectors. *Workforce 2000* (Johnston & Packer, 1987), a report commissioned by the U.S. Department of Labor, outlined anticipated changes in the work environment such as the globalization of markets, the growth of the service sector, technological advances, and demographic shifts in the labor force. This report projected that minorities and immigrants would become an ever larger share of the labor force. It is estimated that over the next 10 to 15 years the labor market will become smaller, older, and significantly more diverse. Only 15% of new entrants into the job market will be native-born White males, although this group traditionally has accounted for 47%. People of color will constitute 29% of the future workforce, women 42%, and immigrants 22%. The workplace will include a diverse group of individuals differing in gender, age, race, religion, and ethnicity.

Somewhat to their surprise, managers are finding that increasing diversity is a quite positive development. A human resources executive explained,

> We have learned that cultivating differences in our workforce is a key competitive advantage for our company. The differences among people of various racial, ethnic, and cultural backgrounds generate creativity and innovation as well as energy in our workforce. Differences between men and women, [when] managed well, have similar benefits. (quoted in Bureau of National Affairs, 1986, p. 93)

A *Harvard Business Review* article on diversity was even more specific in addressing the question of why organizations should encourage greater diversity. The article pointed out that, until recently, the answer to that question was simply that discrimination is wrong, both legally and morally. Today's managers are voicing a second notion—that a more diverse workforce will increase their organizations' effectiveness.

> It will lift morale, bring greater access to new segments of the marketplace, and enhance productivity. It is our belief that there is a distinct way to unleash the powerful benefits of a diverse workforce. Although these benefits include increased profitability, they go beyond financial measures to encompass learning, creativity, flexibility, organizational and individual growth, and the ability of a company to adjust rapidly and successfully to market changes. (Thomas & Ely, 1996, p. 79)

We also are experiencing the effects of globalization as we have greater and more significant interactions with people from all around the world. The emerging global economy, as well as the increasing interdependencies among nations with respect to issues such as environmental quality, means that public administrators increasingly will engage with those from other cultures. In so doing, they will need to be sensitive to the important cultural differences among nations. Famed anthropologist Edward Hall (1959, 1976) said that "culture is communication and communication is culture, so a multicultural world requires better understanding among the individuals and the groups who nurture different "symbols, heroes, rituals, and values" (Hofstede & Hofstede, 2005, p. 6). "The main problem is not the presence of these cultural diversities, but the way to deal with them in intercultural communication" (Baraldi, 2005, p. 65). Intercultural communication is complex because it includes learning new and "different kinds of human activity" (Hall, 1976, p. 61).

An important part of understanding a different culture is learning how things are organized and how one goes about learning them in *that* culture. But intercultural communication also requires unlearning. "As soon as certain patterns of thinking, feeling, and acting have established themselves within a person's mind, he or she must unlearn these before being able to learn something different, and unlearning is more difficult than learning for the first time" (Hofstede & Hofstede, 2005, p. 3). As public administrators, we will need to interact effectively with people from many different places and do so in a manner that respects their cultures as well as our own. That will require learning and unlearning.

Learning Cultural Awareness

Given these trends, public managers would be well advised to increase their cultural awareness and sensitivity. Learning about culture begins with cultural self-awareness. Yet according to Stewart and Bennett (1991, p. x), cultural self-awareness is not always easy since culture is internalized patterns of thinking and behaving that are believed to be natural (or simply the way things are). Awareness of their subjective culture is particularly difficult for Americans since they often interpret cultural factors as characteristics of individual personality. This view of internalized cultural patterns, disregarding their social origins, is a characteristic of American culture. It is not a universal point of view.

Bennett (1993) described the cognitive changes that occur as we change our frame of reference by distinguishing between ethnocentric thinking and ethnorelative thinking (Figure 9.6). In typical ethnocentric thinking, culturally different behavior is assessed in relation to one's own cultural standards. In ethnorelative thinking, "cultures can only be understood relative to one another, and particular behavior can only be understood within a cultural context. Cultural difference is neither good nor bad; it is just different" (Bennett, 1993, p. 26). People who are able to make this shift increase their ability to empathize and experience greater ease in adapting to changes in organizations and in dealing with those from other cultures. Realizing that behavior, values, and identity are not absolute but rather constructed by culture frees one to more fully appreciate the ongoing process of living life (Diller, 1999). These skills not only transform how we think but also prepare us for working more effectively with our culturally different colleagues.

Increasing Cultural Competence

Public managers increasingly are engaging with people from many different cultures, both in this country and abroad. In so doing, these managers are coming to recognize that they need to make important adjustments in their normal way of doing things so as to operate effectively in a cross-cultural context. The capacity for doing so sometimes is called "cultural competence," a "set of congruent behaviors, attitudes, and policies that come together in a system, [in an] agency, or among professionals and enable that system, [that] agency, or those professionals to work effectively in cross-cultural situations" (Cross, Bazron, Dennis, & Isaacs, 1989, p. 13). Moving to cultural competence is hard emotional work that involves shifts

Ethnocentric Characteristic	Ethnorelative Characteristic
Denial: Individual denies that a cultural difference exists	*Acceptance:* Individual recognizes and values cultural differences without evaluating them as positive or negative
Defense: Individual acknowledges the existence of certain cultural difference as threatening to his or her reality	*Adaptation:* Individual develops and improves skills for interacting and communicating with people from other cultures
Minimization: Individual acknowledges cultural differences but trivializes them, believing that human similarities far outweigh any differences	*Integration:* Individual not only values a variety of cultures but constantly defines his or her own identity and evaluates behavior

Figure 9.6   Characteristics of Ethnocentrism Versus Ethnorelativism

SOURCE: Adapted from "Towards Ethnorelativism: A Developmental Model of Intercultural Sensitivity," by M. Bennett, in *Education for the Intercultural Experience* (pp. 21–71), by R. M. Paige (Ed.), 1993, Yarmouth, ME: Intercultural Press. Used with permission.

in awareness and attitudes as well as the development of new skills. Cross and colleagues identified five basic skills areas necessary for effective cross-cultural service delivery.

Awareness and acceptance of differences. Cultural differences exist in values, styles of communication, the perception of time, the meaning of health, community, and so on, and managers must become aware of those differences. But equally critical is to be accepting of those differences (Diller, 1999). It is no surprise that cultural values that are at odds with our own will be the most difficult to accept. For example, punctual northern Europeans might have difficulty in accepting the tardiness of more flexible and inexact cultures. Accepting individuals are able to broaden their perspective so as to understand that the simultaneous existence of differing realities requires neither comparison nor judgment. Further along the continuum, one is able not only to accept differences but also to value them for the richness, perspective, and complexity they offer.

For example, Hall (1976) describes high-context and low-context cultures, based on the way in which information is perceived and transmitted by those from different cultures. In Hall's model, people from high-context cultures rely on nonverbal communication more than on verbal or written communication.

> A high-context communication or message is one in which most of the information is either in the physical context, or internalized in the person, while very little is in the coded, explicit, transmitted part of the message. A low-context communication is just the opposite; i.e., the mass of the information is vested in the explicit code. (p. 79)

Moreover, people from high-context cultures do not speak openly, but they expect to be understood. They would not tell directly what bothers them, but when talking they would still expect their peers to realize what the problem is. Obviously, those from different cultural orientations would have difficulty communicating effectively. Imagine the problems as people from Western cultures, such as the United States, Germany, and Scandinavia, which are predominantly low context, attempt to communicate with those from Eastern cultures such as China, Japan, or Turkey, which are high context.

Further, Hall extends his model to difference in the temporal orientation of different cultures, distinguishing monochronic time, or M-time, and polychronic time, or P-time. P-people (polychronic), who tend to belong to high-context cultures, are almost never alone, and they prefer to do more than one activity at a certain point in time. M-people, most likely to be found in low-context cultures, are individualists, appreciate punctuality, exactness, and scheduling, and prefer to do only one activity at a time. Again, imagine the difficulties as those from different cultural orientations attempt to communicate.

Self-awareness. It is necessary to be in touch with one's own culture to appreciate the impact of culture on the lives of others. Culture is the glue that gives shape to life experience, promoting certain values and experiences as optimal and defining what is possible (Diller, 1999, p. 14). Yet according to Cross (1988, p. 2), many people never acknowledge how their day-to-day behaviors have been shaped by cultural norms and values and reinforced by families, peers, and social institutions. How one defines family, identifies desirable life goals, views problems, and even says hello are all influenced by the culture in which one functions.

For example, have you ever noticed the differences between the ways in which Latinos and Anglos greet each other?

Dynamics of differences. This notion requires knowing what can go wrong in cross-cultural communication and how to get it right. Cultural miscommunication has two general sources. The first is related to past experiences that we have had with members of a group or the nature of current political relations between the two groups. The second involves differences in cultural style. The latter may be illustrated by the example of the professor who interprets direct eye contact as a sign of respect when, in fact, the student might be from a culture that teaches its members to avert eye contact as a sign of deference.

Knowledge of the client's culture. Interpreting the behavior of someone who is culturally different without considering cultural context is fraught with danger, as is demonstrated by the following incident:

> Several years ago, during a period of particularly heavy immigration from Southeast Asia, Children's Protective Services received a rash of abuse reports on Vietnamese parents whose children had come to school with red marks all over their bodies. A bit of cultural detective work quickly turned up the fact that the children had been given an ancient remedy for colds called "cupping," which involves placing heated glass cups on the skin, leaving harmless red marks for about a day. The resulting fallout was a group of irate Vietnamese parents, always hyperattentive to the needs of their children, deeply insulted by accusations of bad parenting. And several workers feeling rather foolish about their cultural ignorance. (Diller, 1999, pp. 15–16)

Novinger (2001, pp. 23–24) suggests that we be attentive to (a) differences in perception, (b) differences in verbal behavior, and (c) differences in nonverbal behavior. Perceptions might include broad cultural considerations (see Figure 9.7) and personal traits specific to a given culture—for example, one's adaptability or attitudes toward uncertainty. Verbal processes might include one's accent, cadence, or use or tolerance of silence. Nonverbal processes might include eye contact, appearance, or attitudes toward interpersonal space.

It might not be reasonable to expect individuals to be knowledgeable of all cultures and subcultures, particularly as diversity and cultural interaction increase. Nonetheless, it is possible to learn to identify the type of information that is required or at least to be able to identify the cultural experts with whom to consult. Hofstede and Hofstede (2005) provided us with a checklist to begin looking at characteristics of culture (Figure 9.7). As we saw in the previous chapter, people from different cultures have different expectations with regard to power, and obviously those with different perspectives would have difficulty communicating. The same would be true of differences in individualism–collectivism, masculinity–femininity, uncertainty avoidance, and temporal orientation.

Adaptation of skills. The final skill area involves adapting and adjusting generic service practices that, in reality, have their roots in the dominant cultural paradigm. For example, the definition of a family member can vary greatly from culture to culture. African Americans might include multiple generations as well as nonbiological family members, such as good friends and neighbors, as members of their families. As organizations hold functions for employees and "their families," adjustments may be made to accommodate the expanded group.

In conclusion, greater sensitivity to cultural differences is increasingly important to those in public organizations. Not only are the workforce trends such that this issue cannot be ignored, but greater cultural (and other forms of) diversity enhances the productivity and achievements of the group. We have learned that, once again, we must begin with self-awareness. We must learn about our culture and how our culture influences us before we can attempt to learn about someone else's culture. As a public manager, you will have opportunities to improve the working conditions and living conditions of all, regardless of sex, race, ethnicity, or cultural heritage. Opportunities for inclusion of all in formal and informal activities will increase the success of your organization. Remember that this might not come naturally and might require learning how to initiate and develop effective communications with people who are different from you.

Power Distance: This is the extent to which the less powerful members of institutions and organizations within a country expect and accept that power is distributed unequally.

Individualism–Collectivism: Individualism denotes that the individual is *not* integrated into strong cohesive groups, as would be the case is a collective society.

Masculinity–Femininity: Masculinity pertains to societies in which social gender roles are distinct. In feminine societies, social gender roles overlap (e.g., both men and women are supposed to be modest and caring).

Uncertainty Avoidance: This is the extent to which members of a culture feel threatened by uncertain or unknown situations.

Long-Term/Short-Term Orientation: Members of a culture emphasize values associated with the future versus values focusing on the past or present.

Figure 9.7   Dimensions of National Cultures

SOURCE: From *Cultures and Organizations: Software of the Mind,* by G. Hofstede, and G. J. Hofstede, 2005, London and New York: McGraw-Hill. Used with permission.

Ways of Acting

We have discussed a variety of approaches to communicating more effectively. But remember that understanding communication skills and putting them into practice are two different things. It is easy enough to learn the skills of effective communication intellectually, but under the pressures of the moment in the "real world," it also is easy to revert to old and less effective communication techniques. As in many areas of organizational behavior, it is not just what you *know* that counts but also what you can *do*. In any case, the following guidelines might be helpful as you seek to improve your communication skills.

1. *Remember that effective communication involves creating meaning, transmitting meaning, and deciphering meaning.* At any of these points, the communication process can break down. We see the world in different ways, and we shape our own communication and respond to the communication of others based on the way in which we see the world. Many messages are ambiguous, in part because some communication serves different functions. But we are human in what we try to communicate; we communicate both our ideas and our feelings, and both must be appreciated for others to fully understand our meanings.

2. *Recognize the many barriers that inhibit effective communication.* There are obvious distortions through semantic differences and through mechanisms such as filtering. But there also is the question of which medium or channel of communication is the best for a particular situation. For various reasons, some may be "noisier" than others. Finally, the psychological state of the recipient of any message will affect what is heard.

3. *Practice supportive communication.* Strive to focus on problems and solutions rather than people. Try to resist immediate evaluation. Be as specific as possible. Try to relate to what has been said before. Help others feel accepted and validated through your communication. Take responsibility for what you are saying. Finally, listen carefully to the other person and encourage feedback in both directions.

4. *When speaking, consider your audience and make sure that your content, tone, and approach fit the situation.* Think about what other people need to know and what they want to know. Be empathetic to the feelings and dispositions of others. Engage in appropriate self-disclosure.

5. *When you wish to persuade someone to accept your position, consider your credibility and work to improve it.* If the issue is one of facts, then expertise will be important; if the issue is one of values, then you will be more effective if you share similar experiences with those you are trying to persuade. Choose the communication strategy that best fits the situation.

6. *Listen, listen, listen!* Practice active listening. Have a reason or purpose for listening. Suspend immediate judgments or evaluations. Resist distractions,

whether the distraction is a part of the environment or a characteristic of the one with whom you are talking. Wait before responding; let the other person finish before you start making your response. Rephrase what you hear in your own words; let the other person know you understand, and if you do not, then give him or her a chance to clarify. Listen for themes rather than details or specifics. Use the thinking–speaking differential to reflect on what the other person is saying and to look for themes.

7. *Remember that body language communicates as much as, or more than, what we actually say.* Be especially sensitive to the differences that exist across various cultures in nonverbal communication. Know your audience and consider any differences that might affect your message.

8. *Take advantage of electronic communication, but use electronic channels only when they are appropriate.* When the issue is clear and straightforward, you can use a lean medium such as e-mail. But when the issue is complex or ambiguous, use a richer medium such as face-to-face conversation. This will increase the opportunities for feedback and clarification.

9. *In specialized forms of communication, always consider the receiver or audience and the norms and expectations embedded in the situation.* In counseling employees, be specific and stay on target. Do not advise with respect to personal problems, but do refer employees to other sources of help. In conducting meetings, clarify your purposes and keep the meetings on track with respect to those purposes. In preparing written reports, know your topics, know your audiences, plan your papers, and then be attentive to the six C's of effective writing.

10. *Remember to consider the ethics of communication.* Your ethics and integrity are most clearly on display when you communicate with others. The truth of what you say obviously is important, but the way in which you communicate is important as well. Many people will measure your credibility by how you communicate. An honest, open, and straightforward way of communicating will significantly enhance your credibility. A devious and cunning way of communicating eventually will destroy it.

Thinking in Action

An Exercise in Supportive Communication

Read the following portion of a conversation between Frank Banks, head of a small internal audit unit in a state department of social services, and Mary Ann Burke, one of his employees.

Frank: I've asked you to come in because we've had some serious complaints about your work from some of the division directors. Generally, they say

	that you are rude and abrasive in your conversations with them. I'd like an explanation.
Mary Ann:	I really don't know what you are talking about, but it sounds like the old rumor mill has been working overtime and that you've gotten caught up in it.
Frank:	Don't try to deny that there's a problem. You can't get out of it that easily.
Mary Ann:	There's *not* a problem—except that you don't trust your employees. And you're too blind to see the way some of the division directors perceive our office—and your leadership—or rather the lack thereof.
Frank:	Mary Ann, you won't get anywhere with personal attacks on me. I'm not the one who's on trial here.
Mary Ann:	Frank, give me a break. This isn't a trial. Except that you're really trying my patience. Good-bye.

Analyze this conversation in terms of the principles of supportive communication that we have presented in this chapter. Show examples of how Frank and Mary-Ann violated each of the principles. Then create groups of three individuals. Let one person play Frank and another play Mary Ann, with the third person acting as an observer. Try to demonstrate how the same conversation might go if both Frank and Mary Ann made an effort to use supportive communication. How would the conversation differ? How might the outcome differ?

Turmoil in the Community Development Department

Read the following conversation fragments, and then pick up and role-play the conversation that is beginning between Bob and Patti. Try to use the principles of effective communication that we have discussed in this chapter.

Robert Gentry is director of the planning department in a large metropolitan community. Patti Lazard recently joined the department as associate director. Freddie King and Linda Graham both are planners in the lab.

One day, as Robert is walking down the hall, he is pulled aside by Freddie and Linda. Freddie begins the conversation:

Bob, we've been wanting to talk with you about your new assistant. I know she has some impressive degrees and all, but I'm not sure she really knows what we're all about in this lab. You know, this is hard work, and we have to be very careful to get everything just right. We also have to make sure that our clients are being brought along. But Patti seems to be concerned that we are moving too slow. In fact, a couple of times, she's actually come into my work area and pushed me out so she could show me how to do the job faster. Frankly, it's really getting on my nerves.

Linda continues the conversation:

There's no question that Patti knows what she's talking about technically, but she just doesn't understand the culture of this organization. Maybe it's because she previously worked in the private sector where it didn't matter whether she talked with anyone else. But if we get too far out in front of our clients, we're in big trouble. Sometimes we have to sacrifice a little efficiency in order to be responsive to what citizens in the neighborhoods are saying. And that takes time. Bob, I really think you need to rein her in—or maybe just put her out. She's trouble.

Robert is taken aback by the conversation. He was terribly impressed with Patti when she was hired and has not heard anything negative about her prior to this conversation. After giving the matter some thought, he walks over to Patti's office and asks to come in. He closes the door behind him and begins to speak:

Patti, I've heard a couple of concerns expressed about your approach to the work we're doing and wanted to talk about it a little. Specifically, some people seem to feel that you want to move too fast and are neglecting the time it takes to work with clients. Also, there seems to be some concern that you are pushing them aside and showing them how to do their work.

Patti replies as follows:

That's silly. We have some people in this office who just don't understand what efficiency means. They take forever doing things that can be done in a matter of a few hours. When I've been asked how the job could be done more quickly, I've shown them. But I certainly haven't pushed anyone aside to do that. I'm afraid there are just some people working here who are too lazy even for government work.

SOURCE: From "Intergroup Dialogue: Democracy at Work in Theory and Practice," by S. H. Schoem, T. Sevis, M. Chester, and S. H. Sumida, in *Intergroup Dialogue* (pp. 1–21), by D. Schoem and S. H. Schoem (Eds.), 2001, Ann Arbor: University of Michigan Press.

One-Way Communication Versus Two-Way Communication

In this exercise, give one student (in communication terms, the *sender*) a complex figure such as the combination of rectangles shown in Figure 9.8. Then give instructions to other students (the *receivers*), who will stand at the front of the room and try to reproduce the figure on the board. (The figure also can be

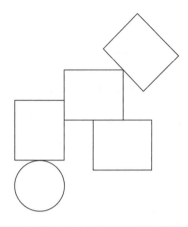

Figure 9.8   Figure for One-Way/Two-Way Communication Exercise

given to the rest of the class, with a request that the students stay quiet during the exercise.)

In the first case, the sender faces the class and those who are drawing stand at the board, listening to the sender's oral instructions and trying to draw the figure as accurately as possible. Except for the sender's directions, there are no communications between the sender and those doing the drawing. This is an example of one-way communication. In a second case, using a different but comparable drawing, the sender continues to face away from those who are doing the drawing, but they may ask questions of the sender. This is an example of two-way communication. In a third case, using still another comparable drawing, the sender faces the board and is able to watch the studets doing the drawings as well as to hear the questions and comments from those who are drawing. This is a case of enhanced two-way communication.

After the exercise is over, the senders and receivers should talk about how they experienced the exercise. What pattern was most effective in accurately reproducing the drawings? (This answer should be obvious.) But those involved in the exercise also should be asked about how they felt during the exercise. What was most frustrating? What was most helpful? What was most awkward? Under what circumstances is one-way communication necessary? Under what circumstances is two-way communication possible? (Typically, class members not directly involved in the exercise will have suggestions about how the instructions should have been given to communicate most effectively. Let them try.)

A variation of this exercise is to have pairs of students seated back-to-back. The first student is given a figure and asked to give the other student instructions as to how to draw the figure. Then the second student, with a new diagram, gives instructions to the first student. Typically, the second student will be more successful, demonstrating that those who previously have been on the "receiving" end and have a better idea of the receiver's situation can give more effective directions.

A Strange Meeting: A Case Study

Sergey Vladimirovich, formerly a Russian budget analyst, was in the United States only 6 months when he was employed by the department of budget planning and analysis in a large American city. His work duties were similar to those he had been performing in Russia. Still, he was experiencing some "strange" situations. One of the strangest happened at a meeting his boss was conducting last Monday.

He had earlier received an e-mail from the head of the department, Laura White, informing him about the meeting for next Monday morning at 10. There was an agenda attached. They were going to discuss the possibility of making changes in the current strategic plan. Instead of a 3-year plan, Laura wanted people to think about an alternative 5-year plan that would include some performance indicators and be monitored in order to control the efficiency and the effectiveness of the city's departments.

When the meeting started, Laura told the group that the council wanted the department to review the strategic plan. She favored the idea of extending the planning period and felt that the plans should include performance indicators for all departments. Her argument was that this department should have a clear picture of how and why money was spent by city agencies.

Although Sergey thought that the department should have more control over spending, he was not convinced that the department should be responsible for performance indicators for programs that other agencies were performing. And he was not sure whether a 5-year plan, no matter how carefully prepared, would be accurate.

While he was thinking about Laura's proposal, another employee, Ben Hall, started an argument with Laura, pointing out the same concerns with which Sergey was preoccupied. And Ben was not only talking about his concerns openly; he was suggesting that the department should continue with 3-year planning, with the same indicators. He was even suggesting that they should be more flexible and only be reviewed annually.

Sergey thought Ben was right, but how could he oppose his boss so openly and in front of all these people? Employees are not supposed to do that! And Laura surprised Sergey, too. Instead of being offended, she said that Ben made a very good point and that at the next meeting they would discuss both alternatives and see what to accept. Americans are so strange, Sergey thought!

Questions:

Why couldn't Sergey understand the behavior of his fellow workers?

What, according to Sergey, was "strange" at this meeting?

Are our bosses always right? If not, what should we do?

SOURCE: This case was contributed by Ljubinka Andonoska.

Trends in Electronic Communication

Earlier in this chapter, we listed the following hypotheses about the influence of electronic technology on organizational communication that were developed by

O'Connell (1988) two decades ago. Review the list and then develop a discussion of which of these hypotheses have proven to be true during the intervening time.

1. Opportunities for face-to-face contact will be diminished, and information from nonverbal cues will be reduced. Consequently, opportunities for random spontaneous information sharing will be reduced.

2. More informal messages and "short-circuiting of the hierarchy will occur. . . ." Organization structure and formal information flow will be redefined.

3. Messages of affect and value will decrease. Ambiguity in interpreting information will increase. Managers will have to seek new ways of communicating the affective component of messages.

4. Trust develops with shared experience, values, give-and-take, and the result of human communication. Satellites, electronic mail, and networks could reduce the dimensions of trust to which we are accustomed.

5. The computer imposes a discipline of linear thinking. Organizations . . . will need to find ways to encourage and protect nonlinear thinking and communicating.

6. Expectations of work performance may be machine driven. Employees in some organizations will perceive this as dehumanizing and coercive. (pp. 480–481)

CHAPTER 10

Working in Groups and Teams

You have a bond. You have a bond that's so thick that it is unbelievable! It's the pull, it's the team, the work as a team, the team spirit! You'll do it because of the team, for the team, with the team, and because the team has the same focus.

—A Canadian soldier, quoted in
Harrison & Laliberte (1994, p. 28)

Questions related to teams and teamwork seem to permeate our lives these days. No matter where you are (e.g., on the athletic field, in a classrooms, in other settings), and no matter who you are (e.g., a public manager, a nonprofit employee, a student), it is almost impossible to avoid being part of a team. Increasingly, and for various reasons, organizations are moving to team-based operations. That is, they are organizing around various types of teams as opposed to organizing around the traditional organizational hierarchy and horizontal division of labor. Our discussion of teamwork in this chapter is applicable to many settings outside of the workplace. However, the focus here is on teams and teamwork in public and nonprofit organizations. In this chapter, we see how teams are formed, what types of teams there are, how teams can be implemented in work settings, how teams develop over time, and how the effectiveness of teams can be measured.

We define a team as a group of people with a high degree of interdependence geared toward the achievement of a goal or the completion of a task. According to Smith and Katzenbach (1993), all teams must have "a meaningful purpose, specific performance goals, common approaches, complementary skills, and mutual accountability to work" (p. 45). Typically, teams are considered different from groups. Basically, without a commitment to achieving a goal or completing a task, a group is not a team. Kinlaw (1998) further distinguished between work groups and teams in terms of their functional and qualitative characteristics. Work groups typically have single supervisors or leaders and are best described by what they produce. On the other hand, teams have a considerable degree of self-management, share responsibility, and have authority for assessing their own performance. In general, work groups lack the level of consistency, intensity, and restless dissatisfaction found in teams. Functionally, work teams manage more of their own work processes and performance, undertake more systematically the ongoing tasks of team development, and (as a result) usually produce superior results.

The current interest in teams and teamwork began during the 1980s with the idea of quality circles and a growing interest in the effectiveness of well-trained teams. More recently, the idea of total quality management has raised the awareness of managers and executives about the strategic value of teams in continuous improvement. Consequently, Lawler, Mohrman, and Ledford (1995) found a well-documented growth rate in the number of teams in organizations by 1993. W. Edward Deming, one of the founders of the quality movement, stated, "Isn't it logical? If you work together, you should end up with something better than if you work apart" (quoted in Koehler & Pankowski, 1996, p. 17). Today, teams are considered vital to organizations. Consequently, Manz and Sims (1993) estimated that 50% of the workforce would be in teams by the year 2000.

It is becoming clear that, with the increasing influence of technology, the importance of innovation, and the new focus on the stakeholders, teams are becoming more and more popular. Be that as it may, there still is some resistance to moving beyond individual roles and individual accountability in our culture. Studies have demonstrated that in individual cultures such as the United States, perceptions of individual efficacy are higher than perceptions of collective efficacy (Earley, 1993, 1994; Lawson & Ventriss, 1992). This mindset presents a challenge during an era when team building, diversity, and use of teams have escalated to meet new demands on public (and other) organizations (Guzzo & Dickson, 1996; Katzenbach & Smith, 1993; Lawson & Shen, 1998; Marks & Mirvis, 1992). As the workplace becomes more diverse, so do work groups and teams. A "culturally heterogeneous" work group is a group that comprises members who are different on the basis of ethnicity, race, value, and cultural backgrounds (Ayoko & Hartel, 2006).

Indeed, the failure to engage in team-based solutions to problems can be disastrous. Straus (1986), then president of the American Arbitration Association, illustrated that point in telling of his involvement in the acid rain controversy. In this case, individuals developing their own agendas rather than a collective agenda obviously would impede progress in this area. Straus believed that our ability to collaborate effectively in developing and implementing concrete responses to the problems of acid rain lagged far behind our technical ability to detect the environmental damage and document the increasing severity of the problem (Larson & LaFasto, 1989). In other words, technical solutions might mean little if we lack the capacity to act together, in teams and other organized groups, to implement those solutions.

Teams are used in public organizations for a variety of reasons, not the least of which is that teams outperform individuals acting alone or in larger organizational groupings, particularly when performance requires multiple skills, judgments, and experiences. Maier (1967) argued that teams are more effective than individuals for five reasons. First, teams produce a greater number of ideas and pieces of information than individuals acting alone. Therefore, decision making and problem solving are more fully informed. Second, teams improve understanding and acceptance among individuals involved in problem solving and decision making due to the participation of each team member in the process. Third, teams have higher levels of motivation and performance than individuals acting alone due to the effects of "social facilitation"—that is, the reinforcing effect of each member "pushing" the others in the groups. Fourth, teams offset personal biases and blind spots that inhibit effective problem analysis and implementation but that might be overlooked by individuals. Fifth, team members are more likely to entertain risky alternatives and take innovative action than individuals working alone. In general, team judgments are superior to those of individuals working alone. Team members tend to be more motivated and creative, make more risky decisions, and learn faster.

Teams also seem to perform better under some circumstances than larger organizational groupings. For example, studies have found that schools that have team-based management outperform schools that have hierarchical management (Chubb, 1988). Teamwork also has proven to be a powerful tool for shifting social values, including racism. During the 1970s, several research projects demonstrated that the least prejudiced students were those who participated in sports teams and school bands with members of other races (Parker, 1990).

Examples of effective teamwork may be found at all levels of government and in the nonprofit sector. For example, the Chicago Community Trust's Government Assistance Project provided models of excellence (MOEs) to the city of Chicago's administrative agencies. The MOE project cultivated employee participation at every level by creating agency-wide problem-solving teams. The teams were purposely "multirank" and brought in members to represent the city's diversity in all areas. Rategan and O'Hare (1996) found that problems were solved faster, better, and with more creativity than when they were solved by a more homogeneous group of managers. In keeping with the team tradition in the city of Chicago, the director of the children's services division began a practice of empowering employees to make their own decisions about the agency. This led to their feeling like responsible members of the team instead of responsive members of a hierarchy.

Another example is the Sacramento Animal Control Center, which responded to the budget cutbacks of 1996 by implementing change through a team-based approach for maximizing the efficiency of the organization while experiencing a tighter budget. By making employees an integral part of the plan, the Sacramento Animal Control Center was able to find new ways of improving operations (Lee & Caughran, 1996). Finally, Coleman (1996) noted that the various components of public safety (police, fire, and emergency medical professionals) increasingly are forming cross-functional teams. During times of crisis, the citizens they serve rely on them interchangeably. The fact that public organizations today require more and more cooperation suggests that those organizations should be more attentive to developing teams and teamwork.

Where Do We Begin?

The best way to understand teams is to look at teams themselves and determine what makes them successful. But before we get into that discussion, you should begin by examining your own experience with teamwork.

Assessing Team Performance

Think of a group of which you are (or were) a part, whether in a classroom, personal, or workplace setting. How do (or did) members of your team address the following issues?

1. Purpose of team
   a. What is the purpose of the team?
   b. What are its goals and objectives?

2. How does the team fit into the overall management structure of the organization, classroom, and so on?

   _____

   _____

   _____

3. Membership
   a. How were members selected to join the team?
   b. Will new members be welcomed?
   c. How will members be allowed to rotate out of the team if they so desire?

4. What is the role of the leader?
   a. How will the leader be selected?
   b. Will there be one assigned leader?
   c. Will leaders rotate periodically?

5. How will the members be held accountable?

6. Do you currently have a "team agreement"?

7. Do you generate agendas with the dates, places, and times for the next meetings?

Getting to Know Your Team

Use the following exercise, adapted from Amachi and Wade (1996), to get to know your team better and to assess your team's development.

Assess the Team

How effective is the current team?

_____

_____

_____

Interview Team Members

What is the perception that members have of the team?

_____

_____

_____

Gather feedback from the team's designated leaders. Do their views differ from those of the team members?

_____

_____

_____

Interview any other key members of the organization. For example, who organized the team originally? Who is getting feedback on the team's work? How are the team's recommendations being used in the organization?

_____

_____

_____

Help the Team Define Its Mission, Values, and Roles

How do members envision the "ideal team"?

_____

_____

_____

Compare the current team to the "ideal team."

_____

_____

_____

Have ground rules been established for the team?

_____

_____

_____

Are these written ground rules?

_____

_____

_____

Are the rules readily available?

_____

_____

_____

Have issues been prioritized?

_____

_____

_____

Has the team been empowered to prioritize the issues?

_____

_____

_____

Has the priority order been provided by someone else?

_____

_____

_____

Have roles been defined and assigned?

_____

_____

_____

How are members held accountable for serving in the assigned roles?

_____

_____

_____

Communication and Conflict Management

Is "how things are said" consistent with "what is said"?

_____

_____

_____

Is what is spoken or communicated in writing consistent with the actions of the team?

_____

_____

_____

Are conflict management processes implemented in the event of conflict among members?

_____

_____

_____

Analysis and Feedback

After completing this chapter, design an effective and specific action plan for use by individual team members to improve overall team performance.

Team Agreements

If you do not currently have a "team agreement," then you might want to create one. Team agreements are formulated around the issues of values, norms, and team processes. These should be developed early in the process of team development. For example, the Internal Revenue Service virtual team that we discuss later in this chapter agreed on the following values, norms, and processes for operating as a team (Ferrero & Lewis, 1998, p. 183). Look at each set and then ask which values, norms, and processes you would like to see as part of your team's agreement.

- Values

  Integrity
  Trust/respect
  Freedom/autonomy
  Challenging/stimulating work
  Professional/personal balance
  Personal/team excellence
  Experiment/risk taking

What values would you include in your team agreement?

_____

_____

_____

- Norms

  Work as partners together
  Own our perspectives
  Take personal responsibility
  Feedback on task/behavior
  Respectful confrontation
  Contributions by everyone
  Have fun

What norms would you include in your team agreement?

_____

_____

_____

- Process approach

  Collaborative teamwork
  Build on past successes
  Participative decision making
  Mutual agreement and discussion
  What am I supposed to do?
  Self/peer assessment
  Learning organization—On the leading edge

What process approach would you include in your team agreement?

_____

_____

_____

Ways of Thinking

Teams have been used to perform work for thousands of years, even before the Great Pyramid at Giza was built. However, not until the 20th century were work teams studied by behavioral scientists, and our understanding of team behavior has increased (Guest, 1986). As we saw in Chapter 1, the Hawthorne studies uncovered the importance of teams and the power of the informal system in the workplace. Elton Mayo concluded from these experiments that it was a major responsibility of management to foster the conditions that promote effective teams. Extending from his conclusions, the fields of group dynamics and laboratory education next contributed toward building theories and methods for using groups as a basis for organizational change. Schein and Bennis (1965), for example, outlined procedures for using groups successfully to introduce changes at both the individual and organizational levels. Especially since World War II, there has been a tremendous increase in the attention paid to groups and group members. McGrath and Altman (1966) conducted a synthesis and critique of the literature on small groups, and their bibliography contained 2,699 entries. Certainly, this burgeoning research on group dynamics, group processes, and the conditions for effective teamwork has had a considerable impact on the design of team development programs (Dyer, 1977).

As mentioned earlier in the chapter, not all groups should be considered teams. Hackman (1990), for example, studied a variety of teams—top management teams, task forces, professional support groups, performing groups, human service teams, customer service teams, and production teams—to specify the notion of teams. He concluded that teams could be defined through the following three characteristics:

Teams are intact social systems, complete with boundaries, interdependence among members, and differentiated member roles.

Teams produce some outcomes for which members have collective responsibility and whose acceptability is potentially assessable.

Teams operate in an organizational context.

In a similar way, Katzenbach and Smith (1993), after talking with more than 50 teams in 30 public and private companies, defined a team as "a small number of people with complementary skills who are committed to a common purpose, set of performance goals, and approach for which they hold themselves mutually accountable" (p. 112). Katzenbach and Smith concluded with the following differentiating characteristics found in groups versus teams:

Work Groups	Teams
Strong and clearly focused leader	Shared leadership role
Individual accountability	Individual and mutual accountability
Group's purpose the same as the organizational mission	Specific team purpose that the team itself delivers
Individual work products	Collective work products
Runs efficient meetings	Encourages open-ended discussions and active problem-solving meetings
Measures its effectiveness indirectly by assessing its influence on others	Measures performance directly by collective work products
Discusses, decides, and delegates	Discusses, decides, and does real work together

SOURCE: From *The Wisdom of Teams: Creating the High-Performance Organization,* by J. R. Katzenbach and D. K. Smith, 1993, Boston: Harvard Business School Press. Copyright © 1993 by the President and Fellows of Harvard College. Reprinted with permission. All rights reserved.

Benefits of teams include the ability to select appropriate skills for a particular project; the creativity and synergy they create, particularly in the handling of non-routine work; flexibility of structure; and the ability to disband or reorganize the team (Van Wart, 2005).

Types of Teams

Now that we have established the difference between teams and groups, what do we need to know before we implement a team in our organization? First, we should recognize that there are many different types of teams that may operate even within one organization. Indeed, in organizations that emphasize the team concept, we might find up to six different types of teams: top management teams, project teams, cross-functional teams, process-improvement teams, self-directed work teams, and virtual teams. Even though we make a distinction among these types of teams, all teams use similar approaches for organizing, decision making, and continual improvements. Each team distinguishes itself by fulfilling a specific purpose.

Top management teams. A top management team is responsible for establishing the overall mission of the organization and for selecting the overall management system. The top management team sets the course for the organization, but it rarely is involved in the day-to-day operations of the organization. Members of this type of team tend to be visionaries and try to keep their eyes on the "big picture." In team-based organizations, the top management team becomes a process-improvement team concentrating on the needs of the whole system as opposed to a particular process.

Project teams. A project team typically is formed by management and given a specific mission. Membership on the team is based on individual expertise and experience. A project team functions only so long as is needed to solve the assigned problem and is discontinued once the problem is resolved. As opposed to process teams that do not have deadlines, project teams often must work within a time frame. "Management reserves the right to approve or disapprove [project teams'] recommendations" (Koehler & Pankowski, 1996, p. 32). The project team's role is to advise, not to implement. Typically, the project team will make a recommendation to top management, which may or may not decide to implement the recommendation.

Cross-functional teams. A cross-functional team serves the purpose of breaking down the barriers that exist in a hierarchical organization with a long history of division of labor and division of tasks. The cross-functional team may bring together representatives from several divisions "to improve the hiring process," or it may be as complex as a cross-functional team whose mission is to develop a single process for administering unemployment benefits and securing employment (Koehler & Pankowski, 1996, p. 35).

Process-improvement teams. A process-improvement team is a small group of individuals who interact with each other for the purpose of improving those work processes in which they engage. For example, a process-improvement team might explore the way in which checks sent to a state government are processed and deposited. By speeding up that process, the team might significantly increase the interest that the state earns on those funds. Koehler and Pankowski suggested the following principles for a process improvement team.

Organize the team around organizational processes: To increase effectiveness, organizational processes must be improved. Koehler and Pankowski recommended that the team be structured around processes by those who are most familiar with the process. Examples of processes that the team can improve within government might include job placement, financial reporting, vendor payment, leasing, or records management (1996, p. 20). The team is formed around the organizational processes, keeping in mind that many of these processes will include members from several programs. Changes made in work processes may substantially improve services for a variety of internal and external stakeholders.

Control the process, not the team: Once the process is clearly defined, it should be the responsibility of the team to control the process. If the system is producing desired goals and is continuously improving, then the team should be empowered to take the initiative to improve the process.

Maintain process partnerships: It is the responsibility of the team to develop and maintain partnerships with those affected by the process.

Continually improve the process: The focus of each team meeting should be to improve the process that the team has been charged with examining.

Require team participation: To achieve quality in a team-based organization, everyone must participate.

Data-driven team decisions: Data are collected and analyzed to improve the process.

Empower teams: Empowerment refers to the authority that the team is provided to make the changes necessary to improve the process.

Develop and train team members: Each employee should be trained and educated for the betterment of the organization.

Self-directed teams. Organizations are increasingly using self-directed or self-managed teams. In fact, any of the previously mentioned teams may function as a self-directed team. The notion of the self-directed team was promoted by Hammer and Champy (1993), who indicated that a team performing process-oriented work inevitably is self-directing. Within the boundaries of its obligations to the organization, including agreed-on deadlines, productivity goals, and quality standards, the self-directed team itself decides how and when work is going to be done. If the team has to wait for supervisory direction of its tasks, then it is not a self-directed team. There are several misconceptions about self-directed teams (Caudron, 1993). The first is that *self-directed teams do not need leaders.* There is a definite need for leaders to serve the function of coaches or facilitators so as to transfer what traditionally has been left to management to these team members. The second misconception is that *leaders lose power in the transition to teams.* Power is not a zero-sum game; rather, it is an expandable and flexible resource. The third misconception is that *newly formed teams are automatically self-directing.* As we have seen, team development is an evolutionary process that takes considerable time and effort. Describing new teams as self-directed might establish unrealistic expectations. The fourth misconception is that *employees are waiting for the opportunity to be empowered.* Not everyone will welcome the empowering effect of self-directed teams. With empowerment comes responsibility, and some will not want more responsibility than they already have. The fifth misconception is that *if employees are grouped in a team structure, then they will function as a team, and the organization will reap the benefit of teamwork.* As discussed earlier, a team must go through a developmental process. In addition, team members will need training in areas such as group problem solving, goal setting, and conflict resolution.

Although self-directed teams have a leader, they do not receive direct supervision. These teams are trained and provided expectations for the quality and quantity of their work. Several conditions have been found to be crucial to the success of self-directed teams (adapted from Deep & Sussman, 2000, p. 123):

1. Management wants to give employees greater emotional ownership for the tasks they perform.

2. Management is willing to relinquish control and to trust the team to make decisions.

3. The team is provided with the resources it needs to meet expectations.

4. The team is trained to function without direct supervision.

5. Members are highly motivated to take control of their work.

6. Team members respect and trust each other.

7. Team members are equally committed to the success of the team and to the success of the larger organization.

Virtual teams. Virtual teams are a new phenomenon aiming to deal with the issue of communicating with team members who might be a distance away. The virtual team makes use of newly available information technology including videoconferencing, satellite television, and the Internet. For example, the Internal Revenue Service has virtual team meetings every other Monday morning by way of a 90-minute conference call (Ferrero & Lewis, 1998). A formal agenda is sent by way of electronic mail (e-mail) to the team two working days prior to the call. Team members rotate the role of facilitator. In addition to phone conferences, the team uses facilitated teleconferences on an electronic bulletin board. Team members and clients are connected by way of e-mail, may access the Internet, and may access the voice mail system nationwide through a toll-free number. Four key factors make these teams unique (Gibson & Gibbs, 2005; Gibson, 2005):

1. Electronic dependence—technology alone does not make a virtual team. It is the degree of reliance on electronic communication that increases virtuality.

2. Geographic dispersion—requiring that members not take for granted that other members share their contextual knowledge, culture, and common values. Cramton and Orvis (2003) found that virtual team members need to share more information about context and in much greater detail than they would if working in the same location.

3. Cultural diversity—in highly virtual teams, it is often necessary to create a hybrid culture, structure, and set of operating policies that represent a compromise among the various alternatives preferred by different team members.

4. Dynamic structure—due to the nature of the teams, the team structure is dynamic and evolving.

Implementing Teams

Implementing a team concept in a public organization requires careful advance planning, starting with a clear commitment to the team concept on the part of senior management. In considering the implementation of work teams, managers should consider the long-term needs and goals that they wish to achieve through the use of teams and carefully determine the role and importance of the teams within the larger organization. Wellins, Byham, and Wilson (1991) recommended an organizational culture readiness assessment prior to implementing teams. Such an assessment can help in predicting the possibility of success in using teams. According to Jones and Beyerlein (1998), the following conditions must be met for a productive team:

- A clearly articulated need for change in the organization
- Interdependence among individuals as necessary to perform the work or provide the service
- Clarity of goals as provided or developed by the team
- Commitment to goals on the part of the team and senior management
- A shared mental model or conceptual model of how things work among team members
- Similar values, including those that are compatible with work teams; valuing what others have to offer, possibility thinking, involvement, fairness, equality, responsibility, and accountability
- Opportunity for teamwork as created by senior management or other individuals
- Protected space and time free from interference so that the team can do its work
- Norms of self-regulation, with the team being allowed to create its own mechanism to manage its own behavior
- Established boundary management, with clarification of the boundaries for membership and the limits on the types of decisions the team can make
- Feedback based on strategy and performance measurement to keep the team on target
- Challenges from customers, competition, and changing work requirements used to galvanize the team into action
- Support systems aligned with the needs of the team including evaluation, training and development, and other personnel issues

A good balance between managerial and team authority is necessary but difficult. "Managers should be unapologetic about the direction—the end state the team is to pursue—and about outer limits constraints on team behavior—the things the team must always do or never do" (Hackman, 1990, p. 496). Katzenbach and Smith found that "most successful teams shape their purposes in response to a demand or [an] opportunity put in their path, usually by higher management" (1993, p. 112). This advice is consistent with other findings suggesting that teams benefit from carefully interacting with their environment so that the greatest number of demands and opportunities will be recognized. Research conducted by Katz and Allen (1988) on team development and performance found that the higher performing teams were the ones that had significantly more communications with people outside their labs. The lower performing teams isolated themselves from information (see also Kouzes & Posner, 1995).

Team Effectiveness

How can a manager be sure that implementing a team concept will be successful? As we already have seen, a team is more effective if it is well designed and if the organization is designed to support it (Mohrman, Cohen, & Mohrman, 1995). Successfully implementing a team requires keeping the focus on the larger organization, obtaining buy-in at all levels, developing a solid team structure, establishing ground rules, and fostering team bonding (Magee, 1997). In addition, research has found that the success of the self-managing team greatly depends on its external leader. (Conditions necessary for success were outlined earlier in this chapter.) Multiple case studies have found that external leaders who struggle with their role usually exert too much control, undermining the ability of the team to do its work (Urch Druskat & Wheeler, 2007).

Other issues to consider include performance evaluations, the structure of the team, the size and life expectancy of the team, the diversity of the team, and the training of team members. We discuss each of these issues in terms of its contribution to team effectiveness.

One important issue for managers introducing the team concept in the workplace is how to evaluate the performance of a team. Obviously, reward systems that are based on individual performance will work against the goals of the team. For this reason, the traditional style of *performance evaluations,* which focuses on the individual, is not well suited to the evaluation of a team. Although it is difficult to implement, finding a way of focusing on the team's performance is important. One way of doing this is to involve the team itself in establishing the performance appraisal system that eventually will be used to evaluate its work. Involving the team in the performance appraisal not only can lead to effective ways of measuring team performance but also models the value of teamwork in the organization. Another way of developing an evaluation system is to create circumstances in which various teams participate in evaluating each other's work. Such peer evaluation means that those doing the evaluating understand some of the special circumstances faced by teams and team members and that they can take those special circumstances into account in their evaluation.

Another factor differentiating between high- and low-performing teams is the *structure* of the team, especially the relationship between the team's structure and its overall purpose. But a key point is that one structure is not necessarily better than another in all cases. What is important is "identifying the appropriate structure for the achievement of a specific performance objective" (Larson & LaFasto, 1989, p. 40). Indeed, Larson and LaFasto found that the same performance objectives could be supported by different structural designs so long as the designs provided adequate support for the team in moving toward a desired objective. Three designs are commonly found: problem resolution, creativity, and tactical execution. A *problem-solving* team would be set up to solve a specific problem statement. For example, how can we provide the most nutritional and cost-effective food to inmates? A *creativity* team would be established to come up with more innovative ideas. For example, how can we vary the menu for inmates and make use of their services to cut costs? A *tactical* team would be set up to deal with specific problems of implementation. For example, how do we schedule the inmates on a regular basis to work the three meals of the day on a 7-day-per-week basis?

The *size of the team* also influences team effectiveness. A team can be too small or too large. A small team does not have sufficient breadth and variety to see all sides of an issue. A large team often is unwieldy and ineffective. Parker (1994) found that this fundamental principle for team effectiveness often is violated. He recommended 4 to 6 members, with no more than 10, for an effective team. Along the same lines, Gardenswartz and Rowe (1994) recommended 7 to 12 members. We recommend about 7 members to a team.

The *duration of the team,* or how long the team is expected to be "in business," is important in deciding on the amount of time and energy that the organization will invest in team development. A team can vary along a continuum, from permanent to temporary. A permanent team will have sufficient time to work out its own leadership patterns. But during the early stages of team implementation, short-duration teams might need more formal leadership. Of course, people who have been team members in one place will adapt more quickly to a new team. For these reasons, as the organization becomes more proficient in the team process, it is easier to establish a self-managing, short-duration team (Parker, 1994).

Team diversity, and how differences are managed, also will influence the effectiveness of a team. Diversity in teams has "the potential to increase the creative power of teams, one of their most valuable features, as well as ensure adequate representation and fairness" (Van Wart, 2005, p. 217).

Gardenswartz and Rowe (1994) suggested four layers for examining the diversity that individuals bring to the organization. The first layer is personality, permeating the other layers. Teams have used the Myers-Briggs Type Inventory, mentioned in Chapter 2, as a way of understanding the preferences of other team members. Another helpful source is Parker's (1990) Team Player Survey, which identifies the team members' preferred roles and the impact of these roles during the various stages of team development, a topic we return to later in this chapter. The second layer is the group's internal dimensions, including age, gender, sexual orientation, physical ability, ethnicity, and race. The third layer is the external dimensions, including geographic location, income, personal habits, recreational habits, religion, educational background, work experience, appearance, and parental and marital status. The fourth layer is organizational dimensions, including functional level/classification, work content/field, division/department/unit/group, seniority, work location, union affiliation, and management status. Differences in any of these dimensions can affect the group either positively or negatively. But the key is to be mindful of differences and to use them in a positive fashion. For example, a group with members whose personality types differ dramatically might "fight" more initially. But if the members can get past the "fighting," they are likely to be better at problem solving because they will see all sides of any particular issue.

A fifth layer that may be considered is the degree of individualism or collectivism exhibited by the team members. The majority of the world's people live in collective societies "in which people from birth onward are integrated into strong, cohesive in-groups, which throughout people's lifetimes continue to protect them in exchange for unquestioning loyalty" (Hofstede & Hofstede, 2005, p. 76). Examples of countries with these orientations include those in Latin America and Saudi Arabia. On the other side are the individualistic societies "in which the ties between individuals are loose: everyone is expected to look after himself or herself and his or her immediate family" (Hofstede & Hofstede, 2005, p. 76). Examples of these countries are the United States, Australia, and the United Kingdom. As immigration, multinational organizations, and globalization increase, Hofstede and Hostede's classification of nations as individualistic or collectivist may not be particularly useful to understanding the group when forming cross-national teams consisting of individuals from different countries, ethnicities, and social backgrounds. However, it will provide some understanding of the individual's position.

Finally, the *training of team members* will contribute to the effectiveness of the team. Wellins et al. (1991) suggested three categories of training: (1) job skills (including all of the technical knowledge and skills that team members need for success on the job), (2) team/interactive skills (including all of the interpersonal and communication skills necessary for team members to be effective in their roles), and (3) quality/action skills (those necessary for team members to identify problems and make improvements). The initial training, *job skills,* usually is conducted by in-house personnel and is highly job dependent. This training will need to include reference to the appropriate processes and procedures of the organization. To whom will the team ultimately be accountable? What process will be used to evaluate team participation? How will members be selected to join a team? The second training, *team/interactive skills,* should include general training in communication skills, meeting management, listening, assertiveness, conflict resolution, goal setting, and other topics that provide the skills necessary to be an effective team player. These skills, which may be taught either in-house or by a trained consultant, should emphasize developing interpersonal skills and team cohesion. The last skill set, *quality/action skills,* requires that the team learn how to identify opportunities for improvement and be able to make recommendations to team members. For example, in the case study of a Florida county corrections division discussed later in this chapter, eight dimensions were used to evaluate team performance: (1) encouragement of risk taking; (2) interaction as equals and sharing leadership; (3) use of verbal and nonverbal listening skills; (4) adherence to the mission, vision, and values of the division; (5) engaging in team building or the development of the team; (6) use of formal decision making and consensus building; (7) use of formal conflict resolution to resolve issues; and (8) accountability by holding team members responsible.

To summarize the attributes of successful teams, we can examine research on effective teams and their defining characteristics. Hackman (1990) listed as "process criteria" for team performance the requirements that team members devote sufficient effort to accomplish the task at an acceptable level of performance, that team members bring adequate knowledge to bear on the task, and that the team employ performance strategies that are appropriate to the work and to the setting in which the work is being performed (p. 13). Similarly, Kinlaw (1992) found the following four sets of characteristics distinguishing superior teams, characteristics that may be used to rate team development and to identify opportunities for improvement:

Team results: Superior teams are productive and achievement oriented.

Informal process: Superior teams are successful in communication and contacting, responding and adapting, influencing and improving, and appreciating and celebrating.

Positive team feelings: Members of superior teams share feelings of inclusion, commitment, loyalty, pride, and trust.

Leadership: The roles of leaders of superior teams include those of initiator, model, and coach. As initiators, leaders might propose procedures, tasks, goals, or actions. As models, leaders might need to model appropriate behavior for team members by inviting participation and by being friendly and warm, responsive to others, and accountable to team members. As coaches, leaders might need to reduce tension in conflict situations, keep communication channels open, provide training and encouragement to participants of the team process, and (most important) help teams to solve their own problems.

Finally, Katzenbach and Smith (1993) found that, for success, the team requires technical and functional expertise, problem-solving and decision-making skills, and interpersonal skills. Interestingly, Katzenbach and Smith's research concluded that teams are powerful vehicles for developing the skills needed to meet teams' performance challenges. Therefore, they encouraged the selection of team members as much on potential as on proven skills.

In an effective team, the behavior of team members is interdependent and personal goals are subservient to the accomplishments of the team goals. The team has a clear understanding of the goal to be achieved and a belief that the goal embodies a worthwhile or important result (Larson & LaFasto, 1989). A commitment to, and a desire for, team membership is present. Even though individuals might be formally designated as a team, if they do not have the commitment to team membership and are unwilling to forgo personal objectives and exclusive credit, then they will not function as a team regardless of what they are called. For this reason, managers and team members should be aware of how team members take responsibility for the work of the team.

Figure 10.1 shows Magin's (1994) set of indicators and experiences that will make the difference between positive and negative team experiences.

Measuring Team Effectiveness

In implementing a team concept in a public organization, it is helpful to have some idea of how to measure the effectiveness of the various teams. There are several criteria that may be used to judge a team's effectiveness (Hackman, 1990). The first is the degree to which the team's "productive output (product, service, or decision) meets the standards of quality, quantity, and timeliness of those who receive,

Indicator	Good Team Experience	Not So Good Team Experience
Members arrive on time?	Members are prompt because they know others will be.	Members drift in sporadically, and some leave early.
Members are prepared?	Members are prepared and know what to expect.	Members are unclear of the agenda.
Members are organized?	Members follow a planned agenda.	The agenda is tossed aside, and freewheeling discussion ensues.
Members contribute equally?	Members give each other a chance to speak. Quiet members are encouraged.	Some members always dominate the discussion. Some are reluctant to speak their minds.
Discussions help members to make decisions?	Members learn from others' points of view, new facts are discussed, creative ideas evolve, and alternatives emerge.	Members reinforce their beliefs in their own points of view, or their decisions were made long before the meeting.
Any disagreement?	Members follow a conflict resolution process established as part of the team's policies.	Conflict turns to argument, angry words, emotion, and blaming.
More cooperation or more conflict?	Cooperation clearly is an important ingredient.	Conflict flares openly and also simmers below the surface.
Commitment to decisions?	Members reach consensus before leaving.	Compromise is the best outcome possible. Some members do not care about the result.
Members' feelings after team decision?	Members are satisfied and are valued for their ideas.	Members are glad it is over and are not sure of the results or the outcome.
Members support decision afterward?	Members are committed to implementation.	Some members second-guess or undermine the team's decision.

Figure 10.1   Indicators of Positive and Negative Experiences in Teamwork

SOURCE: From *Effective Teamwork,* by M. D. Magin, 1994, Chicago: Irwin. © 1994 Irwin Professionals, Inc. Reproduced with permission of the McGraw-Hill Companies.

review, and/or use the output." The second is the degree to which the "process of carrying out the work enhances the capability of members to work together interdependently in the future." The third is the degree to which the team experiences "contribute to the growth and personal well-being of team members" (p. 6).

A comprehensive framework for team effectiveness must include both process and personnel outcomes (Gibson, 2007). Possible process outcomes are goal achievement, productivity, timeliness, customer satisfaction, organization learning, innovation, and cycle time. Personnel outcomes include team member attitudes (an example would be commitment to the team as demonstrated through performance), cohesion and longevity, and the capacity to work together in the future.

As an example of how one organization dealt with the question of measuring team effectiveness, we examine how teams in the Division of Corrections in one Florida county developed a team concept that measured the performance of the teams so as to increase their effectiveness. The division formed teams as an integral part of the move toward participatory management during the late 1980s. Each level of management in the organization was grouped as a team, and other teams (both cross-functional and self-directed) were organized throughout the organization. Each team received training on team building from a consultant. Part of the training involved team agreements that defined behavior for the group and its members. The agreements of teams throughout the organization contained similar elements. A small evaluation committee then used the team agreements to define broad goals (called "dimensions") and specific behaviors related to each of those. This information ultimately was used to measure performance. Eight dimensions were identified to be of critical importance for the performance of teams:

- Encouraging risk taking among members
- Interacting as equals and sharing leadership
- Using verbal and nonverbal listening skills
- Adhering to the mission, vision, and values of the division
- Engaging in team building or the development of the team
- Using formal decision making and consensus building
- Using formal conflict resolution to resolve issues
- Holding team members accountable or responsible

For each of these dimensions, the evaluation group developed descriptive behaviors that were measured using a Likert-type scale. These scales were then used to measure the performance of 14 teams: 11 departmental teams (some were cross-functional by design) and 3 management teams. The purpose of the measurement was as follows:

- To determine the effectiveness of the team as defined by the dimensions and descriptive behavior
- To use the results of the study to establish action plans for team improvements

The instrument was designed, pretested, and used for interviews and observations. The results of the interviews and observations varied greatly. Although the dimensions and behaviors were those reached through the team agreement, the results of the measurement demonstrated that the teams were at different levels of development and that some had not made the transition from group to team.

In keeping with Katzenbach and Smith's (1993) observations, the most successful teams were those that exhibited high levels of trust and commitment. The highly effective teams also were observed encouraging risk taking and valuing members' opinions. Team members in these groups interacted as equals and shared leadership among various members. Conflict itself was not viewed as a problem in the effective groups, and formal conflict resolution was included in later training as needed. On the other hand, those scoring lower in the evaluation process tended to exhibit a lack of commitment and involvement in team building and also did not hold themselves or individuals in the group accountable for the performance of the group.

We can learn the following lessons from this experience:

- Trust and commitment are necessary for effective teams.
- Training is not a substitute for commitment or an assurance of learning. Perhaps Senge's (1990) description of the learning organization is the best description of the learning necessary for team performance:

> At the heart of a learning organization is a shift of mind—from seeing ourselves as separate from the world to connected to the world, from seeing our problems as caused by someone or something "out there" to seeing how our actions create the problems that we experience. A learning organization is a place where people are continually discovering how they create reality. And how they can change it. (pp. 12–13)

- Decisions made within the team matter. Acknowledgments and celebrations of success are necessary components of team performance and accountability.
- Commitment to the team process requires team building. Some of the more effective team building occurs on an informal basis.
- Trust is more difficult with a large group, particularly one with an influx of new members. Nonetheless, trust is necessary for team effectiveness.
- Performance measures may be used as a tool for continuous improvement of teams. The overwhelming success of the performance measures in this organization was that by defining behaviors, the teams began dialogue toward continuous improvement in processes.

Commitment from top management is imperative. The director of this organization strongly supported the team activities and measurement process, viewing the measurement activity as a learning opportunity for the teams and as a tool to improve communications and performance.

Individual Styles and Team Development

To effectively build, lead, or participate in a team, one must understand the stages of development that teams undergo in coming together and carrying out their assigned responsibilities. Interestingly, there are certain fairly predictable stages in the development of teams, whatever the setting. Understanding these stages and the way in which different types of people act during the different stages can be very helpful in understanding the dynamics of team development. Research has shown that teams tend to develop through four separate states or stages that were first labeled by Tuckman (1965) as *forming, storming, conforming,* and *performing.* Later research by Greiner (1972) and Cameron and Whetten (1981) reversed the order of the second and third stages so that the stages became forming, conforming, storming, and performing.

It also is important to understand that individuals bring their own personality styles to the team. That is, different people react to and engage in the team experience in different ways. Parker's (1990) research indicated that there are four primary styles of team players:

Contributor: This is a task-oriented member who enjoys providing the team with good technical information and data, does his or her homework, and pushes the team to set high performance standards and to use its resources wisely. As a team member, the contributor is viewed as dependable.

Collaborator: This is a flexible, goal-oriented member who sees the vision, mission, or goal of the team as paramount but who is flexible and open to new ideas. He or she is willing to share the limelight with others and is viewed as a person who sees the big picture.

Communicator: This is a process-oriented individual with good listening and facilitative skills. He or she is viewed as a good people person who is able to resolve conflict and build informal relaxed relationships.

Challenger: This person openly questions the goals and methods of the team and is willing to disagree with the leader. This person encourages risk taking and is appreciated for his or her candor and openness.

Each style contributes in different ways to the success of the team, and the unique contributions that each type makes to the development of the team should be acknowledged. But the orientation and behavior of each type will vary by the different stages of team development. We can examine what happens in each of the different stages.

The Forming Stage

You might recall that on first entering a team as a potential member, you asked questions such as the following. Who are these people? What are their expectations of me? How do I fit in? Will everyone be a "team player"? How much work will this involve? If one or all of these questions surfaced in your mind, then you are not alone. Our first questions on forming a team have to do with establishing a sense of security and direction, getting oriented, and becoming comfortable with the new situation. Sometimes team members articulate these questions, and other times team members fail to articulate these feelings but still experience them as a vague sense of discomfort and disconnectedness. How a person reacts during this stage is a reflection of his or her style. Refer to Figure 10.2 for a short description of the concerns and positive actions of the different styles during the forming stage of team development.

The Conforming Stage

Once the issues of the forming stage have been resolved, team members enter a new stage of development, the conforming stage (Figure 10.3). When a team begins to function as a unit and team members become comfortable in their setting, team members experience pressure to conform to the emerging norms. The concern of team members shifts from overcoming uncertainty and increasing clarity during the forming stage to becoming unified and identifying roles that can be played by each member during the conforming stage. Typical questions in the minds of team members during this stage include the following. What role will I be allowed to perform? Will I have the support of my team members and management? How much time and commitment should I give to this team? What are the norms and expectations of team members? During the conforming stage, team members become content with team membership and begin to value the team's goals more than their personal goals. This is facilitated if the team has reached a team agreement during the forming stage. But as we saw, the reactions of different types of individuals will vary during the forming stage.

	Contributor	Collaborator	Communicator	Challenger
Concerns	My role Expectations of me Time commitment My tasks	Mission of team Goals Leader's vision	Membership Acceptance Inclusion Resources of members	Is the team serious? Openness Receptivity of leader
Positive Actions	Discuss tasks and roles. Ask leader for direction. Offer to take on an assignment.	Ask the leader's view. Discuss team mission and goals.	Ask how members were selected. Ask that members introduce themselves. Suggest a team "talent bank."	Ask if team is satisfied with mission. Express reservations. Suggst a discussion of member concerns.

Figure 10.2　Forming Stage and Reaction Among Team Members by Style

SOURCE: From *Team Players and Teamwork,* by G. M. Parker, 1990, San Francisco: Jossy-Bass. Copyright © 1990, Jossey-Bass. Reprinted by permission of Jossey-Bass, Inc., a subsidiary of John Wiley & Sons, Inc.

	Contributor	*Collaborator*	*Communicator*	*Challenger*
Concerns	Will the standards be maintained? Will all resources be used?	Will the team stay focused on goals? Will we continue to make progress?	Is drive for consensus masking real disagreement? Will emphasis on process go too far?	Will tough questions continue to be asked? Will risk taking be reduced?
Positive Actions	Insist on high-quality work. Push for priority setting. Take responsibility; do not wait to be asked.	Keep the team focused on the big picture. Ask the team to revisit goals periodically.	Remind the team that consensus does not eliminate disagreement. Suggest an assessment of team process. Use feedback skills.	Ask tough questions and encourage others to do the same. Confront groupthink. Encourage risk taking.

Figure 10.3   Conforming Stage and Reaction Among Team Members by Style

SOURCE: From *Team Players and Teamwork*, by G. M. Parker, 1990, San Francisco: Jossy-Bass. Copyright © 1990, Jossey-Bass. Reprinted by permission of Jossey-Bass, Inc., a subsidiary of John Wiley & Sons, Inc.

The Storming Stage

The differentiation that begins to occur during the conforming stage leads to conflict and counterdependence in the team (Figure 10.4). During this stage, members question the legitimacy of the team, the leader, the roles and actions of the other members, and the team's objectives. The long-term success of the team will depend on how well it manages this storming stage of development. During this stage, the team must learn to cope with conflict, differences, and disruptions. If it does not, then the team might disintegrate. Typical questions that arise during this stage include the following. Do I want to remain a team member? How can we make decisions amid disagreements? Is there someone else who would be a better leader? Can this team make the necessary changes? During this stage, the team must learn to deal with adversity, especially adversity produced by its own members. If it is to be effective, then the team's focus must not be simply on maintaining harmony at all costs. Rather, the differences that emerge must be confronted directly and openly. Efforts must be made by team members to solve problems and accomplish tasks so as to be effective in the long run. This is a natural phase of development in the team, and again, team members play different roles and develop different perspectives.

The Performing Stage

When the team reaches the performing stage of development, it is able to function as a highly effective and efficient unit. It has been able to work through issues

	Contributor	Collaborator	Communicator	Challenger
Concerns	More heat than light? Will any work get done? Can we be objective?	Can we move forward? Will conflicts lead to failure to help others? Will conflict dilute commitment?	Will members listen? Will members attack each other? Will members look at both sides?	Will team be receptive to minority opinion? Will leader allow differences to surface? Will team be open to revising its mission?
Positive Actions	Ask for data to support opinions. Remind team of need for homework. Remain objective.	Be willing to help others. Ask how opinions affect team mission. Be open to new ideas.	Model good listening. Suggest norms for resolving conflict. Encourage the expression of all views.	Model positive confrontational behavior. Be willing to back off when a consensus emerges. Push the team to take well-conceived risks.

Figure 10.4 Storming Stage and Reaction Among Team Members by Style

SOURCE: From *Team Players and Teamwork,* by G. M. Parker, 1990, San Francisco: Jossy-Bass. Copyright © 1990, Jossey-Bass. Reprinted by permission of Jossey-Bass, Inc., a subsidiary of John Wiley & Sons, Inc.

of lack of trust, uncertainty, unclear expectations, lack of participation, and self-centeredness—issues characteristic of the forming stage. It has clarified a mission, team members' roles, the degree of personal commitment to the team, and the leader's direction—questions characteristic of the conforming stage. The team also has overcome tendencies toward counterdependence, conflict, polarization, and disharmony—questions typical of the storming stage. It now has the attributes necessary to become a high-performing team. The questions that team members have at this stage include the following. What further improvement may be made to our processes? How can we continuously improve? What do we need to do to continue to be creative and innovative? How do we maintain this level of energy? A team during this stage of development relies less on strong directive leadership and begins to function more like a self-managing team, and once again, the team members make different contributions, as shown in Figure 10.5.

Team Conflict

At any stage in the development of teams, conflict may occur, and the causes of the conflict must be known before it can be resolved. The sources of team conflict might include the following (Topchik, 2007):

- *Intrapersonal, or conflict from within oneself.* In this case, the team member's internal conflicts often influence his or her working relationships with other

	Contributor	*Collaborator*	*Communicator*	*Challenger*
Concerns	Will team slip on responsibilities? Will team react quickly? Will members stay current on issues?	Is it time for a new mission? Does the team need to revise goals?	Will the team take the time to acknowledge success? Will members revert to lack of concern for process?	Will the team react poorly to changes? Will members confront signs of stagnation?
Positive Actions	Push to maintain standards. Propose an examination of needs and resources. Recommend new and challenging assignments.	Facilitate brainstorming sessions focusing on the future.	Initiate positive celebrations of accomplishments. Challenge the team to maintain norms. Give feedback to members.	Confront the team with indicators of stagnation. Initiate discussion of environmental changes. Question the assumption of success.

Figure 10.5   Performing Stage and Reaction Among Team Members by Style

SOURCE: From *Team Players and Teamwork*, by G. M. Parker, 1990, San Francisco: Jossy-Bass. Copyright © 1990, Jossey-Bass. Reprinted by permission of Jossey-Bass, Inc., a subsidiary of John Wiley & Sons, Inc.

team members. For example, consider the young employee who does not feel that he is in the right profession and participates without interest in the team assignments.

- *Interpersonal, or conflicts that occur between two or more people on the team.* For example, consider a team of six where five of the six team members work hard to collect data for their assigned project by conducting interviews, yet one fails to do any of the interviews assigned, reducing the sample size considerably.
- *Structural, or conflicts that are innate to the organizational structure or the work.* For example, consider a team at a school who is told that they are not to address curriculum issues because those can only be handled at the district level.
- *Values/beliefs, or differences attached to deep-seated emotions.* Consider a team member who values collectivism and is explicit about this being a priority in his decision-making style. However, he is in a team with members who value individualism and do not believe that the good of the whole should be prioritized over the good of the individual.
- *Personality differences in style and behavior.* For example, consider the team member who always completes assignments on a timely basis and has

a colleague on the team who treats deadlines as a suggestion, and on time who time is when she gets around to it.

- *Perceptions or differences in view or perspective of the situation or issue.* Consider the team that attributes a lack of time for the project as the reason for delay when the leader views the lack of progress as a lack of dedication on the part of the team members.

- *Work methods or disagreements about solving problems.* For example, consider the team member who believes the best solution to the problem will require a systematic evaluation, yet another team member believes that an intuitive solution will suffice.

Solutions to the conflict include "creative collaboration, giving in, controlling, workable compromise, and avoiding" (Topchik, 2007, p. 107). All are valuable and can be highly effective depending on the situation. More may be found on conflict resolution in Chapter 11.

Ways of Acting

In this chapter, we have learned that teams often are used in public organizations to achieve important assignments. The performance of a team typically is greater than what can be accomplished by an individual. Individuals bring different personalities to the group, and those personality differences will affect their concerns during different stages of team development, and conflicts may occur at any of the stages. When they work at their best, teams can add significantly to the quality and productivity of the organization. And, of course, the team experience can create positive bonds among individuals. (Recall how the Canadian soldier quoted at the beginning of this chapter felt about the bond that is created through teamwork.)

We also have seen that a successful team needs the commitment of the organization as reflected in a culture that allows for interdependence, allows for group decision making, and rewards teamwork. Other measures of success such as establishing goals are contingent on factors that are within the control of the team. Overall, this chapter should help you in determining a team's stage of development, in becoming familiar with the attributes of high-performing teams and incorporating these into your own team, in understanding the different roles that team members play during each stage of team development, and in helping your team to progress through the different stages of development by managing challenges and issues that predominate at particular stages. As a review, it might be useful to return to the exercise that you completed in the "Where Do We Begin?" section. You might then try to design an effective and specific action plan for use by the individual members of your team to improve the team's overall performance.

We have discussed a variety of issues regarding teamwork. The success of the team will depend on skills, practice, and management commitment. You might find the following recipe proposed by the U.S. Department of Labor (1996) to be helpful in improving your team's effectiveness.

1. *Have clarity on the goals of the team.* You should seek agreement on the team's mission, see the mission as workable, have a clear vision, progress steadily toward its goals, and be clear about the larger project goals and the purpose of individual steps, meetings, discussion, and decisions.

2. *You should develop an improvement plan.* You should create a work plan, have a flowchart or similar document describing the steps you will take, refer to these documents when discussing what directions to take next, and know what resources and training are needed to support your work on the team.

3. *You should clearly define roles.* Start by having formally designated roles so that each team member knows what is expected. When roles are shared, be clear about how the shared roles are assigned and used. Use each member's talents and involve everyone in the team's activities so that no one feels underused, left out, or taken advantage of.

4. *Communicate clearly.* Team members should speak with clarity and directness. They should be succinct, avoiding long anecdotes and examples. They should listen actively, exploring rather than debating each speaker's ideas. They should avoid interrupting and talking when others are speaking. They should share information on many levels.

5. *Keep in mind these beneficial team behaviors.* There always is a need to initiate discussions, to seek information and opinions, to suggest procedures for reaching a goal, to clarify or elaborate on ideas, and to summarize and test for consensus. One or more people should act as gatekeepers or conversational traffic cops. They should try to prevent simultaneous conversation and should throttle dominant talkers, make room for reserved talkers, keep the discussion from digressing, try to ease tension in the group and work through difficult matters, get the group to agree on standards, refer to documentation and data, praise and correct others with equal fairness, and allow both praise and constructive complaints. The group should seek a standard that allows members to compromise and be creative in resolving differences.

Thinking in Action

The following three exercises, used to improve the relationships among team members, have been adapted from Koehler and Pankowski (1996, pp. 70–71).

A Team-Building Exercise

Divide the group into teams of seven or eight that eventually will be asked to make recommendations to the dean of your college about improving student services.

1. Ask team members to come up with a team name and perhaps even a song or logo that represents them as a team.

2. Take time to understand the jobs of all team members. The team also might wish to discuss life outside of the workplace. Members may share what they do for

entertainment, information about their families, and so on with the goal of getting to know each other better and helping all members to feel part of the team.

3. The team's assignment is to come up with three major recommendations to improve the services offered to the students in your college. Each team member is instructed to take a few minutes and list what he or she would do. Then each member is asked to read his or her top three recommendations to the group. All the recommendations are listed on a flip chart. The team's charge is to develop one list with consensus reached on the recommendations.

The Case of Guard Uniforms

The guards of a jail in a southwest Texas county decided that the uniforms they had used for years were grossly inadequate for the environment in which they currently worked. The guards had brought up the issue to their respective supervisors. Prior to the request, the jail had gone through a major leadership transformation, changing from a paramilitary facility to one that advocated empowerment and participatory decision making. Cross-functional, self-directed teams were found throughout the department. These cross-functional teams often were named to deal with issues that might be affecting specific stakeholders.

It is Monday morning and you, Pat Reynolds, assistant director of the jail, are having your weekly meeting with the division directors. The issue of guard uniforms is brought up. Apparently, the guards are interested in something more casual and cooler for the Texas heat. John James, the division director from food services, suggests that a team be named to look into the issue. The group decides that it would be best to name a new team from the various divisions (a cross-functional team) to look into the issue. The new team is named, and you are part of the team. The team's first meeting is scheduled for the following Monday.

Respond to the following questions:

1. What will need to be included in the agenda for the first meeting?
2. How will the team select a leader?
3. What may be the goal of the team?
4. What will the "team agreement" contain?

Relocating a State Reformatory School

The department of education in a northeastern state has decided that the state boys' school is grossly inadequate and a dangerous firetrap. After some struggle, the state legislature has appropriated $8 million for a new reformatory.

The department wishes to build the reformatory in a state forest. Such a location would provide attractive surroundings, isolation from cities, and constructive work for the boys. Besides, the property already is owned by the state.

(Continued)

(Continued)

> Recently, conservation groups have issued vehement protests and threatened court action to block the move. They also have started a public campaign to force the governor and the state department of education to reverse the decision. The community where the present reformatory is located has organized a committee to keep it in their community.
>
> The secretary of education wants to form a team within the department to study the situation and make recommendations. She has asked for your recommendations on what type of team to use and how to organize it.

Respond to the following questions:

1. What factors would determine what type of team is appropriate to look into the situation?

2. What type of team would you recommend?

3. Who would the members be?

4. Who would lead the group?

5. What information would the team members need?

A Team Exercise on Gender and Pay[1]

Scenario: The state government's office of personnel management has informed the governor of a gender gap in salaries of professional state employees. The governor thanks the office of personnel management for bringing this to her attention and calls a meeting with department heads to inform them that she will be establishing self-directed, cross-functional teams to study and define the issue and provide recommendations. The governor asks each team to make a presentation to a committee of legislators addressing state compensation.

Individual salary adjustments will be beyond the scope of the teams. The office of management and budget offers to provide research to the teams on women's earnings, occupation, and the labor market.

Assignment: Five cross-functional teams have been assigned; please make sure that you represent different interests and occupations in the state. The team of legislators will also serve the role of experts on teams, assist with team protocol, and evaluate the team on its performance. As legislators, they will be asked to establish criteria to select the team whose recommendations they would like to pursue.

---

1. Preparation for this exercise requires time out of class to research gender and salary issues.

Instructions: Team members: Drawing on discussion and reading materials on communication, decision making, interpersonal skills, and teams: (a) Establish an agenda for the meeting, (b) select a team leader, (c) discuss team agreement, (d) establish a goal for the team, and (e) prepare your findings to be presented to the legislators and the governor.

Experts: Please use the form for "Assessing Team Performance" in this text to evaluate the performance and be ready to assist the team as needed.

Legislators: Establish the criteria that you will use to evaluate the work of the teams. Please work with the other legislators to reach consensus on the criteria.

Cross-functional, self-directed teams will meet. Experts will work with the teams to offer advice and evaluate their team's performance. At the end of the time allotted, the legislators will come together to reach agreement on the criteria that they will use to evaluate the proposals.

Each team will have 10 minutes to define the issue and provide possible solutions to the legislators. Then, legislators, the governor, and the audience will ask specific teams for clarification and further discussion. Finally, the legislators will decide which team solutions they would like to pursue and why. The team of experts will discuss the readings and their evaluations of the teams.

Discussion Questions

What were the issues and solutions proposed by each team?

Which team solution is more likely to be pursued and why?

Did the groups function as a team?

Were members encouraged to participate?

What was the role of the team leader? How was he or she selected?

CHAPTER 11

Managing Conflict

We often hear that conflicts can be mitigated by "walking a mile" in the shoes of another. I offer that it's decidedly more complicated. The entire picture must be understood. What needs are answered, and what needs will be left unsatisfied if resolution occurs? From what source has the conflict grown and created such passion? Is the conflict minor or fundamentally intractable? Can a resolution be reached, or will judicial intervention be required? These questions demonstrate the inextricable link between conflict and psychological intent, motivation, interpersonal relationships, the nature of perceptions, and justice.

—Barbara Male, Director,
Office of Management and
Information, U.S. Department of Energy

C onflict management is an important part of any relationship, any group, or any organization. You may experience conflict with a friend, a classmate, a coworker, a supervisor, or a subordinate. Conflict may be about personal preferences, political differences, or organizational policies and procedures. Conflict may reside largely below the surface, but it also may break into the open—sometimes at the oddest times—and, on occasion, latent conflict may explode into sheer nastiness. In interpersonal conflict (the type that we are primarily concerned with),

the people are interdependent; the people perceive that they seek different outcomes or they favor different means to the same ends; the conflict has the potential to negatively affect the relationship if not addressed; and there is a sense of urgency about the need to resolve the issue. (Lulofs & Cahn, 2000, p. 5)

In any case, as Barbara Male reminded us in the introductory quote to this chapter, conflict always is more complicated than it may appear.

Most students of organization view conflict as inevitable (DeVoe, 1999a). They argue that so long as there are humans, deadlines, and things that do not work, there is going to be conflict. Public administrators are especially open to conflict because they are, by the very nature of their work, required to deal with uncertainty, ambiguity, and differences of opinions. In addition, the current trends toward workforce diversity, globalization, and partnerships with other organizations are making the way in which managers from different organizations and cultures deal with conflict increasingly important (Seybolt, Derr, & Nielson, 1996). In a nutshell, conflict arises whenever interests collide, and the public sector is one place where interests inevitably collide.

Many people think that conflict is a negative force and dysfunctional—that it makes people feel uncomfortable and, consequently, makes them less productive. Yet, when conflict is properly managed, it can be extremely beneficial to the work-place (Caudron, 1999). We already have noted that the environment in which public organizations operate is highly turbulent and often chaotic. Organizations in which there is little disagreement are less likely to do well in such environments. Members are either so homogeneous that they are ill equipped to adapt to chang-ing environmental conditions or so complacent that they see no need to improve the status quo. Indeed, some argue that conflict is the very lifeblood of vibrant, pro-gressive, and stimulating organizations because it sparks creativity, fosters innova-tion, and encourages personal improvement (Pascale, 1990; Wanous & Youtz, 1986; Gruber, 2006). Drucker (1967) went so far as to advise his readers to create conflict in their decision-making process if it does not already exist. Drucker claimed that the most effective American presidents would cultivate disagreement among their advisers to gain a better understanding of the issues involved (pp. 148–149). The ability to generate disagreement might be a hallmark of the effective decision maker, but we should note that generating conflict requires considerable maturity and self-confidence on the part of the manager; many managers feel too insecure to stir up conflict among their subordinates.

By managing conflict properly, an administrator can mobilize disparate pieces of information and diverse perspectives into productive solutions. For this reason, conflict presents opportunities for mobilizing ideas and approaches in the organi-zation and can promote increased creativity, innovation, flexibility, and responsive-ness as well as generally improve the overall effectiveness of the organization. Conflict forces a person to test and assess him- or herself and, as a result, stimulates interest and curiosity in others, promoting productive change. External conflict helps to generate internal cohesion and group loyalty.

Whereas conflict is inevitable and desirable in organizations, a high level of unresolved conflict can be destructive. Ideally, managers are proactive in creating an environment in which the likelihood of dysfunctional conflicts is minimized as diversity of contributions and talents of others are appreciated (Van Wart, 2005). When conflict is not resolved, administrators risk letting differing perspectives go undirected, often resulting in tension and dysfunction rather than creative and pro-gressive change. Kaatz, French, and Prentiss-Cooper (1999), for example, found that conflict among city councils was the primary cause of burnout and turnover among city managers. High levels of conflict on city councils were associated with stress, diminished performance, and ultimately failure on the part of the managers. When city managers became discouraged by poorly managed conflict, many quit, forcing their cities to find new managers willing to tolerate the struggle until they too burned out.

Administrators interested in effectively managing conflict would do well to focus on the closely related issues of communications and trust. According to experts, the most common source of internal conflict in an organization is insufficient or unsatisfactory communication (DeVoe, 1999a). As we saw in Chapter 9, effective interpersonal communication is based on trust. Thus, it should come as no surprise that the variable with the greatest impact on other conditions of conflict is the amount of trust we have in other people. The more we trust other people, the more certain we will be of their motives in conflicts. When there is trust, we are more likely to think that other people have our best interests at heart and will not use power to hurt us (Lulofs & Cahn, 2000).

An important step in moving from theories of conflict to better conflict management is to adopt a mindset that embraces conflict as an opportunity while recognizing the risks involved in it. Wagner and Hollenbeck (1998) listed the following benefits to conflict:

- It lessens social tensions and helps to stabilize and integrate relationships.
- It provides opportunities to readjust valued resources.
- It helps to stimulate innovation and serves as a motivation for change.
- It supplies feedback regarding the state of interdependencies and power distributions within an organization.
- It provides a sense of identity and purpose as differences and boundaries are clarified within groups.

So, public managers need to understand both the positive and the negative aspects of conflict. By using strategies that aim to enforce an environment without conflict, an administrator is shutting off valuable channels of communication. According to Weiss and Hughes (2005), "clashes between parties are the crucibles in which creative solutions are developed and wise trade-offs among competing objectives are made" (p. 93). On the other hand, if an administrator can learn to mobilize seemingly opposing points of view, then he or she can increase the effectiveness of the organization. But learning to manage conflict starts with the way in which people think about conflict.

Where Do We Begin?

We all learn different ways of responding to and handling conflict. Most of this learned behavior comes from observing others around us. These observations lead us to deal with conflict by fighting back, running, yelling, or simply remaining quiet. Some of us have more than one style and have the ability to use different styles depending on the situation. Others tend to rely on one style and might have trouble practicing another style; they choose one style over the others because it tends to work for them.

How Do You Behave During Conflict?

The following questions provide additional insight on how you behave in conflict situations (Lulofs & Cahn, 2000, p. 36). Answer each question as to the extent that you think or believe that the statement is true—*always, usually, occasionally, seldom,* or *never true.*

1. Do you believe that in every conflict situation, mutually acceptable solutions exist or are available?
   __ always __ usually __ occasionally __ seldom __ never true

2. Do you believe that in each conflict situation, mutually acceptable solutions are a desirable thing?
   __ always __ usually __ occasionally __ seldom __ never true

3. Do you favor cooperation with all others in your everyday activities and disfavor competition with them?
   __ always __ usually __ occasionally __ seldom __ never true

4. Do you believe that all people are of equal value regardless of age, race, religion, culture, or gender?
   __ always __ usually __ occasionally __ seldom __ never true

5. Do you believe that the views of others are legitimate (i.e., genuine, accurate, true) expressions of their positions?
   __ always __ usually __ occasionally __ seldom __ never true

6. Do you believe that differences of opinion are helpful and beneficial?
   __ always __ usually __ occasionally __ seldom __ never true

7. Do you believe that others are worthy of your trust?
   __ always __ usually __ occasionally __ seldom __ never true

8. Do you believe that others can compete but that they also can choose to cooperate?
   __ always __ usually __ occasionally __ seldom __ never true

9. Do you believe that how one thinks and how one feels are factors in deciding how one behaves?
   __ always __ usually __ occasionally __ seldom __ never true

After answering these questions, go back and reflect on your answers. For example, are you more likely to accommodate or avoid confrontations? What else did you learn? (You might want to revisit these questions after you have finished reading this chapter.)

How Do Relationships Affect Conflict?

Think back over the past 5 years and recall conflicts that you had with three different people: (1) a personal friend, (2) a coworker, and (3) a roommate. Respond to the following questions.

1. What happens to conflicts as relationships become closer, more personal, and more interdependent?

2. Did you find that as relationships become closer and more interdependent, there are more opportunities for conflict, the more trivial complaints become significant ones, and feelings become more intense ?

Ways of Thinking

As the industrial revolution brought about significant changes to the workplace, the question of how to manage conflict began to receive attention (Gleason, 1997). But from that time until the 1940s, a fairly harsh and "traditionalist" view of conflict held sway. During this period, conflict was viewed as destructive and a result of flaws in individuals' personalities. The role of the manager was to eliminate conflict in the workplace, usually by punishing the perceived initiators.

During the 1950s, the disciplines of sociology and human relations began to influence the way in which conflict was perceived. During this period, known as the "behaviorist period" in conflict resolution, managers began to view organizational conflict as inevitable. No longer were they interested in eliminating conflict completely. Instead, they were interested in finding ways of managing conflict effectively. Strategies were developed to train employees and managers to reduce conflict where possible and to deal with the inevitable conflict they would encounter.

Thomas (1976) built on these ideas by describing two behavioral dimensions that determine how an individual approaches conflict. The first is *assertiveness,* which is defined as taking action to satisfy one's own needs and concerns. The second is *cooperativeness,* which is defined as taking action to satisfy the other party's needs and concerns. Based on varying combinations of these factors, Thomas (1977) went further and presented five approaches that the individual may take (although we should note that different approaches may be more or less appropriate depending on the circumstances).

Competition. This approach is high on assertiveness and low on cooperation. Individuals who consistently use this approach are interested in their own positions and view the world as a zero-sum game with winners and losers. The reason for engaging in conflict is to win. Although this is a common approach for handling conflict, it is not viewed as beneficial to individuals or groups that have repeated interaction. But it might be appropriate when an unpopular action needs to be implemented for the greater good of the organization (Faerman, 1996).

Collaboration. This approach is high on assertiveness and high on cooperation. The assumption is made that most conflicts emerge as a result of interdependence, not incompatible goals. The reason for engaging in conflict is to find a solution that is in both parties' best interests. Collaboration normally takes more time than the other approaches, but the long-term gains of a collaborative solution may well be worth the extra time. This approach is discussed further later in this chapter.

Compromise. This approach is characterized by a moderate amount of assertiveness and a moderate amount of cooperation. As in competition, conflict is viewed as a zero-sum game where, through compromise, each party gets some benefit but also must give up something. Although this approach allows parties to work together, in the long run they will focus on what they have given up rather than on what has been gained. Still, compromise might be the only solution when there truly are not enough resources to provide for another solution (Faerman, 1996).

Avoidance. This approach is low on assertiveness and low on cooperation. It is used when individuals do not want to explore the issues behind the conflict. Individuals avoid conflict by withdrawing or creating a physical separation to avoid discussing the issues. This approach may be useful in the short run in that it allows individuals time to cool off and regain perspective, but it can be quite harmful in the long run. For example, individuals might resent having to suppress their feelings about the conflict, and they might find other dysfunctional ways of dealing with the issues.

Accommodation. This approach is low on assertiveness but high on cooperation. It is used when one or more of the parties do not wish to confront or explore the issues behind a conflict. In this approach, one of the individuals decides that the issue at hand is not as important to him or her as it is to the other person. The individual doing the accommodating is able to build credibility for the next conflict. Accommodation may be useful in the short run but harmful in the long run. If one party continuously accommodates while the other party has its needs and concerns met, then the accommodating party eventually will begin to resent the other party (Faerman, 1996).

Theories of Conflict

Before we continue our discussion of sources of conflict and techniques that may be used to deal with conflict, we should take a look at some of the theories that have been developed to explain conflict.

Systems Theory

Systems theory, which is discussed in more detail in Chapter 12, urges that conflict be viewed as one aspect of a larger system of interactions. Assessing conflict may be accomplished by (a) assessing the working of the overall system, (b) determining recurring patterns inside the system, and (c) identifying individual contributions to the overall functioning of the system. Systems theory urges that we understand conflict by looking for patterns, interlocking sequences, the role and function of the various parties, and typical methods of processing information (Hocker & Wilmot, 1995).

In the view of systems theory, conflict and adaptation are inseparable concepts. Conflict is essential for growth, change, and the evolution of living things. It also is a system's primary defense against stagnation, detachment, entropy, and eventual extinction (Ruben, 1978). Three assumptions guide our thinking about conflict within systems. First, we expect that organizations will experience growth and decay and, by the same token, will experience other aspects of the growth cycle such as cooperation and conflict. Second, conflict is predominantly viewed as a process of reducing alternatives (or limiting options) as one adapts to the environment. This adaptation can be the result of expected behaviors that may or may not reduce the conflict.

Third, processes within a system are interrelated and interconnected. Therefore, decisions that are made to alter one part of the system will affect other parts as well (Lulofs & Cahn, 2000).

Attribution Theory

Attribution theory assumes that the way in which people act in conflict situations is due, in large part, to their individual dispositions and ways of thinking. In other words, the individual in a conflict plays a major role in determining the direction that the conflict will take. For example, the literature shows that dissatisfied individuals are more likely to attribute the causes of their problems to flaws in other parties or in their situations. As opposed to evaluating events objectively, actors attribute negative characteristics to the other actors. For example, an actor might claim that the other person involved in the conflict is "mean-spirited" by nature. In the event of a conflict, an actor also might make attributions about the ability of the other person to handle conflict. For example, if a person leaves the room during the conflict, then he or she might be labeled as unable to handle conflict when, in fact, the person left to simply collect his or her thoughts.

Most of us consider ourselves to be reasonable individuals. Yet it is not uncommon for us to think of other people as unreasonable in conflict situations. Understanding others' points of view requires time, patience, compassion, and skills. Sillers (1981) indicated that "actors tend to over-attribute responsibility for conflict to the intentions and personality characteristics of their partners or adversar[ies]" (p. 280). But when attributing their own behavior, actors tend to give reasons such as unstable causes, judgments, and environmental conditions rather than recognize that their own behavior is contributing to the conflicts. Therefore, an actor might attribute his or her own behavior in a conflict to stress because of a pressing deadline, whereas the behavior of a colleague might be attributed to irrationality. In more theoretical terms, one actor engaged in conflict with another may interpret the other actor's behavior in the situation based on the assumption that (a) something is wrong with the other's personality, (b) the behavior would occur in any situation, or (c) the behavior has been in place since childhood and cannot be changed (Lulofs & Cahn, 2000).

Social Exchange Theory

Social exchange theory, developed by Thibaut and Kelley (1959), holds that people evaluate their interpersonal relationships in terms of their value, which is based on the costs and rewards associated with the relationships. In other words, a relationship is assessed in terms of the amount of effort put into the relationship (costs) compared with what is received as a result of the relationship (rewards).

Conflict occurs when the rewards received are perceived to be small compared with the costs of the relationship. Conflict occurs in close relationships because interdependent parties share outcomes and depend on the actions of others to achieve valued resources. According to social exchange theory, conflict will occur most frequently in relationships that lack personal reward or in those that are characterized by inequity. On the other hand, conflict is least likely to occur in relationships that are both rewarding and equitable.

Sources of Conflict

Whetten and Cameron (1998, p. 323) suggested four sources of interpersonal conflict (shown in Figure 11.1): personal differences, information deficiencies, role incompatibility, and environmental stress.

Personal differences are influenced by the personality and culture of the individual. Conflicts based on personal differences tend to be highly emotional and difficult to resolve. For example, a devout Catholic might have difficulties recommending funding for a Planned Parenthood clinic where abortions are performed. A disagreement about funding may turn into a bitter argument about who is morally correct.

Personal differences also may arise from *information deficiencies* in the organization's communications pattern. This type of conflict is common in organizations and is relatively easy to resolve. As an example, employees in a local government garbage collection unit believed that promotions were given only to those who belonged to the after-hours bowling team. A management audit revealed that there was absolutely no correlation between promotion and bowling but that there definitely was a problem with communication from supervisors. To remedy this information deficiency, work teams were organized and weekly meetings were scheduled to delve into the situation.

Role incompatibility also may lead to conflict and, in turn, to poor performance. Employees not comfortable with their assigned roles and responsibilities are less likely to be productive. A manager might remedy this problem by reassigning these employees to areas for which they are better suited and where they are more comfortable.

Sources of Conflict	Focus of Conflict
Personal differences	Perceptions and expectations
Informational deficiency	Misinformation and misrepresentation
Role incompatibility	Goals and responsibilities
Environmental stress	Resource scarcity and uncertainty

Figure 11.1 Sources and Focus of Conflict

SOURCE: From *Developing Management Skills* (4th ed.), by D. A. Whetten and K. S. Cameron, 1998. Reprinted by permission of Pearson Education, Inc.

Environmental stress also may create conflict. For example, social service organizations with workers with heavy caseloads have unusually high turnover rates. The stress of the nature of the work and the heavy caseloads and limited resources are ideal conditions for incubating interpersonal conflict. Uncertainty in the workplace also may lead to environmental stress. In today's public organizations, downsizing, or "right-sizing" (as it sometimes is called), is causing some of this stress as employees feel anxious about the specter of unemployment. But even when the downsizing has occurred, those left in the organization might suffer as they feel guilt in having jobs while others do not. This type of "frustration conflict" often stems from rapid repeated change (see Chapter 12). Although this type of conflict generally is intense, it dissipates once the new way of doing things becomes routinized and individuals' stress levels are lowered.

From an organizational perspective, Katz (1964) identified three organizational bases of conflict. The first identified by Katz is "functional conflict induced by various subsystems within the organizations" (pp. 105–106). In the public sector, conflict among subsystems can occur not only within the organization but, with the increasing movement toward privatization, contracting out to nonprofit and for-profit organizations, and devolving responsibility from federal, to state, to local government, also among the government organizations and other groups interacting with the agency. A second basis for conflict occurs when different units have similar functions that may result in "hostile rivalry or good-natured competition" (Katz, 1964, p. 106). Organizations often set up boundaries to avoid this conflict. For example, in local government, internal audit departments might conduct financial audits, whereas management audits are conducted out of an office of management and budget. Unhealthy conflict can easily arise out of "forced" competition. The third basis for conflict in organizations is "hierarchical conflict stemming from interest group struggles over the organizational rewards of status, prestige, and monetary reward" (Katz, 1964, p. 106). Here the conflict may involve equity issues (e.g., an unfair distribution of rewards) and equality issues regarding basic status differences (Kabanoff, 1991). In the public sector, this sometimes is witnessed in the allocation of merit raises.

Today's rapidly changing work environment is also contributing to conflict (Susskind & Cruikshank, 2006). Let's examine some of the changes we are experiencing: First, organizations are flatter and more networked than ever before. For example, consider the way that social services are provided by your state government. If your state is like most, it is increasingly devolving its social service delivery to nonprofit organizations. This creates a situation in which state officials are ultimately responsible for social services that they fund nonprofits to provide, creating conflict as responsibility is extended well beyond the authority of the state. Second, organizations are organized as matrix- and team-based. Consider, for example, the breaking down of silos as university academic programs are being asked to work together across disciplines to contribute to degree programs. Third, organizations are increasingly forced to adapt to rapidly shifting environmental constraints. For example, consider the school principal struggling to meet the No Child Left Behind Act requirements while addressing the needs of a more diverse student body. Fourth, organizations are under pressure to "do more with less," contributing to conflict as subunits compete for scarce resources. For example, consider the community where small nonprofit organizations provide transportation services to an increasing elderly population while energy costs continue to rise and funding is not raised to cover increases in population or expenses. Fifth, organizations are struggling to manage increasing diversity, as their workforces incorporate staff with unfamiliar cultural norms. For example, consider the teacher from a culture that values punctuality working with one that has little regard for time.

Diversity and Conflict

Despite progress over the past several decades, issues of diversity in the workplace continue to pose challenges and conflicts in today's organizations (Combs & Luthans, 2007). In previous research we find evidence that (a) conflicts continue in interactions among various demographic groups; (b) policies and procedures promoting a more diverse workforce continue to generate opposition from traditional employees (Kidder, Lankau, Chrobot-Mason, Mollica, & Friedman, 2005; Plantenga, 2004); (c) diversity programs continue to be criticized with perceptions of preferential treatment (Combs & Nadkarni, 2005; Kravitz & Klineberg, 2000); (d) minorities and women continue to have lower job involvement and satisfaction (Roberson & Block, 2001); and (e) covert, subtle, aversive discrimination continues to stigmatize groups (Brief et al., 2002).

Findings also include organizations fostering a positive diversity climate by selecting, developing, and promoting talent regardless of origin, ensuring that pluralistic perspectives are welcomed and heard; demonstrating improved understanding of diverse stakeholders; emphasizing and creating an organizational culture that avoids stereotypes, biases, and prejudices that hinder the individual's development and achievement of organizational goals; and making a conscious effort by formulating strategic organizational goals to successfully manage diversity (Combs & Luthans, 2007; Bell, 2006; Cox, 2000; Kidder et al., 2005; Wiethoff, 2004; Wentling & Palma-Rivas, 2000).

Globalization has had a significant impact on international companies, national private companies, and public organizations as the migration of people brings different cultures to one organization. Differences in cultural beliefs and practices provide examples of how people rely on assumptions and misperceptions as interaction takes place. Baraldi (2006) states that "when diversity becomes a primary value . . . the problem is through which form of communication to coordinate incommensurate cultural forms" (p. 66). Yet, knowing how to manage the conflict in these organizations is the first step for coordinating "incommensurate cultural forms." Diversity requires comparative and nonjudgmental management, where a true/false approach will be replaced with appreciation of dialogue and increased participation. "Dialogue creates communicative conditions of welfare and safety for participants" (Baraldi, 2006, p. 67).

Culture represents the normative and expected ways of thinking and ways of behaving that are passed on from generation to generation within a given group (Axelrod & Johnson, 2005). These authors view all communications and therefore all conflicts as taking place within the context of culture and define culture as it relates to conflict: "culture is the way in which a group of people perceives and responds to conflict" (p. 114). Yet, culture is not a stagnant concept; it evolves over time as we gain knowledge and abilities and as environments influence individuals.

The social identity theory postulates that group members establish a positive social identity and confirm affiliation by feeling more comfortable around and identifying with members of their social category (Billig & Tajfel, 1973; Tajfel & Turner, 1986). This is often reinforced in a fundamental principle emphasized in North America known as the "golden rule," where one would treat others as one would wish to be treated. The application of this rule can lead to discrimination and self-segregation (Jehn, Northcraft, & Neale, 1999; Ayoko & Hartel, 2006). In diverse societies, a more applicable response may be the "platinum rule": "Treat others as they wish to be treated" (Axelrod & Johnson, 2005, p. 133). This rule allows for differences in beliefs, desires, interests, and needs and requires an understanding of these differences.

Individuals' dispositions are rooted in their early social and cultural experiences, and, because conflict is an interpretive behavior, culture shapes people's interpretation of behavior and their style of interaction with others. Therefore, cultural values create a social environment that encourages members to select some behaviors over others. Social status and gender will also influence individuals' choice of conflict management strategies (Tinsley, 2001). For example, avoiding disputes or refraining from direct confrontation with conflict issues in a formal or public sphere has been found to be a prevailing mode of conflict management by low-status individuals and members of minorities (Desivilya & Yagil, 2005). Korabik's (1992) work on gender and conflict resolution found that femininity was significantly related to the use of an accommodative style in conflict resolution, while masculinity was related to the competitive style.

It thus is not surprising that previous research has also found that modal practices relating to strategies for negotiating conflict vary according to one's cultural background and cultural values (Triandis, 1994; Tinsley, 2001). Collectivist cultures such as those of Asian, Middle Eastern, and Latin American countries tend to adopt a harmony perspective of conflict (Kamil, 1997); individualistic cultures in English-speaking countries are more likely to use a confrontational approach (Ayoko & Hartel, 2006); eastern European and Iberic countries are likely to adopt a regulative model of conflict, which relies on bureaucracy and organizational structure to contain conflict (Kamil, 1997).

In a study of 104 businesspeople in Japan, Germany, and the United States, Tinsley (2001) examined values that created observed differences in behaviors within these cultures. What she found was that individualism, egalitarianism, and polychronicity encourage parties to use interest strategies, values for explicit contracting encourage parties to use regulation strategies, and values for collectivist, hierarchy, and low explicit contracting encourage parties to use power strategies. More specifically, Tinsley's findings include the following:

- Japanese used power strategies more than Germans, who used more power than Americans.
- Americans and Germans used interest strategies more than Japanese, but Americans did not use interests more than Germans.
- Germans used regulations more than Americans and Japanese, but Americans did not use regulations more than Japanese. (p. 590)

A word of caution is found in Tinsley's research as she concludes that "each culture uses a variety of strategies to avoid stereotypic models of conflict management behavior" (p. 592).

Stages of Conflict

Thomas (1976) described four stages of conflict: frustration, conceptualization, behavior, and outcome. During the *frustration* stage, one or both parties believe or perceive that their goals or plans have been (or will be) interrupted or frustrated in some way. As the parties become aware of their frustration, they move to the *conceptualization* stage. During this stage, each party attributes intentional and unjustifiable acts to the other party. This may lead to an emotional reaction such as anger, hostility, frustration, pain, or anxiety. During the *behavior* stage, parties are likely to take action. This is when a person's style of conflict resolution—competition, collaboration, compromise, avoidance, or accommodation—will be exhibited. Parties might even escalate the conflict to get others to take sides. The actions taken during the behavior stage will determine whether the *outcome* is positive or negative. Positive outcomes might include a better understanding of the issues underlying the conflict as well as improved relationships among individuals and work groups. Negative outcomes might include resentment, reduced communication, possible withdrawal, and (in extreme cases) exit from the organization. They also might provide the basis for conflict in the future.

Obviously, in many cases, conflict that starts with minor disagreements can build into much more significant difficulties. What has been called the escalation model (Jordan, 2000), a model emphasizing the situational pressures acting on people in a conflict situation, is a way of sensitizing people to how this occurs. Understanding the mechanisms of conflict escalation may lead to a greater awareness of the steps that one should take to avoid a conflict spinning out of control.

Stage 1: Hardening. The first stage of conflict escalation develops when a difference over some issue or frustration in a relationship proves to be difficult to resolve. When progress fails, individuals sometimes cannot just walk away from the situation. Although hostility is created between the parties, they remain committed to finding a solution. The threshold to Stage 2 is crossed when one or both parties lose faith in arriving at a resolution through straight and fair discussions.

Stage 2: Debates and polemics. Discussions tend to develop into verbal confrontations. The dispute no longer is confined to a well-defined issue, and the parties start to believe that their general well-being is at stake. Attention is now diverted to appearances; parties are interested in being perceived as successful, strong, and skillful rather than compliant, insecure, and incompetent. The threshold to Stage 3 surfaces when either party feels that further discussion is useless and starts acting without consulting the other party.

Stage 3: Actions rather than words. Common interests and the prospect of resuming cooperation recede into the background, and each party views the other as a competitor. The most important goal now becomes to gain one's own interests. The parties lose trust in what is being said verbally; action and nonverbal communication now dominate the course of events. The threshold to Stage 4 occurs when attacks are made on the other party's social reputation, general attitude, position, or relationships with others.

Stage 4: Images and coalitions. The conflict no longer is about concrete issues; instead, it is about victory or defeat and defending one's reputation. The parties actively try to enlist support from bystanders and make their confrontations public so as to recruit supporters. The causes of the conflict are now viewed by each party as being rooted in the very character of the other party. The threshold to Stage 5 results from public loss of face on the part of one or both parties.

Stage 5: Loss of face. The transition to this stage is particularly dramatic as the basic status of a person in a community is threatened. During this stage, the counterpart is viewed not only as annoying but as an incarnation of moral corruption. Incidents leading to loss of face usually are followed by dedicated attempts by the parties to rehabilitate their public reputations. When the parties start to issue ultimate and strategic threats, the conflict enters Stage 6.

Stage 6: Strategies of threats. Because all alternatives are viewed as closed, each party to the conflict will resort to threats of damaging actions so as to force the other party in the desired direction. One would expect the other party to yield to the pressure, but instead the threatened party usually sees the damaging consequences of the threat and rallies to issue a counterthreat. The media may be used as an outlet during this stage. Feelings of powerlessness might lead to fear and possibly rage. When each party actively seeks to harm the other side's ability to impose sanctions, the conflict enters Stage 7. The threshold to Stage 7 usually arises from fear of the consequences that might ensue if the threats are carried out.

Stage 7: Limited destructive blows. No longer is it possible to see a solution that includes the counterpart. The other party is now a pure enemy with no human qualities. There no longer is any communication, and each party is concerned only with expressing his or her own message. There is no concern for how the message is received or the response it elicits. The main goals of this stage are surviving and suffering less damage than the other party suffers. The threshold to Stage 8 is reached when attacks are directed at the core of the counterpart. These attacks are intended to shatter the enemy or destroy his or her vital systems.

Stage 8: Fragmentation of the enemy. The main goal of this stage is to destroy the very existence of the adversary and to maintain one's own survival. The threshold to Stage 9 is reached when the self-preservation drive is forfeited. At this point, there is no check on further destruction.

Stage 9: Together into the abyss. At this point, not even self-preservation counts. The enemy must be destroyed even at the price of one's own very existence as an organization, group, or individual. The only remaining concern is that the enemy be destroyed.

In general, this model suggests that there is an internal logic to conflict that transcends individual differences. Instead of seeking to blame the individuals involved, participants in the conflict might recognize the pattern in which they are engaging and therefore be able to design interventions that would prevent further escalation. Conscious efforts are needed to resist the escalation mechanisms, which are viewed as having momentum of their own. Note that the stages of escalation can be easily seen in a conflict between two individuals, but they apply to groups and organizations as well. Fortunately, there are a variety of strategies that can aid in resolving conflicts, but before we discuss strategies, let us consider another theory to help us understand the adoption of conflict management style.

The dual concern model (Blake & Mouton, 1964; Pruitt & Rubin, 1986; Rahim, 1983; Desivilya & Yagil, 2005) helps us to understand our reaction, and that of others, to conflict. The basic tenet of this model is that the conflict-management mode adopted by the individual stems from two underlying motives, concern for self and concern for the other party, and the dominance of the underlying motive will have a bearing on the style that is adopted:

- We will most likely adopt a *dominating* style if we have high concern for self and low concern for the other(s) in the situation causing the conflict.
- We will opt for an *obliging* style if we have a low concern for self and high concern for the other(s).
- We will resort to an *avoiding* style if there is low concern for self and low concern for the other(s).
- And finally, we will engage in a *compromising* style if there is moderate concern for self and moderate concern for the other(s) in the conflict.

Strategies for Negotiation and Conflict Management

There is a wide variety of approaches that are used to manage conflict in the workplace. "Thousands of businesses and government agencies have appointed ombudspersons, people whose full-time job is to help employees, sometimes on a confidential basis, [to] resolve their disputes with management and one another" (Ury, 2000, p. 9). Similarly, mediation, once confined to settling union–management contractual disputes, is increasingly used to resolve employee and citizen grievances. And inside the organization, of course, trained facilitators work with individuals and teams to overcome interdepartmental and interpersonal conflicts. Even more important, the skills employed by these conflict "professionals" are being learned by managers throughout organizations. Public and nonprofit managers are learning to mediate among their teammates, employees, and (often) stakeholders. The success of an organization often is dependent on its ability to handle those conflicts that do arise.

A first step in managing conflict is understanding the strategies that the parties are employing. A number of organizational scholars have noted the similarities between conflict management and negotiation strategies (Smith, 1987). Negotiation strategies are commonly divided into three types: integrative, distributive, and avoidance. Negotiations that focus on dividing up a "fixed pie" typically use *distributive* bargaining techniques, whereas parties interested in *integrative* outcomes search for collaborative ways of expanding the pie by avoiding fixed incompatible positions (Bazerman & Neale, 1992). Others might simply prefer conflict *avoidance*. We should note that culture also biases alternative conflict resolution styles. For example, the Japanese seek to avoid conflict, withdraw when confronted by conflict, or accommodate when unable to withdraw. The American approach to conflict typically is competitive in nature, resulting in either winning or losing. Certain European cultures tend to favor compromise. The strategies and tactics most frequently identified for conflict management are provided in Figure 11.2.

Another question that scholars have addressed is when various strategies are most likely to be employed. Again, using essentially the same three conflict strategies—collaborative/integrative, competitive/distributive, and avoidance—we can examine the possible reasons to employ one strategy rather than another (Canary & Cupach, 1988; Witteman, 1988).

A *collaborative/integrative* strategy is more feasible if the person making the conflict choice perceives a common ground between the parties and, therefore, believes that there is a likelihood of finding an alternative that suits both individuals.

A belief in one's ability to solve problems, success in using problem solving, and a perception that the other party is ready to focus on problem solving contribute to the selection of a *collaborative* style.

A *competitive/distributive* strategy is more likely if the other person shows some resistance to the situation or "if the other's aspirations (however high they may be) seem relatively easy to dislodge" (Pruitt & Rubin, 1986, p. 39).

An *avoidance* strategy is

preferred when the problem of confronting the issue outweighs the problem of avoidance; when it is simply not worth the effort to engage the other in conflict; when postponement to another time would be more advantageous; when

Conflict Strategy	Conflict Tactics
Collaborative/ integrative strategy	Involves a cooperative mutual orientation, seeking areas of agreement, expressing trust, seeking mutually beneficial solutions, showing concern
Competitive/ distributive strategy	Involves competing, insulting, threatening, using sarcasm, shouting, demanding
Avoidance strategy	Involves minimizing discussion, avoiding issues, shying away from a topic

Figure 11.2   Conflict Strategies and Tactics

SOURCE: From *Conflict: From Theory to Action* (2nd ed.), by R. S. Lulofs and D. D. Cahn, 2000, Boston: Allyn & Bacon. Copyright © 2000 by Allyn & Bacon. Reprinted by permission.

one's communication skills are not equal to the task of confronting the other person; or when there will be sufficient time to deal with [the] problem later, when conditions are more conducive. (Lulofs & Cahn, 2000, p. 105)

Pruitt and Rubin (1986) argued that people use these various styles based on a "perceived feasibility or the extent to which the strategy seems capable of achieving the concerns that give rise to it and the cost that is anticipated from enacting each strategy" (p. 35). In other words, we try what we think will work.

Blake and Mouton (1973), among others, favor a collaborative style of conflict resolution. This model is chosen when both parties view their relationship and the goal of the conflict as equally important. Again, a collaborative approach is one that seeks a win–win solution for all parties. This is achieved through the skillful use of a process that affirms all parties and allows their interests to be met. Among the advantages of this model are that (a) all parties have a say in the outcome, (b) the parties are empowered to make decisions for themselves, (c) each person gains a better understanding of the other's needs and point of view, and (d) each person is building confidence in him- or herself to handle future conflicts.

Faerman (1996, pp. 639–640) suggested several specific steps to take in conflict situations that call for collaboration:

Face the conflict: Do not allow yourself to become overwhelmed by the situation.

Get the other party to face the conflict: Do not assume that the other individual will be as ready to collaborate as you are.

Schedule a meeting in a neutral environment: Neither party should feel trapped or threatened by the location.

Establish a collaborative context: Reinforce the notion that you and the other party are there to learn and that you both need each other to come up with a solution. Establish ground rules that will foster positive communication (e.g., no personal attacks, no interrupting, active [reflective] listening).

Discuss your position until you reach a mutual definition of the conflict: Make sure that you and the other individual understand each other's position. Provide relevant facts, information, and theories to support your position. Ask questions about each other's position until it is clearly understood.

1. Discuss the nature of your interdependence, and identify your mutual goals. Some direction for generating potential solutions might readily emerge.

2. Try to think "outside the box" to develop several potential solutions. Doing so requires that you turn off the natural evaluator in you and engage in divergent thinking. You need to reserve judgment and eliminate any other barriers to creative thinking.

3. Integrate several solutions to create a mutually beneficial solution. This might require that you return to the evaluator in you. Examine all of the proposed solutions and find the best elements of each. Discuss how the various

solutions complement each other and how they may be designed to meet multiple needs. Keep in mind the overarching goals and the longer term.

4. Make a commitment to this solution. Sometimes a handshake might be all that is necessary, whereas other times a written agreement outlining the specific terms as agreed on might be needed.

Perhaps the most sophisticated contemporary approach to conflict resolution is that developed by the Harvard Negotiation Project during the 1990s. Leaders in that project inspired the development of a new theory of conflict resolution referred to as the "principled" approach (Gleason, 1997). This approach views conflict as essential in keeping an organization competitive but as being beneficial *only* if it is managed correctly. The principled approach to bargaining and negotiation is contrasted with what the negotiation project's leaders call the "positional" approach. That approach is a familiar one. Whether the negotiation concerns a contract, a family quarrel, or a peace settlement among nations, people routinely begin their negotiations by taking positions. In this approach, each side comes up with his or her own desired solution, argues for it, and ultimately makes concessions to reach a compromise. Fisher, Ury, and Patton (1991) contended that arguing over positions is inefficient, endangers ongoing relationships, and produces unwise agreements. They offered an alternative—principled negotiation or negotiation on the merits. There are four points to their alternative.

People. Separate the people from the problem. A basic fact about negotiations, yet not one easily remembered, is that we are dealing with humans who have emotions, deeply held values, and different backgrounds and viewpoints. "A working relationship where trust, understanding, respect, and friendship are built up over time can make each new negotiation smoother and more efficient" (Fisher et al., 1991, p. 19). The opposite, which is failing to deal with others sensitively as humans prone to human reactions, can be disastrous for negotiations. We suggest the guidelines of (a) trying to understand how the other party perceives the dispute and how he or she might feel about it, (b) suspending judgment, (c) recognizing and legitimizing the emotions at work (yours as well as the other person's), (d) allowing people to let off steam without reacting to emotional outbursts, and (e) building a relationship with an adversary by getting to know the person's interests, likes, and dislikes and by not characterizing the other party.

Interests. Focus on interests, not positions. The basic problem in a negotiation lies not in conflicting positions but rather in the conflict between each side's needs, desires, concerns, and fears. At this stage, you need to ask the *why* and *why not* questions. In addition to eliciting information about the other party's interests, you need to communicate information about your own. By identifying where these interests overlap or are compatible, you can begin to move to the next stage.

Options. Generate a variety of possibilities before deciding what to do. Brainstorming (discussed in Chapter 9) is a good technique to arrive at as many options as possible. Decisions should not be made until all options have been exhausted. Fisher and colleagues suggested that you can convert ideas into options by using different perspectives or "invent[ing] agreement of different strengths" (Fisher et al., 1991, p. 70). Look for mutual gains in the options.

Criteria. Insist that the result be based on some objective standard. Once the objective criteria and procedures have been identified, frame each issue as a joint search for objective criteria. Ask others what objective standards would be most appropriate for dealing with the issue. Reason, and be open to reason, as to which standards are most appropriate and how they should be applied. If you need to yield in the negotiation process, then choose to yield to principle, not to pressure.

By accurately identifying individual needs as well as the sources of conflict, the principled approach can result in positive growth of the individuals involved and the organization as a whole.

> The method of *principled negotiation* . . . is to decide issues on their merits rather than through a haggling process focused on what each side says it will and won't do. It suggests that you look for mutual gains wherever possible and that, where your interests conflict, you should insist that the result be based on some fair standards independent of the will of either side. The method of principled negotiation is hard on the merits [and] soft on the people. It employs no tricks and no posturing. Principled negotiation shows you how to obtain what you are entitled to and still be decent. It enables you to be fair while protecting [yourself] against those who would take advantage of your fairness. (Fisher et al., 1991, p. xviii)

The Program on Negotiation (PON) at Harvard Law School and the Consensus Building Institute (CBI) offer a workshop for managing conflict inside the organization that replaces the emphasis on top management as the problem solver (which they believe only treats the symptoms) for what is referred to as the Consensus Building Approach (CBA), seeking to involve all stakeholders. This integrated model stresses "(1) diagnosing the source of conflict, (2) building consensus from differences, (3) selling agreements and overcoming resistance, and (4) pushing back on the organization (to encourage institutional learning)" (Susskind & Cruikshank, 2006, p. 207). The CBA model has been found to provide longer lasting solutions and to build more lasting organizational capabilities than the traditional top-down methods.

Conflict and the Public Sector

Conflict certainly is not a foreign notion in public administration. The fact that public organizations are part of a governance system that in part plays an important role in mediating conflicts in society means that those organizations often are caught between competing values. For example, one might find conflicting views on how public services are to be defined and a lack of agreement on who is entitled to such services. This typically is compounded by the fact that resources are scarce and, for that reason, choices have to be made as to which programs are funded and which are not. The public administrator often is placed in the role of deciding among conflicting priorities. In this process, legislation is not always helpful, given that it tends to be vague and conflicting in and of itself. The administrator is drawn into the center of the conflict.

Other factors also contribute to conflict. According to Rourke (1992), matters that traditionally were considered internal issues facing public bureaucracies have been opened to much greater outside scrutiny since the 1960s. In the wake of these developments, the political environment of the agencies has become less supportive and more adversarial. The number of groups interested in what the agencies do has multiplied, while the information available to these people about the agencies has increased. Rourke viewed this situation as creating an increasingly hostile environment for administrators. These changes in public scrutiny combined with an increasingly diverse constituency breed a very complex and conflicting environment.

Consider these examples. The National Park Service deals with contradictory policy objectives on a daily basis. On the one hand, the agency must promote public use of parks; on the other, it must preserve and protect the national parks. Often these values collide, as when traffic in national parks becomes excessive and begins to spoil the natural beauty of the area. Other situations that may lead to conflict in public management include issues such as economic development versus environmental protection, increased social wealth versus problems with poverty and crime, low compensation versus the requirement for high-quality public service personnel, democratic demands for responsiveness versus efficiency and effectiveness, special interests versus the public interest, national homogeneity versus cultural diversity, and nationalism versus internationalism. Lan (1997), in fact, viewed these opportunities for conflict in public administration as the rule rather than the exception.

Recent trends in the public sector also have increased the points of contact and potential conflict among the public, private, and nonprofit sectors. Government agencies are having to forge new partnerships with nonprofit organizations and private entities (Frederickson, 1996). The new players have provided a newfound flexibility for the provision of services that are provided by government and may provide greater efficiency and responsiveness (Pynes, 1997). But the increased contacts also provide opportunities for potential conflict. This conflict may provide vibrancy and positive change if managed properly, but it also may result in dysfunction and disruption of services if not managed properly.

Conflicts also arise among different agencies within government. For example, many environmental disputes involve not only a variety of interest groups but also multiple government agencies at the federal, state, and local levels. Consider the controversy over water pollution problems in the Patuxent River in Maryland (Bingham, 1986). At the heart of this dispute was a disagreement over whether the pollution control strategy for the river should emphasize the reduction of phosphorus or nitrogen in the river. The dispute not only pitted upstream counties against downstream counties but also angered fishermen, farmers, environmental groups, and other civic associations. The controversy involved seven counties through which the river flows, three Maryland state agencies, and one federal agency. Each had overlapping jurisdiction over the Patuxent River, and numerous private parties were interested in either the river itself or the use of adjacent lands. Initial meetings to handle the dispute involved 18 scientists and engineers whose differing studies had been used as evidence by both sides of the controversy. The mediators were able to develop consensus on a nutrient control strategy on the river by bringing together approximately 40 people representing all the stakeholders in this controversy.

We cannot begin to provide "one size fits all" solutions to conflict management. It is imperative that we be cognizant of sources of conflict, different styles for responding to conflict, and various conflict resolution strategies. Conflict not only is inevitable in public organizations but also may be necessary for their success. As Barbara Male reminded us at the opening of this chapter, conflict involves a variety of challenges as well as motives. Besides the typical interpersonal and interorganizational conflicts such as personal grievances and labor disputes, public agencies are being challenged by privatization, technological advancement, diversity, and globalization. Any or all of the latter may serve as a source of conflict. For public agencies to remain competitive and function effectively, they must incorporate new approaches to solving conflicts in a cooperative and creative way.

Ways of Acting

In this section, we review some strategies for conflict resolution and discuss the skills necessary to turn strategies into action. We begin by reemphasizing the importance of viewing conflict as a natural part of life for individuals and organizations. Conflict, when properly managed, can provide an opportunity for positive change. But remember that understanding someone else's point of view requires time, patience, compassion, and skills in negotiation and conflict resolution. Ury (2000) provided us with 10 possible problems for conflict and 10 practical roles we can play at home, at work, and in the world.

First Ask Why Conflict Escalates	*Then Use This Role to Transform Conflict*
1. Frustrated needs	Act as provider
2. Poor skills	Act as teacher
3. Weak relationships	Become the bridge builder
4. Conflicting interests	Resolve through mediation
5. Disputed rights	Resolve through arbitration
6. Unequal power	Act as equalizer
7. Injured relationship	Become the healer
8. No attention	Act as the witness
9. No limitation	Become the referee
10. No protection	Act as the peacekeeper

SOURCE: From *The Third Side*, by W. Ury, 2000, New York: Penguin.

This process may be used by individuals seeking to resolve problems or by mediators assisting others. The process requires that at least one person have the necessary skills to execute each step. This person may serve as a model and teacher and help others to attain the same skills. In addition, we suggest the following.

Air all viewpoints. Each party should have uninterrupted time to describe the problem. This might involve some history, but the goal of the process should be to maintain a future-oriented view. While the first party is speaking, the other party is playing the role of active listener (see Chapter 9). This requires maintaining good eye contact and body language, showing respect, and not interrupting. The listener may take notes if there is something that he or she would like to come back to and comment on later. Depending on the intensity of the situation, this step might prove to be difficult. It will require that the listener keep his or her emotions in check and focus on the other person. Next the parties are asked to exchange roles. The listener now has the opportunity to tell the story of the conflict from his or her point of view during an uninterrupted time. The first speaker must assume the role of active listener as just described. During this stage, it is very important not to jump to firm positions prematurely.

Clarify the problem and the interests involved. Once all the views have been heard, the parties may start an "exchange." Emphasis should be placed on separating the people from the problem (Strom-Gottfried, 1998) and on formulating a problem statement. You also should try to clarify the interests that the parties bring to the table. In any case, agreement must be reached on the problem before looking for solutions.

Brainstorm solutions. Brainstorming includes four basic rules. First, set a time limit. Second, no idea is too crazy. Third, everyone participates. Fourth, no one evaluates or comments on any suggestions during the brainstorming process. Premature criticism and closure must be avoided because "judgment hinders imagination" (Fisher et al., 1991, p. 58). When the ideas have been generated and listed, establish some criteria for evaluating solutions. For example, there may be limits on time, money, personnel, and so on. All constraints should be identified. The next step will require eliminating the solutions that will be impossible to fulfill. The remaining ideas that are viable should then be evaluated.

Reach agreement. Once solutions have been agreed on, they should be written down in as detailed a manner as possible. Questions such as who, what, when, and where should be included in the agreement. All parties need to understand what they are agreeing to. There also should be agreement on how the parties will notify each other of problems and how they will behave if there is another problem.

Be aware of your own biases. In addition to the skills and methods just described, you need to be aware of your biases. You might be biased against certain people and biased in favor of others. In recognizing your biases, you need to be aware of the assumptions that you make, often subconsciously, and you need to check these assumptions with the other party before you act.

Thinking in Action

Asking Questions

The most basic method for promoting mutual understanding is to ask questions. Sometimes others are hesitant to ask questions because they might be perceived as criticism. By providing structure, this exercise will help you to understand that questions are not intended as attacks (adapted from Kaner, 1996, pp. 173, 175).

1. Ask for a volunteer to be the "focus person" and another to be the facilitator. The focus person in the group is invited to speak on any controversial problem facing the country. This person starts with "Here is the point I want to make" and is given 3 minutes to speak.

2. When the speaker is done, the facilitator asks the group, "Can you explain why?" or "What did he or she mean by that?"

3. The questions are answered by the group.

4. If the answers are clear to all participants, then go to Step 5. If they are not, then ask those who are unclear about what was said exactly what they still find to be unclear. For example, someone might say, "I heard the person say that we should all share the assignment equally. But I am not sure why he feels so strongly about it. In my view, if we divide up the tasks according to skill, the work may not be equally divided, but the product may be more effective." Give the focus person a chance to respond.

5. When both the group and the speaker feel understood, ask for someone else in the group to take a turn as the focus person.

The goal of this exercise is to promote understanding, not to resolve differences. This should be emphasized beforehand and throughout the activity.

Individual Needs

Have you ever been in a situation where the arguing just kept going around in circles? It will be helpful if the parties can stop arguing over the proposed solution and start talking about their individual interests instead. For an example of a possible situation that might cause this type of discussion, look at the budget surplus case study in the next section, where two parties are interested in the same pot of money. It will become easier to develop proposals that meet a broader range of needs when those needs have been made explicit and understandable to all. Assume the roles of the two parties vying for the funds. Allow each group to make a case for its viewpoint.

1. Make sure that group members understand the difference between their proposed solutions and what they need. For example, beautifying downtown is a proposed solution, whereas honoring a prior commitment for safe sidewalks for pedestrians is a need or an interest. Take time, if necessary, to clarify this distinction among group members.

2. Ask everyone to answer the question, "What are the needs and interests in this situation?"

3. Continue until everyone is satisfied that his or her own needs and interests have been stated clearly, then ask the group to generate new proposals that seek to incorporate a broader range of everyone's needs.

Budget Surplus Case Study

A small midwestern city has a $1 million budget surplus. Two groups immediately begin vying for the funds. One of the requests comes from downtown businesses requesting to use the money to beautify downtown by adding brick sidewalks and planting areas with the goal of attracting customers. As city manager, you are aware that the downtown area has not been doing as well as predicted and that the small businesses are necessary for the development of a "vibrant downtown" as stated in the city's goals. The other request comes from the city's police department wanting to begin a unit to pursue "career criminals." You are familiar with the statistics and know that repeat offenders commit an overwhelming number of crimes. There is an apparent trend in police departments to address this issue separately.

The two groups are competing for limited resources. Both causes are considered worthy of city funding, but decisions must be made given that $1 million will not fully fund both requests. Both crime control and economic development are of vital interest to your community, and both have active constituents who will come to the city council meetings with their requests.

Respond to the following questions:

How will you, as city manager, handle these requests?

What recommendations will you make to the city council?

What role will you play with the constituents of both groups to satisfy their requests?

Parks and Recreation Case Study

Pace is a beautiful, peaceful, and rapidly growing county in the heart of the Sunbelt. One winter day, Joseph Andraseli, MPA, an assistant city manager in a northeastern town, decided that he would answer an ad for a new county manager in Pace. The county commission liked him, and he liked what he saw of the area.

At 9 A.M. on his 10th day on the job, his secretary, Meg, came into the office and said, "Mr. Andraseli, there are five park employees here waiting to see you. They seem angry." Andraseli had a busy schedule, and besides, he was six organizational levels removed from the park employees. But he reconsidered, as he had interviewed on the notion that he had an "open door" policy. He asked Meg to send them in.

(Continued)

(Continued)

Parks and recreation workers were among the lowest paid and least skilled workers on the county's payroll. Their occupation most of the time involved working outdoors. These five workers, all of whom were older employees, wished to complain that their supervisor, who was much younger, always assigned them to the worst parks in the county. The younger employees, who also were "friends" with the supervisor, were able to choose the parks in which they worked. The older employees never were given any say on their assignments, and they wanted this changed.

Andraseli obviously was in a tough position. The grievance had clear overtones of discrimination and had the potential to escalate. Yet he did not want to undermine the authority of the managers and supervisors that stood between him and the five angry men seated across from him. He had not met the supervisor and had only had a limited introduction to the department director.

The union that represented the parks and recreation workers also was a possibility for these employees, but Andraseli did not want the union to represent these workers if he could solve the problem. These workers obviously had not gone through the chain of command, but what could he do to keep this from escalating?

You are Andraseli. What will you do next?

Bayshore Child Development Center

Tanya R. Li has been promoted to director of the Bayshore Child Development Center. The children serviced by the center are racially and ethnically diverse and from low-income families. The White teachers are in the minority and feel isolated. The teachers of color feel that the White teachers do not understand the children. In addition, James, a veteran teacher, has been discovered to have had a criminal record prior to employment at the Center. The state that funds the nonprofit Center does not allow anyone with a criminal record to work in direct contact with children, but he was employed prior to the law going into effect.

Tanya has identified three problems: (1) How can she make the teachers gain better understanding of each other's cultures? (2) How can she help the teachers gain better understanding of the children's culture? (3) How does she deal with James, whose performance has been stellar since he joined the Center 15 years ago? She also understands the shortage of preschool teachers in her area and is interested in creating a more satisfying work environment.

How would you advise Tanya to prioritize the problems that need to be addressed?

What do you believe is at the root of the problem?

How would you address the problems that make up the situation?

What methods would you find most useful in trying to deal with the conflict?

CHAPTER 12

Organizational Change

Change is bad.

—Contemporary management aphorism

Change is good.

—Contemporary management aphorism

I
f there is one constant in public organizations today, it is change. The environment of public and nonprofit organizations, as well as those in the private sector, is rapidly changing, bringing new requirements and demands almost daily. Citizens are becoming more vocal with respect to what they expect from public organizations, especially with respect to the quality of service they receive. Moreover, technology is moving so quickly that today's work practices may become outdated almost overnight. Similarly, there are changes in the workforce and the expectations of workers, leading to thoughtful consideration of previously "radical" ideas such as family medical leave, telecommuting, and job sharing. There is the impact of the new global economy and the constant pressure on public institutions to do more with less. Finally, especially in the public sector, there are increasingly complex demands for ethics and accountability as government is called on to respond to a wider range of interests in society. As one county government department head told his staff,

> If you are aware at all of those changes that are going on, how could you not expect that those would impact your workplace? You are going to be constantly buffeted by a changing world. So, you might as well prepare yourself to embrace change because change is going to be part of your life. (quoted in Denhardt & Denhardt, 1999, p. 20)

Those organizations that develop the creativity and flexibility to adapt to changing circumstances will be those that will thrive during the coming decades.

But as much as we recognize the importance of change in public organizations, we also have to recognize that change is very difficult for most people, whether in their personal lives or in their work lives. When new ideas come forward about how the organization might improve, especially when those ideas fundamentally challenge the existing organization, people might very naturally be apprehensive and cling to the status quo. Some of this resistance to change might be based on objective reasoning. That is, people might truly believe that the proposed changes will not work or that they will undermine an important part of the organization's mission or philosophy. But much of the resistance will be based on more emotional and psychological reactions. People develop standard ways of coping with their environments, and proposed changes may be seen as undermining the security that their past practices afforded. That which is well known and comfortable will be seen as giving way to something that is less clear and therefore a little scary. People also may experience change in terms of personal or psychological *loss*. As familiar surroundings and ways of acting are replaced by new ones, people may long for times past and experience great sadness at what they have lost. Under these circumstances, people might formally challenge the new system or might engage in less formal objections, often through increased "hall talk" and rumors. In either case, their productivity might drop and the organization might suffer.

As we will see in this chapter, there are several ways in which people's normal resistance to change may be overcome and in which change may be implemented more successfully (Nadler, Shaw, Walton, & Associates, 1995, pp. 51–54). Three ideas seem central to bringing about change effectively. First, managers or other "change agents" need to clarify and communicate the problems inherent in the current situation. The goal here is to have people recognize that the existing way of doing things is flawed and, consequently, to open their eyes to the possibility of change. In some cases, public dissatisfaction with the organization's operations will make the need for change abundantly clear. For example, those in organizations that experience massive fiscal crises or even crises in public confidence likely will understand the problem. In other cases, especially those in which change is needed to keep pace with an environment that is changing in subtle but significant ways, specific data or other information might need to be provided to demonstrate the difficulties with current operations.

Second, managers should involve people throughout the organization in the change process. Having people participate in diagnosing the existing situation, in planning new strategies and approaches, and in implementing the changes typically facilitates communication and builds ownership in the change process. Those who are part of the change process usually feel more comfortable with that process.

Third, managers must recognize that people involved in change simply need time. They need an opportunity to disengage from the current state, they need a period of adjustment, and they need to become accustomed to a new way of working. As we noted earlier, change involves loss, and people need time to let go of the past and embrace the future. Change often leads to feelings of stress and insecurity, problems that must be recognized and addressed before the organization can move on.

We should recognize that there are several different types of change that occur in public organizations. For example, we can distinguish between *incremental* change and *discontinuous* change. Even during periods of relative calm, a public organization is constantly changing. Managers and others make improvements in work processes, they experiment with new reporting relationships, and they modify the organization's strategies and approaches to meet changing demands. But these changes take place within the context of the organization's existing framework and orientation; they involve solving problems or tinkering or fine-tuning ongoing operations. Each effort builds on the existing work of the organization and occurs in relatively small increments. These changes might be called *incremental* (Nadler et al., 1995, p. 22).

On the other hand, public managers increasingly are finding it necessary to make more fundamental and dramatic changes in their organizations. For example, a city government facing major increases in population might find it necessary to completely rethink how it operates. Similarly, a state agency whose mission has been completely revised by the legislature might have to make equally dramatic changes in its work. In cases such as these, the organization will not just be trying to adjust its relation to the environment; it also will be seeking a whole new strategy or configuration. Changes of this type will involve almost a complete break with the past and a major reconstruction of every element of the organization's work. These changes might be called *discontinuous* (Nadler et al., 1995, pp. 22–23). Obviously, discontinuous change is far more difficult for those in the organization than is incremental change. Discontinuous change will involve a shock to the system; people will have to learn new ways of thinking and acting, and they will have to "unlearn" past approaches. But given the dramatic changes in the environment of public organizations, such fundamental changes are more and more likely to be required.

Similarly, we might differentiate between *strategic* change and *grassroots* change (Galpin, 1996, pp. 1–13). Strategic change refers to those choices made by executives, senior managers, consultants, and others whom they involve in planning activities leading to changes that are both broad range (typically organization-wide) and long term. Strategic changes often are developed in the course of a strategic planning process that considers the mission, vision, and values of the organization; those forces acting on the organization from the environment; the strengths and weakness of the existing organization; desired future states or "scenarios of the future"; and tactics that might be employed to move the organization in the desired direction. Although this phase of the change effort is highly analytical and often quite technical, it also begins to establish the momentum for change. Grassroots changes, on the other hand, are those that take place at the local or street level and involve middle-level and supervisory-level managers as well as workers on the front line of the organization. These changes are concerned with implementing and sustaining the changes envisioned at the strategic level. Obviously, for comprehensive change to occur in any organization, attention must be given to both strategic change and grassroots change.

A final way to look at change in organizations is to consider the dynamic rhythm of organizational change. For example, Huy and Mintzberg (2003) talk about dramatic, systematic, and organic change in the organization. Dramatic change is initiated in times of crisis, systematic change is slower and less ambitious (and is often promoted by staff groups and consultants), and organic change usually arises from the ranks without being formally managed. While they argue that each change considered separately can be chaotic, they suggest an advantage in creating a rhythm of change, where these three changes are functioning in a "dynamic symbiosis" (p. 80), something that requires managing change with an appreciation for continuity. In other words, at any particular time, there are a variety of changes occurring in the organization, stimulated by quite different forces. The trick for the manager is to be able to comprehend and manage the complexity of these forces for change in a positive way.

Where Do We Begin?

Work through the following two cases and the questionnaire that follows to assess your orientation to change.

To Change or Not to Change?

Read each of the following cases and then write a two-page essay responding to the question at the end of each case.

Case 1. You have just been appointed city manager in a suburban community of about 20,000 people. (The previous manager was fired after questions were raised about his handling of the city's finances.) Although the community is fairly affluent overall, there are significant pockets of poverty and growing concerns among the minority community about the lack of responsiveness of local government. The main issues in the rest of the community seem to be continued economic growth, expansion of city services into newly annexed parts of the city, and how to receive a proportionate share of state funding for education and transportation. How will you spend your first 6 months on the job?

Case 2. You have worked in state government for a number of years, rising steadily to the position of deputy director of the Office of Budget and Management, where you developed a reputation as a strong and diligent manager. Somewhat to your surprise, you were asked to become secretary of the Department of Youth Services. After a long series of conversations with people in the governor's office, with legislators (who urged you to take the position), and with friends in state agencies (many of whom said, "Don't go near that job"), you have decided to accept the position. The Department of Youth Services, originally designed to focus on the problems of troubled youth, has been racked with turmoil over the past several years. There are questions about what the department is supposed to do, how it relates to the Department of Social Services, how it handles federal money, and how it is managed in general. Indeed, if there is agreement on anything having to do with the department, that agreement is that the department is the worst managed in state government. How will you spend your first 6 months on the job?

Your Orientation Toward Change

Choose which endings to the following questions best represent your preferences.

1. Do you prefer
   a. doing a job that you are comfortable with and know well?
   b. doing a job that presents a new challenge every day?   _____

2. Do you find change
   a. invigorating?
   b. stressful?   _____

3. In terms of your career, do you think you are or will mostly be
   a. fixed in place?
   b. always moving?   _____

4. Do you consider yourself
   a. mostly focused on the future?
   b. mostly focused on the present?   _____

5. Would you prefer a job that
   a. is pretty much the same from day to day?
   b. changes constantly?   _____

6. When change occurs, are you
   a. typically out in front leading the way?
   b. typically holding back and waiting to see what will happen?   _____

7. Do you like to
   a. go with the flow?
   b. make things happen?   _____

8. Do you tend to see
   a. the possibilities in a situation?
   b. the realities of a situation?   _____

9. In terms of style, are you
   a. solid and mainstream?
   b. always on the cutting edge?   _____

10. Are you
    a. a leader?
    b. a follower?   _____

Total your scores by giving yourself one point for each "a" answer on questions 2, 4, 6, 8, and 10 and for each "b" answer on questions 1, 3, 5, 7, and 9. The total score represents your orientation toward change. Discuss the results with others in your class. Does the result sound like you? Are there particular questions that you found troublesome? Does this scale really measure an orientation toward change, or is it just a trigger for discussion?

Discussing Your Experiences With Change

Be prepared to talk about your answers to the following questions. Think of a specific change, preferably in a group or organization of which you are a part; if necessary, it can be a change in your personal life. How did the change come about? Who were the people that triggered the change? How did they bring the change forward? What did they do? What did they say? Did they force the change on others, or were others involved in the change and agreeable to it? How did others in the group or organization react to the proposed change? Which members of the group or organization were most resistant to the change? What were the reasons for their resistance? How was their resistance overcome? How did you feel about the change? Were you an early convert to the new way of operating or one of the last to give in? What were the reasons for your conversion or resistance? Was your reaction in this case typical of your reactions in situations involving change? If the change has been in place for a while, how is it working out? If you had been the one managing the change process, how would you have done things differently?

Ways of Thinking

Approaches to Understanding Change

The first step in bringing about organizational changes is for the manager to understand something about the process of change. Over the years, there have been a number of different efforts to conceptualize change and to suggest strategies for change based on these basic ideas. We can begin with a discussion of some of the classic approaches to change and some of those that are more recent.

Classic Approaches

Most contemporary approaches to understanding organizational change have their roots in the early work of social psychologist Kurt Lewin. Lewin (1951) wrote, "Group life is never without change, merely differences in the amount and type of change exist" (p. 199). If this is the case, then one way of understanding the dynamics of organizational behavior is to examine the interplay of forces affecting social change. In any given field of human endeavor, whether in an organization, a social group, or a family, there are both forces trying to bring about change and forces trying to resist change. To use a football analogy, at any given point in the game, the position of the ball on the field actually is the result of many plays by each team and many moves by individual players. There is an offensive team, whose players employ force to try to bring about change in the position of the ball, and there is a defensive team, whose members try to resist or restrict change. Although at any point prior to a new play the ball appears to be at rest, its resting place really is the balance of fiercely contending forces moving back and forth on the field.

Think about an organization facing a question about moving to a new accounting system. The situation "on the field" at any time (with respect to this issue) is determined by some forces that seek to bring about change and others that resist or restrict change. Lewin called these "driving" and "restraining" forces. For example, one force driving change might be the additional information that will become available if the new system is implemented. On the other hand, a restraining force might be that conversion to the new system will be costly. Similarly, another driving force might be that the new system will be easier to use. On the other hand, another restraining force might be that people understand the old system and are accustomed to using it. At any given point, the driving and restraining forces may appear to be in equilibrium, although in actuality there are a variety of contending forces for change and stability that balance themselves from moment to moment. One way of using this understanding in real-life situations is to conduct a "force field analysis"—that is, listing in one column the driving forces at play in a particular change opportunity and in a second column the restraining forces. Once these are apparent, it might be easier to see what strategies, affecting what forces, are most likely to be successful. Used in this way, force field analysis becomes a useful tool for evaluating a large number of interrelated forces and tracking their likely effects in the future (Bruce & Wyman, 1998, p. 125).

In any case, for change to occur, there must be a shift in the balance of forces at play in any given organizational "field." Either those forces propelling change must be increased or those forces restricting change must be lessened. (Interestingly, in many cases, the latter is easier to accomplish than the former.) In either case, according to Lewin, the first step is *unfreezing* the existing situation or shaking loose the current condition of equilibrium. For example, people must come to recognize the need for change and begin to loosen their normal resistance to change. The second step is the *change* itself. The new program—say, the new accounting system— is implemented, and the new knowledge and behaviors that are required to make it work are learned. The third step is *refreezing* the situation. Here an effort is made to "institutionalize" the change, or make it part of the organization's routine way of operating, something that may be accomplished through training, encouragement, and new reward systems.

One stream of theory and practice closely related to Lewin's model, a stream that undergirds much contemporary work on organizational change, is the "action research" model. The action research model involves a cyclical process in which initial research in the organization provides information to guide further action and eventually evaluation. In the action research model, there usually is significant collaboration between group members and an external consultant, with the role of the latter primarily focused on helping members to uncover the most important information and to design strategies for change based on that information. As such, action research itself models the importance of involving organizational members in the change process. As we will see, many of the more contemporary ways of understanding and bringing about organizational change rest on the assumptions of early force field analysis and action research.

Organizational Culture

One more contemporary way of understanding organizational change relies on a concept borrowed from anthropology—the concept of culture. Although anthropologists themselves disagree on the exact meaning of culture, the term generally is taken to embrace those norms, beliefs, and values expressed by members of a particular culture and manifest in their typical behaviors and in the artifacts they produce. The term is used in a similar fashion in studies of complex organizations. The idea is that members of an organization share certain ideas about everything from the appearance of their offices, to the overall values they hold, to the basic assumptions they have about the work they do.

Edgar Schein (1985), whose early work on organizational culture was groundbreaking, actually distinguished among three levels of organizational culture (pp. 14–21). First, there are "artifacts and creations" of the culture, the social and physical environment, things such as physical layout, technological preferences, typical language patterns, and the day-to-day operating routines that guide people's behavior. Second, there are the "values" of the organization, ideas about the way in which the organization *ought* to be. Presumably, if the values of the organization are fully accepted by the organization's members, then their behavior will reflect those values. But as Argyris and Schön (1974) pointed out, many times certain values will be "espoused" by those in the organization but will not actually guide the behavior of members in real-life situations. Third, there are the "basic underlying assumptions" of the organization, those patterns of believing or acting that are taken for granted to the point where they are not even questioned. For example, someone from a Western culture might place an emphasis on problem solving, whereas someone from an Eastern culture might emphasize saving face. In either case, the belief is so basic that, although it affects behavior daily, it is not even a subject of conscious discussion. Schein ultimately took this latter category to be the core definition of culture: a pattern of basic assumptions—invented, discovered, or developed by a given group as it learns to cope with its problems—that has worked well enough to be considered valid and, therefore, to be taught to new members as the correct way to perceive, think, and feel in relation to those problems (1985, p. 9).

In a somewhat more direct fashion, Ott (1989b, p. 50) outlined six elements of the notion of organizational culture on which he found general consensus:

1. Organizational culture is the culture that exists in an organization, something akin to a societal culture.

2. It is made up of such things as values, beliefs, assumptions, perceptions, behavioral norms, artifacts, and patterns of behavior.

3. It is a socially constructed, unseen, and unobservable force behind organizational activities.

4. It is a social energy that moves organization members to act.

5. It is a unifying theme that provides meaning, direction, and mobilization for organization members.

6. It functions as an organizational control mechanism, informally approving or prohibiting behaviors.

As we will see, the last three features of organizational culture tie directly to the question of organization change, suggesting that culture plays an important role in either bringing about change or preventing change.

But before we explore that issue, we should say a word about how organizational culture comes into being and is transmitted throughout organizations. Within public organizations, many important aspects of a specific organization's culture are derived from the larger societal culture, specifically its standards and expectations concerning the role of public organizations in the governance system and the desired behavior of those engaged in public service. But in addition, the cultures of public organizations are likely to be affected by their founding legislation, by political sentiment concerning their work, and by the imprint of early and important leaders within the organizations. Whatever their derivation, the cultures of public organizations, like those of other organizations, are likely to be transmitted overtly to members through the processes of hiring, orientation, performance appraisal, and promotion as well as more subtly through conversations and communications concerning "the way things are done around here." The result may be organizations with widely varying norms, beliefs, and values. For example, some public organizations place a high value on stability and permanence, whereas others emphasize change and innovation.

With respect to organizational change, of course, the key idea is that the culture of an organization will shape the values and attitudes and, in turn, the *actions* of the organization's members. If this is the case, then changing the organization's culture may be a key step in changing the behavior of the organization's employees. For example, many public organizations recently have sought, with considerable success, to create a "culture of innovation" in which members will discard their traditional aversion to risk and innovation in favor of experimentation and change. When asked about their new orientation, they might respond, "That's just the way we do things around here"—a sure indicator that new beliefs and assumptions have become fully embedded in the culture of the organization.

As an example, a decade ago, the city of Phoenix undertook a lengthy process of clarifying its values. After involving people throughout the organization in coming up with the central commitments of the organization, the city established "Our Vision and Values," a statement including the following items:

We are dedicated to serving our customers.

We work as a team.

We each do all we can.

We learn, change, and improve.

We focus on results.

We work with integrity.

We make Phoenix better!

Having such a clear and straightforward statement, and having these ideas communicated throughout the organization, clearly has contributed to the city's culture of innovation and its reputation as "America's best run city."

Latham (2003) has focused on some practical issues in achieving cultural change by focusing on behavior, then identifying a five-step approach to behavior change. The first step is establishing a superordinate goal, the purpose of which is "to capture the imagination, hence to galvanize people to take action" (p. 309). Latham argues that the primary effect of the superordinate goal is affecting people's emotion (e.g., Martin Luther King: "I have a dream" [p. 309]). The second phase is goal setting, establishing goals, which will make the superordinate goal concrete. Latham points out that the goal must be SMART: "specific, measurable, attainable, relevant and have a time-frame" (p. 311). The importance of the SMART goal for the organization is to "obtain goal commitment" by the employees (p. 311). The next two steps, ensuring integrity and accessibility of the managers in the organization, are especially important for overall performance and reaching goals as a result. Latham argues that leaders have to make sure that their words match the organizational superordinate and SMART goals. "Leaders need to take a look in the mirror to see whether their words are consistent with the superordinate and SMART goals" (p. 314). And he also points out that leaders' accessibility is a key for achieving the goals successfully. "It is difficult to be an effective leader when you are inaccessible to the people who are on your team" (p. 314).

But at best an organization's culture is far from simple, and there are disagreements in the literature on organizational change about how successful managers can be in employing a cultural approach to change. Because the organization's culture is socially constituted (i.e., the result of a constant stream of interactions and negotiations among people at all levels), there might be actors scattered throughout the organization who are strong enough to resist the planned changes that management would like to see in the organization's culture. On the other hand, situations do occur in which managers can decisively influence the core beliefs and values of organizational members and, consequently, reorient the entire organization. When thinking about seeking cultural change, managers should at least recognize several possible limitations to this approach. First, cultural norms are deep-seated and may be quite resistant to change. Second, successful changes in an organization's culture typically occur over a long period—5 to 15 years, according to some estimates (Bluedorn & Lundgren, 1993). Third, important ethical questions may arise as managers attempt to "manipulate" the norms and values of those in the organization. Schein (1997) recognized the limitations of efforts to change culture in writing that managers seeking to change an organization's culture must "build on and evolve the culture one has rather than wishing for some dramatic changes or some other cultural forms" (p. 243).

In any case, the cultural perspective provides important insights into the operation of complex organizations, as illustrated in an extended public sector case study of the Washington State ferry system by Ingersoll and Adams (1992). The ferry system began as a private family-owned business but eventually fell on hard times and was bought by the state of Washington and assigned to the highways department and eventually the Department of Transportation (DOT). During its early days, the culture of the ferry system was much like that of a large, extended, and quite happy family. People joked, socialized, and celebrated together. Their interactions were guided by friendship and family ties as much as by managerial systems and detailed accounting standards.

But the DOT prided itself on the strength of its management systems and eventually found it necessary to recommend "the establishment of a mission statement, development of means to measure the achievement of objectives consonant with the mission, and the creation of a performance monitoring and reporting system" as well as to move toward more automated technical systems (Ingersoll & Adams, 1992, p. 228). Although the approaches put forth by the DOT certainly were consistent with images of high-performing public organizations held by the larger culture, they clearly were at odds with the traditional culture of the ferry system, and indeed, much of Ingersoll and Adams's account detailed the difficulties brought about by the resulting clash of cultures. Certainly, the meanings that people hold, or those beliefs and values that are deeply embedded in their ideals and practices, constitute important sources of stability and resistance to change. But acknowledging their importance may cause managers to recognize the need to take culture into account in attempting to bring about organizational changes.

Open Systems and Organizational Learning

Another way of viewing organizational change, one closely related to and often overlapping with the cultural approach, is sometimes called "organizational learning" and is sometimes described as building a "learning organization." In either case, organizational learning starts with individual learning; organizations cannot really learn, but individuals within them can. Public organizations clearly have an interest in encouraging individuals to learn as much as they can about their work, the political context within which it occurs, and their own energies and ambitions. But although individual learning is essential, it is not enough. "An organization may be staffed by authentic, well-informed, capable, self-knowing, and self-developing individuals. But unless it takes steps to allow individual insights and perceptions to blossom outward into a greater whole, no true organizational learning may emerge" (Canadian Centre for Management Development, 1994, p. 58). Contemporary approaches to organizational learning derive from several sources, but most notably early work on organizational learning, particularly the work of Chris Argyris and Donald Schön and what is called "open systems theory."

Argyris and Schön (1987) began by noting how the theories that people hold shape the way in which they actually behave. In terms of guiding action, a theory offers a set of guidelines for practice that will lead to the results the person desires. But there are different types of theories of action. For example, Argyris and Schön pointed to a distinction, which we already have noted, between "espoused theories" and "theories-in-use." An espoused theory is one to which we give conscious allegiance; it is the one we describe when people ask us what ideas govern our actions. But the theory that *actually* governs our actions is called the theory-in-use (chap. 1). Obviously, there may be differences between those ideas or approaches we espouse and those we actually follow. We might not do what we say; we might not "walk the walk."

In either case, there are two ways in which we can learn. We can first learn new strategies that will lead to our desired goals, whether those goals are objective and achievable (e.g., greater productivity) or more personal (e.g., achieving a more integrated personality). Or we can learn to change our goals, or what Argyris (1999) more formally called "governing variables," the preferred states that individuals strive to attain when they are acting (p. 68). Learning new strategies is called "single-loop" learning; learning new governing variables is called "double-loop" learning. (The single-loop/double-loop terminology is borrowed from engineering. A thermostat can be set at a particular desired temperature, programmed to detect temperatures that are too hot or too cold and then to turn the heat on or off to correct the situation. This is single-loop learning. If the thermostat were able to ask why it was set to a certain temperature or why it was programmed as it was, then it would be able to engage in double-loop learning.)

Both types of learning are required in organizations, although single-loop learning is by far the more common type. Where organizational members face routine or repetitive issues, and where the desired end states are clear, single-loop learning is appropriate. Where members face decisions that are more complex and "nonprogrammable," double-loop learning is more appropriate. But these issues themselves never are completely clear. For example, there is the danger that issues will be taken as routine or that end states will be taken as clear, when in fact neither is the case. There also is the possibility of differences between an espoused theory and a theory-in-use, as in the case where a person says that the goals are clear but acts as if they are not. Or there may be conflicts between those theories held by one person or group and those held by another person or group, something that can easily lead to defensive behavior and even outright conflict. Sorting out any of these potential confusions requires double-loop learning, examining the assumptions that underlie our actions, and changing the governing variables that guide them.

As we will see, contemporary approaches to the issue of organizational learning build on the Argyris and Schön approach by exploring conditions under which more effective learning might take place. But before moving to that material, we should note the parallel contribution of what is called open systems theory to recent ideas about organizational learning. Systems theory emerged in the social and organizational sciences during the 1960s and 1970s after enjoying success in areas such as biology and cybernetics before that. In all cases, the basic systems model showed the system (whether biological, political, or organizational) first receiving various "inputs" from the environment either in the form of "resources" (e.g., human or financial resources, information, technology) or "demands" (e.g., legal or political mandates, customer or citizen expectations). These inputs pass through the system and are converted into "outputs" (e.g., products, services, regulations, ideas). These outputs flow into the "environment," where they may affect customers, clients, citizens, political leaders, families, other organizations, or society in general. The response of these individuals and groups to the organization's outputs becomes "feedback" to the organization (e.g., requesting more or fewer services, requesting more or fewer regulations). The system then takes this information into account along with other new inputs, and the cycle begins again (Figure 12.1).

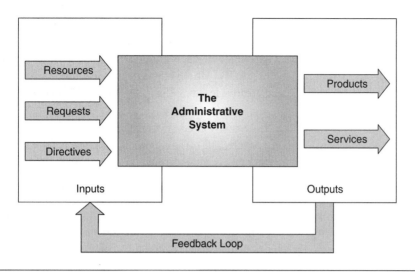

Figure 12.1   Basic Systems Model

Basically, systems theory (as applied to an organization) emphasizes (a) the relation between an organization and its environment and (b) the inter-dependence of all elements of the organization. In this way, systems theory guards against our natural tendency to see immediate problems as being independent of the setting in which they reside and largely unaffected by (and not affecting) other parts of the system. The systems approach can be applied to a wide variety of focal organizations, including organizations, subunits, or sets of organizations, any one of which can be analyzed in terms of the flow of inputs, the processing of these, and the production of goods or services that are the outputs of the system. This approach also helps to clarify the relationships between the focal organization and actors in the environment as well as the relationships among various organizational components such as technology, structure, behavior, and culture. The systems approach is therefore seen as a way of ensuring attention to the "big picture."

Earlier work on organization change and open systems theory has been brought together in ideas about organization learning. Most notably, Senge's (1990) book *The Fifth Discipline* brought the idea of learning organizations to prominence. Senge suggested five "disciplines" in which individuals can engage to build a learning organization.

Personal mastery. This discipline focuses on our sense of self and basic capacity to focus on what is most important while ensuring that our view of reality remains clear and truthful. This discipline connects personal skills—especially skills of individual learning, spiritual growth, and self-mastery—with organizational learning (Senge, 1990, pp. 141–143).

Mental models. This discipline focuses on the way in which we see the world, including our assumptions of how things work, with innovation and learning. Our mental models may pose substantial barriers to new ideas, especially when those ideas conflict with our existing version of "reality." However, mental models also may become sources of new knowledge and creative learning (Senge, 1990, pp. 174–178).

Shared vision. This discipline is concerned with how a compelling vision or ideal becomes part of the whole organization's culture. The organization that has such a shared vision is "connected [and] bound together by a common aspiration" (Senge, 1990, pp. 206).

Team learning. This discipline is concerned with the capacity of a collection of individuals to come together and combine their individual energies in an integrated team effort. The team remains connected primarily because members hold a shared vision of their work, thereby ensuring that individual learning is translated into group and organizational learning (Senge, 1990, pp. 234–235).

Systems thinking. This discipline enables people to see how human actions are connected through a system of interrelated events. Following the systems view outlined previously, this discipline is focused on recognizing the interconnectedness of our actions and their consequences for broader systems. Those who are able to evidence this type of thinking embody the notion of individual and organizational learning. Because it is built on the preceding four disciplines, Senge called this the fifth (and key) discipline.

How these ideas about organizational culture and organizational learning might guide the work of public managers interested in bringing about substantial changes in the quality and productivity of their organizations is explored in Denhardt's (2000) book *The Pursuit of Significance.* Based on interviews and conversations with highly regarded public managers in Australia, Canada, Great Britain, and the United States, his study examined the way in which managers approach the question of change in their organizations, particularly the values that they wish to instill as a matter of culture. Among the themes that emerged in the work of the various managers are the following.*

A commitment to values. The manager seeks organizational change less by attention to structure than by developing a pervasive commitment to the mission and values of the organization, especially the values of professionalism, integrity, service, and quality. Values are clearly articulated by the chief executive and shared throughout the organization.

Serving the public. The manager gives priority to service to both clients and citizens. That priority is supported by high standards of performance and accountability and by a constant emphasis on quality. Most important, the manager recognizes that technical efforts alone will fail unless equal or greater attention is given to the human side, especially to building a sense of community within the organization and a sense of cooperation outside of the organization.

Empowerment and shared leadership. The manager encourages a high level of participation and involvement on the part of all members of the organization in efforts to improve the quality and productivity of the organization. Leadership from the top is complemented by empowering individuals throughout the organization to assume leadership within their own realms.

Pragmatic incrementalism. Change occurs through a free-flowing process in which the manager pursues a wide variety of often unexpected opportunities to move the organization in the desired direction. The manager views change as a natural and appropriate feature of organizational life and employs a creative and humane approach to change, taking into account the personal concerns and interests of members, clients, and others.

A dedication to public service. People throughout the organization understand and appreciate the special character of public service, especially the role of public organizations in the process of democratic governance. The manager insists that members of the organization maintain high ethical standards and encourages them to make the organization a model of integrity for similarly situated groups.

---

*From The Pursuit of Significance, R. B. Denhardt, 1993 (reissued 2000), Prospect Heights, IL: Waveland Press. Reprinted with permission of Waveland Press, Inc. All rights reserved.

In a similar but more recent set of books, Jim Collins, an author well known in the business management field, first explores in *Good to Great* (2001) why some companies are only good, while others, similarly situated, achieve levels of greatness. In his subsequent book, *Good to Great and the Social Sector* (2005), he makes it clear that public organizations are different and that they should not blindly follow business practices for a simple reason: The achievements of public and nonprofit organizations cannot be measured though earned profit. While for the "great" private companies, it is perfectly legitimate to measure the input and the output in monetary terms, for the "great" public organizations, money is a measure of input, but delivering "superior performance" and "a distinctive impact over a long period of time" are better measures for assessing output (2005, p. 5).

Collins (2005) offers five essential elements for building "great" public organizations:

Defining "great"—Calibrating success without business metrics (p. 4). Public organizations should strive for excellence in delivering services. "What matters is not finding the perfect indicator, but settling upon a *consistent and intelligent* method of assessing your output results, and then tracking your trajectory with rigor" (p. 8). His advice to organizations in the social sector is to concentrate on great outputs.

Level 5 leadership—Getting things done within a diffuse power structure (p. 9). The Level 5 leader is the leader able to "build enduring greatness through a paradoxical blend of personal humility and professional will" (p. 12). True leaders are those who empower people. These leaders are followed by the people when people have the freedom not to follow them (p. 13).

First who—Getting the right people on the bus, within social sector constraints (p. 13). True leaders also know who should be "on the bus" and how to attract the right people to "get on the bus"—that is, they know how to overcome social sector constraints and recruit motivated and competent "great" (not good or average) people.

The hedgehog concept—Rethinking the economic engine without a profit motive (p. 17). In order to be effective with all the constraints in the social sector, social sector managers should concentrate on three elements: "passion," "best at," and "resource engine" (p. 19). "Passion" refers to the organization's values and core mission; "best at" refers to the activities that are unique to the organization; "resource engine" refers to the appropriate combination of time, money, and brand.

Turning the flywheel—Building momentum by building the brand (p. 23). Organizations in the social sector should build a brand by which they are recognized in a positive manner. In other words, while the sector itself may face huge challenges, social sector organizations should recognize that which is their particular advantage and work on building and advancing their "pocket of greatness" (pp. 28–31).

In the next section, we examine some of the ways in which the cultural perspective and the learning organization culture are translated into specific strategies and techniques for change. For now, the important lesson is that thinking about organizations in terms of paying attention to organizational culture—the norms, beliefs, and values of organizations—and to building the learning capabilities of their members and the learning organizations provides a useful way of envisioning organizational change.

Approaches to Bringing About Change

Whether we conceive of organizational change in terms of an interplay of driving and restraining forces, building or remodeling an organization's culture, or building a capacity for organizational learning, there are several specific strategies or techniques that may be helpful in bringing about organizational change.

Change Through Management Action or Reorganization

Historically, most organizational changes have been brought about by fairly unilateral action on the part of the managers, and indeed, many organizational changes continue to occur in this way. Certainly, such an approach is consistent with centuries of organizational practice, especially the hierarchical practices of traditional military and industrial organizations. In this view, the person holding a higher position in the organizational system is assumed to have the prerogative of basically "telling" others what to do. In this model, orders contained in memos, policy declarations, or verbal commands flow downward through the hierarchy, and the expectation is that they will be obeyed. Change of this type tends to be formal, impersonal, and task oriented. Although contemporary management thinking has cast doubt on this approach to organizational change in favor of approaches that are characterized by openness, involvement, and shared decision making, many managers continue to use this approach, especially in situations where tasks are somewhat routine, highly structured, and easily programmed.

Many managers also seek to bring about changes in their organizations through restructuring or redesigning their organizations' structures, their basic work processes, and their core systems. Such efforts are deeply rooted in the history of organizational change; reorganization is a familiar refrain in most public organizations. But there are more contemporary approaches that suggest greater flexibility on the one hand and greater attention to detail on the other. In either case, organizational structure—the arrangement of the organization's human resources so as to best meet its objectives—is considered to be closely connected to the behavior of individuals within the organization. Presumably, all else being equal, people operating under one structure will behave differently from those operating under a different structure. Moreover, many believe that changes in the basic strategy of the organization must be reflected in the structure of the organization.

Traditionally, discussions of organizational structure have centered on several key questions. The most important of these is how various functions and the employees associated with those functions should be grouped in units such as departments, divisions, and sections. Early on, Mooney and Reiley (1939), two former General Motors executives, suggested several types of organizational groupings, including what they termed the "scalar" principle (the vertical division of labor such as that between a general and a private in the military), the "functional" principle (the horizontal division of labor such as that between infantry and artillery), and a distinction between "line and staff" (with line offices representing a direct chain of command or the structure through which authority flows, and staff offices serving as advisers to the chief executive but holding no direct authority over line offices).

Early writers on public administration were similarly preoccupied with questions of organizational design. Luther Gulick (1937), the first city administrator of New York and a founder of the American Society for Public Administration, offered four steps that should be taken in creating a new agency: (1) defining the job to be carried out, (2) selecting a director, (3) determining the nature and number of units required, and (4) establishing a structure of authority through which the director can coordinate and control the activities of the unit (p. 7). In turn, Gulick suggested that work can be divided (or functions grouped) on the basis of the following:

Purpose: Work may be divided on the basis of the major purpose being served by an agency, such as issuing food stamps or providing indigent health care.

Process: Work also may be organized around the major process employed by the agency, such as engineering, law, or medicine.

Persons or things: Work may be divided on the basis of those persons or things dealt with by the unit. For example, the Veterans Administration deals with all problems of veterans, including financial, medical, and legal problems.

Place: Work may be organized according to the geographic location of those being served, such as in regions or districts with defined boundaries. (pp. 21–29)

In addition to answering the central question of how organizational units are to be organized, those interested in structural change must ask other questions such as the following. Who will report to whom? What is the appropriate span of control (i.e., how many people can one manager reasonably have reporting to him or her)? How will the assignment of duties and responsibilities for each task or functional area be determined? How will the various units of the organization interact with one another?

Most managers seeking structural change even today answer these questions merely on the basis of the advice of other practitioners and on sheer intuition. But recently scholars and practitioners have begun to investigate the question of organizational structure more systematically and have identified a much wider range of structural possibilities. For example, a distinction sometimes is made between "mechanistic" and "organic" structures. Mechanistic structures are highly formalized, specialized, standardized, and centralized. They rely primarily on traditional top-down hierarchical authority. Organic structures, on the other hand, emphasize horizontal rather than vertical relationships and are much "looser"—more flexible, adaptable, and responsive. Such organizations, which are becoming more and more common, are especially well suited to dealing with rapidly changing environments and to promoting change and innovation.

There are a variety of other organizational approaches that are being tried today as organizations seek greater flexibility and adaptiveness. Certainly, many organizations are becoming "flatter"—that is, having fewer levels from top to bottom. Many organizations are seeking to overlay the traditional organizational structure with self-managed work teams or other such groups that are empowered to come up with solutions to organizational problems independent of their place in the organizational hierarchy. As one example, the "matrix" organization superimposes a project structure on a traditional functional structure, in some cases establishing permanent project teams but, in the public sector, more often depending on task forces or interdepartmental teams brought together for a specific purpose. For example, at the local level, employees from a neighborhood services department, a housing department, a police department, and an economic development department might come together in seeking to expand youth services. As more and more governmental activities require the participation of many different agencies, this form of interdepartmental coordination transcending the traditional "silos" represented by parallel agencies probably will be more and more frequent. And, of course, advanced information technology makes it considerably easier for people throughout the organization to communicate with one another regardless of their positions in the formal structure.

Many managers believe that they can come up with plans for reorganization by locking themselves in their offices and experimenting with assorted organizational charts drawn on their walls. Unfortunately, that approach often spells disaster. More recent explorations of how to bring about organizational change through organizational redesign recognize the greater complexity of the issue. Nadler and Tushman (1997), for example, used an open systems approach to suggest that a key to organizational success will be the extent to which the various components of the organization "fit" together. That is, the degree to which the organization's strategy, its work processes, its people (and their capabilities), its structure, and its culture are aligned will determine the organization's effectiveness (p. 34). The key is to engage in a careful and systematic analysis of these various components with an eye toward their "congruence."

Interestingly, Nadler and Tushman (1997) argued that the design of organizational "arrangements" should not be limited to questions of organizational structure—those decisions reflected in that standard organizational chart. Rather, there are three categories: (1) structures (the formal patterns of relationships between groups and individuals), (2) processes (specifically designed sequences of steps, activities, and operational methods), and (3) systems (applications of either physical or social technologies that enable the performance of work such as human resources systems or information systems) (p. 47–48). Nadler and Tushman's approach to organizational design, then, is comprehensive:

> Organization design involves decisions about the configuration of the formal organizational arrangements including the formal structure, processes, and systems that make up an organization. The goal is to develop and implement a set of formal organizational arrangements that will, over time, lead to congruence, or good fit, among all the components of the organization: strategy, work, people, the informal organization, and the formal organizational arrangements. (pp. 48)

Those undertaking organizational design efforts would be well advised to think systematically about how all of the different elements of the organization might fit together in the future.

Despite these advancements, we should note that recent writers have called into question changes in the organizational structure as a way to improve performance (Oxman & Smith, 2003). Although they confirm the ameliorative effects structural change can have on cost efficiencies, they argue that organizational communication and performance management no longer depend heavily on the organizational hierarchy. They emphasize that the new technologies (e-mail, voice mail, text messages) "prevent the miscommunications associated with the handoff of messages from person to person across the levels" (p. 78). They further point out that the increasing knowledge and competitiveness of the employees together with project-by-project evaluations and individual project consolidation make less significant the levels in the organizational hierarchy. They suggest focusing on what they call "nonstructural issues such as *people, process* and *rewards*" in order to achieve flexibility in the organization (p. 79). "Flexibility is trumping structure as the governing principle behind organization design" (p. 80).

Organization Development

Another approach to organizational change that has received widespread attention and application over the past several decades is organization development (OD). This is an approach to planned change in the organization that is (a) based in the behavioral sciences; (b) aimed at systemwide improvements in the functioning of the organization; (c) conducted primarily with a focus on improving individual human capabilities, especially "process" skills—that is, *how* things are done as opposed to *what* is being done (typically issues such as communications, power and authority, and motivation); and (d) guided by an external consultant or interventionist hired to "facilitate" the group's development. In each case, the goal of an OD intervention is to help members of the organization themselves to bring about needed organizational changes. (A variety of different definitions of OD are discussed in French and Bell [1999].)

The role of the OD consultant is quite different from other consulting roles. A consultant, for example, may be hired to provide *expertise* to the organization. That is, a manager may identify a need for competencies, such as skills in survey research or financial analysis, not contained in the organization or already assigned to other tasks. Although the manager and consultant may work together to define or diagnose the problem, in the end the consultant basically tells the manager what should be done. A consultant also may be hired into a *doctor–patient* relationship. That is, the consultant is brought into the organization to figure out what is wrong with the patient and then to prescribe a course of action for the patient to follow. Here both the diagnostic role and the prescriptive role lie largely with the consultant, making the relationship particularly dependent on a complete and accurate flow of information between the consultant and the client and on the accuracy of the consultant's recommendation and the ability (and willingness) of the client to follow that recommendation. OD relies instead on what sometimes is called *process consultation*, an approach that assumes that "the client must learn to see the problem for himself and be actively involved in generating a remedy" (Schein, 1988, p. 9). The OD consultant neither tells the client what to do nor prescribes a remedy. Rather, the consultant recognizes the client's autonomy by working with the manager and those throughout the organization in identifying issues, developing solutions, and implementing those that are proposed.

In a classic portrayal of the interventionist's role in OD, Argyris (1970) suggested the importance of having solutions generated from within the organization rather than imposed from outside of the organization. In keeping with this approach, he recommended that the consultant's role be to generate valid and useful information, to promote free and informed choice on the part of the client group, and to help build internal commitment to the choice that is made. Argyris explained each point as follows.

Valid and useful information. "Valid information is that which describes the factors, plus their interrelationships, that create the problem for the client system" (1970, p. 17). Such information not only must be valid but also must be capable of being used by the client group to change the system.

Free choice. "Free choice places the focus of decision making in the client system. . . . Through free choice, the clients can maintain the autonomy of their system" (1970, p. 19).

Internal commitment. "Internal commitment means the course of action or choice that has been internalized by each member so that he experiences a high degree of ownership and has a feeling of responsibility about the choice and its implications" (1970, p. 20).

Whereas the OD consultant aids the client system in exploring problems and in designing solutions to those problems, the interventionist is, in this view, largely neutral with respect to the solutions chosen so long as the group is committed to those solutions.

But other OD consultants bring a set of fairly explicit values to their consultation. Robert Golembiewski (1972), probably the leading OD theorist in public administration, suggested that OD represents a particular philosophy at odds with traditional top-down tendencies. According to Golembiewski, this philosophy includes the following values:

- Mutual accessibility and open communications
- A willingness to experiment with new behaviors and to choose those that seem most effective
- A collaborative concept of authority that emphasizes cooperation and willingness to examine conflicts openly
- Creation of a mutual helping relationship involving a sense of community and acceptance of responsibility for others
- Authenticity in interpersonal relationships (pp. 60–66)

In this less neutral view, the bias clearly is toward democratic approaches as opposed to authoritarian ones. The interventionist comes into the organization believing that certain behaviors are more likely to produce positive results than are others (Figure 12.2).

To create an open problem-solving climate through the organization so that members can confront problems rather than fight about or flee from them

To build trust among individuals and groups throughout the organization

To supplement or even replace the authority of role or status with the authority of knowledge and competence

To locate decision-making and problem-solving responsibilities as close as possible to information sources

To make competition, where it exists, contribute to meeting work goals as opposed to win–lose competition

To maximize collaboration between individuals and units whose work is interdependent

To develop a reward system that recognizes both the achievement of the organization's mission and the growth and development of the organization's members

To increase self-control and self-direction for people within the organization

To create conditions where conflict is surfaced and managed appropriately and positively

To increase awareness of group process and its consequences for performance

---

Figure 12.2   Major Objectives of Typical Organization Development Programs

SOURCE: Adapted from *Public Administration: An Action Orientation*, by R. B. Denhardt, 1999, Fort Worth, TX: Harcourt Brace.

Whatever their philosophies, OD practitioners typically employ a variety of strategies and techniques to help facilitate organizational change. These include the following.

T-groups. The earliest (and still most controversial) OD interventions evolved from the T-group (with *T* standing for *training*) or sensitivity group movement of the 1960s. T-groups involve 10 to 12 members and a facilitator brought together for an extended period in an unstructured group situation where the group must create its own agenda, its own norms and expectations, and its own models for appropriate behavior. Advocates of T-group training suggest that such training can increase members' sensitivity to and competence in dealing with behavioral issues, their understanding of group and intergroup dynamics, and their skills in dealing with uncertainty and ambiguity.

Process consultation. As mentioned earlier, process consultation is concerned with helping a client or client group understand more clearly and act on those process issues that arise in organizational settings. These process issues include but are not limited to communications, the roles and functions of group members, group problem solving and decision making, the development and maintenance of group norms and expectations, and the role of leadership, power, and authority in groups and organizations.

Third-party interventions. Conflict or competition occasionally arises in groups and organizations. Third-party interventions are designed to bring the parties together in the presence of a facilitator to identify problems and begin to develop ways of dealing with them in a constructive way, often reaching solutions that are consistent with the basic interests of both parties to the conflict.

Survey feedback. Perhaps the most widely used OD technique, survey feedback involves the consultant collecting data from a broad cross-section of the organization (or its entire population) through questionnaires, interviews, or focus groups and then analyzing the resulting data and feeding back the data to the members so that they can work together to interpret the information and design corrective actions. Typically, members of the organization hold a great deal more information about the organization and its problems than is apparent in their day-to-day interactions. Having such information collected and presented to them often helps members to assume ownership not only for existing problems but for their solutions as well.

Quality of work life. Traditionally, quality of work life programs alternated between improving the social and psychological conditions of work for individuals and involving lower-level participants in organizational decision making, both of which seem to contribute at least indirectly to enhanced organizational performance (Cummings & Huse, 1989, chap. 11). Among the approaches that might be undertaken in a quality of work life intervention are creating flatter and leaner organizational structures emphasizing employee involvement, developing job designs that provide employees with high levels of discretion and involve them in a variety of tasks, and opening communications throughout the organizations horizontally, vertically, and diagonally.

Team building. Much of the work of the modern organization is done in groups or teams, so it is not surprising that OD practitioners have been especially attentive to building effective teams. Again, a facilitator may work with a specific team to identify elements of individual behavior and group dynamics that might impede the group's functioning and then to develop strategies for overcoming those problems. The content of such sessions probably will include attention to the purpose of the group, how comfortable members are with one another, how open the pattern of communication within the group is, how various members play different and important roles in the group, and how leadership in the group is shared among members (Parker, 1990, p. 33).

We should note that although OD in its classic sense involves the use of external consultants, many elements of the OD philosophy and even the techniques used by OD practitioners have been appropriated by managers for their own use in the workplace. Certainly, the central OD commitment—that of involving people throughout the organization in the analysis, interpretation, and solution of organizational problems—has become a key tenet in contemporary management. Largely because of OD theory and practice, managers today agree that involving employees in organizational change is an essential contributor to success in bringing about change and that improving the social and psychological circumstances of work life can have enormous benefits in terms of organizational productivity.

Change Through Six Sigma

Six Sigma is one of the most recent and most widely heralded organizational change and quality improvement strategies. Originally designed to increase business profitability, the Six Sigma approach was developed in the mid-1980s by Dr. Mikel Harry, then a senior staff engineer at Motorola, and used by executives such as George Fisher and Richard Schroeder of that company to produce both improvements in quality and reductions in cost, with savings due to operations improvements alone of over $2.2 billion. From Motorola, the Six Sigma methodology was taken by Schroeder and Harry to such companies as ABB (Asea Brown Bovari), an international engineering firm, and later to Texas Instruments, Allied Signal, and General Electric, in each case producing documented savings of hundreds of millions of dollars within a relatively short time period (1 to 2 years). Having shown such impressive results, Six Sigma is being employed by hundreds of companies and an increasing number of public and nonprofit agencies as well.

What is Six Sigma? Six Sigma is "a comprehensive and system for measuring, achieving, sustaining business success" (www.6-sigma.com/index.html; retrieved June 2007). More specifically, Six Sigma begins by employing statistical analysis to locate process errors that produce defects in a product line. A "sigma rating" is then determined, based on the number of defects per million products. Strategies are developed for correcting errors and in turn improving quality and reducing cost.

Six Sigma itself performs at the level of 99.9997% perfection, meaning that the organization delivers its services with only 0.0003% defects among 1,000,000 transactions. This means that only three to four customers are not satisfied by the service (or they receive services with defects). For example, a state-level Office of Cash and Debt Management could decide to implement Six Sigma methodology and establish a goal of achieving 99.9997% perfection with domestic cash transactions. That would mean that the Office of Cash and Debt Management would allow only 3 to 4 defective transactions out of 1,000,000 total. On the one hand, this will reduce the extra costs that the unit is paying because of the errors that occur while making the payments, and on the other it will increase the satisfaction of the customers because they would be paid on time and without any inconvenience.

Advocates of Six Sigma claim that their techniques and approaches can turn around poor performance, improve public perception of a company's products, develop an improved financial rating, create a competitive barrier, corner markets, and improve the cycle time of new product development. Six Sigma uses statistical tools, but it is focused on the customers. "The measures of Six Sigma performance begin with the customer" (Pande & Holpp, 2002, p. 214); it helps managers to decide which data and information they need and how this data and information can be best used. Using the Six Sigma methodology, managers in the organizations can define clear goals and act on events in advance—they can be proactive.

The implementation of Six Sigma starts with a management decision on what the organization needs to achieve: a full-scale change (business transformation), strategic improvements limited to one or two critical needs, or solving persistent problems within the organization. Once this decision has been made, many employees and managers in the organization are trained for different roles: Black Belt, Green Belt, Master Black Belt, Champion, and Implementation Leader. The people acting in these roles have specific tasks that should be successfully implemented. The Black Belt works with a team on a specific Six Sigma project and is "responsible for getting the team started, building their confidence, observing and participating in training, managing team dynamics, and bringing the project to successful results" (Pande & Holpp, p. 25). The Green Belt brings the new Six Sigma tools into day-to-day activities. Most employees in the organization are trained to perform this role. The Master Black Belt is an expert in Six Sigma analytical tools, who trains Black Belts and their teams. The Champion is the person in the organization who provides the resources, informs the management on the Six Sigma progress, and makes sure that ongoing projects are in accordance with organizational goals. "The ultimate goal of the Implementation Leader is to drive Six Sigma thinking, tools, and habits across the organization and to help the effort reap financial and customer benefits" (p. 25).

All Six Sigma roles can be successfully performed if the actors are adequately trained. Six Sigma involves cultural change as well, and the people in their new roles have to act to facilitate that change. These new roles definitely require abandoning the well-rooted saying "That's the way things are done here." Changing habits and establishing new statistical tools in order to improve the quality of processes and to achieve almost perfect performance is a hard task. Management has to know how to energize the employees and most of all has to be persistent in meeting the established high goals. Six Sigma, if appropriately established and implemented, can be a powerful tool to motivate employees. "When the company is committed to improving its processes, to meeting customer expectations, to cutting cost, employees will naturally feel motivated to do better" (Brue, 2002, p. 30). The fact that they actively participate in the implementation of the changes and ultimately in achieving the goals of the organization motivates the employees to give their best to the organization.

The Six Sigma methodology follows five steps (DMAIC) in establishing goals, tools, and measures:

D—Defining the projects and goals. The project(s) should be meaningful and manageable, which means that the team can get the project(s) done.

M—Measuring the current performance. The units of measurement are the outputs or outcomes, the process itself, and the inputs.

A—Analyzing and determining the roots of the problems or defects.

I—Improvement of the outputs or outcomes, the process, and the inputs.

C—Control. Control means "developing a monitoring process to keep track of changes . . . ," "creating a response plan for dealing with problems that may arise . . . ," and "helping focus management's attention on a few crucial measures." (Pande & Holpp, 2002, p. 54)

The DMAIC steps can be briefly explained by using our example of the Office of Cash and Debt Management transactions. Once the managers have decided to use Six Sigma methodology, they have to define what would be the goal. As used in the example, let us suppose that the goal of the project is to reduce the number of errors made in their cash flow transactions to 3 to 4 in 1,000,000. After establishing the goal, a project team has to be formed and the people on that team should be trained. The other employees who will not be part of the project team have to be trained to perform day-to-day operations in order to achieve the goal. The next step is measuring the current performance.

The project team should gather data, such as how many transactions a day this office is doing per certain time unit (daily/monthly/semiannually/annually), how many defects are occurring, where in the process the defects occur, the amount of fees that this office is paying because of the repeated transactions, whether there are any other consequences induced by these errors, and so on. The data then must be carefully analyzed in order to find the source of the problem. In our case, the analysis might show that one part of the problem is outdated software that cannot adequately support the increased number of transactions, and another part of the problem lies in the lack of training for employees. The improvement step has to solve these two major problems by providing new software and organizing training for the employees. The final step of DMAIC is control, or the phase where the Office of Cash and Debt Management would ensure that the results of the project will last in the future.

The ultimate goal of Six Sigma is to reach almost perfect performance in the organization, to satisfy the customers, and finally to save money by reducing the defects in the production phase and the delivery of goods and services. This is possible only if the whole organization is aware of the goal and is willing to implement the necessary changes in the organization. Six Sigma establishes the goals and explains how the changes should be made. It changes the mission and the culture of the organization and the roles of the employees, it requires the whole organization to be involved in the new process, and it also requires support from the managers who play the major role in the success of this new method.

The organizations that have decided to use Six Sigma methodology are faced with great challenges. They have to be prepared to implement all necessary steps properly, they have to train their employees in how to perform new roles, and they have to be persistent with the established goals if they want to enjoy the benefits. Producing and delivering goods and services with the greatest customer satisfaction, avoiding the defects, and saving money are goals of both private companies and public organizations.

Obviously, the language of Six Sigma is currently the language of business. And even though Six Sigma advocates claim successes in service industries as well as product-oriented concerns, the greatest gains based on Six Sigma to date have been in large manufacturing companies. But that is not to say that the techniques and approaches of Six Sigma cannot be adapted to the public sector generally and to human service agencies in particular—for example, through the use of outcome measurement or balanced scorecard techniques.

The Management of Change

Public managers often are called on to bring about substantial change in their agencies. Some managers are specifically hired to "fix" existing agencies. But even for managers who have been in place for some time, new legislative mandates, a public crisis of confidence, dramatic changes in the environment, or a vague feeling that things could be working much better might lead managers to think in terms of a systemwide organizational transformation. We already have examined some of the approaches and strategies that managers might employ in specific situations, but we also should ask how managers might bring about systemwide improvements in quality and productivity in their organizations.

Steps in Organizational Transformations

Studies have shown some agreement concerning the steps that managers should take to bring about organizational change. For example, a study by Denhardt and Denhardt (1999) explored the question of how local government managers bring about change, based on case studies of three highly regarded local government leaders. Briefly, Robert O'Neill's approach in Fairfax County, Virginia, has been to emphasize open communications throughout the organization, significant involvement of county employees in major decisions, and the building of more effective linkages with the community. Descriptions of Phil Penland's work in Altamonte

Springs, Florida, tend to center on two or three especially important or signal efforts that helped to set a tone or establish the culture of change and innovation that characterizes Altamonte Springs today. But what is most striking is the way in which Penland has encouraged a culture in which change is seen as a positive value rather than as something to be feared and in which all employees are actively involved in pursuing innovations that make the city work better. Jan Perkins in Fremont, California, has led a transformation that has centered on building more effective customer service, working internally and externally through the use of interest-based bargaining, and significantly involving citizens in every aspect of the city's governance (see case study later).

Based on these case studies, Denhardt and Denhardt (1999) developed a model of leadership for change that posits a series of five steps undertaken by those wishing to successfully bring about change in their communities. Successful public managers hoping to lead change must (1) assess the organizations' environments and the need for change, (2) plan for change both strategically and pragmatically, (3) build support for the change process both through conversation and through modeling the change process in the managers' own behavior, (4) implement specific changes while at the same time encouraging a broader positive attitude toward change and innovation, and (5) institutionalize the changes. Cutting across these issues, Denhardt and Denhardt also pointed out the importance of managers' learning capacities, especially with respect to knowing themselves and their values, knowing their communities, knowing their organizations, and knowing their governing bodies. Finally, the authors suggested that the form of leadership exhibited by these managers differs significantly from the traditional top-down, internally focused approach frequently employed in public administration in that the former is much more open, free-flowing, engaging, and collaborative than the latter, yet it is firmly committed to the ideal of service to the community.

Although public sector change activities are likely to be considerably more attuned to public engagement than those in the private sector, these findings are consistent with those of scholars examining change in the private sector. Nadler and colleagues (1995, chap. 6), for example, suggested five phases in the change process.

1. *Diagnosis.* This is a thoughtful assessment of the current state—its strengths, weaknesses, and embedded aspirations. Diagnosis should not be complex or cumbersome; its primary purpose is to identify the resources available for developing the new organization. Therefore, the focus is on clarity, simplicity, and communicability.

2. *Clarification and coalition building.* The objectives during this phase are to refine and clarify the vision of the future state and to recruit key change agents and interventions. Here activity picks up; staff members are involved in articulating the future state and describing the specific changes to take place.

3. *Action.* The major changes are launched, and the organizational identity and architecture are communicated. At the end of this phase, the major pillars of the new organization should be in place.

4. *Consolidation and refinement.* During this phase, there are several activities ranging from assessment and checking to moving people who are not working out. The key output at the end of this phase is the broad-based implementation and acceptance of change.

5. *Sustainability.* During this phase, the challenge is to reflect on how the organization is working and what refinements, if any, are required to achieve the original design intent. Typically, the executive team collects data and uses them to evaluate the new organization's strengths and weaknesses. In fact, one of the outputs of this phase might be to launch incremental change or refinements to the now current state. The purpose is to build the new organization into a high-performance mode.

Kotter's (1996) work *Leading Change* added an interesting dimension to the transformational process, suggesting that too much complacency is the death knell of organizational change. He argued that managers often overestimate their own influence in organizations and underestimate how difficult it is to get people to change. According to Kotter, "Without a sense of urgency, people won't give that extra effort that is often essential" (p. 5). He even recommended that managers create crises by allowing financial losses to occur or allowing errors to blow up instead of being corrected. Although such tactics seem especially questionable in public organizations, they at least emphasize Kotter's recommendation that managers begin the change process by creating (or at least communicating) a sense of urgency.

Change and Innovation in Public Organizations

Public organizations present unique problems and opportunities for managers seeking organizational changes. For example, although politics plays a role in all organizational changes, the politics of change are considerably more complex in public organizations than in private ones. In a democratic political system, power is widely shared, meaning that many constituencies will need to be involved and many approvals might be required. As noted earlier, this aspect of change in public organizations is likely to become even more important in the future as the most pressing problems cut across agency and jurisdictional boundaries. Under these circumstances, Popovich (1998) and his writing team colleagues recommended that public managers be especially attentive to the politics of change. Among other things, the contributors to that volume noted that nearly every move public managers make will have political implications. Political leaders will want to know what is going on and will resent surprises. Moreover, managers should remember that government agencies are the way they are because somebody at some time wanted them to be that way. Nearly all barriers to effective agency performance (i.e., those burdensome rules and regulations) started out as reforms, and this political history is important to consider. For example, the state of Maryland has particularly rigid procurement rules that one might be inclined to change except that those rules are the result of a series of scandals that became important politically. So, any change-oriented public manager, in Maryland or anywhere else, needs to consider how proposed changes will be viewed by elected officials, citizens, and others.

Another important concern is that leadership in political offices and appointed offices can turn over quite rapidly. This means that changes that appear extremely important to one group might, for political or other reasons, appear quite "out of touch" to another group. Numerous changes in public organizations have garnered enthusiasm and support when they were introduced, only to be quickly discarded as the next administration came on board. But this is not always the case. The state of Oregon, for example, began a broad-based strategic planning process in 1988 that established several hundred benchmarks for assessing the progress of state government. Three consecutive gubernatorial administrations have embraced those benchmarks and maintained the momentum set two decades ago. (One variation of this issue is, of course, that organizational changes are influenced by political cycles, especially the calendar of elections. Beginning major changes during the final year of a particular administration is not likely to receive strong support. Instead, this is the time to secure and institutionalize those changes that already have been made.)

Whether because of political constraints or because of other considerations, public managers seeking change in their organizations often make progress only through what Behn (1988) called "groping along" and what Denhardt (2000) called "pragmatic incrementalism." Behn argued that change in public organizations often is not so much a matter of rational planning in which a manager considers all courses of action and then settles on a strategy that guides all of his or her future actions. Instead, "an excellent manager has a very good sense of his objectives but lacks a precise idea about how to realize them" (p. 645). But Denhardt pointed out that these managers are not moving forward randomly or without insight. Rather, they have a very clear idea of where they want to go, even though they might lack specific steps to reach those places. They do not have step-by-step plans, but they do have strategies, and from day to day and from moment to moment, they take advantage of opportunities to move in the desired directions. They might talk with citizen groups, encounter legislators in restaurants, or hold formal staff meetings. But in all of these settings, their messages remain much the same and fully consistent with the directions in which they want to move their organizations (Denhardt, 2000, chap. 5).

Another issue that has received increasing attention in the literature on public administration is how to create organizational norms where experimentation and innovation are not feared but rather valued. Light (1998) studied 26 public and nonprofit organizations in which innovation had become a way of life. Light found that these organizations followed many of the same prescriptions for organizational change that we already have discussed but that they were particularly adept at encouraging creativity. Among Light's recommendations for creating "the freedom to imagine" were to stay "thin" (minimize organizational layering), create room to experiment (by granting groups the freedom to think "beyond the box"), push authority downward, lower the barriers to internal collaboration, democratize (by shifting from centralized rule to a more participatory style), prime organizations for innovation (by creating separate funding to implement creative new ideas), create a marketplace of ideas (in which ideas rise or fall on their own merits rather than on the basis of power or politics), prepare for stress (because change can be discomforting), maximize diversity (internally but especially in relation to the community), and age gracefully (while maintaining an interest in innovation) (Light, 1998, chap. 4).

Similarly, Denhardt and Denhardt (1999) found that many in public organizations, like their counterparts in business organizations, are "risk averse" in that they place a high value on not "rocking the boat." This means that managers interested in encouraging innovation must take special measures to encourage employees to experiment, to value change, and (under the right circumstances) even to take risks. Indeed, a significant part of building a culture of innovation is setting expectations with respect to risk and opportunity. Change-oriented public managers want their employees to understand that there is no penalty for taking risks so long as they are taken for the right reasons. In any case, although managers can bring about some changes "from the top," in the long run many more innovations probably will occur if those throughout the organization know that change and innovation are valued, that they have been empowered to act, and that calculated risks will be supported by top management.

Finally, Borins (1998) reviewed a sample of semifinalists' applications for the Ford Foundation–Kennedy School of Government's state and local government innovation awards. Consistent with what we have just said, a large portion of the innovations that occurred were initiated by public servants at the middle management level or on the front line. Borins argued that as public organizations devolve authority and responsibility throughout the organizations, we are likely to experience even more innovation. Moreover, in contrast to other findings, Borins did not find that public servants needed crises before they acted. Instead, they usually solved problems before they became crises. Borins wrote, "Politicians initiate in times of crisis, agency heads [do so] when they take over the reins or in an organizational change context, and middle-level and frontline public servants develop innovative responses as needed to solve internal problems or take advantage of opportunities" (pp. 284–285). Creating a culture in which persons throughout the organization are encouraged to experiment with new ideas is important in actually bringing about change and innovation, a conclusion also reached in a study of the city of Phoenix, considered one of the best run local governments in the world (Denhardt & Denhardt, 2001).

Finally, we should note that many in government think of innovation in terms of generating new practices or adapting new practices. Those governments or nonprofits that establish a culture of innovation will likely have success in generating and implementing new ideas. Others, however, can benefit from the established "best practices" of other organizations. For this reason, groups such as the Alliance for Innovation (www.transformgov.org) are engaged in research into best practices in local government and ways of implementing those best practices in other settings. There are also other resources for advancing the study and practice of public sector innovation, including the *Innovation Journal* (www.innovation.cc).

A Final Note on Personal Change

To be successful in changing public organizations, managers must develop a fairly specific set of skills necessary to the change process. As we have mentioned, many of these skills are what are called process skills—skills related to *how* things are done as opposed to *what* things are being done. A given task can be completed in a variety of ways, depending on the manager's orientation; the difference largely lies in the area of process skills. As traditional modes of change that depend on authority and expertise give way to a growing need to generate the support and commitment of organizational members, these skills will become even more important. As we already have seen in this chapter, the success of organizational change efforts depends not only on what the manager does but also on how he or she does it.

We have, of course, already covered many process skills in this book—communications, motivation, negotiation, power and authority, and so on—but several of these skills deserve special attention in connection with the process of organizational change. First, change often is dependent on the manager's (or the consultant's) capacity for *effective listening*—that is, his or her ability to hear exactly what is being said by those throughout the organization and those outside who interact with the organization. The first stage in any organizational change effort is diagnosis, and that requires careful listening. Second, a manager interested in change will be aided by his or her ability to pick up behavioral clues that might not be apparent on the surface. Indeed, the manager's capacity for *empathetic understanding* may be essential to effecting positive change. Third, we already have pointed out the importance of employee participation and involvement in the change process. But participation does not just happen. It requires the manager to act affirmatively to encourage open dialogue. The manager must feel secure in his or her own position so as to trust the suggestions that others make. Indeed, if the manager is insecure, then employees probably will not trust the manager.

As Judson (1991) wrote,

> Process skills have to do with the dynamics and quality of interaction among members of management and between managers, supervisors, and employees. The cultivation and development of effective process skills depend on having a supportive atmosphere in the organization, on personal willingness to take risks in trying new modes of interpersonal behavior, and on personal sensitivity to the behavioral clues offered by others. (p. 148)

Developing such skills demands much of the manager and even suggests that, to change the organization, the manager might need to change him- or herself. That deep and personal change required of the managers might, in the final analysis, be the single most important determinant of successful organizational change.

Ways of Acting

The following guidelines for action may help you to use the information contained in this chapter in your day-to-day work in public and nonprofit organizations.

1. *If you are seeking to lead change, then consider carefully the emotional and psychological components of resistance to change, both your own and that of others.*

People may oppose change for rational and objective reasons, but resistance also may indicate the play of emotional and psychological forces. People generally are more comfortable with patterns of behavior that are familiar to them. Changing those patterns requires a psychological adaptation, which often is quite difficult. In part, people must become accustomed to the new situation; in part, they must learn to accommodate the loss of what they had before. In either case, they need time to work through the important issues that often accompany change.

2. *If you are seeking to lead change, then try to clarify and communicate throughout the organization the problems associated with the current way of operating and what benefits might accrue if you tried something else.* When people operate in one way for along period of time, they come to think that is the only way of operating. That is why people justify keeping things as they are by saying, "We've always done it that way." That might be true, but there also might be other ways of operating that will be far more effective.

3. *If you are seeking to lead change, then try to involve people throughout the organization in the change process.* People are more likely to accept changes if they fully understand what is going on and if they feel a sense of "ownership" of the changes that are being made. Even more important, as one state productivity improvement director commented, "The people who do the work know the work best and know best how to improve the work." For this reason, involving a wide range of people in the change process is likely to yield better ideas for how to improve the system.

4. *Think about the forces that are driving change and those that are resisting change.* A careful analysis of these factors often will indicate ways in which change can be introduced more effectively. Be especially careful to consider not just how to increase the pressure to change but also—and often even more important—how to reduce resistance to change. Be sure to match your approach to change—whether OD or Six Sigma or whatever—to the particular environment in which the changes will occur.

5. *Consider the culture of the organization.* Understanding the existing norms, beliefs, and values of those in the organization is an important first step in bringing about change. Cultural attributes typically are deep-seated in any organization (or any culture) and will represent substantial forces restraining change. On the other hand, by exposing the existing norms of the organization and by carefully developing a new statement of the organization's vision and values (hopefully with broad participation from those in the organization), you might be able to set course for a new culture. Just remember that it will take a long time before any new culture becomes fully accepted as part of the very fabric of the organization.

6. *Listen, listen, listen.* The first step in bringing about change is to fully understand the organization and its stakeholders. Take time to listen to citizens, employees, clients, legislators, and those in various interest groups. Find out what they think about the organization and how it might be improved. Heed the advice of a local government budget officer who said, "If our city manager comes up with ten ideas a year,

that's good. But if a thousand people in the organization each come up with one, that's even better. And besides, he probably won't come up with ten anyway." You might be that manager. Listen to the advice of those throughout the organization.

7. *Think of building a capacity for learning in the organization.* Although only individuals, and not organizations, are capable of learning, it is possible for you to affect the conditions under which learning that is helpful to the organization might occur. Individual insights and perceptions must be allowed to flow out into the larger organization where their impact will be greatest.

8. *Remember the difference between "single-loop" and "double-loop" learning (learning new strategies vs. learning new basic assumptions).* Where those in the organization are facing decisions that are routine or repetitive, single-loop learning probably will be sufficient; where they are facing more complex and "nonprogrammable" decisions, double-loop learning will be required. Remember that sometimes single-loop learning appears to be double-loop when it really is not. Be sure that your learning processes engage the most basic and preciously unchallenged assumptions of the organization.

9. *If changes in the organization's structure appear necessary, then think twice.* Make sure that the real issues are structural and not behavioral. If they still appear to be structural, then make sure that they require changes in the organization's structure as opposed to work processes or core systems (e.g., technology). If structural changes still appear necessary, then proceed with caution and with the involvement of those affected.

10. *Remember that today's public organizations reside in a complex world of diverse policy networks.* This means that for organizational changes to be effective, they often must involve citizen groups, stakeholders of the organization, and other public, nonprofit, and private organizations. Consider ways of involving all the relevant players in the design and execution of organizational changes, especially those that will affect other participants in the network.

11. *To encourage change and innovation throughout the organization, consider employing a more organic, democratic, or participatory way of operating.* Creating a culture in which people throughout the organization feel comfortable in proposing changes and feel confident that they will not be "killed" if well-considered risks do not pan out eventually will pay great benefits in terms of innovation. A key to innovation is to create spaces for innovation to occur. That is, give people the freedom, authority, and responsibility to propose and carry out needed changes. Encourage and reward innovation. Let people know that calculated risks sometimes are necessary for positive change to occur. Share leadership.

12. *Be attentive to the politics of change.* Remember that whatever changes you make in a public organization, there will be political implications. The existing system is the way it is because others—often political leaders of some consequence—thought that it should be that way. Recognize that changing something that others have invested political capital in has political ramifications.

Thinking in Action

Reasoning Processes in Organizational Change

Imagine a conversation in which Gina Leonard, the supervisor, called Peter Brown into her office to talk about Peter's recent performance. Gina had observed several recent lapses in Peter's performance and had received complaints from others who were concerned as well. Moreover, she was concerned that Peter's disdain for others was affecting the performance of the work group as a whole. Gina really wanted to keep Peter in the organization because he was a highly skilled technician. But she also recognized that if things did not change, then she would have to build a case for his dismissal. Among the things Gina said in the conversation were the following:

Peter, your performance simply hasn't been at the level we expect here.

People at your level have to set an example for others.

You seem to have a chip on your shoulder.

I don't want to talk about what happened in the past that has led to these problems. That's history. We have to deal with the future.

Let's clear the air once and for all.

We need to be clear about your work and your impact on others.

I've heard several people describe you as "disruptive," "uncaring," and "detached."

Others have even complained that you have been downright rude to them.

What is your reaction to Gina's approach and her language? How would you diagnose what was happening here? What advice would you give to Gina in handling situations like this?

Assume that you met Gina in the hall later and that she asked what you thought of her approach as she explained it in a memo about her meeting with Peter. Write out a conversation between Gina and you using the right-hand side of several sheets of paper. On the left-hand side, write any thoughts or feelings that you might have during the conversation that you would not, for whatever reason, want to communicate to Gina. Following is an example:

Let Gina commit herself first so I can see what she thinks happened.

Gina: Did you read my memo on meeting with Peter?

You: Yes, I saw it. Must have been tough.

Gina: I just don't know how to get through to a guy like Peter.

"A guy like Peter." There's a clue.

Write out your version of the conservation from here on. Trade your written conversations with another class member and analyze the hidden assumptions that person made in talking with Gina. Did that person consider Gina effective? If not, then why not? How close were the inferences that person made to the actual observable data? What actions might flow from such inferences? Is it necessary to create more abstract inferences to deal with the problem? If so, then how does the process of inference affect that of organizational change? How does all this connect to the idea of double-loop learning? (This exercise is adapted from Argyris [1999]. See pages 71–87 in the original for a detailed examination of the factors at play here and their connection to the question of double-loop learning.)

Leading Change in Local Government

Read and be prepared to discuss the following two case studies.

Case Study No. 1

Excellence in local government does not come about automatically but rather requires public managers to be highly skilled in leading change. When Jan Perkins became city manager of Fremont, California, in 1992, Fremont, like many other California cities, was suffering from both economic difficulties and the state's efforts to pull back the property tax as a source of local government revenue. Yet while city employees were being laid off and services were being curtailed, citizen demand for quality public services remained high. More important, in Perkins's mind, was the fact that citizens had lost confidence in their government. For both of these reasons, Perkins and other city officials in Fremont recognized that something dramatically different had to be done.

The change process started early in Perkins's tenure, as one of her council members proposed bringing in an outside consultant (at a cost of $500,000) to diagnose what might be done. Especially because a neighboring city had just done the same thing and failed to adopt a single recommendation, Perkins believed that greater benefits could be obtained by working with those within the city to figure out how the quality and productivity of the city might be improved. A facilitated workshop session, involving top elected and appointed officials, was devoted to understanding "what we do, how we do it, and why we do it." From there, the question became, "How can we do it better? Or, more specifically, how can we become fast and flexible, customer oriented, focused on results, and engaged in important partnerships internally and externally?" During the 5 years following the workshop, Perkins led a dramatic change in Fremont's city government, a change built around delivering high-quality services to citizens, creating an internal culture built around continuous and employee-driven improvement, a highly collaborative approach to decision making and problem solving, and the creation of partnerships within the city and with surrounding communities.

The city's interest in customer service was given initial impetus by complaints from local developers about how long it took to get permits and other approvals to undertake construction in Fremont. During a time when economic development was a key issue, these concerns were heard loud and clear, and the permitting process was improved significantly. Similar

(Continued)

(Continued)

concerns were raised in other areas, to the point where Perkins and her top staff began to concentrate on developing a serious philosophical and practical commitment to service quality. In part, Perkins described the philosophy as the Nike slogan: "Just do it." That is, the message to employees was that if they saw a way in which the citizens of Fremont could be better served by city government, then they should take action. "Just do it." But the philosophy also reflected an approach similar to the Nordstrom department store service philosophy—of being interested not only in the transaction (the specific product or service being delivered) but also in building a relationship (between customers and the business or, in this case, between citizens and government).

The city's capacity to innovate has been aided by a much more collaborative approach to decision making and problem solving, an approach cutting across traditional organizational boundaries. Whatever their positions, employees are encouraged to think of themselves as representatives of the city and to do what is necessary to provide citizens with the answers they need. For example, if a planning department employee sees a streetlight malfunctioning, then that employee is encouraged to take action rather than just passing off the problem as one for the street maintenance people to discover and correct. Similarly, any employee receiving a phone call about any topic is encouraged to "own" that question until it has been answered satisfactorily.

This attitude also is supported by a strong emphasis on partnerships (or collaborative problem solving) at many different levels in the organization. Early in the process of labor negotiation, Perkins created joint labor management committees to consider "quality of work life" issues through a structured problem-solving process known as "interest-based bargaining." This collaborative process encourages participants to identify their basic interests (before jumping to solutions) and then to engage in collaborative problem solving to find a way of accommodating the varied interests represented. Interest-based bargaining was so highly successful in labor–management relations that the same approach has been encouraged throughout city government. Training in the process has been offered to all employees of the city, and interest-based bargaining has become a standard way of doing business in Fremont.

The same approach to building partnerships through collaborative efforts is used as the city relates to citizens and to other nearby governmental entities. City employees do not just inform citizens about what is going to be done to them; they also go out and ask citizens what they want and then balance those interests with those of the city. Beyond that, city employees and citizens engage in interest-based problem solving even around issues of how to design a *process* to involve the public. The city engineer commented, "We do more than tell them what we are going to do. We go out now and involve them in the design of the process itself. The process is laid out by the people involved." Perkins described the shift in thinking as a shift from government as a "vending machine," where one puts his or her money in the slot and takes out the product or service (or kicks the machine when it does not work), to government as a "barn raising," where many people come together to combine their efforts to produce a product or service that all can feel good about.

Perkins described the change process in Fremont as involving waves of change, with each wave building over time the quality of the city's work. Wave I involves recognizing the need to change; building trust and relationships internally; specifying the mission, vision, and values of the organization; gathering "low-hanging fruit"; and beginning education and training around these concerns. The key question here is, "Why do we do what we do?" Wave II involves deepening knowledge and skills, improving work processes, reforming the administrative system, building trust and relationships internally, and exploring more entrepreneurial activities.

The key question here is, "How can we best serve our customers?" Wave III involves rethinking the organization's structure, making the boundaries between departments more permeable, providing seamless service delivery, and deepening trust and relationships both internally and externally. The key question here is, "Who does what?" Finally, Wave IV involves forming partnerships with other agencies and groups, integrating the community's vision and the organization's vision and creating interdependencies between the community and the organization, steering and rowing, and asking the question, "What is next?" In this case, Perkins's waves of change have become an integral part of managing the city's business.

(This real-life case study is drawn from a larger study by Denhardt and Denhardt [1999] of leading change in American local government. The entire report is available either in hard copy from the IBM Center for the Business of Government or online at www.businessofgovernment.org.)

Case Study No. 2

In 1993 a newly elected county treasurer in Maricopa County (Arizona) came forward and essentially told top administrators and the board of supervisors, "Well, guess what, you guys are out of money. You have no cash. Not only that, but you are probably $100 million in the hole." According to Tom Manos, the current chief financial officer, "It was bad that we were that bad off. But it was worse that that we didn't know. I've looked at monthly financial reports from that time and from those you'd think everything was peachy." But financial games were being played and the county was nearly out of money. Not surprisingly, *Governing* magazine described Maricopa County as a "poster child for bad government."

According to then chairman of the board of supervisors Betsey Bayless, there began a series of very intense sessions that first resulted in the termination of the county administrator and the chief financial officer. All employees were put on a 5-day furlough—that is, unpaid leave for 1 week, in order to cut the payroll down. There were also major job cuts. It was a very difficult period, one in which, according to one interviewee, "You'd turn over a rock and something ugly would crawl out." Sandra Wilson, deputy county administrator, who came to the county about this time, recalls sitting with Betsey Bayless "cutting budgets and having people scream at us." Eventually, however, with the cooperation of the chairman, the board, and the county administration, a new strategic plan was put into place, efforts were made to gain control of the financial situation, and a search for a new county administrator was undertaken.

The board ultimately hired David R. Smith as county administrator. When Smith arrived in Maricopa County, he discovered that the county "just had no financial recording systems that they could trust. All the departments had their own shadow systems and they couldn't get their main financial accounting system to work properly at all, so they were kind of in the dark as to what their real budgetary numbers were telling them. When I got here they were still losing money on a monthly basis, going deeper into the red." Addressing the financial issue was paramount during this period. Ross Tate, now county auditor, commented, "Most departments ran off a shadow system. The system wasn't good at variances." Working with the board and with a new set of financial managers, Smith got the main system working and generating monthly

(Continued)

(Continued)

budget reports. These reports were important so that Smith and the board would always know where things stood financially. Smith commented, "I always want to see the actual less than the budget and be sure we're showing a positive budget variance as far as the totals go."

The result was a set of budget metrics that were centrally generated and used in making every budget decision for the county. The idea was that the managers in the county would constantly be driving positive budget variances and the budget against which those variances would be measured was "cast in stone." According to Smith, "I would say, 'This is the data we're going to make decisions on. If you want to run your shadow system be my guest, but it has no relevance for our discussions. We are going to rely on this information we believe in, and that will be what we circulate through the county. When we call up and say your revenues are off, or your expenditures are too high or something, you're in negative variance, well, this is the information we're going to be using.'"

At about the same time, Smith made several significant changes in top management as well as put both a capital expenditure and job freeze in place. New managers were brought in who were, as Joy Rich of the Regional Development Services Agency put it, "invigorated and energized, then encouraged to go out and implement their ideas with as few impediments as possible." It began to work. By March of 1995 the county actually broke even, in April and May there was a little positive variance, and by the end of June the county finished the fiscal year "slightly to the good."

The county's "Managing for Results" system has evolved to a fully integrated system of strategic planning, budgeting, and performance measurement, one of the most sophisticated in the country. In an effort to ensure greater accountability to the public, the county began a series of steps in 1998 to incorporate performance-based budgeting into its operations. That effort began with the development of strategic plans integrated with performance measures in six pilot departments. The board passed a "Managing for Results" policy in September 2000, requiring that participation in the program would be a necessary for future funding. Today the "Managing for Results" system integrates planning, budgeting, reporting results, evaluating results, and making decisions about future actions. In 2002, *Governing* magazine in cooperation with Syracuse University identified Maricopa County as one of the two best-run county governments in the United States.

(This case study was completed by Robert and Janet Denhardt and published in 2005 under the title, "Maricopa County: A Case Study in Rapid Organizational Change," by Arizona State University's School of Public Affairs and Maricopa County, Arizona.)

Based on your reading of these cases and your own experience, answer the following questions. How do public managers assess the need for change in their communities? How do they envision change? How do they lead change? How do they create a culture of change—that is, a culture in which change and innovation are valued and not avoided? How do the two cases differ in the approach to organizational change that was taken?

CHAPTER 13

Representing the Organization "On the Outside"

Elected officials bring a very different set of perspectives and values than we bring. The sharper the divide between the policy/political context and the administrative, the quicker you get in trouble.

—Robert O'Neill, Executive Director,
International City/County Management
Association and former city manager

Unless you are trying to hide something, the press should be your ally.

—Jay E. Hakes, Director,
Jimmy Carter Presidential Library

Much of what we have discussed to this point has focused on the management of organizational behavior *within* public and nonprofit organizations. But leadership, communication, motivation, and other such issues also are very much at the center of the relationship between any particular public agency and the individuals, groups, and organizations surrounding it. A significant and increasing part of the success of any particular public organization will depend on the effectiveness of its members in working with others—citizens, the governing body, other public agencies (at various levels of government), private and nonprofit groups and associations (including interest groups), and the media. In this chapter, we examine some of the special circumstances that those in public organizations face in representing their organizations "on the outside" as well as the special skills and abilities that will aid them in that process.

An early formulation by Thompson (1967) suggested three different levels of organization: technical, managerial, and institutional. The *technical* level is concerned with the actual task of the organization, the *managerial* level mediates between the technical group and top management, and the *institutional* level is concerned with the relationship between the organization as an institution and the wider social system of which it is a part. In this traditional view, those at the executive or institutional level were most likely to represent the organization externally. They would be the ones to represent the organization before the legislature and the executive, to bargain with representatives of other governmental and nongovernmental groups, and to address the media. But during the past 30 years, this situation has changed. Although today those at the top probably still play more of an external role than others, managers throughout public organizations today are likely to be called on to represent their organizations externally.

What we are describing is an important theoretical development, but one with direct implications for the skills required of today's public managers. Basically, the argument is as follows: We are experiencing a dramatic change in the way in which the rules and regulations, as well as the programs and processes, that guide society are being developed—or, to put it somewhat differently, a change in the way in which public policy is being developed. In the past, government played a predominant role in what some have called the "steering of society" (Nelissen, Bemelmans-Videc, Godfroij, & deGoede, 1999). That is not to say that other interests were not represented as well, but in the past government played a decisive role.

To use a sports analogy, the playing field on which the game of public policy formation occurred was one proscribed by government, and the primary players were elected public officials and policy advisers throughout government agencies. In turn, public administrators, playing on the same field (but often somewhere near the sidelines), were largely concerned with the implementation of public policies. They were primarily concerned with managing their organizations so that the proper things would get done.

But time and circumstances have changed. The game of public policy formulation and implementation no longer is played primarily by those in government. Indeed, one might even say that today the audience no longer is in the stands but rather is right there on the field, participating in every play. To put this more formally, there has been a reformulation of the steering mechanisms of society. Many groups and interests today are directly involved in the development and implementation of public policy.

In fact, what we are witnessing is the development of many different policy networks, with each serving its own substantive interests (e.g., transportation, social welfare, education). Each network focuses on its own policy area and, in many ways, defines the way in which policies will be developed in that area. That is, one set of rules might define how the "defense" game is played, whereas another set of rules might define how the "social welfare" game is played. But in each arena, major developments in public policy and in the steering of society are likely to occur through a difficult and convoluted process of bargaining and negotiation within that particular policy network.

Under these circumstances, the role of government and the role of the public manager are changing. As we witness a fragmentation of policy responsibility in society, we also must recognize that the traditional mechanisms of governmental control no longer are workable or even appropriate. Traditional hierarchical government is giving way to a growing decentralization of policy interests. Control is giving way to interaction and involvement.

As the steering of society has changed, the role of public administrators and the standards by which administrative performance will be judged also have changed. Public managers—at all levels—are becoming actors in the process of designing and implementing policies, requiring the involvement of many different actors, both within government and outside of government. Increasingly, elected officials and managers need to respond to the ideas of citizens not just by saying "yes" or "no" but also by saying things such as "Let's work together to figure out what we're going to do and then make it happen." In a world of active citizenship, public officials will increasingly play more than a service delivery role; they will play a conciliating, mediating, or even adjudicating role vis-à-vis public, private, and nonprofit groups and organizations (and others). Where the traditional role of public administrators was primarily (but not exclusively) the management of the internal affairs of their organizations, the time and attention of all public managers increasingly is becoming occupied by external matters.

Today and in the future, public managers at all levels will need to be attentive to the traditional external skills of interacting with the executive and the governing body, making effective public presentations, and dealing with the media. But given the changing world around them, they also will find it necessary to improve their skills in listening to the voices of citizens, clients, and "customers"; to increase their understanding of how to involve citizens in the work of government; and to become more adept at building collaborative relationships with other groups and organizations.

Where Do We Begin?

Networks and Relationships

Focus on one particular agency—a federal agency, a state-level department or division, a city department or division, or a nonprofit organization. Construct a chart showing the major actors in the agency's environment that agency personnel must deal with on a regular basis. Put the agency in the middle of the chart and then represent other groups and organizations with circles spread around the page. Vary the size of the circles according to the importance of the external agents (with the largest being the most important), and vary the length of the lines connecting the agencies to the focal agency (with those "closest to" or most friendly with the focal agency having the shortest lines). Use this chart to discuss the importance of the focal agency's relationships with various actors in its environment. Compare the various charts created in the class to examine how the external relations of different agencies can be quite distinct. Your chart should look something like the one in Figure 13.1.

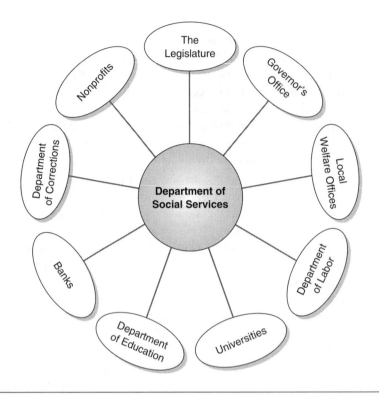

Figure 13.1   The External Relations of a Specific Agency

Working With the Media

The following is a simulation involving interactions between a city manager and the local media.

John Brown is the city manager of Blackberry, Iowa, a community of about 80,000 people. Brown has established a practice of weekly news briefings with the local media. Media representatives who attend typically include someone from the local newspaper, a student reporter from an alternative local newspaper produced by the school of journalism at a local university, and occasionally someone from a local radio or television station. On this particular occasion, the local newspaper is represented by Cynthia Fox, a highly regarded local reporter with many years of experience covering city hall. The university alternative newspaper is represented by Gene Washington, a senior journalism major who counts Woodward and Bernstein among his investigative journalism heroes. The local television station is represented by Marilyn Sullivan, who hosts an early-morning talk show typically devoted to food and fashion.

Several things have occurred in the city this week that are sure to be topics of discussion at this week's briefing. First, the city has received a federal grant of $350,000 to help construct a new senior center that is very much needed in a rather poor area of town. There is no question that the center is needed, but the city will have to come up with $150,000 out of its already tight budget to match the federal grant. Second, the mayor has been accused by another member of the city council of misusing city funds by traveling with his wife to interesting places and asking the city to reimburse their trips as "city business." For example, they spent a weekend in Seattle, Washington, supposedly to attend the National League of Cities meeting—but the meeting took place after they returned. They also went on an economic development trip to Asia and then charged the city for an extra weekend in Singapore. Third, the quarterback of the university's football team was arrested for drunk driving following the team's last victory, a win putting them in line for a bowl bid.

Divide the class into four groups, one representing each of the people who will attend this week's news briefing. Each group should spend 10 minutes discussing the situation from its character's point of view and selecting a person to play the character. Then conduct a complete simulation of the city manager's briefing, videotaping the session if possible. Then replay the briefing and discuss both the way in which the manager played his role and the approaches taken by the various media representatives. What recommendations would you make for improving Brown's approach to the media?

(As an alternative, the simulation can be repeated, changing the names to match genders of new participants in the simulation and rotating people through the various roles. Those not participating in the first simulation can act as observers and then discuss, or they can tape their own session without watching another one. The class as a whole can then watch all of the recorded sessions and discuss the different approaches taken by various actors.)

Ways of Thinking

As we noted earlier, public managers at all levels are likely to be involved in external relations of one type or another and need to develop new skills that go beyond those required for them to manage the internal operations of their organizations.

The Traditional Skills of External Relations

Managers at all levels increasingly are being asked to take on the responsibility of representing their organizations on the outside. As they do so, they will need to develop the traditional skills of working with the legislature, working with the media, and making formal presentations as well as develop new skills in relating to citizens and external groups. In the following subsections, we consider the traditional skills.

Developing Effective Relations With the Legislature

There are a variety of ways in which those in public agencies interact with elected officials, especially members of the legislative body. First, of course, most agencies owe their very existence—and their continuation—to legislative action, either the action of creating or terminating agencies or that of deciding on levels of funding for agencies' activities. The legislature not only sets the tasks of agencies but also defines the limits and boundaries of their activities. Agency personnel have an obvious stake in seeing that the outcomes of the legislative process are consistent with the objectives of the legislature.

Second, legislators exercise "oversight" of agency activities, making sure that agencies are operating within the bounds of legislative intent and in a way that responds to citizen concerns.

> Legislators often see themselves as watchdogs of the public purse and guardians of the public trust. At the national level, each congressional committee is formally required to continuously oversee the programs under its jurisdiction, and many committees have established oversight subcommittees whose sole responsibility is to perform this task. (Sperry, 1989, p. 185)

Third, members of the legislature, acting on behalf of their constituents, often will make requests (or demands) of those in the agencies of government. Inquiries that come from members of the legislature acting on behalf of their constituents—often the result of legislative "casework"—are matters requiring special attention by administrators. Establishing quick and appropriate response mechanisms to deal with such inquiries can help to set a positive tone for legislative relations in general.

Fourth, members of the legislature depend on those in public agencies for advice concerning emerging policy issues. Those in public agencies often are the real "experts" in their field and can provide helpful assistance in developing policies and even in writing legislation to implement those policies. Moreover, they often are staffed and equipped to conduct the type of background research that is essential to develop effective public policies. Acting in this role, administrators have an opportunity to "shape" the resulting policies and legislation in a way that is consistent with their ideas and beliefs.

Finally, agency personnel often are called before the legislative body to provide testimony. Such testimony can range from providing advice on new policies and programs to defending agency practices that appear to have gone astray. The effectiveness of such testimony can help to build trust and confidence in agencies and their personnel, often leading to more ready acceptance of future recommendations.

These various interactions create some tension between public agencies and the legislature, tension that has become even more intense during recent years. But that tension serves important purposes in a democracy and should not just be seen as a source of annoyance. After all, our democratic process builds in tension (not a dichotomy) between politics and administration, evidenced here in efforts to balance legislative accountability and oversight with administrative discretion. "Relationships between legislatures and public agencies are defined by an ongoing tension between the need to ensure accountability and the need to provide administrators with the flexibility to effectively carry out their responsibilities" (Khademian, 1996, p. 171). The tension between accountability and flexibility can be quite difficult and demanding for some administrators, but recognizing the importance of that tension will at least make the situation more understandable.

At the federal level, the tension actually has increased over the past 20 years or so, as oversight has become a more central role of legislators. In part, that change can be attributed to changes in the political culture. For example, public distrust of government probably has increased the attention that legislators pay to agency activities. Moreover, government activity takes place in even greater public view given freedom of information laws, on the one hand, and increasing mass media attention, on the other. Finally, the increasing influence of special interest groups means that legislators are called on more frequently to look into the activities of specific agencies. "Thousands of organizations, using ever more sophisticated methods to influence the legislature, have come to dominate some public policy issues. The use of political action committees and grassroots lobbying efforts increases the pressure on legislators" (Sperry, 1989, p. 181). And that, in turn, increases the pressure on agency personnel.

In any case, administrators should carefully think through their relationships with the legislature and take steps to improve those relationships. Actually, there are a variety of fairly straightforward guidelines that should help in developing more effective relationships with the legislature.

1. *Establish trust and build confidence.* You are well advised to keep legislators informed of your activities so that there are no surprises and to respond to legislative inquires quickly and accurately. It is important to provide technical information and advice promptly, accurately, and in a thoughtful manner. You also can help with legislative casework. "Helping legislators respond to constituents' needs in ways that are not inconsistent with legitimate program objectives can go a long way toward facilitating a good relationship and moving needed legislation forward" (Sperry, 1989, p. 187). All of these activities create an atmosphere of trust, something that is essential for effective legislative relations.

2. *Develop an agency protocol for dealing with legislative relations.* You should know who will respond to certain types of inquiries, decide the manner in which particular types of inquiries will be addressed (e.g., in writing, on the phone, through visits to legislative offices), and develop a tracking system for inquiries so that messages do not get "lost" along the way. By developing such an agency protocol, you can eliminate mixed messages, ensure greater accuracy and timeliness in your responses, and minimize the disruptive effects of inquiries.

3. *Understand the legislative process and the preferences of specific legislators.* Legislators must satisfy their constituents to stay in office. This means that you should have some understanding of what various interests or constituencies are saying. In this way, you often will be in the position to quickly respond to a legislative inquiry on behalf of a disgruntled constituent. You also must become familiar with the legislative process. Not only do you need to track legislation so that you will be aware of potential legislative actions that might affect your agency, but you also need to know where various legislators stand on issues of concern to you and your agency. But in all cases, you should avoid partisanship. "It is important to establish a reputation for fair dealing—regardless of one's party affiliation—and to live up to that reputation in both routine and nonroutine dealings with legislators" (Khademian, 1996, p. 191).

There will likely be times when you will be called on to testify before the legislature, something that many find quite difficult. In fact, Sperry (1989) wrote,

> There is probably no more potentially traumatic activity associated with legislative activity than making a formal statement before a congressional committee, a state legislative committee, or a city council. But administrators should consider it an opportunity. If the witness knows what he or she is talking about, acts in a professional manner, and provides honest and forthright responses to members' questions, the chances of coming out ahead are quite good. (p. 188)

Obviously, there are many ways of preparing for testimony, with the most important being to research the topic thoroughly so that you know the subject inside and out. You also can anticipate potential questions and prepare thoughtful responses that you might even practice with coworkers or colleagues. You can obtain information about the committee and be especially prepared to adjust to any last-minute developments. At the hearing itself, you should present a brief fact-based opening statement, be straightforward and direct in your answers to questions, and be respectful to those legislators who are present. You should be as brief as possible, because there are likely to be others in the room waiting to testify. Avoid repeating what others have already said or at least try to approach the same issue from a different angle. (www.omunileague.org/Legislation/TESTIFY%20TIPS%20WEB.pdf, downloaded June 2007) If mistakes have been made, admit to them but focus on the corrective actions that have been taken. As one public relations expert put it, "Stand your ground if you feel you are right, but remember it rarely pays to be argumentative with someone wielding a gavel" (Meek, 1985, p. 37).

Working With the Media

Obviously, the news media play an extremely important role in a democratic society. But many public managers find that working with the media is one of their most difficult and frustrating tasks. For administrators wanting to present the work of their agencies in the most favorable light, those in the media seem bent on telling only the negative side of things. For administrators trying to serve the public under difficult circumstances, those in the media seem only interested in uncovering scandals and wrongdoing. For administrators wishing to explain the work of their agencies fully and in great detail, those in the media seem only interested in the briefest "catch phrases" or the cleverest "sound bites." Yet according to Wheeler (1994),

> to be or not to be involved with the news media is not a choice that is open to government officials. The role the media play in the democratic process necessitates a relationship between media representatives and representatives of . . . government. The quality of the relationship is often determined by the . . . official's respect for the role of the media in a democracy and their willingness to be active partners in the relationship. (p. 91)

Obviously, the media communicate both from government to citizen and from citizen to government. Certainly, the media inform the public about the activities of government and how the public is affected by those activities. They tell the public about those things that government is doing right and those things that government is doing wrong. On the other hand, the media also inform government officials about the public. They let officials know what the public is thinking and allow for feedback with respect to policies and programs. But the role of the media in a democratic society is not only to be a conduit of information. The media play an important role in holding government accountable to the people. "Indeed, one of the first indicators of real progress in the transition to democratic governance is the existence of a free and open press" (Washington, 1997, pp. 29–30). For this reason, the very existence of a free press is protected by the Constitution, and the role of the media is preserved by judicial interpretation. "Among other things, the court [has] held that the public media's vigorous pursuit of public wrongdoing [is] essential to the well-being of a democratic society and that this pursuit must not be weakened by the threat of court action" (Conner, 1993, p. 41).

Because the media play such an important role, and because the media are not going to go away soon, public administrators are well advised to develop a positive attitude toward media relations, learn all they can about how to interact most effectively with the media, and practice effective media relations. There are several general guidelines that public administrators should be aware of as they interact with the media.

1. *Create a media relations plan.* A media relations plan begins by defining the goals and objectives that you are seeking. Are you concerned with presenting a positive image to the public by way of the media? Are you most interested in letting the public know about upcoming events? Are you concerned with "damage control" when things go wrong? What are the specific goals that your government or agency has that might differ from those of others? Following a definition of goals and objectives, you should assign the responsibility of communicating with the media to a specific individual, perhaps a public information officer (Wheeler, 1994, p. 92). This will give reporters and editors a source to contact when they need information and also will give the agency some control over its media relations. (Others probably will be contacted as well, but most contacts should come through the public information officer.) The designated contact person should become familiar with legal issues affecting media relations, including attention to privacy issues, libel and slander statutes, and copyright laws, and they should learn the full range of media terms such as "background only" and "off the record." But be aware that the use of these terms does not guarantee the safe handling of information. "If the information you have requires special handling, you probably shouldn't be talking to the press about it anyway" (Conner, 1993, p. 30). Finally, your plan should include your best advance thinking about how to handle crisis situations. For example, you should decide when to respond and when to let the situation pass, recognizing that sometimes reacting inappropriately just makes matters worse. In all you do, be dignified but also realistic. "You can't determine whether a story runs, where or when

it will be placed, and what the headline, content, or tone will be" (Corporation for National Service, 1997, p. 10).

2. *Establish positive relationships with reporters.* By developing effective two-way relationships with representatives of the media, you are more likely to be rewarded with fair and substantive coverage of those matters that are important to you. Above all, be honest and credible; tell a reporter that you do not know the answer if that is the case. Be consistent by communicating with reporters whether the news is good or bad. Be available to all (and do not play favorites), be sincere, and have a positive attitude. Be sure to return calls from reporters as soon as possible. You also should recognize that reporters are human too and that their mission is to find "stories." Recognize that they are loyal to their readers or listeners and that they face pressures regarding accuracy of information, timeliness, newsworthiness, and competition (Conner, 1993, pp. 3–15). Occasionally recognizing the pressures and deadlines that reporters face actually will work to your advantage.

3. *Be proactive in your relations with the media.* Involve the media in the policy process at an early stage. If you are able to establish positive relations with media representatives, then they might, in fact, be able to offer advice on questions such as the most conducive environment in which to launch policies. But this approach must be balanced given that media considerations cannot be a reason for public officials to postpone or avoid making unfavorable announcements (Washington, 1997, p. 34). You also should remember that the media are not the only source of information that the public has. For example, you can disseminate important information through a Web site or through advertising, consultations, or public events. (But here you must be careful not to exceed the limits of justifiable expenditures or excessively self-serving public relations.)

4. *Be prepared and be precise.* When you are preparing a press release, be sure that you have a genuinely interesting story to tell. Don't get a reputation for spreading trivia. Keep the message simple with one or two main points and some supporting arguments. Begin with the key points: What is happening? Why is it important? Where is it taking place? Who is doing it? When will it happen? and so forth. When you have your message worked out, be sure that anyone who is likely to encounter a reporter understands the message. (Retrieved June 2007 from www.civilservant.org.uk/c28.pdf)

When you are going to be interviewed yourself, begin by learning as much about the reporter as you can. Read what he or she has written, or watch or listen to one of the reporter's shows. Prepare answers in advance to questions that you think the reporter might ask. Decide on a couple of points that you want to convey in the interview and figure out how you can work them into the interview. Ask in advance what questions will be asked and let the reporter know if there are things that you would like to talk about. Remember to speak in plain English and not to get angry. Finally, in an interview or in a more casual conversation, do not forget that when you are in the presence of a reporter (who may or may not identify himself or herself as such), always assume that what you say could become public information.

Whereas these four guidelines may be helpful in developing an overall approach to media relations, there are several considerations that are specific to particular types of media.

Television. You should recognize not only that more people get their news from television than from any other media source but also that television provides a variety of means to get a message out—news programs, public affairs programs, talk shows, editorial commentaries, and public affairs programming. All of these may be broadcast by national networks, local news organizations, and public television. The key to approaching television is to remember that television messages must be short and simple. Even quite complex stories often are reduced to 30- to 60-second segments. Television reporters and producers, therefore, are likely to look for the brief summary statement or a catchy phrase (sound bite) that summarizes or expresses your viewpoint. In approaching television appearances, follow the rules of interviews mentioned above. Obtain information about the format of the program and the interviewer's name and style so that you will know what to expect. Learn about what other guests will be on the program with you. Dress appropriately so that your clothing does not overpower your message. Arrive early to meet the producer, the interviewer, and others involved in the show. State your main point first and then follow it with supporting material. Try to stay on track, even if there are efforts to interrupt and divert you (General Services Administration, 1999, pp. 6–10).

The print media. The print media (including newspapers and magazines) typically provide more in-depth coverage of stories than other media sources and are read by people who want more detailed and complete information than might be included in a television news show. Consequently, they provide an opportunity for you to go into much greater detail about the work you are doing. In general, reporters for the print media spend a lot of time learning about the issues and will be somewhat better at "staying with" the complexity of a story. They also will appreciate all of the documentation and facts and figures that you can provide. Establishing effective relationships with print journalists and regularly providing information, even detailed information, on the work of your agency should result in more accurate treatment of the stories in which you are interested. If reporters know the background of the story, something that has to be developed over time, then they will be more likely to agree with your ideas about what is important and what is not.

Radio. In many ways, approaching relationships with radio reporters and personalities is like dealing with television journalists. However, radio audiences are much more diverse and specialized than television audiences. Most radio formats target a particular group or "market segment."

> The diversity of radio station formats provides opportunities for targeting specific audiences. A radio station's format—whether rock, classical, country, urban contemporary, all-news, all-talk, or Spanish language—. . . provides the opportunity to direct the . . . government's message to a particular age cohort or interest group within a community. (Wheeler, 1994, p. 102)

Press conferences. Most experts agree that press conferences (or news conferences) should be used only when absolutely necessary and should be used for specific purposes.

> The general rule is that when you need to give the same information at the same time to everyone in the media, and when it is information they want and need quickly, then a news conference is in order. When in doubt about calling a news conference, don't. (Wheeler, 1994, p. 113)

When a press conference is necessary, try to achieve a smooth and concise tone. Start and end on time, have sign-in sheets and press kits available, respond to questions honestly and directly (promising to get back to reporters if you do not know the answers to particular questions and then doing so quickly), and politely end the press conference after a reasonable number of questions (but providing the opportunity for reporters to follow up with more questions).

Making Effective Presentations

During your work in a public organization, you often may be asked to make formal presentations. You may be asked to present a reorganization proposal to top management. You may be asked to explain a newly developed policy to a legislative committee. Or you may be asked to speak at a civic club or neighborhood organization. In any case, your ability to deliver an effective presentation will have an impact on your agency's work as well as on your own reputation. In this subsection, we consider some of the elements that go into making a formal presentation—the planning stage, the pre-presentation stage, the presentation, the question-and-answer session, and using technological support.

The planning stage. During the planning stage, you first should try to be clear about the purpose of your presentation. You should know why you were asked to speak and what the audience expects from you. (This will shape not only your speech but also your attire.) You should decide exactly what major points you want to get across. And you should think about the purpose of your presentation. Are you informing (e.g., providing information, demonstrating a technique, delivering a report), or are you trying to persuade or motivate the audience to do something or take a specific action? You also should think about your audience. How much do audience members know about the subject? (If they know a great deal, then an elementary presentation will bore them; if they know practically nothing, then you need to start with the basics.) You also should think about the audience's frame of reference. One speaker developed a presentation and handouts using baseball as an analogy. After asking some questions of the audience, he found out that about half of the people there were from outside North America and knew nothing about baseball (Abernathy, 1999, p. 22).

Once you believe that you have a good understanding of the audience, you should let that knowledge shape not only the content but also the language of your presentation. We know, of course, of the tendency of those working in a particular field to rely on the jargon—and even the acronyms—of that field. But if you are speaking to others outside of your field, then they might not understand what the words and letters mean. One speech expert complained, "When government workers toss off acronyms, abbreviations, and other jargon, people duck and miss the point. The way federal workers talk sounds like gibberish to outsiders" (Kogan, 1996, p. 53). But that is easy to correct. Naturally, you should research your topic thoroughly and know the material very well. In addition, you should organize your presentation carefully. A message that is well organized is more likely to be retained and to influence listeners than one that is not. Moreover, careful organization improves your credibility as a speaker. The old recommendation to tell the audience what you are going to say, then tell them, and then tell them what you have said has considerable merit. For presentations dealing with new policies or ideas, as with many public sector presentations, one standard way of organizing is to (a) gain attention, (b) show a need, (c) present a solution, (d) describe what will happen if the proposal is implemented, and (e) call for support or action on behalf of the proposal. In any case, begin with some attention-gaining material and then state the purpose of the presentation. Limit the content of the presentation to a few (three to five) main points. Support your points with research, anecdotes, experiences, statistics, and the like. Then summarize and conclude with something memorable. Remember that audiences remember best what they are told first and last, so be sure to end on a strong point, perhaps even reserving a "prepared" conclusion for after the question-and-answer session (Davidson & Kline, 1999, p. 63).

The pre-presentation stage. This stage includes those activities that take place just before the presentation. You should, of course, rehearse your presentation several times and, if at all possible, practice aloud so that you can assess questions of clarity and timing. If you tend to have excess nervous energy prior to presentations, then do something to work off that energy. Go for a walk, go swimming, or just be sure to be mentally active just before the presentation. If possible, arrive early so that you can take care of any last-minute problems with the layout of the room or with your slides or handouts. Greet participants as they come in; that way, you will be speaking to an audience with whom you already have a connection. Most important, get excited about the presentation. Remind yourself of how important your message is and how honored you are to be making the presentation.

The presentation. During this stage, you should try to begin on time if that is under your control. If you are not introduced to the audience, then introduce yourself, telling audience members of your background and credentials that are relevant to the presentation. If possible, interact with the audience or provide interactive handouts. "The more the audience is involved in the presentation, the easier and more fun it is for the presenter, and the more effective it is for the audience" (Robert Pike, quoted in Abernathy, 1999, p. 24). During the presentation, try to maintain eye contact and use conversational language spoken clearly and loudly enough for everyone to hear. End on time, and be sure to save time for questions.

The question-and-answer session. This stage encourages people to ask questions, even difficult ones (for which you should be prepared). Restate each question before answering. This gives you time to think about the response and helps the audience to understand the question. Answer those questions that you can, but do not bluff in response to those that are more difficult. If you do not know the answer, or if you believe that the question is beyond the scope of your presentation, then feel free to say so. If the question is a good one and you do not know the answer, offer to get back to the questioner and take his or her name and address. Remember that although you are an expert on this topic, that does not mean that you know everything there is to know. You will be better off giving an apology and a promise to find out the answer than providing a wrong answer.

Using technological support. This is increasingly expected by today's audiences, although that does not mean that every presentation needs to have lots of animation or audiovisual support. If you do use such aids, then be sure that they are employed to enhance the presentation and not to take it over. For example, do not use too much text on your slides or handouts; graphics, pictures, and charts are more effective. Also, do not use too many slides. One slide every several minutes is plenty. Whatever you use, carefully proofread your work, including checking your spelling. Rehearse the full presentation, including slides, so that you are comfortable in changing slides and sure that the timing will work. Try to get to the location of the presentation in advance to make sure that the presentation style fits the venue and to make sure that everything is working. Just in case there are power problems or equipment failures, have backups on paper. In any case, plan the presentation so that it will be effective whether technology is used or not.

The New Skills of External Relations

In addition to the traditional skills of external relations, today's public managers must develop skills in listening to the voices of citizens, clients, and "customers"; in understanding how to involve citizens in the work of government; and in becoming more adept at building collaborative relationships with other groups and organizations.

Listening to Citizens, Clients, and "Customers"

Over the past couple of decades, those in both the public and private sectors have become more attentive to providing high-quality service. Most such efforts, even those in the public sector, have adopted the language of the private sector and are referred to as attempts to improve "customer service." Under such a banner, employees are urged to identify their "internal" and "external" customers, to determine the needs and desires of those customers, to be responsive to those needs and desires, and to measure levels of (hopefully improved) customer satisfaction.

Clearly, those in government should provide the highest quality service to citizens and clients. And there have been a wide variety of efforts to improve service quality in public and nonprofit agencies. For example, a federal executive order required federal agencies to define more clearly their internal and external customers and to establish and meet higher standards of service quality. In Great Britain, the citizens' charter movement not only has required higher standards of service quality but also has required "compensation" to citizens when those standards are not met. Similarly, many state and local governments in the United States and abroad have undertaken efforts to improve service quality, often using the language of "customer service" to describe their efforts.

But there are several difficulties with the term *customer service* in a public sector context. Obviously, the varied functions of government do not represent uniform products or even a "product line" as one might encounter in business. Rather, the work of government is extremely diverse in the ways in which it originates, is performed, and is received. Of course, some services, such as receiving traffic citations and being put in prison, are not even services that the immediate recipients want. For these reasons, the relationship between those in public organizations and their "customers" is far more complex than the relationship between those behind a hamburger stand and their customers (Denhardt, 2000, pp. 79–82).

Similarly, the diversity of government activities means that even the first step in a service improvement effort, identification of the agency's "customers," can be quite difficult. For example, private sector customer service efforts often distinguish between internal and external customers. One part of an organization might manufacture components used by another division of the company (an internal customer), which then puts together the final product for the market (external customers). But the issue is somewhat more difficult in government. Among the categories of those dealt with by government might be those who immediately present themselves (and their available resources) for the service, those who are waiting for the service, relatives and friends of the immediate recipient, those who need the service even though they are not actively seeking it, future generations of possible service recipients, and so on.

Of even greater importance, some who approach government for services have greater resources and greater skill in bringing their demands forward. In business, that fact would justify special attention. But in government, it surely does not. In fact, an emphasis on "customer relations" in government might create a climate in which special privileges are granted inappropriately. In addition, a business customer is free to go elsewhere when his or her demands are not met; that is less likely in government. And of course, many public services (e.g., schooling and environmental quality, police protection) are designed to have a collective benefit rather than an individual one. Finally, in the public sector, the "customer" of any government service almost always is, at the same time, a citizen—in a sense, the boss. As a citizen, the individual has a stake in *all* services that are delivered, not just those that he or she consumes directly.

Despite these concerns, many public organizations have adopted the language of "customer service" and, whether using that label or some other, have developed impressive service-quality programs. But some of the most carefully thought-out programs have sought to clarify the language used in their efforts. In one such program, "clients" are considered to be the direct recipients of government services. Clients may be divided into internal and external clients, with the first group receiving service from other governmental employees who, in turn, provide service to external clients. In this formulation, the term *citizen* is reserved for those who receive only an indirect benefit from the service. For example,

> a *citizen* may not collect employment insurance and yet has an interest in how the system functions; the actual recipient of an employment insurance payment would be an *external client*. A regional employment insurance office that depends on a central agency to distribute the employment insurance payments to [its] office would be an *internal client*. (Schmidt, 1998, pp. 2–3)

In any case, a well-grounded service quality program would include several different steps (Blythe & Marson, 1999, pp. 6–12). First, you should ask citizens about their service expectations. What standards of service excellence do citizens and clients expect? How does the agency currently rate in terms of meeting those expectations? There are, of course, a variety of tools available to assess expectations and current levels of service quality. These tools range from those that are fairly precise (e.g., comment cards, surveys, questionnaires) to those that are more open-ended (e.g., focus groups, other consultations). For example, several years ago, the city of Daytona Beach, Florida, conducted a citizen survey to determine levels of satisfaction with various city services as well as citizens' views of what services they would be willing to pay more for to improve (Glaser & Denhardt, 1999). Other cities have conducted focus groups to comment on the quality of city services and to provide more of a dialogue about how improvements might be made. And many agencies, even police departments, have used comment cards to assess the satisfaction of citizens with their interactions with officers. (Imagine getting a traffic citation and then a comment card.)

The key issue here is not just to measure levels of satisfaction but also to identify what factors would raise those levels. For example, citizens or clients might be asked about typical "drivers" of satisfaction, such as courtesy, timeliness, and accessibility. How courteous was the person with whom you spoke? How long are you willing to wait to get a driver's license? How convenient are the license bureaus? One technique for analyzing the resulting data is to create a grid showing levels of importance on one dimension (How important is this service to you?) and levels of performance on the other (How well are we doing?).

When a service is rated high in terms of importance but low in terms of performance, this indicates that service improvements are required. If a service is rated low in terms of importance but high in terms of performance, this represents an opportunity for reallocating resources to services that clients deem more important (Blythe, 1999, p. 7).

Second, you should establish a system for measuring progress toward service improvement objectives and ensuring accountability for results. You need to have some system in place for measuring how well you are doing in closing gaps between expectations and performance. A performance measurement system is needed to measure progress over time, and some type of benchmarking might be helpful in determining how your organization stacks up against others that are similarly situated. Again, a citizen survey undertaken over 2 years or so and using the same or similar questions will show increases (or decreases) in citizen satisfaction with local government services. If that information can be correlated with similar information for other cities, a practice know as "benchmarking," then it may become even more valuable. (Standard formats are being developed for measuring service quality. For example, the International City Management Association's Center for Performance Measurement has the mission of helping local governments to measure, compare, and improve municipal service delivery. Similarly, the Canadian Institute for Citizen-Centered Service offers a benchmarking service utilizing an anonymous database against which users can quantitatively measure their levels of service rank against peer organizations [Retrieved June 2007 from www.iccs-isac .org/eng/benchmarking.htm].)

Improving service quality, of course, requires the active support of staff throughout the organization. It is important to establish goals or targets with respect to service improvements and to review the performance of staff with respect to those goals. Staff expected to achieve improvements must know exactly what goals they should strive to attain. But they also should be given the freedom to act. Interestingly, research has shown that employee satisfaction is linked to client satisfaction. That is, if employees do not have the proper tools to get the job done, or if they suffer from low morale, then they are not as likely to provide the best quality service to clients and citizens. Undertaking internal organizational improvements, based on employee-identified priorities, is essential to improving the service performance of the organization. Staff must be held accountable for improvements in service quality, but they must be fully equipped and empowered to bring about those improvements.

Third, you should recognize and employ the variety of tools that are available to improve service quality. In many cases, applications of technology can be used to improve service quality. For example, Human Resource Development Canada has developed a network of several thousand kiosks across the country through which Canadians can access information on job openings, file employment insurance applications, and provide suggestions. Other public agencies are quickly exploiting the possibilities of using the Internet to service citizens. For example, a few years ago, the Arizona Division of Motor Vehicles started an online vehicle registration renewal system. Comments from clients have been overwhelmingly positive. In other cases, technology can be combined with reorganized delivery systems. The city of Montreal's *Acces Montreal* gives residents of that city access to municipal one-stop service centers located throughout the city as well as access to services through telephone, Internet, and public access terminals.

It is important, of course, that improved service delivery options actually meet the public's needs. Many local governments have developed Web sites that are structured around the traditional local government organizational chart. That is, there is a section on planning, one on public works, one on human resources, and so on. But a citizen accessing that site to find out how to have an abandoned vehicle removed from a vacant lot might well find such a site bewildering. Is the problem one for public works or for code enforcement? Although the Web site might make sense to those within the organization, it might be a mystery to those outside of the organization. But the Web site could easily be redesigned around an inventory of city services and be much more helpful to citizens seeking to access those services. In designing new approaches to service delivery, it often is helpful to consult in detail with the clients and citizens who ultimately will access the system.

One interesting question that arises during discussions of service quality in the public sector is how public services compare with those delivered by business. In general, the public seems to think poorly of government services. But when they are asked about specific services or specific interactions with those in government, the public's assessment rises considerably. One study comparing the satisfaction ratings of both public and private institutions in the United States found that people ranked private mail carriers first, followed by the fire department, grocery stores, the U.S. Post Office, banks, public health clinics, and so on. In other words, when ranking specific institutions, the public rates both public and private institutions highly—not just one or the other (Poister & Henry, 1994). A similar study in Great Britain ranked supermarkets first, followed by postal services, doctors, primary schools, refuse collection, and customs. Again, the study showed that both public and private institutions ranked high (Dinsdale & Marson, 1999). So, although the public may be critical of public institutions in the abstract, specific institutions rank comparably with private sector organizations.

A major study sponsored by the Canadian Centre for Management Development summarized some of the most important findings on what citizens expect from government:

1. Contrary to popular belief, [citizens] rate the quality of many government services as high [as] or higher than many private sector services.

2. Overall, citizens rate the quality of *specific* government services higher than government service *in general*. Failing to differentiate . . . has led to unrealistically low estimates of government service quality in the past.

3. Citizens understand that government has a more difficult role than the private sector, balancing efficiency with the public interest. However, they still expect the quality of government services to be as high [as] or higher than that of private services.

4. Citizens' assessments of service quality are determined primarily by five factors: timeliness, knowledge and competence of staff, courtesy/comfort, fair treatment, and outcome.

5. The need to contact multiple government offices for a single service issue arises most frequently around certificates, license, [and] registration. These contacts are often triggered by milestones in life such as getting a new job, going away to [a] university, getting married, [experiencing] a death in the family, or moving. (Erin Research, 1998, p. iii)

It is clear that citizens have high expectations of those in government. But it also is clear that specific and significant steps can be taken to listen and respond to the needs and interests of citizens.

Involving Citizens in the Work of Government

Involving citizens in the development, and even the implementation, of public policy has long been an important concern for public administrators. Especially since the mid-1960s and the War on Poverty's call for the "maximum feasible participation" of the poor, those in public organizations have sought to reach out to and involve citizens in many different ways, using techniques such as advisory boards, hearings, and community forums. The issue of citizen involvement recently has taken on great urgency as scholars and practitioners have become more and more concerned about the substantial decline in the public's trust in government. The call for greater responsiveness on the part of government has led directly to efforts to improve the relationship between citizens and their government, many based on more substantial citizen involvement in both policy and administration (Thomas, 1995).

But the question of citizen involvement has both benefits and costs associated with it (Washington, 1997, pp. 9–11). On the benefit side, involving citizens in discussion and decision making offers the possibility of sensitizing people to emerging problems and possible solutions. For example, those involved in a planning department forum may come to understand the need for new traffic patterns in a high-density area. Moreover, policies or programs developed in consultation with citizens are likely to be more effective than those developed "in private," in part because officials can gain more information about the conditions being addressed and in part because they can target programs to specific needs. Such policies and programs also are more likely to be accepted by the public. Moreover, according to Boyte (2005), involving the public in problem-solving situations and policy implementation increases the accountability and the responsibility of public and nonprofit organizations and ultimately advances the well-being of the whole community. Similarly, people who have had a role in developing solutions to problems are more likely to "buy in" to the resulting solutions. Finally, consultation and involvement improve the openness or "transparency" of government and, in turn, increase accountability. Public participation requires sharing information and revealing the reasoning that underlies the resulting decision.

On the other hand, involving the public in policy development and implementation can be extremely time-consuming and cumbersome. In addition, unless programs of public involvement are carefully planned and managed, the views that ultimately are expressed might not be representative of those of the majority in a given area. Especially where the issues are technical or the procedures for involvement are highly formal, those with greater resources and expertise might have a significant advantage. For example, those favoring a new business development might have advantages over those being displaced by the project. Some have also suggested that the character of public organizations and the fact that public and nonprofit managers deal with social relations that are highly formalized, make decisions that are supposedly objective, and give "little empowerment and much control" to the administrator make it difficult for managers to find a way to involve citizens (Alkadry, 2003, p. 185). In any case, the various benefits and costs of involvement should be carefully thought out so as to address the possible concerns or biases that could prejudice the outcome.

There are a variety of reasons why programs of public involvement might be initiated by government and corresponding differences in the amount of power that is assumed by the public (Washington, 1997, p. 12). Such activities might include the following:

Information: Government wants to educate the public on a particular policy issue, especially where compliance is an issue.

Dialogue: Substantive input is desired from citizens, either to define the problem and explore solutions or to comment on proposed actions that are under consideration.

Partnership: Citizens or citizen groups engage in joint problem solving and decision making. This strategy implies far more influence on the part of the public than do the first two strategies.

Delegation: The task of setting an agenda and developing policy options is essentially handed over to representatives of the public who, in turn, may solicit the ideas and opinions of others.

Control: The public is empowered to determine the outcome. For example, a referendum may be called for citizens to vote yes or no on a specific issue.

Again, the relationship between the purposes to be served and the particular device for enlisting citizen involvement needs to be carefully thought out.

There are, of course, a variety of mechanisms that those in public and nonprofit organizations can employ to encourage greater citizen input and involvement. We already have mentioned some of the techniques that are appropriate to gathering citizen input, such as surveys and focus groups, activities that are employed primarily to find out what the public is thinking about a particular issue. But more active forms of citizen involvement might include *civic education* programs (in which people, often young people, are brought into government to learn about its operation and their avenues for participation), *volunteer opportunities* (which give citizens an up-close look at government while actually working on specific projects), *leadership development* programs (which offer citizens the information and resources to help solve their own problems at a grassroots level), *citizen advisory panels* (which either advise specific agencies on special topics or provide government in general with the views of a particular neighborhood), *boards and commissions* (on which citizens provide input and advice to particular agencies over an extended period of time), *community workshops* or "charettes" (which enlist the help of citizens in planning and designing neighborhood projects), *public hearings* (formal sessions in which proposed activities are subjected to examination and critique by citizens and interest groups), *impact assessment studies* (studies of the economic and social impact of possible government actions, especially in the area of environmental protection and urban development), and *referenda* (yes/no votes of the people on specific policy issues). In some cases, public opinion polls may also be a very useful tool, especially in the early stages of the implementation of a new public policy. Public managers may decide to use public opinion polls in situations that involve uncertainty about the implementation of the new policy and in situations that indicate potential conflict during the implementation phase (Van Slyke, Horne, & Thomas, 2005, p. 337).

The results of all of these efforts may give the administrator a good indicator of whether the population for whom public policy is intended is supporting or opposing the policy. They also can be used to reveal whether the population needs training and public education about the policy before implementation. Finally, these efforts may be used to point at populations that are interested "in becoming partners in implementation" (Van Slyke et al., 2005, p. 337).

Beginning during the 1970s, a number of local governments in the United States developed broad-scale programs to continuously elicit citizen participation. In 1975, Dayton, Ohio, established seven priority boards (representing the interests of 93 neighborhood associations throughout the city) as the official voice of Dayton's neighborhoods. The priority boards identify and prioritize the needs, goals, and objectives of the citizens, working up from the neighborhood level and then making strategic choices at the priority board level. These priority boards have access to the highest levels of government and are the citizens' voice in all decisions about strategic initiatives and choices about priorities for the future.

In Portland, Oregon, district coalition boards are city-funded nonprofit organizations created to represent neighborhoods within their districts. Each board sets its own policies and priorities and can be as "strategic" as it wishes to be in the allocation of those resources. Typically, the district board provides technical assistance to neighborhood associations (e.g., design and content of newsletters), information and referral on issues such as land use and economic development, crime prevention services, and neighborhood mediation services. It also acts as a conduit between citizens and city government.

St. Paul, Minnesota, has a similar system, with 17 district councils that plan and advise the city on the physical, economic, and social development of their areas as well as on citywide issues. Each district council has a city-paid community organizer, jurisdiction over zoning decisions, authority over the distribution of certain funds and services, and considerable influence over capital expenditures. Because these district councils have both authority and resources, they can be effective mechanisms for strategic planning on a district-by-district basis. Their standing, combined with the citywide nature of the program, also makes the district councils the logical conduit for citizen input into citywide strategic planning efforts.

Many other cities have established structures known as *neighborhood planning councils*. They vary greatly in how much planning they actually do, but the existence of such councils can be an important opportunity for city officials seeking citizen input into strategic planning or visioning efforts. Existing neighborhood organizations were used in a community visioning process in Denver, Colorado, where representatives of the city's planning department and others, such as a traffic engineer and a representative from parks and recreation, assisted the staff in working with the neighborhoods in envisioning their future and in identifying strengths and weaknesses of the community. Ultimately, a plan was developed and a neighborhood steering committee was established. The neighborhood plans were adopted by the city council as amendments to Denver's comprehensive plan.

More recently, many communities, and even individual state and federal agencies, have undertaken *visioning or strategic planning projects* involving a wide variety of citizens in their planning processes. Several localities have developed citizen-based strategic planning programs that seek citizen information through citizen surveys, through focus groups (involving neighborhood groups, elected officials, and even high school students), and through workshops involving the county board of commissioners and the top management team. In many cases, the result has been a set of ordered priorities that the local government then used as a guide for its day-to-day activities over the next several years.

As King and Stivers (1998) noted, all of these efforts to involve citizens in the work of government imply a different role for the administrator and, in turn, different "habits of mind" and different skills. The active and involving administrator's habits of mind include seeing citizens as citizens, sharing authority, reducing personal and organizational control, trusting in the efficacy of collaboration, and balancing experiential knowledge with scientific and professional knowledge (King & Zanetti, 2005). As noted earlier in this chapter, the skills required of the administrator to fully engage the public are not the old skills of organizational management and control but rather the new skills of bargaining, negotiating, facilitating, resolving conflict, and listening. Involving citizens in the work of government—in a meaningful and authentic way—is a real challenge for those in public organizations, but it is a challenge that must be met if government is to restore citizens' trust and confidence and build what has been termed a "new public service" (Denhardt & Denhardt, 2007).

In a sense, the involvement of citizens in the work of government is part of a larger movement toward a broad-based system of governance that is emerging. In a recent article, Boyte (2005) pointed out that citizens are no longer only voters or clients to public administrators; they also actively participate in creating public policy and in decision-making processes. Boyte talked about the importance of shifting from a "democratic state" to "democratic society," accentuating the symbiotic relationship among governments and citizens. "This shift holds the potential to address complex public problems that cannot be solved without governments, but that governments alone can never solve" (p. 537).

Indeed, as we noted above, many are now emphasizing the importance of talking about "governance" rather than just "government." The notion of governance implies that public policies are no longer made merely by government but through a complex process of interaction among many different parties, including those in government, but also those in business and those in nonprofit organizations. Decentralization of politics and the empowerment of the ordinary citizen to participate in policy making and implementation are now considered democratic rights in many countries. But they also represent an important new way of doing the public's business.

Collaborating With Others

As we noted earlier, public agencies today are facing issues that are not easily solved by a single agency acting alone. More and more, major developments in the design and execution of public policy are occurring through a difficult and convoluted process of bargaining and negotiation within some particular policy network. Traditional hierarchical government is giving way to a growing decentralization of policy interests. Control is giving way to interaction and involvement.

For those in public agencies concerned with "getting the job done," this new way of operating means that they no longer can simply think in terms of organizational improvements that will enhance the work of their agencies. Rather, they must shift their thinking to ask, first, what the missions they are trying to achieve are and, then, how they can bring together the right actors so that, acting together, they can achieve those missions. For example, in many states, those concerned with issues relating to children and their families recognized that the difficulties faced by troubled youth often are connected to larger issues faced by their families. A child falling behind in school might come from a family living in substandard housing with a father who has just lost his job and a mother who has developed problems with drugs and alcohol. In such a case, multiple interventions might be called for, yet those interventions must come from as many as six or seven state agencies as well as numerous local and nonprofit organizations. The work of those agencies clearly would be aided by sharing information and coordinating service delivery, to say nothing of designing more holistic approaches to the problems at hand.

Similarly, in many communities, officials have recognized that the delivery of services to previously underserved neighborhoods requires the cooperation of many different agencies. A poverty-stricken area might evidence high crime rates, perhaps related to drugs and gang activity, but it also is likely to need infrastructure improvements, social services, employment assistance, and assistance in economic development. Of course, these different problems traditionally are the "turf" of different local and state agencies—the police, public works, social services, economic development, transportation, and so on. But in specific neighborhoods, a coordinated effort to meet the needs of the community makes sense. And in many communities, just such a coordinated effort has taken place.

In situations such as these, efforts to improve the capabilities of a single organization that is part of the network are important, but equally important are efforts that focus on the overall ability of the network to provide the needed services in a clear and coordinated way. Or, to put it differently, efforts at organizational change must give way to change efforts that affect the network or "system" as a whole. Such an idea has, of course, gained some currency in the business world as well, as many businesses have recognized the increasingly "fluid" interactions of various firms and have begun to talk about "virtual" organizations that bring together, at least on a temporary basis, firms that can engage in mutually beneficial partnerships.

The inevitable connections of the public agency or the nonprofit organization with individuals and institutions from the outside have become a norm and a necessity. But, as networks develop, the question of their effectiveness becomes an issue. Provan and Milward (2001) suggest that there are at least three levels of network effectiveness: the community, the network (itself), and the organizational and participant level (pp. 415–423). Network effectiveness at the community level "must be judged by the contribution they [the networks] make to the communities they are trying to serve" (p. 416). Evaluation of the total outcome for the served population should be measured together with the costs imposed for reaching the component outcomes. The problem arises when defining what the goals are for the community and what a successful implementation means. The community has many different stakeholders, and while they may agree on some goals, there certainly will be cleavages. In this case, effectiveness should be measured in the context of the group that is a target of the program. Community-level networks may also compare their work with similar networks in other communities. And, certainly, one of the major issues for these networks is the contribution that they make to building social capital generally.

The second level is the network itself. The effectiveness of one network, according to Provan and Milward, may be measured through "the ebb and the flow of agencies to and from the network" (2001, p. 418). But the number of agencies that enter or exit the network should be considered from the standpoint of the services that these agencies are providing to the community. Multiplexity, or the strength of the ties within the network, may also be an indicator of network effectiveness. And, finally, the level of successful coordination among the myriad agencies is a very important indicator for an effective network.

The third level, according to Provan and Milward (2001, p. 420), is the organizational and participant level. Client outcomes, legitimacy, resource acquisition, and costs are always important for an organization. Agencies enter a network because the management of the organization believes that being a part of the network will advance some of these criteria, although the benefit will vary from organization to organization. While for some organization the main reason for joining a network might be lowering its costs, for another it might be increasing its legitimacy or providing better service for its clients.

Provan and Milward argued that network efficiency on one level does not automatically imply effectiveness on the other two levels. And rarely can the stakeholders at every level be fully satisfied at the same time. But, regardless of the fact that there are differences in the goals and the methods of measuring a network's effectiveness, it will be increasingly important to measure and control the effects of public and nonprofit networks.

Forms and techniques for successful collaboration. Efforts to bring together many of the groups and agencies in a particular policy network may take many shapes. But several approaches provide good examples of how systemic collaboration can be brought about. For example, Milward and Provan (2006) describe four types of networks:

> The first type is a *service implementation network* that governments fund to deliver services to clients. Collaboration is critical because these networks are based on joint production of services, often for vulnerable citizens like the elderly, families on welfare, or the mentally ill. Integration of services is critical so clients will not fall through the cracks.

> The second type of network is an *information diffusion network,* whose central purpose is to share information across governmental boundaries to anticipate and prepare for problems that involve a great deal of uncertainty, such as earthquakes, wildfires, and hurricanes.

The third type of network (which often grows out of an information diffusion network) is a *problem-solving network.* The purpose of this network is to solve a proximate problem—for example, the response to the attack on the World Trade Center and the Pentagon on 9/11.

The fourth type of network is a *community-capacity-building network,* whose purpose is to build social capital in a community so that it is better able to deal with a variety of ongoing and future problems, such as substance abuse among youth.

At a practical level, we can examine several different examples of collaboration among government agencies and between government agencies and private and nonprofit organizations.

Agencies and nonprofits may also engage in community-involvement strategies. We have pointed out that organizational changes are increasingly likely to involve many groups, ranging from citizens, to nonprofit organizations, to private sector groups. Approaches to change that still are bound to the idea of a single bounded hierarchical organization simply will not work in situations where no one is, or can be, in charge. Rather, what probably is required are forums, arenas, or conferences bringing together many different "stakeholders" and engaging them in a carefully designed process of policy development and change (Bryson & Crosby, 1992; see also Chrislip & Larson, 1994). As we mentioned in Chapter 7, Luke (1998, p. xv) suggested that what is needed in such circumstances is "catalytic leadership," a process involving four interacting tasks: (1) focusing attention on an issue (thereby getting it on the public policy agenda), (2) engaging or convening the diverse set of people needed to address the issue, (3) stimulating different strategies and options for action, and (4) sustaining action by managing the interconnections among various groups especially through rapid information sharing and feedback.

Finally, we should note that bringing together various public, private, and nonprofit organizations to meet publicly defined objectives is fashionably called "partnering." One of the ways in which organizations can increase their effectiveness in meeting public goals is to engage with other groups. These partnerships may be of several types—*cooperating* (using resources to assist other agencies), *coordinating* (organizing or combining resources to reach a mutual goal more effectively), or *collaborating* (collectively applying resources to problems that lack clear ownership). These three types of partnerships vary in terms of power sharing (cooperating involves less; cooperating involves more) and in terms of sharing resources (Light, 1998, pp. 76–77). In any case, agencies wishing to work together must resolve a variety of issues, and these may involve substantial changes in the way in which those in the organization think about their work as well as the way in which they interact with others in doing their work.

According to Imperial (2005), these collaborative activities may be confusing because they take place at many different levels: operational, policy making, and institutional (pp. 288–289). "Collaborative activities at the operational level vary and largely consist of government service delivery" (p. 289). Collaboration at the operational level, depending on the services that the government agency is delivering, may include actions that will improve environmental conditions, educate the public and the decision makers, and monitor the activities of delivering the service.

Collaboration on the policy-making level, however, does not have direct effects on the "real world," but it affects the actions undertaken on the operational level (p. 293). Knowledge and resource sharing among the collaborating organizations is typical for this level. Since the problems that public and nonprofit agencies are dealing with are complex, it is necessary in some instances for agencies not only to share their knowledge and resources but also to develop common policies, regulations, or even social norms.

The third level of collaboration, which, according to Imperial (2005), is the highest level of collaboration, is institutional, or developing "collaborative organizations." Once the organizations institutionalize previously shared policies, regulations, and social norms, they begin to operate as a different organization. Goal establishment and decision-making processes are no longer operations that depend only on one organization. Common goals and practices become a priority for every member (organization) of the group. While in collaborative organizations every member is supposed to have equal or almost equal impact on goal establishment, policy making, and policy implementation, still there are many cases in practice where one organization in the group is paramount. This organization usually puts more of its own resources at stake and consequently has more power in the overall collaboration processes.

Interested in researching the dilemmas that arise in multi-partner alliances, Zeng and Chen (2003) looked into the relationships among different organizations in order to predict when organizations are more likely to cooperate and when the cooperation is more likely to be loose. Although their analysis is based on private companies' partnerships, parts of their analysis are beneficial because they point out certain aspects that are equally important for public and nonprofit organizations. For example, if partners develop higher levels of communication (e-mails, phone calls, meetings), the cooperation among them is likely to be on a higher level. Frequent communication enhances trust among the partners, and trust is very important for cooperation. Identification with the alliance and establishing long-term goals are other factors that advance cooperation among the organizations. If the various organizations perceive that they belong to the group, then their contributions will be higher. And finally, partners' cooperation will depend on the "reciprocity" principle, which basically means that if others in the group work on mutual goals, it is more likely that each organization will strive to follow that principle. On the other side, if some organizations impede cooperation, then it is predictable that this will have negative future influence on the other organizations in the alliance. In a practical sense, how might you go about building effective collaborative efforts in any of these realms? Hargrove (1998, chap. 3) suggests that first you have to reinvent yourself as a "lateral" leader, one who recognizes the importance of interdependence and who is willing to think "outside the box" of hierarchical thinking. Next, you must seek out competent people strategically placed to help move the project forward. You must work with those people to build a shared vision of collaboration and then designate clear roles and responsibilities (being careful not to impose restrictive controls or boundaries). After that, you must spend lots of time in dialogue grounded in real problems and, in the process, develop shared models of the creation you seek. Finally, you must be sure the project is loaded with what Hargrove called "zest factors"—those elements such as challenge, urgency, and high spirits that create excitement and enthusiasm for the project.

Ways of Acting

Increasingly, public managers at all levels will be asked to represent their organizations "on the outside." They will be asked to testify before congressional committees or other legislative bodies. They will be asked to build networks with other public, private, and nonprofit organizations. They will be asked to find creative ways of involving citizens in the work of government. These activities will require that public managers master both the traditional skills of external relations and some that are now emerging. If you find yourself in such a position, there are several points that you should keep in mind.

1. *In representing your agency before the legislature, remember the importance of the relationship between the agency and the legislative body.* Be sure to understand the legislative process, develop an agency protocol for responding to legislative inquiries, and (most important) work to establish trust and to build confidence. Provide advice and information in a timely fashion, be clear about what you are doing, and be accurate in what you say.

2. *In working with the media, try to develop and maintain a positive attitude.* You should create a media relations plan, you should develop a good working relationship with members of the press, and you should be proactive by providing information as soon as possible and in the most complete fashion. You should target your interactions with various members of the press based on their backgrounds, their interests, and the media source they represent.

3. *In making presentations, know your audience and be clear about what you are trying to accomplish.* Research your topic thoroughly, organize your presentation carefully, be enthusiastic about your topic, and involve the audience wherever possible. If you do not know the answer to a question, then just say so—and promise to get the answer.

4. *Whether you use the term "citizen," "client," or "customer," be attentive to improving the quality of the service you provide.* Find out what standards of service people expect of your agency. Establish a system for measuring indicators of service quality and tracking progress toward your desired goals. Develop techniques that will allow your agency to move toward those objectives. Remember that public expectations for the quality of service are high—and they should be.

5. *You should do whatever is possible to involve citizens in the development and implementation of policy in your agency.* There are a variety of techniques you can use, such as civic education programs, volunteer opportunities, leadership development efforts, citizen advisory panels, boards and commissions, community workshops, impact-assessment studies, and referenda. Choose the approach that will

secure the greatest input and involvement and then monitor the process carefully as you work through the issues you face.

6. *Seek out opportunities to collaborate with other groups and organizations to meet shared goals.* Bring together the right people, stimulate a variety of action opportunities, and sustain action by managing the connections among the various parties. Remember that successful public policies today rely on successful interactions among many different actors—including public agencies, private businesses, nonprofit organizations, and citizens groups, just to name a few.

Thinking in Action

Improving Relationships With the Legislature

You are an administrative assistant to the cabinet secretary who heads the state's Department of Youth Services, an agency created 5 years ago to give special focus to the problems of children, youth, and their families. During its short life, the agency has been buffeted by controversy. Several instances of severe child abuse have occurred in families with whom child protective services workers already were in touch. The charge has been that the state should have known about these problems and done something about them before they escalated into violence against children. These dramatic public revelations have been played out against a backdrop of general public and legislative mistrust of the agency as lacking focus, as playing fast and loose with public money, and as being somewhat of a "lone ranger" with respect to other state agencies involved in similar social service work.

The secretary has asked you to develop a plan for public and legislative relations that will help to build confidence in the work of the agency. This plan should consist of two parts. First, you should develop general guidelines and recommendations for how the agency should engage with the public and the legislature. This part of the report should deal not only with the specific messages that you would like to convey but also with how your message might be transmitted—periodic news releases, press conferences, formal testimony by the secretary and others before the legislature, meetings with individual legislators, legislators addressing questions to the department, and so on. A second part of the report should detail a public relations strategy for dealing with specific incidents, such as those cases of severe child abuse mentioned above, if they occur in the future. What should be the response of the agency, and how should that response be communicated most effectively? In each part of the report, you not only should offer your plan but also provide a rationale for why you have chosen the approach that you have.

Improving Service Quality

Earlier in the chapter, we noted that citizens' assessments of service quality are determined primarily by five factors: timeliness, knowledge and competence of staff, courtesy and comfort, fair treatment, and outcome. Think of a recent time when you have had an extended interaction with a government organization—for example, when getting a driver's license, applying for a job, or registering for classes at a university. (Your college or university itself should provide plenty of good examples for this exercise.) Write several paragraphs describing in detail the nature of your interaction with the organization. Then develop a detailed service quality improvement plan that you would be willing to send to the organization as a set of suggestions for improving its service quality. What obstacles do you think might be encountered by the organization in trying to improve the quality of its service? If possible, take your suggestions to the head of the agency and see what problems its managers would see in implementing your suggestions.

Exploring the World of Networks

As a class, try to identify a network operating in your community involving at least a government agency and one or more nonprofit organizations. If you don't have other "leads," you might start with a local (city or county) social services agency or an agency involved in health services. Once you have identified the network, have members of the class interview the heads of the major partners in the network. Then discuss the strengths and weaknesses of this particular collaboration. What does the network do best? What are the chief problem areas? What facilitates collaboration? What makes collaboration more difficult? What is the degree of power or influence each partner has in the relationship? How is the network likely to evolve in the future? As an alternative, invite the leaders of each of the organizations involved to come to class to discuss these same questions.

Community Involvement in Changing Priorities

Read and be prepared to discuss the following case.

Through the midnineties, the government of Orange County, Florida (the county surrounding Orlando), experimented with a Targeted Communities Initiative, an effort to use a citizen-based collaborative process to identify and address the needs of traditionally underserved communities. The county's first effort along these lines took place in South Apopka, a predominantly African American and highly disadvantaged community in northwest Orange County. Since then, the program has moved to other communities as well, most notably the communities of Bithlo (a predominantly White mobile home community in east Orange County) and Winter Garden (a predominantly African American community in west Orange County).

The first formal step in both Bithlo and Winter Garden was to conduct widely publicized town meetings to introduce the initiative and to obtain initial input from residents regarding community needs and concerns. The county chairman attended both meetings and talked with citizens about their current frustrations as well as about their hopes for the future. In both cases, citizens voiced considerable distrust of government based on their previous experiences. It was clear that overcoming this level of distrust was critical. The chairman recognized this issue and explained

(Continued)

(Continued)

that the county was ready to commit new resources to the communities and to redirect existing resources so that they might be used more effectively and in a way that was consistent with the residents' own needs and priorities. But she also pointed out the importance of having those in the communities become involved and active in this process.

During these initial sessions, citizens outlined a general list of needs and priorities. Based on these conversations, county staff members were able to provide some immediate remedies to certain problems in the communities by using existing resources and delivery systems. But other problems required more extensive discussion and planning. This planning occurred over a period of about 2 months, with the same pattern being followed in both Bithlo and Winter Garden.

At the first of a series of six biweekly meetings, citizens were asked to discuss the current image of their communities and then to construct a vision of what they would like their communities to be. Citizens worked in groups of about 10 to 12, with their work being facilitated by trained staff members from the county. Their images of current reality and their hoped-for future both were created as a series of drawings on flip charts, a device that proved to be fun for the participants and also addressed a potential literacy issue.

More important, these discussions brought out some extremely important issues. The citizens first drew pictures that expressed all of the problems and deficiencies they saw in their communities. Next, they drew pictures expressing their visions for the future. These visions, which might be considered modest by some standards, included things such as playgrounds, a community center, places to shop, and decent housing. But to the residents of Bithlo and Winter Garden, these crude drawings with stick figures represented their dreams in highly emotionally charged expressions. The session in Bithlo was particularly poignant as the eyes of grown men welled with tears as they were reminded of their current situation of hopelessness and despair but also of their dreams for their own as well as their children's futures.

After the visioning exercise, the citizens became more focused on actually solving the problems they had identified. To accomplish this, at the second and third meetings, attendees were asked to choose one of eight working groups built around issues in the communities: (1) crime and safety; (2) code enforcement; (3) education; (4) health and social services; (5) housing; (6) parks, recreation, and youth programs; (7) public works; and (8) planning and land use. (Code enforcement and planning ultimately were combined, leaving seven groups.) Each working group or task force identified problems that needed to be addressed within its issue area and then developed a set of priorities for addressing those problems. For example, the public works group in Bithlo identified three major needs to receive attention in the next 3 years: road paving and sidewalks, traffic signal and intersection improvements at a particular location, and improved ditch maintenance. Similarly, the housing group in Winter Garden focused on housing rehabilitation and alternative uses for older structures, a home ownership/down payment assistance program, and elderly and rental housing assistance. In both communities, the need for a community center emerged as a major priority. Again, in all cases, the community residents were the primary participants, with county staff members acting as group facilitators and providing some technical assistance where necessary.

A final set of three meetings allowed the residents to bring their work group reports back to the larger community group and then to begin discussion of priorities across the various areas. At this point, county staff members were able to provide information about available government resources and services and about how those might be accessed. Obviously, the solution to many of the problems identified in this process lay outside of county government, involving other local government jurisdictions or nonprofit organizations. But the strategy was to help empower residents to take action on their own and, with the assistance of the county staff, to identify and enlist the help of whatever individuals and organizations were needed.

Based on these discussions, formal action plans were developed. These plans described the overall visions of the communities that the residents themselves desired and then laid out the detailed action steps that would be required to make the visions reality. For example, one action item related to crime and safety had to do with the installation of streetlights. A series of 14 different tasks was created, ranging from streetlights being approved, to obtaining funding, to actual installation. For each task, an implementation schedule was developed, a projected budget was developed, and a responsible individual (either a county staff member or a resident of the community) was listed (with a phone number). The action plans were submitted to the county commission for approval, and work now is under way to implement the various ideas in the communities.

SOURCE: From "Targeting Community Development in Orange County, Florida," by R. B. Denhardt and J. E. Gray, 1998, *National Civic Review, 87* (Summer/Fall), pp. 227–235. Reprinted by permission of Jossey-Bass, Inc., a subsidiary of John Wiley & Sons, Inc.

14

Managing Behavior in the Public Interest

Let the public service be a proud and noble profession.

—John F. Kennedy

W hen we talk about the management of organizational behavior in the public sector, we always must begin and end with the question, "How can we manage our own behavior and influence the behavior of others in a manner that is consistent with the public interest and the values of democratic governance?" We have talked about ways of thinking and acting to motivate ourselves and others, be a good team member, lead and inspire others, make effective decisions, use power constructively, be creative, manage conflict, and communicate effectively. As we consider these and other perspectives, skills, and behavioral guidelines, it is important to remember that they cannot, and should not, be viewed in a normative vacuum. The values of democratic governance and public service call on us to recognize that what we do and how we do it have important implications for the relationship between citizens and their government, the long-term capacity and effectiveness of public organizations to address societal problems, and the very nature of our service to the public. Our own behavior, and our attempts to influence the behavior of others, always must be elevated to focus on meeting public objectives and community needs. In short, in the field of public administration, we not only need to find the best way of accomplishing tasks but also need to be cognizant of the fact that both the goals we pursue and the manner in which we pursue them are of critical importance to democratic governance.

There are several central issues in organizational behavior that need to be addressed as we work toward the realization of these ideals. First, if management in the public interest involves open participative processes within and outside of organizations, then those processes must be designed to foster the involvement of all types of people with all types of perspectives and worldviews. As our nation becomes more diverse and we increasingly interact with other nations around the globe, it is imperative that public administrators become culturally competent so as to better understand and serve the changing needs of communities and citizens. We have explored the ideas of diversity and multiculturalism throughout this book, but we should be reminded of their importance as we think about the values of public service.

The second issue, which we explore in this chapter, is ethics. There are a number of key ethical factors and perspectives that are critical in our efforts to realize and reflect the values of democracy and the public interest in public organizations. In a very real sense, there are normative issues involved in almost everything that public organizations and public administrators do. How can we manage organizational behavior in a manner that respects the rights of the individual, adheres to democratic principles, and engenders trust, commitment, and involvement? What ethical standards should guide our behavior and create the context for our work?

The third issue, one also explored in this chapter, involves the manner in which we define the nature of public service and the role that both individual public servants and public organizations play in democratic governance. We describe the normative foundations for what we call the "new public service," marked by a commitment to serving citizens, broad-based involvement in goal setting and decision making, and respect for all people. In so doing, we suggest that the public service plays a vital and profound role in realizing the ideals of democracy. In playing this role, the question of how we exercise leadership and manage organizational behavior is a central and enduring theme.

The Ethics of Managing Change

Although many consider management to be a fairly technical endeavor, there are important value questions that affect almost everything that managers do. Managers deal with humans and play a significant role in shaping the lives of those within and outside of their organizations. In so doing, they bear a special responsibility to their employees and the citizens they serve, a responsibility to engage in behavior that is not only efficient and effective but also ethical. In this section, we consider some of the values that enter into managers' relationships with their employees.

Earlier, we reviewed some of the ways in which the manager tries to bring about change in the organization, including change through management action or reorganization and change brought about by reshaping the culture or learning capacity of the organization. But in any effort in organizational change, the wishes of the manager are, to some extent, imposed on other people in the organization. If these people were left to their own devices, then they might act in quite different ways. But because of their roles and commitments within the organization, they act in the way that their manager desires.

Obviously, most efforts at organizational change involve attempts to maximize efficiency, effectiveness, and productivity in the organization. But these values are the values of management and might not necessarily be those of employees. For this reason, most attempts to transform organizations require managers to change the value system of the organization and its members in some way. That is, as Woodall (1996) put it, "It has become received wisdom that high levels of commitment and performance require employees to espouse values that are aligned with the managerial vision" (p. 28). In this view, the question becomes one of how the manager can persuade, entice, or co-opt others into following his or her vision of the organization and its future.

McKendall (1993) argued that most organizational change efforts actually serve to increase the power of management relative to others in the organization. This occurs for several reasons. First, planned change, especially strategic change, typically is initiated by top management and implicitly bears the message that top management not only is in control but also has a "right" to be in control. Second, as we saw in Chapter 12, planned change creates uncertainty and ambiguity in the organization. Under these conditions, employees might seek stability through conformity to the wishes and desires of those who appear to be "in charge." Third, efforts at organizational change involve management defining a new "reality" for the organization's members. "It reaffirms the right of management to define the 'order' of the organization" (McKendall, 1993, p. 99). The basic question becomes one of how managers can secure compliance with their wishes.

Obviously, stating the problem in this way makes more apparent the possible ethical dilemmas that the managers may confront in attempts to change or transform the organization. At some point, change can become coercion, and influence can become manipulation—and there might be a very fine line between the two. Even though modern management expresses distaste for the old authoritarian biases of past management practices, there still are activities that managers engage in that have the effect of devaluing, and even dehumanizing, their employees. Being aware of some of the potential ethical dilemmas that are inherent in management and especially organizational change can help the manager to be more sensitive to the concerns of others in the organization and to be more likely to act in a consistently ethical manner. There are two areas that deserve our attention. First, who determines the need for change, the intended outcomes, and the organization's values? Second, how can managers instill change in a way that is both effective and ethical?

The first question—who determines the need for change—may be addressed by thinking through the various obligations that public administrators have. Obviously, a manager (whether in a public or private organization) who pursues organizational change for his or her own self-interest would be acting in an unethical manner. But public administrators have a further obligation—to undertake change only as it is consistent with their obligations as public servants. Public agencies and their managers are, first and foremost, accountable to the public. As Cooper (1998) put it, "It seems reasonable to expect that someone who accepts employment in a public fiduciary role [will] act generally in accordance with the values of the citizenry as expressed through a political system and direct citizen participation" (p. 69). More specifically, public administrators are expected to behave in a way that is consistent with the wishes of elected officials, especially as reflected in legislation. This means that a public administrator who changes the value system of his or her organization in such away that it no longer is consistent with legislation has acted in an unethical manner. Moreover, if an administrator acts outside of the law or his or her delegated authority in planning or implementing change, then this also would be considered unethical (Svara, 2006).

Beyond their obligations as public servants, public managers (indeed all managers) must face the question of the extent to which their imposing their values on others or their directing the behavior of others represents a violation of their employees' freedom and autonomy. Lippitt and Lippitt (1978), in a well-known book on organizational consultation, wrote,

> In the eyes of those persons who hold the enhancement of man's freedom of choice as a fundamental value, any deliberate influencing of the behavior of others constitutes a violation of their basic humanity. On the other hand, effective behavior change involves some degree of utilization of power and control and a potential imposition of the change agent's values on the client system. (p. 70)

Certainly, we typically assume that by involving ourselves in organizations, we give up some of our decision-making autonomy. But we also recognize that there are limits on the extent to which those in positions of power and authority can impose their will on others. Some such restraints are formal and specific, and they protect the rights of employees (e.g., prohibitions on sexual harassment). Others are more general. For example, the current emphasis on empowerment in organizations presents a significantly different answer to the question of power and control in organizations than that given by the early proponents of top-down "scientific management." Moreover, we recognize that some organizations are more open and involving of lower-level participants than are others. In either case, merely by asking the question, we acknowledge that there is an ethical question concerning the extent to which managers can impose their values on employees. This goes to the second question—how managers can bring about change in a way that is both effective and ethical.

We can begin to address this issue by noting when managers' activities would be unethical. For example, we generally would label as unethical actions that would coerce employees into certain behaviors. "Coercion takes place when one person or group forces another person or group to act or refrain from acting under threat of severe deprivation" such as the loss of one's life, job, or well-being (Warwick & Kelman, 1973). Obviously, we would find overt acts of coercion to be objectionable, but in fact coercion is not always overt. Again, although most contemporary management theories favor more open and involving styles of management, there still are situations in which employees are told essentially to "shape up or ship out." Whether these actions are unethical is perhaps only possible to judge within the context of particular activities, but they certainly raise not just technical issues but ethical ones as well. (We should, of course, point out that in addition to the ethical question that coercion raises, in the long run coercion is not likely to be effective anyway. At a minimum, it generates resentment, but beyond that it can lead to strikes, employee turnover, or even sabotage.)

Many of the same issues that we associate with coercion also can be raised with respect to manipulation. Although manipulation is a somewhat vaguer concept, it generally is taken to mean a type of interpersonal influence in which the manipulator intentionally deceives the target. Seabright and Moberg (1998) suggested that manipulation can be classified in two categories: (1) *situational manipulation* (in which the circumstances within which the target acts are so structured that the target sees no apparent alternatives) and (2) *psychological manipulation* (in which the target's efforts to make sense of a situation are confused or misdirected). "Manipulation operates by robbing the victim of autonomy either in choice (situational manipulation) or in self-definition (psychological manipulation) for the sole purpose of advancing the perpetrator's objective" (Seabright & Moberg, 1998, p. 167). The results are actions that are not freely undertaken.

We can easily think of examples of manipulation in organizations—fooling someone into doing something by the use of flattery or lies, playing on the emotions of someone to get one's own way, making the target think that the agent's way was his or her own idea, and so on. In any case, as with coercion, manipulative tactics that involve deception, threats, fear, secrecy, and dishonesty should be considered unethical. But manipulation sometimes is difficult to identify because it is so closely related to persuasion and facilitation, neither of which has quite the same negative connotation as manipulation. But in terms of organizational change, White and Wooten (1983) argued, "Basically, manipulation and coercion can occur when the organizational development effort requires organizational members to abridge their personal values or needs against their will" (p. 691). As with coercion, there may be practical negative consequences as well in that manipulation is likely to breed anger, fear, resentment, and hostility.

The question of autonomy leads to a final consideration—that organizational change efforts can become dehumanizing and therefore ethically questionable. Basically, this argument would hold that efforts at organizational change that suppress human development or limit the individual's pursuit of meaning, autonomy, and independence raise substantial ethical issues. Many, of course, have argued that modern organizations, by their very nature, have tendencies toward dehumanization. What often is termed the rational model of administration primarily focuses on the organization achieving its objectives with the greatest possible efficiency. Efficiency becomes the key value in that model. But it does so by disregarding the question of human meaning. Individual members of the organization are not valued per se but only as means to given ends. Indeed, a major justification of the rational model is that it can help to eliminate those bothersome human qualities—such as feelings, emotions, and values—that might interfere with the efficient pursuit of the organization's objectives. The individual is not granted autonomy or meaning but rather is viewed in an instrumental fashion—valued only as a contributor to the organization's objectives. Employees are forced into narrowly defined roles in the hierarchy so that their contributions can be regulated and controlled.

As with coercion and manipulation, dehumanization raises not only important ethical issues but also practical ones—dissatisfaction, lack of innovation, groupthink, and the creation of an overly conformist culture in which productive conflict cannot be found. Woodall (1996) summarized the ethical issues in organizational change in this way:

> The role of change agents, and above all the process whereby a cultural change is introduced, are surrounded by ethical dilemmas. These do not just concern the inherent worth of the exercise or its benefit to the organization. They also include the impact on individual motivation to comply and above all the infringement of individual autonomy, privacy, self-esteem, and equitable treatment. (p. 35)

Reviewing the ethics of organizational behavior leads us to ask how public managers can bring about change while still maintaining a sense of democratic responsibility and whether efforts at organizational change can be carried out in a way that avoids coercion, manipulation, or dehumanization. In either case, an appropriate response is to suggest that doing those things that promote the autonomy and independent involvement of individual citizens or employees provides the best possible ethical response. Indeed, one of the most significant ethical issues facing public managers is how they can fully involve all of those individuals both within and outside of the organization who should play a role in decisions concerning the work of the public service (Svara, 2006). Public administration is, of course, different in the sense that, because public servants are involved in the governance process, they must constantly deal with issues such as justice, fairness, and equity. Every act of every public servant, whether in the formulation or implementation of public policy, is permeated with ethical concerns.

The New Public Service

As public administrators, the values and assumptions that we hold about our roles and responsibilities in a democracy set the parameters for our actions. How we behave, and how we seek to influence the behavior of others in the public service, is inherently and fundamentally grounded in how we see government and our role in government. What are the key elements of a normative foundation for the field of public administration, and how do those elements speak to the management of organizational behavior in the public interest?

There is considerable disagreement about this question. This disagreement is important and interesting in its own right but also has implications for how we manage organizational behavior. Some have suggested, for example, that public administration can best serve citizens by reinventing government and following the tenets of the "new public management" (Kaboolian, 1998; Osborne & Gaebler, 1992; Osborne & Plastrik, 1997). This view suggests that public administrators should take actions to rid government of hierarchical controls and bureaucratic models of management in favor of a view of government in which the relationship between public agencies and their "customers" is understood as based on transactions similar to those that occur in the marketplace. In this view, public administrators should see themselves as public entrepreneurs creating mechanisms for citizens to make choices based on their self-interest, creating efficiencies by privatizing and contracting out functions, and concentrating on accountability and high performance, streamlining agency processes, and decentralizing decision making.

Using the tools and approaches of new public management, many public organizations and jurisdictions have succeeded in making important and positive changes. They have increased efficiency by privatizing previously public functions, held top executives accountable for performance goals, established new processes for measuring productivity and effectiveness, and reengineered departmental systems to reflect a strengthened commitment to accountability (Aristigueta, 1999; Barzelay, 1992; Boston, Walsh, Martin, & Pallot, 1996; Kearns, 1996).

Others have suggested that these and other prescriptions for enhancing governmental performance ought to be considered within the normative context of democratic values. We believe that this view of the role of public administration has been neglected during recent years and should be given a more forceful voice in the debate. For example, Denhardt and Denhardt (2000, 2007) proposed a series of principles that they argued ought to frame what they call the "new public service." They suggested that we, as public administrators, should not define our role or gauge our actions based on the values of traditional command-and-control bureaucracies. Nor should we base public service solely on business values and the market-based approaches of new public management. Rather, we should define our field and ground our actions in a new public service based on the values of democratic governance.

The new public service begins with the idea that democratic principles and values such as citizenship, community, and participation in decision making are paramount. So, although the importance of traditional organizational perspectives, the need for attention to public sector efficiency, and the contributions of market-based approaches are not questioned, Denhardt and Denhardt (2000, 2007) contended that these tools and approaches must be considered within the larger context of democracy and citizenship. The main tenets of the new public service can be summarized as follows:

1. *Serve rather than steer.* An increasingly important role of the public servant is helping citizens articulate and meet their shared interests rather than attempting to control or steer society in new directions. Although in the past government played a central role in what has been called the "steering of society" (Nelissen, Bemelmans-Videc, Godfroij, & deGoede, 1999), the complexities of the modern world sometimes make such a role both inappropriate and impossible. Rather than being based only on a singular governmental decision-making process, public policies and programs today are the result of the interaction of many different groups and organizations as well as the mixture of many different opinions and interests. Government has a very important role to play within this complex set of interactions involving multiple groups and multiple interests. Government works in concert with other institutions, groups, and organizations to seek solutions to the problems that communities face. So, government does not singularly control the decision. Rather, it sets the agenda, fosters participation, facilitates dialogue, negotiates conflict, and "brokers" solutions to public problems.

2. *The public interest is the aim, not the by-product.* Public administrators must contribute to building a collective shared notion of the public interest. The goal is not to find quick solutions driven by individual choices. Rather, it is the creation of shared interests and shared responsibility. Widespread public dialogue and deliberations are central to the process of establishing a vision or direction based on shared values (Crosby & Bryson, 2005; Luke, 1998; Stone, 1988). The public service should play an active role in creating processes and arenas in which citizens can engage with one another. As a result, citizens come to better understand each other's interests and adopt a longer range and broader sense of community and societal interests. Based on this dialogue, a broad-based vision for the community, the state, or the nation can be developed to provide a set of goals and ideals for the future. It is less important that this process result in a single set of objectives than that it engage administrators, politicians, and citizens in a process of thinking about a desired future for their community and their nation. In participating in this dialogue, government also so has a moral obligation to ensure that solutions that are generated are consistent in both substance and process with norms of justice, fairness, equity, and the public interest (Ingraham & Ban, 1988; Ingraham & Rosenbloom, 1989; Svara, 2006).

3. *Think strategically, act democratically.* Policies and programs meeting public needs can be achieved most effectively and responsibly through collective efforts and collaborative processes. The problems facing society and our communities today cannot be solved by public servants and public organizations acting alone. Solving these problems requires not only that there be widespread involvement in developing policies and programs but also that citizens and communities be engaged in their implementation. Government actions that involve citizens and community organizations can stimulate a renewed sense of civic pride and responsibility. Citizen pride and responsibility can evolve into a greater willingness to be involved at many levels. Although government cannot create community, it can lay the groundwork for effective and responsible citizen action by being open, accessible, and responsive.

4. *Serve citizens, not customers.* The public interest is the result of a dialogue about shared values rather than the aggregation of individual self-interests. Therefore, public servants do not merely respond to the demands of "customers." Rather, they focus on building relationships of trust and collaboration with and among citizens. The new public service recognizes that the relationship between a government and its citizens is not the same as the one between a business and its customers. Government has many "customers" but also must be attentive to the needs of the broader community and the nation as a whole. In government, considerations of fairness and equity often are much more important considerations than the desires of the immediate customers. So, government should not first or exclusively respond to the selfish short-term interests of "customers." Rather, it should work to facilitate citizenship. Citizens, unlike business customers, are committed to matters that go beyond their short-term interests and are willing to assume personal responsibility for what happens in their neighborhoods and communities. Public servants should take actions that encourage more and more people to fulfill their responsibilities as citizens and for government to be especially sensitive to their voices.

5. *Accountability is not simple.* Public servants should be attentive to more than the market; they also should attend to statutory and constitutional law, community values, political norms, professional standards, and citizen interests. The matter of accountability is extremely complex. Despite the popularity of numerical performance measures, they alone are inadequate as a measure of accountability in the public sector. Public servants are and should be influenced by and held accountable to a complex mix of institutions and standards including the public interest, statutory and constitutional law, other agencies, other levels of government, the media, professional standards, community values and standards, situational factors, democratic norms, and citizens. Those in public organizations must recognize the reality and complexity of these responsibilities. Because of this complexity, accountability is enhanced when public administrators do not make these decisions alone. Instead, the balance between these values should be made part of the dialogue, brokerage, citizen empowerment, and broad-based citizen engagement process. Doing so not only makes for realistic solutions but also builds citizenship and democratic accountability.

6. *Value people, not just productivity.* Public organizations and the networks in which they participate are more likely to be successful in the long run if they are operated through processes of collaboration and shared leadership based on respect for all people. The new public service emphasizes the importance of "managing through people." Productivity improvement, process reengineering, and performance measurement are seen as important tools in designing management systems. But the new public service suggests that such systems are likely to fail in the long term if, at the same time, insufficient attention is paid to the values and interests of individual members of an organization. Public servants are more likely to treat citizens with respect if they also are treated with respect by those who manage public agencies. Despite the conventional wisdom that public employees crave the security and structure of bureaucratic jobs, public servants are people who are motivated by their desire to make a difference in the lives of others (Denhardt, 2000; Perry & Wise, 1990; Vinzant, 1998). Public administration must develop opportunities for employees and citizens to affirm and act on public service motives and values. Shared leadership, based on the values of mutual respect, accommodation, and support, should be used to enhance and reinforce the public service motivation of workers.

7. *Value citizenship and public service above entrepreneurship.* The public interest is better advanced by public servants and citizens committed to making meaningful contributions to society than by entrepreneurial managers acting as if public money were their own. Public administrators are not like the owners and entrepreneurs of business enterprises where the goals are to maximize productivity and satisfy customers. Public programs and resources do not belong to the people who work for the government. Rather, as King and Stivers (1998) reminded us, government is owned by the citizens. Public administrators accept a responsibility to serve citizens by being stewards of public resources (Kass, 1990), conservators of public organizations (Terry, 1995), facilitators of citizenship and democratic dialogue (Box, 1998; Chapin & Denhardt, 1995; King & Stivers, 1998), catalysts for community engagement (Denhardt & Gray, 1998; Lappé & Du Bois, 1994), and street-level

leaders (Vinzant & Crothers, 1998). Accordingly, public administrators not only must share leadership, work through people, and broker solutions; they also must accept and act on their role as responsible participants in the governance process. This means that public servants must avoid limiting their knowledge and willingness to respond to citizens to narrow programmatic boundaries. Citizens' needs and problems typically do not mirror our organizational charts. So, effective public service requires knowledge of other public programs and community resources as well as a willingness to assist citizens in finding what they need. It also means that risk taking for public administrators is different from risk taking for business owners or entrepreneurs who know that, in making decisions, the consequences and the success or failure will fall largely on their own shoulders. In the public sector, the risks and opportunities reside within the larger framework of democratic citizenship and shared responsibility. Although some situations might require quick action, the benefits of a public administrator taking a risk or making a decision without consulting others must be carefully weighed against the costs to trust, collaboration, and the sense of shared responsibility.

Although debates among theorists will continue, and although administrative practitioners will test and explore new possibilities, we believe that the new public service model offers an important and viable alternative to both the traditional and the now dominant new public management models. Although a concern for democratic citizenship and the public interest might be subordinated in the current debate, it has been and always will be a central concern in the field of public administration. In the most fundamental sense, the central issue here echoes the potential clash between the values of bureaucracy and democracy that was articulated by Woodrow Wilson (1887) during the late 1800s—a tension that continues to be a vital force in our efforts to define and realize a normative basis for the field of public administration.

The question here is how we can balance these values in the management of organizational behavior. Although some of us might lean more heavily in one direction or another, virtually all would agree that both sets of values are important. Concerns with efficiency and productivity should not be lost, but neither should we lose sight of the larger context of democracy, community, and the public interest. Our approach to managing organizational behavior is central to the realization of both sets of values. But in our view, the literature and dialogue within the field of public administration too often neglects the importance of the democratic side of the equation in evaluating the use of various management approaches. In simple terms, we argue that it is not enough to employ approaches to managing organizational behavior that "work" in terms of efficiently meeting short-term objectives. Rather, we should employ approaches to the management of organizational behavior that not only "work" but also foster the development of skills, leadership approaches, techniques, motivational models, and standards of success that are consistent with democratic values and the public interest.

How do we know that we are acting and influencing others in a manner consistent with the public interest? To which democratic values should we be most attentive in managing organizational behavior in the public sector? We suggest that the public interest may be best thought of as the *process* of engagement or dialogue between citizens and public servants through which we discover and articulate common values, shared interests, and long-term goals. The public interest is not merely the aggregation of individuals' self-interest, nor is it something that can ever be fully and finally defined. Rather, it is through the process of *searching* for the long-term interests of a community and a nation that we realize the ideals of democratic governance and the public interest. So, in our view, it is less important that the public interest be empirically verifiable and more important that we, as public administrators, recognize it as an ideal that can and should guide how we interact with others within our organizations, how we involve citizens and respond to their needs, and how we define ourselves as public servants.

In short, the normative context of organizational behavior in the public sector is founded on democratic values and the ideals of public service in the public interest. Accordingly, as public servants, we should not only understand but also act on these values in our interactions with people both inside and outside our organizations. For example, acting on these values suggests that when we define goals, we do so through a highly participative process. We already have noted the many ways in which participative goal setting promotes sound management and individual performance in terms of enhancing motivation, encouraging creativity, reducing destructive organizational politics, facilitating change, and reducing stress. It also is a core value in the management of organizational behavior in the public interest that reflects our commitment to human dignity and the democratic process. Acting on these values also would suggest that we work to model democratic values within organizations and treat employees as we want them to treat citizens. If we understand how participation, engagement, and empowerment enhance responsibility and commitment, and if we accept how being open to divergent views contributes to the development of effective solutions to problems, then the argument for modeling democratic values in public organizations is even more compelling.

With regard to the skills needed to practice the management of organizational behavior in the public interest, it would seem clear that the ability to facilitate involvement, manage conflict, and communicate effectively with a wide variety of individual groups and individuals is critical. Democratic norms make it incumbent on public administrators to avoid simply deciding what the "right" answer is or deciding what is "best" in terms of providing service to citizens and instead to take responsibility for ensuring that those effected by administrative decisions have a voice in the process. The skills needed to do so involve facilitating broad-based participation, listening effectively, brokering alternatives, fostering creativity, and being responsive to the priorities and values expressed in the process. Leadership skills should focus on sharing power, being open to divergent views, trusting and empowering others, and (as a result) articulating a shared vision based on long-term goals and democratic values.

Conclusion

In our earlier discussion of diversity and multiculturalism, in our discussion of the ethics of managing change, and in our discussion of the new public service in this chapter, we find one theme recurring—inclusion and involvement. Certainly, our interest in diversity is based on a concern for incorporating people of different cultures and backgrounds into the work of our organizations. Similarly, to act in an ethical fashion in bringing about organizational change, one important issue is securing the participation of people throughout the organization. And as we have seen, the new public service places a premium on citizen participation or civic engagement. But of course, given the role of public administration in a democratic system of governance, we should expect no less.

In the context of managing organizational behavior in a manner consistent with democratic values and public interest ideals, the compelling nature of work in the public service becomes particularly significant. Public service values and motivations are what make public sector work exciting, worthwhile, meaningful, and satisfying. People in the public service want to know that they are making a difference—that the programs they work on, the policies they create, the services they provide, and the work they do somehow contribute to making the world a better, safer, cleaner, and more peaceful place. Public service work is difficult, and as managers, supervisors, and coworkers, we can work to make that public service motive more visible and important. Organizational behavior in public administration is, in the final analysis, shaped and motivated by the distinctiveness and inherent value of public service.

References

Abernathy, D. J. (1999). Presentation tips from the pros. *Training and Development, 53*(10), 20–25.

Adams, G. T. (1987). Preventive law trends and compensation payments for stress-disabled workers. In J. C. Quick et al. (Eds.), *Work stress: Health care systems in the workplace.* New York: Praeger.

Adams, J. S. (1965). Inequity in social exchange. In L. Berkowitz (Ed.), *Advances in experimental psychology.* New York: Academic Press.

Aldefer, C. (1972). *Existence, relatedness, and growth.* New York: Free Press.

Alkadry, G. M. (2003). Deliberative discourse between citizens and administrators: If citizens talk, will administrators listen? *Administration & Society, 35*(2), 184–209.

Allison, G. (1971). *The essence of decision: Explaining the Cuban missile crisis.* Boston: Little, Brown.

Allison, G. T., & Zelikow, P. (1999). *Essence of decision: Explaining the Cuban missile crisis* (2nd ed.). New York: Longman.

Amabile, T. (1983). *The social psychology of creativity.* New York: Springer-Verlag.

Amabile, T. (1987). The motivation to be creative. In S. G. Isaksen (Ed.), *Frontiers in creativity: Beyond the basics.* Buffalo, NY: Bearly Limited.

Amabile, T. (1988). A model of creativity and innovation in organizations. In B. M. Staw & L. L. Cummings (Eds.), *Research in organizational behavior.* Greenwich, CT: JAI.

Amabile, T. (1997). Motivating creativity in organizations: On doing what you love and loving what you do. *California Management Review, 40*(1), 39–58.

Amabile, T. M., Barsade, S. G., Mueller, S. J., & Staw, B. M. (2005, September). Affect and creativity at work. *Administrative Science Quarterly, 50*(3), 367–403.

Amachi, R. N., & Wade, L. (1996, September). Government employees learn to work in sync. *Personnel Journal,* 91–95.

Anderson, C. R. (1977). Locus of control, coping behaviors, and performance in a stress setting: A longitudinal study. *Journal of Applied Psychology, 62,* 446–451.

Anderson, P. A. (1983). Decision making by objectives and the Cuban missile crisis. *Administrative Science Quarterly, 28,* 201–222.

Andrews, F. M., & Farris, G. F. (1967). Supervisory practices and innovation in scientific teams. *Personnel Psychology, 20,* 497–515.

Argyle, M. (1988). *Bodily communication.* London: Methuen.

Argyris, C. (1964). *Integrating the individual and the organization.* New York: John Wiley.

Argyris, C. (1970). *Intervention theory and method.* Reading, MA: Addison-Wesley.

Argyris, C. (1999). *Organizational learning* (2nd ed.). Oxford, UK: Blackwell.

Argyris, C., & Schön, D. A. (1974). *Theory in practice: Increasing professional effectiveness.* San Francisco: Jossey-Bass.

Aristigueta, M. P. (1999). *Managing for results in state government.* Westport, CT: Quorum Books.

Armour, N. (1995). The beginning of stress reduction: Creating a code of conduct for how team members treat each other. *Public Personnel Management, 24*(2), 127–133.

Armstrong, M. (2004). *How to be an even better manager: A complete A–Z of proven techniques & essential skills.* United Kingdom: Kogan Page.

Arnold, J. D. (1978). *Make up your mind.* New York: Amazon.

Atkinson, J. W. (1964). *An introduction to motivation.* New York: Van Nostrand Reinhold.

Axelrod, L., & Johnson, R. (2005). *Turning conflict into profit: A roadmap for resolving personal and organizational disputes.* Alberta, Canada: The University of Alberta Press.

Axtell, R. E. (1991). *Gestures.* New York: John Wiley.

Ayoko, O. B., & Hartel, C. E. J. (2006). Cultural diversity and leadership: A conceptual model of leader intervention in conflict events in culturally heterogeneous workgroups. *Cross Cultural Management: An International Journal, 13*(4), 345–360.

Baldwin, J. N. (1984). Are we really lazy? *Review of Public Personnel Administration, 4*(2), 80–89.

Balfour, D., & Weschler, B. (1990). Organizational commitment: A reconceptualization and empirical test of public-private differences. *Review of Public Personnel Administration, 10*(3), 23–40.

Bandura, A. (1986). *Social foundations of thought and action: A social cognitive view.* Englewood Cliffs, NJ: Prentice Hall.

Baraldi, C. (2006). New forms of intercultural communication. *International Communication Gazette, 68*(1), 53–69.

Barendsen, L., & Gardner, H. (2007). Three Elements of Good Leadership in Rapidly Changing Times. In J. C. Knapp (Ed.), *For the Common Good,* pp. 21–32. Westport, CT: Praeger.

Barnard, C. (1948). *The function of the executive.* Cambridge, MA: Harvard University Press.

Barnett, C. C. (1984). The ox and me: A view from atop an organization. *Public Administration Review, 41*(6), 525–529.

Barney, J. B., & Griffin, R. W. (1992). *The management of organizations.* Boston: Houghton Mifflin.

Barron, F. B., & Harrington, D. M. (1981). Creativity, intelligence, and personality. *Annual Review of Psychology, 32*, 439–476.

Barzelay, M. (1992). *Breaking through bureaucracy.* Berkeley: University of California Press.

Bass, B. M. (1985). *Leadership and performance beyond expectations.* New York: Free Press.

Bass, B. M. (1990). *Handbook of leadership.* New York: Free Press.

Bass, B. M., & Avolio, B. J. (Eds.). (1994). *Improving organizational effectiveness through transformational leadership.* Thousand Oaks, CA: Sage.

Bazerman, M. H., & Neale, M. A. (1992). *Negotiating rationally.* New York: Free Press.

Beach, L. R. (1990). *Image theory: Decision making in personal and organizational context.* Chichester, UK: Wiley.

Beehr, T. (1995). *Psychological stress in the workplace.* London: Routledge.

Behn, R. D. (1988). Management by groping along. *Journal of Policy and Management Review, 7*(4), 643–663.

Behn, R. D. (1991). *Leadership counts.* Cambridge, MA: Harvard University Press.

Behn, R. D. (1995). The big questions of public management. *Public Administration Review, 55*(4), 313–324.

Bell, M. (2006). *Managing diversity in organizations.* Mason, OH: Thomsen South-Western.

Bennett, M. B. (1993). Towards ethnorelativism: A developmental model of intercultural sensitivity. In R. M. Paige (Ed.), *Education for the intercultural experience.* Yarmouth, ME: Intercultural Press.

Bennis, W. (1983). The artform of leadership. In S. Srivastya (Ed.), *The executive mind*. San Francisco: Jossey-Bass.

Bennis, W. (1997). *Managing people is like herding cats*. Provo, UT: Executive Excellence Publishing.

Bennis, W., & Nanus, B. (1985). *Leaders: The strategies for taking charge*. New York: Harper & Row.

Beyle, T., & Williams, J. O. (Eds.). (1972). *The American governor in behavioral perspective*. New York: Harper & Row.

Bierstedt, R. (1950). An analysis of social power. *American Sociological Review, 15*, 730–736.

Billig, M., & Tajfel, H. (1973). Social categorization and similarity in intergroup behavior. *European Journal of Social Psychology, 3*, 27–52.

Bingham, G. (1986). *Resolving environmental disputes: A decade of experience*. Washington, DC: Conservation Foundation.

Blake, R. R., & McCanse, A. A. (1991). *Leadership dilemmas: Grid solutions*. Houston, TX: Gulf Publishing.

Blake, R. R., & Mouton, J. (1964). *The managerial grid*. Houston, TX: Gulf Publishing.

Blake, R. R., & Mouton, J. S. (1973). The fifth achievement. In F. E. Jandt (Ed.), *Conflict resolution through communication*. New York: Harper & Row.

Blau, G. J. (1987, Fall). Locus of control as a potential moderator of the turnover process. *Journal of Occupational Psychology*, 21–29.

Block, P. (1987). *The empowered manager: Positive political skills at work*. San Francisco: Jossey-Bass.

Block, P. (1993). *Stewardship: Choosing service over self-interest*. San Francisco: Berrett-Koehler.

Bluedorn, A., & Lundgren, E. (1993). A culture-match perspective for strategic change. *Research in Organizational Change and Development, 7*, 137–179.

Blumenthal, W. M. (1983). Candid reflections of a businessman in Washington. In J. L. Perry & K. L. Kraemer (Eds.), *Public management: Public and private perspectives*. Palo Alto, CA: Mayfield.

Blythe, D. M., & Marson, D. B. (1999). *Good practices in citizen-centered service*. Ottawa: Canadian Centre for Management Development.

Bolman, L. G., & Deal, T. E. (1995). *Leading with soul: An uncommon journey of spirit*. San Francisco: Jossey-Bass.

Bolman, L. G., & Deal, T. E. (1997). *Reframing organizations: Artistry, choice, and leadership* (2nd ed.). San Francisco: Jossey-Bass.

Boone, L., & Hollingsworth, A. T. (1990). Creative thinking in business organizations. *Review of Business, 12*(2), 3–12.

Borins, S. (1998). *Innovating with integrity*. Washington, DC: Georgetown University Press.

Boston, J., Walsh, P., Martin, J., & Pallot, J. (1996). *Public management: The New Zealand model*. New York: Oxford University Press.

Bowman, J. S., West, J. P., Berman, E. M., & Van Wart, M. (2004). *The professional edge: Competencies in public service*. New York: M. E. Sharpe.

Box, R. (1998). *Citizen governance*. Thousand Oaks, CA: Sage.

Boyte, C. H. (2005, September/October). Reframing democracy: Governance, civil agency, and politics. *Public Administration Review, 65*(5), 536–546.

Brewer, M. B., & Gardner, W. (1996). Who is this "we"? Levels of collective identity and self-representations. *Journal of Personality and Social Psychology, 71*, 83–93.

Brief, A. P., Buttam, R. T., Reizenstein, R. M., Pugh, S. D., Callahan, J. D., McCline, R. L., & Vaslow, J. B. (2002). Beyond good intentions: The next steps toward racial equality in the American workplace. In P. J. Frost, W. R. Nord, & L. A. Krefting (Eds.), *HRM reality*. Upper Saddle River, NJ: Prentice Hall. Reprinted from *Academy of Management Executive, 11*, 47–58

Brown, J. S. (1961). *The motivation of behavior.* New York: McGraw-Hill.

Brownell, J. (1990). Perceptions of effective listeners: A management study. *Journal of Business Communication, 27*(4), 401–415.

Bruce, R., & Wyman, S. (1998). *Changing organizations.* Thousand Oaks, CA: Sage.

Brue, G. (2002). *Six Sigma for managers.* New York: McGraw-Hill.

Bryson, J. M. (2004). *Strategic planning for public and non-profit organizations.* San Francisco: Jossey-Bass.

Bryson, J. M., Broiley, P., & Jung, V. S. (1990). The influences of context and process on project planning success. *Journal of Planning Education and Research, 9*(3), 183–195.

Bryson, J. M., & Crosby, B. C. (1992). *Leadership for the common good.* San Francisco: Jossey-Bass.

Bunce, D., & West, M. (1996). Stress management and innovation interventions at work. *Human Relations, 49*(2), 209–231.

Bureau of National Affairs. (1986). *Affirmative action today: A legal and practical analysis.* Washington, DC: Author.

Burke, J. P. (1996). *Administrative discretion and responsibility: Another look at moral agency and democratic politics.* Paper presented at the Annual Meeting of the American Political Science Association, San Francisco, August 29–September 1.

Burns, J. M. (1978). *Leadership.* New York: Harper & Row.

Burns, J. M. (1984). *The power to lead.* New York: Simon & Schuster.

Burton, F. G., Chen, Y. N., Grover, V., & Stewart, K. (1992–1993). An application of expectancy theory for assessing user motivation to utilize an expert system. *Journal of Management Information Systems, 9*(3), 183–198.

Cameron, K. S., & Whetten, D. A. (1981). Perceptions of organizational effectiveness in organizational life cycles. *Administrative Science Quarterly, 27*, 525–544.

Camic, C. (1985). The matter of habit. *American Journal of Sociology, 91*, 481–510.

Campbell, D. (n.d.). *Center for Creative Leadership assessment device.* Retrieved from www.assessments.ncs.com/assessments/tests/cli.htm

Canadian Centre for Management Development. (1994). *Continuous learning.* Ottawa: Minister of Supply and Services Canada.

Canary, D. J., & Cupach, W. R. (1988). Relationship and episodic characteristics associated with conflict tactics. *Journal of Social and Personal Relationships, 5*, 305–325.

Caro, R. (1974). *The power broker: Robert Moses and the fall of New York.* New York: Knopf.

Cartwright, D., & Zander, A. (Eds.). (1960). *Group dynamics.* Evanston, IL: Row & Peterson.

Cartwright, S., & Cooper, C. (1997). *Managing workplace stress.* Thousand Oaks, CA: Sage.

Caudron, S. (1993, December). Are self-directed teams right for your company? *Personnel Journal,* 76–84.

Caudron, S. (1999). Productive conflict has value. *Workforce, 78*(2), 25–28.

Cavanaugh, M. E. (1988, July). What you don't know about stress. *Personnel Journal,* 53–59.

Chapin, L. W., & Denhardt, R. B. (1995). Putting "Citizens First!" in Orange County, Florida. *National Civic Review, 84*(3), 210–215.

Cherrington, D. J. (1994). *Organizational behavior.* Boston: Allyn & Bacon.

Cherrington, D., & England, J. L. (1980). The desire for an enriched job as a moderator of the enrichment-satisfaction relationship. *Organizational Behavior and Human Performance, 25*, 139–159.

Chesbrough, H. (2003). The logic of open innovation: Managing intellectual property. *California Management Review, 45*(3), 33–58.

Chrislip, D. D., & Larson, C. E. (1994). *Collaborative leadership.* San Francisco: Jossey-Bass.

Chubb, J. E. (1988, Winter). Why the current wave of school reform will fail. *Public Interest,* 28–49.

Coates, J. (1994). Organizational politics: A key to personal success. *Employment Relations Today, 21*(3), 259–262.

Cohen, M. D., March, J. G., & Olsen, J. P. (1972). A garbage can model of organizational choice. *Administrative Science Quarterly, 17*, 1–25.

Coleman, T. L. (1996). Citizens, cops, and city hall: Creating an inclusive team. *Public Management, 78*(12), 1–4.

Collins, J. (2001). *Good to great: Why some companies make the leap . . . and others don't.* New York: Harper Business.

Collins, J. (2005). *Good to great and the social sector, a monograph to accompany* Good to great. New York: HarperCollins.

Combs, G. M., & Luthans, F. (2007). Diversity training: Analysis of the impact of self-efficacy. *Human Resource Development Quarterly, 18*(1), 91–120.

Combs, G. M., & Nadkarni, S. (2005). A tale of two cultures: Attitudes towards affirmative action in the United States and India. *Journal of World Business, 40*, 158–171.

Committed co-workers, creativity rank high. (1998, March 16). *Industry Week*, 14–16.

Conger, J., & Kanungo, R. (1988). The empowerment process: Integrating theory and practice. *Academy of Management Review, 13*(3), 471–482.

Conner, J. (1993). *Meeting the press.* Washington, DC: National Defense University.

Contu, D. (2002). How resilience works. *Harvard Business Review, 80*(5), 46–55.

Cook, G. D. (1989, August). Employee counseling session. *Supervision*, 3–5.

Cooper, C. L., & Smith, M. J. (1985). *Job stress and blue collar work.* New York: John Wiley.

Cooper, P. J. (1996). Understanding what the law says about administrative responsibility. In J. L. Perry (Ed.), *Handbook of public administration* (2nd ed.). San Francisco: Jossey-Bass.

Cooper, T. L. (1998). *The responsible administrator* (4th ed.). San Francisco: Jossey-Bass.

Corporation for National Service. (1997). *A guide to working with the media.* Washington, DC: Author.

Côté, S. (2005). A social interaction model of the effects of emotion regulation on work strain. *Academy of Management Review, 30*(3), 509–530.

Covey, S. R. (1991). *Principle-centered leadership.* New York: Summit Books.

Cox, T. H. (2000). *Creating the multicultural organization: A strategy for capturing the power of diversity.* San Francisco: Jossey-Bass.

Cox, T. H., & Beale, R. L. (1997). *Developing competency to manage diversity.* San Francisco: Berrett-Koehler.

Crampton, S., Hodge, J., Mishra, J., & Price, S. (1995). Stress and stress management. *SAM Advanced Management Journal, 60*(3), 10–18.

Cramton, D. C., & Orvis, K. L. (2003). Overcoming barriers to information sharing in virtual teams. In C. B. Gibson & C. G. Cohen (Eds.), *Virtual teams that work: Creating conditions for virtual team effectiveness* (pp. 214–230). San Francisco: Jossey-Bass.

Crosby, B., & Bryson, J. (2005). *Leadership for the common good* (2nd ed.). San Francisco: Jossey-Bass.

Cross, R., Baker, W., & Parker, A. (2003). What creates energy in organizations? *MIT Sloan Management Review, 44*(4), 51–56.

Cross, T. L. (1988). Services to minority populations: What does it mean to be a culturally competent professional? *Focal Point, 3*(1), 1–3. (Portland, OR: Portland State University, Research and Training Center)

Cross, T. L., Bazron, B. J., Dennis, K. W., & Isaacs, M. R. (1989). *Toward a culturally competent system of care.* Washington, DC: Georgetown University Child Development Center.

Cummings, A., & Oldham, G. (1997). Enhancing creativity: Managing work contexts for the high-potential employee. *California Management Review, 40*(1), 22–38.

Cummings, T. G., & Huse, E. F. (1989). *Organization development and change* (4th ed.). St. Paul, MN: West.

Cyert, R., & March, J. (1963). *A behavioral theory of the firm.* Englewood Cliffs, NJ: Prentice Hall.

Daft, R. L., & Lengel, R. H. (1984). Information relatedness: A new approach to managerial behavior and organizational diagnosis. In B. M. Staw & L. L. Cummings (Eds.), *Research in organizational behavior* (Vol. 6). Greenwich, CT: JAI.

Dahl, R. (1957). The concept of power. *Behavioral Science, 2*, 201–215.

Damanpour, F. (1991). Organizational innovation: A meta-analysis of effect of determinants and moderators. *Academy of Management Journal, 34*, 555–590.

Dass, P., & Parker, D. (1996). Diversity, a strategic issue. In E. E. Kossek & S. A. Lobel (Eds.), *Managing diversity: Human resource strategies for transforming the workplace.* Cambridge, MA: Blackwell Business.

David, K., & Newstrom, J. W. (1985). *Human behavior at work.* New York: McGraw-Hill.

Davidson, W., & Kline, S. (1999). Ace your presentations. *Journal of Accountancy, 187*(3), 61–63.

de Bono, E. (1992). *Serious creativity: Using the power of lateral thinking to create new ideas.* New York: HarperCollins.

Deci, E., Connell, J., & Ryan, R. (1989). Self-determination in a work organization. *Journal of Applied Psychology, 74*, 580–590.

Deci, E. L., & Ryan, R. M. (1987). The support of autonomy and the control of behavior. *Journal of Personality and Social Psychology, 53*, 1024–1037.

Deep, S., & Sussman, L. (2000). *Act on it! Solving 101 of the toughest management challenges.* Cambridge, MA: Perseus Publishing.

Denhardt, J. V., & Denhardt, R. B. (2001). *Creating a culture of innovation: Lessons from America's best run city.* Arlington, VA: PricewaterhouseCoopers Endowment for the Business of Government.

Denhardt, J. V., & Denhardt, R. B. (2007). *The new public service* (Expanded ed.). Armonk, NY: M. E. Sharpe.

Denhardt, R. B. (1993). *The Pursuit of Significance.* Belmont, CA: Wadsworth.

Denhardt, R. B. (1999). *Public administration: An action orientation.* Fort Worth, TX: Harcourt Brace.

Denhardt, R. B. (2000). *The pursuit of significance: Strategies for managerial success in public organizations.* Long Grove, IL: Waveland Press.

Denhardt, R. B., & Aristigueta, M. P. (1996). Developing intrapersonal skills. In J. L. Perry (Ed.), *Handbook of public administration.* San Francisco: Jossey-Bass.

Denhardt, R. B., & Denhardt, J. V. (1999). *Leadership for change: Case studies in American local government.* Arlington, VA: PricewaterhouseCoopers Endowment for the Business of Government.

Denhardt, R. B. & Denhardt, J. V. (2000). The New Public Service: Serving Rather Than Steering. *Public Administration Review* 60(6): 549–559.

Denhardt, R. B., & Denhardt, J. V. (2005a). *The dance of leadership.* Armonk, NY: M. E. Sharpe.

Denhardt, R. B., & Denhardt, J. V. (2005b). *Public administration: An action orientation* (5th ed.). Belmont, CA: Wadsworth Publishing.

Denhardt, R. B., & Gray, J. E. (1998, Summer–Fall). Targeting community development in Orange County, Florida. *National Civic Review*, 227–235.

De Pree, M. (1992). *Leadership jazz.* New York: Currency Doubleday.

Desivilya, H. S., & Yagil, D. (2005). The role of emotions in conflict management: The case of work teams. *International Journal of Conflict Management, 16*(1), 55–69.

DeVoe, D. (1999a, August 9). Don't let conflict get you off course. *Info World*, 69–72.

DeVoe, D. (1999b, March). Employers can help workers with personal problems. *Info World, 29*, 92.

Diamond, M. A. (1993). *The unconscious life of organizations.* Westport, CT: Quorum Books.

Diller, J. V. (1999). *Cultural diversity: A primer for the human services.* Belmont, CA: Wadsworth.

Dillman, D. L. (2002). The paradox of discretion and the case of Elian Gonzalez. *Public Organization Review, 2*(2), 165–185.

Dimock, M. (1986). Creativity. *Public Administration Review, 46*(1), 3–7.

Dinsdale, G., & Marson, D. B. (1999). *Dispelling myths and redrawing maps.* Ottawa: Canadian Centre for Management Development.

Doig, J. W., & Hargrove, E. C. (Eds.). (1987). *Leadership and innovation.* Baltimore: Johns Hopkins University Press.

Drazin, R., Glynn, M. A., & Kazanjian, R. (1999). Multilevel theorizing about creativity in organizations: A sensemaking perspective. *Academy of Management Review, 24*(2), 286–307.

Drucker, P. (1967). *The effective executive.* New York: Harper & Row.

Dunphy, S. M. (2004). Demonstrating the value of diversity for improved decision making: The "wuzzle-puzzle" exercise. *Journal of Business Ethics, 53*, 325–331.

Durant, F. R. (Ed.), Kramer, R. (Assoc. ed.), Perry, J., Mesch, D., & Paarlberg, L. (2006). Motivating employees in a new governance era: The performance paradigm revisited. *Public Administration Review, 66*(4), 505–514.

Dweck, C. (1986). Motivational processes affecting learning. *American Psychologist, 41,* 1040–1048.

Dyer, W. G. (1977). *Team building: Issues and alternatives.* Reading, MA: Addison-Wesley.

Earley, P. C. (1993). East meets West meets Mideast: Further explorations of collectivistic and individualistic work groups. *Academy of Management Journal, 36*, 319–348.

Earley, P. C. (1994). Self or group? Cultural effects of training on self-efficacy and performance. *Administrative Science Quarterly, 39*, 89–117.

Eden, D. (1988). Pygmalion, goal setting, and expectancy: Compatible ways to boost productivity. *Academy of Management Review, 13*(4), 639–652.

Edwards, G. C., III, & Wayne, S. J. (2005). *Presidential leadership: Politics and policy making* (7th ed.). New York: St. Martin's.

Eisenberg, E. M. (1984). Ambiguity as a strategy in organizational communication. *Communication Monographs, 51*, 227–242.

Eisenberg, E. M., & Goodall, H. L. (1993). *Organizational communication.* New York: St. Martin's.

Eisenhardt, K., & Zbaracki, M. T. (1992). Strategic decision making. *Strategic Management Journal, 13*, 27–37.

Elbing, A. (1970). *Behavioral dimensions in organizations: A framework for decision making.* Glenview, IL: Scott, Foresman.

Elias, M. (1996, July 8). Epidemic of violence on the job at all-time high. *USA Today,* p. A1.

Emerson, R. (1962). Power-dependence relations. *American Sociological Review, 27*, 31–41.

Erikson, E. (1959). *Childhood and society.* New York: Norton.

Erin Research. (1998). *Citizens first.* Ottawa: Canadian Centre for Management Development.

Esser, J. K. (1998). Alive and well after 25 years: A review of groupthink research. *Organizational Behavior and Human Decision Processes, 73*(2/3), 116–141.

Estlund, C. (2003). *Working together.* Oxford: Oxford University Press.

Etzioni, A. (1988). Normative affective factors: Toward a new decision-making model. *Journal of Economic Psychology, 9*, 125–150.

Faerman, S. R. (1996). Managing conflict creatively. In J. Perry (Ed.), *Handbook of public administration.* San Francisco: Jossey-Bass.

Fairholm, G. (1993). *Organizational power politics: Tactics in organizational leadership.* Westport, CT: Praeger.

Ferrero, M. J., & Lewis, D. (1998). Reach out and touch your team: Development of a high-performing virtual team. In S. D. Jones & M. M. Beyerlein (Eds.), *Developing high-performance work teams.* Alexandria, VA: American Society for Training and Development.

Ferris, G., Frink, D., Galang, M., Zhou, J., Kacmar, K. M., & Howard, J. (1996). Perceptions of organizational politics: Prediction, stress-related implications, and outcomes. *Human Relations, 49*(2), 233–266.

Fiedler, F. (1967). *A theory of leadership effectiveness.* New York: McGraw-Hill.

Filipczak, B. (1997). It takes all kinds: Creativity in the work force. *Training, 34*(5), 32–40.

Fisher, R., Ury, W., & Patton, B. (1991). *Getting to yes: Negotiating agreements without giving in.* New York: Penguin.

Flanders, L. R., & Utterback, D. (1985). The management excellence inventory. *Public Administration Review, 45*(3), 403–410.

Fligstein, N. (1992). The social construction of efficiency. In M. Zey (Ed.), *Decision making: Alternatives to rational choice models.* Newbury Park, CA: Sage.

Forsyth, D. R. (1990). *Group dynamics.* Pacific Grove, CA: Brooks/Cole.

Foster, R. (1995). Do creativity workshops work? *McKinsey Quarterly, 3*, 186–187.

Foundation for Research on Human Behavior. (1958). *Creativity and conformity.* Ann Arbor, MI: Edwards Brothers.

Frederickson, H. G., & Hart, D. K. (1985). The public service and patriotism of benevolence. *Public Administration Review, 45*(5), 547–553.

Frederickson, P. J. (1996). Community collaboration and public policy making: Examining the long-term utility of training in conflict management. *American Behavioral Scientist, 39*(5), 552–570.

French, J. R., Jr., & Raven, B. (1989). The bases of social power. In J. S. Ott (Ed.), *Classic readings in organizational behavior.* Belmont, CA: Wadsworth. (Original work published 1959)

French, W. L., & Bell, C. H., Jr. (1999). *Organization development* (6th ed.). Upper Saddle River, NJ: Prentice Hall.

Frick, D. M., & Spears, L. C. (Eds.). (1996). *On becoming a servant-leader.* San Francisco: Jossey-Bass.

Friedrich, C. J. (1963). *The philosophy of law in historical perspective* (2nd ed.). Chicago: University of Chicago Press.

Fromm, E. (1939). Selfishness and self-love. *Psychiatry, 2*, 507–523.

Galpin, T. J. (1996). *The human side of change.* San Francisco: Jossey-Bass.

Gandz, J., & Murray, V. (1980, June). The experience of workplace politics. *Academy of Management Journal,* 244.

Gardenswartz, L., & Rowe, A. (1994). *Diverse teams at work: Capitalizing on the power of diversity.* Chicago: Irwin.

Gardner, H. (2006). *Five minds for the future.* Boston: Harvard Business School Press.

Gardner, J. (1987). Remarks to the National Conference of the National Association of Schools of Public Affairs and Administration, Seattle, WA, October 23.

General Services Administration. (1999). *Communicator's sourcebook.* Washington, DC: U.S. General Services Administration.

Gerth, H. H., & Mills, C. W. (1946). *From Max Weber: Essays in sociology.* New York: Oxford University Press.

Gibb, J. R. (1961). Defensive communication. *Journal of Communication, 11*(3), 121–128.

Gibson, C. B. (2005). Virtuality and collaboration in teams. In J. S. Osland, M. E. Turner, D. A. Kolb, & I. M. Rubin (Eds.), *The organizational behavior reader* (pp. 325–337). Upper Saddle River, NJ: Pearson/Prentice Hall.

Gibson, C. B., & Gibbs, J. (2005). *Unpacking the effects of virtuality on team innovation* (Working paper). University of California, Irvine.

Gilbert, J. A., Stead, B. A., & Ivancevich, J. M. (1999). Diversity management: A new organizational paradigm. *Journal of Business Ethics, 21*(1), 61–76.

Glaser, M. A., Aristigueta, M. P., & Payton, S. (2000). Harnessing the resources of community: The ultimate performance agenda. *Public Productivity and Management Review, 23*(4), 428–448.

Glaser, M. A., & Denhardt, R. B. (1999). When citizen expectations conflict with budgetary reality. *Journal of Public Budgeting, Accounting, and Financial Management, 11*(2), 276–310.

Gleason, S. E. (1997). Managing workplace disputes: Overview and directions for the 21st century. In S. E. Gleason (Ed.), *Workplace dispute resolution*. East Lansing: Michigan State University Press.

Goldsmith, R. (1989). Creative style and personality theory. In M. J. Kirton (Ed.), *Adaptors and innovators*. London: Routledge.

Goleman, D. (1995). *Emotional intelligence*. New York: Bantam.

Goleman, D., Boyatzis, R. E., & McKee, A. (2002). *Primal leadership: Realizing the power of emotional intelligence*. Cambridge, MA: Harvard Business School Press.

Golembiewski, R. T. (1972). *Renewing organizations*. Itasca, IL: F. E. Peacock.

Goodman, P. S. (1977). Social comparison processes in organizations. In B. M. Staw & G. E. Salancik (Eds.), *New directions in organizational behavior*. Chicago: St. Clair.

Goodrich, E., & Salancik, G. (1996). Organizational discretion in responding to institutional practices: Hospitals and cesarean births. *Administrative Science Quarterly, 41*, 1–28.

Goodsell, C. (1992). The public administrator as artisan. *Public Administration Review, 52*(3), 246–253.

Gordon, W. (1961). *Synectics*. New York: Harper.

Gough, H. G. (1979). A creative personality scale for the adjective check list. *Journal of Personality and Social Psychology, 37*, 1398–1405.

Green, R., & Reed, B. J. (1989). Occupational stress among professional local government managers. *International Journal of Public Administration, 12*(2), 265–303.

Greenberg, J. (2004). Stress fairness to fare no stress: Managing workplace stress by promoting organizational justice. *Organizational Dynamics, 33*(4), 352–365.

Greenleaf, R. K. (1998). *The power of servant leadership* (L. C. Spears, Ed.). San Francisco: Berrett-Koehler.

Greenleaf, R. K. (2002). *Servant leadership, anniversary edition*. New York: Paulist Press.

Greenstein, F. I. (Ed.). (1988). *Leadership in the modern presidency*. Cambridge, MA: Harvard University Press.

Greiner, L. E. (1972, July–August). Evolution and revolution as organizations grow. *Harvard Business Review*, 37–46.

Group, S. R. (1997). How to stay on track. *Association Management, 49*(1), 76–77.

Gruber, H. E. (2006). Creativity and conflict resolution. In M. Deutsch, P. T. Coleman, & E. C. Marcus (Eds.), *The handbook of conflict resolution*. San Francisco: Jossey-Bass.

Guest, R. H. (1986). *Work teams and team building*. New York: Pergamon.

Gulick, L. (1937). Notes on the theory of organization. In L. Gulick & L. Urwick (Eds.), *Papers on the science of administration*. New York: Institute of Public Administration.

Gundry, L., Kickul, J., & Prather, C. (1994). Building the creative organization. *Organizational Dynamics, 22*(4), 22–37.

Guyot, J. F. (1960). Government bureaucrats are different. *Public Administration Review, 22*(4), 195–202.

Guzzo, R. A. (1982). *Improving group decision making in organizations*. New York: Academic Press.

Guzzo, R. A., & Dickson, M. W. (1996). Teams in organizations: Recent research on performance and effectiveness. *Annual Review of Psychology, 47*, 307–339.

Hackman, J. R. (1990). *Groups that work (and those that don't): Creating conditions for effective teamwork*. San Francisco: Jossey-Bass.

Hackman, J. R., & Oldham, G. (1980). *Work redesign.* Reading, MA: Addison-Wesley.

Hackman, J. R., & Porter, L. (1968). Expectancy theory predictions of work effectiveness. *Organizational Behavior and Human Performance, 3,* 417– 426.

Haire, M. (1989). The concept of power and the concept of man. In J. S. Ott (Ed.), *Classic readings in organizational behavior.* Belmont, CA: Wadsworth. (Original work published 1962)

Hall, E. T. (1959). *The silent language.* Garden City, NY: Anchor Press.

Hall, E. T. (1966). *The hidden dimension.* Garden City, NY: Doubleday.

Hall, E. T. (1976). *Beyond culture.* Garden City, NY: Anchor Press/Doubleday.

Hall, R. H. (1999). *Organizations: Structures, processes, and outcomes.* Upper Saddle River, NJ: Prentice Hall.

Hammer, M., & Champy, J. (1993). *Reengineering the corporation: A manifesto for business revolution.* New York: Harper Business.

Hargrove, R. (1998). *Mastering the art of creative collaboration.* New York: McGraw-Hill.

Harland, L., Harrison, W., Jones, J., & Reiter-Palmon, R. (2005). Leadership behaviors and subordinate resilience. *Journal of Leadership & Organizational Behavior, 11*(2), 2–14.

Harrison, D., & Laliberte, L. (1994). *No life like it: Military wives in Canada.* Toronto: James Lorimer.

Harrison, E. F. (1975). *The managerial decision-making process.* Boston: Houghton Mifflin.

Harrison, M., & Phillips, B. (1991). Strategic decision making: An integrated explanation. *Research in the Sociology of Organizations, 9,* 319–358.

Harter, S. (1978). Effectance motivation reconsidered: Toward a developmental model. *Human Development, 21,* 34–64.

Harvey, J. (1988). *The Abilene paradox and other meditations on management.* Lexington, MA: Lexington Books.

Hatry, H. P. (1999). *Performance measurement: Getting results.* Washington, DC: Urban Institute Press.

Hatry, H. P., Blair, L., Fisk, D., & Kimmel, W. (1987). *Program analysis for state and local governments.* Washington, DC: Urban Institute Press.

Hawkins, C. (1999). The "F" words for effective meetings. *Journal for Quality and Participation, 22*(5), 56–57.

Hearty, K., & Oakes, K. (1986, January–February). Preventive medicine for report writers. *CA,* 85–88.

Heifetz, R. A. (1994). *Leadership without easy answers.* Cambridge, MA: Harvard University Press.

Heifetz, R. A., & Linsky, M. (2002). *Leadership on the line.* Boston: Harvard Business School Press.

Helgesen, S. (1996). Leading from the grassroots. In F. Hesselbein, M. Goldsmith, & R. Beckhard (Eds.), *The leader of the future.* San Francisco: Jossey-Bass.

Hendricks, J. A. (1985, May–June). Locus of control: Implications for managers and accountants. *Cost and Management,* 25–29.

Hersey, P., & Blanchard, K. H. (1988). *Management of organizational behavior* (5th ed.). Englewood Cliffs, NJ: Prentice Hall.

Herzberg, F. (1968, January–February). One more time: How do you motivate employees? *Harvard Business Review,* 53–62.

Hesselbein, F. (1996, Summer). A star to steer by. *Leader to Leader.* Retrieved from www.pfdf.org/leaderbooks/l2l/summer96/fh.html

Higgins, J. M., & McAllaster, C. (2002). Want innovation? Then use artifacts that support it. *Organizational Dynamics, 31*(1), 74–84.

Hirschorn, L. (1997). *Reworking authority.* Cambridge: MIT Press.

Hitt, M. D. (1993). *The model leader.* Columbus, OH: Battelle Press.

Hocker, J. L., & Wilmot, W. W. (1995). *Interpersonal conflict.* Dubuque, IA: William C. Brown.

Hofstede, G., & Hofstede, G. J. (2005). *Cultures and organizations: Software of the mind* (2nd ed.). London and New York: McGraw-Hill.

Holli, M. G. (1999). *The American mayor: The best and the worst big-city leaders.* University Park: Pennsylvania State University Press.

Hollingsworth, A. T. (1989). Creativity in nonprofit organizations: Preparing for the future. *Nonprofit World, 7*(3), 20–22.

Holmer, L. L. (1994). Developing emotional capacity and organizational health. In R. H. Kilmann & I. Kilmann (Eds.), *Managing ego energy: The transformation of personal meaning into organizational success.* San Francisco: Jossey-Bass.

Holmer, L. L., & Adams, G. B. (1995). The practice gap: Strategy and theory for emotional and interpersonal development in public administration education. *Journal of Public Administration Education, 1*(1), 3–22.

Holmes, T. H., & Rahe, R. H. (1967). The social readjustment rating scale. *Journal of Psychosomatic Research, 11*, 213–218.

House, R. J., Hanges, P. J., Javidan, M., Dorfman, P. W., & Gupta, V. (2005). *Culture, leadership, and organizations: The GLOBE study of 62 societies.* Thousand Oaks, CA: Sage.

House, R. J., & Mitchell, T. R. (1974). Path-goal theory of leadership. *Journal of Contemporary Business, 3*, 81–97.

Houston, D. (2005). "Walking the walk" of public service motivation: Public employees and charitable gifts of time, blood, and money. *Journal of Public Administration Research and Theory, 16*(1), 67–86.

Huy, Q. N., & Mintzberg, H. (2003, Summer). The rhythm of change. *MIT Sloan Management Review*, 80–84.

Imperial, T. M. (2005). Using collaboration as a governance strategy: Lessons from watershed management programs. *Administration and Society, 37*(3), 281–320.

Ingersoll, V. H., & Adams, G. B. (1992). *The tacit organization.* Greenwich, CT: JAI.

Ingraham, P. W., & Ban, C. (1988). Politics and merit: Can they meet in a public service model? *Review of Public Personnel Administration, 8*(2), 1–19.

Ingraham, P. W., & Rosenbloom, D. H. (1989). The new public personnel and the new public service. *Public Administration Review, 49*(2), 116–125.

Jackson, S., & Schuler, R. (1985). A meta-analysis and conceptual critique of research on role ambiguity and role conflict in work settings. *Organizational Behavior and Human Decision Processes, 36*, 16–78.

James, K., & Arroba, T. (1990). Politics and management: The effect of stress on the political sensitivity of managers. *Journal of Managerial Psychology, 5*(3), 22–27.

Janis, I. L. (1971, November). Groupthink. *Psychology Today.*

Janis, I. L. (1982). *Groupthink* (2nd ed.). Boston: Houghton Mifflin.

Janis, I. L., & Mann, L. (1977). *Decision making.* New York: Free Press.

Jehn, K. A., Northcraft, G. B., & Neale, M. A. (1999). Why differences make a difference: A study of diversity, conflict and performance in workgroups. *Administrative Science Quarterly, 44*(4), 741–763.

Jex, S. (1998). *Stress and job performance.* Thousand Oaks, CA: Sage.

Johnston, W. B., & Packer, A. E. (1987). *Workforce 2000: Work and workers for the twenty-first century.* Indianapolis: Hudson Institute.

Jones, S. D., & Beyerlein, M. M. (1998). Implementation of work teams: An overview. In S. D. Jones & M. M. Beyerlein (Eds.), *Developing high-performance teams.* Alexandria, VA: American Society for Training and Development.

Jordan, T. (2000). Glasl's nine-stage model of conflict escalation. *CADRE Consortium for Appropriate Dispute Resolution in Special Education.* Retrieved from www.mediate.com/articles/jordan.cfm

Judson, Arnold S. (1991). *Changing behavior in organizations.* Cambridge, MA: Blackwell.

Jung, C. (1971). *Psychological types.* Princeton, NJ: Princeton University Press.

Kaatz, J. B., French, P. E., & Prentiss-Cooper, H. (1999). City council conflict as a cause of psychological burnout and voluntary turnover among city managers. *State and Local Government Review, 31*(3), 162–172.

Kabanoff, B. (1991). Equity, equality, power, and conflict. *Academy of Management Review, 16,* 416–441.

Kaboolian, L. (1998). The new public management. *Public Administration Review, 58*(3), 189–193.

Kamil, K. M. (1997). Culture and conflict management: A theoretical framework. *International Journal of Conflict Management, 8,* 338–360.

Kaner, S. (1996). *Facilitator's guide to participatory decision-making.* Gabriola Island, British Columbia: New Society.

Kanfer, R., & Ackerman, L. P. (2004). Aging, adult development, and working motivation. *Academy of Management Review, 29*(3), 440–458.

Kanter, R. M. (1977). *Men and women of the corporation.* New York: Basic Books.

Kanter, R. M. (1979, July–August). Power failure in management circuits. *Harvard Business Review,* 65–75.

Kanter, R. M. (1994, July–August). Collaborative advantage: The art of alliances. *Harvard Business Review,* 98–108.

Kao, J. (1996). *Jamming.* New York: HarperCollins.

Kass, H. (1990). Stewardship as fundamental element in images of public administration. In H. Kass & B. Catron (Eds.), *Images and identities in public administration.* Newbury Park, CA: Sage.

Katz, D. (1964). Approaches to managing conflict. In R. L. Kahn & E. Boulding (Eds.), *Power and conflict in organizations.* New York: Basic Books.

Katz, D., & Kahn, R. L. (1966). *The social psychology of organizations.* New York: John Wiley.

Katz, R., & Allen, T. J. (1988). Investigating the Not Invented Here (NIH) syndrome: A look at the performance, tenure, and communication patterns of 50 R&D project groups. In M. L. Tushman & W. L. Moore (Eds.), *Readings in the management of innovation* (2nd ed.). New York: Harper Information.

Katzenbach, J. R., & Smith, D. K. (1993, March–April). The discipline of teams. *Harvard Business Review,* 111–120.

Kearns, K. (1996). *Managing for accountability.* San Francisco: Jossey-Bass.

Keirsey, D. W. (1998). *Please understand me II.* Del Mar, CA: Prometheus Nemesis Books.

Khademian, A. M. (1996). Developing effective relations with legislatures. In J. L, Perry (Ed.), *Handbook of public administration.* San Francisco: Jossey-Bass.

Kidder, D. L., Lankau, M., Chrobot-Mason, D., Mollica, K. A., & Friedman, R. A. (2005). Backlash towards diversity initiatives: Examining the impact of diversity program justification, personal and group outcomes. *International Journal of Conflict Management, 15,* 77–102.

Kilpatrick, F. P., Cummings, M. C., Jr., & Jennings, M. K. (1964). *Sourcebook of a study of occupational values and the image of the federal service.* Washington, DC: Brookings Institution.

Kim, H. P., Pinkley, R., & Fragale, A. (2005). Power dynamics in negotiation. *Academy of Management Review, 30*(4), 799–822.

King, C. S., & Stivers, C. (1998). Strategies for an anti-government era. In C. S. King & C. Stivers (Eds.), *Government is us.* Thousand Oaks, CA: Sage.

King, C., & Zanetti, L. A. (2005). *Transformational public service.* Armonk, NY: M. E. Sharpe.

King, N., & Anderson, N. R. (1990). Innovation in work groups. In M. West & J. L. Farr (Eds.), *Innovation and creativity at work.* Chichester, UK: JohnWiley.

Kinlaw, D. C. (1992). *Continuous improvement and measurement for total quality.* San Diego: Pfeiffer.

Kinlaw, D. C. (1998). *Superior teams.* Brookfield, VT: Gower.

Kipnis, D., & Schmidt, S. (1985, April). The language of persuasion: Hard, soft, or rational. *Psychology Today,* 40–46.

Kirton, M. (1976). Adaptors and innovators: A description and measure. *Journal of Applied Psychology, 61,* 622–629.

Kirton, M. (Ed.). (1989). *Adaptors and innovators: Styles of creativity and problem-solving.* London: Routledge.

Kleinginna, P., & Kleinginna, A. (1981). A categorized list of motivational definitions, with a suggestion for a consensual definition. *Motivation and Emotion, 5*(3), 263–291.

Knapp, J. C. (2007). Introduction. In J. C. Knapp (Ed.), *For the common good* (pp. xi–xviii). Westport, CT: Praeger.

Knickerbocker, I., & McGregor, D. (1942). Union-management cooperation: A psychological analysis. *Personnel, 19*(3), 520–539.

Knippen, J. T., & Green, T. B. (1994). How the manager can use active listening. *Public Personnel Management, 23*(2), 357–359.

Koberg, C., & Chusmir, L. (1987). Organizational culture relationships with creativity and other job-related variables. *Journal of Business Research, 15*(5), 397–409.

Koehler, J. W., & Pankowski, J. M. (1996). *Teams in government: A handbook for team-based organizations.* Delray Beach, FL: St. Lucie.

Koestler, A. (1964). *The act of creation.* New York: Macmillan.

Kogan, M. (1996). Blah, blah, blah. *Government Executive, 28*(9), 53–57.

Kohlberg, L. (1971). From is to ought. In T. Mishel (Ed.), *Cognitive development and epistemology* (pp. 151–235). New York: Academic Press.

Konrad, A. M., Prasad, P., & Pringle, J. K. (Eds.). (2006). *Handbook of workplace diversity.* Thousand Oaks, CA: Sage.

Korabik, K. (1992). Sex-role orientation and leadership style. *International Journal of Women's Studies, 5,* 328–336.

Kotter, J. P. (1977, July–August). Power, dependence, and effective management. *Harvard Business Review,* 125–136.

Kotter, J. P. (1996). *Leading change.* Boston: Harvard Business School Press.

Kotter, J. P., & Cohen, D. S. (2002). *The heart of change.* Boston: Harvard Business School Press.

Kouzes, J. M., & Posner, B. Z. (2007). *The leadership challenge: How to get extraordinary things done in organizations* (4th ed.). San Francisco: Jossey-Bass.

Kouzes, J. M., & Posner, B. Z. (2003). *Credibility* (Rev. ed.). San Francisco: Jossey-Bass.

Kouzes, J. M. & Posner, B. Z. (1995). *The Leadership Challenge: How to Get Extraordinary Things Done in Organizations.* San Francisco: Jossey-Bass.

Kravitz, D. A., & Klineberg, S. L. (2000). Reactions to two versions of affirmative action among Whites, Blacks and Hispanics. *Journal of Applied Psychology, 85,* 597–611.

Kruglanski, A. W., Friedman, I., & Zeevi, G. (1971). The effects of incentive on some qualitative aspects of task performance. *Journal of Personality, 39,* 606–617.

Kujala, J., & Pietilainen, T. (2007). Developing moral principles and scenarios in the light of diversity: An extension to the multidimensional ethics scale. *Journal of Business Ethics, 70*(2), 141–150.

Lakein, A. (1973). *How to get control of your time and your life.* New York: Signet.

Lan, Z. (1997). A conflict resolution approach to public administration. *Public Administration Review, 57*(1), 27–36.

Lappé, F. M., & Du Bois, P. M. (1994). *The quickening of America: Rebuilding our nation, remaking our lives.* San Francisco: Jossey-Bass.

Larkey, L. (1996). Toward a theory of communicative interactions in culturally diverse work-groups. *Academy of Management Review, 2*(2), 402–433.

Larson, C. E., & LaFasto, F. M. (1989). *Teamwork.* Newbury Park, CA: Sage.

Larson, C. U. (1992). *Persuasion* (6th ed.). Belmont, CA: Wadsworth.

Latham, G. P. (2003). A five-step approach to behavior change. *Organizational Dynamics, 32*(3), 309–315.

Latham, G., & Baldes, J. J. (1975). The "practical significance" of Locke's theory of goal setting. *Journal of Applied Psychology, 60*(1), 122–124.

Lawler, E. E. (1973). *Motivation in work organizations.* Pacific Grove, CA: Brooks/Cole.

Lawler, E. E. (1990). *High involvement management.* San Francisco: Jossey-Bass.

Lawler, E. E., III, Mohrman, S. A., & Ledford, G. E. (1995). *Creating high performance organizations: Practices and results of employee involvement and total quality management in Fortune 1000 companies.* San Francisco: Jossey-Bass.

Lawrence, T., Mauws, M., Dyck, B., & Kleysen, R. (2005). The politics of organizational learning. *Academy of Management Review, 30*(1), 180–191.

Lawson, R. B., & Shen, Z. (1998). *Organizational psychology: Foundations and applications.* New York: Oxford University Press.

Lawson, R. B., & Ventriss, C. L. (1992). Organizational change: The role of organizational culture and organizational learning. *Psychological Record, 42*(2), 205–220.

Lazarus, R. S., DeLongis, A., Folkman, S., & Gruen, R. J. (1985). Stress and adaptational outcomes. *American Psychologist, 49*, 770–779.

Lee, R., & Caughran, B. (1996). Team approach at Sacramento Animal Control Center. *Public Management, 78*(4), 3–4.

Lewin, K. (1951). *Field theory in social science.* Westport, CT: Greenwood.

Light, P. C. (1998). *Sustaining innovation.* San Francisco: Jossey-Bass.

Likert, R. (1961). *New patterns of management.* New York: McGraw-Hill.

Likert, R. (1967). *The human organization.* New York: McGraw-Hill.

Lindblom, C. E. (1959). The science of muddling through. *Public Administration Review, 19*(2), 79–88.

Lindblom, C. E. (1979). Still muddling, not yet through. *Public Administration Review, 39*(5), 517–526.

Lippitt, G., & Lippitt, R. (1978). *The consulting process in action.* LaJolla, CA: University Associates.

Lipsky, M. (1980). *Street-level bureaucracy: Dilemmas of the individual in public services.* New York: Russell Sage Foundation.

Locke, E. (1968). Toward a theory of task motivation and incentives. *Organizational Behavior and Human Performance, 3*, 157–189.

Locke, E. (1978, July). The ubiquity of the technique of goal setting in theories of and approaches to employee motivation. *Academy of Management Review*, 594–601.

Locke, E. (1996). Motivation through conscious goal setting. *Applied and Preventive Psychology, 5*, 117–124.

Locke, E., & Latham, G. (1990). *A theory of goal setting and task performance.* Englewood Cliffs, NJ: Prentice Hall.

Locke, E., Shaw, K., Saari, L., & Latham, G. (1981). Goal setting and task performance: 1969–1980. *Psychological Bulletin, 90*, 125–152.

Lowi, T. (1985). *The personal president: Power invested, promise unfulfilled.* Ithaca, NY: Cornell University Press.

Lubit, R. (2006). The tyranny of toxic managers: Applying emotional intelligence to deal with difficult personalities. In J. S. Osland, M. E. Turner, D. A. Kolb, & I. M. Rubin (Eds.), *The organizational behavior reader.* Upper Saddle River, NJ: Prentice Hall.

Luke, J. S. (1998). *Catalytic leadership.* San Francisco: Jossey-Bass.

Lukes, S. (1974). *Power: A radical view.* London: Macmillan.

Lulofs, R. S., & Cahn, D. D. (2000). *Conflict: From theory to action.* Boston: Allyn & Bacon.

Luthans, F., & Kreitner, R. (1985). *Organizational behavior modification and beyond.* Glenview, IL: Scott, Foresman.

Maccoby, M. (1981). *The leader.* New York: Simon & Schuster.

Machiavelli, N. (1947). *The prince* (T. G. Bergin, Ed.). New York: Appleton-Century-Crofts.

Magee, Y. S. (1997). Teams: Avoiding the pitfalls. *Public Management, 79*(7), 26–29.

Magin, M. D. (1994). *Effective teamwork.* Chicago: Irwin.

Maier, N. R. (1967). Assets and liabilities of group problem solving: The need for an integrative function. *Psychological Review, 74,* 239–249.

Mangini, M. (2000). Character and well-being: Towards an ethic of character. *Philosophy and Social Criticism, 26*(2), 79–98.

Manz, C. C., & Sims, H., Jr. (1993). *Business without bosses: How self-managing teams are building high-performing companies.* New York: John Wiley.

March, J. G. (1994). *A primer on decision making: How decisions happen.* New York: Free Press.

March, J. G., & Simon, H. A. (1958). *Organizations.* New York: John Wiley.

Marcum, J. (1999, Autumn). Out with motivation, in with engagement. *National Productivity Review,* 43–46.

Marks, M. L., & Mirvis, P. H. (1992). Rebuilding after the merger: Dealing with "survivor sickness." *Organizational Dynamics, 21,* 18–32.

Maslow, A. (1943). A theory of human motivation. *Psychological Review, 50,* 370–396.

Maslow, A. H. (1962). *Toward a psychology of being.* Princeton, NJ: Von Nostrand.

Mastrofski, S. D., Ritti, R. R., & Snipes, J. (1994). Expectancy theory and police productivity in DUI enforcement. *Law and Society Review, 28,* 113–148.

Maynard-Moody, S., & Musheno, M. (2003). *Cops, teachers, counselors: Stories from the front lines of public service.* Ann Arbor: University of Michigan Press.

McClelland, D. (1985). *Human motivation.* Glenview, IL: Scott, Foresman.

McConnell, C. R. (1997). Effective employee counseling for the first-line supervisor. *Health Care Supervisor, 16*(1), 77–86.

McGrath, J. E., & Altman, I. (1966). *Small group research.* New York: Holt, Rinehart & Winston.

McGregor, D. (1957, November). The human side of the enterprise. *Management Review,* 22–28, 88–92.

McGregor, D. (1960). *The human side of the enterprise.* New York: McGraw-Hill.

McKendall, M. (1993). The tyranny of change: Organization development revisited. *Journal of Business Ethics, 12,* 93–104.

Meek, J. M. (1985). How to prepare your client for government testimony. *Public Relations Journal, 41*(11), 35–37.

Merriam-Webster. (1987). *Webster's ninth new collegiate dictionary.* Springfield, MA: Author.

Metcalf, H. C., & Urwick, L. (Eds.). (1940). *Dynamic administration: The collected papers of Mary Parker Follett.* New York: Harper & Row.

Michailova, S., & Husted, K. (2003, Spring). Knowledge-sharing hostility in Russian firms. *California Management Review, 45*(3), 59–77.

Milgrom, P., & Roberts, J. (1988). An economic approach to influence activities in organizations. *American Journal of Sociology, 94*(Suppl.), S154–S179.

Miller, K. (1999). *Organizational communication.* Belmont, CA: Wadsworth.

Miller, W. (1987). *The creative edge: Fostering innovation where you work.* Reading, MA: Addison-Wesley.

Millett, J. D. (1966). *Organization for the public service.* Princeton, NJ: Von Nostrand.

Milliken, F. J., & Martins, L. J. (1996). Searching for common threads: Understanding the multiple effects of diversity in organizational groups. *Academy of Management Review, 21*(2), 402–433.

Milward, H. B., & Provan, K. G. (2006). *A manager's guide to choosing and using collaborative networks.* Washington, DC: IBM Endowment for the Business of Government. (http://www.businessofgovernment.org/pdfs/ProvanReport.pdf)

Mintzberg, H., Raisinghani, D., & Theoret, A. (1976). The structure of unstructured decisions. *Administrative Science Quarterly, 21*(2), 246–275.

Mohrman, S. A., Cohen, S. G., & Mohrman, A. M., Jr. (1995). *Designing team-based organizations: New forms for knowledge work.* San Francisco: Jossey-Bass.

Mooney, J., & Reiley, A. C. (1939). *The principles of organization.* New York: Harper & Row.

Mor Barak, M. E. (2005). *Managing diversity, toward a globally inclusive workplace.* Thousand Oaks, CA: Sage.

Morehead, G., & Griffin, R. W. (1992). *Organizational behavior.* Boston: Houghton Mifflin.

Morehead, G., Neck, C., & West, M. (1998). The tendency toward defective decision making within self-managing teams: The relevance of groupthink for the 21st century. *Organizational Behavior and Human Decision Processes, 73*(2/3), 327–351.

Morgan, D. L. (1997). *The focus group guidebook.* Thousand Oaks, CA: Sage.

Morgan, D. L. (1998). *Planning focus groups.* Thousand Oaks, CA: Sage.

Morgan, J. S. (1968). *Improving your creativity on the job.* New York: American Management Association.

Mosher, F. C. (1968). *Democracy and the public service* (2nd ed.). New York: Oxford University Press.

Mowday, R. (1993). Equity theory predictions of behavior in organizations. In R. Steers & L. Porter (Eds.), *Motivation and work behavior* (5th ed.). New York: McGraw-Hill.

Munsterberg, H. (1913). *Psychology and industrial efficiency.* Boston: Houghton Mifflin.

Murray, M. (1986). *Decisions: A comparative critique.* Marshfield, MA: Pitman.

Nadler, D. A., Shaw, R. B., Walton, A. E., & Associates. (1995). *Discontinuous change.* San Francisco: Jossey-Bass.

Nadler, D. A., & Tushman, M. L. (1997). *Competing by design.* New York: Oxford University Press.

Nahavandi, A., & Malekzadeh, A. R. (1999). *Organizational behavior: The person-organization fit.* Upper Saddle River, NJ: Prentice Hall.

National Safety Council. (1990). *Accident facts.* Chicago: National Safety Council.

Nelissen, N., Bemelmans-Videc, M.-L., Godfroij, A., & deGoede, P. (1999). *Renewing government.* Utrecht, The Netherlands: International Books.

Neustadt, R. E. (1960). *Presidential power: The politics of leadership.* New York: John Wiley.

Neustadt, R. (1987). Foreword. In *Leadership and innovation* (J. W. Doig & E. C. Hargrove, Eds.). Baltimore: Johns Hopkins University Press.

Neustadt, R. E. (1990). *Presidential power and the modern presidents.* New York: Free Press.

Northouse, P. G. (2001). *Leadership: Theory and practice* (2nd ed.). Thousand Oaks, CA: Sage.

Novinger, T. (2001). *Intercultural communication.* Austin: University of Texas Press.

Nutt, P. C. (1997). Better decision-making: A field study. *Business Strategy Review, 8*(4), 45–52.

Nutt, P. C. (1999a). Public-private differences and the assessment of alternatives for decision making. *Journal of Public Administration Research and Theory, 9*(1), 305–349.

Nutt, P. C. (1999b). Surprising but true: Half of the decisions in organizations fail. *Academy of Management Executive, 13*(4), 75–90.

Nutt, P. C. (2001). Decision debacles and how to avoid them. *Business Strategy Review, 12*(2), 1–14.

Nutt, P. C. (2002). *Why decisions fail: The blunders and traps that lead to decision debacles.* San Francisco: Barrett-Koehler.

Nutt, P. C. (2005). Decision aiding search during decision making. *European Journal of Operational Research, 160,* 852–876.

Oakley, J., & Cocking, D. (2001). *Virtue ethics and professional roles.* Cambridge: Cambridge University Press.

O'Connell, S. E. (1988). Human communication in the high tech office. In G. M. Goldhaber & G. A. Barnett (Eds.), *Handbook of organizational communication.* Norwood, NJ: Ablex.

Oldham, G., & Cummings, A. (1996). Employee creativity: Personal and contextual factors at work. *Academy of Management Journal, 39*(3), 607–634.

Osborne, D. (with Plastrik, P.). (1997). *Banishing bureaucracy.* Reading, MA: Addison-Wesley.

Osborne, D., & Gaebler, T. (1992). *Reinventing government.* Reading, MA: Addison-Wesley.

O'Toole, J. (1995). *Leading change.* San Francisco: Jossey-Bass.

Ott, J. S. (Ed.). (1989a). *Classic readings in organizational behavior.* Belmont, CA: Wadsworth.

Ott, J. S. (1989b). *The organizational culture perspective.* Pacific Grove, CA: Brooks/Cole.

Oxman, J. A., & Smith, B. D. (2003, Fall). The limits of structural change. *MIT Sloan Management Review,* 78–80.

Pande, P., & Holpp, L. (2002). *What is Six Sigma?* New York: McGraw Hill.

Parker, G. M. (1990). *Team players and teamwork: The new competitive business strategy.* San Francisco: Jossey-Bass.

Parker, G. M. (1994). *Cross-functional teams: Working with allies, enemies, and other strangers.* San Francisco: Jossey-Bass.

Pascale, R. T. (1990). *Managing on the edge: How the smartest companies use conflict to stay ahead.* New York: Simon & Schuster.

Pastor, L. H. (1995). Initial assessment and intervention strategies to reduce workplace violence. *American Family Physician, 52*(4), 38–48.

Pearce, C. L., & Conger, J. A. (2003). *Shared leadership.* Thousand Oaks, CA: Sage.

Perry, J., & Wise, L. (1990). The motivational bases of public service. *Public Administration Review, 50*(3), 367–373.

Perry-Smith, J. E., & Shalley, C. E. (2003). The social side of creativity: A static and dynamic social network perspective. *Academy of Management Review, 28*(1), 91–96.

Pescosolido, A. T. (2002). Emergent leaders and managers of group emotion. *Leadership Quarterly, 13*(5), 583–599.

Peterson, D. (1984). *Human-error reduction and safety management.* New York: William Morrow.

Pettinger, R. (1996). *Introduction to organizational behavior.* Padstow, UK: T. J. Press.

Pfeffer, J. (1981). *Power in organizations.* Cambridge, MA: Ballinger.

Pfeffer, J. (1992). Understanding power in organizations. *California Management Review, 34*(2), 29–50.

Pfiffner, J. P., & Davidson, R. H. (2006). *Presidential leadership.* New York: Longman Press.

Philip, T. (1985). *Improving your decision-making skills.* Maidenhead, UK: McGraw-Hill.

Pinder, C. C. (1998). *Work motivation in organizational behavior.* Upper Saddle River, NJ: Prentice Hall.

Plantenga, D. (2004). Gender, identity, and diversity: Learning from insights gained in transformative gender training. *Gender and Development, 12,* 40–46.

Pless, N. M., & Maak, T. (2004). Building an inclusive diversity culture: Principles, processes, and practice. *Journal of Business Ethics, 54*(2), 129–147.

Plunkett, D. (1990). The creative organization: An empirical investigation of the importance of participation in decision-making. *Journal of Creative Behavior, 24*(2), 140–148.

Poister, T. H., & Henry, G. T. (1994). Citizen ratings of public and private service quality. *Public Administration Review, 54*(2), 155–160.

Popovich, M. G. (Ed.). (1998). *Creating high-performance government organizations.* San Francisco: Jossey-Bass.

Porter, L., & Lawler, E. (1968). *Managerial attitudes and performance.* Homewood, IL: Irwin.

Pressman, J. (1973). *Implementation.* Berkeley: University of California Press.

Provan, G. K., & Milward, H. B. (2001). Do networks really work? A framework for evaluating public-sector organizational networks. *Public Administration Review, 61*(4), 414–423.

Pruitt, D. G., & Rubin, J. G. (1986). *Social conflict: Escalation, stalemate, and settlement.* New York: Random House.

Pynes, J. (1997). *Human resources management for public and nonprofit organizations.* San Francisco: Jossey-Bass.

Quick, J., Quick, J., Nelson, D., & Hurrell, J. (1997). *Preventive stress management in organizations.* Washington, DC: American Psychological Association.

Quinn, R. E. (1996). *Deep change.* San Francisco: Jossey-Bass.

Rahim, A. M. (1983). A measure of styles of handling interpersonal conflicts. *Academy of Management Journal, 26*, 368–376.

Rategan, C., & O'Hare, K. (1996). The debureaucratization of Chicago. *Training and Development, 50*(5), 95–97.

Raudsepp, E. (1987). Establishing a creative climate. *Training and Development Journal, 45*(1), 50–53.

Rawlinson, J. G. (1981). *Creative thinking and brainstorming.* New York: John Wiley.

Reddin, W. J. (1978). *Values inventory.* La Jolla, CA: Learning Resources.

Redmond, M., Mumford, M., & Teach, R. (1993). Putting creativity to work: Effects of leader behavior on subordinate creativity. *Organizational Behavior and Human Decision Processes, 55*, 120–151.

Rickards, T. (1988). *Creativity at work.* Hants, UK: Gower.

Riley, A., & Zaccaro, S. (Eds.). (1987). *Occupational stress and organizational effectiveness.* New York: Praeger.

Roberson, L., & Block, C. J. (2001). Racioethnicity and job performance: A review and critique of theoretical perspectives on the causes of group differences. *Research in Organizational Behavior, 23*, 245–325.

Roberts, N. C. (2002). Calls for dialogue. In N. C. Roberts (Ed.), *The transformative power of dialogue* (pp. 3–26). Amsterdam: JAI.

Roethlisberger, F. J., & Dickson, W. (1939). *Management and the worker.* Cambridge, MA: Harvard University Press.

Rogers, C. R. (1961). *On becoming a person.* Boston: Houghton Mifflin.

Rogers, C. R. (1991, November–December). Barriers and gateways to communication. *Harvard Business Review,* 105–107.

Rogers, C. R., & Farson, R. E. (1976). *Active listening.* Chicago: University of Chicago Press.

Rogers, R. E., Li, E. Y., & Ellis, R. (1994). Perceptions of organizational stress among female executives in the U.S. government: An exploratory study. *Public Personnel Management, 23*(4), 593–609.

Rosch, P. J., & Pelletier, K. R. (1987). Designing worksite stress management programs. In L. R. Murphy & R. G. Schoenborn (Eds.), *Stress management in work settings.* Washington, DC: National Institute for Occupational Safety and Health.

Rotter, J. B. (1966). Generalized expectancies for internal versus external control of reinforcement. *Psychological Monographs, 80*, 1–28.

Rourke, F. E. (1992). Responsiveness and neutral competence in American bureaucracy. *Public Administration Review, 52*(6), 539–546.

Ruben, B. (1978). Communication and conflict: A system-theoretical perspective. *Quarterly Journal of Speech, 64*, 202–210.

Russell, B. (1938). *Power: A new social analysis.* New York: Norton.

Salancik, G., & Pfeffer, J. (1989). Who gets power—and how they hold onto it: A strategic-contingency model of power. In J. S. Ott (Ed.), *Classic readings in organizational behavior.* Belmont, CA: Wadsworth. (Original work published 1977).

Sandwith, P. (1992). Better meetings for better communication. *Training and Development, 46*(1), 29–31.

Schein, E. H. (1978). *Career dynamics: Matching individuals and organizational needs.* Reading, MA: Addison-Wesley.

Schein, E. H. (1985). *Organizational Culture and Leadership.* San Francisco: Jossey-Bass.

Schein, E. H. (1988). *Process consultation.* Reading, MA: Addison-Wesley.

Schein, E. H. (1997). *Organizational culture and leadership* (3rd ed.). San Francisco: Jossey-Bass.

Schein, E. H., & Bennis, W. G. (1965). *Personal and organizational change through group methods.* New York: John Wiley.

Schermerhorn, J. R., Hunt, J. G., & Osborn, R. N. (1994). *Managing organizational behavior* (5th ed.). New York: John Wiley.

Schmidt, F. (with Strickland, T.). (1998). *Client satisfaction surveying: Common measurements tool.* Ottawa: Canadian Centre for Management Development.

Schoem, S. H., Sevis, T., Chester, M., & Sumida, S. H. (2001). Intergroup dialogue: Democracy at work in theory and practice. In D. Schoem & S. H. Schoem (Eds.), *Intergroup dialogue* (pp. 1–21). Ann Arbor: University of Michigan Press.

Schön, D. (1983). *The reflective practitioner: How professionals think in action.* New York: Basic Books.

Schott, R. (1986). The psychological development of adults: Implications of public administration. *Public Administration Review, 46*(6), 657–667.

Schutz, W. C. (1958). *FIRO: A three-dimensional theory of interpersonal behavior* (3rd ed.). New York: Holt, Rinehart & Winston.

Scott, W. E. (1965). The creative individual. *Journal of the Academy of Management, 8*(3), 211–219.

Seabright, M. A., & Moberg, D. J. (1998). Interpersonal manipulation. In M. Schminke (Ed.), *Managerial ethics.* Mahwah, NJ: Lawrence Erlbaum.

Seeman, M. (1962). On the personal consequences of alienation in work. *American Sociological Review, 32*, 273–285.

Senge, P. (1990). *The fifth discipline: The art and practice of the learning organization.* Garden City, NY: Doubleday.

Seo, M. G., Barrett, L. F., & Bartunek, J. M. (2004, July). The role of affective experience in work motivation. *Academy of Management Review, 29*(3), 423–439.

Seybolt, P. M., Derr, C. B., & Nielson, T. R. (1996). *Linkages between national culture, gender, and conflict management styles* (Working paper). University of Utah.

Seyle, H. (1956). *The stress of life.* New York: McGraw-Hill.

Seyle, H. (1974). *Stress without distress.* Philadelphia: J. B. Lippincott.

Seyle, H. (1975). Confusion and controversy in the stress field. *Journal of Human Stress, 75*(1), 37–44.

Shafritz, J. M., & Russell, E. W. (2000). *Introducing public administration* (2nd ed.). New York: Addison Wesley Longman.

Sillers, A. L. (1981). Attributions and interpersonal conflict resolution. In J. H. Harvey, W. Ickes, & R. F. Kidd (Eds.), *New directions in attribution research* (Vol. 3). Mahwah, NJ: Lawrence Erlbaum.

Simon, H. A. (1976). *Administrative behavior* (3rd ed.). New York: Macmillan.

Simon, H. A. (1977). *The new science of management decision* (2nd ed.). Englewood Cliffs, NJ: Prentice Hall.

Singh, P. (1985, Spring). Creativity and organizational development. *Abhigyan,* 108–119.

Skinner, B. F. (1971). *Beyond freedom and dignity.* New York: Knopf.

Sluss, D. M., & Ashforth, B. E. (2007). Relational identity and identification: Defining ourselves through work relationships. *Academy of Management Review, 32*(1), 9–32.

Smith, C. G., Hindman, H. D., & Havlovic, S. J. (1997). A discriminant analysis of employee choice in a multi-union representation election. *Canadian Journal of Administrative Sciences, 14*(3), 235–245.

Smith, D. K., & Katzenbach, J. R. (1993). *The wisdom of teams.* New York: McGraw-Hill.

Smith, J. (1993). *Understanding stress and coping.* New York: Macmillan.

Smith, W. P. (1987). Conflict and negotiation: Trends and emerging issues. *Journal of Applied Social Psychology, 17,* 631–677.

Sparks, S. D. (1999). *The manager's guide to business writing.* New York: McGraw-Hill.

Spector, P. E. (1982). Behavior in organizations as a function of employees' locus of control. *Psychological Bulletin, 91*(3), 487–489.

Sperry, R. (1989). Developing effective relations with legislatures. In J. L. Perry (Ed.), *Handbook of public administration.* San Francisco: Jossey-Bass.

Stahl, O. G. (1971). *Public personnel administration.* New York: Harper & Row.

Starbuck, W. H. (1983). Organizations as action generators. *American Sociological Review, 48,* 91–102.

Starling, G. (1993). *Managing the public sector.* Belmont, CA: Wadsworth.

Steel, P., & König, C. (2006). Integrating theories of motivation. *Academy of Management Review, 31*(4), 889–913.

Stewart, E. C., & Bennett, M. J. (1991). *American cultural patterns: A cross-cultural perspective.* Yarmouth, ME: Intercultural Press.

Stogdill, R. (1948). Personal factors associated with leadership. *Journal of Psychology, 54,* 259–269.

Stogdill, R. M. (1974). *Handbook of leadership.* New York: Free Press.

Stohl, C. (1995). *Organizational communication.* Thousand Oaks, CA: Sage.

Stone, D. (1988). *Policy paradox and political reason.* New York: Harper-Collins.

Straus, D. B. (1986). Collaborating to understand without being a "wimp." *Negotiation Journal, 2*(2), 155–165.

Strom-Gottfried, K. (1998). Applying a conflict resolution framework to disputes in managed care. *Social Work, 43*(5), 393–402.

Strunk, W., & White, E. B. (1979). *The elements of style* (4th ed.). New York: Macmillan.

Susskind, L. E., & Cruikshank, J. L. (2006). *Breaking Robert's rules: The new way to run your meeting, build consensus, and get results.* New York: Oxford University Press.

Sussman, L., & Depp, S. (1984). *COMEX.* Cincinnati, OH: South-Western.

Svara, J. H. (2006). *Ethics primer for public administrators in government and nonprofit organizations.* Sudbury, MA: Jones and Bartlett Publishers.

Svara, J. H. (2008). *The facilitative leader in city hall.* London: Taylor and Francis.

Swap, W. C., & Rubin, J. Z. (1983). Measurement of interpersonal orientation. *Journal of Personality and Social Psychology, 44,* 208–219.

Sylvia, R. D., Sylvia, K. M., & Gunn, E. M. (1997). *Program planning and evaluation for the public manager.* Prospect Heights, IL: Waveland.

Tajfel, H., & Turner, J. C. (1986). The social identity theory of intergroup behavior. In S. Worchel & W. G. Austain (Eds.), *Psychology of intergroup relations* (pp. 7–24). Chicago: Nelson.

Takahashi, N. (1997). A single garbage can model and the degree of anarchy in Japanese firms. *Human Relations, 50,* 91–109.

Tannen, D. (2001). *You just don't understand.* New York: William Morrow.

Taylor, F. (1911). *Principles of scientific management.* New York: Norton.

Taylor, F. (1997). Scientific management. In J., Shafritz & A. Hyde (Eds.), *Classics of public administration* (4th ed.). Orlando, FL: Harcourt Brace. (Original work published 1912)

Taylor, S., Klein, L., Lewis, B., Gruenewald, T., Gurung, R., & Updegraff, J. (2000). Behavioral responses to stress in females: Tend-and-befriend, not fight-or-flight. *Psychological Review, 107*(3), 411–429.

Terry, L. D. (2002). *Leadership of public bureaucracies: The administrator as conservator* (2nd ed.). Thousand Oaks, CA: Sage.

Terry, L. D. (1995). *Leadership of Public Bureaucracies.* Thousand Oaks, CA: Sage.

Thibaut, J. W., & Kelley, H. H. (1959). *Social psychology of groups.* New York: John Wiley.

Thomas, D. A., & Ely, R. J. (1996, September–October). Making differences matter: A new paradigm for managing diversity. *Harvard Business Review,* 79.

Thomas, J. C. (1995). *Public participation in public decisions.* San Francisco: Jossey-Bass.

Thomas, K. W. (1976). Conflict and conflict management. In M. D. Dunnette (Ed.), *Handbook of industrial and organizational psychology.* Chicago: Rand McNally.

Thomas, K. W. (1977). Toward multi-dimensional values in teaching: The example of conflict behaviors. *Academy of Management Review, 2*(3), 484–490.

Thompson, J. D. (1967). *Organizations in action.* New York: McGraw-Hill.

Tichy, N. M., & Devanna, M. A. (1986). *The transformational leader.* New York: John Wiley.

Timney-Bailey, M. (1987). Psychological development of adults: A comment. *Public Administration Review, 47,* 343–345.

Tinsley, C. (2001). How negotiators get to yes: Predicting the constellation of strategies across cultures to negotiate conflict. *Journal of Applied Psychology, 86*(4), 583–593.

Tjosvold, D., & Haifa, S. (2006). Effects of power concepts and employee performance on managers' empowering. *Leadership & Organization Development Journal, 27*(3), 217–234.

Topchik, G. S. (2007). *The first time manager's guide to team-building.* New York: AMACOM.

Torrance, E. P. (1988). The nature of creativity as manifest in its testing. In R. J. Sternberg (Ed.), *The nature of creativity: Contemporary psychological views.* Cambridge, UK: Cambridge University Press.

Tosi, H. L., Mero, N. P., & Rizzo, J. R. (2000). *Managing organizational behavior* (4th ed.). Malden, MA: Blackwell Business.

Tracey, W. R. (1988). *Critical skills.* New York: American Management Association.

Triandis, H. C. (1994). Cross-cultural industrial and organizational psychology. In H. C. Triandis (Ed.), *Culture and social behaviour.* New York: McGraw-Hill.

Trompenaars, F., & Wooliams, P. (2003). *Business across cultures.* Chichester, UK: Capstone.

Tubbs, M. (1986). Goal setting: A meta-analytic examination of the empirical evidence. *Journal of Applied Psychology, 71*(3), 474–483.

Tucker, R. C. (1995). *Politics as leadership.* Columbia: University of Missouri Press.

Tuckman, B. W. (1965). Developmental sequence in small groups. *Psychological Bulletin, 63,* 384–399.

Urch Druskat, V., & Wheeler, J. V. (2007). How to lead a self-managing team. In J. S. Osland, M. E. Turner, D. A. Kolb, & I. M. Rubin (Eds.). *The organizational behavior reader* (pp. 338–348). Upper Saddle River, NJ: Pearson/Prentice Hall.

Ury, W. (2000). *The third side.* New York: Penguin.

U.S. Department of Labor. (1996). *Team kit: Tools for setting up successful teams.* Washington, DC: Employment and Training Administration.

Vaillant, G. E. (1977). *Adaptation to life.* Boston: Little, Brown.

Van Slyke, D. M., Horne, C. S., & Thomas, J. C. (2005). The implications of public opinion for public managers, the case of charitable choice. *Administration and Society, 37*(3), 321–344.

Van Wart, M. (2005). *Dynamics of leadership in public service: Theory and practice.* Armonk, NY: M. E. Sharpe.

Van Wart, M. (2007). *Leadership in public organizations.* Armonk, NY: M. E. Sharpe.

Vasu, M., Stewart, D., & Garson, G. D. (1990). *Organizational behavior and public management* (2nd ed.). New York: Marcel Dekker.

Vaughn, J., & Otenyo, E. (2007). *Managerial discretion in government decision making: Beyond the street level.* Sudbury, MA: Jones and Bartlett.

Venolia, J. (1998). *Write right.* Berkeley, CA: Ten Speed Press.

Vinzant, J. (1998). Where values collide: Motivation and role conflict in child and adult protective services. *American Review of Public Administration, 28*(4), 347–366.

Vinzant, J., & Crothers, L. (1998). *Street-level leadership: Discretion and legitimacy in frontline public service.* Washington, DC: Georgetown University Press.

Virtanen, T. (2000). Changing competencies of public managers: Tensions in public commitment. *International Journal of Public Sector Management, 13*(4), 333–341.

Vrendenburgh, D., & Brender, Y. (1998). The hierarchical abuse of power in work organizations. *Journal of Business Ethics, 17,* 1337–1347.

Vrendenburgh, D. J., & Maurer, J. G. (1984). A process framework of organizational politics. *Human Relations, 37*(1), 47–66.

Vroom, V. (1964). *Work and motivation.* New York: John Wiley.

Vroom, V. H., & Jago, A. G. (1988). *The new leadership.* Englewood Cliffs, NJ: Prentice Hall.

Vroom, V. H., & Yetton, P. W. (1973). *Leadership and decision making.* Pittsburgh, PA: University of Pittsburgh Press.

Wagner, J. A., & Hollenbeck, J. R. (1998). *Organizational behavior: Securing the competitive advantage.* Upper Saddle River, NJ: Prentice Hall.

Wanous, J. P., & Youtz, M. A. (1986). Solution diversity and the quality of group decisions. *Academy of Management Journal, 29*(1), 149–159.

Warwick, D. P., & Kelman, H. C. (1973). Ethical issues in social intervention. In G. Zaltman (Ed.), *Processes and phenomena of social change.* New York: John Wiley.

Washington, S. (1997). *Consultation and communications.* Paris: Organization for Economic Cooperation and Development.

Watson, D. J., & Watson, R. J. (2006). *Spending a lifetime.* Athens, GA: Carl Vinson Institute.

Watson, W., Johnson, L., & Merritt, D. (1998). Team orientation, self-orientation, and diversity in task groups. *Group and Organization Management, 23*(2), 161–188.

Weisbord, M. R. (1987). *Productive workplaces.* San Francisco: Jossey-Bass.

Weiss, J., & Hughes, J. (2005, March). Want collaboration? Accept and actively manage conflict. *Harvard Business Review,* 93–101.

Wellins, R. S., Byham, W. C., & Wilson, J. M. (1991). *Empowered teams: Creating self-directed work groups that improve quality, productivity, and participation.* San Francisco: Jossey-Bass.

Wentling, R. M., & Palma-Rivas, N. (2000). Current status of diversity initiatives in selected multinational corporations. *Human Resources Development Quarterly, 11,* 35–60.

Wesenberg, P. (1994). Bridging the individual-social divide: A new perspective for understanding and stimulating creativity in organizations. *Journal of Creative Behavior, 28*(3), 177–192.

West, J., & Berman, E. (1997). Administrative creativity in local government. *Public Productivity and Management Review, 20*(4), 446–458.

West, J., & West, C. (1989). Job stress and public sector occupations: Implications for personnel managers. *Review of Public Personnel Administration, 9*(3), 46–65.

West, M. (1997). *Developing creativity in organizations.* Leicester, UK: British Psychological Society Books.

Wheeler, K. M. (1994). Working with the news media. In K. M. Wheeler (Ed.), *Effective communication: A local government guide.* Washington, DC: International City Management Association.

Whetten, D. A., & Cameron, K. S. (1998). *Developing management skills* (4th ed.). Reading, MA: Addison-Wesley.

White, H. L., & Rice, M. (2005). The multiple dimensions of diversity and culture. In M. F. Rice (Ed.), *Diversity and public administration: Theory issues and perspectives.* New York: M. E. Sharpe.

White, L. P., & Wooten, K. (1983). Ethical dilemma in various stages of organization development. *Academy of Management Review, 8*(4), 690–697.

Whyte, W. H., Jr. (1952). *Is anybody listening?* New York: Simon & Schuster.

Wiethoff, C. (2004). Motivation to learn and diversity training: Application of the theory of planned behavior. *Human Resource Development Quarterly, 15,* 263–278.

Wilson, J. Q. (1989). *Bureaucracy: What government agencies do and why they do it.* New York: Basic Books.

Wilson, P. (1995). The effects of politics and power on the organizational commitment of federal executives. *Journal of Management, 21*(1), 101–118.

Wilson, W. (1887). The study of administration. *Political Science Quarterly, 2,* 197–222.

Witte, E. (1972). Field research on complex decision making process—the phase theory. *International Studies of Management and Organization, 56,* 156–182.

Witteman, H. (1988). Interpersonal problem solving: Problem conceptualization and communication use. *Communication Monographs, 55,* 336–359.

Wofford, J. C., Goodwin, V. L., & Premack, S. (1992). Meta-analysis of the antecedents of personal goal level and of the antecedents and consequences of goal commitment. *Journal of Management, 18,* 595–615.

Woodall, J. (1996). Managing culture change: Can it ever be ethical? *Personnel Review, 25*(6), 26–40.

Woodman, R., Sawyer, J., & Griffin, R. (1993). Toward a theory of organizational creativity. *Academy of Management Review, 18*(2), 293–321.

Wright, A. T., & Cropanzano, R. (2004). The role of psychological well-being in job performance: A fresh look at an age-old quest. *Organizational Dynamics, 33*(4), 338–351.

Wrong, D. (1968). Some problems in defining social power. *American Journal of Sociology, 73,* 673–681.

Wycoff, J. (1995). *Transformation thinking.* New York: Berkley Books.

Xie, J. L., & Johns, G. (1995). Job scope and stress: Can scope be too high? *Academy of Management Journal, 38,* 1288–1309.

Yates, D. (1985). *The politics of management.* San Francisco: Jossey-Bass.

Yerkes, R. M., & Dodson, J. D. (1908). The relation of strength of stimulus to rapidity of habit formation. *Journal of Comparative Neurology and Psychology, 18,* 459–482.

Yukl, G. (1998). *Leadership in organizations* (4th ed.). Upper Saddle River, NJ: Prentice Hall.

Zaleznik, A. (1977, May–June). Managers and leaders: Are they different? *Harvard Business Review,* 67–78.

Zeitz, G. (1990). Age and work satisfaction in a government agency. *Human Relations, 43*(5), 419–438.

Zeng, M., & Chen, X.-P. (2003). Achieving cooperation in multiparty alliances: A social dilemma approach to partnership management. *Academy of Management Review, 28*(4), 587–605.

Zivnuska, S., Kacmar, K. M., Witt, L. A., Carlson, D. S., & Bratton, V. K. (2004). Interactive effects of impression management and organizational politics on job performance. *Journal of Organizational Behavior, 25*(5), 627–640.

Index

About the Authors

Robert B. Denhardt is Lincoln Professor of Leadership and Ethics and director of the School of Public Affairs at Arizona State University and Visiting Scholar at the University of Delaware. Dr. Denhardt is a past president of the American Society for Public Administration and a member of the National Academy of Public Administration. Dr. Denhardt has published eighteen books, including *The Dance of Leadership, The New Public Service, Managing Human Behavior in Public and Non-profit Organizations, Theories of Public Organization, Public Administration: An Action Orientation, In the Shadow of Organization, The Pursuit of Significance, Executive Leadership in the Public Service, The Revitalization of the Public Service,* and *Pollution and Public Policy.*

Janet V. Denhardt is a professor of public administration in the School of Public Affairs at Arizona State University. Her teaching and research interests focus on organization theory, organizational behavior, and leadership. Her most recent book, *The Dance of Leadership,* was preceded by *The New Public Service, Managing Human Behavior in Public and Non-profit Organizations,* and *Street-Level Leadership: Discretion and Legitimacy in Front-Line Public Service.* Prior to joining the faculty at Arizona State, Dr. Denhardt taught at Eastern Washington University and served in a variety of administrative and consulting positions.

Maria P. Aristigueta is a professor in and director of the School of Urban Affairs and Public Policy and policy scientist in the Institute of Public Administration at the University of Delaware. Her teaching and research interests are primarily in the areas of public sector management and include performance measurement, strategic planning, civil society, and organizational behavior. She is the author of *Managing for Results in State Government,* coauthor *of Managing Behavior in Public and Non-profit Organizations,* and coeditor of the *International Handbook of Practice-Based Performance Management.*